Finance in Asia

Asia's demand for second-generation financial intermediaries and markets needs to be met in order for the region's further development to be sustained. This book provides a compelling, fact-based assessment of current practices, law and regulations in Asia's financial markets, and carefully documents the exciting opportunities and challenges that lie ahead in the region's financial systems.

This book differs in design from typical treatments of financial intermediaries and markets because its focus is on Asia, rather than using a US model (in terms of market configurations or products) as a benchmark, and takes a contemporary and forward-looking view of financial markets.

Examples of practice from Asia are used to illustrate major accepted themes in finance and financial regulation. To the extent that Asia's main economies share characteristics that are distinct – for example, in the relationship between government and the banking sector, or in aspects of corporate governance – the book discusses the consequences for market operation and intermediation.

The book's carefully structured facts and rigorously argued analysis carry important implications both for students in business and law and for professionals new to financial markets in Asia. It will change the approach to teaching Asian financial markets and institutions in universities, as well as providing a valuable resource for professionals working in finance in Asia.

Qiao Liu is Professor of Finance and Economics in the Guanghua School of Management at Peking University.

Paul Lejot is Visiting Fellow at the Asian Institute of International Financial Law at the University of Hong Kong.

Douglas W. Arner is Professor and Head of the Department of Law in the Faculty of Law at the University of Hong Kong.

Routledge advanced texts in economics and finance

Finance in Asia

Institutions, regulation and policy

**Qiao Liu, Paul Lejot and
Douglas W. Arner**

LONDON AND NEW YORK

First published 2013
by Routledge
2 Park Square, Milton Park, Abingdon, Oxon OX14 4RN

Simultaneously published in the USA and Canada
by Routledge
711 Third Avenue, New York, NY 10017

Routledge is an imprint of the Taylor & Francis Group, an informa business

British Library Cataloguing in Publication Data
A catalogue record for this book is available from the British Library

Library of Congress Cataloging in Publication Data
Liu, Qiao.
    Finance in Asia: institutions, regulation and policy / Qiao Liu, Paul Lejot and
Douglas W. Arner.
        p. cm.
    Includes bibliographical references.
    1. Financial institutions – Asia. 2. Finance – Government policy – Asia.
    3. Finance – Law and legislation – Asia. I. Lejot, Paul. II. Arner, Douglas W.
    III. Title.
    Hg187.A2l58 2012
    332.1095 – dc23   2012032772

ISBN: 978-0-415-42320-5 (hbk)
ISBN: 978-0-415-42319-9 (pbk)
ISBN: 978-0-203-59773-6 (ebk)

Typeset in Times New Roman
by Cenveo Publisher Services

Contents

Illustrations

Boxes

Figures

Tables

Table of cases, statutes and conventions

Cases

England and Wales

US

Statutes

Cambodia

China

Commonwealth of Australia

England and Wales

EU

Germany

Hong Kong

India

Indonesia

Japan

South Korea

Malaysia

Philippines

Treaties and conventions

Acknowledgements

No book is solely the effort of its authors. This book grew out of our research, teaching, and consulting experiences at different institutions in Asia over the past ten years. We have benefited tremendously from the suggestions, comments, encouragement and support of many people, even long before we began this project in 2006. It is impossible to thank them all individually. Still, there are a few without whom this book would never have been written. Although we take full ownership of any remaining errors in the book, we would like to extend our thanks to them.

We are grateful to our co-authors throughout our professional careers for stimulating conversations, constructive debates, and more importantly, inspiration and friendship. Part of the book has drawn on our collective works. We owe both personal and intellectual debts to many more than we can possibly acknowledge. We wish to thank in particular Chong-en Bai, Ross Buckley, Hongbin Cai, Bradford Cornell, Michael Darby, Qiang Kang, the late Joe Lu, Joe Norton, Rong Qi, Alan Siu, Frank Song, Keith Wong, Zhongfei Zhou, and Yuande Zhu.

We have benefited enormously from our interactions with colleagues in the Faculty of Business and Economics and the Faculty of Law at the University of Hong Kong, and the Guanghua School of Management at Peking University. Several of our friends and students have either assisted with research for this book, shared research or archival material with us, or provided helpful comments on draft chapters. To list all of them will greatly lengthen the book. However, there are some individuals who have been especially helpful, and they deserve special mention: Uzma Ashraf, John Board, Charles Booth, Jiangchun Cai, Elizabeth G. Chan, Ivy Chan, Matthew Edmondson, Daniel de Lange, Amar Gill, Qiang Hu, Helen Huang, Michael Lawes, Connie Leung, Flora Leung, Leung Mei-wah, Zhigang Li, Jingyi Liu, Nick Minogue, David Mordecai, Kingsley Ong, Nick Prior, Pu Lifen, Lotte Schou–Zibell, Nick Thomas, Frédéric Valle, Wang Wei, Marlene Wittman, Alex Woo Kam-wah, Jenny Wu, Steve Xu, Wen Xu, Joy Yang, Ying Zheng, Xianmin Zhou, and Anthony Zolotas. In addition, we want to thank Yong Wei for his outstanding research assistance throughout the development of the book.

Equally importantly, we would like to thank numerous students we have taught at the University of Hong Kong and other places in the past ten years. Part of the book had been used in Qiao Liu's *Current Asian Finance* course, which drew more than 200 students for seven consecutive years, and selected chapters have been used as a primary text in Paul Lejot's *Law of International Finance* and *Current Issues in Financial Law* courses. The materials in the book have also been used extensively in various executive training programs. We would like to thank the participating executives for their suggestions and questions, which helped to shape the book's content. We also want to extend our thanks to the Executive Education Centres in the Guanghua School of Management and at the University of Hong Kong for providing us with such opportunities.

Several organizations provided us with generous support during different stages of this book's preparation. All three authors were supported by the University of Hong Kong's Strategic Research Themes. In addition, Qiao Liu acknowledges the support of the Research Grants Commission of the Hong Kong Special Administrative Region and the Guanghua School of Management at Peking University; Douglas Arner acknowledges the support of the Research Grants Commission of the Hong Kong Special Administrative Region, the University of Hong Kong, and Asian Development Bank.

We also want to extend our thanks to the Routledge team. In particular, we thank Rob Langham and Simon Holt, our editors at Routledge, for their patience, encouragement, and support throughout the project.

Finally, we own more than we can say to the support and love of our families. Qiao Liu in particular wants to thank his mother for teaching him how to stand firmly on sound principles, and his wife, Tingting, and two sons, Alan and Nick, for everything. Paul Lejot wishes to acknowledge the memory of his grandparents, from whom he inherits the notion that finance is exciting. Douglas Arner would particularly like to thank his wife Chantal and daughter Audrey for constantly bearing with the demands of writing.

Qiao Liu, Paul Lejot, Douglas Arner
Beijing and Hong Kong, October 2012

About the authors

Qiao Liu is Professor of Finance and Economics, JiaMao Distinguished Professor, and Assistant Dean in the Guanghua School of Management at Peking University. Before he joined Guanghua in late 2010, Qiao Liu taught in the Faculty of Business and Economics at the University of Hong Kong, first as an assistant professor, and then as a tenured associate professor in finance. Qiao Liu also worked at McKinsey & Company's Asia-Pacific Corporate Finance and Strategy Practice from December 2001 to July 2003, where he advised various MNCs and leading Asian companies on issues related to corporate finance and strategies. Qiao Liu has published dozens of academic articles in leading academic journals including *Journal of Financial Economics*, *Journal of Financial and Quantitative Analysis*, *Journal of Accounting Research*, *Management Science*, *Economic Journal*, *Financial Analysts Journal*, etc. Qiao Liu holds a Ph.D. in financial economics from UCLA (2000), an MA in international finance from the Graduate School of People's Bank of China (1993), and a BS in Economics and Mathematics from the Renmin University of China (1991).

Paul Lejot is a doctoral candidate in law at the University of Hong Kong, a Visiting Fellow with its Asian Institute of International Financial Law, and is engaged in course design and instruction for its Faculty of Law's LLM Corporate and Financial Law programme. He is also a Visiting Research Fellow at the ICMA Centre, Henley Business School, University of Reading, UK. Paul Lejot was for many years a banker involved in client coverage and product management, with a wide transactional command in fundraising and debt strategy for issuer and fund management clients, first in Europe and later throughout Southeast and South Asia. Since resuming his academic career Paul Lejot has authored, co-authored or edited over 50 books, book chapters, journal articles and working papers.

Douglas W. Arner is Professor and Head of the Department of Law of the University of Hong Kong. Prior to becoming Head of Department in 2011, he was Director of the HKU Faculty of Law's Asian Institute of International Financial Law from 2006–2011. He is the author, co-author or editor of 11 books and over 100 journal articles, book chapters and reports. He has worked on financial sector law reform in Asia, Europe and Africa, with the Asian Development Bank, European Bank for Reconstruction and Development, and the World Bank, and has been a visiting professor at the Universities of London, McGill, Melbourne, Singapore, New South Wales and Zurich, as well as the Shanghai University of Finance and Economics and the Hong Kong Institute for Monetary Research.

Introduction

This book tells a simple story that has many technical components and multiple outcomes. We first describe Asia's modern economic development, then explain intermediation, and finally show and question how that process operates in important Asian settings. That anything related to modern finance can be simple seems odd in this age of financialization, especially in the wake of the global financial crisis of 2007–9, when the complexities of modern financial market practice became widely known for the first time in history, if not properly understood.

But the objective of the transformations that are central to financial activity is truly simple: to provide a means by which savings are channelled into investment in capital goods, new commercial ventures or funding for infrastructure. The complexity begins when we realize that those transformations are highly demanding in terms of risk management, and that financial intermediation can take several different elemental forms and an almost infinite number of contractual variations.

We come from three continents and three differing backgrounds and perhaps coincidentally approach our common subject from three perspectives. First, we live in a significant financial hub. Hong Kong's domestic economy is small, but as an offshore financial centre the territory is host to a large population of banks and investors, many using the city as a location for inward or outward investment with parties in Mainland China, where restrictions exist on transnational capital flows. Finance therefore has our close attention.

Second, the academic formalities and professional approaches of economics, finance and law are unalike, even when investigating identical topics. This leads to incomplete coverage or a limited understanding of the hinterland of specialist concerns, an overall understanding of which can be extremely valuable academically and for finance practitioners. We therefore attempt a synthesis in this field that acknowledges the lack of formal demarcations in the real financial world. The value of instruments traded in one market is never wholly independent of activity elsewhere, and contractual or regulatory innovation is quickly adopted by users regardless of national borders. Copyright is almost unknown in finance. In the work that follows, we thus endeavour to assist economists and financial professionals in understanding how the law impacts their interests and to improve the familiarity of financial and commercial lawyers with finance and economics.

I.1 Finance in Asia

If this is our central objective and narrative, then the reasonable reader's first thought may be to ask how this differs from many other discussions of international finance, banking or financial law and regulation? Our answer is given by the deliberate ambiguity of our title.

Finance in Asia means at least two things. It first describes the creation of modern financial markets and practice in Asia from 1949 to the immediate post-crisis period, using an explanation that specifically looks at the legal, regulatory and other institutional factors that influenced those decades of development. We set out to explain Asia's financial markets, customs and outcomes, and how they may change over time. Here, our main theme is that Asian finance has its own character that is not merely a transitional phase in an inevitable global evolution towards a uniform model of finance. Nor is it a function of the urgency of its development needs, as argued by early banking scholars (Gerschenkron 1962).

Central to our view is that institutions, in the sense of rules of law, regulation or entrenched aspects of common practice, are important determinants of commercial systems and behaviour. 'Institution' is used throughout the book in this sense. Unless stated, we refer to banks and similar organizations as *financial intermediaries* and to investors such as pension funds or insurers as *non-bank intermediaries*. As we will show, the bank describing itself as a 'prominent financial institution' hopes to raise its reputational capital by projecting intangible ideas of safeness and stability, often with imposing headquarters to match. As we will also examine, the global financial crisis showed that the result can be a disastrous chimera.

The title's second meaning is more subtle, to illustrate the main forms of financial intermediation with Asian examples, or more accurately examples that are not predominantly European or North American and thus subject to institutional influences that are not necessarily universal. Financial intermediation and its outcomes are influenced by institutional drivers such as national law, regulation and established practices, by local or transnational customs, and by supervisory rules that are adopted internationally so as to become harmonized among adopting or acceding states or territories. It has results that vary in different settings even in a highly globalized world where goods and capital flow easily across national borders.

Path dependence is especially important in finance, so that events in history bear heavily on today's outcomes. Financial systems and custom in today's markets in New Zealand, India or Colombia have certainly been affected by foreign commercial or legal influences, not least because of the impact of colonial practice and waves of globalization, but their nature and operation owe much also to local circumstances and institutions. Similarly, we believe it mistaken to identify intermediation as practised in the most sophisticated financial centres of London, New York or Hong Kong as fully representative of markets or instruments globally. In each case custom and practice is path dependent, so that the functioning of the tax-based US municipal bond market or Japan's recently privatized Kampo life insurance system, for example, are sizeable and highly significant in their respective domains but must be distinguished from comparable forms of intermediation elsewhere.

Understanding practice in the United Kingdom or United States is important from a technical perspective, but we are wary of illustrating intermediation by treating the operational quirks of those states as generic. Most writing on finance and law customarily describes intermediation using Anglo-American examples, and so neglects the extent to which US or British models are functions of local or exceptional circumstance. We see the world's leading financial markets as technically influential but not absolute precedents for systems or behaviour elsewhere, even in a highly globalized world.

I.2 Financial intermediation

This book's central concern is financial intermediation, which is most often associated with the processes by which savings are channelled into investment. Such flows and mechanics are the technical heart of both sophisticated and emerging economies. Intermediation consists of arrays of contracts and organizations that can be simple or so complex as to be deceptive in relation to their cost or risk. We consider intermediation to be the result of generations of financial innovation and worthy of the detailed descriptions contained in this book, but we acknowledge a more cynical view expressed by an elder statesman of international finance, Paul Volcker, who in the context of the global financial crisis declared that the only valuable innovation in finance that he could recall from the previous 20 years was the automatic teller machine (*Wall Street Journal* 2009).

Financial intermediation more broadly, in a non-technical sense, refers to vital links between the constituent parts of every modern economy, however sophisticated and regardless of political orientation. What mechanisms connect the consumer with the saver, or the corporate sector to the state, and how does the overseas sector meld with the national economy? Without these links the adjective 'modern' would be misplaced, because growth and prosperity would be limited. As the world experienced during the global financial crisis, they can be highly complex and interdependent but are often simple in construction or use. All represent processes of financial intermediation. They facilitate every aspect of commerce, trade, savings and capital formation, tax collection, foreign investment, pension provisions, gift giving, house purchase, infrastructural development, foreign aid, consumer credit, military spending, charitable donations and disaster relief, academic research, and deficit finance and borrowing by states, companies, consumers and investors. Further, since we prepared this book during a graphic period of financial trauma, intermediation must include financial speculation, gambling and less desirable links associated with fraud, trafficking or terrorism. Whether beneficial to society or individuals, all these activities require some contractual or organizational medium of financial intermediation, that is, the means by which money and credit move between participants in national economies and around the globe.

Intermediation is always a contractual process, but can be undertaken in two broad ways: through established organizations or by means of open markets or exchanges. This distinction explains the pattern of our book and is shown in simplified form in Figure I.1. A saver might choose to make a deposit with a commercial bank, or instead to buy securities such as shares or bonds in a more open arena where transactions are reported shortly after being made and are generally observable by third parties. This reflects a choice available in many competing ways to savers and investors, and the result is important in an institutional analysis of law and economics. Whether the saver finds the bank deposit more attractive than the

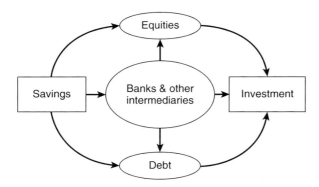

Figure I.1 Simplified financial intermediation.

traded security is partly a matter of resources, but more importantly of personal preference as to expected risk and return. It also illustrates how transaction costs make it feasible for public markets to co-exist as alternative mediums of intermediation with financial organizations such as banks.

The real world is more complicated than our simple bifurcated model, just as the savings and investment channel works in two opposing directions to allow the proceeds of investment to return into savings. Banks intermediate between the deposits they collect and the loans they extend both as internal risk management processes and through transparent securities markets, but the contract–organization distinction is critical to our analysis.

Accordingly, our method is to describe intermediation in Asia's principal economies and try to use examples from within the region to illustrate our analysis, as well as describing non-Asian practices that indirectly impact the region, as with large-scale merger and acquisition transactions. This serves another purpose, which is to learn how finance contributed to Asia's modern economic renaissance. Our book is not a guide to national markets of the type found in databases or country survey material, but an attempt to induce an understanding of transaction and organizational practice, and to illustrate what is done from day-to-day by banks and other financial counterparties that operate around us.

I.3 Convergence?

Our aim is to examine financial intermediation in a way that questions the role of institutions, law and regulation on transaction formation and performance and the behaviour of financial sector commercial parties such as banks or pension funds. Almost all attempts to examine intermediation use traditional examples from Western settings, most commonly Europe or North America, and in particular rely on practice and custom in the United States or United Kingdom, where financial markets have long histories and are well-developed.

But how applicable globally are examples of London or New York practice, especially when national laws are often rooted in local politics? US federal law makes illegal all option or futures contracts based on onions, a prohibition that owes more to the lobby power of American farming than anything connected with intermediation such as the onion's lack of intrinsic value in derivative trading. And does the evolution of finance and banking across the Atlantic or within France, Germany or Japan have universal lessons? Some scholars believe so but we are unconvinced of the single model.

In this respect, our years of research, teaching, transacting and travel in East Asia have produced one unusual observation of our surroundings: that the region's major airports look increasingly alike. Norman Foster or Renzo Piano are magnificent architects with powerful global footprints, and their styles are seen or imitated everywhere in modern Asian transport hubs, from the sweep of a projecting steel roof to the lines of interior furniture. Frequent flyers may find this homogeneity comforting. Many others feel the imprint to be disappointingly mundane, as if intended to stifle differing regional cultures. Some scholars of modern banking have argued that the configuration of global finance would become steadily similar with all states and markets gravitating to a near-uniform model of intermediation (Rybczynski 1997), especially in the way that credit is provided to borrowers.

We are sceptical of this evolutionary model of financial structure, and believe that our view has been vindicated by the global financial crisis. Unlike its airports, the architecture of finance in Asia appears not to be converging towards matching styles drawn from elsewhere, and considerable differences exist between practice within national markets. These extend beyond the traditional distinction between economies of the Continental European model that depend more on banking intermediation than their Anglo-American competitors in Australia, Canada or the United States.

Our architectural analogy has a precedent among political economists. Some years ago, scholars of economic development in Asia imagined a process of take-off and eventual convergence taking place serially: first in Japan; then in South Korea, Hong Kong, Singapore and Taiwan; next in Malaysia and Thailand; and on to the behemoths of China and later India. This procession was pictured as a flock of flying wild geese in a staggered V-formation, first used metaphorically in 1930s Japan (Akamatsu 1961; Cumings 1984) and referred to a succession of processes associated with industrialization.

The concept described a product cycle mode of development, with states successively moving from contract manufacturing of simple goods relying upon inexpensive labour, through the growth of substantial corps of original design or original equipment manufacturers (ODM and OEM, respectively) making and exporting unbranded products of steadily increasing complexity, and eventually to a substantive corporate sector that itself outsources production to low-cost centres, and derives increasing returns and economic rents by creating and sustaining owned brands, especially in technologically demanding goods for export. Often the state led the process by designating sectors to receive strategic commercial support, of which steel or shipbuilding may be the most prominent historic examples. Growth in East and Southeast Asia was consistently predicated on this model after 1949, even in small states and territories such as Singapore or Hong Kong that later abandoned large-scale manufacturing to become service sector hubs.

This product cycle process is yet unfinished. A large share of manufacturing production in Southeast Asia and China's coastal provinces is today associated with contract manufacturing and ODM companies, and although the resources of these installations may be technologically high, product design capabilities are sited elsewhere, within or outside the region. Thus East Asia makes most of the world's notebook computers, merchant ships and mobile phones, but in each case the design content is global. The flying geese image is attractively simple and has yet to be fully contradicted. Later analysts suggested a more complex picture that we also endorse, which recognizes a richer mix of regional and sub-regional forces as being influential in economic and financial development (Bernard & Ravenhill 1995).

Two connected points from these descriptions are relevant to this book. The provision of finance has been vital to Asia's development narrative but in ways that may not always resemble market practice in Europe or North America. Our conclusion is simple: finance in Asia is different. At times this can be problematic, as with the 1997–98 Asian financial crisis which involved rapid market dislocations and shattered confidence, soon followed by profound losses of output and employment in Southeast Asia and South Korea. At other times it may be beneficial, as with a faster than predicted regional recovery commencing from 1999, or in Asia's relatively healthy financial condition following the global crisis.

The structure and operation of finance in Asia seem therefore to accrue benefits but may also raise questions and concerns, especially as to sustainability. For example, one reason for Asia's unprecedented accumulation of foreign currency reserves after 2000 is an institutional deficit that directs savings into highly-rated OECD investments, combined with historically poor standards of financial intermediation and governance within the region. We examine these questions, and ask how Asian savings can be channelled more often into investible opportunities closer to home.

I.4 The future of finance in Asia

The book's third purpose is to consider how finance in Asia differs from other regions and the consequences of this for the future of finance. Our epilogue speculates on the post-crisis outcomes for finance sector behaviour and financial regulation, and asks whether the changes underway globally through the Group of 20, and regionally by members of East Asia's ASEAN+3, represent a cyclical downturn in financial activity or a more significant shift towards a 'post-financialized' world.

This would represent a new phase of modern globalization, in which commerce and manufacturing continue to be conducted globally but finance becomes subordinate to the needs of the real economy. Such a world would allow less leverage of financial risks compared to the period of deregulation that began in the late 1970s. Can the financial world become simpler and less prone to systemic risks, or will it be unable to renounce those sophisticated instruments and concepts upon which the profits of many banks have been based for a generation? If the sceptical view of innovation in finance has merit, can the world's bankers, investors and traders unlearn the complex techniques that we describe in the second part of the book (Chapters 6–12)? Post-crisis re-regulation may make this inevitable unless finance can demonstrate its value in terms of economic development and general welfare.

Intermediation is not merely a process of connection or the transfer of value between parties, but is crucially about transformation, or contracts that allow the exchange of value in ways that suit the preferences of the parties involved. This applies both to instruments sold by one party to a second, and within an organizational setting when a bank elects how to apply funds amassed in the deposits of thousands of savers. Intermediation concerns transformations in the location, risk, duration and liquidity of monetary resources. In functional terms it includes money transmission, exchange and the provision of credit. All other functions are incidental to these. In many cases, the informational demands made by intermediation processes will be high, so that valuing a financial contract at any time will be complex and time sensitive, but intermediation can appear to be intuitive as with *hawala* or other forms of informal finance and money transmission that is conducted according to long-established but unconventional practices. One historic feature of finance in Asia is that informal banking has subsisted alongside the dominant modern forms of organization since the nineteenth century, and continues to be widely valued as an efficient form of money transmission.

Asia has far lesser endowments of non-renewable resources compared to Africa or the Middle East, and its renewable endowment is mixed. Some of the most successful East Asian economies have been relatively resource scarce except for human capital, including Japan, South Korea and Taiwan. How has Asian finance contributed to that broad success? To what extent is finance in Asia associated with economic development, and with crises, recoveries and general stability, either in a general way or through strong causal chains? What is Asia's financial future, and what can other regions learn from its progression? We seek to address all these questions.

I.5 Structure of the book

There are two distinct parts to the book and a short concluding chapter. Text boxes are scattered throughout to explain technical concepts or illustrate aspects of financial intermediation with local or regional examples. The first part consists of five chapters dealing with

Asia's modern economies, the nature of finance, and the virtues and challenges associated with the region's post-1949 development model. It also considers the institutional foundations of finance. We consider Asia's modern economic history to have had three major phases:

- Serial industrialization and embedded finance, 1949–1980.
- From economic miracle to mismanaged asset bubble, 1981–1998.
- Post-crisis reform and risk management, 1999–2009.

At the same time, three characteristics had a consistent and regional importance:

- State guidance of national development, even in Hong Kong and Singapore where a market orientation is assumed to prevail.
- A strong orientation towards production for export.
- Relatively high precautionary savings by consumers and corporations.

The narrative begins in 1949 to signify a series of sudden transformations, some of which would have financial results only decades later with the reopening of China to trade and inward investment. A narrative written in 1948 would have placed Calcutta (Kolkata), Rangoon (Yangon) and Shanghai among the region's leading commercial centres and suggest a very different modern outcome. The occupation of Japan and its forced replication of US laws and practices upon domestic industry and commerce included restrictions on monopoly that contributed to the reform of corporate governance and ownership, the adoption of finance and securities regulation similar to those instituted in the United States after 1929, and a re-orientation of the economy to export-driven manufacturing. The 1949–1980 period saw a succession of accelerated growth in per capita incomes among the industrializing states.

A second phase starts around 1980, following the end of the Bretton Woods system of capital and exchange controls and marking China's adoption of growth policies after Deng Xiaoping sanctioned economic reform. This was the beginning of Asian trade integration, with transnational capital flows becoming increasingly more prominent. Growth continued, notably with no general increase in income inequality, a mix described as the Asian economic miracle (World Bank 1993), and distinguishing the region from Africa and Latin America. The phase ended in mid-1997 with the bursting of inflated asset prices, a rush withdrawal of capital to OECD lenders and a collapse in Asian bank balance sheets and general confidence.

The final phase, through to the global financial crisis of 2008, was notable for rapid economic recovery and a profound risk adjustment, with significant foreign reserve accumulation and decided but partial reforms in financial markets.

Within this framework, Chapter 1 describes the modern economic setting and history. We use 1949 as a starting point for our analysis since it coincides with Japan and China's transformation and predates the Korean War. Asia's development model was reflected in the active and coercive functions of the state, and in a constrained model of corporate ownership. The financial sector was limited in technical and geographical scope. Both Asian and colonial banks concentrated on trade finance and money transmission but provided little finance in the sense of medium-term credit. Only in early industrializing Japan was finance functionally embedded with large corporate groups, or *keiretsu*, as had prevailed before 1940.

To what extent was the financial sector consciously associated with Asia's post-1949 industrialization? Chapters 2 and 3 outline savings and investment intermediation and the financial links between sectors in national economies. Chapter 2 looks more closely at phases in finance and development in the region, and Chapter 3 questions the operations and risks of that model.

Chapter 4 then describes modern financial systems and regulatory practice, central banking, risk management and other institutions and customs that allow intermediation to function, as well as dictate its style. The activities of central and commercial banks meet in national monetary policy, and many aspects of prudential supervision. Chapter 5 then examines certain institutional variables and the value in financial intermediation of property rights, provisions for insolvency, the creation and enforcement of contractual obligations, and the functions and comparative value of collateral and taking security.

In the second part (Chapters 6–12), we review all important forms of intermediation, starting with the most common and well-understood in the simple organizational model of commercial banks, which perform the utility finance functions of money transmission, deposit taking, and making simple loans. Beyond the elemental model, banking practice quickly becomes complex, with structured finance and infrastructural transactions using many advanced techniques in traded securities, contract formation and risk management. The structure and related analysis is shown in Table I.1.

Chapter 6 discusses the operations and functions of utility or commercial banks, including the credit-related activities and trends most commonly found in Asia, as well as project finance and simple securitization. The region's major commercial banks have often acted as arms of the state, regardless of ownership allegiances or the responsibilities adopted in any single jurisdiction. Chapter 7 considers the nature and interests of investment banking and its use of elemental forms of capital in debt, equity and derivatives contracts. These instruments are traded and exchanged in national or transnational markets, the organization and regulation of which are described in Chapters 8 and 9, and used by non-bank intermediaries of the kinds outlined in Chapter 11. Chapter 7 also suggests an explanation for the creation of new financial instruments or contracts, and some of the results among the intermediaries that become their inventors.

Chapter 8 explains the main forms of debt capital that facilitate contractual intermediation, including bonds and money market instruments, complex transactions and structured finance, and discusses the use of derivative contracts in funded or unfunded risk transfer. Chapter 9 concentrates on equities, or ownership participatory contracts, the third form of elemental capital. It considers organized exchanges where shares are bought and sold, the features of Asia's important equity markets, and links between corporate structure and ownership and Asia's prevailing forms of commercial governance in both private and public sectors.

Chapter 10 extends the corporate finance themes by examining modern takeover and merger practice, and uses a notorious example to illustrate the dichotomy of a good deal gone wrong, a skilfully devised and executed transaction that caused an enormous loss of value after completion. The chapter also asks how Asia presents opportunities for both internal and outward transaction opportunities.

Chapter 11 deals with organized non-bank intermediaries, including the traditional in the form of asset managers, pension funds, insurers and private equity, and the less conventional, as seen in sovereign wealth funds, infrastructural funds and hedge funds. Finally, the chapter introduces the principles and functioning of Islamic finance and its relationship to conventional forms of intermediation.

Table 1.1 Financial intermediation: topics and arrangement of chapters

Contracts & instruments	Intermediaries	Organized markets	Supervision & regulation	Institutions & risks
Credit lines, bank loans, bonds, shares, insurance contracts, promissory notes, Islamic finance contracts, bills of exchange, guarantees	Central banks, commercial banks, investment banks, insurers, mutual funds, provident funds, hedge funds, sovereign wealth funds, private equity funds, infrastructure funds	Stock exchanges, over-the-counter derivative markets, organized futures exchanges, insurance markets, commodity markets	Securities law, stock exchange listing rules, banking regulation, financial disclosure law, laws on sales of investment products, laws on market manipulation	Credit risk, interest rate risks, operational risk, legal risk, foreign exchange risk, agency risk
Chapter 6 Loans & credit facilities Cash securitization Covered bonds, Contingent capital Non-recourse finance	Chapter 4 Central banks	Chapter 8 OTC derivatives markets OTC debt capital markets	Chapter 6 Bank regulation Capital adequacy Basel Committee rules Chapter 8 Derivative market regulation & ISDA practices	Chapter 5 Property rights Contractual rights Collateral rights
Chapter 8 Bonds, notes & bills OTC derivatives Credit derivatives Exchange traded funds	Chapter 6 Commercial banks, trade finance banks Private banks Central counterparties	Chapter 9 Stock exchanges Futures & options exchanges	Chapter 9 Securities regulation & IOSCO guidelines	Chapter 5 Risk management
Chapter 9 Equities Equity derivatives	Chapter 7 Investment banks Securities brokers & dealers	Chapter 10 Mergers & acquisitions Corporate finance advisory	Chapter 10 Corporate governance Takeover & monopoly regulation	Chapter 6 Credit risk management
Chapter 11 Insurance contracts Shari'ah compliant contracts	Chapter 11 Non-bank intermediaries, Sovereign wealth funds, Islamic funds, Hedge funds, Private equity & infrastructure funds	Chapter 12 Chiang Mai Initiative	Chapter 11 Regulation of non-bank intermediaries National rules on foreign ownership	Chapter 8 Credit rating agencies Credit risk transfer Derivative uses

Chapter 12 ends the descriptive portion of the book by tracing the recent increase in financial integration in Asia, partly among central banks engaging in shared or common monetary policy cooperation, and partly among intermediaries and organized exchanges through alliances and new forms of transnational intermediation.

Finally, Chapter 13 reflects on the commonalities and differences of finance in Asia, and looks forward into the future of its finance.

Parts of this book have appeared in earlier forms as journal articles and working papers, which are cited when necessary. The entire content draws on our programmes of courses given in the Faculty of Business and Economics and the Faculty of Law at the University of Hong Kong, Guanghua School of Management at Peking University, and elsewhere in the region and around the world.

Qiao Liu, Paul Lejot, Douglas W. Arner
Beijing and Hong Kong, October 2012

1 Asia's development model

Asia is moving into a leadership role in the world economy[1]

We live in Asia's century. If neither China nor any other Asian state dominates the twenty-first century in the way that Britain and the United States were successive geopolitical leaders in the preceding 200 years, the region as a whole will still influence world affairs as never before in modern times. The twenty states and territories that we take to comprise East and South Asia are home to over 3.6 billion people or 53 per cent of the world's population. This region is host to many hundreds of indigenous languages and its cultural roots include important Austro-Asiatic, Austronesian, Dravidian, Indic, Japonic, Sino-Tibetan and Tai-Kadai traditions, each of which is distinct. Western influences have impacted the region at recurring intervals but only embedding in the former settlement colonies of Australasia. Breadth of scale in resource endowments, institutional origins and culture means that it is often difficult to generalize about Asia or its economies. Yet two factors of interest to us are widely shared, a supervening concentration on economic development and a strong desire for social stability, two preferences that can sometimes conflict.

Asia has huge disparities of wealth and income, for as China and Japan are ranked second and third among world economies measured by nominal national output, so several are among the most modest. Thirty years of unusually rapid and consistent growth led China to overtake the United States during 2010 to become the world's leading producer of manufactured goods (IHS Global Insight 2010). China's economy has doubled in terms of annual output every seven to eight years since the early 1980s with striking results in those regional economies with which it engages in trade (Arora & Vamvakidis 2010) – today almost every economy in the region and world. In 2008, a major study supported by the World Bank and several OECD governments sought to identify conditions conducive to growth since 1945 among 13 selected developing economies (Commission On Growth & Development 2008; Lin & Monga 2010). It hoped to encourage similar policies elsewhere to lessen poverty. Nine of the sample were East Asian: China, Hong Kong, Indonesia, Japan, South Korea, Malaysia, Singapore, Taiwan and Thailand, with only one each drawn from Africa, the Americas, Europe or the Middle East. Five broad factors were said to be common to the group:

- Openness to the global economy;
- Macroeconomic stability;
- High rates of saving and capital investment;
- Market-based resource allocation; and
- Effective political leadership and governance.

A number of contrasting factors were said to be negative for development. We will explore the findings at greater length below. The report and its findings have been highly influential, reflecting a pragmatic approach to development and one deviating strongly from the Washington Consensus, which we discuss in Chapter 2. Only Cambodia, Laos and Vietnam are ranked by the IMF as low income East Asian countries if Myanmar (Burma) and North Korea are excluded from analysis (IMF 2010a).

Asia's post-1949 record shows a pattern of state-influenced development but with an increasing market orientation, typically with less reliance on official aid or concessionary finance than other regions, a trait considered unconventional by the traditional developmental literature. So despite the region's wealth and income diversity, common features exist among Asia's economic successes that we shall highlight in this chapter and throughout the book. We also detail systemic limitations in the region's development model and their implications for future policy. The global financial crisis of 2008 increased interest in Asia's world standing, not least because China and the neighbouring economies with which it shares trade, investment and manufacturing links became the principal sources of global post-crisis growth after 2009. At the same time, we will argue that Asia may usefully consider institutional reforms to strengthen its domestic and regional financial systems. A lack of realizable and prudent investment channels leads capital to be diverted elsewhere, and an accumulation of foreign currency reserves since 2000 signifies a relative incompleteness in domestic and regional finance and a profound opportunity cost to domestic welfare.

Our purpose in this chapter is to establish a setting in terms of modern economic history and growth theories for the more detailed studies of financial systems and activity that form the core of the book. The analysis covers a territory that varies slightly from topic to topic, although this will always be clear from each section's context. Equivocation about Asia's components is common in several academic disciplines, especially when discussing political and economic alliances (see Section 12.4). Some regional groups cover many more states or territories than others as Figure 1.1 shows.

Although the EU has expanded periodically since 1972 'Western Europe' is more fixed as a concept than East Asia. In terms of scope, *Finance in Asia* covers the territory south from China and Japan to Indonesia and latitudinally between Malaysia and the Philippines. Our analysis excludes the poorest economies and those with insignificant financial sectors, notably Brunei, North Korea, Macau, Myanmar and Timor-Leste. In some instances we use examples of financial practice in India or Australia and from the West, and in common with market custom we occasionally discuss financial activity in non-Japan Asia, that is, East Asia but excluding Japan. This is usually to avoid the immense Japanese financial sector distorting our presentation of other domestic markets that are far smaller in scale. Our focus is with the nine principal members of ASEAN+3 together with Taiwan and Hong Kong, a combined population of 2.09 billion compared to 1.56 billion in South Asia (CIA 2010).

Finally in these opening remarks, three points of language are important. First, the geographical scope of the book is with states and territories in the eastern sections of the Eurasian land mass. We use 'Asia' and 'East Asia' interchangeably to refer to that area, and not to something larger, either topographically or conceptually. Second, no reference to 'Asia' should be taken to infer dependency in any context. Last, some commentators have described certain recently industrialized economies as 'tigers' but we use the term sparingly. The economies we examine are not feline or near extinction, even though they may be notably powerful.

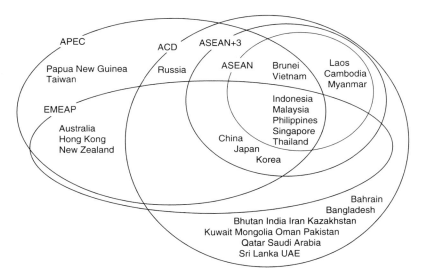

Figure 1.1 Regional political and economic groups.
Key: ACD – Asia Cooperation Dialogue; APEC – Asia Pacific Economic Cooperation forum; ASEAN – Association of Southeast Asian Nations; ASEAN+3 – ASEAN plus China, South Korea and Japan; EMEAP – Executives' Meeting of East Asia Pacific Central Banks (see Box 4.1). APEC's American members are not shown.
Source: Lejot, Arner & Liu (2006b).

Our detailed narrative begins in 1949, partly for convenience, partly to mark four transforming events:

- The passing of economic control in Japan from the occupying administration and an end of the 'deconcentration' period of corporate reorganization (Hadley 1949; Hadley 1970).
- The creation of the People's Republic of China and the effective closure of the Chinese financial sector and external economy.
- US military withdrawal from South Korea, which became a preface to the Korean War of 1950–53.
- International acceptance of Indonesia's independence from the Netherlands.

This was the beginning of Asia's post-colonial era and of its serial industrialization and acceleration in growth. We focus on the common economic narratives in this chapter and elsewhere in this book. This is not to imply that there is a uniform model of regional economic development, although the term 'Asian development model' is widely used to refer to those characteristics that are held broadly in common.

1.1 Divergent results from development

Why have some states or regions of the world grown richer and others lagged? What explains relative shifts or declines in long-term national economic welfare? These questions are central to modern growth theory and have long bedevilled economists and policymakers.

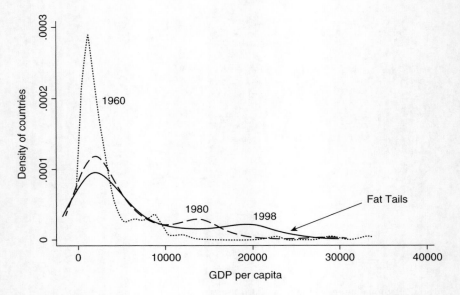

Figure 1.2 Distribution of economies by GDP per capita, 1960, 1980 and 1998.
Sources: Maddison (2006); authors' calculations.

Figure 1.2 plots the distribution of GDP per capita, a common measure of national economic development, across the available set of countries in 1960, 1980 and 1998. The result shows continuing large cross-country inequalities. The three plots represent different time periods and together show that inequalities in the outcomes of development have increased over time, as demonstrated by the much fatter tails in the 1998 curve. At first glance this contrasts with the conclusion of a seminal World Bank study, which described how eight East Asian economies achieved a mix of rapid growth in 1965–90 without increased inequality. It called the result an Asian economic miracle and suggested that the sample states were 'unusually successful at sharing the fruits of growth' (World Bank 1993). Even neglecting important distributive questions, the World Bank's assessment was fulsome, stating that no other group of states had grown more rapidly or consistently since the late 1950s. The report used comparisons of relative income disparities using Gini coefficients (we show recent data in Tables 1.2–1.13), which contrast the shares of national income or accumulated wealth of the richest and poorest percentiles of population. The positive emphasis given to the study's results has since been criticized for methodological reasons as we show in Section 1.3, but the report gave an accurate characterization of how many observers regard the region's progress.

Noted economic historian Angus Maddison (2006) took a far longer view of the dynamics of economic growth across countries, attributing differences in performance over the past millennium to three interactive processes:

- Conquest or settlement of relatively empty land areas that were fertile, contained new resources for husbandry or cultivation, or the potential to accommodate transfers of population, crops and livestock;
- International trade and capital movements; and
- Technological growth and institutional innovation.

Maddison's work suggests that modern variations in economic performance are largely due to differences in resource endowments. In addition, states that adopt policies favouring external trade and capital mobility exhibit generally more favourable results measured by output growth. Finally, Maddison argues that sound institutions and technological growth are consistently important drivers of economic performance.

Economists and policymakers took decades to acknowledge and accept the factors identified by Maddison, in spite of economics having a tradition of exploring the fundamental determinants of economic growth. For over half a century this has been a particular focus of macroeconomics. In 1956 Robert Solow published a path-breaking and Nobel Prize-winning article introducing his eponymous growth model. This offers a simple and clear way to understand the relation between aggregate output, that is, a measure of economic performance or growth, and its main inputs, including capital stock, total employment and technological change. Empirical research later found evidence that the Solow model is a useful starting point for understanding variations in economic performance. For example, many economists use the model to explain the Asian growth 'miracle' and argue that relatively high growth in the region is attributable to increasing deployment of the factor inputs of labour and capital (Krugman 1994; Kim & Lau 1994).

The Solow growth model helps in understanding cross-country income differences and the process of growth but labour inputs, physical and human capital formation and technological progress are arguably only proximate causes of differences in national economic performance (Acemoglu 2008). More specifically, these are not wholly independent factors but variables affected by each other (Romer 1990), or by one or more other fundamentals. This implies a need to search further for the root causes and mechanics of growth. Institutional scholars Douglass North (another Nobel laureate) and Robert Paul Thomas were among the first to criticize growth theory for mistaking proximate causes for fundamental factors:

> Economic organization is the key to growth: the development of an efficient economic organization in Western Europe accounts for the rise of the West. Efficient organization entails the establishment of institutional arrangements and property rights that create an incentive to channel individual economic effort into activities that bring economic growth.
>
> (North & Thomas 1973)

They add that 'the factors we have listed (innovation, economies of scale, education, capital accumulation etc.) are not causes of growth; they are growth' (North & Thomas 1973: 2).

The hunt for primary causes of economic growth continues. Later research has argued from several perspectives that other factors such as geographical conditions, institutions, financial structure, law, state regulation or cultural ties are more basic causes of variations in economic outcomes. Distinguished anthropologist Jared Diamond provides a sophisticated treatment of geographical and endowment theories of development (Diamond 1997), suggesting that geographic differences such as the availability of a variety of seeds or animals influence the timing of crop cultivation and thus the possibility of forming societies in complex settlements. Proponents of geographical theories (Sachs 2001) also argue that continuing factors such as temperate or tropical zone technologies and the incidence of debilitating disease are determined by location, climate and other physical conditions. These ultimately decide the feasible level of productivity and resulting territorial economic performance. The emphasis in geographical theories on endowments in economic development is conceptually appealing, although resource endowments best account for variations in pre-industrial development before the twentieth century and may be less consistently relevant to modern development (Morris 2010).

Culture and religion have also been held to contribute to or constrain economic performance. The importance of such factors is especially associated with sociologist Max Weber in *The Protestant Ethic and the Spirit of Capitalism*, published early in the last century (Weber 1930). Weber argued that post-Reformation ethics influenced the development of nineteenth-century capitalism by condoning the pursuit of economic gain through the individual's self-sacrifice and labour. Commercial activities could thus have a positive spiritual and moral purpose. This contrasted with doctrines found in Catholic canon law and the Islamic Shari'ah which had both traditionally proscribed certain commercial activities, especially in finance and credit.

We shall see in Section 11.4 in discussing contemporary transactions in Islamic finance that the result over hundreds of years was to create incentives for new financial instruments to avoid specific religious restrictions, for example against the charging of interest or speculation by gambling. It also led to financial activity migrating to cities or states that allowed some religious diversity, an observation with which Weber himself was familiar. A flaw in the Weberian argument concerns the importance of intent, in that the dedication of an immoral act to a moral purpose allows the pirate a healthy living, for example. Nonetheless, there have been periods when foregoing consumption in favour of future investment has been popular among policymakers, especially if they face no electoral threat as a consequence – for example, Asia's post-1949 serial industrialization often took place in authoritarian states.

Weber's view of a causal connection between Protestantism and the industrial success of certain states in nineteenth-century Europe later drew him to connect Confucianism as a doctrine favouring cooperation, piety and self-sacrifice with certain national outcomes. He seems not to have identified any economic miracles, in Asia or elsewhere. Weberian theories are unable to explain time differences in the acceleration of growth in Asia after 1949 without taking religion as endogenous to political factors. We must also stress that Protestantism has never been a precondition to hard work or personal endeavour. Landes makes this point in relation to Japan both before and since the economic modernization that followed the 1868 Meiji Restoration, noting that Japanese scholars refer to an 'Industrious Revolution' that preceded industrialization (Landes 1998: 363), while Morris makes the point more generally in relation to comparing Western and Eastern development (Morris 2010).

Another line of research places the nature and quality of institutions as central explanations of economic performance, although it is difficult to achieve consensus in defining 'institutions' or quantifying institutional quality within a state. Should institutions include only formal laws enacted by a state authority or derivative legislation applied by agencies of the state, or can they include informal rules of well-established societal practice? North defines institutions as formal constraints, or 'rules that human beings devise' and informal constraints 'such as conventions and rules of behaviour' (North 1990).

Both formal and informal institutions shape human interactions and help structure incentives in human exchanges, whether political, social or economic. States with effective institutions such as secure property rights or less distorting policies tend to obtain greater investment in physical and human capital, and use those factors more effectively to achieve higher levels of income. Informal institutions such as identifiably strong social ties have been shown to have similar effects. Institutions might therefore be the most fundamental determinant of economic performance.

Although the institutional hypothesis is theoretically sound and intuitively appealing, empirical evidence supporting the effect of institutions on economic performance is hard to isolate, both because of the difficulty in defining and quantifying institutions and due to problems in testing their causal relationships with economic performance. This practical issue may help account for law's impact in the economy being neglected until comparatively recently, a suggestion made by an economic historian of the European Industrial Revolution before the publication of North's pioneering work (Hartwell 1971), and contrary to Marx's view of law as a derivative of economic outcomes rather than a contributor (Freeman 2001: 958–63).

One noted study cleverly tries to overcome these empirical difficulties and provide evidence that institutions have a causal effect on economic growth (Acemoglu, Johnson & Robinson 2001). This examines the effect of institutions on economic growth by using, as a proxy, differences in historic settler mortality rates from indigenous disease measured among European colonialists.[2] The authors argue that rates of mortality dictated settlement policies adopted within different colonies, which in turn produced early institutions of varying quality. Colonies where disease was prevalent were less likely to be comprehensively settled. They became instead 'extractive' economies with strong control structures to subdue indigenous or slave labour but with persistently weak institutions. Little incentive existed for the colonial power to introduce strong institutions since to do so would involve unnecessary costs. By contrast, colonies with lower incidents of disease favoured significant settlement, which acted as an inducement for the introduction or transplant of effective institutions such as the rule of law or effective property rights. Thus:

> the control structures set up in the non-settler colonies during the colonial era persisted, while there is little doubt that the institutions of law and order and private property established during the early phases of colonialism in Australia, Canada, New Zealand, the US, Hong Kong, and Singapore have formed the basis of the current day institutions of these countries.
>
> (Acemoglu, Johnson & Robinson 2001: 1376)

Settler mortality was shown as correlated with today's institutions but exogenous to present economic performance, and is a good guide to current institutions in a sample of former colonies. Using this approach to control for endogeneity in measures of institutions, Acemoglu, Johnson and Robinson show that institutions have a large and robust effect on economic growth and per capita incomes, and claim a causal relation between institutions and economic performance. One concern with the study's method is its use of a restrictive definition of institutions covering only the threat of expropriation by the state, which represents a narrow proxy for individual property rights. The study relies on estimates of local conditions rather than the policy preferences or established legal system of the colonial power. Australia is thus a former settlement colony, for example, despite its foreign occupation being associated with deported criminals.

Landes (1998) makes a similar argument, but suggests that the quality of institutions in former colonies is related to the nature and effectiveness of home institutions in the colonial power, which it is said to have transplanted abroad. Other evidence also supports the importance of institutional factors. Easterly and Levine (2002) test various endowment, institution and policy theories using cross-country data. They find that resource endowments affect development through institutions but identify no evidence of a direct effect between such endowments and growth in income. Independently, Rodrik, Subramanian and Trebbi (2002) reach an identical conclusion: that institutional quality is the most significant determinant of income while resource endowments have at best only a weak and indirect effect. Note that these and similar empirical studies of modern colonial influences using cross-country data have a strong Western orientation and exclude, for example, data relating to Japan's influence on institutions in South Korea or Taiwan. In both cases occupation led to the introduction of elements of civil law, some of which persisted into the modern era.

So the search for explanations of economic growth has generated a wealth of interesting findings. Empirical studies show that resource endowments, human capital, geographical features, religious custom, cultural factors and formal or informal institutions all help explain cross-country differences in income. However, recent evidence seems to indicate that the most significant explanation for development in the modern era can be found in institutions. Although the debate as to differences in long-run economic performance is ongoing, national variations in institutions appear the most promising explanation of differences in development. We ask more specific questions in Chapters 2 and 5 of how institutions affect behaviour within financial systems, and in particular examine the relationships between finance and development (Section 2.1) and law and finance (Section 5.1).

1.2 Asia's modern economic history

The foregoing summary of recent theoretical and empirical research is reflected in Asia's economic history and is useful to help identify commonalities in the region's modern development experience since 1949.

Pre-modern development

Agricultural civilizations and economies developed in China and India at roughly the same time (a period of a few thousand years) as in Arabia and North Africa. In the early classical period, around the fifth century BCE, trade became established between developed parts of East and Central Asia, West Asia and the Mediterranean, with extensive commercial networks and semi-permanent channels of commerce formed between East and South Asia, Arabia and the Eastern Mediterranean. Most notable were the Silk Roads and the coastal shipping routes that predated the invention of transoceanic navigation.

Economic development in Asia was considerably more consistent than in Europe from around the fifth to at least until the late fifteenth century, primarily due to efficient irrigation. Asia was the world's richest region from the period following the collapse of the Roman Empire until the Industrial Revolution took effect in Western Europe, and so led global development for around 1,000 years (Morris 2010). If China was always the Middle Kingdom, so Asia was then at the centre of the world (Glenn 2007: 326). Maddison (2006) estimates that Asia accounted for 70 per cent of global GDP in 1000 CE, compared to Europe's 9 per cent share; China and India took turns as the world's largest economy between 1 CE and 1800 CE.

Asia was then eclipsed. Its agricultural and extractive economies declined steadily in relation to the mass output that resulted from industrialization in Europe and parts of North America. Prior to 1937 most East Asian states were subjected to colonial rule, with only a handful remaining relatively unconquered, notably China, Japan and Thailand. At that time, Japan was the first Asian state to undergo profound change of the kind known in Europe. From the start of the Meiji Restoration, Japan experienced considerable institutional reforms and development, and saw its economy industrialize in a comparable fashion to Western states. Output expanded effectively until the mid-1930s but Japan became increasingly beset with resource constraints, both of primary goods and through a shortage of manufacturing labour, which was mitigated through gains in productivity only much later in the 1950s. Japan's military expansion partly sought to secure resources unavailable at home that were essential to continued growth, although the later military capture of territories in South and Southeast Asia and the Western Pacific were driven equally by power ambitions.

China's economic performance was lacklustre during the same period. In 1800 per capita income was comparable to that of leading Western countries (Bairoch 1993; Maddison 2006), but by 1945 average per capita income among the industrialized economies had grown to six times the level in China. Once the world's leading economy, China was over-taken by Japan in terms of per capita income as early as 1820. At the same time Southeast Asia was prospering through an increasing integration with the global trading system. Intercontinental trade growth accelerated with the opening of the Suez Canal in the 1860s: Malaya was the world's leading supplier of tin and rubber; Singapore became a prominent entrepôt in trade between East Asia and the West; and colonial Indonesia was prolific in timber and spice production. Only in India was semi-skilled manufacturing a significant source of export earnings. Asia's trade was based for an extended period largely on the export of extractive and renewable resources, and became increasingly rebalanced towards manufactured exports only in the modern phase begun in 1949. Wartime occupation was clearly destructive to regional commerce and trade with the West but also represented a severe dislocation, the reverberations of which continue to haunt regional politics and economic cooperation today, even if it hastened the later withdrawal of Western colonial powers after 1945.

Serial take-offs 1949–97

Post-conflict reconstruction led to growth in output and per capita income beginning to rise significantly faster than all mature industrialized economies (except the former Federal Republic of Germany), first in Japan, and then in the four industrializing economies known to some as the Asian tigers: Hong Kong, South Korea, Singapore and Taiwan. Japan maintained an unprecedented 10 per cent annual GDP growth in 1955–73, while Singapore's economy grew on average each year in 1966–90 by a remarkable 8.5 per cent. South Korea, Hong Kong and Taiwan achieved similarly consistent high growth rates as shown in Figure 1.3.

This speed of expansion has drawn continuing attention from both scholars and policy-makers. Except in China, which was a closed economy until the late 1970s, the post-1949 geopolitical environment tended to favour Japan and its neighbouring economies. US policy supported Japan's rapid growth as a bulwark against Soviet expansionism (Das 2005), and Hong Kong, South Korea, Singapore and Taiwan also gained from both this stance and directly from US military consumption and supply needs. More conventionally, a growing and increasingly open US consumer market encouraged the development of labour-inten-sive, then resource-intensive, and finally capital-intensive export industries in Japan and elsewhere, many becoming successful in the global markets for manufactured goods.

Four policy aspects account for the expanded output of Japan and the other industrializing economies:

- Mobilizing foreign and domestic resources to support exporting sectors;
- Human capital development;
- Deferral of domestic consumption; and
- Limiting access to imports of finished goods.[3]

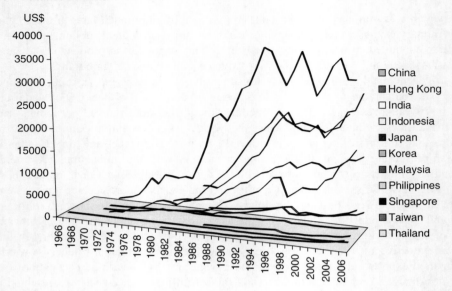

US$

Figure 1.3 Successive take-offs in growth (GDP per capita).
Source: CEIC (undated).

The employed share of Singapore's population rose from 27 to 51 per cent between 1966 and 1990. Educational standards also increased, leading to improved literacy, more workers with completed secondary education and the number of university graduates rising as a share of total population. Singapore's financial system channelled private sector savings effectively into fixed capital formation, in many cases at the state's direction, and fiscal incentives were provided for foreign direct investment (FDI) in export industries. Capital investment remained at 30–40 per cent of GDP throughout almost all of this industrializing period.

The region's success can be largely attributed to increases in measured factor inputs such as resources, physical capital and labour participation (Krugman 1994; Young 1995) but generally sound and consistent macroeconomic conditions helped in almost all cases, especially the pervasive adoption of export-led development, a benign and young demographic profile, and improving labour productivity through investment in human capital. This provided a model that other Asian economies came to emulate in the 1970s and thereafter. Malaysia, Thailand, the Philippines and Indonesia followed similar development paths: that is, an export orientation focused on foreign and domestic resource mobilization, consumption suppression and a degree of domestic protectionism, coupled with generally sound macroeconomic policies. These states also achieved impressive rates of growth after institutional reforms had been effected.

Until the late 1970s, China was a state-directed, centrally controlled, command economy similar to the Soviet bloc model of the 1950s. China could mobilize huge resources to develop traditional heavy manufacturing and chemical industries and achieved moderate success, but development was disrupted from time-to-time by political dislocation and central capriciousness, especially in relation to the agricultural sector. This poor performance was stark when compared to China's smaller neighbours, notably in terms of per capita income. Before the abrupt switch to reform policies in the late 1970s, per capita GDP was a fraction of that in Hong Kong or South Korea. Largely as a result of the failure of the Soviet model to support adequate development, China formally launched a reform and 'open door' policy in 1978, since when it has progressively and cautiously endorsed and adopted many components of the Asian development model, notably in allowing FDI and promoting exporting industries. The result is unique and profound. China had become, by 1990, an energetic part of a rapidly growing and globalizing region, and is now the main driver of regional and global growth.

Despite its representative political system, India was also influenced by the Soviet model and immediately upon independence in 1947 adopted centralized planning policies involving investment in heavy industry, protectionism and economic nationalism. This constrained output growth to a pejoratively termed 'Hindu rate' ceiling. Although India undertook limited reforms in the mid-1980s, it was only after an external payments crisis in the early 1990s that the limits of the long-standing policy model were acknowledged by national political leaders. Reform was essential, not least to allow India to compete with the obvious success of China, a strategic and commercial rival. India began deregulating many industry sectors and in the new millennium has become one of the fastest growing and most powerful economies in the region. Unusually early for a developing economy, India has also experienced notable service sector growth, especially in pharmaceuticals, systems design, high technology and consulting. Protectionism is still prevalent in manufacturing and India sustains more comprehensive outward capital controls than all other economies in the region. Finally, Vietnam was the last of the region's principal economies to adopt an export-led policy orientation, beginning economic reforms soon after restoring political ties with the United States. A take-off in manufacturing output and per capita income followed in 1995.

Thus the period from 1949 was one of rapid development for an increasing number of economies. Although Japan began a deflationary stagnation period in the 1990s, and the Asian and Russian financial crises of 1997–98 were profoundly disruptive across the region, growth returned soon after 1999, centred on China's manufacturing sector, for which most other economies now act as suppliers or subcontractors, and some (chiefly Hong Kong, Japan, Singapore, South Korea and Taiwan) have provided inputs of capital and technology.

Development has improved the lives and welfare of hundreds of millions of citizens and increasingly suggests that Asia is returning to economic-scale parity with the West (Morris 2010). It is less clear that Asia wishes to relinquish its strong export-orientation in the short term, so an uncertain co-dependence may prevail for the immediate future based on sustained external imbalances in trade, savings and capital flows. A growth rate similar to that of the past 25 years will allow China to overtake the United States as the world's largest economy during the 2020s, putting North America, the European Union (EU) and China in approximate economic equivalence. Measured by GDP at purchasing power parity (PPP), China now has the world's second largest domestic economy and will grow to exceed the United States within a decade. If India follows, then within a generation China, India, North America and the EU may be broadly equal in terms of gross income and output. Even though China and India will lag in terms of per capita GDP, the result will be a global economy very different to that of the last 200 years, resulting in a new geopolitics and patterns of consumption, finance, health and welfare that are new to many. At the very least, two of the world's three largest economies are now located in East Asia.

It is tempting to use such trend projections to forecast the future. However, our analysis will show that rapid development comes with costs. Growth in most Asian economies rests on relatively weak institutional and infrastructural foundations, forcing states to employ distorted policies so as to stimulate high levels of investment and labour participation, and maximize other factor inputs for growth. This inevitably leads to domestic and external imbalances and may ultimately be destabilizing. A sudden unwinding of these imbalances would risk triggering an unfavourable dynamic between the real economy and the financial sector in all too many cases.

The collapse of Japan's real estate bubble in the early 1990s and the shock of the regional financial crisis in 1997–98 demonstrate such a result, with major lasting disruption to output and employment, and severe social costs, even in a highly sophisticated setting. Those crises marked the end of the mythical ever-expanding Asian economy. Even with no such shocks, there are incalculable environmental costs to prolonged growth maximization that relies upon continually massing resource inputs. Growth may not be synonymous with improving quality of life.

1.3 Features of the development model

An expanding number of Asia's economies developed impressively after 1949, both collectively and (for the most part) individually. High growth-rates often seemed unstoppable. Figure 1.4 shows that average real GDP growth rates in 1980–2009 for China, India, Japan and our group of exporting economies were 9.89, 6.0, 1.98, and 5.47 per cent, respectively. These rates would have been still higher if the post-1997 recession is excluded.

This remarkable success has prompted two contrasting analyses. The first is that all is well – indeed, the true picture may be brighter than often realized and these favourable trends might continue indefinitely with only minor policy adjustments. Asia's economies are characterized as 'miracles', epitomizing the virtues of market-based, state-influenced, capitalism, although this capitalist system differs in many respects from that prevailing in developed states elsewhere. A relative openness to trade (especially in exporting), high domestic savings and investment, emphasis on human capital development, a disciplined productive workforce, comparatively cheap and plentiful labour, and development-oriented policies have all been cited as building blocks of the Asian development model. Believers in the miracle are committed to the view that the future lies with this beneficent template.

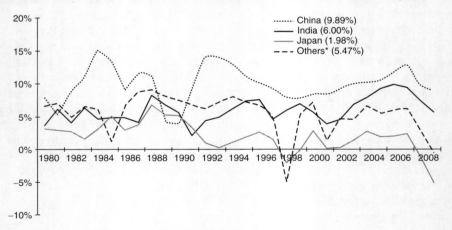

Figure 1.4 Real GDP growth, 1980–2009.

Note: Data in parenthesis indicate average real GDP growth rates. 'Others' are Hong Kong, Indonesia, South Korea, Malaysia, the Philippines, Singapore, Taiwan and Thailand. Vietnam is excluded.

Sources: IMF (undated c); authors' calculations.

The competing view is that Asia's rapid expansion was built on too weak and inefficient an institutional base. This might crumble suddenly – indeed, such a calamity may have occurred unrecognized in Japan in the early 1990s. Weaknesses such as underdeveloped financial sectors, poor corporate governance and narrow corporate ownership, incomplete legal systems and inconsistent judicial enforcement, and widespread cronyism or political corruption that erode the rule of law are continuing vulnerabilities. So also is active exchange-rate management as a deliberate or residual policy, by exaggerating transnational capital and trade imbalances. The 1997 Asian financial crisis was a sign of these systemic limitations.

Certain scholars argue further that a unique Asian model has no empirical support. Studies of total factor productivity (TFP, explained in Box 1.1) by Kim and Lau (1994) and Young (1995) show that growth was, for a long time, driven by commitments of inputs or factor accumulation, and was not due to improved efficiency, at least as measured by TFP. In this view the Asian development model differs little in concept from policies claimed as previously successful elsewhere, for example, in former Soviet or Warsaw Pact states. The true explanation of past growth is instead an extraordinary mobilization of resources, and a willingness to sacrifice current satisfaction for future gain (Krugman 1994) that by implication would not be feasible in most OECD (Organisation for Economic Co-operation and Development) states. Young was in turn attacked for using poor data, Krugman for selective

---

Box 1.1 Total Factor Productivity

Total factor productivity (TFP) is a concept used to measure productivity at disaggregate level (within a firm or industrial sector) or aggregate level (the economy as a whole). The most commonly used method to compute TFP starts with a neoclassical production function, which assume the following:

$$Y_{it} = F(K_{it}, L_{it}, M_{it}) \tag{1.1}$$

where Y_{it} refers to the output in year t for firm i or economy i; K_{it}, L_{it}, and M_{it} are capital input, labour input and the intermediate inputs respectively. Economists usually use the so-called Cobb–Douglas equation to capture the production function in an economy:

$$Y_{it} = A_{it} K_{it}^{\alpha} L_{it}^{\beta} M_{it}^{\gamma} \tag{1.2}$$

where A_{it} measures the contribution of technology, and the three parameters α, β, and γ respectively measure the relative importance of capital, labour and intermediate inputs. Based on equation (1.2), the total factor productivity for economic unit i in year t can be expressed as:

$$lnTFP_{it} = lnY_{it} - \alpha lnK_{it} - \beta lnL_{it} - \gamma lnM_i \tag{1.3}$$

Clearly, *TFP* measures the output components that cannot be accounted for by capital, labour and intermediate inputs. It is thus a good overall proxy for productivity. In practice, *TFP* can be estimated at the level of individuals firms, industrial sectors or sub-sectors, or within an entire national economy.

methodology, and a new alternative suggested reiterating that productivity growth had been important in most, but not all, of the miracle economies (Drysdale & Huang 1997).

Our view is more neutral. Rather than defend or dispute the Asian development model, we acknowledge the difficulty of grouping heterogeneous states under one analytical umbrella, however it is named. However, identifying the common features of post-1949 Asian economic successes is not outrageous:

- Systems were structured to support high rates of savings, including suppressed consumption and investment, both domestic and foreign.
- Export-led growth combined with early stage import protection.
- Surplus labour that evolved from unskilled to highly skilled.
- Sound, stable macroeconomic policies and benign external environments.
- Continuing improvements in productivity.

We will examine these factors in turn.

Investment

A prominent feature of real economies in the region is their customarily having kept investment at high rates so as to drive economic development. Sceptics such as Krugman or Young argue that Asian economic development was merely the application of voluminous inputs, especially in physical capital. Thanks to high savings rates that stem from a culture willing to forego current for future consumption, and with limited choice in financial intermediation available to savers, economies such as Japan, South Korea, Singapore and more recently China have mobilized physical, human and financial resources almost without limit to support development. In one sense, Krugman and Young are correct: the region's economic narrative has always centred on investment. Figure 1.5 shows that average savings rates in China, Japan, India and the exporting economies of Hong Kong, Indonesia, South Korea,

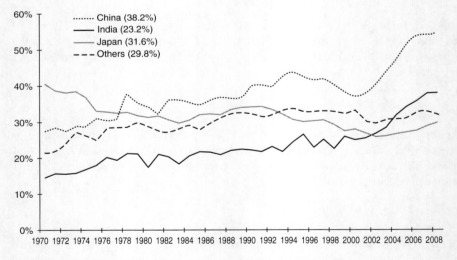

Figure 1.5 Gross national savings as a share of GDP, 1970–2008.

Note: Data in parenthesis indicate average national savings ratios.

Sources: CEIC (undated); authors' estimates.

Malaysia, the Philippines, Singapore, Taiwan and Thailand taken together for the period 1970–2008 were 38.2, 23.2, 31.6 and 29.8 per cent, respectively. India's observed savings rate is traditionally lower than elsewhere, partly from a propensity to hold precious metals, but is significantly higher than those prevailing in the United States and most of Europe. Most importantly, Figure 1.5 shows how savings ratios trended higher over an extended period.

High savings are associated with increased investment, although that investment may not necessarily be fully productive and may lead to overinvestment in specific assets or sectors, as with the real estate bubble created in the approach to the Asian regional crisis in 1997. Focusing on high rates of investment might be misleading in that it downplays the contribution of realized technological advancement. Productivity tends to increase with economic growth; Japan was the exemplar of this trend, which has been repeatedly observed in other parts of the region.

Nonetheless, the headline economic narrative most closely concerns investment at the expense of consumption. Fixed asset formation, especially spending on infrastructure and construction, has consistently driven overall growth. Figure 1.6 shows fixed asset investment as a share of GDP in 1980–2009 and demonstrates the significance of investment volumes. Although Japan's fixed asset investment as a share of GDP fell steadily over the period, it always exceeded 20 per cent, while Hong Kong, Indonesia, South Korea, the Philippines, Singapore, Taiwan and Thailand show fixed asset formation regularly in excess of 40 per cent of GDP.

China has maintained a spectacular investment rate since the early 1980s. The economy is volatile and susceptible to hazardous asset price-cycles, but fixed capital asset investment has remained at high levels and been a primary driver for economic growth. Investment as a share of GDP was higher than 40 per cent in the five years to 2009. India maintained relatively low levels of fixed asset formation until the early 1980s, but this has since increased following large-scale liberalization measures. In the past five years fixed asset investment has been greater than in most of the exporting economies and exceeded 30 per cent of GDP.

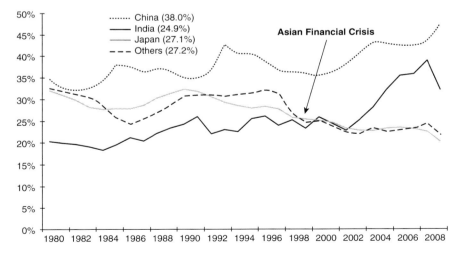

Figure 1.6 Investment as a share of GDP, 1980–2009.
Sources: World Bank (undated b); authors' calculations.

Any analysis dealing only with investment data is clearly incomplete, and proper account needs to be made of savings, consumption and the behaviour of consumers. Some observers claim that Asia might expect a consumer 'take-off' because of generally increasing affluence and lifestyle changes manifested in the propensity to consume (Cookson 2010). The basis of this suggestion is twofold, with middle-income groups growing as a share of total population, and the projection onto East Asia of spending habits of certain mature non-Asian economies. Domestic consumption would thus partially replace fixed asset investment and exports as a major future driver of the regional economy. Others dispute this view (Anderson 2006), and suggest that it represents an external 'non-Asian' analysis requiring the region to adopt non-traditional commercial and savings behaviour. This shift has largely failed to occur in Japan, as the region's first industrializing economy and developmental leader, and instead the most discernable transition has been an increase in contractual savings by consumers at the expense of saving by volition, a sign of greater choice and sophistication in financial intermediation that will gradually be followed elsewhere in the region. We incline to the view that:

- Significant changes in savings and consumption will require a long transition.
- Such changes cannot be forecast from past observations outside Asia.
- If such changes do occur, they will result partly from domestic institutional factors and financial development, including greater savings choices for consumers and companies.

Any profound changes in consumption patterns that did occur would have implications for the broad functioning of the main economies, but seem not to have begun, as Figure 1.7 shows. We see no obvious upward trend in consumption as a share of total national output. For Japan and the Asian export economies ('others' in Figure 1.7), consumption as a share of GDP was fairly stable in 1980–2008. Domestic demand has not yet broken above that long-standing trend, and any forecast take-off must therefore be speculative. The share of consumption in GDP declined steadily across this period in China and India, two fast-growing

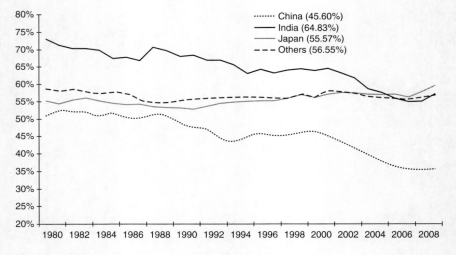

Figure 1.7 Private consumption as a share of GDP, 1980–2009.
Sources: CEIC (undated); authors' estimates.

economies now seen as engines of the global economy. This pattern is more pronounced for India where in the last 25 years the share of consumption in GDP decreased from 75 per cent to below 60 per cent. India's economy has many distinct features but, in common with East Asia, it saves and invests more than most.

Box 1.2 GDP Accounting

In an open economy, total output in any given time period is commonly measured by gross domestic product (GDP), consisting of four components:

$$GDP = C + I + G + X - IM \qquad (1.4)$$

where C is consumption (sometimes known as private consumption), I stands for investment (including domestic and foreign), G is government spending (or consumption), X is exports, and IM is import. Thus $X - IM$ is also called net exports or the trade balance. If exports exceed imports then the economy is in trade surplus for the period measured. If exports are smaller than imports, then a country is said to run a trade deficit. GDP takes no account of income derived from overseas investments or foreign-owned domestic assets, whether positive or negative in aggregate, which are included in measures of gross national product (GNP). States that are heavily invested overseas and receive sizeable flows of interest and dividends will show considerable differences between GDP and GNP.

One inference of Equation (1.4) is that GDP growth could be driven by any of its four main components: consumption, investment, export or government spending. In complex 'real' economies the components work together to drive GDP growth.

Two implications flow from this analysis. First, economic development continues to be driven above all by investment. Figure 1.6 demonstrates this point from a different angle, showing a drop in fixed asset formation after the region's 1997–98 financial crisis that exceeded 5 per cent among the exporting economies. This led to a malaise that negatively affected all of Asia except China and India for nearly a decade. Second, since investment is so vital to economic development, three important tests can be applied in considering the future of the main economies:

- Can fixed asset investment be sustained at high levels?
- How efficient is the resulting investment?
- What are the internal and external sources of funds for investment?

Export-led growth

Trade is consistently important to the region. Only Laos is not a member of the World Trade Organization (WTO) among the states and territories that we assess, as shown in Tables 1.1–1.13. Figure 1.8 shows the ratio of exports to GDP for 1980–2009 as an indication of the importance of the external sectors in our sample.

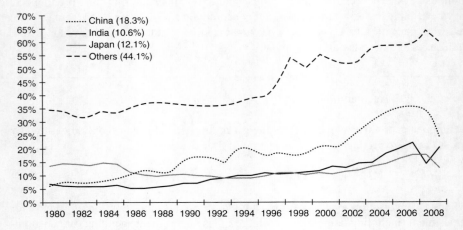

Figure 1.8 Exports as a share of GDP, 1980–2009.
Source: CEIC (undated); authors' calculations.

There is a clear upward trend in the ratio of exports to GDP in the smaller economies ('others' in Figure 1.8). Despite a slight decline in the ratio after the 1997–98 regional crisis, the contribution of exports gradually recovered and has exceeded its pre-crisis levels. Figures 1.9A–D show the trend in exports as a proportion of GDP in the group of other exporters – Japan, China and India – together with annual changes in exports in each case. Thus Figure 1.9A shows that with limited yearly exceptions, exports by the smaller group grew by more than 10 per cent year-by-year.

In its early stages of development, Japan relied heavily on export growth but later became sufficiently large that domestic spending evolved into a major contributor to GDP. Nonetheless Japan's export to GDP ratio of over 15 per cent suggests that the exposure of the economy to external factors over which it has little or no policy influence remains significant, similar to that of the United States but less than for most EU states, and so is sensitive to unforeseen exogenous changes in global markets. Figure 1.9B shows Japan's exports recovering before the global financial crisis, with year-on-year growth rising to 11.1 per cent in 2007. This propensity explains the catastrophic collapse of imports and exports across the region in 2009. Even though Asia was relatively unaffected by credit losses and the purely financial consequences of the global financial crisis, the shattering of confidence in its traditional export markets quickly led to output losses through the region's external sectors. Much of Asia effectively idled until the shock passed and stimulative monetary policy measures had been taken in the West and by China. A recovery began in 2010 but has been highly volatile in some cases – for example, quarterly changes in Singapore GDP since 2008 have included startling gains and losses.[4]

China and India are powerful, fast-expanding, domestic-oriented economies that were until recently largely insulated from the global cycle. An upward trend in exports as a share of GDP can now be seen in both cases in Figures 1.9C and 1.9D. Until the 1980s China was effectively closed to external commerce, but reforms led exports to grow rapidly. Since 1987 China has maintained year-on-year export growth of nearly 20 per cent other than in years when shocks occurred at home or overseas, notably 1989 (political instability), 1993 (credit restrictions), 1998–99 (regional crisis), 2001 (IT and telecom bubbles) and more recently in 2009 with the impact of global recession.

In terms of current shares of exports in GDP, China and India are not closely comparable to traditional exporters such as Hong Kong, Singapore or Taiwan, but resemble most EU states far more than Japan or the United States. China's total exports in 2008 were US$1,217 billion or 36 per cent of GDP. It is naïve to believe that the export sector is the only driver of China's development, but its importance is undeniable. India's exports have gradually increased after the stagnant 1980s and accounted for over 22 per cent of GDP in 2008. This may suggest that India has partly emulated East Asian traditional development strategy, perhaps influenced by China's performance. Figure 1.9D shows that year-on-year export growth has since 1990 risen above that of China.

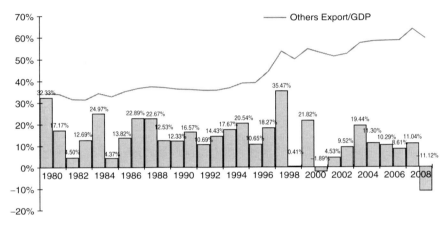

Figure 1.9A Changes in 'other' economies' exports.

Sources: CEIC (undated); authors' calculations.

Others in Figure 1.9A means Hong Kong, Indonesia, South Korea, Malaysia, the Philippines, Singapore, Taiwan and Thailand.

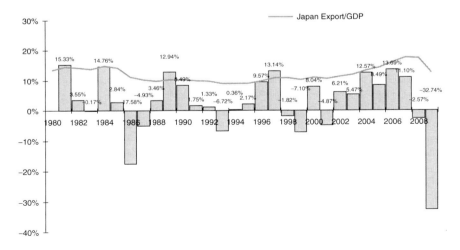

Figure 1.9B Changes in Japanese exports.

Sources: CEIC (undated); authors' calculations.

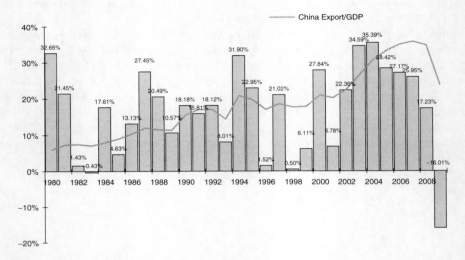

Figure 1.9C Changes in Chinese exports.
Source: CEIC (undated); authors' calculations.

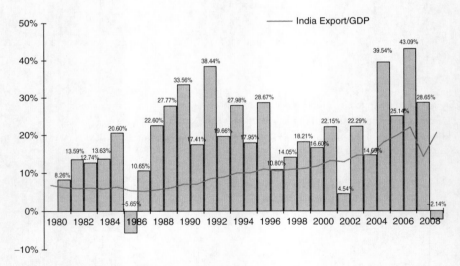

Figure 1.9D Changes in Indian exports.
Source: CEIC (undated); authors' calculations.

There are consequences to this narrative. We see that most Asian states adopt export-oriented policies, including Vietnam as the most recent example. In turn this may induce a similar approach by others, including Cambodia, Laos and the several states in South Asia whose developmental path has been disrupted by recurring political instability. The first policy steps in each case need not be state-expenditure intensive but rather associated with lowering trade and capital barriers. In these cases export-led growth will not only hinge upon OECD demand for goods but on increasing intra-regional trade and the effects of globalization on regionally integrated manufacturing, with the smaller emerging economies providing supply chain output for centres of assembly in China, Malaysia or Thailand.

The long-term implications of export-favouring policy are threefold. First, this emphasis leaves its practitioners vulnerable to exogenous shocks, in particular a historic sensitivity to events in the EU and United States. A recent example is the impact of the 2008 global financial crisis. While domestic conditions were relatively stable and benign (strong growth, generally low external debt, few fiscal deficits, and large capital exports to OECD states), the region's real economy was quickly and strikingly affected by the global crisis and the consequent collapse in Western consumption. Japan was less severely impacted due to the scale of its home economy; similar conditions may in future protect China or India.

Second, because Japan is Asia's second largest economy and importer, its recovery after a decade of stagnant growth and recurring deflation is potentially important for all regional suppliers. Japan's imports are relatively small but large in nominal terms. Furthermore, Japan's promotion of regional trade is important for stable future development. While China and India represent fast-growing economies, they are only now emerging as independent economic engines. Both are comparatively domestic in their overall orientation and China's trade data are swollen by the overwhelming bias of its export sector to a sophisticated assembly function. Over half of imports are applied to manufacturing, value-added processing and re-export, so that China's net purchases from smaller neighbouring suppliers exaggerates the headline trade data (Anderson 2006).

Third, an export orientation has contributed to an accumulation of foreign reserves since 2000, bringing unwanted political pressure from the EU and United States and greatly restricting the effectiveness of domestic monetary and exchange policy (see Sections 4.3 and 12.5). At the same time, high savings and investment, both domestic and foreign, may lead to problems in capital allocation, with the rising possibility of asset price inflation, as seen in Japan's burst bubble and the Asian financial crisis. This is compounded in some cases where impediments exist to prevent individual or corporate savings from leaving the domestic economy, as in China and India, or when individuals have little choice in intermediation but to deposit savings with local banks. It is ironic that states that so often abjure consumption today for future saving have yet to develop mature financial systems that can intermediate savings safely and efficiently. In effect, the region has a lack of investible opportunities, despite being well-resourced with savings and holding a long wish list of infrastructural needs.

Policy conservatism

Most Asian governments have exercised considerable caution since 1949 in designing their economic and financial structures and implementing fiscal, monetary and exchange rate policies. A stable macroeconomic and policy environment is imperative for effective investment and export-oriented growth strategies. Governments in emerging economies are often assumed to be highly active, both in controlling state enterprises and in spending heavily on education, infrastructure or defence. At the same time there are constraints on both tax revenues and the capital available for governments to mobilize through the domestic financial system. The stereotypical conclusion is that states are tempted into sustaining high noncyclical budget deficits, whether financed at home or from foreign borrowing. Whether because of caution or some form of domestic or external pressure, few of these policies have been adopted for sustained periods in Asia.

Asian governments have generally been unusually self-restrained spenders compared to other developing and emerging market economies. Figure 1.10 gives their central fiscal

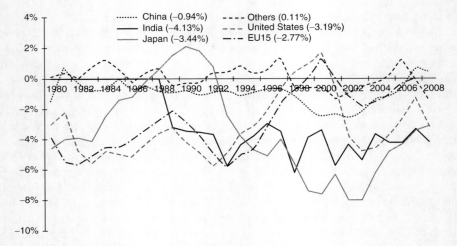

Figure 1.10 Fiscal balance as a share of GDP, 1980–2009.

Others means Hong Kong, Indonesia, South Korea, Malaysia, the Philippines, Taiwan and Thailand. Singapore is excluded since its fiscal balance was predominantly positive in the sample period. Data for India start at 1990.

Sources: CEIC (undated); authors' calculations.

balances and those of the EU and United States as shares of GDP, showing that deficits in Asia are generally below those of the United States and elsewhere. The roots of this outcome are as complex as the sources of growth that we examined in Section 1.1, but the characteristics are easily identified:

- Fiscal and economic systems that are either deliberately or by omission structured to mobilize high levels of savings.
- Central government policies which hitherto have not engaged in provisions for health, pensions and welfare that are more than basic, if they exist at all.

Even defence spending has been relatively modest in most states as a share of GDP.

Inflation has also been generally low, as Figure 1.11 shows. Price inflation has been held in single digits for most of the period since 1980. The average inflation rate for our group of exporting economies ('others' in Figure 1.11) measured by national consumer price indexes (CPI) is about 5.5 per cent. Although this is higher than that in the developed economies of the EU and United States, it is significantly lower than prevailing and historic rates in Latin America. Inflation rates systemically higher than OECD levels has a theoretical justification. Productivity in growing economies improves faster in the labour-intensive manufacturing and export sectors, which puts pressure on prices for agriculture, services and other industries as incomes rise. Average inflation in a growing economy should be high enough as to avoid deflation in sectors where productivity is rising most rapidly. This is the 'Balassa–Samuelson effect' and indicates that differentials in productivity growth are drivers of inflation (Balassa 1964; Samuelson 1964).

Taking into account the generally fast-growing and exporting nature of most Asian economies, inflation has to date generally kept within reasonable bounds and is comparable to that of most developed economies. This has provided a relatively stable macroeconomic and

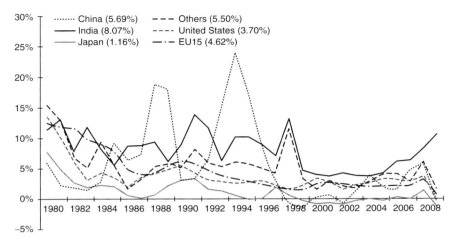

Figure 1.11 CPI comparisons, 1980–2009.

Parentheses contain data averages.

Sources: IMF (undated c); CEIC (undated); authors' estimates.

policy environment that is generally conducive to development. The exception to this overall stability was the 1997 regional crisis. Given a cultural concern for stability, it was unsurprising that subsequent policies indirectly boosted foreign reserve accumulation and controlled external debt levels to help guard against similar shocks, even if there were feasible policy alternatives associated with institutional reform.

Since the 1980s, managing exchange rates has been integral to macroeconomic policies. We discuss this stance by beginning with the features of the Asian growth model. Asia needed to expand rapidly into labour-intensive manufacturing so as to support general growth. Exports contributed significantly to Asia's economic growth, and since 1949 the developed Western countries have been the main destination for those exports. This gave a continuing incentive to sustained competitive exchange rates, producing a powerful mix of relatively low wages at home and cost-competitiveness in global markets. The strategy resulted in Asia's current account surpluses, especially after 2000, and corresponding current account deficits among the major export consumers in North America and Europe.

The net export proceeds accumulate in US dollars or euros as part of foreign exchange reserves, most notably in states such as China that maintain controls over foreign capital flows. This arrangement has frequently worked to Asia's advantage. As long as export growth subsists and developed economies choose to import goods and services, the trade imbalance need not be debilitating, and is matched by an equivalent ongoing capital surplus in favour of the importing economies. However, the strategy can be sustained globally only if confidence does not fail, as we saw after 2007. Imbalances linked to global trade and capital flows have been associated with fundamental problems in both emerging and developed economies, and resulted in a crisis of confidence that paralyzed the EU credit markets in 2010. In this case, it is immaterial whether the world's imbalances resulted from globalized manufacturing and aggressive exports, or excessive import consumption and credit growth.

Low-cost labour

East Asia's relatively young demographic profile (see Tables 1.2–1.13) has, in most cases since 1949, provided an abundant supply of low-cost labour to support national waves of industrialization. The region's share of global GDP is far less than its contribution to world population, especially if Japan's large high-income economy is excluded. Most states in our analysis are classified as middle or low income economies.[5]

A report by consultants McKinsey compares rates of pay for manufacturing workers in selected countries (Farrell, Puron & Remes 2005). Average compensation for manufacturing workers in 2003 in the United States, Canada and Mexico were US$21.3, US$18.0 and US$2.1 per hour, respectively, while in China, the Philippines and India the equivalent rates were all below US$1, at US$0.70, US$0.70 and US$0.40, respectively. Mexico's labour cost is three times that of China and almost five and a half times that of India, despite being seen in North America as a centre of low-cost production. Other South and Southeast Asian states have even lower cost structures and more sizeable populations. From the narrow view of demographics, the Asian model of development seems sustainable for the foreseeable future except in limited cases, with no cost constraints affecting the region as a whole, even if manufacturing resources begin to shift from one state to another or from high- to low-cost hubs within any single economy. A further constraint to growth through industrialization may arise from transnational migration by well-educated workers, most extensively from the Philippines and Indonesia.

We are not making a moral case for these apparently harsh circumstances, but relating the feasibility of the development model to available resources. The capacity of labour to sustain the model will ultimately depend on its human capital and levels of education, which links to future growth in productivity. Development economists have long described the exhaustion of inexpensive labour resources as provoking a turning point for policymakers: Can rapid growth be continued in a more mature open economy (Lewis 1954)? The experience of Japan in the 1930s and after 1949, when labour could no longer migrate from farming to industry, is an example of such a transformation through technological growth and increasing productivity, but it also relied on Japanese manufacturers outsourcing production to lower-cost facilities overseas. The same tactic became important in the 1980s for Hong Kong, South Korea, Singapore and Taiwan, the first economies to industrialize after Japan and then relocate production as a result of labour cost factors.

Educational attainment has improved over time, allowing some economies to gradually transform their focus from low-cost industries to the service or high value-added manufacturing sectors. In 2003 China had around 9.6 million professional graduates with up to seven years' work experience and an additional 97 million people who could qualify for support-staff jobs. China has about 1.6 million young engineers, and one third of university students in China study engineering compared to 20 per cent in Germany. Based on numbers alone the talent pool is vast. Since income disparities are large across the region, a familiar series of economic events has been repeatedly observed, with all economies beginning expansion in simple, labour-intensive industry and over time increasing skills and capabilities to compete in more profitable areas of the value chain, including marketing, research and development, product design and logistics.

Productivity

We saw at the start of Section 1.3 that productivity is arguably the most controversial factor in Asia's modern development. For some years the accepted view was that productivity growth had been extraordinarily high, especially in the manufacturing sectors of the first post-1949 industrializing states. In a comparative study of labour productivity, Lewis (2004) reports that Japan had distinct parts, those sectors where labour productivity was significantly lower than in the United States – for example, retail, housing construction and food processing – and others such as steel, automotive parts, metalworking, car manufacturing and consumer electronics with markedly higher labour productivity. The sectors in which Japan boasts higher productivity are also those in which Japan has a competitive edge over the United States, indicating that improvements in productivity are significant for development.

Some Asian economies clearly achieved that goal, although it would be incorrect to regard productivity as a form of permanent accumulated capital. What accounts for such gains in productivity, and what might lead to a secular drop in productivity from a previously high level? Many factors have been identified in empirical studies or suggested in theoretical research. They include:

- A benign fiscal and macroeconomic environment;
- A commitment to education;
- Reasonable and stable input factor prices;
- Appropriate levels and distribution of income;
- Clear employment laws and effective rules for union participation;
- The availability of skilled workers;
- Effective incentive mechanisms and culture;
- Regulation over product competition and restrictive practices;
- Trade barriers; and
- Industry specific capital intensity and operational efficiency.[6]

Educational attainment is particularly important. Young (1995) analyzes the education background of the working population in four economies in 1966 and 1991 (Table 1.1), an interval marking a period of high growth, and shows that education attainment levels also improved significantly in that 25 year phase. In South Korea, for example, the percentage of the working population with no education dropped from 31 to 6.4 per cent, while about 75 per cent had at least completed secondary schooling. Such human capital accumulation directly accounts for part of labour productivity gains.

Sceptics of the World Bank's 'miracle' believe improvements in productivity have been misperceived. Young (1995) purports to demonstrate a striking finding buried in official data: that while the growth of output and manufacturing exports in Hong Kong, South Korea, Singapore and Taiwan was unprecedented, it was not accompanied by unusual growth in total factor productivity. Over the period 1966–91, productivity growth in the aggregate

Table 1.1 Educational attainment of the working population (%)

	Hong Kong		Singapore		South Korea		Taiwan	
	1966	*1991*	*1966*	*1991*	*1966*	*1991*	*1966*	*1991*
None	19.2	5.6	55.1	Nil	31.1	6.4	17.0	4.5
Primary	53.6	22.9	28.2	33.7	42.4	18.5	57.2	28.0
Secondary	27.2	71.4	15.8	66.3	26.5	75.0	25.8	67.6

Self-taught is included in sub-primary standard. The data excluded the share of the population whose educational attainment is unknown.
Source: Young (1995).

non-agricultural economy of these newly industrializing economies ranged from 0.2 per cent in Singapore to 2.3 per cent in Hong Kong. This is unimpressive by comparison to the United Kingdom, France or Italy, all of which displayed comparable productivity growth in the same period. Young (2003) recently applied a similar analysis to China and claimed that its development model was no different to that of its predecessor industrializers. Asia's productivity measured by total factor productivity is unspectacular.

The debate is ongoing. Scholars such as Hotz (2005) point to Young's reliance on problematic databases, and a consensus as to both method and outcome is lacking. The only safe conclusion may be that productivity matters considerably in terms of the sustainability of Asian economic development, and would thus be one of its most fundamental drivers in the future.

1.4 Asia's economy today

More than a decade since the regional crisis, doubts about Asian development linger, both in the West and in East Asian capitals and colleges. They appear sporadically in a hesitant regional politics, in the marshalling of state resources to invest massively outside the region, and in the protracted response to the 1997 crisis, with institutional reforms of all kinds taking many years to cement. Have banks and regulators made progress sufficient to prevent another home-grown crisis? With China and India becoming engines of development, can regional growth support the long-term fortunes of the world economy? Is the Asian development model real or fiction, or a phenomenon of a certain period? What improvements should be made to overcome the boom-and-bust cycles inherent in Asian economies? Questions such as these are probably inexhaustible.

Asia lags Europe and North America in aggregate economic scale (see Figure 1.12), and the level of development is uneven within the region. Japan and China together dominate East Asian output. While per capita gross national income (GNI) in Japan and Singapore in 2009 was close to the global average for high-income economies, the remaining states include several where income on the same basis is US$1,000 or less. Media and investor attention generally focuses on only a dozen economies, all but India located in East and Southeast Asia. Tables 1.2–1.13 summarize the true state of these core economies, covering economic, socio-economic and financial indicators.

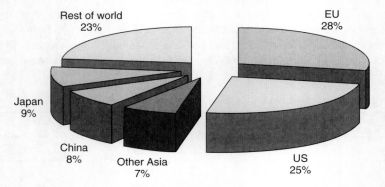

Figure 1.12 Asia in the world economy, 2009.
Global GDP 2009 = US$58 trillion.
Sources: IMF (undated c); authors' estimates.

What lessons can be drawn from the success narratives presented in this chapter? Do they relate only to a narrow mercantilist view of economic development as being strongly associated with growth? In addition to preferences for growth and social stability, the high income and industrializing economies in our review have been characterized by a common approach to development coloured by a strong pragmatism. That approach may soon begin to influence a consensus in development policies elsewhere as a direct result of Asia's experience, especially with China becoming highly influential as a strategic trading partner and FDI supplier in Africa and Latin America. The Growth Report cited in our introductory paragraphs (Commission on Growth and Development 2008) gave five persistent factors as common to the group of 13 economies that it examined, which we will expand upon here:

- All were characterized by a successful leveraging of the global economy for lengthy periods. These economies were open to trade and capital flows; they imported knowledge through education and FDI. At the same time they exploited global demand, adopting an export promotion rather than import substitution approach to trade. Effective policies became gradually embedded in appropriate national institutions.
- Second, policies and institutions tended to support macroeconomic stability, especially in modest inflation and sustainable public finances.
- Third, development was given a forward-looking orientation, with growth sustained through relatively high rates of savings and investment rather than a reliance on external finance. Savings and investment were encouraged through institutional incentives and policies in which the state was directly or indirectly involved.
- Fourth, reflecting a twentieth century battle of ideas between market economics and command models, national economies were organized largely but not wholly through a market allocation of resources. Land use, industrial finance and export sector credit were the most frequent exceptions. In most cases the price mechanism was allowed to guide resource allocation rather than state discretion, even in the frequent cases where central planning was an accepted policy tool.
- The fifth, and most significant, factor was committed, credible and capable leadership and governance, that was seen to adopt a pragmatic approach to policy formation and practice over a long-term time horizon. States made commitments to growth, employment inclusion and capable administration, which often had a specific nationalist taint but was widely understood and accepted, both at large and by professional elites.

The overall picture is of a pragmatic state, working to support balanced market economic development, implementing policies through institutional reform. This may have entailed deficits in representative democracy, but this is a topic for a separate discussion. Let us make two points from outside our brief. First, Asia's period of heightened growth has generally coincided with a gradual move towards greater political or economic freedom across the region. Second, political and economic freedom have been found empirically to be generally associated with high levels of economic development. These two points refer back to our discussion of the importance of institutions to development. In this context, Japan's prolonged phase of slow growth and incipient deflation may be rooted in matters of political structure that are not strictly financial or a product of the domestic financial system, but are easily associated with the effectiveness of national institutions.

Beyond these high-level factors, the Commission on Growth and Development (2008) cited technical policies thought to encourage growth. These include measures embedded in appropriate institutional frameworks that favour resource accumulation, especially in technology and human capital, and in innovation through technological growth and transfer, competition and structural reform.

1.5 Conclusions and questions

What is special about Asia? In this chapter we have presented an overview of economic history and analyzed the commonalities of successful economic narratives. We identify five factors that largely account for these outcomes:

- High savings rates that result in high levels of investment;
- Export-led growth strategies;
- Generally disciplined fiscal, monetary and exchange rate policies;
- Abundant low-cost labour; and
- Continuing gains in productivity.

Most of the five factors are associated with finance, the subject of the remainder of our book and which begins in the next chapter with a discussion of the links between finance and development. The narrative can be controversial and is not always one with a positive short-term outcome, as we know from at least one recent crisis.

Table 1.2 China, end-2009

Macroeconomics	
GDP ($ billion)	4,814
GDP per capita ($)	3,615
PPP GDP per capita ($)	6,600
Exports ($bn/% of GDP)	1,194/25
Imports ($bn/% of GDP)	922/19
FDI inflow ($bn/% of GDP)*	108/2.2
FDI outflow ($bn/% of GDP)*	52/1.1
Foreign currency reserves ($bn/% of GDP)	2,399/50
External debts ($bn/% of GDP)	347/7
Investment ($bn/% of GDP)	2,287/48
Top 3 trading partners	EU, US, Japan
Number of firms in Global Top 500	37
GATT/WTO accession date	11 Dec. 2001
Socio-economics	
Population (million)	1,335
Number of households (million)	480
Mobile phones per 100 people*	53
Internet subscribers per 100 people	29
Literacy rate (%, aged over 15, 2002)	90.9
Gini Index*	45
% of population above 65 years old	8.6
Capital markets & banking	
Number of listed firms	1,718
Equity market capitalization ($bn/% of GDP)	3,573/74
Trading volume ($bn/% of market cap)	7,836/219
Life insurance premium volume/GDP (%)*	2.3
Non-life insurance premium volume/GDP (%)*	1.1
Private bond market capitalization/GDP (%)*	16.5

Table 1.2 (Continued)

Capital markets & banking

Public bond market capitalization/GDP (%)*	32.3
Private credit by deposit money banks and other financial intermediaries/GDP (%)**	135.3
Financial system deposits/GDP (%)**	164.8
Financial derivatives traded on exchanges	Yes
Ratio of non-performing loans (%)*	2.4
Number of ATMs per 100,000 people**	3.8
Number of bank branches per 100,000 people**	1.3

Table 1.3 Hong Kong, end-2009

Macroeconomics

GDP ($billion)	211
GDP per capita ($)	29,910
PPP GDP per capita ($)	42,700
Exports ($bn/% of GDP)	317/150
Imports ($bn/% of GDP)	345/164
FDI inflow ($bn/% of GDP)*	63/30
FDI outflow ($bn/% of GDP)*	59/28
Foreign currency reserves ($bn/% of GDP)	257/122
External debts ($bn/% of GDP)	655/310
Investment ($bn/% of GDP)	38/18
Top 3 trading partners	China, EU, USA
Number of firms in Global Top 500	3
GATT/WTO accession date	23 Apr. 1986

Socio-economics

Population (million)	7.0
Number of households (million)*	2.5
Mobile phones per 100 people*	152
Internet subscribers per 100 people*	75
Literacy rate (%, 2002)	93.5
Gini Index (2007)	53.3
% of population above 65 years old	13.3

Capital markets & banking

Number of listed firms	1,319
Equity market capitalization ($bn/% of GDP)	2,305/1092
Trading volume ($bn/% of market cap)	1,502/65
Life insurance premium volume/GDP (%)*	12.3
Non-life insurance premium volume/GDP (%)*	1.1
Private bond market capitalization/GDP (%)*	14.9
Public bond market capitalization/GDP (%)*	8.3
Private credit by deposit money banks and other financial intermediaries/GDP (%)*	126.5
Financial system deposits/GDP (%)*	285.2
Financial derivatives traded on exchanges	Yes
Ratio of non-performing loans (%)*	0.9
Number of ATMs per 100,000 people**	NA
Number of bank branches per 100,000 people**	NA

Table 1.4 India, end-2009

Macroeconomics

GDP ($billion)	1,095
GDP per capita ($)	934
PPP GDP per capita ($)	3,100
Exports ($bn/% of GDP)	165/15
Imports ($bn/% of GDP)	254/23
FDI inflow ($bn/% of GDP)*	42/3.8
FDI outflow ($bn/% of GDP)*	18/1.6
Foreign currency reserves ($bn/% of GDP)	288/26
External debts ($bn/% of GDP)	224/20
Investment ($bn/% of GDP)	350/32
Top 3 trading partners	EU, China, US
Number of firms in Global Top 500	7
GATT/WTO accession date	1 Jan. 1995

Socio-economics

Population (million)	1,173
Number of households (million)	NA
Mobile phones per 100 people	46
Internet subscribers per 100 people*	6.9
Literacy rate (%)	61
Gini Index**	36.8
% of population above 65 years old	5.3

Capital markets & banking

Number of listed firms	6,408
Equity market capitalization ($bn/% of GDP)	2,531/231
Trading volume ($bn/% of market cap)	1,050/41
Life insurance premium volume/GDP (%)*	3.9
Non-life insurance premium volume/GDP (%)*	0.6
Private bond market capitalization/GDP (%)*	4.0
Public bond market capitalization/GDP (%)*	30.3
Private credit by deposit money banks and other financial intermediaries/GDP (%)*	47.9
Financial system deposits/GDP (%)*	63.3
Financial derivatives traded on exchanges	Yes
Ratio of non-performing loans (%)*	2.3
Number of ATMs per 100,000 people**	NA
Number of bank branches per 100,000 people**	6.3

Table 1.5 Indonesia, end-2009

Macroeconomics

GDP ($billion)	521
GDP per capita ($)	2,150
PPP GDP per capita ($)	4,000
Exports ($bn/% of GDP)	116/22
Imports ($bn/% of GDP)	87/17
FDI inflow ($bn/% of GDP)*	8/1.5
FDI outflow ($bn/% of GDP)*	6/1.2
Foreign currency reserves ($bn/% of GDP)	63/12

Table 1.5 (Continued)

Macroeconomics

External debts ($bn/% of GDP)	151/29
Investment ($bn/% of GDP)	141/27
Top 3 trading partners	Japan, Singapore, EU
Number of firms in Global Top 500	0
GATT/WTO accession date	1 Jan. 1995

Socio-economics

Population (million)	243
Number of households (million)*	62
Mobile phones per 100 people	57.9
Internet subscribers per 100 people	12.3
Literacy rate (%)**	90.4
Gini Index (2005)	39.4
% of population above 65 years old	6.1

Capital markets & banking

Number of listed firms	398
Equity market capitalization ($bn/% of GDP)	215/41
Trading volume ($bn/% of market cap)	94/44
Life insurance premium volume/GDP (%)*	1.6
Non-life insurance premium volume/GDP (%)*	0.5
Private bond market capitalization/GDP (%)*	2.0
Public bond market capitalization/GDP (%)*	18.0
Private credit by deposit money banks and other financial intermediaries/ GDP (%)*	22.8
Financial system deposits/GDP (%)*	33.6
Financial derivatives traded on exchanges	Yes
Ratio of non-performing loans (%)*	3.2
Number of ATMs per 100,000 people**	4.8
Number of bank branches per 100,000 people**	8.4

Table 1.6 Japan, end-2009

Macroeconomics

GDP ($billion)	5,108
GDP per capita ($)	40,250
PPP GDP per capita ($)	32,600
Exports ($bn/% of GDP)	516/10
Imports ($bn/% of GDP)	491/10
FDI inflow ($bn/% of GDP)*	24/0.5
FDI outflow ($bn/% of GDP)*	128/2.5
Foreign currency reserves ($bn/% of GDP)	1,049/21
External debts ($bn/% of GDP)	2,132/42
Investment ($bn/% of GDP)	1,032/20
Top 3 trading partners	China, US, EU
Number of firms in Global Top 500	68
GATT/WTO accession date	10 Sep. 1955

(*continued*)

Table 1.6 (Continued)

Socio-economics	
Population (million)	127
Number of households (million)	NA
Literacy rate (%, 2002)	99
Gini Index (2002)	38.1
% of population above 65 years old	22.6

Capital markets & banking	
Number of listed firms	3,656
Equity market capitalization ($bn/% of GDP)	3,534/69
Trading volume ($bn/% of market cap)	4,162/118
Life insurance premium volume/GDP (%)*	6.8
Non-life insurance premium volume/GDP (%)*	2.1
Private bond market capitalization/GDP (%)*	37.9
Public bond market capitalization/GDP (%)*	165.7
Private credit by deposit money banks and other financial intermediaries/GDP (%)*	94.9
Financial system deposits/GDP (%)*	182.7
Financial derivatives traded on exchanges	Yes
Ratio of non-performing loans (%)*	1.7
Number of ATMs per 100,000 people**	113.7
Number of bank branches per 100,000 people**	10.0

Table 1.7 South Korea, end-2009

Macroeconomics	
GDP ($billion)	810
GDP per capita ($)	16,800
PPP GDP per capita ($)	28,000
Exports ($bn/% of GDP)	355/44
Imports ($bn/% of GDP)	313/39
FDI inflow ($bn/% of GDP)*	8/0.1
FDI outflow ($bn/% of GDP)*	13/1.6
Foreign currency reserves ($bn/% of GDP)	246/30
External debts ($bn/% of GDP)	334/41
Investment ($bn/% of GDP)	228/28
Top 3 trading partners	China, EU, Japan
Number of firms in Global Top 500	14
GATT/WTO accession date	14 Apr. 1967

Socio-economics	
Population (million)	49
Number of households (million)*	19
Mobile phones per 100 people	94.3
Internet subscribers per 100 people (2006)	77.1
Literacy rate (%, 2002)	97.9
Gini Index (2007)	31.3
% of population above 65 years old	11.1

Table 1.7 (Continued)

Capital markets & banking

Number of listed firms	1,788
Equity market capitalization ($bn/% of GDP)	835/103
Trading volume ($bn/% of market cap)	1,559/187
Life insurance premium volume/GDP (%)*	8.7
Non-life insurance premium volume/GDP (%)*	4.2
Private bond market capitalization/GDP (%)*	64.0
Public bond market capitalization/GDP (%)*	48.2
Private credit by deposit money banks and other financial intermediaries/GDP (%)*	89.8
Financial system deposits/GDP (%)*	55.8
Financial derivatives traded on exchanges	Yes
Ratio of non-performing loans (%)*	1.1
Number of ATMs per 100,000 people**	90.0
Number of bank branches per 100,000 people**	13.4

Table 1.8 Malaysia, end-2009

Macroeconomics

GDP ($billion)	210
GDP per capita ($)	8,150
PPP GDP per capita ($)	14,800
Exports ($bn/% of GDP)	156/74
Imports ($bn/% of GDP)	120/57
FDI inflow ($bn/% of GDP)*	8/3.8
FDI outflow ($bn/% of GDP)*	14/6.7
Foreign currency reserves ($bn/% of GDP)	98/47
External debts ($bn/% of GDP)	48/23
Investment ($bn/% of GDP)	38/18
Top 3 trading partners	US, Singapore, EU
Number of firms in Global Top 500	1
GATT/WTO accession date	24 Oct. 1957

Socio-economics

Population (million)	26
Number of households (million)	NA
Mobile phones per 100 people	104
Internet subscribers per 100 people	65
Literacy rate (%, 2002)	88.7
Gini Index (2002)	46.1
% of population above 65 years old	5.1

Capital markets & banking

Number of listed firms	959
Equity market capitalization ($bn/% of GDP)	286/136
Trading volume ($bn/% of market cap)	86/30
Life insurance premium volume/GDP (%)*	3.4
Non-life insurance premium volume/GDP (%)*	1.6
Private bond market capitalization/GDP (%)*	57.5
Public bond market capitalization/GDP (%)*	35.9
Private credit by deposit money banks and other financial intermediaries/ GDP (%)*	96.4

(*continued*)

Table 1.8 (Continued)

Capital markets & banking	
Financial system deposits/GDP (%)*	109.4
Financial derivatives traded on exchanges	Yes
Ratio of non-performing loans (%)*	4.8
Number of ATMs per 100,000 people**	16.4
Number of bank branches per 100,000 people**	9.8

Table 1.9 Philippines, end-2009

Macroeconomics	
GDP ($billion)	161
GDP per capita ($)	1,630
PPP GDP per capita ($)	3,300
Exports ($bn/% of GDP)	37/23
Imports ($bn/% of GDP)	46/29
FDI inflow ($bn/% of GDP)*	2/1.2
FDI outflow ($bn/% of GDP)*	0.2/0.1
Foreign currency reserves ($bn/% of GDP)	44/27
External debts ($bn/% of GDP)	53/33
Investment ($bn/% of GDP)	23/14
Top 3 trading partners	US, Japan, China
Number of firms in Global Top 500	0
GATT/WTO accession date	27 Dec. 1979

Socio-economics	
Population (million)	100
Number of households (million)	NA
Mobile phones per 100 people (2006)	68.1
Internet subscribers per 100 people*	14.1
Literacy rate (%, 2002)	92.6
Gini Index (2006)	45.8
% of population above 65 years old	4.2

Capital markets & banking	
Number of listed firms	248
Equity market capitalization ($bn/% of GDP)	86/53
Trading volume ($bn/% of market cap)	21/24
Life insurance premium volume/GDP (%)*	0.9
Non-life insurance premium volume/GDP (%)*	0.5
Private bond market capitalization/GDP (%)*	1.1
Public bond market capitalization/GDP (%)*	31.2
Private credit by deposit money banks and other financial intermediaries/ GDP (%)*	27.1
Financial system deposits/GDP (%)*	51.0
Financial derivatives traded on exchanges	Yes
Ratio of non-performing loans (%)*	4.5
Number of ATMs per 100,000 people**	5.3
Number of bank branches per 100,000 people**	7.8

Table 1.10 Singapore, end-2009

Macroeconomics

GDP ($billion)	165
GDP per capita ($)	35,212
PPP GDP per capita ($)	50,300
Exports ($bn/% of GDP)	269/163
Imports ($bn/% of GDP)	245/148
FDI inflow ($bn/% of GDP)*	23/14
FDI outflow ($bn/% of GDP)*	9/5.5
Foreign currency reserves ($bn/% of GDP)	188/114
External debts ($bn/% of GDP)	19/12
Investment ($bn/% of GDP)	49/30
Top 3 trading partners	EU, Malaysia, China
Number of firms in Global Top 500	2
GATT/WTO accession date	20 Aug. 1973

Socio-economics

Population (million)	4.7
Number of households (million)	NA
Mobile phones per 100 people	136
Internet subscribers per 100 people (2006)	72.3
Literacy rate (%, 2002)	92.5
Gini Index (2008)*	48.1
% of population above 65 years old	9

Capital markets & banking

Number of listed firms	773
Equity market capitalization ($bn/% of GDP)	481/292
Trading volume ($bn/% of market cap)	245/51
Life insurance premium volume/GDP (%)*	7.5
Non-life insurance premium volume/GDP (%)*	2.5
Private bond market capitalization/GDP (%)*	14.9
Public bond market capitalization/GDP (%)*	39.3
Private credit by deposit money banks andother financial intermediaries/ GDP (%)*	90.9
Financial system deposits/GDP (%)*	115.9
Financial derivatives traded on exchanges	Yes
Ratio of non-performing loans (%)*	1.4
Number of ATMs per 100,000 people**	37.9
Number of bank branches per 100,000 people**	9.1

Table 1.11 Taiwan, end-2009

Macroeconomics

GDP ($billion)	362
GDP per capita ($)	15,010
PPP GDP per capita ($)	29,800
Exports ($bn/% of GDP)	204/56
Imports ($bn/% of GDP)	175/48
FDI inflow ($bn/% of GDP)*	5/1.4
FDI outflow ($bn/% of GDP)*	10/2.8
Foreign currency reserves ($bn/% of GDP)	352/97

(*continued*)

Table 1.11 (Continued)

___

Macroeconomics

External debts ($bn/% of GDP)	80/22
Investment ($bn/% of GDP)	68/19
Top 3 trading partners	China, Japan, US
Number of firms in Global Top 500	6
GATT/WTO accession date (Chinese Taipei)	1 Jan. 2002

Socio-economics

Population (million)	23
Number of households (million)	NA
Mobile phones per 100 people	110
Internet subscribers/100 people*	68.2
Literacy rate (%, 2003)	96.1
Gini Index (2006)	NA
% of population above 65 years old	10.8

Capital markets & banking

Number of listed firms	755
Equity market capitalization ($bn/% of GDP)	658/182
Trading volume ($bn/% of market cap)	905/138
Life insurance premium volume/GDP (%)*	15.2
Non-life insurance premium volume/GDP (%)*	2.7
Private bond market capitalization/GDP (%)*	22.4
Public bond market capitalization/GDP (%)*	28.4
Private credit by deposit money banks and other financial intermediaries/ GDP (%)*	NA
Financial system deposits/GDP (%)*	NA
Financial derivatives traded on exchanges	Yes
Ratio of non-performing loans (%)	NA
Number of ATMs per 100,000 people**	NA
Number of bank branches per 100,000 people**	NA

___

Table 1.12 Thailand, end-2009

___

Macroeconomics

GDP ($billion)	270
GDP per capita ($)	4,054
PPP GDP per capita ($)	8,100
Exports ($bn/% of GDP)	151/56
Imports ($bn/% of GDP)	132/49
FDI inflow ($bn/% of GDP)*	10/3.7
FDI outflow ($bn/% of GDP)*	3/1.1
Foreign currency reserves ($bn/% of GDP)	138/51
External debts ($bn/% of GDP)	66/24
Investment ($bn/% of GDP)	57/21
Top 3 trading partners	Japan, EU, US
Number of firms in Global Top 500	1
GATT/WTO accession date	20 Nov. 1982

Socio-economics

Population (million)	66
Number of households (million)	22
Mobile phones per 100 people	93.9

Table 1.12 (Continued)

Socio-economics

Internet subscribers per 100 people (2006)	24.4
Literacy rate (%, 2002)	92.6
Gini Index (2006)	43
% of population above 65 years old	9

Capital markets & banking

Number of listed firms	535
Equity market capitalization ($bn/% of GDP)	177/66
Trading volume ($bn/% of market cap)	126/71
Life insurance premium volume/GDP (%)*	1.8
Non-life insurance premium volume/GDP (%)*	1.5
Private bond market capitalization/GDP (%)*	17.0
Public bond market capitalization/GDP (%)*	40.0
Private credit by deposit money banks and other financial intermediaries/GDP (%)*	77.9
Financial system deposits/GDP (%)*	84.5
Financial derivatives traded on exchanges	Yes
Ratio of non-performing loans (%)*	5.7
Number of ATMs per 100,000 people**	17.0
Number of bank branches per 100,000 people**	7.2

Table 1.13 Vietnam, end-2009

Macroeconomics

GDP ($billion)	93
GDP per capita ($)	1,040
PPP GDP per capita ($)	2,900
Exports ($bn/% of GDP)	57/61
Imports ($bn/% of GDP)	69/74
FDI inflow ($bn/% of GDP) *	8/8.6
FDI outflow ($bn/% of GDP) *	0.1/0.1
Foreign currency reserves ($bn/% of GDP)	15/16
External debts ($bn/% of GDP)	31/33
Investment ($bn/% of GDP)	40/43
Top 3 trading partners	China, Japan, US
Number of firms in Global Top 500	0
GATT/WTO accession date	7 Nov. 2006

Socio-economics

Population (million)	90
Number of households (million)	NA
Mobile phones per 100 people	78.1
Internet subscribers per 100 people (2006)	23.2
Literacy rate (%, 2002)	90.3
Gini Index**	37
% of population above 65 years old	5.5

Capital markets & banking

Number of listed firms	304
Equity market capitalization ($bn/% of GDP)	33/36
Trading volume ($bn/% of market cap)	24/73
Life insurance premium volume/GDP (%)*	0.7

(continued)

Table 1.13 (Continued)

Capital markets & banking	
Non-life insurance premium volume/GDP (%)*	0.6
Private bond market capitalization/GDP (%)*	NA
Public bond market capitalization/GDP (%)*	NA
Private credit by deposit money banks and other financial intermediaries/GDP (%)*	90.6
Financial system deposits/GDP (%)*	73.5
Financial derivatives traded on exchanges	Yes
Ratio of non-performing loans (%)	NA
Number of ATMs per 100,000 people	NA
Number of bank branches per 100,000 people	NA

All tables. * 2008 data; ** 2004 data.
Sources: All tables: CEIC; CIA (2010); IMF; World Bank, Fortune; World Bank; authors' calculations.

2 Finance in Asia

One important test of a scientific claim is whether it can be disproven, something that can happen long after a theory in chemistry or physics has been accepted as truth (Popper 1959). The world of science thought for centuries that Newtonian physics contained universal truths, only to be shown their incompleteness by Einstein in the early twentieth century. We enjoy the study of finance enough to regard it as art and experimentation, so perhaps the maxim of disproof cannot be strictly applied here, but there is a paradox about finance and its place in the modern world that is almost as striking as Popperian logic. Two statements make it clear:

- *Finance matters.* This is shorthand for contemporary thinking about finance and generally reflects the approach of this book.
- *Financial activity is not a focus of scholarly work.* This reflects academic thinking until the late twentieth century.

Each statement is largely true *of its time*. Our characterization is not precisely like Einstein's refutation of Newton, for the reality is that the functioning and nature of financial systems in economic development was largely ignored by academics until the 1960s and only widely studied in the last three decades. In Chapter 3, we return to address important questions raised in this chapter and to reflect on the future and value of finance.

Whatever their importance in history, factors identified as supporting economic development have received increasing attention since the early 1990s and especially following the 1997–98 Asian financial crisis. Financial sector development has been highlighted by both writers and policymakers in Asia and around the world. We begin this chapter with a discussion of financial development and economic growth, suggesting that there is a consensus as to the importance of financial development in economic growth and general welfare. It then discusses finance in Asian economic development and the Asian developmental model, before turning to the regional financial crisis. This shock fundamentally challenged the organization of the region's finance of the previous 40 years. We then begin a narrative of the results of that crisis for financial and monetary reform. This continues in Chapter 3 and at intervals throughout the book. Last, we review the onset and results of the 2007–9 global financial crisis, a profound and severe disruption that challenged not only the role of banking and extent of financial activity and leverage in the global economy, but also the consequences of Asia's focus on export-led growth.

2.1 Finance and development

Whether financial development is crucial for economic growth began as a small controversy but has been hotly debated in more recent times. The question can be better understood by focusing on three related aspects:

- Is there a correlation between financial development and economic development?
- Does causation exist in any such relation between financial development and economic growth?
- In addition to the level of financial development, does the structure of the financial system matter?

By the level of financial development we mean the relative scale of financial assets in any economy, a factor that can be defined or measured in many ways and will typically include banking sector assets, equity and bond market capitalization, and in some cases cross-border financial claims held by non-bank intermediaries such as pension funds or insurers. We begin with a survey of the academic literature on these three issues, and then draw implications for the Asian economy and financial systems.

Financial sophistication

Among the potential causes of economic development, proximate or fundamental, financial development has been singled out as one important determinant and has drawn particular attention from both researchers and policymakers over the past 20 years. Financial markets and financial intermediaries perform important functions in the growth process in that they channel funds towards the most productive uses. Effective financial intermediation is thought to address adverse selection and moral hazard problems and thus promote capital formation. It facilitates risk sharing, the monitoring of risks, and the allocation of wealth and other resources within an economy. Box 2.1 lists the benefits customarily associated with well-functioning financial systems. Note that certain of these theoretical attributes have become muddied in the fall in reputation of the financial sector associated with the global financial crisis.

Box 2.1 Benefits of Effective Intermediation

Most research and policy experiments conducted since Raymond Goldsmith's 1960s work on financial systems and economic performance show a causal relationship between well-developed financial systems and economic development, measured conventionally as per capita national income. Until the shock that followed Lehman Brothers' collapse in September 2008, the majority of economic and financial analysts agreed that, in principle, effective financial intermediation has three beneficial effects: fuelling economic growth, fostering more stable financial systems and encouraging national integration into international markets for trade and finance. The global financial crisis encouraged more critical views but the consensus has been as follows.

First, effective domestic intermediation promotes growth:

- Encouraging overseas investors and suppliers of capital to participate in the domestic market, augmenting a relatively small local investor base;
- Enabling a more diversified interest rate term structure for investing and funding, importantly including long-term fixed rate debt;
- Allowing access to investment funds for a growing number of corporate borrowers;
- Improving capital allocation and corporate governance through increased market discipline and transparency; and

- Helping to mobilize domestic savings and providing more diversified investment choices for individual investors and organizations.

Second, effective financial intermediation assists stability:

- Enhancing risk management. Effective intermediation decreases systematic risk by lessening reliance on banks as a dominant financing channel. It also allows better management of transaction risks, improved corporate governance through greater market discipline within the banking sector, and introduces broad access to hedging instruments.
- Assisting the pricing of credit and trading risks. This helps avoid structural imbalances, given improved transparency for sovereign and corporate debt issues, more consistent price discovery, and stable risk-free benchmark interest rates.
- Lessening moral hazards. Failing or bankrupt borrowers are less likely than banks to jeopardize the failure of the financial infrastructure or create a collapse in general confidence.
- Facilitating corporate workouts. Debtors and creditors are encouraged to negotiate practical solutions and new terms for outstanding debt claims that are delinquent or in default.
- Separating business and corporate risks. Securitization is a contractual tool that allows banks and other enterprises to raise long-term funds secured against specific future cash flows.

Third, effective intermediation encourages national integration with global markets:

- By adopting common minimum standards for governance and reporting that allow companies to raise funds and issue shares in global markets; and
- By improving the functioning and transparency of domestic financial markets, allowing greater access to foreign users, and lessening price and other disparities with global markets.

Critics of this traditional analysis have been more prominent in the dislocations of the global crisis of 2008, especially those questioning links from financial sophistication to stability. These include neo-Marxian scholars such as Giovanni Arrighi, earlier sceptics of the machine of capitalism such as Hyman Minsky, and analysts who view the juxtaposition of banking regulation and finance as creating false incentives and being ultimately destabilizing (Shin 2010).

Theoretical interest in the structure and operation of financial systems was largely absent from legal and financial studies before the 1970s, and in schools of economics was confined to political economy. This indifference has vanished, due in large part to the influence of two trains of scholars. First, Goldsmith sought ways to test whether financial structure could be related to levels of economic development (Goldsmith 1969), with results that later became a foundation of the law and finance school. Second, North (1990) and others synthesized separate concepts from law, finance and economics in what has become modern institutional economics, which stresses the nature and effect of core rights, duties and incentives.

It has long been held by theoreticians that finance will spur economic growth. Schumpeter (1934), Gurley and Shaw (1955), Goldsmith (1969) and McKinnon (1973) all pointed to the importance of financial development in explaining economic growth. More recent work by Romer (1986, 1990) and Grossman and Helpman (1991), emphasizes the positive effects of financial development on capital accumulation and savings, and on technological innovation. Early analyses considered mainly the scale of financial activity, but more recent work looks into the nature of the financial system. Many empirical studies have also sought to establish a relationship between financial development and economic growth. This literature arguably traces its origin to observations made in Japan by Patrick (1966), but one important aspect of the work can be faulted as we explain in Box 2.2. This also points to a questioning prompted by the global crisis, regarding the societal value of highly developed financial sectors of the kind seen in the United States and parts of the EU.

Box 2.2 How Important is Finance?

There are two reasons for mentioning the philosopher of science Karl Popper at the start of this chapter: to highlight the risk of looking in the wrong place for intellectual support, and to show how recent is the analysis of financial sector activity. Hugh Patrick is a distinguished scholar of economic development and Japanese economic history who published a discursive article in 1966 that was among the first to ask how an enhanced financial sector might contribute positively within developing states. The article was soon influential among financial and development specialists, and from the 1990s for both advocates and critics of the law and finance school. Patrick begins by quoting the words that Keynesian economist Joan Robinson wrote in an essay collection in 1952:

> It seems to be the case that where enterprise leads finance follows. The same impulses within an economy which set enterprise on foot make owners of wealth venturesome, and when a strong impulse to invest is fettered by lack of finance, devices are invented to release it ... and habits and institutions are developed.
>
> (Patrick 1966: 174)

Robinson's essay looks at long-run constraints on growth in aggregate output and employment. She considers the supply of finance in a highly stylized form and concludes that capital investment and growth are not generally hampered by limited access to funding (Robinson 1953: 80–7). If policymakers wish to generate employment, they must worry not about the flow of savings for investment but about other factors related to aggregate demand. The passage from which Patrick takes his quotation describes behaviour at the micro level of the capitalist or financial decision-maker who, when wishing to invest, will devise an innovative transaction solution and use it to fund creditworthy capital investment. This is similar to the investment bank function that we examine in Chapter 7. Even if Robinson's picture does not translate to the aggregate economy, it supports the case that the nature of finance induces development rather than the converse. The quoted words were taken out of context, and form no part of a wider view of growth or development having a causal effect on finance, which was in any event not Robinson's concern.

Robinson's quotation hints at a creative function for finance, but she wrote little of financial practice. Her work was theoretical, dealing variously with imperfect competition, unemployment, capital formation and interest rate determination, and only rarely and briefly with markets for finance. First, she was sceptical that funding in a developed economy could either be quantified or assessed by the conditions upon which it is made available, because the credit risk of users was varied or 'very amorphous' (Robinson 1965: 402). Second, she was interested in banks as participants in monetary policy rather than intermediaries that lend or invest (Robinson 1965: 227–9). Third, she saw share markets as subject to 'notorious instability' (Robinson 1979: 156–61) and observed that capital formation is instead largely financed from company profits. Fourth, she suggested that bankers seek always to 'assert the authority of finance over industry' (ibid: 161). Finally, she was hostile to finance as a purely profit-seeking activity, which like Marx she saw as speculative and providing no societal value (ibid: 159). This last view echoes in the post-crisis thinking of several prominent financial regulators including Paul Volcker in the United States (*Wall Street Journal* 2009), Andrew Haldane (2010) and Adair Turner in the United Kingdom (2009b, 2010a), Andrew Sheng in Hong Kong (2009) and Jacques de Larosière for the EU (de Larosière Group 2009). We explain this discussion in Section 2.5.

The Patrick quotation has been used many times since 1966 despite Robinson's intention. The result is that Robinson's supposed 'theory' is almost ubiquitous in writings on finance and development. For example:

> numerous influential economists believe that finance is a relatively unimportant factor in economic development. Notably, Robinson [1952] contends that financial development simply follows economic growth.
>
> (King & Levine 1993: 717)

Or:

> prominent researchers [such as Robinson] believe that the operation of the financial sector merely responds to economic development, adjusting to changing demands from the real sector, and is therefore overemphasized.
>
> (Demirgüç-Kunt 2006: 1)

And

> It's a long-held view, most famously associated with Joan Robinson, that where industry leads, finance follows.
>
> (Roe & Seigel 2009: 787)

These are mischaracterizations. Robinson's was a casual remark in a dry argument about interest rate determination and supply bottlenecks. She states controversially later in the same essay that finance does not constrain output growth because it flows from a bottle with 'an elastic neck' (Robinson 1953: 128) and generally leans to the view that she is now famously said to oppose. The idea that financial structure or sophistication is primarily a function of economic growth, that is, the converse of

Hugh Patrick's and Raymond Goldsmith's observations, has been stated by few schol-ars, notably Max Weber. Robinson's non-theory became a straw-man argument in false opposition to a growing finance and development literature, as though refuting her 'argument' gave credence to new ideas.

It is certainly true that since the 1960s a growing number of empirical studies sought to identify causal links between financial sector growth or sophistication and general economic development. It is also true that this investigation began as a new concern for a handful of theoreticians. Yet analysts of financial markets often look for explanations of practice, and scholars search the relevant literature in case they are not the first along a particular research seam before venturing a conclusion. In this exam-ple the first descriptions of a causal impact of finance on development were genuinely new and not the subject of prior research except in very different disciplines. And more generally the nature of finance or how funding was provided to governments, industry or commerce was, before the 1960s, a subject limited to narrative historians of banking and securities markets. Only in the increasingly financialized post-Bretton Woods world of the 1980s did the nature of financial activity and financial systems become a subject of its own. This leads to some intriguing questions:

- Did we notice finance only after it seemed to grow more prominent, especially with constant media coverage of stock market prices and bank bonuses?
- Is modern finance a truly innovative force, or something that has more societal costs than benefits?
- Did we look for a causal impact on development because of the resources that finance now consumes?

We return to these issues in Chapter 13.

Goldsmith (1969: 390) further emphasized the importance of finance by saying:

> One of the most important problems in the field of finance, if not the single most important one, almost everyone would agree, is the effect that financial structure and development have on economic growth.

Goldsmith's analysis covered 35 economies and showed a positive correlation between financial development and the level of economic development, drawing on previous theoretical work (McKinnon 1973; Shaw 1973). Since then, the finance–growth literature expanded steadily so that the relation between growth and financial development has been empirically investigated in different contexts and with varying data samples. King and Levine (1993) use data for 80 countries over the period 1960–89 to show that the level of financial develop-ment is positively and strongly associated with economic growth. They find that a rise in financial depth measured by the ratio of liquid financial liabilities to GDP from the mean of the slowest growth quartile of countries (0.2 per cent per annum) to the mean of the fastest growing quartile of countries (0.6 per cent per annum) would be expected to increase annual per capita growth by almost one percentage point. There is also evidence of this observation at the industry or firm level. Rajan and Zingales (1998a) use cross-country analysis to show that industry sectors relying more on external finance than retained earnings grow faster in countries with better financial development. This evidence also supports the positive effect of financial development on economic growth. Demirgüç-Kunt and Maksimovic (1998) provide evidence at firm level that finance spurs firm growth. Wurgler (2000) shows that efficient financial intermediation promotes more efficient capital allocation among investible opportunities. The positive relation between financial development and economic development is illustrated in Figure 2.1.

Related work includes a considerable body of empirical studies in the style pioneered by Goldsmith and following the methods adopted by King and Levine and the law and finance scholars La Porta, Lopez-de-Silanes, Shleifer and Vishny (LLSV) in seeking evidence of causal relationships between financial market, institutional sophistication or structure (including the nature of legal conditions and national sources of law) and economic development (commonly measured by growth in national output). While not unanimous, these generally suggest that finance often has a positive effect on growth.

Although the positive relationship between financial and economic development has been well-documented empirically, it remains controversial whether such a relation is *causal*. For example, in one study, Levine, Loayza and Beck (2000) try to use an array of empirical methods to control for potential simultaneity biases, measurement errors, and missing variable problems, and so establish a causal relationship.

Important exceptions have also been raised to question the role of finance in economic development. For example, some economists believe that China's fast economic growth in the past quarter-century has been achieved largely without strong support from its financial sector. Allen, Qian and Qian (2005) even argue that informal finance has been more important

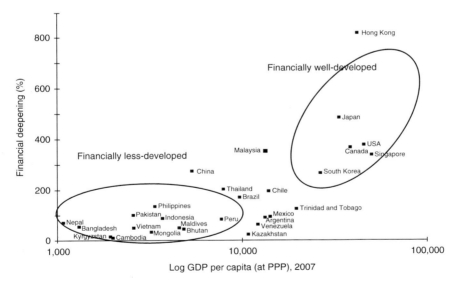

Figure 2.1 Financial deepening and per capita GDP (PPP basis), 2007.

Financial deepening is the ratio of the sum of outstanding financial claims or market capitalization in the form of equity and debt, which is bonds, private loans and other credit at market value to output (GDP at PPP). Hong Kong is an outlier in the result with financial deepening of 817% and per capita GDP at PPP of US$42,180, which probably derives from it being an offshore finance centre.

Sources: World Bank (undated b); authors' estimates.

than the formal financial system in driving economic growth. Although this puzzle challenges the conventional wisdom that stems from more recent growth theories and empirical evidence, it seems that informal financial intermediation has effectively relieved the financing constraints imposed on the Chinese economy. This means that finance still matters, and is an intrinsically important driver of growth. The trouble here is that we do not know how to correctly quantify the size of finance in emerging economies such as China, whether formal or informal.

2.2 Finance in the Asian development model

As noted in the introduction, this book has two aims: to explain and discuss important contemporary issues that Asia faces in the early twenty-first century in the fields of banking, finance, financial regulation and economic development; and to assess global aspects of today's financial world with illustrations from Asian markets, rules and practices. This demands an understanding of the historical and institutional factors that shaped the region's dominant post-1949 growth model and its relationship with financial intermediation. The narrative begins relatively recently as we explained at the beginning of Chapter 1, but some features of Asian finance have older roots, especially those involving trade finance, corporate governance and informal intermediation.

Global financialization

Globalization appeared in the English language only in the late 1950s, but elements in the process it signifies are in no sense new. Adam Smith regretted that distance made disregard for fairness or compassion inevitable, suggesting that even a 'man of humanity' in Europe would be indifferent to the suffering caused by a distant earthquake in China, and might instead choose to speculate on its commercial outcome (Smith 1759: III.3 § 4).

Two analyses of modern globalization refer to its result as 'the death of distance' (Cairncross 2001) and 'the end of geography' (O'Brien 1992). Yet critics link globalization to cultural conflicts among industrialized and developing states in matters of trade, corporate governance and employment practice, with national norms vulnerable to functional outsourcing of manufacturing production, intrusive or coercive trades in goods or extractive resources, the demands of foreign shareholders, and the loyalties of transnational companies. Asia's place in the global economy is a significant part of that process, arising from an export orientation adopted after 1949 and its importance as a centre of manufacturing, especially with ODM (original design manufacturer) and OEM (original equipment manufacturer) operations.

Modern globalization is often associated with Anglo-American capitalism and challenges developed states that value the Rheinish model of the 'coordinated market economy' associated first with post-1945 Germany (Hall & Soskice 2001: 8), with its emphasis on stakeholder capitalism. This means that large companies are required by law and their internal constitutions to be responsible to the interests of employees and customers as well as their shareholder owners. Most Asian economies share similar characteristics but seem unthreatened by globalization and almost certainly have benefited from the process in terms of economic growth.

Globalization is associated above all with shifts in relative transnational demand for labour. This was anticipated by an early twentieth century anti-imperialist scholar, who foresaw East Asia becoming the world's centre of manufacturing due to its comparative advantage of inexhaustible and inexpensive labour (Hobson 1902: 334–5). Hobson also feared that the 'driving force of the competing Imperialism of Western nations has been traced to the interests of certain small financial and industrial groups within each nation, usurping the power of the nation and employing the public force and money for their private business ends' (ibid: 332), a view echoed in today's hostility to Wall Street or the City of London (but less so, however, in Hong Kong).

Modern globalization is a new process that in two respects is significant for Asia:

- First, it represents a form of manufacturing integration or fluid 'complex interdependency' (Keohane & Nye 1989: 3–11), which begins with commercial production and affects states and individuals culturally, economically and ethically.
- Second, since the mid-1980s an intense financial orientation has grown in the global economy, characterized by high leverage of assets and credit risk, the commoditization of risks, complex transactions, and intermediation occurring through specialist vehicles outside the traditional financial sector.

The process of financialization and the growth of a 'shadow banking system' (McCulley 2007) was stimulated and made lucrative by transnational regulatory arbitrage, mainly in the developed Anglo-American economies, as we show in Section 2.5. Asian finance did not generally follow these extremes, but the region's real economies soon suffered in the global crisis as a result of excesses elsewhere. The region's function as global manufacturer depended upon globalization trends, but involved risks from globalization's financial aspects that became popularly known only in the wake of the global financial crisis, to some accounting for immense 'creation and destruction of value' (James 2009), and ensuring that the deflation of US property prices that began in 2006 was highly contagious.

Financial structure

It is useful in reviewing finance's roles in Asia to consider first the conceptual structures that have prevailed at various times since 1949. At one extreme is the government-controlled financial system. Financial resources are allocated purely on the basis of government direction, which may be either planned or dictated. The former was first seen in the Soviet model of central planning, ownership and control, and was the dominant rival to market-based economic organization and finance during much of the twentieth century.

This model had considerable influence in Asia until the 1980s, especially in China and Indochina. The dictatorial model with central control by an individual or family has been less common in Asia and often more characteristic of African and Middle Eastern states, but regimes dominated by the military subsisted in Asia for extended periods after 1949, partly encouraged by Cold War fears of state communism, and were entrenched in Indonesia, South Korea, the Philippines and Taiwan as each entered the early phases of rapid growth. Both control models have generally proven significantly constrained in supporting long-term economic development. Neither has great influence today.

At the other extreme is a securities-based financial system, with widely dispersed ownership and market allocation of financial resources. This model is identified most strongly with the Anglo-American economies and has been adopted less frequently in Asia. Hong Kong may be the leading example, at least superficially, for its economy has long-standing features such as land-use rights that are highly centralized. The market model was popular until the Asian financial crisis, and was the dominant influence in China until the global financial crisis.

With this exception, the Anglo-American model ceased to have unqualified appeal in Asia after 1998, when even a supposedly libertarian Hong Kong government acquired very substantial commercial shareholdings to deter destabilizing speculation. In its most extreme form of unfettered finance the model has been questioned again following the recent global financial crisis.

Between these extremes is a range of structural alternatives that are best described as market-based but not free-market oriented. Governments and other interest groups control or influence economic activity and financial allocation but without detailed central planning or direction. State policy operated indirectly in a setting that generally favours market activity, although the state may often retain reserve powers in respect of foreign ownership of key commercial sectors, and may influence activity through the active use of fiscal and monetary policy or credit incentives. Commercial banks may be central in financial allocation, as in the Rheinish model adopted in certain European states after 1945, and which was critical to Germany's economic development until the 1990s. In such government- and bank-centred systems, the state exerts economic influence through an administrative involvement in financial allocation. This may happen through designated intermediaries or specialist infrastructural lenders such as Germany's Kreditanstalt für Wiederaufbau (KfW) or the long-term credit banks of Japan, all established in the 1950s, and continues through policy banks or development lenders in China, South Korea, Thailand and elsewhere. The system combines elements of both the bank-centred and government-controlled system, and generally allows the state considerable influence over finance in the context of a market economy.

This developmental state model was pioneered in Japan, has been influential in most parts of the region, and characterized the position of its financial sectors prior to the 1997 crisis (Chang 1999). In some cases an oligopolistic family-dominated system prevailed, with the allocation of financial resources determined largely by small numbers of wealthy families, usually operating through complex conglomerates with control of large segments of industry and commerce. This leaves the state market-oriented, but subject to significant monopolized activities. This model was common in parts of Continental Europe, especially Belgium and Italy, and for decades throughout Asia and Latin America. Family groups together own or control to differing degrees the heights of the economies of Hong Kong, India, Indonesia, the Philippines, Singapore, Taiwan and Thailand. In some cases this model allows governments to have strategic influence over finance through its close connection with wealthy elites, a system known pejoratively as crony capitalism.

Post-1949 finance

The long history of finance in Asia has led to certain influential innovations. These were manifested in trading instruments, retail savings and small-scale investment mechanisms, and generally characterized as informal finance (Ray 1995). The system was especially developed in areas of China and India and continue in a variety of forms today. Developments in modern finance have generally evolved state by state but with certain clear themes shared among several economies since 1949, which we divide into three periods.

- 1949–80. This encompasses reforms instigated in post-war Japan, the adoption of the Soviet model in China and Vietnam, to the post-Bretton Woods era and the beginning of financial globalization. The period includes the emergence of the developmental state model, first in Japan, then Singapore, South Korea, Taiwan and elsewhere. The model was influential even in Hong Kong where the state's role has traditionally been thought of as modest. Finance in this period was largely subservient to manufacturing and the strategic purposes of the state, with credit to some extent directed to favoured industry sectors.

- 1980–97. The second phase begins with the partial opening and industrialization of China through to the 1997 regional crisis. Finance is central and instructive in this period, and towards the later years in particular provides the impetus for wealth creation in the fast-growing real estate sector.
- 1999–2008. From post-crisis recovery to the global financial crisis of 2008 is a time of intense global financialization. Asia focuses by contrast on widespread privatization of state investments, cautious institutional reforms to assist domestic market development, and a period of self-imposed risk aversion on the part of governments as a hangover to the regional crisis.

Over the period since 1949 as a whole, four additional and persistent themes are evident:

The active role of the state in the direction and use of the financial sector, especially in relation to external sector growth, aspects of directed savings through state-sponsored provident schemes, and the financing of targeted industries.

The importance of informal finance, seen in alternative forms of saving and money transmission, and semi-regulated credit creation.

A general lack of indigenous formal innovation in finance, but instead the adaptation of transaction forms and financial practices developed elsewhere.

Parochial and segmented financial activity from state-to-state, but with transnational and regional financial activity led largely by non-Asian banks and other intermediaries.

The developmental state model seen throughout Asia after 1949 did not generally require transactional innovation of the kind associated with modern investment banking and discussed in Sections 7.3–7.5. Finance was central to the model but subordinated in its purposes to industrialization, and its functions closely observed by government.

The Asian development model 1949–80

Indigenous and colonial banks functioned as intermediaries and trade financiers for generations, but our starting point is the formative period of modern Asian finance and its place in the region's growth model, regardless of an apparent low profile. The immediate post-war period sees the development of two main models of finance in Asia: one originating in Japan and eventually adopted by most states, and the second adapted from the Soviet Union. The first was largely abandoned following the Asian financial crisis, while the other was progressively shunned from the late 1970s. This period is characterized by limited finance with a state orientation in all cases, even where markets were supposedly paramount.

Parts of China's financial system were sophisticated well before 1949 and Shanghai had begun to recover as a hub for Chinese and foreign banks soon after occupation ended in 1945, with at least 50 modern local banks and 20 foreign banks operating in 1946 under the supervision of the nationalist government's central bank (Ahlers 1946: 386–9). This changed suddenly with the founding of the People's Republic and the substantial economic isolation that followed. All commercial interests and financial intermediaries were nationalized and made subject to central control, the nationalist regime's four policy banks were disbanded and the Shanghai stock market closed. The People's Bank of China (PBOC) became China's sole formal intermediary between 1950 and 1978. PBOC, owned by the central government and controlled by the Ministry of Finance, was both central and commercial bank, a 'monobank' system, controlling about 98 per cent of China's financial assets and conducting almost all financial transactions (Allen, Qian & Qian 2005). No material structural changes occurred in China's isolated financial system until after 1978 and the start of an era of economic reform.

Japan's post-1949 banking sector was supervised closely by the state and made to assume a functional position of serving manufacturing industry. Banks began the period largely under private ownership but far reduced in scale and capital compared to 1939. Central government wanted the banking sector to fulfil a particular purpose, in which growth was associated with export-oriented manufacturing. Financial innovation was allowed in certain export credit schemes for heavy industry, such as the financing of ship construction though intricate *shikumisen* transactions. Japan's credit banks and securities firms were comparatively weak. The first reforms to corporate governance in 1948–49, allowing the creation of *keiretsu* conglomerates, were prompted by an occupation administration with a strong US anti-monopoly ethic. The transition from Japan's earlier corporate model is described in Box 2.3.

Box 2.3 From *Zaibatsu* to *Keiretsu*

Japan's *zaibatsu* (literally 'wealthy clique') were large self-financing family owned conglomerates that often held powerful industrial monopolies and great political power. They flourished throughout most of the period from the Meiji Restoration to the end of the Pacific War in 1945, having been formed in a wave of privatization of state businesses soon after 1868. The *zaibatsu* eventually became subject to wholesale dissolution under the allied occupation administration, which at first demanded the introduction of US-style antitrust laws to eliminate Japan's 'monopoly enterprise' system (Hadley 1948: 429) but finally introduced more pragmatic legislation from 1947 and sought instead to remove concentrations of control and introduce a degree of competition. Before the end of the *zaibatsu* era it was said that as few as 56 heads of family controlled 11 corporate groups (Hadley 1948: 433; Fearey 1950: 60–1), which represented the heights of the economy until its widespread destruction in 1943–45.

Powerful commercial groups were never eliminated from Japan's system of 'non-liberal capitalism' (Streeck & Yamamura 2001) that developed after 1949. In the 1950s and 1960s, this evolved into a new form of governance through conjoined industrial and finance conglomerates known as *keiretsu* (meaning 'series' or 'network'). These shared the names of many of their famous predecessors but were far more widely owned than the *zaibatsu*, and looser in their affiliations and dealings between group members.

Each *keiretsu* included a commercial bank which held shares in operating subsidiaries within the network and was itself owned jointly by those companies. The bank was both a preferred lender for *keiretsu* companies and a corporate governance monitor for the entire group. Under this 'main bank' system (Aoki & Patrick 1994) each bank also became a junior partner to its counterparts in other *keiretsu*, thus forming semi-permanent lending syndicates.

Keiretsu could be diversified or vertically integrated. For example, Mitsui is involved in a range of largely unrelated manufacturing, electronics and chemical sectors, while the Toyota group concentrates on integrated automotive production including sourcing and distribution. In all cases a trading company has central control of the logistics of purchasing and exporting across the entire *keiretsu*, and may instigate and coordinate large projects undertaken jointly by group members.

The *shikumisen* ship finance model is an example of project integration. Steel from a *keiretsu* plant is used to build ships in *keiretsu* yards; the main bank provides trade and shipyard credit and loans to a shipowner in Hong Kong; upon delivery, the *keiretsu* trading company charters the vessel to carry goods from a *keiretsu* manufacturer overseas, returning to Japan with inputs for the steel plant. Only the shipowner is separate from the network. A typical diversified example is Mitsubishi. Bank of Tokyo Mitsubishi UFJ is the main bank of the *keiretsu*, which currently includes Kirin Brewery, Mitsubishi Motors, Mitsubishi Trust and Banking, Meiji Mutual Life Insurance, Nikon and Nippon Oil, with Mitsubishi Shoji as the main trading company. Mitsubishi Pencil Co. Ltd. made the pen we used to correct proofs of this book.

External investors may acquire shares in many parts of a *keiretsu* but would remain in minority positions in all cases. The cross-shareholding has two effects, in preventing hostile takeovers and minimizing the shareholding needed for control and continuity. Closely controlled conglomerate structures are not uncommon in Hong Kong, Indonesia, the Philippines and Thailand, but only in Japan has the main bank been central to the *keiretsu* structure. This may have contributed to prolonged weakness in the banking system after the 1990s collapse of property and stock market prices, when main bank capital was depleted by loan and share price losses arising from *keiretsu* partners.

The internal capital market system may lessen financing constraints for member firms, but *keiretsu* also have inherent risks. Limited competition within the *keiretsu* can lead to inefficient investment due to easy access to credit or capital. This might cause operating firms to overborrow and eventually jeopardize the health of banks. Globalization, technological advancement and competition intensity are forcing Japanese firms to rethink the virtues and weaknesses of *keiretsu*, whether the system will adapt to a changing business environment and how significant it will be in a future economy.

In this first phase of reconstruction and structural reform Japan experienced large surplus savings in its consumer sector and a corporate sector deficit. Risk-averse savers were accustomed to using simple bank deposits and the state post office, which were stifled in providing funds to industry. Reforms in the 1950s created several classes of banks, including those intended to conduct public policy (Aoki & Patrick 1994). The state encouraged commercial lending to targeted sectors by persuasion and occasionally with legislative decrees, and participated in the credit process by creating new specialist lenders such as the Japan Export–Import Bank and Japan Development Bank from 1950.

In the reformed *keiretsu* system, each large commercial group included a trading house to conduct commercial dealings overseas and a main bank. This system comprised 'an informal set of practices, institutional arrangements, and behaviour patterns that constitute a system of corporate financing and governance' (Aoki & Patrick 1994). The main bank was not an instigator of group policy or capital investment, but was placed centrally within the *keiretsu* structure and given responsibility for corporate surveillance and support. Main banks provided short-term credit within the group and supplied funds in syndicates to the competing *keiretsu* of their rivals.

Legislation in 1952 established three long-term credit banks, privately owned but with distinct operating objectives of funding industrial investment and mobilizing private savings with the sale of marketable securities away from the traditional commercial bank sector. Thus the financing of Japanese industry took place under a supervisory umbrella held jointly by the powerful ministries of finance and of trade and industry, and was integrated with the state's export–growth objectives.

Like Rheinish stakeholder capitalism in Europe, Japan's developmental state model design was lauded by many Anglo-American scholars in the 1960s, 1970s and 1980s as exemplary in encouraging growth and employment. Even as late as 1996 and in the wake of the Japanese financial crisis emanating from the bursting of the real estate and stock bubbles at the end of the 1980s, Joseph Stiglitz, then World Bank chief economist, applauded the model as a third alternative to the extremes of market capitalism and central planning, suggesting that Japan and its industrializing neighbours had adopted policies that complemented rather than replaced markets, assisted in cases of market failure, and ensured that financial sector activity was regulated (Stiglitz 1996: 155–6), but without specifying the nature of such regulation.

Financial systems in Southeast Asia after 1949 were dominated by colonial intermediaries and imported structures. As these were absorbed or became less prominent and variations on the Japanese or Soviet systems were adopted, with most states choosing the developmental-state model. India followed a similar path but favoured Soviet-style controls.

Washington consensuses 1980–97

The state partially withdrew from close control of finance from the late-1970s in Japan and later in China, India and elsewhere. In the overall export orientation of the Asian growth model, finance remained embedded but gradually broadened its purposes. There was also an influx of modern foreign banks during this period, for the first time since the late 1930s. Policies associated with the Washington Consensus were increasingly adopted after 1980, in line with the precepts explained in Box 2.4. The combination of financial liberalization inspired by the Washington Consensus as it became in the mid-1990s, with institutional structures that had supported the Asian development growth model, were together to lead to the 1997 financial crisis.

Box 2.4 The Changing Washington Consensus

Financial markets thrive on acronyms and labels that may be ambiguous. The Washington Consensus is an example of a term coined by an academic, adopted in popular commentaries, that within a decade came to signify an approach to development that was fully the reverse of its first meaning.

The term refers to a development philosophy and the analysis of economic and financial policy associated for many years with the international organizations established by the Bretton Woods agreements in 1944, the World Bank and the International Monetary Fund (IMF). The World Bank provides funds for infrastructural projects and developmental schemes to assist agriculture, health, education and welfare, while the IMF was originally made to police the newly reformed international financial system, and more specifically to extend bilateral credit when needed by states experiencing temporary acute external payments problems.

Until 2009, when a new and simple IMF facility was introduced, credit was provided by the Fund to member states on strict conditions (see Sections 4.3 and 12.5), which often entailed limits to public sector spending and employment or the use of exchange controls. This approach became widely discredited and resented after the Asian financial crisis because the Fund was thought to have made demands for policy changes in Indonesia and Thailand that trespassed on state sovereignty. They may also have been damagingly deflationary at a time when growth in output was especially needed. IMF practice and its founding laws required it to undertake regular policy surveillance of member states, especially those likely to become its borrowers. The IMF's experience of national surveillance, its standing in international law and the World Bank's immense financing mandate made the two Washington organizations powerful for several decades.

Neither the Bank nor the Fund declared an overt objective philosophy, but their activities from the early 1950s until the mid-1990s were characterized by the following policy measures (Williamson 1990):

- Public fiscal discipline;
- Public spending focused on generating high returns and improved income distribution, especially from healthcare, education and infrastructure;
- Tax reform, lowering marginal rates and broadening the tax base;
- Liberalization of interest rates, trade, and FDI;
- Competitive exchange rates;
- Privatization of state assets and businesses;
- Deregulation of barriers to foreign investors; and
- Secure property rights.

Each was market-oriented and apparently opposed to the state capitalist or command economies of the Soviet bloc in the 1960s and beyond. However, they lacked a rigid ideological core and were tolerant of mixed economies involving significant public participation and a generally favourable view of welfare spending and equitable income distribution, and a positive view of the state's contribution to economic policy, or an 'embedded liberalism' (Ruggie 1982: 392). This was the Washington Consensus, a neo-Keynesian approach intended to assist broad growth without extremes of politics or policy. It was named in 1990 by John Williamson, a Washington economist specializing in Latin American development.

Ten years later, the same writer suggested that the term had found a different meaning (Williamson 2000), no longer of the Keynesian centre but more closely linked to libertarian or neoliberal support for deregulated markets and limited government. One focus of this new approach was institutional reform, especially favouring property rights and the rule of law (see Chapter 5). In effect, the Soviet Union's collapse prompted Washington to upend its consensus from embedded liberalism to a market-oriented 'embedded neo-liberalism' (Wade 2007: 250) based on an Anglo-American model of financial globalization.

Note that both Washington Consensuses have favoured domestic financial market reform (see Chapter 12), for example, to bolster trading in local currency debt and equity securities.

The 1980s was a golden decade for Japan and its financial and economic model. It ended precipitously in 1989 with a collapse of property prices and stock market values from which a full recovery is still awaited. Yet elements of the Japanese model worked to great effect in South Korea and Southeast Asia during this period until becoming discredited in 1997.

Following the introduction and official sanction of a household responsibility system from the late 1970s as its first market-oriented reform, China entered a period of economic change that has subsisted for more than three decades. The early success of rural reforms greatly increased per capita household incomes in the 1980s and encouraged vast numbers of internal migrants to search for employment in coastal cities, an echo of Lewis's developmental model that we mentioned in Section 1.3.

Exports and heavy capital investment became the pillars of China's economic development. This was also a period in which China began to create a modern financial system. Four national state-owned commercial banks were formed in the 1980s: Bank of China, Industrial and Commercial Bank of China (ICBC), China Construction Bank (CCB) and Agricultural Bank of China. They still dominate the financial system in terms of their share of loans and deposits. Several national joint-stock commercial banks were later formed, including Bank of Communications, Everbright Bank, CITIC Industrial Bank, China Merchants Bank and Minsheng Bank. Many regional banks were also created from consolidations of urban and rural credit cooperatives. All these new intermediaries competed aggressively to erode the dominant positions of the big four banks. Capital markets followed, with two stock exchanges opening in 1990 in Shanghai and Shenzhen. Share turnover grew quickly in most of the following decade, interrupted only when state authorities sought to suppress speculative activity by curbs on credit-based margin trading.

China's financial reforms after 1980 were heavily influenced by Japanese and Southeast Asian experience, although this altered when Japan entered a phase of domestic deflation, its 'lost decade' of slow growth and asset price stagnation. India's financial and economic reform process began in earnest only after the early 1990s, when the era of isolation and central planning was acknowledged to have done little to lessen poverty and may have induced an external payments crisis.

2.3 The Asian financial crisis of 1997–98

In this section we dwell on the events and causes of the Asian financial crisis for three reasons:

- Its severity has had profound effects on policy, leading to a conservative approach to domestic financial market development and the dismantling of regional barriers to financial activity.
- The crisis indicated risks to growth and employment resulting from inadequate financial development, providing that an expanded domestic financial sector was associated with sound practices in regulation, governance and risk management.
- Policy caution resulting from this regional crisis tempered the impact in Asia of the global financial crisis of 2008.

Asia's regional crisis began with shocks in Thailand through the deflation of an asset price bubble and the abrupt floating of an overvalued currency. The result might have been confined to one economy, but linkages within the modern financial system can allow shocks to be transmitted rapidly between national markets, so that losses in confidence or unexpected changes in asset prices may reverberate in other market sectors. This is the basis of the contagion that swept from Thailand throughout Southeast Asia, South Korea, Hong Kong and Taiwan. The crisis drew attention to the dangers of financial globalization and the need to develop well-functioning and crisis-resistant financial systems, regardless of the risk preferences of commercial participants or the state. The crisis shows how the developmental state model failed to generate positive dynamics between the real economy and the financial sector when confronting unforeseen shocks. We will also explore how better intermediation could have prevented an isolated crisis becoming contagious.

Weakening confidence in Southeast Asia was first seen from mid-1996 in capital flight, including steep reductions in lending by Japanese and European banks. Lenders that had willingly funded local banks and other borrowers began to scale back their commitments and refuse the renewal of short-term credit lines. This exposed the fragility of states that had come to rely on foreign currency borrowings. Domestic banks lacked dependable funding in US dollars or Japanese yen, that is, their access to central bank lender of last resort (LLR) facilities to cover emergency shortages of liquidity was confined to their home currencies (Section 4.3 explains the LLR function).

This eroded confidence further and encouraged speculative sales of local currencies, especially the Thai baht, Indonesian rupiah, Malaysian ringgit and Korean won. Much of the flight capital had been used by local banks to fund domestic investments in property and other assets without fully hedging the resulting currency or interest basis risks. The effect was a disruptive spiral: the withdrawal of capital removed local access to foreign currency funding, put downward pressure on local exchange rates, and created exchange losses for cross-border borrowers.

The causes of the crisis and ensuing contagion are still debated. Most explanations focus on macroeconomic factors such as vulnerabilities in the financial sector and inconsistently applied policies. In our view the roots of the crisis were at the micro level in high corporate leverage, weak commercial profitability, and inadequate financial sector supervision. In Thailand and elsewhere these conditions had developed at the same time as rapid growth in domestic financial sector activity and buoyant external investor interest in developing Asia.

We focus on Thailand because the beginnings of the crisis were replicated in Indonesia, South Korea and Malaysia, and structural factors considered in the Thai context apply equally elsewhere. Several of the 15 Thai domestic commercial banks had adopted international targets for capital adequacy, but their accounting practices and procedures for reporting and provisioning for delinquent and defaulted loans (non-performing loans or NPLs) were often substandard. Regulatory supervision and internal risk management were patchy, but these were problems masked by rising asset prices and high confidence. These conditions allowed a misallocation of resources to the non-bank financial sector and to property development so that, at times in 1995–96, it seemed as if most of Bangkok was under construction. The notable events of the crisis are shown in Table 2.1.

Thailand's meltdown

The events of 1997 came after years of lax monetary policy, loose governance and sluggish corporate performance. The Thai authorities sought to defend the baht's peg to the US dollar, which until 1997 had been politically favoured (Hall 2005). The Bank of Thailand (Thailand's central bank) began spot and forward sales of US dollars in July 1996 and was largely successful until May 1997 (Tongurai 2005; Nukul Commission 1998). Forward sales of foreign currency were used to conceal the loss in reserves and were both technically illegal and

Table 2.1 Timeline of the Asian financial crisis

January–July 1997	August–November 1997	December 1997	January 1998	May–Sept 1998
Jan.–Apr. Japanese & EU banks increasingly refuse to renew foreign currency loans to Thai borrowers	5 Aug. Thailand agrees economic conditions in consideration for US$17bn IMF standby credit	3 Dec. IMF approves US$57bn support for South Korea, then its largest programme ever	8 Jan. Creditors agree 90-day rollover of external short-term South Korean debt. Indonesian rupiah falls to new low after state budget, ignores IMF terms	21 May. Indonesian President Suharto ousted after 32 years in power
May–Jun. Bank of Thailand exhausts foreign currency reserves in purchasing falling baht	14 Aug. Indonesian rupiah allowed to float	8 Dec. Thailand closes 56 insolvent finance companies, required by IMF conditions. 30,000 white-collar jobs lost. IMF head Camdessus praises Thailand's 'solid progress'	12 Jan. Hong Kong's Peregrine investment bank collapses. Asia's largest investment bank suffered large credit losses on unsold local currency SE Asian loans. Potential rescuers withdrew on sight of Peregrine's accounts	25–26 May. 2-day national strikes in South Korea after 90 days of 10,000 daily job losses
2 Jul. Thai baht allowed to float. External value falls by at least 20 per cent	8 Oct. Indonesia seeks IMF assistance after rupiah collapses by 30 per cent	23 Dec. World Bank makes unprecedented emergency US$3bn loan to South Korea	28 Jan. South Korea agrees rescheduling of US$24bn short-term external debt. US$57bn unprecedented IMF-led aid contingent upon large-scale job losses, agreed 6 Feb. by labour unions	14 Aug. Intense speculation against HK dollar provokes massive government support by bear market squeeze, buying and stabilizing local equity and currency markets
8 Jul. Bank Negara Malaysia sells US dollars to support the ringgit	23 Oct. Hong Kong raises interest rates to 300 per cent to deter short-selling of HK dollar. Hang Seng stock market index falls over 10 per cent	24 Dec. South Korea avoids default on short-term external bank loans with US$10bn loans from IMF and G7 states. Seoul agrees to reforms and allow foreign access to financial markets		19 Aug. Russian government defaults on short-term local currency GKO bills
11 Jul. Philippine peso devalued. Widening of official trading range of Indonesian rupiah	31 Oct. IMF agrees US$40bn standby facility for Indonesia, requiring closure of 16 insolvent banks and wide-ranging policy changes			23 Sept. US Federal Reserve organizes US$3.5bn private sector rescue of hedge fund LTCM to forestall general market panic
24 Jul. Singapore dollar begins steady fall. Malaysian Premier Mahathir attacks hedge fund owner George Soros as a 'rogue speculator'	21 Nov. South Korea requests IMF aid			

Sources: BIS (1997); Nukul Commission (1998); authors' records.

speculative, in that the Bank of Thailand knowingly maintained a fixed exchange rate having exhausted resources for later delivery. Thailand bought US$11 billion in baht on one day in May 1997 (Nukul Commission 1998: s.180). The scale of intervention was kept secret but became subject to mounting rumours in May and June. The Bank of Thailand finally revealed in early July the virtual exhaustion of its currency reserves and allowed the baht to float and find its own value in the foreign exchange markets. It immediately lost over half its value against the US dollar and continued to fall in the following months.

As the baht dropped, so the capacity of Thai banks to service their currency liabilities evaporated. State approval for most foreign currency borrowing was long-standing practice in Southeast Asia and South Korea, but domestic banks were generally given more leeway to raise or renew short- or medium-term debt, and the result was a concentration of external claims against the banking sector. Capital flight from mid-1996 has often been termed speculative, but included a considerable withdrawal of lending by Japanese banks. This credit run was involuntary, for banks were forced to allocate capital to cover domestic loan losses and could not then fund their offshore lending (McCauley 2007). Similar circumstances arose among South Korean banks in late 2008, such that the Bank of Korea (South Korea's central bank) drew on its lines with the US Federal Reserve and Bank of Japan (the US and Japanese central banks, respectively) to provide foreign currency liquidity to the banks it supervised (Bank of Korea 2008: 32–33). We explain these central bank practices in Sections 4.3 and 12.5.

Although Thai lending and deposit-taking was concentrated among four to five of the domestic commercial banks, finance and leasing company quasi-banks had grown prolifically in number in early 1990s. Some were controlled by banks so as to evade prudential lending and leverage limits, and securities houses such as Finance One or Phatra Securities and certain finance companies were sizeable and had considerable corporate influence.

This two-tier system led to a moral hazard within the domestic financial sector based on the state's implicit support for a deteriorating property and lending market. Inflated metropolitan real estate prices peaked in mid-1996. This at once weakened all financial intermediaries as so much of their lending had been made to property developers. This became public in February 1997 when prominent developer Somprasong Land defaulted on payments due on foreign loans, and led to further losses in asset values. The Bank of Thailand tried to fund distressed lenders through a Financial Institutions Development Fund (FIDF) but confidence failed to recover, and foreign investors guessed that the baht could no longer be supported in conditions of slow export growth, weak foreign earnings and domestic financial distress.

The proceeds of many foreign currency borrowings had been used by Thai banks to fund baht loans to domestic clients, including the burgeoning quasi-banks, with the banks retaining an open exchange risk. First informally, but then publicly, the Thai authorities assured the banks that they would support the quasi-bank sector in the event that it experienced credit problems. Such difficulties began immediately and overwhelmed the entire financial sector in 1997, with only two to three large banks having sufficient capital to survive. In June the FIDF was unable to purchase loans of US$3.9 billion made by Finance One, and the Bank of Thailand ended its implicit guarantee and announced that the firm's creditors would be forced to write off their claims. Foreign lenders anticipated similar conditions elsewhere as soon as the baht was freed to float, leading to capital outflows throughout the region. Thai interest rates soared, the state announced capital controls, and the financial sector became largely paralyzed.

Thailand sought financial assistance from regional sources and in Washington. The US refused bilateral assistance, and in August urged Japan not to 'pour money into' Thailand prior to International Monetary Fund (IMF) credit being sanctioned (FOMC 1997: 9–13), the Federal Reserve stating that aid would create 'two elements of moral hazard' due to the risk of the Bank of Thailand defaulting on forward commitments to other central banks (ibid: 13). An emergency US$17 billion emergency credit from the IMF, Japan and several other Asian states was announced the following day, but was effectively pre-committed to meet US$23.4 billion in forward sales of US dollars by the Bank of Thailand (Ito 2007: 25). In 1997–98 the IMF and Asian Development Bank (ADB) eventually provided credit to Indonesia, South Korea and Thailand of US$25.0 billion, US$35.3 billion and US$6.7 billion, respectively. Other states made bilateral commitments totalling US$54.7 billion (IMF undated a). Hong Kong liquidated over US$15 billion in reserves to support its share and equity derivative markets from speculative attack (Yam 1998).

The impact on the Thai economy was devastating. Interest rates doubled to nearly 10 per cent to provide a floor for the baht and control inflation, but the result was a contraction in GDP of 8 per cent in 1998 and a 5 per cent rise in the national unemployment rate by 1999. The asset and collateral quality of the bank sector collapsed and NPLs rose to between 50–75 per cent of total assets. Some banks experienced 'strategic' NPLs, where borrowers ceased payments when the government signaled that it would intervene to support the banks. These NPLs were made possible by ineffective bankruptcy law. At first 56 finance companies were shuttered, but the number of closures eventually reached several hundred. Foreign interests took control of several failed banks.

Run up to the crash

Thailand's reliance on foreign funding to support domestic lending has come to be known as a *carry trade*, meaning a borrowing in a low-coupon currency to buy assets in a second with higher nominal interest rates. The exchange risk to the unhedged trade is obvious and large enough to wipe out any accrued cross-currency interest differentials.

Conventional wisdom holds that cross-border portfolio capital flows are generally volatile because investors are fickle and speculators prone to withdraw at the first sign of trouble. Bank funding is perceived as more stable. Yet Thailand's crisis was driven by foreign lenders rather than free-trading speculators. Financial deregulation led to a credit boom, and a high-yielding currency attracted foreign capital, much of which flowed via domestic intermediaries to risky sectors that could easily absorb funding. More and more funds chased fewer and fewer sound investments, and led to the widespread destruction of corporate value. Eventually the integrity of the financial system depended upon real estate prices remaining high. To understand how the crisis unfolded we examine the dynamics of funds absorbed by the financial sector and channelled into real sectors, drawing on our contemporary analysis and several academic and official narratives (Barton, Newell & Wilson 2003; Corsetti, Pesenti & Roubini 1998; Nukul Commission 1998).

Capital inflows

Thailand steadily deregulated and liberalized its financial sector from 1992, removing interest rate ceilings, lifting exchange controls and drawing offshore finance activity to Thailand through a new Bangkok International Banking Facility. This innovation was made ostensibly to promote Thailand as a regional banking hub, and followed a model used in the Philippines and Bahrain that separated offshore and domestic transactions.

Thai and foreign banks were allowed to establish lightly capitalized subsidiaries for foreign currency borrowing and lending largely free of capital controls and withholding taxes. The result by 1997 was a jump in foreign currency activity but with no tangible gains in the effectiveness of the domestic banking or securities markets. Thailand's part financial liberalization produced a national credit boom. Net foreign liabilities of financial intermediaries rose from 6 per cent of domestic deposits in 1990 to 33 per cent by 1996, and net foreign liabilities ballooned from US$22 billion in 1993 to US$78 billion in 1996 (Nukul Commission 1998). An overabundance of funds from foreign sources could only lead to speculative investment, particularly in the real estate sector. By the end of 1996, the banking system's exposure to the property sector and related equities stood at 41 per cent of total loans compared with 23 per cent for manufacturing. The health of the financial system became dependent upon property prices.

Prudential regulation was generally poor. Bank risk management was influenced by entrenched commercial interests, with credit granted to politically favoured firms and industries and questionable lending allowed within conglomerates. Banks were owned by well-connected families, who were indulgent in financing the operations of affiliated companies – the definition of crony capitalism mentioned in Section 2.2. This led to poor credit decisions and to the misallocation of resources towards poorer and poorly compensated risks. Strains in the financial system were exacerbated by the following structural weaknesses:

- Banks that were isolated from international competition;
- Lack of effective prudential regulation and supervision of all intermediaries;
- Ill-enforced requirements for corporate disclosure;
- Lack of transparency among most financial intermediaries;
- Unreliable bankruptcy law and reconstruction procedures;
- Unenforced bank capital and NPL accounting requirements and little regulation of non-banks involved in lending; and
- Immature capital markets.

Thailand's financial system was overwhelmingly driven by banks and by finance companies dependent on bank funding, much of it from abroad. Bank loans to non-banks accounted for 89 per cent of Thailand's private sector liabilities at the end of 1997, while equity market capitalization accounted for only 15 per cent of GDP in 1997. This was an unstable growth model. Joseph Stiglitz noted early in 1998 that the international financial system had failed to operate in Asia to the standards he had previously praised, and argued that 'too little government regulation (or perverse or ineffective government regulation)' was partly the cause (Stiglitz 1998).

Corporate dynamics

As capital inflows financed domestic investment activity, an overvalued baht led to a growing current account deficit. Large inflows were beyond the economy's capacity for productive deployment and resulted in nothing but excess capacity. Overinvestment helped erode profit margins and led to declining returns on invested capital (ROIC). Private sector credit quality also fell, shown in a fall in interest coverage from 4.6 times in 1992 to 1.9 times in 1996. Table 2.2 shows that in 1992–96 debt-to-equity ratios increased from 71 to 155 per cent. Thailand was not unusual – similar growth in leverage was evident in Indonesia, South Korea and Malaysia. Leverage ratios for Asian firms were consistently significantly higher

Table 2.2 Corporate leverage ratios (%) end-period

Total debt/equity	1992	1993	1994	1995	1996
Hong Kong	26	23	33	36	39
Indonesia	59	54	58	81	92
South Korea	123	129	127	132	NA
Malaysia	31	29	38	45	62
Philippines	81	78	50	49	69
Singapore	37	34	33	45	58
Taiwan	71	73	71	67	65
Thailand	71	81	103	135	155
Latin America	31	35	34	33	31
France	141	133	117	112	111
Germany	61	67	61	59	58
Japan	136	139	139	135	138
US	106	102	97	94	90

China and India were insulated from the 1997 crisis and are excluded.

Source: Pomerleano (1998).

than firms in developed economies in this period, and left the region's entire corporate sector vulnerable to shocks.

High leverage was partly a result of the corporate and governance environment in some states, of which South Korea's *chaebols* are a good example, as explained in Box 2.5

Lower returns on invested capital led to value destruction in most industrial sectors. Poor corporate governance and the dominance of family conglomerates allowed this destruction to continue (Chang 2003). The *chaebol* lacked independent directors and often channelled

---

Box 2.5 Chaebol (재벌): Conglomerates and Governance

South Korea's *chaebol* are diversified business conglomerates, narrowly owned and closely controlled, often by family interests (Chang 2003). They typically comprise many operating and administrative subsidiaries functioning under a single corporate name. Among the largest, best known and most powerful in their commercial and political influence are Samsung, LG and Hyundai. The term derives from the Chinese (财团, or *cai tuan*) meaning money clique or syndicate, and once referred to business groups that commanded vast fortunes, often in secret.

Chaebol have been powerful in the South Korean economy since 1960–61 but became subject to concerns over collusion and anti-competitiveness after the late 1980s. For example, in 1995 the largest 30 *chaebol* by sales accounted for approximately 16 per cent of South Korea's GNP, a share that would have been higher were all group affiliates included (Chang 2003). The *chaebol* share of South Korean output fell slightly after 1998 but still accounted for more than 10 per cent of GNP in 2000, of which the largest five groups provided around three-quarters. As well as standing at the commanding heights of the domestic economy, larger *chaebol* have invested heavily overseas, especially since the late-1980s.

Many analysts argue that unduly inexpensive credit and imprudent government policies contributed to South Korea's asset price inflation before the 1997–98 financial crisis. However, the profitability of *chaebol* investments remained low. Investment returns of most *chaebol* measured by ROIC were lower than total interest costs. The more the *chaebol* invested, the more they appeared to lose. Poor returns were chiefly due to three factors:

- After South Korea's accelerated growth period of the 1980s the corporate sector became steadily uncompetitive in producing both simple ODM goods and high capital-value exports, due to labour cost competition from China and Indonesia, and an appreciation in the South Korean won.
- The *chaebol* responded to changing costs with increased capital spending for plant automation and construction at home and overseas, borrowing heavily from South Korean and foreign banks in won and other currencies (much of the increase in domestic bank lending was funded by cross-border US dollar loans). Growth in post-tax net incomes was disappointing and ROIC failed to improve.
- Many *chaebol* diversified aggressively in the 1990s into non-related businesses (Figure 2.2 shows the pre-crisis subsidiaries of the ten largest groups) which required further infusions of funds.

These strategies had two consequences prior to the 1997 Asian financial crisis. First, many South Korean business groups had sub-optimal capital structures, with too little core capital to support excessive bank liabilities. Figure 2.2 shows leverage ratios for the largest *chaebol* in 1997. Hyundai, then the largest *chaebol*, reported a debt–equity ratio of 437 per cent, and this may have been an underestimate, with the true level of

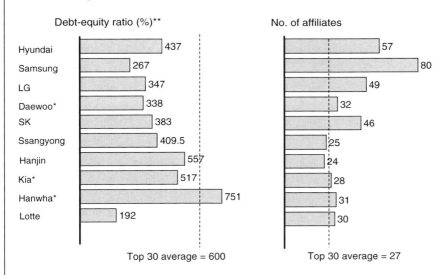

Figure 2.2 Chaebol capital and affiliate structure, 1997.

* Firms that were either bankrupt or reorganized under bank-sponsored workout programmes as of end-1992.

** Financial companies are excluded.

Source: Chang (2003).

leverage hidden by inadequate accounting consolidation. Average leverage among the largest 30 *chaebol* was higher at around 600 per cent.

Clearly, *chaebol* relied heavily on financial intermediaries. This was based on long-standing and often semi-captive relationships, in spite of 1980s legislation to prohibit *chaebol* from controlling interests in commercial banks. The state, family interests and others of influence could exert pressures on local banks to lend or roll over loans to the *chaebol*. In consequence, the risk exposure of the banking sector became more concentrated and prone to payment defaults and delinquent interest. Without concerted supervision, many banks chose to keep their loans current by extending further credit to unprofitable *chaebol*, a failure of risk management, regulation and bank governance that was shown by the 1997 financial crisis to be widespread in Southeast Asia, as well as South Korea. Prior to 1997, investment returns measured by ROIC declined steadily, leading to an accumulation of commercial bank non-performing loans (NPL). This unhealthy interaction between its corporate and financial sectors led eventually to South Korea's financial collapse in late 1997.

The pre-crisis relationship between the *chaebol* and their banks was a typical moral hazard. This once referred to the risk that the existence of a contract would change the behaviour of one or both parties, so that those insured against damage or fire would be less cautions in their custody of the insured property. Here, the moral hazard problem was twofold. *Chaebol* became less prudent in using bank credit, knowing that banks would not withdraw their lines, while banks made and maintained imprudent loans believing that their risk exposure was protected by the unwritten guarantee of the state or highly influential families. The system was unsustainable as soon as asset prices weakened and interbank markets withheld wholesale funding from the lending banks. Nobel economist Paul Krugman (1994) concluded that moral hazard and weak governance were critical problems in Asia's financial and corporate sectors.

investment funds into related companies, taking advantage of institutional deficiencies. They also leveraged government and corporate relationships to protect their market share, enter new sectors on privileged terms, overcome regulatory barriers and gain access to credit. Larger conglomerates often owned or controlled banks, which made credit easy to obtain.

EVA was thus negative for many Asian firms, especially in Thailand. If returns on investment are less than the average cost of raising capital then investment schemes would be best avoided as destroyers of economic value. Institutional deficiencies in financial discipline, information weaknesses and poor corporate governance may have led firms to overinvest. Most Asian emerging economies thus experienced lower levels of investment efficiency. Figure 2.3 shows the differences between average returns on capital employed (ROCE) and interest costs for 11 economies in 1992–96. The average gap between returns on capital and the cost of capital shown in the last column was minus-8 per cent in Thailand, minus-9 per cent in Indonesia and minus-2 per cent for South Korea, with Malaysia a low plus-3 per cent. Widespread investment inefficiency will compromise the balance sheet integrity of financial intermediaries, leading to NPLs at unsustainable levels. The pegged baht policy also reduced apparent currency risks, which itself encouraged the carry trade in foreign borrowing. When cheap capital meets bad investment decisions, it is not hard to guess the result: the Thai economy experienced a sharp and immediate decline in real output with GDP growth dropping from 8.9 per cent in 1994 to minus-0.4 per cent in 1997.

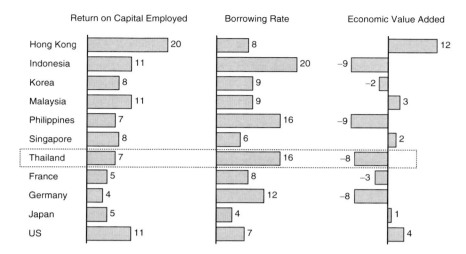

Figure 2.3 Corporate investment efficiency (1992–96 average).

* Economic value added (EVA) is the product of: (i) return on capital employed (ROCE) less the cost of capital; and (ii) total invested capital. Figure 2.3 shows only the gap between ROCE and borrowing rates.

Sources: World Bank (undated b); authors' calculations.

Policy misconduct

The pegged currency policy was questionable in the long term because it resulted in an over-valued baht, reducing Thai competitiveness in global markets, and producing current account deficits and an accumulation of short-term foreign debt. Pre-crisis growth had been largely financed by a rise in the current account deficit, that is, the counterpart of inflows of foreign capital. A thriving economy with a profitable commercial sector could comfortably service the resulting debt but Thai firms were heavily leveraged before the crisis. Overall activity dropped in 1996 with year-on-year import growth slowing from 3 to 2 per cent, and exports declining. The ratio of short-term debt to foreign reserves increased to 99.7 per cent in 1996. In a liquidity crisis with banks unable to renew foreign currency funding, foreign reserves would be insufficient to cover short-term liabilities.

Foreign capital flows

The foreign funding dynamic was central in building imbalances while confidence lasted, both by inducing current account deficits and supporting an overvalued exchange rate. Growing foreign liabilities backed by domestic assets also created a national balance sheet with a vast currency mismatch. Finally, the credit boom encouraged overinvestment in marginal projects by Thai banks and corporations, partly due to poor or unenforced risk management standards by competing lenders. This misplaced funding allowed the destruction of corporate value, eventually resulting in defaulted or delinquent loans that undermined the stability of the domestic financial system.

Asset price dynamics

Speculative investment created an asset bubble as early as in 1992, leading eventually to 1997's collapse of the domestic financial system. Speculative overinvestment in land and real estate was evident in its impact on equity prices, which rose more rapidly in the property sector than all others sectors in 1990–96. When the stock market collapsed in 1997, the percentage drop in property shares was far higher than the market as a whole. Between 1990–93, the stock market rose by 175 per cent compared with 395 per cent for the property segment, but then lost 51 per cent of its value by the end of 1996, compared with 73 per cent for property shares.

By mid-1996 these five structural factors had made Thailand fully vulnerable to instability in both the real and financial sectors. The ensuing loss of confidence in the baht was merely a trigger.

2.4   From regional to global crises

The 1997 crisis has had an enduring impact on national economies and policy formation. The economic and social dislocation provoked in South Korea and Southeast Asia by the collapse of confidence produced concern in the international community that Asia lacked national and regional crisis remedies, since only non-Asian organizations such as the IMF were able to provide credit and help stem the draining of external resources. This view led Japanese officials to propose an Asian monetary fund (Hayashi 2006: 82–102; Lipscy 2003) but the initiative was unsuccessful. Later discussions were vetoed by the United States (Hayashi 2006), and only in 2009 when Asia had gained material influence among the G20 states and IMF shareholders could these ideas be revisited. The crisis also induced a lasting risk aversion among policymakers who now feared reliving similar instability. This helped limited financial market reforms in individual economies but prevented the introduction of significant regional solutions that might involve a sacrifice in state sovereignty.

The first post-crisis reaction of banks in Asia was a herd withdrawal of credit. This squeeze affected almost all corporate borrowers across the region, including the economies least affected by capital flight or losses in confidence. It encouraged loan delinquency by healthy enterprises that might otherwise have relied on customary credit renewals. Many banks quickly became unable to support their untroubled lending due to real loan losses, tougher standards for risk management and regulatory enforcement of capital adequacy, in some cases dictated as part of agreements with the IMF. Corporate demand for loans collapsed. In 2000, with few acceptable financial assets available from traditional sources and the region's property markets in slump, Asia's commercial banks began using liquidity to invest in highly rated, major currency loans and securities issued by non-Asian borrowers, adopting the same portfolio shift as the region's foreign reserve managers. This was the start of the capital export process that saw an unprecedented accumulation of foreign asset holdings by East Asian money managers, both public and private.

Further controversy arose in discussions over capital controls. China and Malaysia maintained or introduced barriers to the movement of capital contrary to Washington Consensus advice: each suffered smaller falls in output and asset prices in 1997–98, while the crisis was most severe in Indonesia, South Korea and Thailand, each of which had minimal controls on capital inflows, although asset prices in China were also protected by a substantial prior currency devaluation in 1994. These examples helped other states to see Washington Consensus policies as deleterious to recovery (Demirgüç-Kunt & Detragiache 1998). Capital mobility was identified by policymakers as a condition that contributed to the financial crisis and the contagion that made its effects so severe.

The crisis exposed a helplessness within Asia's limited regional organizations. No organization based in the region could provide even short-term support to any state needing external aid. One ironic result is that Indonesia, South Korea and Thailand experienced an invasiveness from the IMF in their policymaking contrary to the consensual approach of ASEAN, that encouraged minimal interference by member states in the policies of others. Short-term IMF credit was given on deflationary terms without concern for non-interference in state governance. Thailand first sought liquidity assistance from Japan in early 1997 but no mechanism existed to allow meaningful support, and neither Japan nor the United States wished to abandon the conditionality of funding associated with IMF programmes. Policy changes demanded by the IMF before granting credit to Indonesia, South Korea and Thailand are remembered as unforgivable and counterproductive.

The Asian financial crisis not only revealed weaknesses in national financial systems, but also in imperfect regional economic and financial linkages that made every domestic economy vulnerable to contagion from systemic shocks. Its aftermath produced discrete national reforms intended to bolster recovery and improve crisis avoidance. These sought to improve the effectiveness of national financial systems and alter the extent of state involvement in finance, but with the exception of China, South Korea and Malaysia, most changes were modest, especially in legal and regulatory systems. State influence persists in individual financial sectors and the burgeoning results of currency management have diluted the incentives for domestic or regional financial reform. We return to the regional financial cooperation issues that extend from 1997–98 in Chapter 12.

Foreign reserve accumulation

The most visible part of Asia's medium-term response to its regional crisis was a precautionary accumulation of non-Asian financial assets. This may not have been an overt objective of policy for any single state but is closely connected to deliberate currency and economic management over the period.

No single factor explains the growth in aggregate Asian reserves since 2000 (Cheung & Ito 2008). States control very substantial foreign reserves but the scale of their accumulation has prompted concerns on three main grounds:

- Credit and currency risk concentrations for reserve holders, especially in US dollar denominated or other transferable securities with high credit ratings.
- External concerns as to global financial imbalances and their role in the recent global crisis (Arner 2009; Wolf 2008a, 2008b).
- Whether a portion of the reserves might be allocated to regional assets, or support domestic welfare spending or infrastructural development.

That accumulated savings might be destabilizing has been a theme in recent US policy, with a Federal Reserve chair referring for some time to a global 'savings glut' (Bernanke 2005). Reserves are not free resources but investible foreign currency assets and are matched by domestic currency liabilities. States decide how reserves are invested but this constitutes a portfolio choice rather than full liberty of use, which may have domestic credit or monetary consequences (Lejot 2011a). Furthermore, as we saw in Section 1.3, most Asian economies have comparatively high rates of precautionary savings. Individuals tend to hold much of their savings as deposits, often for lack of choice, but bank liquidity has often been associated with poor risk management or indiscriminate lending. One developmental initiative would focus on creating more transparent financial markets to allow broader use of foreign reserves within the region and apply domestic savings more effectively to support capital investment. Many states have now created semi-autonomous investment vehicles known as sovereign wealth funds (SWF).

Since 1999 Asia has realized sizeable current account surpluses and remarkable levels of international reserves relative to output. There have been periodic exceptions after exogenous shocks or policy corrections and certain states have followed distinct macroeconomic policies with consequences for government and external financing, but the region's modern financial characteristics are long-standing. Malaysia's central government has traditionally been active in direct spending on infrastructural investment, while the Philippines has a comparatively weak national tax base. Both have maintained fiscal deficits over extended periods. Growth recovered unexpectedly soon after the 1997 crisis, though not before considerable permanent losses in national income in Southeast Asia and South Korea. Table 2.3 summarizes the salient characteristics of Asia's contemporary economies, highlighting common aspects of the region's performance since the early 1980s and in the post-crisis recovery.

Structural concerns

The World Bank 2003 *Global Development Finance* report was concerned at Asia's susceptibility to shocks, high leverage, fiscal imprudence and the region's risk preferences in investment. This repeated arguments made widely in 1998 that 'structural and policy distortions' were to blame for the onset of the crisis (Corsetti, Pesenti & Roubini 1998: Part II, 1). Any recovery would be far off, for '[t]here are many reasons to believe that the East Asian cycle will not take the V-shaped form of Mexico [in 1994], and that the contraction in economic activity in the region will last for much longer' (ibid: 26). Yet growth resumed throughout Asia in 1999, although in some economies output losses took some years to make good, particularly in Indonesia. Recently, a different argument has been made, that Asia will lead the recovery from the global crisis but that the region is still in need of structural change, especially to encourage private domestic consumption and lessen a dependence on external spending (IMF 2010a).

The World Bank's 2003 analysis focused on four factors needing long-term attention. As to Asia's systemic vulnerability, the 'extreme openness of the region leaves it vulnerable to global shocks' (World Bank 2003: 29). Historically, the World Bank has been an unlikely proponent of capital controls but the remark conceals a paradox. The great expansion in investment has been funded largely from private sources, but since 1997 private markets are thought to have contributed to the likelihood of destabilizing shocks. What was once felt to favour development became a cause of suffering. Market innovation must be responsive to this problem, especially in relation to risk appraisal for capital investment, risk management in banks, and assisting credit risk appraisal by all financial investors.

Second, on financing risks, leverage and fiscal policy, '[t]here has been a remarkable recovery in the health of much of the region's corporate sector since the dark days of 1998. But levels of corporate leverage remain high' (World Bank 2003). Yet leverage was high well before the 1997–98 crisis and is identified as a threat regardless of duration and currency composition. The importance of changes in leverage also became clear: the 1992–96 increase in corporate leverage was highest in countries most affected by the crisis, that is, Indonesia, South Korea, Malaysia and Thailand (Pomerleano 1998).

Table 2.3 Common features of Asian economies

External trade, current account, international reserves	Historically strong export growth. Rapid expansion of current account surpluses since 1999, partly leading to substantial increases in foreign currency reserves
Output growth	Consistently high rates of growth, except in isolated cases and immediately after 1997
Government fiscal balance	Frequently conservatively managed. No consistent pattern; nor any systematic tendency to counter-cyclical deficit financing. Limited post-1997 crisis reflation measures
External financing	Consistent public and private direct investment from overseas and within the region; portfolio investment cyclical and strongly correlated to domestic US trends. Debt finance more reliant on loans than public issues of securities. Relatively narrow direct tax base
External debt	Comparatively low relative to other regions, to national output, and since 1999 relative to international reserves
Savings	Private and public sector savings have been consistently and appreciably higher than all other regions. Recent establishment of provident funds and growth of institutionalized consumer savings
Investment	Consistently far higher than other regions; relatively large proportion of private sector contribution compared to other emerging markets
Financial intermediation	Relatively concentrated or cartelized banking sectors; non-bank credit providers important in domestic lending prior to 1998. Modest non-bank financial intermediation of private savings. Low liquidity in money market instruments other than in the banking sector and for monetary policy use. High levels of impaired assets (except Hong Kong and Singapore), often poorly reported
Company finance	Internal finance more important than for companies elsewhere. Bond issues used far less than bank loans and equity new issues

Third, on the region's post-crisis portfolio management and risk preferences, the World Bank noted that 'the breadth and amount of central bank reserve accumulation over the past couple of years is striking' (World Bank 2003: 37), and much more was to follow. Precautionary motives have been at play since 1999 with governments building reserves partly in fear of further shocks, a traditional risk-averse strategy. A preference for low-risk assets is widely observed, although high savings partly reflect a lack of forced or contractual savings schemes compared to many advanced economies. It may also echo a scarcity of appropriate investment opportunities of the kind we diagnose in relation to Thailand in 1992–96, or of long-term institutional problems that encourage investment in well-rated OECD markets and penalize low-risk investments at home.

Asia's flows of funds are shaped by historic and cultural dynamics, some of which are relevant to today's financial markets. Dependence on bank credit has roots not only in the region's relative development but in cultural flows of funds similar to those seen in Japan from the 1950s. If financial markets reflect the characteristics of underlying capital flows then Asia's bond markets may have evolved to a limited state to meet limited purposes. Asia's modern orientation has been export-led growth assisted by capital asset formation. The greater part of that investment has been privately sourced and deployed, with a reliance on internal funding and bank borrowing. Governments have generally avoided heavy military spending as a share of national output, and in most cases state welfare or pension schemes are modest or absent. The effect of that stance in encouraging precautionary savings cannot be gauged, but Asian savings rates appear to remain above global averages in the few cases where directed provident schemes are broadly established, such as in Singapore. Home ownership is significantly lower than in advanced economies and the markets supporting private home purchase are sophisticated only in Hong Kong, Malaysia, Singapore and Taiwan. High savings ratios are often thought to indicate more than risk aversion and generally show no inverse correlation with per capita income. They may also be a function of a lack of entrenched welfare systems and underdeveloped institutional savings industries, and although there is some evidence that savings ratios decline marginally when these institutional factors are established, Japan suggests this is not a sufficient explanation. All these conditions dictate borrowing by companies and governments, and may have contributed to inefficient financial markets.

Structural results

The conditions lead to five main characteristics in the region in terms of corporate owner-ship, competition and sources of funding.

Concentrated ownership

Corporate ownership is generally more concentrated than in advanced countries. This pro-motes a primary reliance on internal funding. Secondary debt financing is sourced mainly from banks, from which arises an emphasis on relationship financing, which in turn militates against disclosure and transparency. Investment decision-making and capital allocation are heavily influenced by the innate preferences of the relationship bank. Immediately before the 1997 crisis Asian lenders were more content to finance speculative property development by advancing against collateral, which was very familiar to risk assessors, than credible projects for which whole business cashflow analysis was essential and for which they were histori-cally ill-prepared. Bank preferences heavily influence investment decisions.

Funding

Bank funding depends upon retail and interbank deposits, a narrower base than for banks operating in major markets. Tradable certificates of deposit and regulatory capital debt issues are either trivial or unavailable, in spite of the wishes of all institutional investors. Asia's money markets are dominated by short-term government debt issues, even though they lack much of the liquidity that established markets offer to non-bank participants. The absence of markets in short-term corporate debt similar to the US or eurocommercial paper markets, or the Dutch inter-corporate note market, cramps corporate investing and borrowing culture and limits the options available to all company treasurers. In several cases (including Hong Kong) promising markets for short-term corporate notes have been extinguished by the weight of government money market issuance and regulatory incentives.

Anti-competitive practices

Regulations or cartels in some countries require corporate issues to be guaranteed by a financial party, usually a commercial bank, regardless of the credit standing of the issuer. The practice may spring from investor protection concerns that a robust credit rating culture would ameliorate, but is usually induced by monopolistic banks. Such anomalies question whether the region's young domestic debt capital markets have provided corporate borrowers with any real alternative to bank credit. Some views are optimistic, holding that this was the case in Hong Kong after the crisis when new bond issues 'partially filled the gap' in financing that opened in 1998–99 when total bank lending fell. Yet the amount raised was modest, in 1999 representing only 13.7 per cent of that year's fall in domestic lending, and the buyers of new bonds were mainly banks. A large share of the corporate debt issued in this period comprised securitized floating-rate notes issued by asset-rich companies, structured solely to overcome prevailing bank credit policies.

Informal funding

In its process of reform since the late 1970s China has developed a positive association between growth and financial development, but the non-state corporate sector has not used domestic intermediaries for finance in any direct material way. Most spending by non-state enterprises relies on internal funding, while external financing sources are divided crudely between bank lending for state-owned enterprises and FDI for the non-state sector. However, an unknown but significant share of FDI for non-state enterprises may be more loan than capital in character, disguised to avoid capital controls on cross-border lending. This is observed with enterprises in mainland China controlled and funded from Hong Kong.

Bank lending

Certain aspects of corporate funding behaviour impact both domestic and cross-border debt markets. In the three years before the Asian crisis, sources of credit broadened in several economies, with secondary banks and finance companies lending heavily to companies and consumers. These lenders were typically more lightly regulated than banks and operated to poor risk management standards. Directly and indirectly, this quasi-bank sector was funded substantially with foreign currency loans: the phenomenon is central to the evolution of the crisis. The critical long-term lesson is that the growth of corporate lending by finance and leasing companies suggests that the banking sector is a poor provider for the needs of small- and medium-sized enterprises (SMEs).

   Such structural weaknesses became clear following the Asian crisis. Some large companies with established foreign currency revenues were immune to the regional withdrawal of credit in 1998–99, but all others suffered in funding or refinancing due to a scarcity of bank capital and improvements in regulatory accounting that forced banks to better recognize substandard assets. Alternative sources of corporate funding would not only lessen this problem but encourage bankers to raise their transactional skills beyond the secured lending and trade finance to which they were accustomed.

2.5 The global financial crisis 2007–9

The global financial crisis originated in one obscure segment of the US financial markets. It was to have major negative implications for Asia's real economy, but then lead to a rebalancing of influence among G20 states and an investor reappraisal of Asian risk. While the 1997 regional crisis signalled a need for change in Asia's financial systems, the global crisis shows the vulnerability of the region's traditional development model.

Before beginning a narrative of events in 2007–9 it may be helpful to capture the basic configuration of the world's financial markets as they were at the end of 2006, which was the last normal pre-crisis year and might be seen by history as the final year in the first wave of financial globalization that began in the 1980s.

Figures 2.4A and 2.4B present world finance in three segments, which is a way of allocating elemental financial claims by type. Derivative contracts are excluded as a class of capital and treated where necessary as embedded in other contracts (see Sections 8.2 and 8.3). Claims against governments and companies are of a similar scale, while structured transactions represented by asset-backed securities account for a massive amount that has since collapsed. At its peak in 2006 this amounted to around one quarter of claims against the corporate and government sectors. Asia was somewhat different, with only small aggregate amounts outstanding in structured securities. The timeline in Table 2.4 shows only major events or shocks that impacted heavily on market confidence such as to affect general behaviour. It does not include events relating solely to the Eurozone sovereign credit crisis of 2009–10.

The US housing market's fall

The global crisis followed a lengthy period of excessive borrowing, lending and investment, much of it encouraged by economic and regulatory factors. Excessive borrowing and lending occurred most egregiously in the US market for subprime residential mortgage loans in the five years to 2006. Excessive leverage was also prevalent in commercial real estate and corporate lending, especially for acquisitions and fundraising for the private equity sector.[1] The United States was the focus of the collapse, but risk redistribution had allowed banks and other intermediaries in the EU and Asia to acquire credit interests in its overvalued domestic markets. A startlingly diverse group of global investors found themselves unhappily exposed to collapsing US asset prices.

Simple 'cash' securitization is a form of contractual intermediation that makes traditional lending risks available to third-party investors. A lender sells an accumulation of loans to a

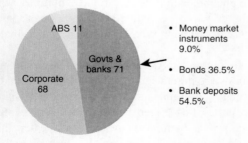

Figure 2.4A Global market composition, end-2006 (US$ trillion).

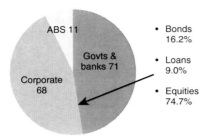

Figure 2.4B Global market composition, end-2006 (US$ trillion).
Source: Bank of England (2007).

legally isolated vehicle or trust. This funds the purchase by selling new securities to investors. The original lender receives cash or funding, and goes on to make more new loans and repeat the process. Investors gain indirect exposure to the securitized loans in the form of claims against the vehicle or trust.

The accounting, capital treatment and transactional integrity of securitization varies by jurisdiction, but the concept grew increasingly popular from the 1980s among US loan originators. Securitization can lower interest costs on the underlying loans and help lenders reduce payment risks. At the same time the structure may offer incentives for abuse, for at the market's peak loans were made purely for redistribution and sale, both by experienced mortgage lenders and new loan aggregators whose transactions were not subject to ongoing supervision. Banks that made and sold home loans in large numbers lost the credit risk incentive to make proper lending appraisals or retain an interest in the loan being properly serviced.

This occurred with no corresponding shift in supervision. A migration of intermediation took place from traditionally capitalized lenders to a locus of contracts without any adjustment to the regulatory setting. Over two decades the demand for new investment channels allowed securitization to become a link between overinvestment in complex securities and excessive borrowing and lending. For the new model to function without eventually becoming a systemic threat, a change in regulatory philosophy was required to emphasize contractual standardization and supervision. Other false incentives arose from the Basel accord rules for bank capital adequacy, and the conflicted involvement of credit rating agencies, topics we discuss in Chapter 8.

Crisis narrative

What began in mid-2006 as a fall in real estate and loan values in the US subprime mortgage lending sector became, by late 2008, the severest global shock and economic downturn since the early 1930s. A sequence of debilitating events in the US financial markets, shown in Table 2.4, spread into a global contagion and for the first time made the most elemental segments of the financial and credit markets broken and dysfunctional. Two events stand out: a retail deposit run at British mortgage lender Northern Rock in September 2007 and the insolvency of US investment bank Lehman Brothers in September 2008. These events caused seizures in the international interbank credit markets, certain domestic money markets in the United States and elsewhere, and US dollar markets in short-term notes and commercial paper.

Table 2.4 Global financial crisis timeline, 2007–9

2006–7	1H 2008	Jul.–Sept. 2008	Oct. 2008	Nov. 2008–2009
29 Aug. 2006. Peak in US subprime mortgage loan market*	11 Jan. Mortgage lender Countrywide sold to Bank of America	11 Jul. Failure of US mortgage lender IndyMac	Run on US money market funds, US commercial paper closed, global credit markets paralyzed	23 Nov. 2008. US Government rescues Citigroup
5 Mar. 2007. Leap in HSBC US subprime mortgage delinquencies	24 Jan. Rogue trading losses at Société Générale	7 Sept. US federal agencies Fannie Mae and Freddie Mac nationalized	Oct. UK government takes control of Royal Bank of Scotland	Mid-Dec. 2008. US$583bn peak use of Federal Reserve central bank swap lines
30 Jul. German bank IKB fails after CDO losses at its Rhineland Funding Capital Corp. conduit	11 Feb. AIG restates accounts after credit derivative valuation errors	14 Sept. Bank of America agrees to buy Merrill Lynch	29 Oct. Federal Reserve grants swap lines to South Korea and Singapore central banks	3 Feb. 2009. Major central bank swaps lines renewed for 6–12 months
9 Aug. BNP Paribas bans investor withdrawals from US subprime money market funds	17 Feb. Northern Rock nationalized	15 Sept. Lehman Brothers declares largest-ever US bankruptcy	Oct.–Nov. Banks recapitalized or fully nationalized in Belgium, Germany, Iceland, Ireland, Netherlands, UK and US	2 Apr. G20 states plan IMF recapitalization and global regulatory reforms
17 Sept. Northern Rock suffers first UK bank deposit run in 150 years.	16 Mar. Insolvent Bear Stearns bought by JPMorgan Chase with help from federal guarantees	16 Sept. AIG rescued with US federal aid	Oct.–Nov. Federal Reserve swap lines to EU, Swiss and UK central banks made limitless. Collapse of Iceland's banking system	17 Apr. US$47bn IMF Flexible Credit Line opened for Mexico
12 Dec. Central banks in Canada, EU, Switzerland, UK and US provide crisis LLR liquidity	Mar.–Jun. OECD central banks allow emergency repos and provide crisis liquidity	18 Sept. OECD central banks agree to unblock interbank markets		
		20 Sept. US government announces US$700bn Troubled Asset Relief Program		

* One synthetic index of single-A rated subprime loans (Markit ABX.HE A-06-2 index) peaked at 115.08 on 28 August 2006, then fell gradually before beginning a precipitous drop in June 2007. When Lehman Brothers failed on 15 September 2008 the index stood at 8.6 (2 July 2007 = 100).
Sources: BIS (2009a; 2009b); Bank of England (2008); Mollenkamp (2007), Federal Reserve Bank of St Louis, Federal Reserve Bank of New York and Markit Group data; authors' records.

Banks and investors suddenly became fearful of further defaults and began hoarding liquidity in cash or government securities, limiting credit transactions to the shortest maturities, and trading only with undoubted counterparties. Markets in all asset-backed and structured securities ceased to function and remained fractured as we concluded this book. Figure 2.5 is an illustration by the Bank of England of how certain securities markets functioned after 2007. No public data exist to illustrate interbank conditions in the same way, but those markets were also subject to prolonged impairment.

The most extreme conditions occurred in the six months that followed Lehman's collapse and the simultaneous rescue from insolvency of insurer AIG by the US government and central bank. Both firms had outstanding arrays of funded and contingent financial contracts with thousands of banks and other intermediaries around the world. The failure of a major intermediary will always disturb sentiment but with Lehman the markets were doubly shaken, having convinced themselves that the US government was certain to organize a

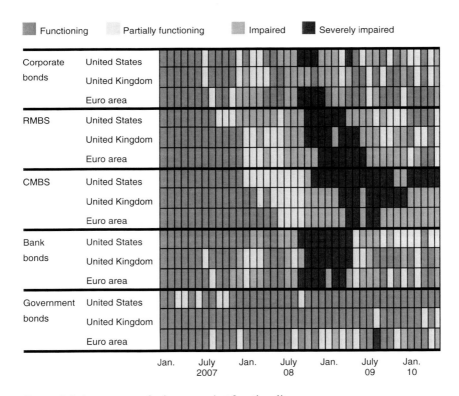

Figure 2.5 Assessment of primary market functionality.

The chart shows the feasibility of new transactions in the debt securities markets in the United States, United Kingdom and Eurozone from 2007 to June 2010, covering simple bank, corporate and sovereign issues and asset-backed securities (ABS) based on residential and commercial property loans (RMBS and CMBS, respectively). The assessments reflect actual issuance in each category relative to GDP and the comparative cost of those issues both expressed as deviations from the average results for the whole period (Bank of England 2010: 18). The 2010 improvement in issue conditions for bank bonds and RMBS relied upon sales to banks encouraged by central bank monetary policy, explained in Section 4.3.

rescue if it became necessary, as it did earlier in 2008 with a smaller (although still substantial) investment bank, Bear Stearns.

We see the reasons for this unprecedented loss of confidence as more complex. Confidence shattered partly for simple credit reasons, driven by a collapse in real estate values and financial assets identical to the fall in the Thai commercial property market a decade earlier. More troubling was a fear of unknown credit risks that can be characterized as unquantifiable 'Knightian' uncertainty. Banks that were unable to assess accurately the creditworthiness of their day-to-day counterparties chose instead to avoid as much risk as possible, and ceased to operate in the most basic credit markets upon which all other markets depend.

Underlying that concern was a qualitative factor in addition to any logical fears of recession impacting credit risk at large. This resulted from the proliferating use of credit risk transfer, which since the mid-1980s had transformed bank intermediation from a process based on organizations to one relying increasingly on contract formation and administration. We describe the mechanics of this transformation in Sections 6.4 and 8.1. The essence is that banks of all types and sizes, that until the 1980s undertook a simple balance sheet exercise in making loans, became increasingly able to manipulate their entire loan portfolios through credit risk transfer in one of three main forms:

- Buying or selling new or seasoned loans in a similar way to trading in securities;
- Selling pools of loans in a securitization process involving new asset-backed securities; or
- Using credit derivatives contracts to alter the risk composition of loan portfolios.

None of these actions is in itself risk preferring or speculative and would often be used for conservative reasons. The first two are examples of funded transfers that usually change the size of the bank's balance sheet, and the third is a simple example of unfunded transfer, which means that the bank's claim alters in terms of credit risk but not in scale. The three techniques can combine to form highly complex or synthetic transactions, and this activity was a sizeable source of revenue for large and sophisticated banks until the crisis erupted – among them Lehman Brothers, a prolific originator of asset-backed securities (ABS), collateralized debt obligations (CDOs), and other complex debt securities. Investment banks and secondary lenders used securitization to access credit markets that previously were controlled by commercial lenders, and all forms of credit risk transfer allowed banks to acquire risks that were formerly as commercially remote as Adam Smith's pre-globalization 'man of humanity' was from China.

Technical advances in credit risk transfer were welcomed by many intermediaries and generally applauded by the Bank for International Settlements (BIS) and other regulators as conducive to better risk management and capital allocation (BIS 2005). In an ideal world, the redistribution of credit risk would have been seen as valuable: better in a downturn to have risk evenly spread among a large number of participants. This bull market logic was exposed as faulty by mid-2007.

Even had no general deterioration in credit risks occurred, each intermediary realized that it could no longer quantify the extent to which its potential counterparties were exposed to failed assets. Perhaps redistribution had spread overall risk more evenly, but no-one could be sure, and if distribution had been increasingly incomplete as markets reached their peaks then certain banks might have concealed masses of unsold risk as inventory, as Lehman's bankruptcy filing would show (Valukas 2010). Markets feared that failures in credit risk distribution would leave the system with high transaction leverage, falling asset prices, and certain banks thus exposed to funding difficulties. Participants became exceptionally risk averse, a caution that was dysfunctional to those essential parts of the financial system that had traditionally been of least concern. Section 7.3 discusses the importance of reputational capital to deal-oriented investment banks in winning new business and allowing successful execution. Effective distribution resources are always valuable and often scarce.

Excessive investment was largely the result of two economic factors:

- Low nominal US interest rates following the technology stock price-correction in March 2001, and in Japan after the banking crisis of the early 1990s; and
- Imbalances in saving and investment between the Anglo-American economies, especially the United States and United Kingdom, and the rest of the world, especially China, Japan and other emerging economies.

Low interest rates and voluminous flows of funds from outside the United States supported the purchase of ABS and other securities of apparent high credit quality with attractive yields. A combination of capital market technology, regulatory incentives, low nominal interest rates and expectant investor demand provided the resources necessary for a crisis. US real estate prices reached unsustainable levels during 2006. Central banks increased interest rates to forestall inflation concerns, and payment defaults quickly began to increase among less affluent US borrowers. New home buyers vanished and a steep fall in property values followed, as shown in Figure 2.6. This downward price spiral was the real economy root of a systemic financial crisis.

Weakened housing conditions were broadcast throughout the financial system by the securitization process. Analysts and participants first asked which lenders would be most impacted by price falls and loan failures, but the question was made difficult by the volume of assets that had been transferred and repackaged through loan sales. This was less a matter of the enforceability of claims than uncertainty as to the ability of investors to carry losses, because residential mortgage-backed security (RMBS) investors customarily share claims in tiers (tranches) against the issuer of their securities rather than any subrogated rights against

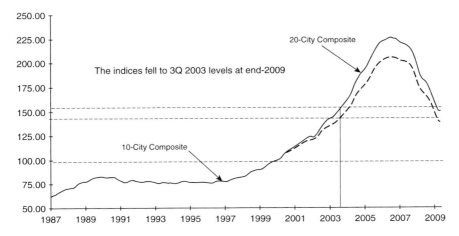

Figure 2.6 US housing market dynamics, 1987–2009.
The figure uses the S&P/Case-Shiller home price indices.
Source: S&P governance scores (2001).

defaulting home buyers. This produced a classic case of adverse selection: no-one could know who held economic interests in the defaulting loans so the markets ceased to deal in instruments whose values were now highly uncertain. Coupled with increasing risk aversion, the core credit markets quickly lost confidence in banks that had been most active in loan origination and securitization since they were likely to hold substantial impaired and unmarketable claims. The new issue and funding process came to an abrupt halt and banks in the United Kingdom and United States such as Northern Rock and Bear Stearns found themselves unable to fund their continuing operations.

Confidence continued to deteriorate with the collapse of Bear Stearns in early 2008. Figure 2.7 shows the changes in major bank market capitalization during this period.

From late 2007 many OECD governments were forced to assist in preventing a general financial collapse, using interest rate cuts, infusions of liquidity or capital, backstop guarantees of credit risk, and facilities for asset repurchases. This prevented the fracture of the financial system but could not forestall the major consequences that would follow in the real global economy.

In December 2007 the Federal Reserve created six-month US dollar swap lines with the European Central Bank (ECB) and Swiss National Bank (SNB) (the Eurozone and Swiss central banks, respectively) to provide certainty of US dollar funding for the banks they each regulate. Ten months later, the shock of Lehman's failure led it to use standing statutory authority to open lines to 14 central banks at a total amount of US$620 billion, including the central banks of Australia, Brazil, Canada, Denmark, Japan, South Korea, Mexico, New Zealand, Singapore, Sweden and the United Kingdom (Goldberg, Kennedy & Miu 2010). In the same period the ECB provided similar lines to non-Eurozone central banks in Denmark, Hungary and Poland; the SNB to the ECB and the National Bank of Poland; and Norwegian

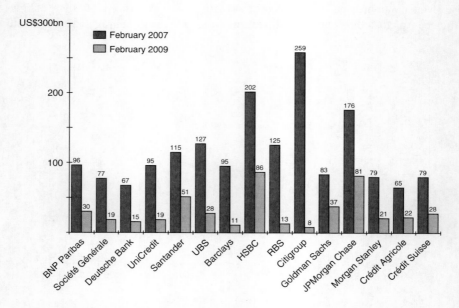

Figure 2.7 Market capitalizations as at February 2007 and February 2009.
Sources: Bloomberg; authors' calculation.

and Swedish central banks to their Icelandic counterpart (Ho & Michaud 2008). Most of these lines were drawn. US lines to the Bank of England, ECB and SNB were made limitless so as to meet any creditworthy demand for offshore liquidity and allow the Federal Reserve's counterparties to fund the US dollar liabilities of the banks they supervise. Usage peaked at US$583 billion in December 2008 (Mersch 2010).

Impact in Asia

The credit market seizure spread to those Asian banking sectors where short-term foreign currency liabilities were relatively high. The Bank of Korea drew over one third of its US$30 billion Federal Reserve line in October 2008 (Bank of Korea 2008: 32–3). South Korea exhausted 23.3 per cent of its international reserves in 2008 (ibid: 56). In other respects the timeline in Table 2.4 contains only passing reference to Asia. The real economy was affected by a collapse in aggregate OECD demand but the region's financial systems were relatively unaffected. The exceptions included events both good and bad:

- Many South Korean and some Japanese banks experienced problems in obtaining US dollar funding. This was relieved when the Bank of Korea drew on credit lines with the Federal Reserve.
- Large and small banks in China, Hong Kong, Malaysia, Singapore and Thailand made embarrassing losses on passive investments in complex securities.
- Many complex securities sold with embedded derivatives to small investors in Hong Kong, Singapore and Taiwan were found to be worthless and led to popular protests.
- Japanese investment bank Nomura Securities bought many of the non-US businesses of the failed Lehman Brothers, with the substantial but uncertain prospect of becoming Asia's first leading investment bank.
- Asian sovereign wealth funds invested heavily in large US and EU banks needing to raise fresh capital, sometimes with success, sometimes not.
- Several large Western banks raised capital by selling strategic minority holdings in large Chinese banks, held since shares were listed in initial public offerings (IPOs).
- Some Western banks shifted resources and capital to Asia for better prospects and increasingly acceptable credit risks.
- A rise occurred in outward direct investment by state and commercial parties, both within the region and more widely.
- Capital raising by new listings and rights issues by Chinese and other Asian companies continued throughout the period and were well-supported by strategic investors.
- Asian states gained influence with the IMF for the first time since 1999.

Common factors in two crises

One significant difference between the Asian and global crises is that no material interbank credit run took place in the former. Precautionary reasons led to the withdrawal of foreign currency lending rather than the funding for that lending, which was the core problem in the post-Lehman dislocation. Other differences are less material and our analysis points to many shared factors, at the core of which is a breakdown of links between the real economy and the financial sector. Table 2.5 proposes a generic framework summarizing the causes of the crises in five dimensions: the real sector, financial sector, asset price dynamics, macroeconomic policies, and fund dynamics.

Table 2.5 Commonalities in two crises

	1997 Asian crisis	2008 Global crisis
Real economy	Overleveraged corporate sector destroyed value by persistently poor capital investments Slowing export growth	Misaligned incentives for US mortgage brokers and lenders Housing bubble and subsequent price correction with major effect on disposable income and spending
Financial sector	Poor performance in real sector resulted in mounting bank NPLs Currency and duration mismatch resulting from domestic assets funded by foreign currency loans	Vast leverage in credit risk via structured debt products Opaque shadow banking system Credit rating agencies compromised and unable to assess risk Banks lose from exposure to CDOs and proprietary structured securities for which no market price is available Extreme credit and balance sheet leverage in the financial system propagated the shocks
Asset price dynamic	Property and stock market price inflation and bubbles, leaving lending banks highly vulnerable to default	Loan defaults and fall in values of RMBS and other CDOs create realizable losses in bank balance sheets, without sufficient capital to support write-offs Vicious cycle of asset price declines. Price falls create pressure for sales; sales then further depress asset prices
Macro policy	Managed exchange rates encouraged capital inflows before the crisis Lax fiscal policies and inefficient government spending	Low nominal interest rates Global imbalances in investment and savings between the surplus exporting economies in Asia and deficit importing economies in Europe and the US
Funding dynamics	Large amounts of foreign funds flowed in before crisis, resulting in mounting foreign debts Foreign banks began to withdraw lending from late 1996, and refused loan renewals when the crises erupted in mid-1997 Central banks exhausted foreign reserves	Confidence collapses in structured securities and investment vehicles. Investor funds withdraw leading to a withdrawal of general credit and liquidity Loss-making banks cease lending, causing a global interbank seizure Widespread run on many intermediaries and markets

Problems in the real economy or the financial sector, when propagated via poorly designed macroeconomic policies, adverse funding dynamics or volatile asset price dynamics, may induce a breakdown of the links between the two sectors and increase the risk of a major crisis. In both cases the five dimensions discussed in Table 2.5 share the blame, although each crisis had its own trigger.

Central to the Asian financial crisis were highly leveraged national corporate sectors making consistently inefficient investments. This led to a rise in banking sector NPLs. The situation was worsened by a collapse of property values in Southeast Asia, inappropriate government policies and fixed exchange rates, and unfavourable foreign capital dynamics. The global financial crisis originated in sophisticated financial sectors. Highly leveraged intermediaries suffered losses due to their credit commitments and unsold inventory of complex securities, positions that after Lehman's collapse and AIG's rescue could no longer be hedged. The loss spiral in financial intermediaries provoked major turmoil and a liquidity crisis throughout the global credit markets. Credit market dysfunction then spread to other asset classes and the real economy.

Since 2009 these events have prompted national policymakers and regulators to consider legislative changes to reform and re-regulate the financial industry, in some cases assisted by popular disquiet as to the worth of the sector. This wave of re-regulation focuses on the G20, led by the US and EU. Our taxonomy of the two crises points leads to several lessons:

- Reducing incentives for excessive transaction leverage and borrowing. One theme common to both crises is high sectoral and transactional leverage. The Asian financial crisis saw overleverage in the corporate sector; the global financial crisis was rooted in leverage within financial intermediaries.
- Deleveraging the corporate sector, financial sector or transactional practices poses a problem for architects of the next generation of financial systems. The era of financial globalization has been credit-based, even in states such as Germany where personal borrowing is less entrenched. Reducing incentives to borrow or invest involves a deep institutional transformation, and the results, if implemented, may differ from state to state.
- Improving governance in the financial sector. Regulatory design must strengthen disclosure, transparency and accountability in financial markets and among intermediaries, including non-bank intermediaries such as hedge funds and private equity funds. This might include enhancing disclosure for complex products and ensuring complete reporting of the financial condition of intermediaries. Some analysts favour forms of intelligent disclosure that would meet the expected needs of investors by emphasizing identified key facts. Managerial incentives may need to be realigned to penalize excessive risk-taking in intermediaries that have access to LLR facilities.
- Improving governance in the corporate sector. Banks need to maintain an arms-length relationship with their corporate clients, even if they function under a Rheinish model as in Germany or Japan, where a lead bank is formally involved in corporate strategy and governance. Limits to lending to connected firms or insiders needs to be enforced. Transparency is required where banks and corporations are controlled by a single interest, which could include disclosure rules or a formal ownership relationship through a public holding company structure. Intermediaries and agents involved in disciplining firms should be encouraged to enhance their roles.
- Regulation of non-bank financial intermediaries. Thailand learned in 1997–98 that non-bank intermediaries can infect the banking sector and the entire financial system.

More recently a shadow banking system of non-bank intermediaries, structured investment vehicles (SIVs) and undercapitalized lending conduits allowed undisclosed leverage for their controlling banks and eventually amplified their losses. All intermediaries must be regulated. Only with an integrated system, that allows for financial innovation in contracts or intermediaries with continual and adequate disclosure, can states realistically expect that financial intermediation will be more likely to absorb than magnify unexpected shocks.

- Strengthen capital requirements and prudential regulation or limit the permissible scale of commercial intermediaries. A moral hazard arises repeatedly in financial crises if liabilities created by reckless intermediation become a burden to the state.
- Improve bankruptcy provisions and mechanisms for creative restructuring. Without credible procedures banks and corporate owners may delay recognizing losses to prevent losing control of assets to creditors or new investors. Both crises showed a need for effective mechanisms to encourage restructuring as an alternative to court directed bankruptcy and the liquidation of assets.

Research has established the important function of financial development in economic development. Theory and empirical evidence point to a causal effect of the level and sophistication of financial development on economic growth. Our two crisis narratives suggest that states which fail to promote effective financial systems are likely to undermine the momentum of economic growth. The general success in Asia's development since 1949 has partly masked structural problems in its core economic model, which is the subject of Chapter 3. The region needs well-functioning, 'second generation' financial systems to deal effectively with these issues, which are distinct from those prevailing before 1997 ('first generation' financial systems). Both the Asian and the global financial crisis have highlighted the centrality of financial design for Asia's future economic development

3 Challenges to development and finance

Post-1949 industrialization in Asia was not achieved without cost, despite raising the living standards of millions in a relatively short period. In Section 1.1 we cited a seminal report that declared Asia's growth performance to be an economic miracle for being notably rapid without widening disparities in income (World Bank 1993), but this unusual cocktail became diluted after the 1997 financial crisis. In the following decade incomes became progressively less evenly distributed as the same time as a general recovery in growth. This may have no single explanation, but we want to consider whether global financialization and rising financial asset prices were important in the change.

The 2000s also brought concerns as to how industrialization affects mass urbanization, climate change, environmental degradation and labour conditions. High finance may seem remote from these issues, but effective financial systems can promote sound commercial governance and corporate responsibility, assist in social welfare through provident schemes and health insurance, help investors achieve their return objectives without unwanted risks, and augment essential infrastructure to relieve poverty. Finance in Asia is far from primitive, but nowhere is it complete in these dimensions. Finance cannot therefore serve its full purpose, and so one aim of this chapter is to question that effectiveness.

We begin by discussing the challenges faced by finance in Asia, and then provide a description of intermediation and its functions. Five elements together characterize all forms of intermediation, whether complex, primitive, constant or constantly changing, and regardless of national preferences in societal goals or forms of governance, for example in the distinction we made in Section 2.2 between Anglo-American and Franco-German models of capitalism. These elements are:

- Contracts made in standardized forms, commonly called *financial instruments*;
- Established, regulated organizations or *financial intermediaries*;
- Organized markets, many of which are known as *exchanges*;
- The regulation and supervision of the first three elements; and
- Risk, in the dimensions associated with its identification, measurement and management.

This chapter points towards Asian finance's future. It plots the changes made to national systems in the post-1999 recovery and ends with a description of the unique, centrally led, market intermediation underpinning China's economy, a system that was not long ago entirely without finance. The paradox of non-hasty financial reform is that Asia's experience of the global crisis was less severe than in the older industrialized world, where after 2000 financial sophistication became increasingly associated with destabilizing leverage and a wanton disregard for risk, especially among complex intermediaries and their investor clients.[1]

Our view is that Asia's fortuitous escape cannot allow its faults and omissions of law and practice to be ignored, nor absolve the region of the need to intensify financial reform while guarding against systemic risks.

3.1 Weaknesses in the development model

The structural problems that made the 1997 crisis so debilitating included:

- Costly intermediation, leading to welfare losses and endangering growth;
- Deteriorating long-term demographics;
- Savings dynamics that limit full access and fail to provide choice for users;
- Unfavourable external changes in the macroeconomic policy environment; and
- A propensity for overinvestment.

If not addressed sensitively these problems will undermine the six central foundations of Asia's growth model discussed below. As one example, some have contributed to the secular decline in Japan's growth since the collapse of its 1980s asset bubble. One further concern is how the region might respond if the global financial crisis has shaken a central feature of the growth model: that is, a continuing dependence on sub-assembly and manufactured exports to developed markets.

We ended Chapter 2 by citing certain institutional and structural problems. These vary by both time and place but became evident during the regional financial crisis. In spite of many institutional reforms they continue to be visible in several national markets, in part because reactions to the crisis were inconsistent. The shock of the contagion and the enforced deflation that followed had profound and cautionary effects on the thinking of policymakers, despite which financial and institutional reforms were debated far more than they were implemented, a theme we address in Sections 12.4 and 12.5.

Policy caution led to massive reserve accumulation rather than a strengthening of domestic banking and securities markets; to a mercantilist export orientation; to a 'glut' of global savings identified by the chairman of the US Federal Reserve rather than to investment in physical infrastructure (Bernanke 2005); and to expressions of institutional intent but too little real momentum. The policy mindset was negative: that stronger financial markets are volatile, incapable of being managed, might weaken the authority of government, and be far too associated with the hated Washington Consensus. One IMF study observed that:

> the region generates substantial net saving … and countries have been accumulating large stocks of foreign reserves. This has resulted in the financial sectors of developed countries in Europe and North America serving as financial intermediaries for the Asian economies, with relatively more stable outbound official flows and more volatile inbound private flows.
>
> (Cowen & Salgado 2006: 11)

These reasons help explain the incremental approach taken to regional cooperation in financial policy described in Chapter 12.

The post-1949 model of development enabled a succession of economies to achieve rapid, seldom interrupted growth, but not without costs. Its sustainability relies on six main assumptions:

- There exists an effective system of financial intermediation that continuously channels capital flows in the form of savings and investment to the sectors of the economy where it is most capable of use and is well-rewarded.
- Reliance on foreign consumption, especially in the EU and United States, as a precondition of development, regardless of the possibility of a deterioration in those markets with the resulting risks of protectionism and weak domestic consumption.
- High levels of personal savings will continue for the foreseeable future, even if corporate savings become volatile or generally decline.
- The supply of low-cost labour will not become constrained in the foreseeable future.
- Existing macroeconomic and structural policies can deliver high growth and an acceptable degree of macroeconomic stability. Opportunity costs and welfare losses associated with the accumulation of foreign reserves can be sustained at a manageable level.
- Regional competition will not generate imbalances and become a source of instability. This applies especially to competition for cheap factor inputs such as labour.

Such lists are inexhaustible, but not all these conditions will prevail at all times and in all economies. Weak or missing links in any one economy could produce less favourable economic dynamics that, through globalization, would spread and have adverse repercussions on growth and welfare, as with the impact in Asia of the global financial crisis.

Transnational financial activity has been important in Asia for generations, at first in domestic or colonial direct investment, then in trade finance provided by merchants and commercial banks, and during the Asian economic miracle through an export orientation and relatively open capital flows guided by the developmental state. The functioning of Asian financial markets is influenced by overseas practices, inward direct and portfolio investment, the penetration by non-Asian firms into domestic markets for investment banking, commercial lending and non-bank intermediation, and the influence of financial innovation from other centres, even where foreign ownership of domestic intermediaries is restricted.

One consequence of a policy resistance to financial integration is that few indigenous intermediaries have a regional spread of businesses, while certain non-Asian banks and non-bank intermediaries are well-represented throughout the territory. The financial organizations seen most frequently in major cities are AIA, ANZ, Citigroup or HSBC, rather than Bangkok Bank, DBS, ICBC or Kookmin Bank. This is often a legacy of long-standing operating licenses granted in colonial times that predate more recent restrictions.

Modern Asian states are inclined to protect their domestic financial markets from foreign participation or ownership, even after an infusion of Western capital into stricken banks after 1997 in Indonesia, South Korea and Thailand. Even the generally open Singapore limits foreign engagement in its domestic retail financial markets, and most states have made very limited liberalization commitments in the context of the WTO framework addressing trade in financial services. Japanese banks were well-represented overseas by the 1980s, but their presence in the region has diminished since the early 1990s after profound domestic loan losses, sectoral cutbacks and forced consolidation. Banking that deals only with large-scale transactions is often managed from major financial centres, but coverage of consumers, SMEs and high net worth (HNW) clients is usually associated with a broad geographical presence – even as cyberbanking becomes widely available – making most indigenous banks regionally constrained.

Costly intermediation

We began Chapter 1 by showing how Asia's economies are characterized by relatively high levels of personal savings and investment in real estate and other fixed assets. Growth would rise and be experienced more broadly if the region were able to encourage savings into more productive areas of activity. The limiting factor to this progression is that most national financial systems remain underdeveloped. The most common measure of the scale of financial sector development relies on the work of Goldsmith explained in Section 2.1, using the ratio to GDP of the sum of market capitalizations of debt and equity securities and the aggregate of private credit extended by banks. Figure 2.1 showed the results of this measure, which is also reflected in the final column of Table 3.5. Most Asian economies are relatively financially unsophisticated even though their equity markets are comparatively well-developed, and the region's banking sector has been subject to considerable administrative reform since the errors that exacerbated the regional crisis.

This high-level conclusion conceals subtle and diverse national differences. Asia's financial systems allocate capital more effectively than in many other emerging economies. Certain commercial and private banks are both efficient and highly profitable in specific market segments such as trade finance, consumer credit and wealth management. The general stock of NPLs has fallen since the Asian financial crisis, not only with the cyclical recovery but for reasons of efficiency, including improvements in accounting and reporting, regulatory supervision and in risk management by banks and other lenders. It also reflects the development in most economies of trading in distressed loans, through commercial investors in distressed debts and government-sponsored asset management companies (AMCs).

The former may be aggressive vulture funds that acquire claims against distressed borrowers at substantial discounts and then negotiate a sale of the claim at a higher price back to the borrower, sometimes with the threat of litigation. Some borrowers welcome this approach as a means to cancel debt cheaply and make a paper profit. It was commonly used in Southeast Asia after 1998 but is contrary to acceptable practice in cases involving many financial creditors, where the ethic is for equally ranked creditors to share the burden of restructuring.

The result is that banks in most economies are now far more likely than in 1997 to recognize and report problem credits, seek solutions with debtors or make appropriate provisions against loan losses. This approach is neither perfect nor infallible, but has increased the willingness of lenders to liquidate their least recoverable claims to specialist investors. The improvement brings regional practice closer to OECD standards, and the reported results are shown in the first two columns of Table 3.1, with NPLs as a share of total lending. In most states the improvement resulted from both cyclical recovery and financial sector reforms. Only in Hong Kong and Singapore has the long-term occurrence of banking sector NPLs been consistently low by global comparisons.

For all these positive qualities, the most productive segments of each national economy are not necessarily fully or effectively funded through the financial system, causing social welfare loss and endangering overall stability. We use as examples the two fast growing large economies, China and India.

China's striking expansion in the past quarter century has resulted largely from fixed-asset investment characterized by three features:

- High gross domestic savings rates and success in attracting FDI mean that investment in real estate and other fixed assets have also tended to be high. This suggests that China is prone to overinvestment, which in turn may provoke inflation and asset bubbles.

Table 3.1 Comparisons of bank soundness (%)

FYE	NPL/total loans		Capital adequacy		Loan loss provisions/ NPLs	
	2000	2009	2000	2009	2000	2009
China	22.4	1.6	13.5	10.0	4.7	115.0
Hong Kong	7.3	1.3	17.9	16.8	NA	NA
India	12.8	2.4	11.1	13.2	NA	52.6
Indonesia	20.1	3.3	21.6	17.4	36.1	127.4
Japan	5.3	1.9	11.7	15.8	35.5	27.1
South Korea	6.6	0.8	6.7	11.4	81.8	125.2
Malaysia	8.3	1.8	11.3	13.5	57.2	95.6
Philippines	15.1	3.0	16.2	16.0	43.6	112.3
Singapore	3.4	2.5	16.4	13.5	87.2	91.0
Taiwan	5.3	1.2	10.8	8.6	24.1	95.7
Thailand	17.7	4.8	7.5	11.7	47.2	99.4
Asia median	8.3	1.9	11.7	13.5	43.6	97.6
Eurozone	NA	2.4	11.7	15.8	NA	NA
US	1.1	5.4	9.4	11.7	146.4	58.3

Data are not available for Vietnam. Capital adequacy ratios shown are based on total regulatory capital except in South Korea, Malaysia, Singapore, Taiwan and the US where Tier 1 capital is used.

Sources: Adapted from Arner & Park (2010); IMF (2010d).

- The majority of fixed asset formation is concentrated in the state or quasi-state sectors (shown in Table 3.2), where productivity and investment efficiency are often relatively low.
- Until recently China's capital market funding for the corporate sector was negligible, making bank lending the main funding source for investment and the entire economy dependent on the health of the state banking sector.

Allocating excess capital within the state sector causes widespread inefficiency in state-owned enterprises (SOEs), reduces overall productivity and often results in substantial bank NPLs. Scholars have identified several sources of inefficiency in corporate investment that they attribute to weak institutions and poor financial development, the foremost being a financial system that systematically allocates capital away from productive sectors or regions to less effective parts of the economy (Brandt & Li 2003; Cull & Xu 2003; Liu & Siu 2011; Boyreau-Debray & Wei 2005). Inefficient SOEs are favoured with access to funds and by regulation, at the expense of more efficient non-state sectors (Huang 2003). It is empirically difficult to map the dynamics between corporate investment behaviour, institutions and financial development, despite anecdotal evidence and economic intuition, but Liu & Siu (2011) try to quantify investment efficiency across different sectors by estimating structural models that characterize the investment behaviour of firms and derive the effective discount rate perceived by managers when deciding capital spending programmes. The starting point for this analysis is the cost of capital, which we explain in Box 3.1.

The implied cost of capital is a hurdle rate used to evaluate investment choices, and may be a function of variables that signify institutional quality and financial development. These will also influence the ROIC based on actual expenditure by individual firms. The results provide robust evidence that:

Table 3.2 China fixed investment and distribution of corporate ownership (Rmb billion)

	2000	2001	2002	2003	2004	2005
SOE	1650.4	1760.7	1887.7	2166.1	2502.8	2966.7
	50.14%	47.31%	43.40%	38.98%	35.51%	33.42%
Collective	489.6	537.3	612.6	819.8	1018.3	1219.9
	14.87%	14.44%	14.08%	14.75%	14.45%	13.74%
Mixed	406.2	566.4	832.9	1273.4	1769.8	2353.6
	12.34%	15.22%	19.15%	22.92%	25.11%	26.51%
Private	470.9	542.9	651.9	772.0	988.1	1389.1
	14.31%	14.59%	14.99%	13.89%	14.02%	15.65%
Hong Kong & Taiwan	129.3	158.3	176.5	237.5	311.4	376.7
	3.93%	4.25%	4.06%	4.27%	4.42%	4.24%
Foreign	131.3	141.5	168.5	253.4	385.4	465.7
	3.99%	3.80%	3.87%	4.56%	5.47%	5.25%
Other sectors	13.9	14.2	19.8	34.6	72.1	105.7
	0.42%	0.38%	0.46%	0.62%	1.02%	1.19%
Total	3291.8	3721.3	4349.9	5556.7	7047.7	8877.4
	100%	100%	100%	100%	100%	100%

Source: National Bureau of Statistics of China (2008).

Box 3.1 Discount Rates

The term 'discount rate' has two meanings. One is a term for the official rate at which central banks lend very short-term funds to banks suffering temporary shortages of liquidity, and comes particularly from practice among the member banks of the US Federal Reserve system. We focus here on the second meaning as an important input to investment decision making.

The discount rate is a variable used in modelling future cash flows, techniques used in all simple or complex financial tasks, including calculations of net present value (NPV) and present value (PV). The concept is to compute an equivalent in today's money of the sum of future payments and receipts discounted to take account of the time value of money. The calculation is based on expected cash flows in the numerator and an adjustment for risk and time in the denominator, that is:

Present value of payoff = Future value of payoff /(1+r)

where *r* is the discount rate.

Discount rates are used in many ways. For example, the value of any financial asset is often taken as the sum of its discounted expected future cash flows. This can be reasonably certain with highly rated debt claims but less easily predicted in the case of corporate equity claims, where dividend payments may vary from year-to-year. The discount rate also guides commercial decisions by manufacturers or financial investors. Proposed capital expenditure or investments are tested to estimate if their expected rate of return is higher than the investor's prevailing discount rate, which is typically computed as its weighted average cost of capital (WACC).

For large companies WACC is a blend of the costs of borrowing and issuing new shares. The discount rate can also be taken as the firm's external financing cost based on prevailing market conditions. No company contemplating an investment will commit resources to a project if its expected return on invested capital is less than the rate of return required by its funds providers, at least without viable non-financial justification.

One popular application of this idea is economic value added (EVA), which proposes that an investment with a return lower than the applicable discount rate will destroy economic value for its sponsors or their shareholders and should not be undertaken. This helps explain why hostile takeovers are often controversial for the acquiring company, for if it is forced to pay more than the future enterprise value of the target based on EVA then the result will be a balance sheet liability known as goodwill, which must usually be written off against future profits.

Choosing the appropriate discount rate for a project has implications for transparency and governance for large companies or the state. While WACC may appear easy to define, it has become complicated in the last two decades by financing techniques such as financial derivatives or securitization. For example, an infrastructural project such as an airport or rail system might be financed by government borrowing, for which the discount rate would traditionally be the prevailing yield on government bonds of a similar maturity to the project, but the rate might now be more accurately taken from the interest rate or credit default swap markets (Sections 8.2 and 8.3). The project could also be tendered to commercial organizations that would each have a WACC derived from their performance and credit rating, or financed through securitization as a stand-alone scheme and different cost base (Section 8.4). A project can thus be feasible for some promoters but not others.

Correctly estimating the discount rate is crucial for sound corporate investment. Managers who underestimate discount rates create an unnecessarily strong incentive to invest or overinvest. China's SOEs tend to apply a sub-market discount rate to guide their investments, which helps explain the sector's widespread investment inefficiency (Liu & Siu 2011).

- Ownership is the primary institutional factor affecting firm-level returns on invested capital; and
- Returns on invested capital for non-state firms tends to be around 10 per cent higher than for similar SOEs.

India's experience over the past two decades has been similar, as it shifted from comprehensive central planning to a broad market-orientation. The most commercially productive parts of its economy historically lacked full access to external funding due to institutional flaws and a state bias imposed upon the financial system.

Most funding was absorbed by central government or state-preferred investments, in some cases by regulatory fiat. Portfolio allocations of insurers or pension funds are closely supervised and banks are required to meet quotas for 'priority sector lending', including the agricultural sector and microenterprises, by the Reserve Bank of India (India's central bank).

Policies that encourage lending among economically disadvantaged sectors are common worldwide, but India's indigenous banks were required until 2007 to meet a priority lending quota of 40 per cent of the prior year's net credit creation, regardless of demand. This was commercially unrewarding since directed loans have relatively high default rates and are costly to administer, and the policy may not of itself have reduced financial exclusion or lack of access to basic banking services. The quota remains in force but now has a more commercial orientation (Reserve Bank of India 2009).

The result of state direction was that in 1999–2005 private companies received less than 45 per cent of total bank credit, with the larger share made available to SOEs and priority lending (Farrell, Lund & Puri 2005). That allocation has since altered with the expansion of the private banking sector and more liberal central bank policies.

Two other conditions limited Indian corporate access to bank credit, and these are traditionally common throughout the region:

- Financial sector productivity and poor risk management have historically lessened the scope for bank lending as a proportion of deposits, even in cases where low-cost retail deposits are readily available; and
- Unsophisticated lending techniques and a reliance on collateral to support much commercial credit have tended to limit leverage.

For example, these factors leave indigenous banks, except those in South Korea, as net suppliers of funds to the interbank markets. Deposit-rich or under-lent banks place their surplus liquidity with competitors or the branches of foreign banks that lack a local currency deposit base, which may be transaction efficient in the short-term but often signifies an underdeveloped financial system that avoids systemic risks by endemic caution rather than capable banking and risk management. Whether or not the 2008 crisis encourages a lasting global reduction of bank leverage, Asia's banking sectors (except for that of South Korea) have sustained lower loans relative to deposits than their OECD peers, as Table 3.3 shows for 2000 and 2009.

Many factors will have influenced this result because the spread of loan-to-deposit ratios within the region is varied, but there is no clear association with per capita income. Comparisons with the United States and the Eurozone suggest a deliberate or unconscious conservatism in lending for which there are four possible explanations:

Table 3.3 Banking sector loan/deposit ratios, 2000 and 2009 (end period)

	2000	*2009*
South Korea	111.5	126.3
Thailand	101.6	95.2
Malaysia	109.4	91.6
Singapore	99.7	77.9
Indonesia	40.6	75.1
China	95.2	72.6
India	63.0	71.4
Japan	83.5	70.1
Taiwan	82.0	60.6
Philippines	82.0	58.6
Hong Kong	66.7	49.1
Asia median	83.5	72.6
Eurozone	135.0	134.7
US	111.5	109.1

Sources: Adapted from Arner & Park (2010). Comparable data are not available for Vietnam. Loans means claims against the private and non-financial sectors.

- National policy or regulation;
- Poor risk management and productivity within banks;
- Weak loan demand from outside the banking sector; and
- Institutional factors that restrict available collateral.

Recent reforms to liberalize India's markets have been introduced only with great caution, an approach shared with Beijing. At the same time India has sustained generally successful equity markets since the early 1990s, partly based on the savings of an expanding middle class and providing a valuable mechanism for private sector fundraising. India also removed obstacles to the private sector sourcing capital from overseas equity funds and non-resident Indians through IPOs or convertible debt issues. China allowed the private sector freer access to foreign and domestic equity markets only in recent years, but the majority of listed Chinese companies measured by market capitalization and amounts raised in IPOs or subsequent issues have been former SOEs. However, the situation is rapidly changing and now private companies account for about 35 per cent of all listed firms (Liu, Zheng & Zhu, 2010).

Demographic challenges

Demographic change is inevitably important to a populous, fast-growing region, but can be expected to have complex and conflicting effects in the coming decades. Asia's population is young but aging, moving to urban conurbations, shedding some of the savings habits of its parents, and making more demands of the financial sector. Much of industrializing Asia relies on labour-intensive export manufacturing, although this is mitigated by Japan and its high-growth followers in Hong Kong, South Korea, Singapore and Taiwan delivering higher-margin products and services.

Demand for labour is almost ubiquitous, but Asia's demographics will cease to work in its favour as the median population ages, the workforce shrinks, or the total population reaches a peak. Of 233 states and territories for which net population growth estimates exist for 2010, Japan ranked 216 with a decline of 0.24 per cent; eight economies in our study had small positive growth rates below the world average of 1.13 per cent; and only India (1.38 per cent), Malaysia (1.7 per cent) and the Philippines (1.93 per cent) were relatively high (CIA 2010). This issue is pressing in Japan, where those aged 65 or more exceed 20 per cent of the population. UN estimates in 2005, reproduced in Figure 3.1, show a share of population over 60 in East Asia at 20.5 per cent, falling slightly to 13 per cent in Southeast Asia. By 2050 the proportion of the population aged over 60 years in East and Southeast Asia will be 30.2 and 22.6, respectively. Labour supply will become strained if industry continues to focus on sectors that are labour intensive.

The social problems of aging are beyond the scope of this book, but the financial consequences are clear. An older society undermines a pillar of the development model by lessening the overall propensity to save, while at the same time becoming more demanding in its need for investment products, contractual savings and insurance.

Life expectancy has increased almost everywhere due to improvements in healthcare and living conditions, and as such the elderly or retired make up an increasing share of the population, so the flow of new savings available at any time for investment or wealth accumulation will dwindle as a share of GDP. Whether individual saving is mandatory, contractual or voluntary, the annual mean addition to individual savings tends to fall after the age of 50. Some governments recognize this threatening pension gap and have introduced compulsory saving plans or opened their national pension funds to private sector

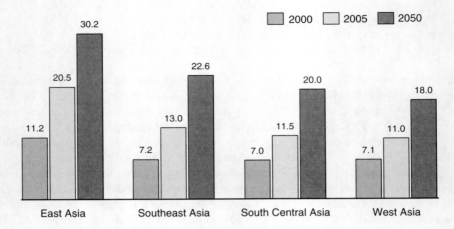

Figure 3.1 Projected share of population aged over 60.
Source: UN (undated).

workers, notably in Hong Kong, Japan, South Korea, Singapore and Taiwan. The matter is further complicated as young workers generally save less than their forebears, knowing little of the hardship that made past generations frugal, and rely instead on a mix of inheritance and the growing availability of consumer credit and home mortgage loans. Household financial wealth will decline as the population mean begins to age. This will challenge the high-investment model, especially if intermediation remains as inefficient as we have shown. All possible policy responses to the new demographics are controversial:

- Increasing overall birth rates. This was tested in Singapore but is counter to contemporary trends in most advanced societies and China's long-standing policy.
- Increasing immigration. This is politically sensitive in comparatively closed societies such as China or Japan, and helps explain the manufacturing sector outsourcing trend of the globalization era. Capital moves freely in a supposedly globalized world, but labour mobility is so constrained that manufacturing facilities tend to migrate towards favourable cost factors.
- Increasing the statutory retirement age. This may delay but not solve the aging problem, especially since Japan is alone in making full provision for health and other state-assisted benefits.
- Increasing the savings propensity of younger workers. This has a short-term cost by depressing consumption. In the long-term it would be favourable to all groups providing that pension provisions were funded rather than paid from general taxation. Such a shift was encouraged by legislation in Australia in the 1990s, producing a massive rise in pension contributions and demand for long-term savings vehicles.

An alternative is to improve the average yield on financial assets (Farrell, Ghai & Shavers 2005). This requires a supportive financial system to offer consumers a range of savings and investment choices. It relies secondarily on innovation and adequate resources for intermediaries to identify and administer risks, including the critical mismatches in amounts, duration and credit risks between the savings they collect and the investments they then acquire.

Global imbalances

Since the 1980s Asian governments have adopted fiscal, monetary and exchange rate policies to promote overall savings, exports and investment. This helped to create a stable environment to support growth and development but also led to massing external imbalances, with a persistent trade surplus between the exporting East and importing West, the transfer of capital from Asia to North America, Western Europe and Australia (but importantly excluding Canada, Germany, Norway, the Netherlands, Sweden and Switzerland), and a massing of foreign reserves by the successful exporting states.

Export-dominant development usually promotes trade imbalances and a reliance on overseas consumption. As Asia's economies grew more complex and integrated with the global commercial and financial system, they became more susceptible to shocks from a collapse of exogenous demand, protectionism, competition for cheap inputs, or tension over political issues such as North Korea, Myanmar or the status of Taiwan.

A reliance on trade may also induce internal imbalances, especially with financial systems that are less than fully effective, so that the orientation of investment finance generates excess capacity in exporting industries, distorts demand and encourages profligate lending and rising NPLs. Exporting industries in China and elsewhere are largely driven by FDI, which often receives fiscal incentives or institutional concessions such as access to land-use rights. The same incentives may be withheld from indigenous firms, and so an exporting focus tends to penalize domestic firms and non-export sectors. This is certainly the case in China (Huang 2003). Skewed incentives may also constrain the development of the financial sector.

Figure 3.2 shows how aggregate reserves have risen since 2000. At end of 2009, China, Hong Kong, India, Japan, South Korea, Singapore and Taiwan together held US$4.7 trillion in reserves, or 58 per cent of the global aggregate. The same group held only US$817 billion in December 1999.

The reasons for this unprecedented shift are several, interrelated and controversial. We are sceptical that rising reserves are necessarily a function of an undervalued currency or a controlled capital regime, nor a primary policy objective. The phenomenon is also a residual

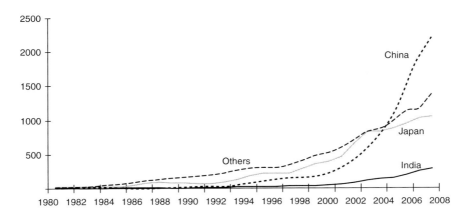

Figure 3.2 Reserve accumulation, 1980–2008 (US$ billion).

Others are Hong Kong, Indonesia, South Korea, Malaysia, the Philippines, Singapore, Taiwan and Thailand. Data for Indonesia, Malaysia and Philippines begin in 2000.

Source: CEIC (undated); authors' calculations.

of weak domestic financial markets and institutions that limit options for domestic investment, and the result of portfolio choices by states that arises from risk aversion, including an overarching wish to avoid crisis circumstances similar to 1997–98. Some regard this view as tendentious (Cecchetti 2010), but we showed in Section 2.4 that substantial reserves are indelibly associated with crisis avoidance and cautious self-insurance by most Asian states, despite reducing welfare at home. Citizens in China, Japan or South Korea are marginally less well off due to the state maintaining this scale of offshore liquidity.

Receipts from exports force central banks to use their resources to buy the foreign currency collecting in the bank accounts of exporters. Domestic liquidity is credited to commercial bank reserves through each trade transaction. For every US$100 that PBOC bought in September 2010 from a commercial bank, it credited ¥670 to the account that it holds for that bank. The bank acquires yuan base money to lend, which represents an increase in domestic money supply. When central banks acquire foreign currency they automatically print money at home unless they take compensating action, and capital controls affect the timing of this process rather than its impact. Banks functioning in an open economy without capital controls can choose when to sell foreign currency collected from clients and may be able to deploy it in other ways by on-lending US dollars or euros, a tactic that led to the creation of the offshore Eurocurrency markets from the late 1950s. All or part of the currency receipts will eventually seep into domestic bank reserves.

Asian central banks have bought huge volumes of foreign currency for a decade and in doing so created domestic liquidity in equivalent and unprecedented amounts, making reserve accumulation a large part of the money stock. With undervalued currencies such as the yuan or won, high inflows may suppress domestic real interest rates, leading to strong credit growth, higher inflation and asset bubbles, a picture that Japan would recognize from its property market collapse from 1990 and which at times threatens China, South Korea and elsewhere. Those economies like Hong Kong that operate a fixed exchange rate and currency board system relinquish control of domestic interest rates and allow net foreign currency inflows to set monetary policy, but this currency stability can be costly in terms of inappropriate monetary conditions and volatile property prices.

Box 3.2 Sterilization

Sterilization means the operations used by a national monetary authority to lessen or eliminate the impact on domestic monetary aggregates of inflows of foreign currency, whether from trade transactions or investment flows. The principal method used is to conduct offsetting domestic borrowing operations to reduce available local currency liquidity. Central banks can choose to sell government bonds from their securities inventory or issue new short-term bills or bonds, increase bank time deposits, or simply freeze domestic liquidity by administrative measures such as changing reserve requirements.

Sterilization eliminates the effects of foreign exchange purchases on the domestic monetary base by withdrawing an equivalent volume of liquidity. The aim of sterilization is usually to stabilize the long-term domestic price level and avoid increasing inflation expectations. As China and Japan have been especially aware in 2009–10, it may have a political cost overseas by appearing to allow currency undervaluation and preventing the correction of trade imbalances. We are sympathetic to this complaint but believe that in both cases it neglects other important factors, especially the domestic demand for foreign financial assets and the institutional reasons underpinning that demand.

Other central banks deal with these problems with sterilization, described in Box 3.2. As we write, this is the prevailing policy in China, India, South Korea, Malaysia, Singapore and Taiwan. Sterilization has noticeable costs, despite its widespread use. Issuing short-term debt to commercial banks to reduce base money requires the central bank to pay a market rate of interest for unwanted funds. The only form of sterilization not to incur direct costs for central banks is to raise commercial bank reserve requirements. This withdraws liquidity from the system and leads to tighter credit conditions. At other times central banks may be able to profit from sterilization by investing in foreign currency securities, or may refrain from sterilization when domestic nominal interest rates are high, as commonly happens in Indonesia and the Philippines.

Even when coupled with sterilization, reserve accumulation is not always favourable:

- Beyond a level required for precautionary and liquidity reasons, it signifies a loss of corporate, national and regional autonomy due to a reliance on exporting. For states that manage their currencies with fixed or sticky exchange rate pegs, this implies a loss of monetary policy independence.
- Reserve accumulation indicates a general welfare loss to the domestic economy. Most of Asia's reserves are held in non-Asian assets and provide no direct value except for accruing foreign-sourced interest income.
- Reserve accumulation may create excess domestic liquidity if sterilization fails or when the cost of sterilization outweighs its benefits. Unchecked domestic liquidity will eventually be destabilizing by leading to lower real interest rates, unwarranted credit growth, inflation and asset bubbles.
- Accumulated reserves are highly visible, and their scale and impact on global commodity and financial asset prices and interest rates can create systemic risks through bubbles and excessive leverage.

Many commentators argue that structural imbalances contributed to the global financial crisis (Stiglitz 2010; Wolf 2008a; 2008b), and in October 2010 the IMF's managing director unhesitatingly described the world at risk of a 'currency war' of competitive exchange rate manipulation.

Even if this view is accurate, blame cannot be attributed solely to reserve or currency policies. Japan has sustained exceptionally low nominal interest rates since 2001–2 to bolster domestic activity, but whenever the yen has been stable against other currencies this resulted in corporate and individual savers borrowing yen and using the proceeds to buy high-yielding foreign currency financial assets. All such leveraged 'carry trades' rely on positive cross-currency interest differentials, and by 2007 had created volatile capital flows of the same order as Japan's total reserves. Unhedged carry trades entail the investor or speculator ignoring the risk of principal loss through currency volatility in pursuit of a positive yield differential. The mass reversal of the carry trade through the sale of foreign currency investments would always tend to destabilize asset prices, and this happened on a large scale in 2008–9, not only among investors in Japan.

One further technical point is often neglected, especially when reserves are wrongly pictured as accrued national profits. Foreign reserves are not freely available resources but are investible assets matched by domestic liabilities, usually in the central bank's balance sheet. A state may decide how its reserves are invested, but this constitutes portfolio choice rather than liberty of use. As a further caution, excess reserves usually signify an underdeveloped financial sector and an overall loss of economic welfare. At the same time we acknowledge that the global crisis had a lesser impact on those states whose reserves were massive and seen as wasteful by most conventional measures. Reserve accumulation is ultimately an inconclusive tactic, while Asia's macroeconomic setting and those policies that supported the region's post-1949 growth now constrain how states are able to deal with future shocks.

3.2 A generic view of intermediation

We begin addressing the future of finance in Asia by revisiting the decomposition of GDP. Total output for any economy in any period is given by:

$$GDP = C + I + G + X - IM \qquad \text{Eq. (3.1) is identical to Eq. (1.1)}$$

where C is consumption; I is investment, including investment made by non-residents; G is government spending; X is exports; and IM is imports; making $(X - IM)$ net exports, or the trade balance. If exports exceed imports in any period, the economy has a trade surplus; in the converse case it runs a trade deficit. Equation (3.1) is a fundamental identity that we can use to characterize financial intermediation within national or regional financial systems. Figure 3.3 shows the composition of GDP in 2006 in the most prominent economies. Consumption is the largest element of output but investment is consistently high by global standards. Net exports tend to be higher in the smaller exporting economies.

Growth requires investment in both physical capital such as property, productive equipment, intermediate or transport resources and information systems, and in human capital resulting from education and vocational training. Figure 3.4 illustrates the relationships between savings, investment and output.

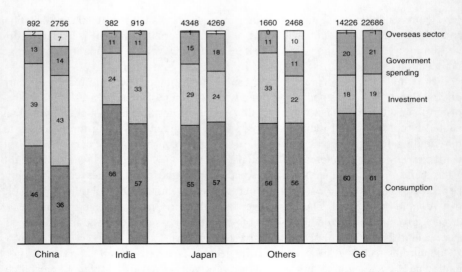

Figure 3.3 Components of GDP, 1996 (left column) and 2006 (right column).

Others are Hong Kong, Indonesia, South Korea, Malaysia, the Philippines, Singapore, Taiwan and Thailand. G6 is Canada, France, Germany, Italy, the UK and US. Data for Canada are incomplete.

Sources: CEIC (undated); authors' calculations.

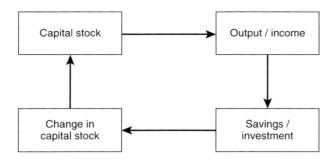

Figure 3.4 Capital, output, savings and investment.

Savings and capital formation help sustain economic growth. Figure 3.3 shows an average ratio of household consumption to GDP of 57 per cent in Asia, compared to 65 per cent in the United States. The typical Asian population is less likely to consume than those of OECD economies, reflecting both cultural and institutional reasons that can be characterized respectively as a series of choices, and a lack of choice.

Equation (3.1) dictates that lower consumption is associated with higher levels of savings, which in turn allow higher investment. This has remained around 30 per cent as a share of output since the late 1980s, and is higher for the smaller exporting states. Investment takes many commercial and contractual forms, from buying financial instruments in an organized market or the purchase of physical capital, to acquiring whole businesses by merger or takeover. It results from activity and non-consumption in the government, corporate, household or foreign sectors. China's gross domestic investment has averaged over 35 per cent of GDP for the past two decades, peaking at nearly 50 per cent in 2005–8. Similar investment booms have occurred in the past throughout the region and recently in India, Vietnam and Cambodia.

The source of funds for investment is given in a second identity shown in Equation (3.2):

$$S - CA = I \tag{3.2}$$

where S is domestic savings; I is domestic investment; and CA is the current account surplus, which can also be taken as the amount of savings held overseas. In a closed economy S will equal I. This was the reality of the Bretton Woods system of fixed exchange rates and restrictions on transnational movements of capital until post-1970s globalization. The shift was important in Asia's development and one to which we return throughout this book. Equation (3.2) is merely an accounting identity and does not describe how savings become investment through the process of financial intermediation, facilitated by systems consisting of intermediaries and markets. We illustrated this mechanism in simplified form in Figure I.1 in our Introduction. Markets and intermediaries are central to any financial system, regardless of the state's political or policy objectives, whether those markets freely allow price discovery, or whether intermediaries are controlled or compete.

Market, instruments and intermediaries

Financial markets are organized structures or continuing arrangements among participants that facilitate the flow of funds between sources and end users. Markets rely on an institutional setting, which means that they are subject to rules ranging from established practice to formal legislation. The law of markets is an important topic in our discussion of organized exchanges in Section 9.3. Markets are commonly classified by the features of the instruments for which they act as forums for exchange. This means that we refer to money markets or capital markets according to the term of the instruments they trade, that is, short- or long-term claims; to equity markets, derivative markets or debt markets according to the claims those contracts represent; and to markets in corporate, government or structured instruments as core types of credit risk:

- Money market instruments are debt claims in the form of promissory notes maturing within 12 months, known as *bills* when issued by governments or banks and *commercial paper* when issued by companies.[2]
- Any debt security with a scheduled maturity at issue longer than one year is a *bond*, although US practice refers to intermediate maturity bonds of up to ten years as *notes*.
- Bonds with a remaining scheduled life of less than 12 months are still bonds but are valued in relation to money market instruments.
- *Equities* or shares are tradable securities representing claims, normally with no contractual maturity but with rights of collective ownership over companies.
- *Derivatives* are claims valued by reference to separate assets or other benchmarks that may be real or manufactured.

Markets can also transact in self-liquidating contracts such as spot foreign exchange, where a trade or bargain is settled almost as soon as it is made, or over forward periods from one or two days to as long as ten or 20 years. Technological change helps create new financial markets and leads others to fade. For example, there is no longer a market to hedge future cotton prices in the English port of Liverpool, while a flourishing global market has developed since the mid-1980s in loan contracts among banks and other intermediaries, and India and China announced in 2010 that they would permit banks to contract credit default swaps referenced to domestic debt obligations.

We assume that all securities are readily transferable, which means crucially that if bills, bonds or shares are repeatedly bought and sold, then successive investors will enjoy the same rights against the issuer until making their sale, whether or not the securities are widely traded and liquid. Reliable and enforceable transfer usually relies on provisions of law rather than commercial agreement. Securities are bought and sold as new issues in primary markets where funds are raised by issuers, or in secondary markets that allow trading in outstanding claims of the same type. We speak of companies being *introduced* to a stock exchange through an IPO of shares, after which the exchange provides a forum for those and other shares to be bought and sold.

These matters are analyzed from an institutional perspective in Chapters 8 and 9. All markets provide a forum for exchange but each has a local jargon and practice, and it is important in buying or selling securities to know the accepted terms of exchange and settlement or standardized contractual terms such as interest accrual calculations. These often differ from place to place because of history, sometimes long forgotten. The flow of funds between real sources and users through organized markets is usually called *direct financing*.

Intermediaries exist because financial markets are always imperfect. This may be due to inherent transaction costs, asymmetries of information between users, or irrational behaviour among savers and investors. It may be impossible for a company to fund perfectly reasonable investments when all investors act similarly in herd fashion, or exporters may be reluctant to ship goods to unknown overseas buyers without some assurance of payment. Intermediaries help fill those gaps. From an elemental perspective there are few financial contracts that are complete because their parties can never perfectly tell the future and prepare an appropriately specific set of terms.

Financial intermediaries are organizations such as banks, insurers or fund managers, most of which have commercial objectives and which collect funds from savers and use the proceeds to acquire financial assets, chiefly loans, securities, or claims against other intermediaries. They organize and administer the claims of savers in the form of deposits or funding securities and the claims they hold as risk assets, and use their resources for money transmission, facilitating trade, and through the creation of credit provide a conduit for the state to conduct its monetary policy. As with markets for direct financing, intermediaries link sources of funds to desired users. Intermediaries are commonly known as *financial institutions* but we choose not to use the term for the reasons explained in the Introduction. The flow of funds through an intermediary is called *indirect financing* because it is contractually discontinuous and identified as two balance-sheet claims that are unrelated and unalike, except in some securitized transactions such as those discussed in Sections 8.2 and 8.3.

The generic intermediary engages in three commercial processes or risk transformations in receiving deposits from savers and lending to users. This is more than a mechanical procedure for all but simple mutual associations that only pay out what they collect from members. Suppose the bank takes a deposit for a contractual period of six months, and on the same day makes a loan in a similar amount to a different party for one month. This involves transformations that impact the bank's balance sheet and which the bank must manage:

- Credit risk. A default by the borrower leaves the bank in need of funds to repay the deposit. Loans and deposits may also be unintentionally concentrated, a particular problem for localized banks or those serving specific industries, because a cyclical downturn may lower deposit funding just as borrowers become more likely to default.
- Duration risk. The loan in our example matures prior to the deposit, leaving the bank with a reinvestment risk if the deposit is unusable. If a loan is longer in tenor than a deposit then the bank faces the converse problem if the deposit is not renewed, which is the basis of liquidity runs of the kind cited in Table 2.4.
- Value risk. If the borrower defaults the bank would collect only a portion of its loan but would be expected to repay the deposit in full.

Real-world intermediaries take many forms according to national custom or law, and deal with different classes of client, risks or business practice. The US banking sector is highly segmented geographically and by function, even after the abolition in 1999 of the Glass–Steagall Act that largely prevented commercial banks from selling and trading in new issues of securities (Banking Act of 1933; and see Chapter 7).

Until relatively recently, US federal or state legislation encouraged sectoral fragmentation by limiting the permissible market shares of banks by deposits or the number of offices that were allowed to function outside their home state or principal location. US intermediaries include commercial banks, 'thrifts' or savings and loan associations and credit unions, housing and agricultural finance cooperatives, community banks, mortgage banks, investment banks, mezzanine funds that invest in high-yield subordinated debt, consumer or instalment finance companies, captive credit corporations that fund car dealer loans, mutual funds that pool resources to fund diversified portfolios, pension funds that offer retirement savings plans, and insurance companies that sell protection against adverse events. EU states such as

Germany and the Netherlands have traditions of public sector infrastructure banks similar to those in Japan or South Korea, or specialist commercial lenders to municipal authorities and capital-intensive sectors such as shipping or property. In Asia only China, Japan and South Korea have a range of specialist intermediaries separated by law or regulatory authority.

Although segmentation exists in many jurisdictions by law or custom, it is especially entrenched in the US for historic reasons relating to finance being popularly disfavoured and identified with unwanted corporate power, in the Great Crash of 1929 for example. Japan's similar functional segmentation of intermediaries into city banks, regional banks, trust banks, long-term credit banks, cooperative banks and a vast public bank based on the postal system was reduced partly by bank failures and consolidation, and partly by a 1981 Banking Law and 1990s legislation that introduced 'Big Bang' reforms to give banks and securities firms far more competitive freedom. Section 3.4 explains the divisions within China's financial sector.

Commercial banks attract funds with current (checking) and savings accounts and fixed time deposits, which they deploy as loans to individuals, firms or arms of government. Deposits are liabilities of the bank and contractual claims for depositors; the loan is a debt obligation of the borrower and an asset for the bank. Section 6.2 explains the commercial and contractual processes in these simple activities. Commercial bank revenue is characterized as derived from the accrual of net interest or trade finance fees so that earnings are normally ongoing. Investment banks have a transactional focus, and regardless of business orientation rely on repeated but discrete transactions for their revenue, including arranging new securities issues, providing corporate finance advice for mergers or acquisitions, and buying and selling bonds or shares for clients. The principles of investment banking are discussed in Chapter 7 and corporate finance in Chapter 10.

In the last three decades a demarcation between these two models has largely dissolved, in part as a trend towards universal banking of the kind traditionally found among large German or Swiss intermediaries that were never subject to the legal fragmentation of their US or Japanese competitors. Conceptually, universal banks resemble industrial conglomerates and mix complementary business streams, in some cases involving non-bank activities such as insurance or asset management, and targeting clients of all kinds. A trend favouring universal banking in the 1990s also sprang from technological change, as techniques common to commercial bank funding and managing deposit–loan transformations require skills once associated mainly with investment banks. Trading functions formerly used for internal purposes similarly became revenue generating when made available to clients.

Insurance companies are liability driven intermediaries, charging premiums for contractual protection and issuing debt claims in the form of policies. Insurers cannot know for certain when or if they might pay under a policy claim, nor can they know the present value of any future claim. Insurers invest premium revenues in securities and other liquid assets and maintain reserves of capital and liquidity to meet regulatory standards. Most jurisdictions require insurers to hold a minimum capital in the form of a risk-based capital ratio or solvency margin represented by an excess of assets over deposits, and in minimum levels of reinsurance depending on the nature of the policies they write. Reinsurers and wholesale markets such as Lloyd's of London provide supervening cover as a form of risk substitution for primary insurers. It is common for regulators to set minimum credit risk criteria for the investments made by insurers, which has important secondary consequences for the growth of national capital markets. Non-bank intermediaries are described in Chapter 11.

Asset managers invest client funds in return for fees based on performance and the volume of their investments. They usually have two main goals: to generate a net return on invested funds that compares favourably with a recognized benchmark, and to maintain a surplus of assets over liabilities. Benchmarking and relative performance are crucial dynamics in asset management for both specialist and broadly based funds, and are explained in Chapter 11. We class these and other non-bank intermediaries according to their target clients, whether large scale, individual, professional or retail, or by investment strategy. They include pension funds, hedge funds or 'alternative' investors, mutual funds, private equity funds and SWFs. Commercial fund managers operate under contracts with their clients as the ultimate investors, and generally owe their clients a fiduciary duty for the money they manage.

Risk transformation

We have pictured a financial system funded by deposits, insurance premiums or investment flows that it manipulates to help create loans, securities or funds for illiquid and non-transferable capital. Financial intermediaries or markets undertake contractual transformations of the source of funds so as to finance a required use. This process requires the assumption of distinct risks. The intermediator is compensated with a risk premium in the form of fees or interest. Within known regulatory parameters, intermediators choose either to absorb the risks inherent in intermediation or transfer those risks to others. Risks differ both through their causal factors and in the way they are estimated and managed. For finance scholars, risk is the volatility associated with the potential outcomes to certain events, as with our conceptual description of deposit taking and lending involving the three risks of credit, duration and value. A more detailed analysis of intermediation risks is given in Table 3.4. These may appear in distinct ways within different intermediaries or markets.

Table 3.4 Risks in financial intermediation

Type	Description
Market risk	Potential changes in the value of a financial asset or portfolio due to price movements – for example, interest rate risk, foreign exchange risk, stock price risk, commodity price risk
Credit risk	Potential losses due to inability or unwillingness of a counterparty to make contractual payments, default risk, migration risk, settlement risk, recovery risk, sovereign risk
Liquidity & funding risk	Potential losses arising from covering payment obligations due to the liquidation of a strategic risk position, and to timing differences in payments leading to funding or reinvestment needs
Behavioural operational risk	Potential losses due to malfeasance or operational error, including documentation failure, errors in funds transfer, reporting or settlement, fraud or non-compliance, taxation or regulatory changes
Business risk	Potential losses in firm value due to changing long-term demand conditions
Insurance risk	Potential losses due to unexpected claims and premium development, mortality, morbidity or lapse of insurance cover, property or casualty risks, risks associated with data collection, fraudulent contracting or claims

The modern financial system is compensated to absorb risk and provide a clearing function for the redistribution of risk. Both functions generate revenue, although intense profit-seeking by banks is a recent phenomenon. Prior to the 1980s, most publicly incorporated banks tended to generate steady 'utility' returns for their shareholders. The shift to targeting higher returns and a broader embracing of risk by banks was encouraged both by commercial competition and a changing regulatory setting. When intermediaries gather deposits, trade in securities or provide insurance they pool and manage risks through diversification. The financial system also engages in risk advisory activities that involve no direct intermediation of cashflow – for example, in assessing credit and market risks for its own purposes or with clients, by managing financial assets, and in corporate finance.

Finance and the real economy

The relationship between the economy's real and financial sectors is one that we will explain by adapting a model associated with the consultancy firm McKinsey to assess financial development in Asia (Barton, Newell & Wilson 2003). The discussion points to a concern voiced since 2008 as to the societal value of a highly developed financial sector, a question referred to at the opening of this book and exemplified in populist American demands that a remote Wall Street be made to act in the interests of Main Street, or the economy familiar to consumers. The financial system intermediates between savings and investment by facilitating risk management and financial contracts. Our model has five facets, and a failure in financial intermediation can spring from specific weaknesses in any of those distinct dynamics, for example:

- Generally poor performance by the corporate sector;
- Poorly performing intermediaries that are badly managed, under-resourced or given insufficient institutional or supervisory support by the state;
- Sub-optimal capital markets without such depth or liquidity to function as a valid pricing mechanism;
- Inadequate macroeconomic policies; and
- Unfavourable funding dynamics.

These are collected in Figure 3.5. Growth occurs only when they successfully interact, and intermediation can then be regarded as effective. In the worst case a financial crisis is more likely to occur when the functional dynamics between the real and financial sectors break down, and will typically be followed by falling output and employment (Reinhart & Rogoff 2009: 143–7).

The first dynamic concerns the real economy. Firms collect and process capital, labour and raw materials to produce goods or services. Generations of economists analyzed GDP to evaluate macroeconomic performance, but many now rely on microeconomic indicators of firm-level behaviour. Do companies create value, so that their return on investments is higher than the associated cost of capital? Are firms maximizing value for their owners rather than pursuing managerial goals? A weak real economy might result from an inefficient financial system, but can also contribute deleteriously to ineffective intermediation.

In the second dynamic, financial intermediaries and markets provide funds needed in real activities. The dynamics of the financial sector can be explained by three aggregated variables:

- Total periodic change in credit volume, comprising new net corporate lending, net proceeds of stock issuance, and net issuance of debt securities after redemptions;

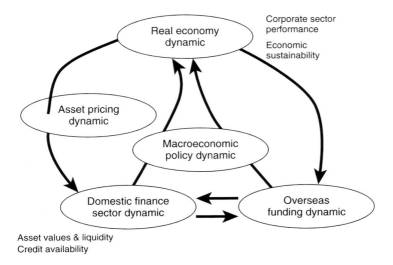

Corporate sector
performance

Economic
sustainability

Asset values & liquidity
Credit availability

Figure 3.5 Financial intermediation under globalization and change.
Source: Barton, Newell & Wilson (2003).

- Periodic liquidity, measured in stock market turnover, debt market trading volume and the volume of loan transfers; and
- Financial asset values, consisting of share, loan and bond prices, and in each case complemented by financial derivative prices.

When the financial sector is healthy, credit volumes, liquidity and asset prices move within normal ranges and the system is thought to serve the real economy effectively. Undeveloped financial systems and ineffective intermediation deprives the real economy of essential support so that its sustainability is compromised. The soundness of the financial sector is conversely affected by the health of the real economy. As output falters so the creditworthiness of intermediaries and securities will deteriorate as loans become delinquent and stock and bond prices fall. Measuring how the real sector affects intermediary balance sheets is difficult, especially in jurisdictions lacking sound reporting or accounting practices, as was almost ubiquitous in Asia prior to 1997, at which time the crisis showed corporate underperformance and high leverage leading to bank failures and collapsing asset values.

The third dynamic involves government policy. Regulators and central banks are important influences on financial intermediation. Central bank decisions affect interest rates, credit creation and the money supply, all of which influence output and prices. Central banks use commercial banks and other intermediaries as conduits for monetary policy, and provide LLR facilities to safeguard general stability. Regulators seek to ensure bank solvency, the integrity of bank governance, and may from time-to-time issue quantitative instructions regarding credit creation, a form of direct intervention that is universally used in Asia despite becoming unpopular among OECD regulators prior to 2008. Direct intervention is likely to be more widely used as a post-crisis measure, with limits to total leverage or ceilings on loans.

Cross-border funding is reflected in the fourth dynamic and is important in a globalized economy. It introduces control risks if policy formation becomes dependent upon foreign inflows that are volatile or prone to a destabilizing withdrawal – as we saw in Section 2.3 in the approach to the Asian financial crisis – or unacceptably costly, as in the Eurozone sovereign debt crisis of 2009–10.

The fifth dynamic concerns asset pricing, driven by the real economy. Financial asset bubbles eventually destabilize confidence and lead to excessive price volatility, but even moderate changes in asset prices can squeeze expected credit creation in a financial system that uses collateral as security for lending (Kiyotaki & Moore 1997). Such effects may have further destabilizing impacts when the institutional setting is weak – for example, in poorly supervised macroeconomic policies, predatory entrenched corporate interests, or inadequate laws or ineffective enforcement of creditor rights.

Our approach shows that insight into the real economy helps assess the effectiveness of intermediation. To understand movements in financial asset prices, we must assess the performance of the real assets that those claims either represent or fund.

3.3 Intermediation in Asia

Our stylized description allows us to assess the functioning of intermediation in Asia, including its distinct characteristics, comprehensiveness and efficiency, the access it provides to households, SMEs and disadvantaged communities such as the rural and urban poor, and recent developments and reforms that have strengthened its operation. Post-1999 developments are both organic and planned, and include:

- Growing sophistication in consumer wants and in the logistical and funding needs of SMEs and other companies;
- Concentration in trade finance and foreign exchange dealing among relatively few very large banks;
- Increasing but inconsistent opportunities for foreign participants to enter selective or segmental markets, either through establishment with new operating licenses or in equity participation in domestic intermediaries;
- Deliberate but not comprehensive reforms to encourage capital market development;
- Entrenched links between Asia and organized investors elsewhere, replacing more speculative or unreliable flows;
- Broadening mechanisms to value and liquidate NPLs, including state AMCs, and debt restructuring or semi-formal negotiations among financial creditors;
- Discrete cooperation in regional financial activity, described in Section 12.5;
- Establishment in Asia or expansion from North America of Asian-specific private equity and hedge funds;
- Entry of new investment vehicles, including Shari'ah compliant models and SWFs, respectively;
- Legislative and commercial efforts to increase financial inclusion among rural communities or the socio-economically disadvantaged, especially in China, India, Malaysia and Thailand; and
- Increasing commercial orientation and competition among stock exchanges.

An improving post-crisis environment brought competition from non-Asian intermediaries in capital market transactions, and through direct entry by both banks and private equity funds. This infusion of contractual and organizational innovation also encouraged more professional management in the financial sector, and has been shown to be influential in improving the risk management of intermediaries throughout the region, especially in Indonesia, Japan, South Korea and Thailand.

Foreign entry helps weaken traditional lending relationships between banks and company owners, with imported products and risk management skills gradually encouraging indigenous banks to avoid adverse selection and corporate cronyism. The consolidation of banks in these four states had similar effects, especially where foreign interests were allowed to buy control of local banks. Such post-1997 crisis investments were not numerous but were influential by being transformative and involving prominent targets, notably the purchase of Bank Central Asia in Indonesia by a US hedge fund, and of Long Term Credit Bank in Japan by a US private equity consortium. Small or strategic stakes of 5–20 per cent were sold by over 30 Chinese banks to foreign banks in the same period, either in transactions encouraged by the state and linked to NPL sales or prefatory to large IPOs or secondary share sales, but in few cases have the bank's operations or risk management altered materially, as we show in Section 3.4. Regulatory and supervisory standards have also been subject to external influence through informal colleges of supervisors, participation by Asian officials in cross-border forums – especially with widened memberships at the Basel Committee on Banking Supervision (BCBS) and International Organisation of Securities Commission (IOSCO) – and in some cases by participation in IMF reviews of financial sector stability.

Shifting demographics, more HNW investors and other conditions cited in Section 3.1 have increased and broadened the demand for financial products. An aging population with increasing retirement needs will require more diverse means of saving, and demographic changes will gradually lead everywhere to fewer workers supporting many retirees. Population aging has a compounding effect, creating difficulties for workers who save for retirement while supporting existing retirees. Widespread population concern with retirement incomes will support high savings rates, and each factor increases the marketing scope for wealth management products.

Demand for financial products was fed more generally after 2000 by a mismatch between rising incomes and narrow product penetration. New instruments have not always been successful, as when the failure of Lehman Brothers led to a collapse in the value of structured securities sold to retail investors in Hong Kong, Singapore and Taiwan. Some cases involved mis-selling, as we show in Chapter 8, but structured notes such as Lehman's infamous Minibonds became popular after 2002–3 by offering high returns to aggressive savers with few other alternatives.

HNW investors are more fortunate, having leverage to negotiate the terms on which they invest through banks or fund managers, or to demand a satisfactory explanation of the mechanics of any investment proposition. The head of one Asian 'family office', or private HNW fund manager, tells of being repeatedly canvassed by Bernard Madoff, who for decades ran a fraudulent investment pyramid in New York. Madoff's representatives abandoned this prospect when asked to explain plainly their fictitious investment strategy. Inward migration since 2000 has led many private banks, hedge funds, private equity and pledge funds and captive fund managers or family offices to establish in Asia, often managing private portfolios from Hong Kong or Singapore. Ownership of financial claims and assets is far more concentrated than in OECD economies, with small shares of the population controlling the great majority of bank deposits or investment media.

The scale of NPLs accumulated after 1997 initially made it difficult for the banking sectors of East and Southeast Asia to be consolidated by mergers. The problem was large but poorly quantified, and some states prevented stricken banks from being acquired by foreign buyers. No Asian economy was immune to this problem, and in the 1997 crisis only Hong Kong operated a consistent regulatory approach to reporting and provisioning for delinquent or defaulted loans of the kind explained in Box 3.3.

Box 3.3 Problem Lending

For a long time, national regulators have set rules to guide how their lenders deal with impaired, delinquent or defaulted loans, a mix usually known as NPLs. Those rules indicate how NPLs must be identified, classified, reported, accounted for, administered and – in some cases – recovered. If we conceptualize the promotion of financial stability, these rules are the rearward facing part of the regulatory regime that governs bank behaviour, with the Basel capital accords intended as the forward-looking component.

Basel guides the national rules that require banks to hold a buffer of accumulated resources judged as sufficient to meet future losses. The treatment of NPLs deals with how capital is used when the probability of a loss increases, turning a balance sheet entry into a deduction to the bank's income statement through loan loss provisioning. Most states allow banks to value loans at cost, which is usually their nominal amount, but claims in bank trading books or intended for sale are typically *marked-to-market*, with their fair value used for balance sheet and risk management purposes.

Modern NPL provisioning began with formulae that were largely subjective, and federal US banking practice was among the first to be codified in 1976. National banks must classify loans according to a credit scale running in five steps from 'normal' to 'loss'. Only the last two categories ('doubtful' and 'loss') required that the loan be placed on 'non-accrual', meaning that net interest received by the bank would not be accounted as operating income but used to write down the outstanding loan principal.

The rules at first allowed discretion in classification, but regulators later imposed a mandatory mechanism to reclassify loans that suffered non-payments lasting for 30 or 90 days. Worsening classification required the bank to increase its general provision for bad loans, that is, a reserve set aside against probable loss, reduce its capital, and make a deduction from operating income. If the bank later recovered the debt by negotiation or through the courts, then the amount received would usually be fully credited to the income statement, making any debt recovery highly lucrative. The picture is often complicated by differential tax treatments of loan losses and recoveries.

Similar processes spread around the world in the 1980s, but most states differed subjectively over classification or provisioning. The rules that apply in Asia today are partly the product of such national discretion, which can be either conservative or lax but are usually opaque and applied to broad international standards negotiated within the BCBS and International Accounting Standards Board (IASB).

The third element or 'pillar' of the Basel II capital accord explained in Section 4.4 sets quantitative standards for the reporting and disclosure of NPLs (BCBS 2006b: 226–42). The IASB introduced Rule IAS 39 in 2002 as a means to classify and value all financial instruments, including loans or other claims likely to become impaired. The IASB hoped to replace IAS 39 in mid-2011 with a stricter formula called IFRS 9, but its implementation has been contentious and protracted.

The treatment of NPLs has always differed from state-to-state, but the quality of supervision and reporting in Asia was shown in 1997–98 to be highly variable and often poor, largely as a matter of weak regulatory practice and bank governance. Banks could decide how to classify or report NPLs and often defeated any rules by making new advances to clear delinquent assets. These practices were overwhelmed by the scale of losses after 1997–98 and led eventually to widespread reforms that make Asia's post-2008 record appreciably better (Angklomkliew, George & Packer 2009). NPL practice is now well-developed and transparent in Hong Kong, India, Malaysia, the Philippines, Singapore and Thailand, and considered sound in China, Japan, South Korea and Taiwan but subject to significant national discretion from the perspective of both BCBS and IASB intentions.

Post-1988 international standards from the BCBS stipulated that banks hold regulatory capital of no less than 8 per cent of risk-weighted loans. That cushion was shown to be deceptively thin during the stresses of 1997 and 2008. A delinquent portfolio of 4 per cent of total loans represents 50 per cent of minimum regulatory capital, so that two years of unre-covered losses leaves the bank technically insolvent and unable to operate. Basel III reforms negotiated in 2010–11 will increase the minimum level and quality of capital and introduce a minimum liquidity requirement. More positively, BCBS rules for bank capital allow many national variations, but we show in Chapter 4 that the non-quantitative aspects of the frame-work dealing with supervisory practice and market discipline will further raise compliance standards. IMF reviews of Asia's banking sectors conducted in 2009–10 suggest that capital adequacy standards were favourable across the region, and only Indonesia, the Philippines, Thailand and Vietnam had poorly capitalized banks within a generally well-protected sector.

After 1999 several states created AMCs to recycle distressed banking claims, using the US Resolution Trust model of the 1980s to expunge NPLs from the savings and loan sectors. The first results were mixed. Impaired assets must be written off or valued appropriately for sale, implying a capital cost either for the original lender or the AMC assisting the process. AMCs in South Korea and Malaysia bought NPLs from the banks at generally realistic dis-counts, but in Indonesia and Thailand the transfer was at first made at book values far above any realistic appraisal, effectively delaying the purpose of the AMC process. China's four AMCs generally acquired bank claims at depressed values but became subject to political pressure when investors that later bought claims from an AMC at distressed levels were able to improve their value and realize profits with a subsequent sale. The AMCs grew reluctant to liquidate their assets, so that the recycling process slowed and was made more reliant on a general recovery. China's NPL process was successful only because the state was willing to infuse new capital into its banks.

Access to finance

Assessing the effectiveness of a financial system is only partly an empirical matter of national scale, market completeness and cost structures. Differences in local or national practice, and between market segments, mean that depth of field is important: banks can be backward while stock markets are efficient; some consumers customarily visit a bank branch to make a deposit while others meet an insurance agent who collects savings at the door of their home. Consumers or corporate borrowers may be well served by systems that depart from OECD norms, even though conventional measures suggest that they face a relatively undeveloped financial sector.

Any assessment must take account of accessibility as well as scale and diversity. We will show that the effectiveness of Asia's various financial systems is deficient in some important respects, but that other factors mitigate this for many individuals and companies, especially economically disadvantaged households. These include: informal money transmission systems or *hawala* (Arabic for transfer and one of many regional names); informal banking based on *hawala*, known widely in South Asia as *hundi* (from the Hindi term for trust) and in China as *fei ch'ien* (飞钱, or flying money); community savings groups; credit unions; chit funds or *yin hui* (銀會); and community based microfinance operators. Together they represent a financial system that has functioned in parallel to 'conventional' banks and markets for more than a century, and has a symbiotic relationship with Western banks in trade finance. We discuss some of these practices here and use 'mitigate' in this paragraph with particular care:

- Informal practices are less amenable to measurement, comparison or assessment than conventional financial systems. By their nature, informal practices or institutions may exist privately or among members of small communities, or be intended to avoid financial regulations or lending rules.
- There is ample evidence of informal finance being efficient for its immediate users and providing low-cost solutions for intermediation or money transmission. *Hawala* is far cheaper at the point of use than money transmission through electronic bank transfer if the funds are not of an interbank scale, or flow from a foreign contract worker in East Asia or the Gulf states to a remote home village. International NGOs use *hawala* extensively in crisis states and when administering emergency relief.
- It is less clear that it is systemically valuable in either developed or emerging economies, and may entail diseconomies of scale so that it assists economic development only to a certain level. Informal finance may assist the poor or rurally disadvantaged but will not help them prosper.
- Governance concerns exist where informal finance is prominent in the economy at large, not for reasons of fraud or criminality but due to adverse selection and transparency. Informal lending has taken place on a large scale in China, and since the early 1980s has provided a source of credit to non-state enterprises that were at times unable to borrow from state sector banks, but this cannot be a model solution.
- Informal finance may offer a use threshold more appropriate for low-income groups than conventional modern intermediation. Household use of financial services and products tends to increase with income but rises and broadens discontinuously in jumps, so that demand for more costly or sophisticated products will rise as incomes reach a series of thresholds.

Asia was successful in mobilizing resources for growth until the mid-1990s, but except in Hong Kong its conventional financial intermediaries and markets were customarily controlled, directed or heavily influenced by the state. Bank management practices were poor and often geared to the interests of large corporate borrowers, and markets were sheltered by restrictions such as directed interest rates, bans on foreign ownership and controls on external capital payments. Banks focused on deposit gathering, trade finance and simple corporate banking, with lending relying either on entrenched relationships or collateral-based allocation, and credit assessment was poor. Incumbents could easily achieve high profits without concern for customer service or the usefulness of their products, protected by the state or close controlling shareholders. It would be wrong to regard Asia as unique in these respects, but until the 2000s its poor financial sector governance was out of step with rapid industrialization.

Research accepts the importance of a developed financial system to the economy as a whole (Arner 2007), although those systems may vary by design or from place to place. When intermediation is effective it tends to provide funding that is less costly and longer in duration to a broader range of users, and can support both growth and poverty alleviation (Beck, Demirgüç-Kunt & Levine 2003; Honohan 2004). It may also contribute to technological progress and innovation (Ayyagari, Demirgüç-Kunt & Maksimovic 2008), and facilitate the creation of new enterprises (Klapper, Laeven & Rajan 2004). Access to financial services not only creates economic opportunities beyond the rich and influential, but may promote democracy and economic development (Rajan & Zingales 2003b) and the well-being of poorer communities (Claessens 2006), but research in this field has yet to identify how household or SME access to finance is impacted by specific institutional obstacles, partly because the outcomes are subject to considerable national variations.

The composition of capital markets in the main global economic groups, and the scale of their respective financial sectors in relation to output, are shown for the end of 2009 in Table 3.5, while Table 3.6 gives a sectoral analysis of each economy's financial systems at the start and end of the post-crisis decade. Taken together, these data show the dominance of the banking sectors across the region compared to the Eurozone or United States – an increasing financialization that is almost ubiquitous, even after the dampening effect of the global crisis – and the jump in value of domestic equity and bond markets, albeit from low beginnings. Hong Kong and Singapore are noticeable financial hubs with banking especially important for the latter.

Table 3.5 Capital market indicators (end-2009) US$ bn

	GDP	Stock market capitalization	Debt securities			Bank assets	Total claims (bonds, equities & bank assets)	Bonds, equities & bank assets/ GDP (%)
			Public sector issues	Private sector issues	Total			
EU	15,373	10,013	10,076	23,480	33,556	41,708	85,277	554.7
Canada	1,336	1,677	1,006	862	1,868	2,712	6,257	468.3
US	14,119	15,077	9,478	22,174	31,652	14,163	60,892	431.3
Japan	5,069	3,396	9,657	2,264	11,921	8,847	24,164	476.7
Newly-industrialized Asian economies[1]	1,604	4,309	724	1,063	1,787	3,569	9,665	602.6
Emerging Asian economies	7,876	5,435	2,449	1,499	3,948	9,945	19,327	245.4
Other emerging economies	10,086	4,475	2,447	1,225	3,671	6,003	14,150	140.3
Others	2,380	2,808	566	3,113	3,680	6,022	12,509	NA
World aggregate	57,843	47,189	36,403	55,679	92,082	92,970	232,241	401.5

[1] Hong Kong, South Korea, Singapore and Taiwan.

Source: IMF (2010d).

Table 3.6 Sectoral analysis of financial systems, 2000 & 2009 (period end) % of GDP

	Banks & deposit taking intermediaries		Other non-bank intermediaries		Stock market capitalization		Local currency bonds outstanding	
	2000	2009	2000	2009	2000	2009	2000	2009
China	157.2	200.6	5.1	5.8	48.9	82.7	16.9	52.3
Hong Kong	505.5	651.7	188.3	459.0	368.3	1,093.9	35.8	68.4
India	64.5	103.5	15.6	29.0	69.9	205.2	24.6	48.8
Indonesia	63.6	34.7	8.7	11.4	16.2	39.8	31.9	18.2
Japan	510.8	541.8	274.7	291.3	67.6	69.7	97.4	189.6
South Korea	130.5	158.6	41.9	67.3	27.8	100.3	66.6	122.7
Malaysia	154.2	211.5	41.4	99.9	120.6	149.5	73.3	96.5
Philippines	99.2	83.1	23.9	20.0	33.3	53.6	27.6	39.2
Singapore	646.3	643.7	76.6	83.9	167.3	271.7	48.0	84.7
Taiwan	256.0	295.4	92.2	75.9	173.5	37.7	37.7	57.5
Thailand	132.3	146.6	10.7	41.1	23.8	67.1	25.3	67.0
Asia median	155.7	206.1	35.4	75.6	68.8	124.9	36.8	67.7
Eurozone	230.9	315.6	157.8	214.5	79.6	56.5	87.9	114.4
US	79.6	107.9	279.3	314.1	152.1	105.8	138.0	175.8

Data not available for Vietnam. Financial asset data for Indonesia as of 2001 and 2008.

Source: Adapted from Arner & Park (2010).

The ratio of private credit to GDP measures funds provided to the private sector, and the ratio of total deposits in the financial system to GDP measures the resources available for lending or credit creation (Djankov, McLiesh & Shleifer 2007). Taken together these gauge the scale of financial intermediation as shown by Table 3.7.

Both developed and some emerging economies maintain financial intermediation comparable to that in Europe or North America. The ratio of private credit to GDP in China in 2004 was 135 per cent, and deposits held by all intermediaries (commercial banks, finance companies, policy banks, credit cooperatives, trust, investment and leasing companies) amounted to 164 per cent of output, similar to Germany or the United Kingdom. In scale terms China has been successful in mobilizing resources derived from high private savings. Measured by the ratio of deposits to GDP, the developed Asian economies and China outperform most European and North American economies except Switzerland, but this should be considered cautiously, for high deposit ratios also indicate a reliance on banking rather than sectorally balanced development. The scale of financial development varies but is especially small in Indonesia, Indochina and the Philippines, where the private credit ratio ranges between 4–51 per cent and the deposit ratio between 14–51 per cent.

While the overall scale of intermediation is comparable to advanced economies elsewhere, this says little of the inclusiveness of any financial system. When individuals or enterprises are denied ordinary access to finance then intermediation fails to serve the economy, regardless of its size. Assessing the efficiency and span of intermediation is empirically difficult due to data limitations. This is particularly the case for differences in national practices or technological change that make cross-border or inter-temporal comparisons unreliable – problems that appear in Table 3.8, which shows four indicators of the distribution and availability of intermediation. The aim is to gauge the accessibility of simple products or services on reasonable terms, rather than the general availability of credit.

Table 3.7 Financial intermediation and output (2007), %

	Private credit/GDP	Financial system deposits/GDP
Cambodia	8.12	14.49
China	135.28	164.81
Hong Kong	147.16	250.06
India	32.83	51.23
Indonesia	20.91	38.73
Japan	99.49	120.79
South Korea	125.57	80.24
Laos	4.99	14.59
Macau	40.29	137.11
Malaysia	121.38	109.69
Philippines	32.73	51.48
Singapore	122.56	107.37
Thailand	95.20	91.28
Vietnam	50.93	47.95
Canada	100.28	74.61
France	88.088	66.96
Germany	112.61	96.25
UK	147.87	115.28
US	237.03	59.19

Source: World Bank (undated b) Financial Structure Database.

Table 3.8 Access to financial intermediation (end-2009 unless stated)

	ATMs	Bank branches	No. of deposits	No. of loans
	(per 100,000 of population)		*(per 1,000 of population)*	
China	3.8*	1.3*	NA	NA
Hong Kong	NA	23.0	NA	NA
India	NA	10.6	NA	NA
Indonesia	14.5	7.7	223	NA
Japan	113.8*	12.5	171	7,099
South Korea	90.03*	18.6	NA	4,384
Malaysia	47.5	10.7	1,492	287
Philippines	13.6	7.5	401	NA
Singapore	53.2	10.5	2,117	915
Thailand	75.0	11.2	1,081	223
Vietnam	15.4	3.4	NA	NA
Canada	219	24.4	NA	NA
France	70.30*	43.23*	1,800	NA
Germany	61.16*	49.41*	NA	NA
UK	42.45*	18.35*	NA	NA
US	175.7	36.3	NA	NA
World median	16.63*	8.42*	529	81

No data are available for Taiwan. * indicates end-2004 data.
Sources: Beck, Demirgüç-Kunt & Martinez Peria (2007); IMF (undated b) *Financial Access Survey*.

Only Japan, South Korea and Thailand have installed ATMs of the same per capita order as Europe or North America. This might indicate generally poor access to banking services, but the conclusion is necessarily qualified:

- Cultural and commercial variations mean that ATMs are free-standing in some economies, especially at transport hubs or shopping malls, but sit mainly within bank offices elsewhere. Fees are standard in some states but not others. A lack of standalone machines may be related to income factors such as the level of crime or availability of electricity, and to cooperation between banks so that their respective machines may serve all users.
- The population density of ATMs is not synonymous with access to a bank account, especially in rural areas or poor communities. Informal financial intermediation such as indigenous savings schemes or *hawala* are often effective in reaching such groups. A lack of conventional banking may be no disadvantage if informal finance is well-established.
- Evidence from very poor developing economies suggests that access to intermediation is undergoing transformation not because of ATMs, bank branches or cyberbanking, but due to money and credit transmission made by cellular phone, where rural communities and market traders make and receive payments by text messages in a similar way to compensating payment mechanisms such as *hawala*.

Asia's incidence of bank branches is also below the sample median. Low-income states are especially poorly served, but this is another variable to be treated with care. The per capita numbers of loans and deposits vary considerably throughout the region, but both indicators underperform the world average.

Figure 3.6 shows the limits of access to financial intermediation measured by the share of households and SMEs with bank accounts (Beck, Demirgüç-Kunt & Martinez-Peria 2007). Accounts are held by only 21 and 23 per cent of households in Indonesia and the Philippines respectively, and 39 per cent of Indonesian SMEs. Singapore is an outlier for household accounts but its population is small, concentrated and urban, in spite of which 37 per cent of

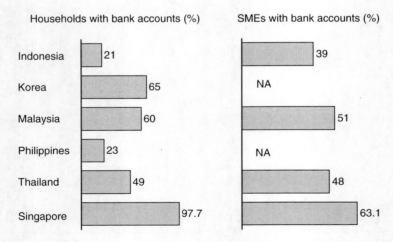

Figure 3.6 Shares of households and SMEs with bank accounts.
Source: Beck, Demirgüç-Kunt & Martinez Peria (2007).

Singapore's SMEs lack access to banks. Conventional financial services are apparently unwanted or not available to many in the region.

These findings are only a guide (Claessens 2006), for households may use formal alternatives to deposit-taking banks such as state postal services, which can be prominent in developed and emerging economies alike, as in Japan, Singapore and Indonesia. A 2009 survey of 10,043 upper-income urban households in 19 Chinese provinces and municipalities found that 85.3 per cent were homeowners for whom property was by far their largest investment, but that 80.5 per cent held bank deposits in an average amount of Rmb65,583 (US$9,850), or twice the level of the sample's reported annual disposable income (Seade & Wei 2010: 299). Around 19 per cent and 11 per cent of households respectively held shares and investments in managed funds (ibid). Even if this relatively affluent group is conservative in using financial products, these results suggest that choice is restricted.

Access to insurance is also highly variable, even though most insurers meet clients through the tied national sales forces of agents, which helps engage small savers and can be very numerous. Life insurance is the most widespread form of non-bank saving, and other forms of insurance such as health and accident cover are growing in scale but are far less established in Asian households, as Figures 3.7 and 3.8 show.

Regional sales of life insurance has risen in the last two decades and in 2009 accounted for 15.4 per cent of global paid premiums (AIA Group Ltd 2010: 107), but is generally more modest as a share of GDP than in the United States or Japan. Non-life premiums have been static by the same measure, although growing in nominal terms. Table 3.9 examines the life insurance sector in more detail, showing the change in household behaviour in the five years to 2009. Density rate measures the average annual premium amount paid for traditional life cover, and in the mature markets of Hong Kong, Japan, South Korea and Taiwan is now higher than, or comparable with, the EU and North America. Insurance products are not widely bought elsewhere in Asia. Moreover, high household penetration in India, Singapore and the four leading markets may not be synonymous with effective financial markets if it indicates high savings, a lack of investment choices for the median income household, or the powerful networking skills of the region's numerous insurance agents.

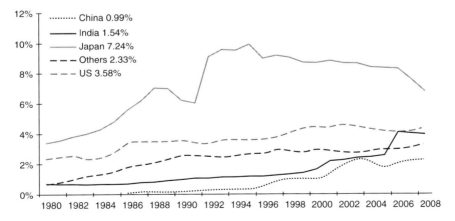

Figure 3.7 Life insurance premiums as a share of GDP, 1980–2007.

Sources: World Bank (undated b); authors' calculations.

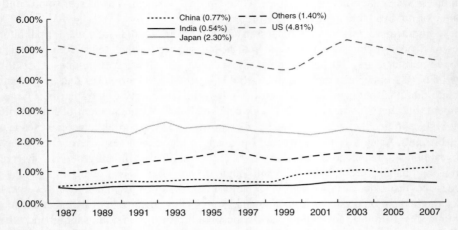

Figure 3.8 Non-life insurance premiums as a share of GDP, 1987–2007.

Values shown are period averages. 'Others' are Hong Kong, South Korea, Malaysia, the Philippines and Thailand.

Sources: World Bank (undated b); authors' calculations.

Table 3.9 Household life insurance sales, 2004 and 2009

	Paid life insurance premiums			Penetration rate (%)		Household savings rate (%)		Density rate (US$)	
	2004 US$bn	2009 US$bn	CAGR 2004–9 %	2004	2009	2004	2009	2004	2009
China	34.4	109.2	26.0	2.1	2.3	31.6	36.7	27	81
Hong Kong	12.6	20.3	9.9	7.6	9.6	27.3	24.9	1,836	2,887
India	17.5	57.1	26.7	2.5	4.6	NA	NA	16	48
Indonesia	2.0	5.1	20.6	0.6	0.9	NA	NA	8	22
Japan	391.2	399.1	0.4	NA	7.8	NA	NA	NA	3,139
South Korea	48.5	57.4	3.4	6.9	6.5	19.2	19.4	1,007	1,181
Malaysia	4.2	5.7	6.2	3.5	2.9	13.9	15.8	167	207
Philippines	0.8	1.6	14.9	0.9	1.0	NA	NA	9	17
Singapore	6.7	6.6	6.2	6.0	5.1	33.0	32.2	1,484	1,912
Taiwan	33.3	52.2	9.4	11.1	13.8	NA	NA	1,495	2,257
Thailand	3.1	6.2	15.0	1.9	2.4	15.3	17.9	51	92
Vietnam	0.5	0.7	7.0	1.4	0.7	NA	NA	7	8
Canada & US	531.0	536.0	0.2	NA	3.4	NA	NA	NA	1,573
EU	696.5	927.7	5.9	NA	5.5	NA	NA	NA	1,911

CAGR is the five year compounded annual growth rate. Penetration rate is national paid life insurance premiums as a share of GDP; density rate is paid per capita life insurance premiums.

Source: AIA Group Ltd. (2010: 109–22).

The composition of finance

National or regional finance can be examined by its availability and impact on users or providers and by its aggregate composition. Each approach must acknowledge idiosyncrasies in local practice, and this is important in Asia for three main reasons:

- Variations in development and per capita income mean that finance is configured differently from state-to-state, not least in our 11 member core group;
- Informal finance involving credit, savings systems and money transmission are prominent everywhere, either complementing or substituting for 'conventional' finance; and
- National financial security is a strong concern of governments due to political and post-colonial rivalry or policy caution rooted in the Asian financial crisis.

Figure 3.9 transposes Table 3.5 into graphical form to show the relative importance in output of four components of the financial systems of Japan, the United States and four regional groups, using the respective capitalizations of the banking sector, government bond market, private bond market (similar to corporate bonds in issue) and equity markets.

Many changes have occurred since 2000, as Table 3.6 suggests, especially in local-currency bond market capitalization reaching significant scales in China, Japan, South Korea and Malaysia. Table 3.6 also shows that aggregate financial activity to the end of 2009 in the four newly industrialized economies of Hong Kong, South Korea, Singapore and Taiwan was higher relative to output than any other country grouping or the United States, largely due to the inclusion of the two large financial city hubs. Figure 3.9 allows us to compare the composition of finance in Asia with other states and regions:

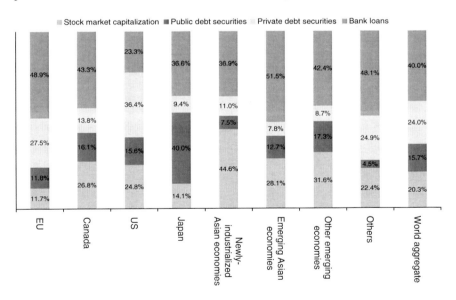

Figure 3.9 Composition of financing as a share of GDP, end-2009.

Newly industrialized Asian economies are Hong Kong, South Korea, Singapore and Taiwan; emerging Asian economies comprise 26 states in East and South Asia and the Pacific; other emerging economies are those in Africa, Central and Eastern Europe, the Commonwealth of Independent States, Middle East and Latin America; 'others' are 39 heavily indebted poor states by World Bank classifications.

Source: IMF (2010c).

- Asia relies on bank financing, particularly in its emerging economies. We cannot prove that bank finance is always qualitatively inferior to direct intermediation through securities issuance, but it is widely believed that a balanced national portfolio of financial assets increases intermediation efficiency and lessens systemic risks. Two related dangers are that when large companies borrow rather than issue bonds or shares they may crowd out SME access to bank credit, and that securities markets fail to develop adequate depth to be effective. This also increases systemic risks among both intermediaries and markets.
- Corporate debt issuance is far less important throughout Asia, even where the government bond sector is large and sophisticated, as with Japan. One distinction here is that few Asian government bond markets are traded as actively as in the United States, Canada, larger Eurozone members, Australia or the United Kingdom, making Asian government bonds largely a vehicle for passive investment, often by banks and sometimes through central bank fiat. In a dynamic sense, Asia's private and public bond markets are modest everywhere.

These conditions prevailed throughout the last decade in spite of financial sector reforms, but our analysis must be read with care for three important reasons:

- Our data point shows stock markets of both newly industrialized and emerging blocs as more valuable in relation to output than in the EU, United States, Canada or Japan, but partly indicates the weakness of major markets in the global crisis;
- Methods of quantification and valuation differ among established markets, for practical reasons explained in Box 3.4. This is acceptable if applied consistently, for example when comparing equity or loan market capitalizations at intervals or within groups of economies or regions; and
- Informal finance is less likely to be measured consistently or accurately within or across states, despite its importance in many economies. This can reflect institutional evasiveness, that informal finance can take place outside the scope of law or regulation, or traditional practices that are officially accepted but vary idiosyncratically from place to place.

Intermediation in China is especially bank-centred, as Figure 3.10 shows. Financial assets held by households totalled Rmb21.6 trillion at the end of 2006, 76 per cent of which was represented by bank deposits.

Discussion of the composition of financial systems often neglects two important variables. First, national systems differ partly for reasons of political and cultural choice, so that one variety of capitalism may favour a prominent banking sector and a second rely more on direct intermediation through securities markets. Differences persist despite globalization and increasingly harmonized regulation, and we see no reason why emerging or newly industrialized economies need to follow one track. Also neglected is the *breadth* of credit provided by banks, in particular through a product range known as trade finance. Asia's reliance on relatively conservative banks has for generations provided capital and liquidity to support overseas trade almost without limit, which has two convenient merits:

- A trade orientation concentrates on short-term self-liquidating transactions, some secured with collateral, and suits the conservative risk preferences and limited product capabilities of indigenous banks of all sizes and domiciles.

Box 3.4 The Hazards of Market Capitalization

Our analysis of the components of modern financial markets is frequently used to compare national or regional systems or track the configuration of financial development over time. We expect Germany and South Korea to differ from Canada or Singapore in the relative importance of their respective banking and capital markets due to their respective long-standing orientations shown in Section 2.2. Time-lapse pictures of a fast developing economy taken at intervals of a decade might also show a financial emancipation – weightier capital markets, non-bank intermediation growing and bank sector assets falling in relative terms, or swings in value between equity and debt securities markets. Care needs to be taken in interpreting the results, for although such panel or cross-sectional time-series data can be useful, it may be hazardous to look closely at any single subset such as the data for one economy, or a selection of data taken on any date. Three particular risks exist with Tables 3.5 and 3.6 and Figure 3.9, even assuming that data are presented uniformly.

First, the results are time sensitive. End-2009 stock market capitalizations in Europe and North America were more heavily depressed by the global crisis than those in many emerging markets. We cannot say whether the effect on the relative composition of financial systems is temporary. A similar but longer-term effect arises because equity markets are usually valued according to differing earnings multiples that alter only gradually over time. For long periods prevailing yields measured by the inverse of price–earnings ratios was higher in New York than London, and higher there than in Hong Kong. This has been attributed to several factors, including depth of investor resources and the intensity of financial regulation, but can apply both to markets at large and to the shares of similar companies.

Second, market practice influences the results. Where bonds or loans are bought and sold actively there will be a tendency for financial assets to be marked to market at their prevailing value from day-to-day. Where trading is uncommon and assets are generally retained to maturity or default, any holder will be far more likely make a valuation at their nominal or purchase price. Most share values are recorded each day, whereas illiquid bonds may be priced less often or only when a sale takes place. In some economies bank loans are always recorded at par, and a separate measure made of NPLs or provisions.

Finally, the capitalization of equity markets is not usually precise, but an estimated value based on a large sample of listed company share prices. Not all shares trade every day, and so commercial data suppliers such as Bloomberg or DataStream extrapolate capitalization data from the proportion of companies whose shares can be reliably priced. They may also exclude non-traded shares of quoted public sector companies, such as China's listed SOEs.

- Banking to facilitate trade matches the region's post-1949 export orientation. This placed banks in sympathy with their major relationship corporate clients and SMEs as well as the policy preferences of the state.

Trade finance products include those of considerable commercial antiquity in bills of exchange or letters of credit, but increasingly rely on electronic platforms for issuance and settlement. In most cases the objectives are clear:

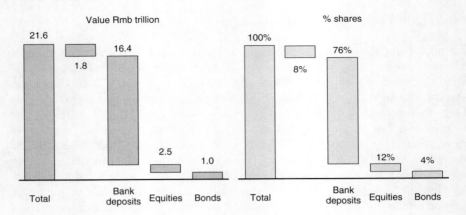

Figure 3.10 China household financial assets, end-2006.
Sources: CEIC (undated); Wang & Yam (2007).

- Provide suppliers with short-term finance for inventory accumulation;
- Improve an exporter's certainty of payment, especially when its foreign importer is remote and unknown as a credit risk;
- Safeguard a foreign importer from making advance payments to a supplier that is remote and an unknown credit risk;
- Provide insurance for the shipment of goods;
- Separate the financing of trade from disputes over the supply of goods;
- Provide cash advances to suppliers based on the discounted value of shipped goods; and
- Indicate through the bank's surveillance of shipping documents that trade transactions are genuine.

These features mean that trade finance is widely used even though its cost erodes export profits. IMF surveys suggest that 35–40 per cent of transnational trade is linked to bank intermediation compared to transactions settled by open account or payment ahead of shipment (Asmundson, Dorsey, Khachatryan, Niculcea & Saito 2011: 18). That share varies by region and industry practice, and tends to increase in recessions for precautionary reasons when sellers are guarded in extending credit.

Common to many trade finance products is the discounting of commercial invoices or bills of exchange, or their use as collateral for advances. The principle of all trade finance techniques is that banks provide funds or payment guarantees when presented with documentary evidence of the shipment of goods, or less frequently of an export contract. The result is to strengthen commercial confidence, with the bank interposing itself between parties that know little of each other's financial condition or intentions, and verifying the trade transaction as genuine. The related techniques of countertrade and medium-term forfeiting used to support Western trade with the former Soviet bloc can also facilitate exports to contentious or dysfunctional economies, especially if controversial goods such as weapons or military materiel are involved.

The availability of conventional trade finance is evidently not hindered by the systemic prominence of Asia's banks.[3] Everyday trade finance is costly to administer but can provide well-resourced non-indigenous banks with low-risk revenue and valuable access to local corporate clients. Indigenous banks compensate for a lack of scale economies by acting for exporter clients, and traditionally had less need to keep overseas networks. Most global trade finance providers have roots in colonial or overseas legacy banks in Europe, Japan or North America that made foreign payments and collections for home companies and governments. They include ANZ, BNP Paribas, BBVA, Bank of Tokyo-Mitsubishi UFJ, Citigroup, Deutsche Bank, HSBC, Raiffeisen Zentralbank Österreich, Standard Chartered and UBS.

Informal finance is often associated with emerging economies but exists throughout the region in parallel with conventional banking, so that its scale and ubiquity make it important, especially in providing access to finance for disadvantaged groups. Informal finance is manifested in both transaction types and organizations, of which the most notable are:

- Microfinance: a widespread form of community lending made famous by Bangladesh's Grameen Bank, introduced in Box 3.5. Practitioners provide very small subsidized or commercial loans to disadvantaged groups whose credit risk is augmented by the institutional cohesiveness of the community. Microfinance has functioned effectively as a mix of commercial and developmental motives but may have inherent scale limitations and governance conflicts.

- Credit unions: loan and deposit cooperatives serving local communities that deal solely with and are governed by their members. They began as simple non-profit associations in nineteenth century Germany but now include substantial and sophisticated quasi-banks, especially in Canada and the United States. Credit unions are usually less leveraged than commercial banks, and their business model simpler. Industry data suggest that at the end of 2009 credit unions functioned in 97 economies and held an average of US$23.2 million in savings (WCCU 2010). Their members represented 7.7 per cent of that group's aggregate adult working population but was far higher at 44.6 per cent in North America, where member savings held by each credit union averaged US$111.1 million. Overall penetration in Asia (excluding China and Japan for which data are unavailable) was 2.6 per cent of the adult working population, but was noticeably higher in South Korea at 14.8 per cent, and over 6 per cent in Singapore and Thailand.

- Chit funds: small savings associations common among Chinese and Hindu communities. They once had connotations of extortion, and since the 1970s have been subject to size restrictions in Hong Kong, Malaysia and Singapore to protect members losing their savings to powerful clan heads. Legitimate chit funds are circular subscription savings vehicles, where members take turns to borrow from the group (Litton & Chang 1971).

- Money transmission and trade credit through *hawala* or *hundi*: this generic form of informal finance includes techniques for money transmission and trade credit that vary regionally and can be as sophisticated as structured finance transactions of the kind explained in Section 8.3. They may mimic conventional trade finance, except that *hawala* involves no single transaction but instructions on behalf of a user that fit into an array of compensating transnational and domestic transfers of money, credit and goods. *Hawala* is paradoxically a complex technique to supply financial services to areas of institutional weakness, including conflict zones and undeveloped or inaccessible territories, often for users lacking any access to finance. It allows states and NGOs to fund regions without infrastructure and where no banks exist, and low income expatriate workers to remit small sums to rural homelands in South or Southeast Asia.

- The essential feature of *hawala* is that no transmission of funds occurs, but a series of compensating transfers creates a credit available to the remote beneficiary, to be settled in due course by one or more transfers elsewhere within the *hawaladar*'s network or family or with a second network. Figures 3.11 and 3.12 show examples of these mechanics. A payment made to a rural village in Southeast Asia on the instruction of a family member working overseas may be settled by the transfer of goods between affiliates of the respective *hawala* networks in two other countries. At times since 2001 *hawala* has been claimed as favouring money laundering or terrorist financing but no convincing evidence supports the assertion any more than with conventional banking, although regulation of *hawaladars* can be hindered by poor record-keeping (El Qorchi, Maimbo & Wilson 2003; Maimbo 2003; Martin 2008).

- Overseas workers give remittance instructions to nearby *hawaladars* and receive codes to pass home by phone or text message, so that their beneficiaries can be identified by the home *hawaladars* and be given cash. Settlement by the home *hawaladar* could be made by one or more mirror transactions but more commonly involves a payment among other members of the two *hawala* networks. The arrangement shown in Figure 3.12 is similar conceptually to transnational parallel lending explained in Chapter 7, typically used to circumvent capital controls. In our example the importer and foreign *hawaladar* are part of one network, and the exporter and home *hawaladar* a second. The importer is over-invoiced for goods shipped in the ordinary course of business, with the excess payment used to settle the creditor *hawaladar*'s claim.
- The utility of informal finance means that it augments conventional finance rather than exists as a competing system, and suggests that continuation is its most likely future.

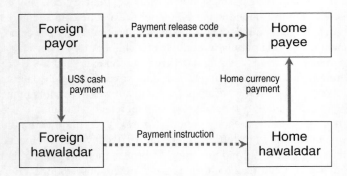

Figure 3.11 Simplified *hawala* transaction.

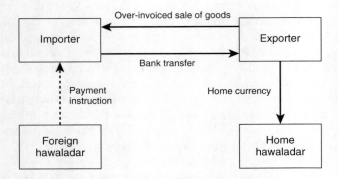

Figure 3.12 Physical *hawala* settlement.

Box 3.5 Muhammad Yunus, Sufiya Begum and Microfinance

In 1976, a Bangladeshi academic called Muhammad Yunus led his students on a village field trip. Among those they interviewed was Sufiya Begum, a homemaker who wove and sold bamboo stools. Sufiya Begum would borrow from a village moneylender to buy small amounts of raw bamboo costing only 22 US cents, but the interest rate she was asked to pay could be as much as 10 per cent per week, or over 14,000 per cent annually, leaving her with a negligible 2 cents. Yunus was shocked by the story.

> I watched as she set to work again, her small brown hands plaiting the strands of bamboo as they had every day for months and years on end.... How would her children break the cycle of poverty she had started? How could they go to school when the income Sufiya earned was barely enough to feed her, let alone shelter her family and clothe them properly?

Were she able to borrow at a more reasonable cost to buy raw materials, Sufiya Begum could contemplate raising her income above a pure subsistence level. Yunus reacted by using his own cash to repay the debts to a moneylender of 42 individual basket weavers, a total cost of US$27. Soon he began an experiment of lending small sums directly to the villagers, both men and women, and then acted as a broker between the village and a local bank. Over time he learned that very small loans not only helped the villagers with their immediate needs but also began a wave of self-initiative that could raise living standards and improve the villagers' bargaining position with suppliers and customers. Yunus continued this small-scale benevolent lending to the consternation of village and town moneylenders and their patrons in government. Despite being warned that the borrowers had no commercial judgment, he found that most loans were promptly and fully repaid. Late payments were almost always attributable to men and Yunus decided to concentrate lending with the women micro-workers.

Yunus sought funding from both conventional banking sources and the state to expand his work, but his plans were generally opposed and he looked instead to developmental donors. In 1983 he established Grameen ('village') Bank to develop his personal philanthropy into a non-profit seeking microfinance venture.

By making small-scale credit available to non-traditional borrowers, Grameen might be thought to rely on luck and charity rather than sound risk management, but the performance of its credit portfolio has often been better than bank lenders in Bangladesh. The success is institutionally driven in that each community exerts a positive influence on borrowers to make payments to schedule, a practice associated with strong informal customs within homogeneous groups (Greif 2006). The goods producers of Sufiya Begum's village share an interest in the renewal of their working credit, and so provide incentives and tangible support to encourage each borrower to remain in good standing with Grameen.

The bank was first assisted by non-governmental development agencies but has raised wholesale funds from commercial sources since the mid-1990s and become successful in attracting retail deposits. Grameen Bank had 2,481 branches dealing with over 80,000 villages at the start of 2008, compared to 1,055 and 35,533 respectively in 1995, and had lent to 7.4 million borrowers, up from 2.1 million over the same period. Its deposits have exceeded its loans since 2004.

Microfinance is not free from criticism, both for commercial and ethical reasons. As lenders expand, their practices and lack of scale economies force reliance on commercial funding rather than concessionary or non-commercial sources. This lessens the developmental function and increases pressure to achieve higher returns, which in turn may encourage usurious interest rates and an aggressive approach to debt collection. Grameen's loan losses rose in the late 1990s as the bank grew and shifted from its early community based lending model, with the result that around 50 per cent of loans were used for productive purposes rather than debt servicing or consumption.

Corrupt or anti-social forms of lending and debt recovery became widespread in 2010 in Andhra Pradesh and other poor Indian states, partly based on preferential lending under central bank requirements, as we describe in Section 3.1. Development analysts have claimed that all small-scale lending is costly to administer and a diversion from general poverty reduction, while feminist economists have suggested that its effect when successful is to draw women from poor communities into the traditional labour force in ways that are far from empowering and neglect their existing needs.

Cooperative and rural finance has been a feature of many economies since 1949, including newly industrialized states such as South Korea and Taiwan and in underdeveloped OECD regions, notably among manufacturing cooperatives in northeast Spain and throughout Italy. Grameen Bank's original approach, using a mix of official and NGO assistance, has been applied widely in other emerging states, and Muhammad Yunus was awarded the Nobel Peace Prize in 2006. Our guess is that successful microfinance requires both informal institutions and benevolent objectives of the kind first associated with Yunus and there may be limits to its continual expansion.

Sources: Collins, Morduch, Rutherford & Ruthven (2009); Rajan and Zingales (2003b); Yunus (1998).

Implications of financial structure

When appropriately managed, funds infused into the real economy will support corporate performance and economic growth, and we saw in earlier chapters that investment has been vital to Asia's post-1949 success. Figure 3.5 illustrates the connectivity between the modern economy's real and financial sectors, so that material problems or gains in one component easily migrate to the other. Those linkages also appear in the profitability of each sector. Higher returns in the corporate and financial sectors are mutually reinforcing and corporate strength or weakness will improve or undermine the condition of the financial sector. Corporate governance is concerned with agency conflicts between managers and shareholders and with balancing the interests of controlling and minority shareholders. Good governance and corporate transparency can be associated with a superior share price performance and lower capital costs, although this is observed infrequently in Asia due to the limited alternatives available to equity investors.

Asia's corporate and financial sectors have tended to be institutionally constrained, a concern we discuss in Chapter 5, and relatively poor governance is common among financial and industrial companies, both public and private, with the closely-held conglomerate model prone to a lack of transparency, oppressive treatment of minority interests, and commercial collusion. These conditions are found throughout the region and contrast with accepted best practice, which generally includes:

- Relatively dispersed ownership in public companies, so that unrestricted control cannot be held by a dominant shareholder, family or the state. This helps protect minorities from oppressive actions by controlling shareholders such as expropriating value ('tunnelling') or benefiting unfairly by committing the company to connected party transactions;
- Board directors being given authority and resources to act independently or on behalf of minority shareholders so as to protect against agency conflicts;
- Accounting and reporting integrity and information transparency; and
- External regulatory and commercial discipline from standard-setting bodies and financiers.

While these conditions apply equally to industrial and financial companies, governance outcomes are influenced both by supervisory or stock exchange requirements and by commercial preferences. These respectively set rules for compliance and influence behaviour through contractual covenants or investor decisions. Such incentives or constraints are inevitably weaker in less sophisticated systems and where government participates forcefully in the financial sector. Dominant owners may appoint senior executives as directors or enlist compliant government or family appointees.

Failing to correct for agency conflicts can lead companies to overborrow or overinvest, encouraged by weak financial sector governance and poor risk management within bank intermediaries. The *chaebol* model described in Box 2.5 demonstrates these moral hazards in the corporate and financial sectors, and similar conflicts persist in Indonesia, Japan, Malaysia, the Philippines, Taiwan and Thailand. This is not to repeat a frequent accusation of non-Asian commentators after 1997 (Chang 2000) that cronyism is ubiquitous in the region, but commercial favouring of 'friendly' parties implies distortions in allocating finance, oppression of third-party interests, and corrosion in national institutions such as the rule of law. Concentrated ownership leads companies to rely on internal funding, with secondary financing sourced mainly from small groups of banks. This militates against disclosure and transparency, leading investment decisions to be strongly influenced by the preferences of those relationship banks.

Asia has lacked a robust investigative credit culture and independent rating companies, reinforcing its reliance on lending. Free availability of bank credit inevitably leads to imprudent uses, a dynamic made clear by the Asian financial crisis. The operations of many South Korean and Thai companies were value-destroying prior to 1997 as their capital costs persistently exceeded their respective ROIC. Even sophisticated stock markets in Hong Kong, Singapore and Tokyo are less demanding in governance in relation to the issuers they host and their own commercial objectives than their global peers. This is especially the case in protecting minority interests, disciplining connected transactions to promote transparency and prevent tunnelling, and requiring independent directors to be sufficiently resourced to perform their responsibilities.

Bank ownership lies with the state or closely controlled family interests to a far greater extent than in OECD economies, even though the jurisdictions in our study, except Japan and South Korea, ostensibly limit the permissible shareholding of any single owner and the aggregate shareholdings of connected parties. A survey conducted before the 1997 financial crisis reflected in Figure 3.13 showed that the share of assets of state banks in total assets to be commandingly high in China, India, Taiwan and Vietnam and significant in the order of 35–45 per cent in Indonesia, South Korea and Singapore.

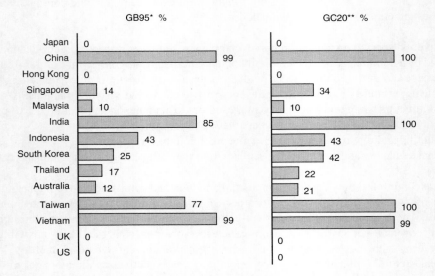

Figure 3.13 Prevalence of state-owned banks, 1995.

* GB95 is state ownership in the banking sector, weighted by bank assets.

** GC20 is the share of state-controlled banks in banking sector assets.

Source: La Porta, Lopez-de-Silanes & Shleifer (2002).

States restrict access to foreign intermediaries in three ways, the first two constrained to some extent by WTO financial services agreements:

- Withholding of operating licenses by national regulators;
- Limiting permissible operations by licensed non-indigenous firms, for example by scale of assets, number of offices, geographical spread or business segment. Some states allow foreign banks to engage only in wholesale transactions with large counterparties; or
- Limiting foreign investment in local banks.

Constrained access to domestic deposits often encourages substantial foreign banks to seek local acquisitions, but limits to foreign control of banks are common and only Hong Kong and Japan have been comparatively open to foreign entry. Singapore maintains a barrier between domestic currency or retail financial activity, which is protected from excessive competition, and a relatively liberal approach to licensing foreign entrants to conduct offshore business. Reciprocal access to the entrant's domicile is demanded almost universally.

Overseas interests were allowed to buy control of insolvent banks immediately after the regional financial crisis, notably in Indonesia, South Korea and Thailand, and in China in one prominent case, but the window closed when the new owners made politically sensitive gains from their investments. Few major changes in foreign ownership limits occurred between 1997 and 2003 (Barth, Caprio & Levine 2006). Majority control is usually prohibited in China, India, South Korea, Malaysia, the Philippines, Singapore, Taiwan, Thailand and Vietnam, and limited to 30 per cent interests in most cases. Indonesia is unique in ASEAN (the Association of Southeast Asian Nations) in permitting almost full foreign control.

China usually enforces a 25 per cent maximum for foreign shareholders but rules can be applied capriciously elsewhere.

Many governments can thus directly influence bank lending decisions, not only through the impartial effects of monetary policy, but in some cases through issuing guarantees for loans and using banks to provide credit for favoured policies. The objectives may be acceptable policy for any state, but the results are often poor for bank profitability, credit quality, asset price inflation and potential NPLs. China stipulated that its state banks increase post-crisis lending to help sustain domestic spending and China Banking Regulatory Commission (CBRC) data show year-on-year nominal growth in total banking sector assets in 2009 and 2010 of 26.3 per cent and 19.1 per cent, respectively. CBRC simultaneously required those banks to maintain dividend payments to help the state recover the cost of past capital infusions, which forced the banks to issue new shares in Hong Kong and Shanghai in 2010–11 to meet a shortage of capital and anticipate growth in NPLs.

The calculation as to the appropriateness of such measures is beyond our scope, but it is reasonable to demand that the state's interest in credit policy at least be fairly applied and made for acceptable purposes, even if the results are commercially deleterious for individual lenders. We see China's recent intervention as not dissimilar from the strategic way that Japan and South Korea directing funding to shipbuilding in the 1960s and 1970s.

Assessing effectiveness in intermediation raises normative questions and is never empirically straightforward. Two assumptions are crucial throughout our narrative:

- We use 'effectiveness' in a conventional commercial sense, as it provides a simple means to compare national financial systems. Unlike 'efficiency', the most common financial metric, it does not suffer from association with the prevailing view prior to the global financial crisis. At the same time, it fails to address outreach or inclusiveness in financial systems. Commercial effectiveness may also neglect positive factors associated with state sector banks or where the state is accustomed to influencing credit policy, as with our examples from China and elsewhere.

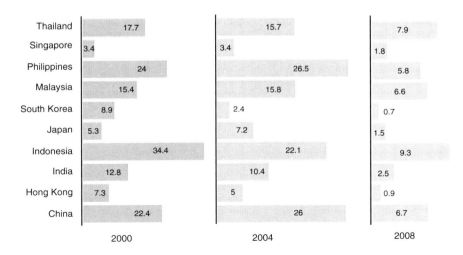

Figure 3.14 NPL ratios, 2000–8.
Sources: World Bank (undated b); IMF (undated c); authors' calculations.

- The effectiveness of the banking sector gives a generally faithful empirical picture of the overall system, since most Asian economies rely so heavily on bank financing.

While our preferred approach relates to 'effectiveness' rather than 'efficiency', the majority of the literature takes the second approach and so we begin from this starting point. One comprehensive study of bank efficiency in 72 economies constructs an index relating banking's commercial output (total earning assets and other non-interest income) to input (costs of funding, physical capital and labour, and loan loss provisions as a proxy for risk management resources) using data averaged from 2005–7, and includes ten of our study group plus Macau but not China, Taiwan or Vietnam (Barth, Lin, Ma, Seade & Song 2010). The top tier of results shown in Table 3.10 is broadly correlated with national income so that OECD banks are dominant, but Asian economies are well-represented and all but two register above average efficiency. The study also suggests that efficiency may be negatively associated with restrictions on banking activities and with government ownership in the bank sector (ibid: 204).

Table 3.10 Index of bank sector efficiency (2005–7 averages)

	Mean
UK	0.94
Belgium	0.92
Switzerland	0.92
Luxembourg	0.91
Spain	0.91
France	0.89
Canada	0.88
Germany	0.87
South Korea	0.87
Singapore	0.86
Japan	0.85
Portugal	0.84
Italy	0.83
US	0.83
Hong Kong	0.82
Australia	0.81
Austria	0.81
Netherlands	0.81
Sweden	0.79
Hungary	0.78
Thailand	0.78
Denmark	0.76
Macao	0.76
Malaysia	0.76
Mauritius	0.76
Total (72 economies)	0.76

The index range is 0–1. Not shown are 47 economies with bank efficiency below the mean, including India ranked 34 and the Philippines ranked 63.
Source: Barth, Lin, Ma, Seade & Song (2010).

Structural change and future drivers

Reading this evidence with our appraisal of financial access shows that intermediation has been far from optimal in terms of scale, diversity, efficiency or effectiveness. Banks long suffered from poor governance and risk management, inadequate capital and inferior asset quality that together constrained their business streams to a narrow credit-intensive model, limited innovation, and with the exception of Japanese banks restricted geographical expansion. Improvements only began after the Asian regional crisis, helped variously by national accession to WTO, competition from foreign intermediaries, sectoral consolidation, and official steps to recapitalize banks and reduce NPLs. Economic recovery was also considerably helpful to commercial lenders, which were thus generally sound when global confidence collapsed in 2008.

That relative shift in fortune has made Asian banks more prominent by asset size and market capitalization, so that four Chinese banks were ranked in 2009 among the largest 25 by total assets in *The Banker* magazine's annual survey, the same number as British, French and US banks, and five were among the 20 reporting the largest pre-tax profits. Similar past results have been ephemeral, for European, Japanese and US banks alternated as the largest by assets or capital in the last two decades, but *The Banker*'s commentary suggests that China's banks display a 'creeping global dominance' (*The Banker* 2010). That trend will continue, more from growth among successful provincial and city banks than the largest state banks. Asian banks outside China and Japan were far less prominent, with the next largest being Development Bank of Singapore, ranked 62 by capital in 2009. However, no Asian bank featured in the most successful 25 by returns on assets. Tables 3.11 and 3.12 show asset and equity yields in order of 2009 results, and Tables 3.13 and 3.14 show the results of the recovery for capital asset ratios over a five year period. The performance of Asian banks in returns on assets and equity since 2006 has been not unlike those of OECD competitors but with less volatility.

Table 3.11 Bank sector return on assets, %

	2005	2006	2007	2008	2009
Indonesia	2.5	2.6	2.8	2.3	2.6
Hong Kong	1.7	1.8	1.9	1.8	1.6
Malaysia	1.4	1.3	1.5	1.5	1.2
Philippines	1.0	0.4	1.0	0.8	1.2
Singapore	1.2	1.4	1.3	1.0	1.1
India	0.9	0.9	0.9	1.0	1.0
Thailand	1.4	0.8	0.1	1.0	1.0
China	0.6	0.9	0.9	1.0	0.8
South Korea	1.3	1.1	1.1	0.5	0.4
Japan	0.5	0.4	0.3	−0.2	0.2
Australia	1.0	1.0	1.0	0.7	0.6
Switzerland	0.9	0.9	0.7	0.3	0.5
France	0.6	0.6	0.4	0.0	0.4
UK	0.8	0.5	0.4	−0.4	0.1
US	1.3	1.3	0.8	0.0	0.1
Germany	0.4	0.4	0.3	−0.3	NA

Source: IMF (2010d).

Table 3.12 Bank sector return on equity, %

	2005	2006	2007	2008	2009
Indonesia	21.4	22.4	23.2	15.5	18.4
Malaysia	16.8	16.2	19.7	18.5	16.1
China	15.1	14.9	16.7	17.1	15.1
Hong Kong	19.1	19.8	25.1	13.9	14.4
India	13.3	12.7	13.2	12.5	12.3
Singapore	11.2	13.7	12.9	10.7	11.0
Philippines	8.6	3.2	8.7	6.9	10.8
Thailand	14.2	8.5	1.2	10.3	9.5
South Korea	18.4	14.6	14.6	7.2	5.8
Japan	11.3	8.5	6.1	−6.9	4.7
Australia	14.7	16.7	17.4	13.7	10.4
France	11.8	14.0	9.8	−1.0	8.2
Switzerland	18.0	17.7	15.4	5.4	8.2
UK	11.8	8.9	6.2	−10.3	2.6
US	12.4	12.3	7.8	0.4	0.9
Germany	13.0	9.4	6.6	−7.7	NA

Source: IMF (2010d).

Table 3.13 Regulatory capital/risk-weighted assets (end period), %

	2005	2006	2007	2008	2009
Indonesia	19.9	20.6	19.2	17	17.6
Hong Kong	14.8	14.9	13.4	14.8	16.9
Singapore	15.8	15.4	13.5	14.7	16.5
Japan	12.2	13.1	12.3	12.4	15.8
Philippines	17.6	18.1	15.7	15.5	15.8
Thailand	13.2	13.6	14.8	13.9	15.8
Malaysia	13.7	13.5	13.2	12.6	15.4
South Korea	13	12.8	12.3	12.3	14.4
India	12.8	12.3	12.3	13.0	13.2
China	2.5	4.9	8.4	12.0	11.4
Switzerland	12.4	13.4	12.1	14.8	17.9
Germany	12.2	12.5	12.9	13.6	14.8
UK	12.8	12.9	12.6	12.9	14.8
US	12.9	13.0	12.8	12.8	14.3
France	11.3	10.9	10.2	10.5	12.4
Australia	10.4	10.4	10.2	11.4	12.0

Source: IMF (2010d).

The region's banking sector in 2010–11 had four notable features:

- Locally domiciled commercial banks dominate their home markets except in Hong Kong. Few are regional in physical presence or cross-border transaction penetration. A small number of Japanese banks are an exception. Those banks and securities houses with developed networks have non-Asian domiciles and many are colonial legacy businesses.

Table 3.14 Bank capital (equity & reserves)/total assets (end period), %

	2005	2006	2007	2008	2009
Hong Kong	13.3	13.0	10.4	11.0	12.7
Philippines	12.0	11.7	11.7	10.6	11.1
South Korea	9.3	9.2	9.0	8.8	10.9
Singapore	9.6	9.6	9.2	8.3	10.5
Indonesia	9.8	10.2	10.1	9.2	10.3
Thailand	8.9	8.9	9.5	9.2	9.8
Malaysia	7.7	7.6	7.4	8.1	9.0
India	6.4	6.6	6.4	NA	NA
China	4.4	5.1	5.8	6.1	5.6
Japan	4.9	5.3	4.5	3.6	4.7
US	10.3	10.5	10.3	9.3	11.0
Switzerland	5.1	4.9	4.6	5.7	5.5
UK	6.1	6.1	5.5	4.4	5.4
Australia	5.2	5.4	4.9	4.4	5.0
Germany	4.1	4.3	4.3	4.5	4.8
France	4.4	4.5	4.1	4.2	4.5

Source: IMF (2010d).

- Other foreign ventures are limited and cautious. This reflects state policy in some cases or the exporting orientation of the banks' clients, which tends to limit direct investment in foreign markets. A general rise in outward FDI might induce banks to expand abroad, although industrial investors have generally relied on internal funds for foreign ventures and given limited opportunities for their house banks. The few exceptions using external finance for overseas investment or acquisitions are either Hong Kong or Singapore companies or in the energy or extractive sectors, and all rely for funding on non-Asian investment banks.
- No indigenous bank has yet appeared among recognized regional surveys of innovative or admired multinational companies, even though manufacturing and non-financial companies have been well-represented for several decades. The improving brand value of finance is limited to domestic commercial banking.
- Few conventional indigenous intermediaries are innovative in introducing new financial instruments, risk management techniques or managerial strategy. A part-exception is the expanded franchise of Nomura Securities, which bought the European and Asian operations of Lehman Brothers in 2008, but the commercial result has been poor: Nomura's revenues accrue mainly at home. *The Banker's* 2009 rankings place Asian banks lower in profitability than in generating income, which points to their narrow credit-based focus. Financial sector innovation has arisen mainly from state development banks and applied both domestically and overseas, from certain sovereign wealth funds, and from non-Asian investment and universal banks.

Asian finance's improving standing has so far led only to a modest diversification in activities or overseas expansion. We associate this lack of innovation with strategic caution or commercial choice rather than a developmental issue, which reinforces our scepticism that Asian finance will evolve towards a mythical global model. China's modern financial system was created in the same years that saw radical changes in Anglo-American 'high finance', producing unprecedented revenue growth, financial leverage and commercial complexity. Can anyone say which model is more successful? If the links shown in Figure 3.5 are weak then intermediation will be disturbed or fail. Financial crises are often examples of intermediation rendered so dysfunctional as to require costly state support. Rather than see financial development converging to a non-existent global benchmark and an Anglo-American paradigm, we prefer to examine how the links within each economy might be strengthened with country specific policies. This leads us to a qualitative assessment of how China has created its financial system.

3.4 Intermediation in China

Global finance began a remarkable period of change in the late 1970s. Responding to commercial innovation and financial deregulation, this gave users steadily greater freedom to deal in financial instruments or invest and borrow transnationally, and by the late 1990s led to a system with claims totalling many multiples of global output. Precisely the same period was used by one leading state to develop a modern financial sector from the most primitive beginnings. Post-1949 China was long without either law or finance, one scholar writing that it 'emerged from an era of lawlessness' with Deng Xiaoping's reforms (Chen 1983: 291). After a plenary session of the Central Committee of the Communist Party in 1978 'legal life in China … rapidly and vigorously revived' (ibid: 292). Similar words could describe the opening of a financial system, built from ground lacking any institutional base. China's banking sector accounted for 51.2 per cent of Asia's core Tier 1 capital in 2009 (*The Banker* 2010). Critics of finance in China need to account for the speed with which a modern financial system and supporting institutions have been established.

The setting for reform has changed several times, ranging from committed liberalization to the form of state-led directed capitalism that prevails today (Huang 2009). Local and foreign banks have grown accustomed to receiving freedom to engage in new businesses after periods of restricted trials, indicating a cautious policy approach informed by both economic objectives and foreign regulatory experience or professional practices. Some early reforms were soon reversed or made subject to stricter limits on use. Dealings in interest rate futures and option contracts began in the early 1990s but were forced to close in 1994–95 for being damagingly speculative, only to be reopened on a more constrained basis after a 2004 State Council endorsement of domestic debt and derivative capital markets.

China's financial system is semi-sophisticated, heavily bank dependent and subject to imbalances, but cautious policy sequencing is crucial to the state's pursuit of stability and the system's faults are generally known at a political level and to regulators.

Post-1980 reforms

The People's Republic of China (PRC) lacked a financial sector in an accepted sense for its first 30 years. Credit creation was minimal and confined to the privileged, and intermediation was limited, centralized, unavailable to the non-governmental sector and isolated from overseas. This makes the current financial system a remarkable achievement regardless of its omissions, and the foremost example of a managed financial system created by the state compared to those developed through the competitive behaviour of participants and licensed by the state. Central government chooses when markets or intermediaries may commence operations and the forms of activity that they may undertake. Some market segments have adapted overseas practices while others rely on domestic solutions, with all strongly influenced by sectoral regulators, the finance ministry or PBOC. Informal financial interme-diation coexists with the state system, not only for small-scale users but assisting in funding for non-state enterprises (NSEs) of all sizes.

The reform era began substantively in 1979–81 with a shift from collectivism signalled by the new household responsibility system. Annual growth in GDP averaged 9.85 per cent in 1980–2008 and was achieved despite the lack of many conventional institutions. This 'China enigma' (Trebilcock & Leng 2006: 1554) is held by some scholars to undermine the predicted causal relationship between finance and economic development explained in Section 2.1 (Clarke, Murrell & Whiting 2008). Attributing the creation of China's financial system to increasing growth and economic sophistication is a reversal of the more accepted causal flow (ibid: 420).

To us this argument neglects the nature of finance and the manner of its introduction in a specific developmental setting. China's state-led design may have created a financial system simultaneously with accelerated growth by relying on both conventional and informal insti-tutions. Formal institutions such as new commercial laws allowed growth and development to entrench, so, for example, 'there is a positive correlation between the development of the formal legal regime and the expansion of bank lending' (Yu 2009: 30). This in turn contrib-uted to economic development and helped sustain high rates of growth. Informal institutions assisted financial development by augmenting or substituting for law and regulation. This phenomenon is recognized in both product markets (Bernstein 1992), and social settings (Greif 2006), where in all cases a cohesiveness among commercial parties takes the place of formal law in establishing property rights, making contracts and resolving commercial disputes. China's conspicuously effective informal institutions include:

- Private socio-commercial networks or *guanxi* (關 係) at local, regional or national level. Connections with the Chinese commercial diaspora were also crucial (Trebilcock & Leng 2006), with Hong Kong and Taiwanese interests providing substantial inward FDI in coastal manufacturing when domestic finance was unavailable.
- The presence of Chinese Communist Party (CCP) cadres throughout the emerging financial sector and regulators has been highly influential on commercial activity, regu-latory impact and senior appointments.

The government first organized a banking sector and later established equity and debt capital markets. The latter are now sizeable in nominal capitalization but enjoy limited day-to-day liquidity and so intermediation relies mainly on banks, as seen in Table 3.6. The sector began as a clutch of national state commercial banks (Agricultural Bank of China, Bank of China, China Construction Bank, Bank of Communications, and Industrial and Commercial Bank of China), none of which were material before 1980,[4] and a handful of sectoral 'policy banks'. State and private interests were later allowed to create joint stock commercial banks, usually with a provincial or sectoral focus. With variable success the bank sector was allowed to expand until 1998–99, when several prominent banks and quasi-banks (trust companies) failed, making a costly reorganization and recapitalization imperative. The state now over-sees a hierarchical system that includes:

- State policy banks;
- National state commercial banks;
- Joint stock commercial banks;
- City and rural commercial banks;

- Rural and urban credit cooperatives;
- A postal savings system;
- Foreign banks licensed to operated in the PRC; and
- Non-bank financial intermediaries, including finance companies (many owned by large commercial enterprises), trust and investment companies, leasing companies, auto finance companies and money brokers.

A legal framework and supervisory system was established in stages. Laws covering banking, company formation and governance, contract, property, financial securities and bankruptcy were enacted, revised and adapted, so that the current financial sector legislation is recent (Commercial Banking Law 2003; Insurance Law 2008; Securities Law 2005), partly due to commitments made as part of WTO accession. PBOC was designated as the central bank in 1983 by decree (a central banking law was enacted only in 1995), taking charge of monetary policy and financial system supervision. CBRC is one of three sectoral regulators, along with China Securities Regulatory Commission (CSRC) and China Insurance Regulatory Commission (CIRC), all of which are arms of government under the State Council. The agencies are inevitably rivals, and enforce stricter divisions in the permissible activities of banks and other intermediaries than many other large economies.

Equity markets were established in 1990–91 in Shenzhen and Shanghai. These now host substantial aggregate capitalizations of listed companies, mainly from IPOs of minority interests in SOEs. Shanghai is significantly larger by market capitalization, ranking fourth among world exchanges in mid-2009 and mid-2010, and of a similar order to Hong Kong, London or Euronext (Amsterdam, Brussels, Lisbon and Paris). Share trading volumes have been disproportionately limited both by poor liquidity and regulation, with many shares listed but allowed not to trade until 2005–6 and the state retaining majority control of listed SOEs.

CSRC opened limited access to foreign equity investors in 2003 through vehicles known as Qualified Foreign Institutional Investors (QFII), and in 2006 Chinese intermediaries became able to invest in overseas share markets as Qualified Domestic Institutional Investors (QDII). Debt capital markets have also become large in relation to GDP, although bond trading is limited by separating users and instruments into distinct sub-markets, which reflects the state's refusal to cede control over interest rates. The insurance sector is modest in terms of funds under management and its contribution to savings intermediation.

Critics argue that intermediation is generally unsophisticated, inefficient and asymmetric in that state banks provide credit mainly credit to SOEs. Yet the system is plainly capable of quickly channelling funds for investment, as shown by the central government's 2009–10 counter-cyclical lending instruction to state banks. New lending exceeded that central target, whereas banks in the Anglo-American model would have chosen to conserve capital during a downturn by withdrawing credit. What share of that infusion of credit will ultimately be productive can only be guessed, reinforcing our view that intermediation is thus simple, often effective, but inefficient and sub-optimal. Can the financial system avoid disruption and provide value in the real economy despite its imperfections? Four particular forces condition the outcome:

- High savings rates by the household and corporate sectors;
- External capital controls;
- Central regulation of interest rates; and
- Incremental reforms in financial policy strategy and functional liberalization.

These control factors protect against exposure to imported risks, so that China has usually been able to guard against sudden external contagion. The controls are asymmetric: for example, inward FDI is freely allowed for designated projects or provinces.

Costs of savings

Savings are high by global standards and rose throughout the 2000s to levels that are historically high for China itself. Even if the reasons are disputed or understandable, it is clear that there are significant costs to savings rates exceeding 50 per cent of GDP. Section 1.3 showed that regional savings rates have been consistently higher than OECD or global levels, yet China's predicament is unique in that savings are high in all sectors: household, corporate and government (Ma & Wang 2010: 5–6).

The head of PBOC has argued that high savings reflect Confucian self discipline, family structure, demographics and China's early and bifurcated stage of development (Zhou 2009a), and suggests that high savings and foreign reserves are also anti-speculative defences learned from the Asian financial crisis. Other explanations for high household savings include the life-cycle theory, that savings rise with the share of those of working age in the total population (Modigliani 1970), and precautionary theories predicting that savings increase with income uncertainty.

Primitive financial development and poor access may be contributory, in that consumers lack investment choices despite their rising incomes. Wei and Zhang (2009) argue that competition for marriage partners due to gender imbalances encourages postponed consumption in favour of wealth accumulation. The rise in the savings ratio above 50 per cent of GDP in 2008 has been attributed largely to low SOE dividends and high corporate savings (Anderson 2009; Kuijs 2006), but others suggest that high corporate savings are not limited to China (Bayoumi, Tong & Wei 2010). Regardless of their provenance, savings are excessive relative to their historic level and compared with other major economies. Any natural or enforced adjustment will be protracted.

Capital controls

The capital account is largely closed and most cross-border flows are closely monitored, which makes the system less susceptible to external shocks. These controls indicate a cautious approach to all aspects of innovation, including foreign financial engagements. The state's massing of US dollar reserves can be seen as a result of the same method, even though the result is an extreme concentration of risk. China's relatively small losses in the global banking crisis resulted mainly from semi-official participation in 2007–8 share issues by foreign intermediaries, including Blackstone Group, Citigroup and Morgan Stanley, before the share prices reached their respective lows (although we note that China's foreign reserves include substantial claims against US federal housing finance agencies Fannie Mae and Freddie Mac, both of which were placed in government conservatorship in 2008 to avoid insolvency).

Interest rate management

The gradual freeing of market sectors has been asymmetric. Most product markets are at least partially liberalized, but factor markets remain tightly controlled. PBOC sets floors and ceilings for bank lending and deposit rates, ensuring a large and stable interest rate spread

(Anderson 2009; Huang 2009). Interest rate regulations have two immediate implications for intermediation in helping commercial bank profitability while reducing incentives for banks to seek non-interest income.

Reform by increment

Caution is also the guiding principle for reform. PBOC or sectoral regulators often use a problem-solving tactic, requesting the National People's Congress to permit pilot projects or model transactions under declarations of intent made by the State Council. This allows the value of any innovation to be demonstrated to conservative interests and help obtain permanent enabling legislation. The process is inevitably protracted, as with the post-1999 reform of the large state banks which began under 'trial' legislation creating AMCs to acquire and process NPLs, provide official infusions of capital and allow commercial reorganizations prior to domestic and overseas IPOs. The opening in 2010–11 of an offshore market in yuan bonds in Hong Kong is a recent example of incremental reform. Allowing approved Chinese and foreign issuers to borrow yuan outside mainland controls is both a non-inflationary use of yuan deposits accumulated in Hong Kong and a trial of currency convertibility.

Structural problems

Global imbalances are determined by uneven investment and consumption that is highlighted in China's growth model. Restating Equation (2.2) as $CA = S - I$ shows that reducing any current account surplus requires cutting the gap between savings and investment $(S - I)$. If investment is high such that further increases are infeasible, then savings must be reduced. China's current growth model has two needs:

- Export-led growth continues, so the savings investment gap is left unresolved. This is ever more difficult to sustain for reasons of both politics and risk, given that China accounts for more than 8 per cent of global exports, holds unprecedentedly large foreign reserves, and is exposed to imported primary goods inflation.
- The savings ratio is encouraged to fall. Even if this becomes a policy aim, the process is subject to a multiplicity of factors, many of which cannot change quickly or without significant structural reforms.

Cutting the savings–investment gap is a substantial challenge for financial intermediation. Delaying resolution of the problem may not jeopardize China's growth prospects, but procrastination may make structural problems more difficult to solve later. In the meantime persistent high savings encourage asset price inflation, as will domestic liquidity created inadvertently as a result of foreign reserve accumulation. Increasing demand for financial assets is also troublesome for underdeveloped capital markets since they lack suitable instruments to absorb excess credit. Each factor increases systemic risk in the financial system. The challenges for intermediation are considerable even when the savings rate is eventually lowered. Commercial banks function in a controlled environment that protects their profit margins, limits competition from foreign banks, and provides fresh capital when NPLs become threatening. Such conditions would be at risk from an intensification of economic and financial reforms.

Household consumption fell from 46 per cent of GDP in 2000 to 35 per cent in 2007. This variable is difficult to influence, being entrenched due to income uncertainty and the absence of a sound welfare system, and because consumption decisions are typically made at household level. Promoting consumption will succeed if resources shift from the state to individuals and effectively increase personal income. PBOC's governor cited this solution as 'deepening the reform of government and [the] state-owned sector' (Zhou 2009b). Effective and accessible intermediation would help redirect financial resources from the state to the private sector, including rural entrepreneurship and household consumption.

More generally, the problem demands that financial resources be allocated to the most productive parts of the economy. We saw that SOE investment is far less efficient than that of NSEs, whether private companies, collectives or foreign-invested firms. State banks were traditionally 'advised' to cap the interest cost of loans to SOEs, partly due to the state sector being a de facto welfare provider. This credit imbalance continues even without central direction, not least because heavy SOE indebtedness itself requires ongoing credit. NSEs are simultaneously starved of funds. Controlled interest rates make it impossible for banks to price loans for the private sector, despite its relative efficiency.

Solving these structural problems demands similar efforts to liberalize the factor markets for land, labour and capital (Huang 2009). This would expose the implicit production costs embedded in the economy, such as low wage rates, cheap land, subsidized capital or environmental degradation, and more faithfully reflect corporate earnings and growth prospects. The result would give more precise guidance for resource allocation. Deregulating interest rates and allowing the yuan to be fairly valued are both essential in this process. State intermediaries will undoubtedly face more volatile conditions in future, and we hope they respond by seeking new sources of revenue to replace guaranteed income from their existing loan-centred model.

Future intermediation

Finance in China must eventually resolve six problems:

- The need for growth or reform;
- Cheap credit or asset bubbles;
- State control or market-based liberalization;
- Financial innovation or the risk of instability;
- The place of informal intermediation; and
- Preserving or reforming the international monetary system.

These are linked rather than mutually exclusive dilemmas that address related themes from different perspectives. The choices made from these factors will determine China's future finance.

Growth or reform?

With rare exceptions, governments at national and regional levels have been certain that a minimum annual GDP growth rate of 8 per cent is essential to maintain employment and keep social problems in check. With this dominant policy objective, finance is treated as a tool to facilitate growth by funding exports and fixed capital formation. A new growth model would involve shifting financial resources to the non-state corporate sectors and households, a task for which the large state commercial banks are poorly equipped. For the foreseeable future the state will want its banks to remain as dominant and profitable lenders, both for control and stability motives and to promote growth by funding large projects and SOEs. The alternative would be for the state-bank business model to be adapted by lessening its reliance on the state, improving competitiveness, credit and risk management, and identifying new sources of product demand. This may be a shift that smaller regional and joint-stock banks are better equipped to make.

Capital market activity is unlikely to rival the banking sector for many years, but effective equity and bond markets will be increasingly important to resource allocation, especially if China is able to cut excessive savings and deregulate interest rates. Functioning capital markets are needed to encourage corporate restructuring, solve industrial overcapacity problems, and provide funds and investor exit options for new businesses, as the economy's sources of growth shift from exporting towards domestic consumption.

Cheap credit or asset bubbles?

Financial intermediation provides credit to the real economy through a spectrum of markets and instruments, their range depending upon the relative sophistication of the system and its institutional setting. Since finance in China is narrow and relatively inefficient, a greater volume of credit is needed to fund any given rate of growth. Future finance must supply abundant credit at lower costs.

The economy is also prone to asset bubbles. Recurrent trade surpluses and the accumulation of foreign reserves tend to add to domestic liquidity which underdeveloped capital markets cannot fully absorb, resulting in persistent inflationary pressures and unstable bubbles in the share and property markets. Further pressure stems from misallocated lending by state banks. Credit is allocated centrally to sectors prone to overinvestment, and may be redirected through informal channels to seek supposedly profitable opportunities in shares or property, and further contributing to price volatility.

A more stable balance of credit creation and asset prices has long-term implications for intermediation. State bank credit that feeds overinvestment by SOEs could usefully be channelled to growth sectors with poorer access to finance, and the scope of intermediation expanded with capital market reform to encourage long-term investment and some form of venture capital.

Control or liberalization?

State control of factor markets allows resources to be readily mobilized for chosen economic goals or social objectives. It also has negative results in a partially liberalized environment. China's asymmetric liberalization of product and factor markets limits the signalling value of the price mechanism by giving incentives to producers. The long-term result of factor prices deviating from their true value is to warp incentives and misallocate resources. Thus interest rate regulation distorts the cost of capital perceived by SOE managers and local government, leading to investment inefficiency and worsening problems of sectoral overcapacity. Control of the exchange rate draws resources to exporting sectors of the real economy, and effectively increases reliance on foreign demand.

On the other hand, the state's traditional administrative approach in economic and financial development appears to have been relatively successful during the global financial crisis. Nationalization, directed lending and state bailouts conducted in 2008–9 by some OECD states may have been chosen by events rather than policy preference, but critics of a heavily financialized capitalism may conclude that China's approach to intermediation is appropriate.

Innovation or stability?

The business model of most Chinese commercial intermediaries is kept simple by decree and has generally avoided the complex problems experienced by many OECD counterparts in the global crisis and collapse of financial confidence. That benign setting will change as the capital account is gradually opened and greater competition allowed at home and abroad.

Weaknesses encouraged by the centrally administered system will need continued reparations, including independent credit risk appraisal, more effective treasury and balance sheet management, consistent NPL policies, and less concentration on corporate lending. The financial system needs innovation to provide incentives for these changes and make finance accessible to a broader population.

We take innovation to mean progressive applications of transaction, marketing and risk management behaviour, not a leap towards high leverage and excessive complexity. Financial innovation must be balanced with the proper containment of risk, especially if the financial sector is to undergo structural reforms. Innovation should improve the sector's value to the real economy and eliminate the flaws in the traditional financial intermediation model. It includes establishing a consistent and transparent regulatory framework across the entire financial system.

The place of informal intermediation?

Informal intermediation has contributed significantly to growth sectors of the real economy (Allen, Qian & Qian 2005). It comprises intermediaries, internal financing within conglomerates, trade credit, and loose but permanent commercial networks among firms, investors and local governments. Informal funding is vital for NSEs that often lack regular access to bank credit despite being the largest sectoral contributor to national growth. Informal intermediation is used by the most vibrant parts of the economy but is riddled with institutional, regulatory and governance problems.

This also indicates a general failure of the formal financial system. The scale and ubiquity of informal finance is a challenge to regulation, and impedes the performance measurement of intermediaries and markets, or the assessing of systemic risk. Informal financing lacks pricing and functional transparency, disguises the true scale of intermediation, and complicates the functioning of monetary and macroeconomic policies. The real sector's reliance on so well-developed an informal sector means that radical reforms will be implemented only with difficulty. China has a significant challenge to introduce a more formal institutional framework for this part of its financial system.

Preserve or reform the international monetary system?

The 2008 financial crisis exposed unforeseen fragility in the international monetary system – especially in the Bretton Woods architecture and the reserve status of the US dollar – and the assumption that the interbank deposit market was a stable utility not susceptible to a rapid loss in confidence. The Federal Reserve's emergency solution of creating liquidity to meet a vast global demand illustrates the dilemma identified by Robert Triffin in the 1960s, that a reserve currency issuer cannot maintain the value of that currency while satisfying world demand for liquidity (Triffin 1978). Supplying US dollars in this way is to jeopardize the risk-free characteristic supposedly associated with a reserve currency.

China is the largest non-US holder of US government securities and faces an inescapable strategic choice. Meaningful diversification from this position is impossible, even though a weak US dollar is not in China's interest. PBOC has called for a new international monetary system (Zhou 2009a), despite China being far from ready for any such reforms. Its closed financial system could not cope with large inflows and outflows, portfolio shifts or more demanding exchange rate risk management. The approach that China eventually adopts will have global implications and a profound effect on domestic intermediation.

Future intermediation, not only in China but in the region and around the world, will be shaped by China's approach to these six dilemmas.

4 Financial systems and practice

Central banking, regulation and risk management

One aspect of finance which the global crisis did not change is that it remains central to growth and development, despite the welfare costs associated with sporadic financial shocks. Financial development is a continuing objective throughout Asia, indeed a post-crisis consensus to support more balanced and sustainable global growth, further domestic and regional financial development in Asia is more vital than ever.

This chapter begins by discussing Asia's alternatives in second generation financial systems, and the underlying principles and reforms that might lead to their introduction. Our approach to these topics is pragmatic, reflecting a mainstream view of financial practice. We are neither in favour of unrestricted markets nor excessive government intervention – we strongly favour the price mechanism in allocation and decision making, but not to the extent of endorsing any single variety of capitalism or a strong bias towards a laissez faire version. In any event, we would acknowledge those who have long held more radical views as to how best to configure financial activity, including Marxian scholars for whom finance is largely non-productive and parasitical, and Austrian school libertarians for whom central banking or state-led commercial activity are value-destroying and inefficient.

Asia's financial reforms will result from its own choices. It is less clear that the region will contribute to global reform except by example. The leading economies are no longer free to decide changes in the world's financial architecture, yet Asian states may be reluctant to steer or initiate reforms (Zhou 2011). This leads us to review central banking, including monetary policy operations and the provision of conventional and emergency liquidity. We also introduce credit lines, a simple universal foundation of banking and securities market practice, and the basis of all activity involving credit, lending and trading. The regulator's concern for stability is expressed through financial regulation, which we explain through the narrative of the Basel capital accords and other cooperative international arrangements, not only in Basel's effects on commercial behaviour but its considerable transnational political and institutional implications. We end the chapter with a review of risk management policies in financial intermediaries – expressing an interaction between the institutional framework and financial intermediary behaviour.

4.1 Second generation financial systems: lessons from law and finance

Economic growth is not the result of conjuring. Chapters 2 and 3 discussed the pitfalls in Asia's economic and financial development, and how links between the real economy and the financial sector can be tenuous. They also considered the proximate causes of the

1997–98 and 2007–09 financial crises: notably excessive leverage; poor risk and liquidity management; poorly hedged maturity and currency mismatches between assets and liabilities; inappropriate macroeconomic policies; unfavourable funding dynamics; and volatile asset price cycles.

These apparent causes concealed deeper structural flaws. All financial systems are tied to stability and growth. Financial development is not an endowment, unlike the assumptions of the growth literature, but an integral part of development shaped by country specific factors. Knowing how best to promote financial development requires an understanding of the determinants of the scale and structure of the financial system. In this section we examine the elemental causes of financial development and apply the results to our assessment of Asian finance to suggest how the links between the region's real and financial sectors might be strengthened.

Legal origins

The law and finance literature introduced in Section 2.1 focuses on the role of law and legal institutions in financial development (La Porta, Lopez-de-Silanes, Shleifer & Vishny 1997; 1998). Evidence from cross-sectional studies showed legal origin as a strong, exogenous determinant of financial development. LLSV suggest that the roots of any jurisdiction signify its propensity and ability to protect private property rights and enforce contracts, and these factors increase the propensity of potential investors to hold financial assets. Common law systems of English origin are thus more suitable than civil law systems of French origin in promoting the development of capital markets, largely because the common law evolved to protect private property while civil law was developed to address judicial corruption and enhance the power of the state. LLSV conclude that effective capital markets are prone to develop faster in states with common law systems than in those with civil law systems.

Law and finance is primarily an empirical literature. Its main protagonists only recently sought to develop a theory to explain their findings (La Porta, Lopez-de-Silanes & Shleifer 2008), and the result is convincing only with very limiting assumptions as to how effective contract formation and enforcement affect commercial outcomes in any state (Lejot 2013). This is one of several grounds on which academic lawyers have faulted LLSV's method and conclusions, but their approach has altered since 2000 from outright criticism to constructive engagement.

Other cross-sectional studies are supportive. Rajan and Zingales (1998b) and Beck and Levine (2002) show that legal institutions affect the availability of financing and firm creation. Beck, Demirgüç-Kunt and Maksimovic (2005) show that firms in states with ineffective protection of property rights face more financial constraints and grow more slowly than those elsewhere. Wurgler (2000), Claessens and Laeven (2002), and Beck and Levine (2002) show that legal institutions affect not only the volume but the allocation of capital among firms and industry sectors. All find that strong investor protection induces a more efficient allocation of capital to growing firms.

The legal origin view argues generally that:

- Finance is better developed in countries with a strong legal framework.
- National differences in financial development may be explained by a range of factors, including the origin of the legal system, exemplified in the treatment of investor or property rights, or how the legal system adapts to commercial circumstances.

- A state's legal tradition has an enduring influence on its approach to private property rights and financial development.
- Differences in endowments shaped initial institutions and these institutions have had lasting repercussions on property protection and financial development.

A narrow summary refines the legal origins argument to linking:

> Creditor rights with financial development by documenting positive correlations between creditor rights and the size of credit markets in cross-country regressions. The major function attributed to law is that it empowers creditors to enforce their contracts. The suggested mechanism through which law affects financial development is by reducing the cost of external financing.
>
> (Haselmann, Pistor & Vig 2010: 549)

Although the legal origins view has intuitive appeal and certain empirical support, it has also prompted intense criticism, some rooted in varying interpretations of legal rules, systems and evolution. For example, LLSV use eight proxies to construct a variable to measure shareholder protection. The variable itself is biased towards the US legal system but the study uses it to measure investor protection across 49 countries. Lele and Siems (2007) use a more comprehensive index to measure shareholder protection and show that there are no significant differences between civil and common law countries with respect to shareholder protection. Indeed, from their analysis France and Germany have provided better shareholder protection than the United States since the 1990s. Looking further back, Bordo and Rousseau (2006) found that the financial systems of civil law jurisdictions were more developed than those of common law states prior to 1914.

LLSV have also been criticized for three main methodological reasons:

- The use of small sample regressions is hazardous, producing results that are sensitive to outliers and not robust.
- The choice of explanatory variables and the specification of models may be incomplete or endogenously related to the objective questions that the analysis seeks to answer. They may also take no account of compensatory mechanisms within different legal systems.
- The analysis is static. It ignores convergence between civil and common commercial law due to political regionalization and financial harmonization, the impact of extensive treaty networks, and informal institutions such as the private ordering activities of international self-regulatory bodies and market practitioners.

State ownership

A growing literature looks at the state's involvement in financial development, where its influence is largely signalled by government ownership of banks. Significant government ownership enables intervention in credit policy and commercial decisions, so that funds may necessarily be channelled to sectors or firms according to political interests rather than sound business and economic judgments. This may eventually undermine economic growth. It is often argued that such a system is insufficiently supportive of innovation and tends to be relatively uncompetitive: La Porta, Lopez-de-Silanes and Shleifer (2002) analyzed bank ownership in 92 countries and provide some empirical support for the critical view. State ownership is globally extensive but more prevalent in poorer countries and those with weaker protection of property rights. State ownership of banks has negative effects on subsequent financial development and growth, which the authors interpret as causal. They conclude that 'financial systems of countries with higher initial government ownership of banks grow less fast' (ibid: 284).

We see these conclusions as fragile due to a small-sample bias, and a failure to control for the effects of initial financial development and variables such as schooling levels. With these variables included in regressions, state ownership of banks becomes statistically insignificant at conventional levels. It seems premature on empirical grounds to claim that public ownership tends to exert a negative effect on financial development, for as we saw in Section 2.2 the state played an important role in shaping Asia's post-1949 financial systems.

Political institutions

The new growth literature highlights institutions as a cause of economic growth (Acemoglu 2008). Institutions help shape the incentives and constraints of economic agents that drive financial development. Acemoglu, Johnson and Robinson (2004) and Acemoglu and Johnson (2005) introduce a dynamic political economy framework to further explore the effects of institutions, arguably that different political environments prompt varying degrees of economic and financial development, and that the effectiveness of institutions might vary considerably with the political support they command.

Acemoglu and Johnson (2005) distinguish two institutions: those that are political (property rights) and regulate the relationship between the state and citizens, and those that are legal (contracting institutions) that regulate commercial and employment relationships between individuals. They then examine the impact of contracting institutions on economic and financial development and find them to have no significant impact unless supported by robust political power. Conversely, even weak or dysfunctional contracting institutions will encourage economic and financial growth if political institutions are able to protect against expropriation by power elites or the state.

This political economy view of financial development has empirical support (Johnson, McMillan & Woodruff 2002), implying that fostering economic and financial development demands institutions that allocate power to groups committed to the rigorous protection of property rights, that create effective constraints on power holders, and which leave few rents to be captured by power holders.

A related view has been formulated by Rajan and Zingales (2003a). They propose an interest group theory where incumbents oppose financial development because it breeds competition. There will be occasions when incentives for incumbents to oppose development is muted, for example, when national borders are open to trade and capital flows, opposition to financial development will be subdued and allow financial sector development to flourish.

Financial structure and economic development

The most important societal function of a financial system is to promote growth through the effective mobilization of savings into productive capital and the channelling of capital to its most effective use. In a market economy this may take place either through open markets or intermediaries. Modern finance has classified the former as a market-based financial system and the latter as a bank-oriented financial system.

An important and long-standing issue in finance has been the relative merits of banks and financial markets as providers of capital. Does the structure of the financial system matter of itself? Most studies have delivered mixed evidence, ranging from the view that financial structure is of no real consequence (Demirgüç-Kunt & Levine 2001) to arguments emphasizing the superiority of the market-based system (Macey 1998) or bank-oriented system (Gilson & Roe 1993).

Beck, Loyaza and Levine (2000) provide evidence that the scale and quality of financial intermediation matter more than the means by which it takes place. This view is built on the understanding that banks and financial markets are complementary and neither is intrinsically more advantageous (Allen & Gale 1999). Tadesse (2002) uses industry level data from a panel of 36 countries to explore how financial structure affects performance in the real economy. He finds that market-based systems outperform bank-oriented systems in states with relatively developed financial sectors, while bank-oriented systems fare better among countries with underdeveloped financial sectors. Furthermore, economies in which SMEs are relatively important achieve faster growth using bank-oriented systems, and those where large firms are dominant grow faster with market-based systems.

Other research is more equivocal. The structure of the financial system matters, and how it matters depends on many institutional conditions, including the legal and contractual system, and business and economic environment (Levine 2004). The relative merits of markets and banks depends on the effectiveness with which they conduct intermediation. Country specific factors decide which system is conducive to economic development. Similarly, capital markets become more active and efficient relative to banks in high-income economies, and financial systems tend to become more market oriented as states grow wealthier (Demirgüç-Kunt & Levine 2001). Common law traditions, strong protection of shareholder rights, reliable accounting regulations, low levels of corruption, and a lack of explicit deposit insurance tend to favour a market-based financial system, consistent with a decentralized pattern of financial intermediation. Demirgüç-Kunt and Levine (2001) also suggest that countries with a French civil law tradition, weak protection of shareholder and creditor rights, a poor contractual environment, higher levels of corruption, inadequate accounting standards, restrictive banking regulations, and higher inflation tend to have underdeveloped financial systems and rely more heavily on banks.

4.2 How does finance matter?

This review suggests that the structure of a financial system may have little impact on economic growth, so that the consequences of financial structure depend on specific factors. Does finance therefore matter in Asia, or how? Our discussion has implicitly taken Western OECD financial systems as a benchmark, but this may neither correspond with what exists in Asia, nor be appropriate in the region's future. What should be the features of a new generation of financial systems? How can Asian states encourage the development of their current financial intermediation practices in a new generation, especially when their modern experience has been largely state-led, with finance generally subordinated to the real economy? The finance and growth literature may provide some elucidation:

- Research on the relationship between financial development and economic growth shows that the level of financial development matters. Most research tends to support the claim that such a relation is causal, that is, a well-developed financial system

contributes to economic growth. We conclude that finance matters significantly for Asian economic development.
- Empirical evidence on the relative merits of bank-oriented financial systems and market-based financial systems is mixed. Financial structure is not an analytically useful way to distinguish the effectiveness of national financial systems.
- The relative advantages of banks or capital markets depend on many country specific factors.
- The nature and extent of financial development are determined by many factors, of which the institutional quality is paramount.

This appraisal has several implications:

- If a robust causal relation exists between financial development and economic growth, developing an effective financial system is crucial for long-run economic development. Our earlier chapters discussed the progress of Asia's economies since 1949 and suggested challenges to the sustainability of regional growth, with many contemporary issues related to financial development because of institutional weaknesses.
- It is questionable whether the Anglo-American financial model is an appropriate paradigm for Asia. National financial development is shaped by both formal and informal conditions, meaning that a single model cannot be successfully adopted without great care and significant variation. States wishing to encourage financial development are more likely to succeed by enhancing their core institutions to allow banks and markets to intermediate effectively.

Effective intermediation

Practitioners and policymakers tend to believe that financial intermediation requires four features to function effectively: depth and diversity, liquidity, efficiency and an absence of inherent systemic risks (Ghosh 2006).

Depth and diversity requires a financial system to host a variety of intermediaries and markets and offer a broad array of instruments and transaction types. Common measures of financial size or depth include the number of intermediaries and organized markets, the value of financial assets, and deposits and private sector credit in nominal terms and as a share of GDP. A more developed financial system is usually more diverse, with non-bank intermediaries and open markets established alongside the banking sector. Liquidity requires a financial system to have equity and bond markets able to absorb large trade volumes with relatively small effects on prevailing prices. Being able to conduct sizeable transactions in financial instruments is an important aspect of liquidity and of importance to professional asset managers. This allows savers to hold financial claims such as demand deposits, equities or bonds that can easily be sold for cash or alternative investments as economic conditions change.

Intermediation is efficient or competitive when financial services are offered by a healthy number of rival suppliers, and are sufficiently diversified to match the supply and demand for funds. Few such systems exist in reality. Competitive financial systems are desirable because they lead to the improved efficiency of participants, lower costs for customers, and produce higher quality services. A competitive system generally improves financial access for less advantaged consumers and SMEs. The costs of products and services provided by the financial system are the key indicators of its efficiency. Quantitative measures in this regard include the total costs of intermediation as a share of total financial assets, and interest rate spreads.

More efficient markets tend to have narrower bid–offer spreads. Price volatility is a further proxy in assessing market efficiency.

Well-functioning intermediation should also lessen systemic risk, which has been described by the G10 as:

> The risk that an event will trigger a loss of economic value or confidence in, and attendant increases in uncertainty about, a substantial portion of the financial system that is serious enough to quite probably have significant adverse effects on the economy. Systemic risk events can be sudden and unexpected, or the likelihood of their occurrence can build up through time in the absence of appropriate policy response. The adverse real economic effects from systemic problems are generally seen as arising from disruptions to payment system, and to credit flow, and from the destruction of asset values.
>
> (G10 2001: 126)

For example, the bankruptcy of Lehman Brothers triggered a systemic crisis in the United States, accelerating a loss of economic value and confidence in the global financial system, which soon led to a systemic global crisis. A financial system is regarded as protected from systemic risks when banks and non-bank intermediaries are well-managed, regulated and supervised, adequately capitalized, have strong balance sheets and are well-provisioned for NPLs, and the financial sector has a sound legal and regulatory framework and strong enforcement capacity. Even such an idealized setting can be prone to failure, as the experience of 2008 showed Alan Greenspan, a former Federal Reserve Board chair, not least because of agency problems and distorted incentive structures in the global banking sector, which may have led to excessive leverage and disregard for risk:

As a significant example, Greenspan recanted before a US congressional committee only five weeks after Lehman Brothers entered bankruptcy proceedings:

> those of us who have looked to the self-interest of lending institutions to protect shareholder's equity (myself especially) are in a state of shocked disbelief. Such counterparty surveillance is a central pillar of our financial markets' state of balance. If it fails, as occurred this year, market stability is undermined.
>
> (Greenspan 2008: lines 384–90)

> I found a flaw in the model that I perceived is the critical functioning structure that defines how the world works, so to speak. CHAIRMAN: In other words, you found that your view of the world, your ideology, was not right, it was not working? Mr. GREENSPAN. Precisely. That's precisely the reason I was shocked, because I had been going for 40 years or more with very considerable evidence that it was working exceptionally well.
>
> (ibid: lines 854–63)

4.3 Monetary policy and central banking

Commercial and central banks are intimate partners – sometimes amicable, sometimes in conflict. Their relationship is important in several ways, including bank and central bank governance, the operations of monetary policy, and in the central bank's interest in domestic stability and international cooperation with its peers. Central banks stand at the core of the

Table 4.1 Central banks and banking regulators

	Principal banking regulator	Central bank
Australia	Australian Prudential Regulatory Authority	Reserve Bank of Australia
China	China Banking Regulatory Commission	Peoples Bank of China
Hong Kong	Hong Kong Monetary Authority	Hong Kong Monetary Authority
India	Reserve Bank of India	Reserve Bank of India
Indonesia	Bank of Indonesia	Bank of Indonesia
Japan	Financial Services Agency	Bank of Japan
South Korea	Financial Supervisory Commission/Financial Supervisory Service	Bank of Korea
Malaysia	Bank Negara Malaysia	Bank Negara Malaysia
Philippines	Bangko Sentral ng Pilipinas	Bangko Sentral ng Pilipinas
Singapore	Monetary Authority of Singapore	Monetary Authority of Singapore
Taiwan	Financial Services Commission	Central Bank of China
Thailand	Bank of Thailand	Bank of Thailand
Vietnam	State Bank of Vietnam	State Bank of Vietnam

national financial system.[1] They are agencies or arms of the state, usually responsible for currency issuance, administration of monetary policy including open market operations, and certain business activities, serving as a bank for bankers and as banker to the state. Most modern central banks are state agencies, but several are privately owned or a public–private hybrid, as with the US Federal Reserve. The central banks in our sample are either state agencies or quasi-ministries, but are subject to varying degrees of political or legislative control. This endows most central banks with wider goals, such as maintaining the external value of the currency, supporting financial stability, and promoting employment and economic growth.

Although the roles of central banks vary, their functions typically include:

- Responsibility for monetary policy and currency stability, as well as reserve management;
- Responsibility for financial stability, which may or may not include supervision of financial intermediaries, addressed in more detail in Section 4.4; and
- Supporting the payment and clearing systems and providing liquidity and lender of last resort facilities.

Table 4.1 lists the main central banks and banking regulators in the region. Six of our sample economies (China, India, Indonesia, Japan, Malaysia and the Philippines) operate single bank supervisory authorities, of which four have a joint role as the central bank (India, Indonesia, Malaysia and the Philippines). The remaining six (Hong Kong, South Korea, Singapore, Taiwan, Thailand and Vietnam) operate multiple bank supervisory authorities, of which four have a joint function as the central bank (Hong Kong, Singapore, Thailand and Vietnam).

Monetary management

For most economies, monetary stability has two interconnected facets, one external (an exchange rate that is not unduly volatile) and the other primarily domestic (a price level that is neither volatile nor rapidly changing). In the twentieth century the domestic goal was often the more visible, giving central banks the core objective of maintaining a relatively low nominal rate of price inflation by influencing the money aggregates, in some cases with specific interest rate or exchange rate objectives, and in others by setting targets for monetary base expansion. Practice in the 1980s focused on money supply control as a proxy for inflation targeting, but most central banks later began treating interest rates or exchange rates as instruments that influence the outcome of monetary growth and price inflation, with specific objectives set across a range of monetary variables and economic expectations. This approach stemmed from ideas developed by scholar and practitioner Charles Goodhart – that explicit monetary policy target-setting leads to a breakdown in the statistical relationship between the policy instrument and the target variable (Goodhart 1989).

Monetary stability is important for all central banks, and is achieved in principle through control of the money supply, or at its most simple by setting the monetary base and required reserves at fixed levels. Central banks create money by accumulating domestic and foreign assets, in the process of which deposits accrue in the commercial banking system, causing the money supply to expand. This process is shown in Equation (4.1):

$$M = mB \tag{4.1}$$

where M is the total money supply in the economy; B is the monetary base or 'high-powered money', including currencies and reserves required by the central bank; and m is the money multiplier. Supplying money is one means by which the state finances its spending and acquires claims to GDP. The claim on national output that the government derives from creating money is known as *seigniorage*, and is usually measured as the change in base money (B in Equation 4.1) as a share of GDP. For example, seigniorage is estimated at around 6–8 per cent of GDP in China, and may be even more valuable when a currency is widely used in international trade or finance.

The money supply is defined in several ways according to the claims that it includes. We often hear about M1, M2 and M3, all of which are measures of money supply, but economies have different specifications for each variable. In the United States, M1 refers to currency plus deposits in current (checking) accounts; M2 is M1 plus the nominal value of overnight repurchase agreements (repos), money market funds, savings and time deposits of under US$100 million; and M3 is M2 plus large time deposits and term repos. A further variable L, represents M3 plus other liquid assets. Table 4.2 shows the three definitions used in Hong Kong, each of which is used in different contexts, with M1 being the narrowest definition and M3 the most broad. Central banks tend to have different targets for monetary control depending on national conditions and expectations – for example, PBOC currently uses M2 as its primary monetary indicator.

The money multiplier (m in Equation 4.1) measures the money supply that can be created through the financial system for a given monetary base. Different multipliers exist for each definition of money, so that $m1$ represents the money multiplier for M1. If $m1$ equals two, then one dollar of high powered money can generate two dollars of M1 in the economy. The multiplier is a function of the ratio of currency to demand deposits, the required reserve ratios for demand deposits, saving and time deposits. Intuitively, m is an inverse function of the required reserve ratios, that is, m declines as required reserves increase.

Central banks control M by manipulating m or B. If a central bank seeks price stability and the preservation of external currency value, it sets the monetary base and reserve ratios

Table 4.2 Hong Kong definitions of money

	Composition
M1	Narrow definition. Transaction money that can be used instantly to pay for goods and services. It comprises: • The sum of legal tender notes and coins held by the public; and • Customer demand deposits in Hong Kong dollars and foreign currencies placed with licensed banks
M2	Broader definition. Reflects actual and potential purchasing power at the disposal of users in both Hong Kong dollars and foreign currencies. It comprises: • M1; plus • Customer saving and time deposits with licensed banks; and • Negotiable certificates of deposits (CDs) issued by licensed banks and held outside the banking sector
M3	The broadest definition. It comprises: • M2; plus • Customer deposits with restricted licence banks and licensed deposit-taking companies; and • Negotiable CDs issued by banks or licensed deposit-taking companies and held outside the banking sector

Source: Hong Kong Monetary Authority <http://www.hkma.gov.hk/eng/> (accessed 1 October 2012).

at fixed levels. Real economic life is usually more complicated, for the money supply is influenced by behavioural choices that influence the magnitude of m: for example, whether funds leave the financial system, whether demand for bank loans changes, or how much lending banks are willing to make available to the non-bank sector. In an economy without external capital controls, m will also be affected by the direction and size of capital flows. Central banks watch changes in M1, M2 or M3 closely, and take actions to influence either m or B. For example, a central bank can expand the money supply to add funds to the financial system during recessions (a reduction in reserve ratios, changing the monetary base through open market operation), or reduce the money supply during booms by adjusting required reserve ratios and open market operations.

Figure 4.1 plots the dynamics of money supply (M2 as a share of nominal GDP), showing upward sloping trends for China, Japan and the smaller exporting economies. The rise in the ratio of M2 to GDP does not necessarily signify excessive monetary growth but at least other two possibilities:

• Demand for money increases due to transaction needs driven by marketization, that is, due to a greater share of economic activity conducted openly in the market place.
• The money velocity steadily declines. As shown in Equation (4.2), money supply (M) multiplied by money velocity (k) equals total output (nominal GDP): $k = M/\text{GDP}$. That is, M/GDP also captures money velocity.

$$Mk = PY \qquad\qquad (4.2)$$

The volume of broad money supply (M2) as a share of GDP is often used to measure financial depth, with a larger value indicating a deeper financial sector. Figure 4.2 shows a cross-sectional comparison of this ratio in 2006, which indicates two divergent groups of

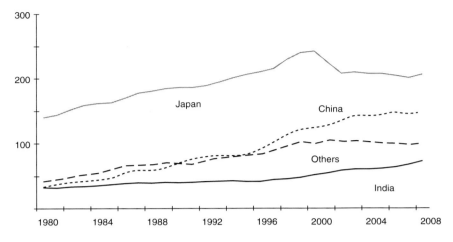

Figure 4.1 Money supply (M2) as a share of GDP, 1980–2008 (%).
Others are Indonesia, South Korea, Malaysia, the Philippines, Singapore, Taiwan and Thailand.
Sources: World Bank (undated b); authors' calculations.

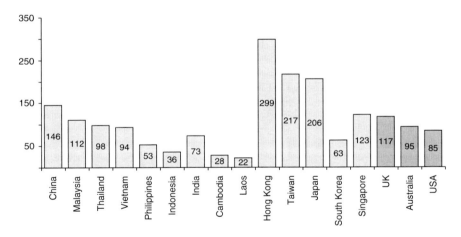

Figure 4.2 Money supply as a share of GDP, 2006 (%).
Sources: World Bank (undated b); authors' calculations.

economies, one with broad money comparable to the leading developed economies, and a second with broad money of less than 25 per cent of GDP.

Payments, liquidity provision and lender of last resort

Central banks generally have primary responsibility for ensuring the effective functioning of the payment system and providing regular and emergency liquidity. This typically takes three forms:

- Holding bank reserves;
- Lending to banks, either as part of day-to-day open market operations or in more extreme cases where liquidity is temporarily restricted; and
- Supervising and in some cases managing national payment and securities settlement systems.

The central bank may also act as commercial bank to the state, and may issue government securities on its behalf and maintain stability in the government bond market, topics discussed in Section 8.1. Central banks are important in ensuring the safety and integrity of the banking and financial system, and may also be responsible for the functioning of government securities markets and for dealer regulation. Many set capital and practice standards for market participants.

Some states now locate financial regulation and supervision in specialized agencies separate from the central bank, partly to delineate duties clearly and lessen conflicts in policy implementation, so for example CBRC supervises China's banks while PBOC is in charge of monetary policy. In spite of this demarcation, bank regulation is complicated without the participation of the central bank. This dysfunction occurred in the United Kingdom in 2007, when the main financial regulator and central bank failed to cooperate and lacked necessary alacrity when LLR access was urgently needed.

A second central bank objective is to encourage financial stability, including standing as liquidity provider or LLR in times of stress. Banks lend and fund their activities in many currencies outside the currency of issue in their main domicile, and this aspect of financial globalization means that the LLR functions in two dimensions:

- Operations conducted in domestic currency to support liquidity available to intermediaries for which the central bank has primary regulatory responsibility; and
- Arrangements with overseas central banks, involving emergency credit or swap lines to fund foreign currency operations with the banks for which the central bank has primary regulatory responsibility.

Lender of last resort

When depositors make a commercial withdrawal of funds, the deposit-taking bank meets that demand using its reserves of liquidity. As reserves are subject to prudential rules and risk management considerations, the bank must *ceteris paribus* withdraw or recall loans to fund a replenishment of reserves. This may take time, while deposit withdrawal may be rapid. The central bank stands ready to provide necessary liquidity in such cases by replenishing reserves in the short term so as to maintain or restore general confidence. When conditions return to normal the bank or banks involved repay the loans and replenish their reserves.

Such a mechanism serves as a protection against bank runs and general panic that may be both unreasonable and debilitating. Victorian economist Walter Bagehot was the first to articulate that a successful LLR will deploy resources in such a manner as to assure depositors and the wider financial markets that the system will continue to function with sufficient liquidity, notwithstanding the immediate stressed conditions (Bagehot 1873). This support for confidence may be costly and radical, Bagehot's rules of conduct for lenders of last resort have survived many decades of practice, increasing financial sophistication and numerous periods of illiquidity and false rumour, with the simple principle that to maintain public confidence and forestall systemic volatility, central banks must lend freely to illiquid but not insolvent banks, and charge penal rates of interest for funds as a deterrent to imprudence.

Liquidity provision and credit lines

A credit line is an allocation of resources to facilitate subsequently defined transactions. It represents a simple institution that may be formal or informal, is part of market practice or influenced by globally harmonized regulation. The allocation is made because of the finite nature of core bank resources, whether prudential risk limits or capital-based ceilings. The line is personal to the providing bank and may be withheld from disclosure to its beneficiary, or disclosed to various degrees of detail. This means that the line's existence may be known but not its scale or other conditions. Lines can be reciprocal if they involve similar or matching constructs between two banks, but reciprocal lines need not be symmetrical.

The simplest line signifies a willingness to consider engaging in transactions from time to time. Its withdrawal for whatever reason is similarly unilateral. In common law terms, no consideration exists to make the line contractual, and more generally it is free of strictly commercial obligation on the part of its provider. Lines can be substantive even when not fully contractual. Disclosure of their existence may create incentives to allow use, including embarrassment or commercial threats, and for central banks a disclosed line may suggest a moral commitment to allow use. These risks tend to encourage mutual confidentiality.

Lines may also be formal, signifying a contractual agreement prior to any transaction being contemplated and allowing compensation for the provider. In most modern states, capital regulation encourages commercial lines to be either unadvised or formal and compensated by small periodic fees. Documents recording formal lines would not represent fully actionable contracts but contain model terms to be adopted by incorporation into any subsequent such contract. They might include pre-contractual representations or undertakings, the making of which would become conditions precedent to later trades. In this way, lines form a spectrum running between five degrees of contractual formality between counterparties (Lejot 2011a):

- Internal and non-disclosed;
- Unilateral but disclosed;
- Bilateral (agreed) but non-committed;
- Bilateral (agreed) and committed; and
- Bilateral and committed according to terms of detail.

The spectrum is analogous to the degree of volition retained by line providers in making loans. Lines of longer duration are more complex, with terms providing a template for contract formation, as with debt issuance programme prospectuses (Section 7.4) or ISDA agreements for derivative contracts (Section 8.2). These require the acknowledgment of the counterparty, although lines will be capable of withdrawal in the broadest circumstances without consultation.

Bank lines cover several transaction types and uses, not all of which involve counterparty credit risk. Most are short term, in that trades made under the line have a life of less than 12 months or shorter than the period remaining prior to the expiry of a non-renewable line. Lines may be renewed, but when disclosed or subject to formal agreement will contain triggers allowing the line to lapse upon expiry. Transactions maturing after 12 months usually require separate internal approval.

The uses of bank lines are inexhaustible but commonly provide for:

- Short-term advances (credit, contingent credit or money market lines);
- Cash and forward dealing in foreign exchange (FX lines);
- FX swap lines combining currency dealing and short-term credit;
- Securities lending or repurchase (repo) lines; or
- Lines for interest rate, currency or commodity swaps, often of longer terms.

Many use a formal umbrella agreement as with ICMA, ISDA or US money market practice to allow collateral to be held against a net market risk position between counterparties that is 'marked' or fluctuates from day to day. Lines may be denominated in a major currency or the currency of issue of the bank's domicile but by agreement also used in several currencies.

The risks associated with bank lines include credit risk, settlement and liquidity risk, legal risks, and market risks (changes in asset prices, interest rates, FX rates, commodity prices or credit spreads). Contingent credit (guarantee, or backup) lines are an unusual credit risk in that they are drawn *in extremis*, or to mitigate market failure when a rational provider might prefer to avoid commitments that increased its funded risk. Like central bank LLR facilities, these often involve penalty charges and collateral. The assessment of a line's credit risk dictates ordinarily:

- Whether to grant a line;
- Whether to advise its existence and terms, if any;
- Automaticity of use;
- Terms for drawings; and
- Collateral requirements.

Credit losses sustained under lines are usually treated as deductions to bank capital and reserves, as with losses and defaults on single transactions.

Central bank practice differs from this description only in terms of purpose, although political and non-commercial factors may influence the granting of central bank lines and credit (Coombs 1976). This occurred frequently in the 1960s when external payment imbalances threatened the global fixed exchange regime and its relationship to gold prices, and in 1997 when US authorities urged Japan not to 'pour money into' Thailand prior to its obtaining IMF credit (FOMC 1997: 9–13), the Federal Reserve having refused to grant a line to the Bank of Thailand (see Section 2.3). Central bank providers of lines concentrate on short-term extension of credit, FX lines for swaps, spot and forward dealing, securities repos, and certain derivative transactions. Many are prolific users of trading lines with commercial counterparties.

Central banks use lines in similar ways to the commercial sector in terms of mechanics and the institutional setting (formal, informal, contractual, disclosed or undisclosed), even if their purposes differ. Their behaviour is analogous, so central banks are concerned with credit and settlement risk and, in the words of a former Federal Reserve chairman, try to limit use to 'those countries whose financial markets are sufficiently sizable and developed that they may expect from time-to-time to be the source or the recipient of funds during periods of uncertainty' (Martin 1967: 961).

Lines between central banks may be associated with crises or crisis prevention but were a mechanical feature of the financial architecture introduced with Bretton Woods. They have commonly been of three kinds: short-term credit lines, FX swap lines and (more rarely) repo lines. The first allow short-term advances in a designated currency, notably US dollars as the dominant post-1945 trade currency, or the currency of the provider. On occasions, these were drawn prior to the cessation of fixed exchange rates in 1971–73, typically as a temporary bridge to IMF or collaborative longer-term financial assistance. Swap lines have been used more frequently when currency convertibility was reintroduced by the industrialized economies from 1958, and act as a liquidity device by facilitating simultaneous spot and forward FX transactions. As liquidity instruments, FX swaps are effectively repos involving foreign currency rather than securities. In the 1960s, the forward unwinding trade was conducted at the same exchange rate as the opening spot trade, but terms became negotiable when the fixed exchange era ended.

In the 2008 global crisis, a new use of swap lines involved transnational funding by central banks to allow others to conduct LLR operations in foreign currencies, essentially to help alleviate paralysis in the global interbank markets. This use had not been widely contemplated prior to 2007, nor cited in analyses of the arrangements described in Section 12.5 that exist between ASEAN+3 central banks, despite their relevance to both the 1997–98 and 2007–9 crises. Modern central bank lines are almost always bilateral, and if credit is provided collaboratively the several claims are channelled through a single agent.

Central bank objectives

Most central banks in Asia are responsible for preserving the value of the currency so that inflation control is their main goal. High or unstable inflation is known to adversely impact socio-economic conditions in the following ways:

- High inflation erodes real incomes and reduces living standards;
- Unstable inflation creates uncertainty in all decision making relating to saving, consumption, investment and production, all of which impedes activity; and
- High inflation causes real domestic interest rates to lose competitiveness, which is likely to force currency depreciation and further add to domestic price inflation through poorer terms of trade.

For example, Bank Indonesia's statute includes the instruction:

> Under Act No.23 of 1999 concerning Bank Indonesia, as amended by Act No. 3 of 2004, the ultimate goal of Bank Indonesia is to achieve and maintain stability in the rupiah (Article 7). This mandate clearly defines the role of the central bank in the economy; enable Bank Indonesia to focus more closely on achievement of its single objective.
>
> (Republic of Indonesia Acts of 1999 & 2004)

Stability in the rupiah is reflected by the inflation rate and exchange rate. Inflation is reflected in overall increases in prices for goods and services. The factors influencing inflation can be grouped into two broad categories: pressure from demand–pull inflation and cost–push inflation. Bank Indonesia is only able to influence pressure from demand–pull inflation, while the effects from cost–push inflation (often related to natural disasters, droughts, or supply distribution bottlenecks) are outside Bank Indonesia's control. The cooperation and commitment of all sectors of the economy are essential to achieve and maintain stable price levels, including government and the private sector. Although the value of the rupiah is determined mainly by supply and demand, Bank Indonesia has some scope to reduce unwanted fluctuations.

Several approaches enable a central bank to preserve currency value and fight inflation. The first is to monitor the monetary base (B), under which the central bank sets a base money target. The relation between money supply and price level is described in Equation (4.2). The effectiveness of this framework depends on short- and long-term stability in the velocity of money, which are never assured. The framework would work if the relationship between base money and inflation were stable, and the central bank able to maintain control over cash held outside the banking sector. Those assumptions are unlikely to be satisfied in most Asian economies due to ongoing structural and developmental change. Another institutional factor that constrains base money targeting is that the main component of currency is held outside the bank system. Some scholars believe that the large amounts of informal or underground financing in Asia referred to in Section 3.3 make it difficult to control base money, most clearly in China (Allen, Qian & Qian 2005).

The second approach is inflation targeting, giving the central bank one overriding objective in monetary policy. The target is determined with regard to a presumed trade-off with growth. The most commonly used measure of inflation is the consumer price index (CPI). To comply with the inflation targeting framework, the central bank adopts a forward-looking approach, in which current policy is guided towards a future inflation target, taking account of a monetary policy lag. In determining its policy stance, the central bank must consider forecasts for inflation, growth and many other variables, including government economic policy. Indonesia, South Korea, the Philippines and Thailand adopted an inflation target approach after the 1997–98 crisis, while others, including the relatively open economies of Singapore and Taiwan, have tended to follow exchange rate targets.

Central bank independence

Only two ASEAN+3 central banks have statutory independence (Japan and South Korea); two are empowered to act with a high degree of autonomy (Indonesia and Singapore); two must accept the directions of ministers (Hong Kong and the Philippines); and the remainder follow policies set by central government and altered from time to time. The arguments for central bank independence are well known. Delegating monetary policy to an agent whose preferences are more inflation averse than society's preferences serves as a commitment device that permits sustaining a lower rate of inflation than would otherwise be possible (Alesina & Summers 1993). According to Stanley Fischer:

> They are arguments from the world of the second best. In a first-best world, monetary and fiscal policy would be perfectly coordinated and chosen, and there would be no need for independent central banks. But in the imperfect world in which most central bankers ply their trade, political systems tend to behave myopically, favouring inflationary policies with short-run benefits and discounting excessively their long-run costs.

An independent central bank, given responsibility for price stability, can overcome this inflationary bias.

(Fischer 1997)

Insulating monetary policy from the political process helps avoid these problems and sustain low inflation expectations, and empirical evidence suggests that countries with more independent central banks have lower inflation, at no cost in terms of growth or the variability of growth. For example, Alesina and Summers (1993) show a significant negative correlation between an index of central bank independence and average inflation rates, and a negative correlation between central bank independence and inflation variance, a measure of the stability of macroeconomic policy.

Despite such performance merits, central bank independence cannot be taken for granted. Real independence depends not only on whether the central bank has legal independence, but on formal and informal institutional arrangements such as the exchange rate regime, the central bank's ability to engage effectively in open market operations, and the state's fiscal policy stance. History matters too. The experience of hyperinflation in Germany may have raised the public's aversion to inflation and its desire to have an independent central bank overwhelmingly committed to price stability.

Asian central banks may be pressured by politicians, government officials and influential commercial interests. The tale of two central banks illustrates this difficulty. In October 2004 the Bank of Korea defied the finance minister's plea to cut interest rates despite his calling for a 'more aggressive, accommodative' monetary policy, a response applauded as a sign that the Bank of Korea was now 'truly independent' (Mukherjee 2004). In January 2007, while market participants expected the Bank of Japan to increase its benchmark rate, the governor surprisingly left the rate unchanged. This came after officials said the bank should consider the government's views when setting rates, and the Bank of Japan's standing was consequently damaged (Kennedy & Benjamin 2007). Independence can also be misunderstood, as with the fraudulent currency intervention of the Bank of Thailand in 1997 shown in Section 2.3.

For the most part, independence aims to assist general confidence, albeit with a possible loss of policy coordination, so that:

> If policy were conducted by benevolent and knowledgeable dictators, monetary and fiscal decisions would be run together. The academic case for central bank independence was avowedly a second best one, in response to what was called the credibility problem. The full inflationary effects of an excessive stimulus might be delayed for a few years, while the favourable effects on output and employment might come much sooner. There was therefore a powerful incentive for governments to stimulate prior to elections ... The central bank ... could make sure that a government behaving in this way was punished by high interest rates that would inhibit the boom.

(Brittan 2010)

No approach is perfect, and this led to severe costs in 2008:

> [N]o major central bank had any inkling of the weakness developing in the world financial system. There was the obstinate refusal to take asset bubbles seriously and the wrong-headed preoccupation with short-term targets for narrowly defined inflation indices.

(ibid)

The impossible trinity

Central banks face an operational constraint, that a lack of independent monetary tools means that it is impossible simultaneously to:

- Maintain stable exchange rates;
- Allow free capital mobility; and
- Conduct an independent domestic monetary policy.

Monetary policy with domestic objectives will lead to a divergence between home and foreign interest rates or shifts in exchange rate expectations that induce capital flows, which then require an adjustment to monetary policy. If the state is unwilling to sacrifice its monetary policy objectives, it must either abandon its exchange rate target or restrict capital flows. Maintaining pegged but adjustable exchange rates has become difficult with the increase in international capital mobility associated with globalization and deregulation. Large volumes of international capital flows require substantial reserves and other funding to support currencies under pressure, making currency stabilization increasingly costly.

This leaves two alternatives, allowing exchange rates to float or be fixed, either through a currency board or the adoption of a common currency, both of which imply the abandonment of independent monetary policy. The stresses experienced in the Eurozone from 2009 suggest that a trend to larger currency blocs may have been interrupted, and at the time of writing there is far more global willingness to contemplate capital controls as a means to lessen currency volatility and external imbalances than at any moment since the 1970s (Buckley & Arner 2011).

4.4 Financial stability, regulation and development

This section considers regulatory design and the impact of regulation and financial supervision in the economy and for intermediaries. In addressing financial development in Asia, the overall objective is to develop a competitive, integrated and efficient financial system that is properly regulated and supervised and effectively mobilizes savings to provide financing to support economic growth and development. A strong financial sector will support economic growth and development while at the same time minimizing the risks of financial crises. This objective has two elements, financial stability and financial development to support economic growth.

The importance of financial stability is generally agreed, emphasizing financial regulation and supervision, and improving operations, compliance and risk management – the subject of Section 4.5. The global financial crisis shows us that, while some causes of instability are beyond the influence of individual banks and better addressed through appropriate macroeconomic policies and the institutional framework, if any single intermediary is managed in a prudentially safe and sound manner, then crises triggered by problems within any single intermediary will be dampened or foreshortened, thereby increasing overall financial stability. Intermediaries should thus be provided with appropriate regulatory or supervisory incentives as well as support for capacity development to encourage improvements in their internal operations. Such changes not only decrease the risks of financial crises but enhance intermediation and resource allocation.

Effective financial intermediation demands that confidence is maintained in the financial system at large, in the network connectivity of the system, in individual intermediaries and in the competence and integrity of regulators, such that there is:

- Sufficient confidence of savers so that they hold deposits domestically and hold their savings within the formal financial system;
- Confidence among borrowers to use the formal financial system for financing; and
- Mutual confidence among intermediaries.

The willingness of market participants to behave in these ways is critically dependent on the general awareness and confidence in the regulatory and supervisory system, which we view as a function of its effectiveness, fairness, consistency and transparency.

Regulation and supervision

Many aspects of commercial activity in the financial sector are subject to regulation, that is, rules governing behaviour supervised by an official agency. While this differs between jurisdictions, there is a generally agreed approach to certain features of regulation that are accepted globally, even if they may be enforced weakly in some cases. Finance is perhaps the most regulated of all industries. Regulation governs activity by intermediaries and other organizations, it directly impacts upon financial contracts and instruments used in all markets, it monitors behaviour and seeks to protect depositors and investors, and it punishes miscreants and tries to safeguard the entire system. In this chapter we describe the design, and in Chapters 6–11 introduce and assess the regulation of each class of intermediary and markets.

Oversight of the financial system encompasses regulation, including the formulation and enforcement of rules and standards governing financial behaviour as well as the supervision of individual intermediaries. Regulation and supervision are essential in fostering stable and robust financial systems, and should seek to support and enhance market functioning rather than displace it by establishing and policing rules (Goodhart, Hartmann, Llewellyn, Rojas-Suarez & Weisbrod 1998).

Prudential regulation and supervision promote public confidence on which decentralized financial systems are based, and complement effective management and market discipline. The requirements of market segments have different motivations and requirements. The task of such regulation and supervision is to ensure that intermediaries operate prudently and that they hold capital and reserves sufficient to support the risk of loss that arise in their operations. Regulation can also be a source of vulnerability to the extent that it is lax, intrusive, poorly designed, outdated or inadequately implemented. Strong and effective regulation and supervision therefore represent a necessary public good.

Regulatory objectives

Regulatory and supervisory authorities generally have three objectives:

- Preventing and addressing systemic risk;
- Promoting reliability, effectiveness and integrity in market infrastructure; and
- Fostering efficient operations and competition in the financial system.

Within this framework:

- Supervisory and regulatory authorities need to be both functionally independent and accountable (Quintyn & Taylor 2002). This applies to central banks, whether or not they have supervisory responsibilities (ibid; Lastra 1996). Ideally this should be established in the law establishing the regulator or central bank and its relationship to government.
- Authorities need to have powers of licensing, prudential regulation and consolidated supervision, and have access to accurate and timely information as well as the ability to engage in remedial action. As a general proposition, this should be provided by the law establishing the regulator or in laws governing specific markets. While regulations will be important in this regard, the general principles should be clearly placed in primary legislation.
- Authorities must have adequate powers and resources to cooperate and exchange information on the health and standing of intermediaries, both with other authorities in their own jurisdiction and with those from outside. This factor is often underemphasized. Financial sector legislation should ideally be viewed as an opportunity to design the overall plan of the financial system, for example, what form of intermediaries will be allowed, what they will be permitted or licensed to do, who will monitor them and how will those responsible authorities relate to one another and to the state?

In order to achieve these general goals, regulation generally seeks to promote financial market efficiency, protect consumers and prevent instability in the financial system through rules and practices intended to address market failure. It is increasingly agreed that from an economic standpoint regulation seeks to address a variety of problems that occur when financial transactions are left solely to market forces, or market failures. With this analytical framework, regulation should address four issues:

- Anti-competitive behaviour (competition regulation);
- Market misconduct (market integrity regulation);
- Information asymmetries, usually referred to as prudential concerns; and
- Systemic instability (financial stability regulation).

Regulatory design

At the heart of the global financial crisis were two serious supervisory failures, both relating to the scope and coverage of regulation, at home, regionally and internationally.

First, in a number of jurisdictions, especially the United States, regulatory gaps, overlaps and divisions presented opportunities for regulatory avoidance and arbitrage. Combined with a general philosophy of regulatory permissiveness, this allowed financial intermediaries to organize their operations to minimize, and in many cases avoid, regulatory scrutiny. At the same time, global markets and financial intermediaries maximized regulatory arbitrage opportunities within individual economies and across jurisdictions, with the result that no single regulator had a clear or complete picture of the activities and risks of any substantial intermediary or market, despite considerable attention being given to consolidated supervision for two decades prior to the global crisis. The crisis also revealed how many finance sector managers lacked a clear understanding of the scope of their organizations' operations, risks and legal structure.

These elements were most clear in the context of the near failure of AIG and the insolvency of Lehman Brothers. Similarly, significant financial markets were organized to minimize regulatory scrutiny and interference, resulting in a lack of transparency for complex banks and other intermediaries and for certain of the markets and products in which they dealt. The clearest examples were the markets for credit risk transfer, including certain forms of securitization, credit derivatives, and shadow banking arrangements such as bank conduits of SIVs.

Second, financial authorities – finance ministries, central banks and regulatory agencies – focused on the safety and soundness of individual intermediaries, or *microprudential supervision*. Whether or not this was conducted effectively, it undoubtedly neglected systemic connectivity, or the linkages between intermediaries, markets and instruments, as part of *macroprudential supervision*. This omission occurred despite many central banks being given, or taking on, specific objectives relating to overall financial stability in the decade before the global crisis.

In addressing related issues, the global financial crisis has shown that the overall design and coverage of a regulatory system are vital to its effectiveness. In Asia and internationally, as highlighted by the G20, there is an urgent need to review and enhance the scope of regulation, focusing on regulatory design to eliminate gaps and implement effective macroprudential financial system oversight. This requires a reshaping of regulatory systems so that authorities may identify and take account of macroprudential risks, with the scope of regulation and oversight extending to systemically important financial intermediaries, instruments and markets, including non-bank intermediaries, and to credit rating agencies to ensure they meet international codes of good practice. In addition, prudential standards must be designed to address cross-sectional dimensions (how risk is distributed across a financial system) and time dimensions (how aggregate risk evolves over time) to build capital and reserve buffers for use in bad times.

For Asia, two lessons can be drawn. The first is the necessity of putting in place appropriate macroprudential arrangements, domestically and regionally, although there is in fact little agreement on how to go about it.

The second is the need to review the design of domestic and regional regulatory structures to address gaps and reduce the potential for regulatory arbitrage. In the context of the financial stability issues which arose during the global financial crisis, given that many arose from regulatory gaps and divisions, an important aspect is to consider the system in a broad and integrated way. Asian jurisdictions would benefit from an analysis of the structure and coverage of their respective regulatory systems, including regional and international reviews through the IMF–World Bank Financial Sector Assessment Program (FSAP) or the Financial Stability Board (FSB), and the Asian Development Bank or organizations such as the emerging Asian Financial Stability Dialogue.

Overall, a number of lessons have emerged in relation to regulatory design. First, individual jurisdictions must examine the advantages and disadvantages of possible change, including the risks inherent in the change process. Second, a number of basic structures are feasible, including:

- The traditional sectoral model with separate regulators for banking, securities and insurance often combined with legal or administrative separation or holding company structures for financial conglomerates;
- The functional model with separate regulators for financial stability, prudential, market conduct and competition regulation, catering to financial conglomerates and product innovation;

- The institutional structure with separate regulators for different types of inter-mediary typically adopted in the context of banks with operations in securities or insurance; and
- The integrated structure with one or more sectors or functions combined in a single agency, often serving a universal banking model.

It cannot be taken for granted that a particular model is better than any other – this depends on jurisdictional circumstances.

To date, international consensus and guidance on structural issues has been limited, with design remaining a domestic matter. Most significantly, in January 2010 the Joint Forum – comprising the BCBS, IOSCO and International Association of Insurance Supervisors (IAIS) – released an initial review of related issues (Joint Forum 2010), which emphasized four fundamental guiding principles:

- Similar activities, products, and markets should be subject to similar minimum supervision and regulation;
- Consistency in regulation across sectors is necessary, although legitimate differences can exist across the three sectors;
- Supervision and regulation should consider the risks posed, particularly any systemic risk which may arise not only in large intermediaries but also through interactions and interconnectedness among actors of all sizes; and
- Consistent implementation of international standards is critical to avoid competitiveness issues and regulatory arbitrage.

The Joint Forum's recommendations included consistency across sectoral financial principles, for example the BCBS Core Principles of Effective Banking Supervision summarized in Table 4.3, and among organizations, for example the BCBS, IOSCO, IAIS and IASB; development of uniform capital standards for insurers and securities dealers; and cross-sectoral standards where necessary, for example in relation to mortgage broking and loan origination or credit risk transfer.

Other recommendations focused on ensuring that all financial groups, particularly those operating across borders, are subject to comprehensive regulation and supervision on the basis of updated international standards addressing conglomerates, that supervisory colleges operate consistently across sectors, and that cross-sectoral issues are appropriately addressed.

Given the problem of regulatory gaps arbitrage in the global financial crisis, these are issues that are likely to be central to future IMF and FSB regulatory reviews, and hence a focus for Asian jurisdictions, especially the G20 and FSB members.

Addressing systemic risk

At its most fundamental, financial stability depends on regulators effectively monitoring, preventing and addressing systemic risk. The global financial crisis confirmed that international and domestic financial regulatory approaches were insufficient to mitigate systemic risk or maintain the stability of the global financial system. Moreover, the crisis demonstrated that addressing systemic risk is fundamental to financial regulatory design, not only at the domestic level but also in the context of the global financial system and the system of international regulatory cooperation. In our opinion, designing a regulatory system to address systemic risk requires that seven core elements are addressed.

First, the system must ensure the existence of a robust financial infrastructure, especially payment and settlement systems. Financial infrastructure is the essential 'plumbing' of any financial system and must be regulated to support stability and effectiveness.

Second, the regulatory system should support the existence of well-managed financial intermediaries with effective corporate governance and risk management. While regulation cannot and should not prevent the failure of financial intermediaries it needs to provide rules and incentives to improve management whenever possible.

Third, financial markets require information, and thus regulation should provide disclosure requirements sufficient to support market discipline and address information asymmetries which may have negative implications for market functioning and confidence. Disclosure requirements should also be sufficient to provide regulators with comprehensive information to allow both microprudential and macroprudential regulation.

Fourth, in addition to reinforcing risk management and market discipline, the regulatory system should provide minimum requirements for the safety and soundness of individual intermediaries, markets and essential infrastructures – what is traditionally known as 'prudential regulation.' These four elements seek to address prevention of systemic financial crises and at the same time establish the primary regulatory elements supporting the effective functioning of any financial system.

Any regime needs to be able to address crises when they occur. The final three elements seek to establish a minimum regulatory framework for such circumstances. First, there should be a liquidity provider (or lender) of last resort to provide liquidity to intermediaries and markets on an appropriate basis. This role is typically filled by the central bank of a given monetary system. Second, in order to allow the possibility of failure, there should be appropriate mechanisms for resolving problem banks and non-bank intermediaries, including insolvency arrangements. Finally, there must be mechanisms to protect consumers in order to maintain market confidence, especially in the event of bank failure.

These issues cannot be addressed solely within individual jurisdictions, but require global coordination and cooperation. The global crisis highlighted significant weaknesses in each of these seven elements, which are being addressed by the G20 and FSB. At the same time, Asia faces issues beyond those highlighted by the global financial crisis. First, payments systems remain underdeveloped in several jurisdictions and cross-border payment systems are at the early stages of development. As a result, while OTC derivatives regulation has been a central focus of the G20, for example, the development of payment systems is perhaps of greater concern in Asia, especially given the limited development of OTC derivatives markets in the region. Effective, robust payment systems are essential to making financial resources available in individual economies and across the region, and in supporting the use of savings and rebalancing financial resources towards regional development.

Second, in relation to corporate governance, it has become evident that many banks have failed to monitor or manage risk. This is certainly one of the central failures in the global financial crisis, but remains a concern in Asian markets dominated by bank financing. In economies dominated by small numbers of banks, effective corporate governance is a fundamental concern, not only for stability but also for development. There is thus a clear need to continue the development of well-managed banks with effective corporate governance and risk management systems.

Third, disclosure requirements were not sufficient to support transparency and market discipline, giving rise to systemic risks due to asymmetric information. Such issues are characteristic of complex structured products, which acted as the transmission mechanism of the excesses preceding the crisis, and led to adverse selection issues during the crisis. The activities of credit rating agencies exacerbated such issues both prior to and during the crisis. In this respect, transparency is fundamental not only to stability, but also to effective market functioning, and should continue to be a major focus, both domestically and regionally.

Fourth, in relation to prudential regulation, systemic risk did not arise from areas that were the subject of regulatory responsibility, but from areas that were largely unregulated. Examples include mortgage broker activities, off-balance sheet activities of banks and securities firms, OTC derivatives, and non-traditional activities of insurers. Risks often arose from regulatory arbitrage as firms shifted activities away from conventional supervision. Such regulatory arbitrage was also made possible by the splintering of financial regulation, with individual regulators usually less concerned about activities falling outside of the scope of their major responsibilities. In addition, systemic risks arose due to improperly designed prudential regulatory standards, especially in relation to capital, liquidity and leverage. In this respect, appropriate coverage of regulation is an essential focus throughout the region, especially with regard to improving the quality, quantity and international consistency of capital, including regulation to prevent excessive leverage and requiring buffers of resources to be built up in good times.

Fifth, systemic risk arose due to the lack of appropriate mechanisms to deal with problems which arose from or unexpected sources. Examples include the necessity of rescuing AIG and the lack of any mechanism for resolving Lehman Brothers. The crisis exposed the limitations of the separation of liquidity provision from prudential regulation, most obviously in the cases of Bear Stearns, Lehman Brothers, Merrill Lynch and AIG. In addition to the need for an effective resolution mechanisms for banks, the lack of a similar mechanism capable of dealing with non-banks or financial conglomerates is a weakness in most regulatory systems.

International financial standards

Since 2008 the G20 has coordinated post-crisis responses and financial regulatory reforms. From 1999 to 2008, it comprised ministers of finance and central bank governors meeting annually, supported by biannual meetings of their deputies. In November 2008, it met for the first time at the heads of government level, since when it has met six monthly at the level of heads of government and among ministers of finance and central bank governors.

While not a traditional treaty-based international organization, and lacking an international legal character, the G20 has become the main policy-directing body for discussions of international financial and economic policy. The impact of the G20 on international financial regulation therefore results mainly from the domestic implementation of internationally agreed approaches, as well as through voting control of the more formal international organizations such as the IMF and World Bank.

In relation to international cooperation and development, and the implementation of international financial regulatory standards, the FSF was renamed and reconstituted as the FSB, with a mandate to coordinate international financial regulatory initiatives and monitor their implementation. Hosted by the BIS, the FSB brings together G20 finance ministries, central banks and regulatory authorities, along with the principal international and regional organizations, the BIS, IMF, World Bank, OECD, European Central Bank and European Commission, and the main international standard-setting bodies, the BCBS, IOSCO, IAIS, IASB, Committee on the Global Financial System (CGFS), and Committee on Payment and Settlement Systems (CPSS).

The 2009 London G20 summit gave the FSB a ten-point mandate detailing its role in supporting international financial regulatory cooperation. In turn, FSB-member jurisdictions, subject to FSB reporting and evaluation, are committed to:

- Pursuing the maintenance of financial stability;
- Maintaining the openness and transparency of the financial sector;
- Implementing international financial standards; and
- Undergoing periodic peer reviews, using (among other evidence) public IMF/World Bank FSAP reports.

The FSB can therefore be seen as the central organization responsible for coordinating the detailed development of the global regulatory reform agenda, and for monitoring its implementation.

In terms of international standards, two main sorts have emerged: overall principles for differing forms of regulation, such as the respective core principles of the BCBS, IOSCO and IAIS, and detailed regulatory standards, of which the Basel capital accords are the most influential. The BCBS core principles are summarized in Table 4.3.

Basel capital accords

Of the various international standards developed to date, the Basel capital accords are the most significant. Financial regulation has increasingly come to be associated with internationally framed accords or principles, negotiated among state officials and adopted in harmony within national statutory or administrative settings. The work of the BCBS is a long-established example of this institutional process (Kane 2005). The Basel process is seen as effective by many scholars of public international law (Kapstein 2006; Kingsbury, Krisch, Stewart & Wiener 2005; Slaughter 2004) but criticized by political economists as secretive and relying on discriminatory 'public–private coalitions' (Underhill 2006: 23), and as usurping of national legislative processes by some administrative lawyers (Barr & Miller 2006). A thorough chronology of the Basel process appears in Alford (2005).

It also represents an example of transnational commercial law, characterized as

> law which is not particular to or the product of any one legal system but represents a convergence of rules drawn from several legal systems or even, in the view of its more expansive exponents, a collection of rules which are entirely national and have their force by virtue of international usage and its observance by the merchant community. In other words, it is the rules, not merely the actions or events that cross national boundaries.
>
> (Goode 1997: 2)

By classifying credit risk and assigning risk weightings in broad strata, Basel I induced increasingly active portfolio management among bank intermediaries and created a new science of regulatory capital management, with a developing array of vehicles and financial

Table 4.3 BCBS core principles for effective banking supervision

Principles	Notes
1 Objectives, supervisory independence, powers, transparency and cooperation	(i) Supervisory bodies to have clear responsibilities and objectives; operational independence, transparent processes, sound governance, adequate resources; and (ii) to be fully accountable. (iii) Suitable legal framework is required for banking supervision (iv) Supervisory bodies to have compliance powers over laws, and banking sector safety and soundness. (v) Legal protection for supervisors. (vi) Provisions for information sharing among national supervisors and for data protection.

Licensing and structure

2 Permissible activities	Permissible activities must be defined. Supervisor must have control over the use of 'bank' in organizational titles.
3 Licensing criteria	Supervisor to set license criteria and be able to reject applications. Process to include assessment of ownership structure, governance (including suitability of directors and senior managers) strategy, operating plans, internal controls, risk management, and projected finances. Consent of home supervisors needed if the owner or parent is foreign.
4 Transfer of ownership	Supervisor may review and veto significant ownership changes.
5 Major acquisitions	Supervisor may review major acquisitions or investments against set criteria (including cross-border operations) and be satisfied that affiliations or structures do not expose banks to undue risks or hinder supervision.

Prudential regulation and requirements

6 Capital adequacy	Supervisors to set prudent and appropriate capital adequacy requirements and definitions of capital. Such requirements not to be less than Basel Accord demands (at least for 'internationally active' banks).
7 Risk management process	Supervisors to be satisfied with comprehensive risk management processes and oversight, suitable for the scale and complexity of the bank.
8 Credit risk	Supervisors to be satisfied with credit risk management processes.
9 Problem assets, provisions and reserves	Supervisors to be satisfied with procedures and application of policies for problem risks, and adequacy of provisions and reserves.
10 Large exposure limits	Supervisors to be satisfied with risk concentration policies and procedures, and set prudential limits for large or connected counterparty exposures.
11 Exposures to related parties	Banks to be required to extend credit to related parties without undue influence, and manage such risks as with third parties.
12 Country and transfer risks	Supervisors to be satisfied with bank policies and procedures for managing and provisioning against country and transfer risks.
13 Market risks	Supervisors to be satisfied with bank policies and procedures for managing and provisioning against market risks, and given power to set limits or capital charges against market risk exposure.
14 Liquidity risk	Supervisors to be satisfied with bank policies and procedures for appropriate liquidity management, including contingency plans for liquidity problems.
15 Operational risk	Supervisors to be satisfied with bank policies and procedures to manage operational risks, suitable for scale and complexity of the bank.

Table 4.3 Cont'd

Principles	Notes
16 Interest rate risks	Supervisors to be satisfied with systems to manage interest rate risks in lending and funding, such strategy to be approved by directors and suitable for scale and complexity of those risks.
17 Internal control and audit	Supervisors to be satisfied with internal controls, including suitability for the scale and complexity of the bank's business, provision for delegating authority, internal functional separations, safeguarding bank assets, and independent internal audit and compliance.
18 Abuse of financial services	Supervisors to be satisfied with policies and procedures to promote high ethical and professional standards and prevent the bank from being used for criminal activity.
Supervision methods	
19 Supervisory approach	An effective system requires supervisors to understand bank operations and the banking sector as a whole, focusing on safety, soundness and overall stability.
20 Supervisory techniques	Bank supervision should be conducted both on- and off-site, and include regular management contact.
21 Supervisory reporting	Supervisors to be able to collect, analyze and independently verify bank prudential reports and statistical returns.
22 Accounting and disclosure	Supervisors to be satisfied that banks maintain adequate records drawn up in accordance with internationally accepted accounting practice and regularly publish information on their financial condition.
23 Corrective and remedial supervisory powers	Supervisors to have adequate tools to demand timely corrective actions, including banking licence revocation.
Consolidated and cross-border banking supervision	
24 Consolidated supervision	Supervision must always be conducted on a consolidated basis.
25 Home–host relationships	Cross-border consolidated supervision requires cooperation and information exchange among home and host supervisors. Local operations of foreign banks to be conducted to the same standard as domestic banks.

Source: Condensed from BCBC (2006a).

instruments. Basel I thus inadvertently led to the proliferation of securitization, which radically altered the costs faced by banks when using structured finance to meet risk, return, or liquidity objectives. This included banks not formally subject to Basel I precepts, resulting either from regulatory competition between markets, or bank lenders being subjected to peer pressure through interbank credit pricing. Such behaviour occurred in Asia prior to the 1997–98 financial crisis, although seldom practised to appropriate standards.

The Basel accord's application of banded weightings to loans and other risk assets – together with standard capital provisioning and the creation of distinct tiers of regulatory capital – immediately became critical in credit preferences, although not in overall credit creation. Capital-intensive instruments such as committed standby lines of credit lost favour, especially where competition eroded compensation for such lines. Banks that had formerly targeted net returns on assets (ROA) as a measure of operating performance found that peer pressure made it essential to manage the accumulation of risk and both actual and regulatory capital according to a series of metrics, including returns on risk-adjusted assets, and on the component layers of regulatory capital set by the Basel Committee.

The result was a profound effect on transaction costs and an encouragement for many banks to separate credit origination from considerations of risk accumulation. Some critics assert that it may have provoked casual standards of credit appraisal and management of the kind associated with US subprime mortgage lending (FCIC 2011). It thus helped intensify the rewards of active organizational and balance sheet management. Basel I also induced portfolio arbitrage and credit distortions, so as to reinforce the development of securitization and credit risk transfer markets. This perspective sees securitization and credit risk transfer as secondary results of harmonized regulatory principles, and a substantial explanation of securitization and other forms of credit risk transfer developed by banks since the late1980s.

Basel II was intended to improve the economic rationality of regulatory incentives for credit risk transfer and require regulatory capital to reflect more closely actual economic risks: regulatory capital and economic capital should become largely equivalent. It also lessened incentives to securitization that arose with Basel I.

Basel III

Asia's implementation of Basel II was uneven prior to 2008, and as a result of the global financial crisis, attention has regulatory interest has switched revising capital standards. In September 2010, the BCBS agreed to the underlying elements of the Basel III capital adequacy regime, with the new system being endorsed by the FSB and G20 in November 2010 for phased implementation by 2019, summarized in Table 4.4.

Basel III's capital hurdles focus on shareholder's equity and retained earnings, which are taken as optimal in absorbing losses. They dispense with the complex tiers of regulatory capital allowed by the earlier accords, mainly because certain forms of subordinated debt failed to be properly loss-absorbing in 2008–9. Basel I and II set a minimum 8 per cent ratio of capital to risk-weighted assets, with at least 50 per cent of capital comprising Tier 1 equity. Credit was given as Tier 2 capital for two bands of subordinated or hybrid instruments, with other forms of regulatory capital (Tier 3) allowed to support market risk. Basel III eliminates Tier 3 on the premise that credit and market risks require capital of equal quality, and simplifies permitted Tier 2 capital into one band comprising relatively robust subordinated instruments, including the contingent capital notes described in Box 6.3.

The minimum overall capital ratio remains at 8 per cent but share capital and retained earnings must be at least 4.5 per cent and all Tier 1 capital at least 6 per cent of risk-weighted assets. Tier 2 subordinated debt, preference shares or contingent capital can supply no more than one quarter of the minimum requirement. A new 2.5 per cent required *conservation buffer* of share capital and retentions lifts the overall minimum capital adequacy ratio to 10.5 per cent; this element is intended to prevent distributions and cause capital to be rebuilt after periods of stress. Basel III also allows national imposition of a further *countercyclical buffer* of 0–2.5 per cent of share capital or 'other fully loss-absorbing capital' (BCBS 2010a). The revised requirements are summarized in Table 4.5.

It is abundantly clear that markets now require banks to hold higher amounts of equity capital. In addition, the global crisis highlighted that subordinated debt, at least when held by other organized intermediaries, is unlikely to provide much in the way of external

Table 4.4 Basel III accord transition

	2013	2014	2015	2016	2017	2018	1 Jan. 2019
Leverage ratio	Parallel run from 1 Jan. 2013 to 1 Jan. 2017. Disclosure begins 1 Jan. 2015					Migration to Pillar 1	
Minimum Common Equity Capital Ratio (A)	3.5%	4.0%	4.5%	4.5%	4.5%	4.5%	4.5%
Capital Conservation Buffer (B)				0.625%	1.25%	1.875%	2.5%
Total A + B	3.5%	4.0%					7.0%
Phasing of deductions from common equity & Tier 1 capital (incl. excesses over DTA, MSR & financials limits)		20%	40%	60%	80%	100%	100%
Minimum Tier 1 Capital	4.5%	5.5%	6.0%	6.0%	6.0%	6.0%	6.0%
Minimum Total Capital	8.0%	8.0%	8.0%	8.0%	8.0%	8.0%	8.0%
Minimum Total Capital plus conservation buffer	8.0%	8.0%	8.0%	8.625%	9.25%	9.875%	10.5%
Existing capital instruments	Non-core Tier 1 or 2 capital phased out from 2013						
Liquidity coverage ratio			New minimum standard				
Net stable funding ratio						New minimum standard	

Source: BCBS (2010a).

Table 4.5 Simplified Basel III capital requirements

	Common equity net of deductions (%)	Tier 1 capital (%)	Total capital (%)
Minimum (A)	4.5	6.0	8.0
Conservation buffer (B)	2.0		
Total A+B	6.5	8.5	10.5
Countercyclical buffer (common equity or other fully loss absorbing capital)	0–2.5		

Source: BCBS (2010a).

monitoring, thereby compromising its value in supporting corporate governance and financial stability. As a result, subordinated debt has become significantly less important as a form of bank capital.

At the same time, crisis re-regulation has included proposals for new capital instruments such as contingent convertible securities ('Cocos'), which convert automatically to equity when bank capital ratios fall to preset levels, and other forms of hybrid securities that commit their holders to make infusions of additional capital following certain commercial events. There is no international consensus as to the specification of these instruments.

The other side of the equation has also changed, including methods for calculating risk asset weightings. While Basel I was overly simplistic, Basel II was overly complex and reliant on external credit ratings and internal valuation models. Both were susceptible to gaming, and before 2008 many regulators took a permissive view of such behaviour. Two UK banks, HBOS and Northern Rock, were granted reductions in minimum regulatory capital shortly before each sought LLR funding in 2007–8. Permissible off-balance sheet treatments have been tightened to avoid a resurgence of shadow banking activity and reduce systemic complexity, and market risks subjected to closer regulation than previously, including valuation policies and how assets migrate between banks' lending and trading books. All such issues are tied not only to regulatory standards, but also to accounting practices.

Basel III is also intended to provide for simple leverage ratios and liquidity standards. The latter were agreed in 2011 (BCBS 2010b) but national implementation of maximum leverage ratios is likely to be varied for some years. Other financial standards setters (namely IOSCO for securities and the IAIS for insurance) are developing parallel capital frameworks to enhance financial stability and reduce regulatory arbitrage.

The development of comprehensive new standards for capital, with much higher requirements for equity capital and the reduction of the role of subordinated debt, is clearly an important development. However, studies suggest that even at Basel III rates, capital would be insufficient to meet the stresses experienced in the global financial crisis. At the same time, systemic complexity has not been significantly decreased, indicating the continuing possibility of market participants seeking to game the new regime, just as they became adept at doing with Basel I and Basel II.

In relation to liquidity, while agreement on a new international approach is significant, the reality of the standards themselves is that they are highly subjective and therefore subject to great variations between markets. At the same time, liquidity regulation must be complemented by work in other areas, especially OTC derivatives and issues relating to overall market liquidity provision.

A simple leverage ratio is an important innovation and has the important potential to not only limit a central aspect of the build-up of the crisis (through leverage and related asset price inflation), but also to limit the potential for gaming the capital framework. Leverage and capital are the most important international prudential regulatory issues. Without an agreed limit on leverage, the G20's reform project fails to meet the test of being able to prevent the last crisis, before even considering the next crisis.

At the same time, given that in most jurisdictions regulation of non-bank intermediaries such as securities firms and insurance companies tends to be weaker than that of banks, there is a need to develop capital, leverage and liquidity standards that apply to non-banks, especially since many such firms engage in similar activities. Significantly, the G20 has made this a priority, but its absence at present is further evidence that international regulatory reforms agreed to date could not have prevented the global financial crisis.

Asia's policymakers face further considerations. Although the region's banks were less disrupted by the global crisis than their US or European counterparts, they equally need to meet new international standards for capital, liquidity and leverage. Conversely, Asia's widely used fiat approach to bank regulation has become influential elsewhere, especially in the form of countercyclical prudential rules such as supervening loan-to-value and sectoral lending limits. Finally, as capital requirements look increasingly at core equity, regulators must consider how local or regional equity markets can absorb new issues, and policymakers how to allocate resources to allow supervisors to meet demanding international norms.

4.5 Financial intermediaries and risk management

At the heart of financial stability and financial development, and a core objective of financial regulation, is that individual financial intermediaries manage risks effectively. While failures in financial risk management and corporate governance were apparent in the global crisis, these issues have received relatively little international attention to date.

This section gives an overview of the risks to which financial intermediaries are exposed, and the general techniques for identifying, monitoring, managing, disclosing and mitigating those risks. We first define various types of risk. We then discuss how to measure and manage risk. Specifically, we discuss the concept of value at risk (VaR) and describe principles financial intermediaries use to manage risk exposure. Finally, we explain the purposes of risk management and explore the relationship between risk management and strategies of financial intermediaries.

Understanding risk

Risk is a measurable deviation from an expected outcome. It is not synonymous with expected losses. When a bank makes loans, for example, it may anticipate from experience that it will fail to recover 1 per cent of the resulting claims. This expected loss is not treated as a risk, which is instead the chance that the lender loses 2 or 3 per cent of the claims, for example, rather than the anticipated 1 per cent. In financial services, risk is defined as the possible deviation – one caused by unexpected variations in underlying factors – of the value or net worth of a position from its expected value.

Based on the potential causes of the deviation from an expected outcome, a typical financial intermediary must manage the following major categories of risk. If an unexpected loss is due to unexpected changes in interest rates, FX rates, commodity prices or equity values, we call the risks involved *market risks*. Other forms of market risk include real estate valuation risk and financial investment risk, both of which stem from changing market conditions. For example, a company might acquire real estate only to discover later that it is worth less than the assessed value.

If an unexpected loss is due to the inability or unwillingness of a counterparty to make contractual payments, then the risks involved are called *credit risks*. Of all the reasons that banks have failed or filed for bankruptcy, credit risk is probably the most significant. Financial intermediaries are also exposed to *liquidity risks*, which may cause unexpected losses from covering cashflow obligations due to liquidation of an illiquid or strategic position. *Business risks* refer to the risks of negative deviation in the value of a business due to unexpected changes in current or future business volumes or margins. Factors driving business risks include the economic cycle, competition, technological shocks and incorrect forecasts. Operational risks refer to the risks of loss resulting from inadequate or failed internal processes, people and systems, or from external events such as legal suits, disasters and reputation loss.

Credit and market risks account for the majority of bank risk exposure. In recent years, financial intermediaries have made greater efforts to manage their risk exposure so that credit derivatives, hedging activities and market liquidity can improve control over credit risk positions.

Value at risk as a metric

Risk measurement has become sophisticated. However, regardless of improvements in risk models, their construction has to be based on four principal factors. The first is the volatility of the underlying risk factor. The value of a fixed rate bond, for instance, depends on market interest rates. The volatility of interest rates is a key determinant of risk. A US treasury bond features lower interest rate volatility than a high-yield emerging market bond. Volatility is usually measured as the standard deviation from an expected outcome.

The second factor is time. The time horizon describes the risk exposure of a position as a function of time. For example, interest rates might change far more over a year than they would in a day. An important concept for the time factor is liquidity: positions that are more difficult to liquidate are more exposed to time-horizon risk.

The third factor is the valuation of the position, which in turn, is highly dependent on leverage. For example, a highly leveraged derivative position, when a small amount of capital is invested to control a much larger volume of an underlying asset, will have a very different proportion of value at risk than a position in highly-rated government securities.

The final factor involves the probability that an unexpected deviation in value is beyond a certain threshold. This is a way for intermediaries to consider the worst-case scenario. If a financial asset's value drops by a certain amount, it may create a serious concern for any particular firm. The probability factor allows a financial intermediary to ask, 'What is the chance that this situation will occur?'

Viewed by many as an indispensable measure of risk, VaR is widely used by financial managers to measure the financial risk of an asset, portfolio, or risk exposure over some specified period of time (Jorion 2001). Despite its simplicity, VaR has the aforementioned four factors inherent in its construction. In its generic form, VaR measures the potential loss in value of a risky asset or portfolio over a defined period at a given confidence interval. For example, if the VaR on an asset is US$100 million over one week, with a 95 per cent confidence level, there is only a 5 per cent chance that the value of the asset will drop more than US$100 million over any given week.

Figures 4.3A and 4.3B is an example of VaR calculations, showing the process that a risk manager will follow to calculate VaR for each portfolio position. Here, the expected return of the position described in the figure is 1.6 per cent per month, and the standard deviation of expected returns is 14.8 per cent. These values are based on historical performance. To calculate standard deviation per annum, we multiply standard deviation per month by the square root of 12 – the number of months in a year. We use the square root because each month is a statistically independent event. The same process is used to obtain average per annum return.

In this example, the return is 19.3 per cent per annum, and the annual VaR is 51.4 per cent. The expected value of the investment is 119.3 per cent of its original amount. Subtracting the VaR gives 67.9 per cent. This is the minimum value we can expect with a 95 per cent confidence interval. In other words, there is a 95 per cent probability that the investment's value after one year will be at least 67.9 per cent of the original investment.

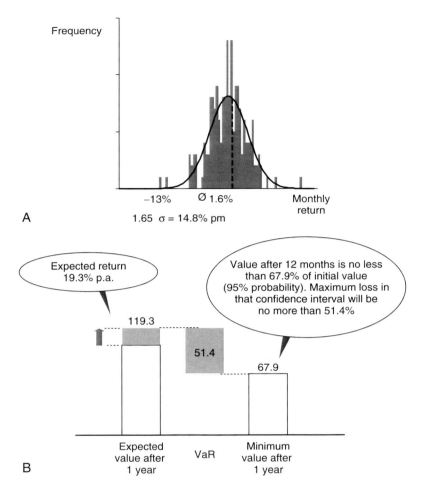

Figure 4.3. Illustrative VaR calculation.

VaR: 51.4% pa = 14.8% pm x √(12)

Average return: 19.3% pa = 1.6% pm x 12

Box 4.1 A Short History of Value at Risk

The impetus for the use of VaR measures came from recurring crises and successive regulatory responses to those crises. In the mid-1970s, New York-based Bankers Trust, later part of Germany's Deutsche Bank, developed the risk adjusted return on capital (RAROC) metric for its main foreign exchange and money market trading units. The weakness of this standard was that it did not address the amount of capital that banks would require to cover losses. Bankers Trust began to apply the RAROC concept in the 1980s to the firm's fixed income and interest rate derivatives business streams, using input data based upon the covariances in historic yields on bonds and interest rate swaps of different durations.

US banks began adopting VaR models in the late 1980s, albeit with variations as to how it was measured. The first mover had been Morgan Guaranty Trust Company (now merged with several other large banks into JPMorgan Chase), whose former chief executive Denis Weatherstone began his career with the bank as a London foreign exchange dealer. Weatherstone instructed Morgan's risk managers to devise a method that would produce a daily assessment of the bank's overall risk position, expressed in terms of its susceptibility to losses based on adverse movements in markets, whether interest rates, exchange rates or asset prices. With the system installed, Weatherstone received at the close of each day one sheet of paper, upon which was given a summary of Morgan's credit position and balance sheet, together with a single number showing the gain or loss that would result from incremental changes in those key variables, a number that came to be known as the 'value at risk'. Morgan Guaranty came to create a comprehensive VaR-based model called RiskMetrics, which began as a proprietary tool but was eventually made available to Morgan clients and then the market at large.

VaR analysis is statistically simple and any organization can purchase the required algorithms. However, the methodology requires substantial volumes of data, such as extended volatility time series. Morgan had assembled this information in association with data supplier Reuters, and in the mid-1990s elected to disseminate it freely. This created an industry standard and effectively prevented Morgan's competition from developing more sophisticated models. Most banks soon adopted Morgan's risk management software and data, but by analyzing the trading patterns of its rivals Morgan could estimate their risk positions. Eventually most major banks developed their own internal models.

European banks followed their US counterparts and implemented VaR in the early 1990s, as did most large Japanese banks. In 1997, Morgan and several investment banks released a model called CreditMetrics for valuing credit risk. Gradually, VaR methodology has become the dominant measure of risk exposure in the financial sector.

International bank regulators also influenced the development and use of risk models. The Basel Committee on Bank Supervision recognized internal models based on VaR in 1995 as part of best risk management practices, and in 1996 accepted the principle of internal VaR models as the basis for calculating equity capital, part of the Market Risk addendum to the first Basel capital accord. The successor Basel II accord was negotiated by national regulators over the following decade and included a regulatory capital regime based upon the approval by national authorities of the internal risk models of the major banks that they supervise. As Chapter 6 shows, this methodology became the industry standard, even though the global crisis that began in 2007 damaged its reputation as a single tool to assess the risk quantum and capital requirements of even moderately complex banks.

Largely because of simplicity and intuitive appeal, VaR and its variants have been popular risk assessment tools. However, as with any other tools, VaR has its own limitations. The 2007–9 global financial crisis highlighted these limitations and necessitated a more comprehensive understanding of risks and more effective tools to manage risks. Four features of the model are especially criticised:

- The purpose of VaR is to protect financial intermediaries against risk under a reasonable set of scenarios. Firms cannot protect against every circumstance, especially against outlier events, or those in the tail of the distribution. For example, VaR measures set in accordance with this analysis would not have protected Bear Stearns or Lehman Brothers from bankruptcy because the stresses they experienced involved such low probabilities of occurring. Before the global crisis, banks believed that they could adequately measure risk factors. The crisis forced a reconsideration, especially as to the use of single-risk metrics. The crisis as an outlier event reduced liquidity well below expectations, and caused a global compression of credit.
- The calculation of VaR is based on assumptions which, when wrong, usually lead to erroneous results. Most VaR measures make assumptions about return distributions. Most measures assume that the returns follow a normal distribution. However, there is substantial evidence that returns are not normally distributed and that not only are outliers more common in reality but are much larger than expected – dramatically highlighted by the global financial crisis.
- All VaR measures use historic data to obtain the estimates of important model parameters, but history may be a poor predictor. Campbell, Lettau, Malkiel and Xu (2001) document that firm-level volatility experienced a noticeable increase in the US stock market in 1962–97. Using historical firm-level volatility to predict the future may be misleading. In addition, VaR measures are conditional on explicit estimates of correlation across risk sources such as those provided by RiskMetrics or implicit assumptions about such correlations. Again, these estimates are usually based on historical data and can be extremely volatile.
- VaR has been often criticized as being conceptually narrow. It was originally designed to assess market risks. Although the concept was later extended to measure credit and other risks, it does not consider political risk, liquidity risk, agency risk or regulatory risk, and as we have seen, it fails to fully consider event risk, especially when the probability of occurrence is small.

Risk assessment

Despite its shortcomings, VaR allows us to explore more general ways of assessing risk. All risk assessment models should focus on the same principle of calculating VaR, and do so by analyzing positions, risk factors and correlations, regardless of what techniques will be finally adopted: that is, historical variance–covariance analysis or more complicated Monte Carlo simulations. Such a framework generally consists of four steps:

- Intermediaries properly aggregate positions for analysis according to classes of credit and other risks, in some cases concentrated and in others diversified.
- Intermediaries adopt empirically validated models to estimate risk factors and loss probabilities (that is, the default probability in the case of credit risk). They can

parameterize directly or derive input parameters from macroeconomic models. These models assess or simulate loss probabilities and allow firms to calculate expected losses differentiated by risk segment. In this process, financial intermediaries must take many risk factors into account and incorporate differentiation by risk segment into their expected loss and volatility calculations. Because many risk factors do not adhere to normal distributions, they must create new distributions for these factors.

- Intermediaries then determine which correlations or probabilities between counterparties or segments can be estimated. This includes consideration of correlations between risk segments, and calculation for concentration risks in undiversified portfolios.
- Based on the results of these three steps, intermediaries then simulate distributions of portfolio losses to obtain an overall VaR.

Stresses are found everywhere, and risk management is therefore of primary importance. The principle guiding corporate risk management is straightforward: to reduce the expected costs of financial distress while preserving a company's ability to exploit any comparative advantage in risk-bearing. The goal of corporate risk management is 'the elimination of costly lower tail outcomes' (Stulz 1996).

Modern finance has established robust empirical evidence showing that risk management, especially in corporate hedging, helps reduce the high variance of a position or portfolio, which consequently improves firm performance and firm value. Smith and Stulz (1985) discuss several channels through which risk management reduces variability and improves firm performance:

- Reducing bankruptcy costs by lessening downside risk, that is, the chance of having negative results:
- Allowing firms to reduce firm owners' risk and hence their required rates of return; and
- Assisting in managing firms' tax liabilities.

However, overemphasizing the role of risk management as reducing variability has its limitations. It understates the importance of risk management as a way to preserve as much of the commercial upside as can be justified by a firm's risk appetite and business model. Risks involve potential losses but also provide a firm with opportunities for profit. A proactive risk management strategy should be built on the principle that it allows a firm to capture those upside opportunities.

Linking risk management to strategy

To achieve its risk management goals, a financial intermediary should use a risk-based planning and performance management process to link its commercial strategy and risk management resources. Intermediaries constantly engage in risk-taking, and must therefore monitor and adjust performance, determine their appropriate appetite for risk, permissible risk profile, and consequent capital requirements, and accordingly allocate economic capital and set performance targets for their business units. When front office commercial units are required in this way to conform with agreed risk profiles, the firm's compliance function will be better able to determine when abuses or breaches of policy are likely to occur. Figure 4.4 illustrates this process.

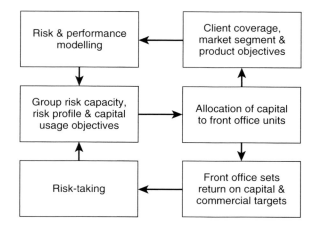

Figure 4.4 Risk management linked with commercial strategy.

A bank must first determine the level of risk to which it is exposed – a level that depends heavily on the bank's business profile, for example, as a retail or universal bank. It must then determine the maximum unexpected loss it can endure before endangering its financial viability. From this point, it must calculate the economic capital it would require to cover this loss. The bank's strategies underlie these fundamental risk management calculations. The bank must determine the attractiveness of its business and its comparative advantages in risk taking: it needs to understand in which areas the bank has the highest profitability and advantages in risk management.

To manage risks, the bank must determine which risks it is willing to take. It should base these decisions on its chosen lines of business. Banks that enter businesses outside the core expertise of management often experience failure. Some might make the mistake of entering high risk businesses, because of potentially enormous profits. However, when these financial intermediaries do not properly consider the amount of earnings they place at risk by entering these businesses, their actions could affect overall profitability, and in the worst scenario, lead to their failure.

It is therefore essential that intermediaries set guidelines at the corporate level about which risks are consistent with their risk appetite, and review new investments according to these policies. Such a risk management process implies that some intermediaries need to hedge all risks, while others need to worry about only certain kinds of risks. When making decisions about whether or not to hedge, management should keep in mind that risk management can be used to better pursue strategic objectives rather than merely reduce variance.

After financial intermediaries determine their default probabilities, they can measure the amount of economic capital they require. The risk manager can calculate the organization's capital requirements by assessing its total risk. However, it is difficult for banks to use this type of analysis at a finer level of detail. An alternative option is to determine VaR for each type of risk individually. VaR and economic capital requirements are then calculated for the company as a whole from these individual VaR calculations. The benefit of this approach is that it can produce more accurate results. However, it can be difficult for organizations to measure the correlation between different kinds of risk, with the potential consequence of over- or under-estimating capital requirements.

The next step is to properly allocate capital. Rating agencies will downgrade borrowers that have insufficient capital reserves for its risk level. A company that has an inappropriately high level of capital reserves may achieve a high credit rating but the market will penalize it for not achieving an appropriate level of return on equity. Organizations must give their individual business units economic capital performance targets.

Throughout the process, the bank will continuously monitor risk and performance and adjust its capital reserves accordingly. The firm's risk-adjusted return on capital (RAROC) is a measurement that accounts for risk as well as returns and is calculated by the formula:

$$RAROC = \frac{Revenues - Costs - Expected\ Losses}{Economic\ Capital} \tag{4.3}$$

RAROC measures returns adjusted for risks (through expected losses and required capital). It therefore provides a common performance measure which can be used across business units, projects, products and geographies. This metric helps managers make sound business decisions and allows them to determine if their respective organizations are behaving in accordance with their target risk profiles. For example, a company can easily obtain higher returns by placing its capital in risky investments: RAROC analysis reveals that this policy exposes the organization to additional risks. The company requires additional capital to meet its target risk profile. On a regular basis, management should review the performance of each business unit and the economic capital each uses and use this information to analyze each unit's risk-adjusted returns.

Risk organization

Firms that excel in risk management and gain an advantage from bearing risk do not do so by accident, for there are several elements that successful risk management organizations have in common:

- They succeed in obtaining a consistent commitment from senior management. Effective managers have a consolidated view of all risk that allows optimal direction of the organization's businesses. The commitment of senior management allows risk management to gain respect based on capabilities. The commitment from senior management also develops a culture within the organization that is conducive to sensible risk bearing and risk management.
- They keep central oversight of risk policies and procedures. The risk management team maintains overall authority for policy setting such as overall risk tolerance, procedures and measurement standards, subject to senior management and board approval.
- A separation is maintained in policy setting, monitoring and control, and risk origination and management execution. Here, risk measurement and analysis largely resides within responsible functions, which ensures an appropriate segregation of duties.
- They maintain formal involvement of risk management in the strategy development process to ensure that risk–return considerations are adequately accounted for. Within these organizations, there is a significant interaction between business units and risk management to ensure a sound understanding of risk in the business units.

- Responsibilities are defined for assuring, managing and controlling risk, tied to individual and group performance measurement and incentive systems. The incentive and control mechanisms in these organizations are designed to punish poor risk taking and encourage good risk taking.

This discussion of the macroeconomic, regulatory and risk management parameters of financial markets and operations is a base for our analysis of a series of specific contexts across Chapters 6–11. Chapter 5 considers the institutional and legal factors that complete that foundation.

5 Institutional foundations of finance

All plays need a stage and setting, whether real or virtual, and the commercial and economic activity facilitated by financial intermediation described in Chapters 1–3 takes place on a stage with two main features:

- The institutional setting, including law and general rules of conduct; and
- Regulation and supervision conducted by the state or by delegation to market participants.

Chapter 4 looked at those national and transnational policies that connect the state to the financial economy and influence that institutional setting. This financial drama is never passive because those rules and principles inevitably have unanticipated second order effects on commercial participants that stem from profit seeking and regulatory arbitrage. The Basel capital regime described in Chapter 4 is an important example. Its introduction and periodic reforms have induced profound and unforeseen changes in commercial behaviour, often influencing the ability of policymakers to encourage financial stability.

The micro-level interplay between finance, law and rules of conduct are the subject of this chapter, which shows how these factors condition the commercial choices of intermediaries and investors.

5.1 Institutional foundations of finance

Financial systems of all types and complexities rely on institutions. Without those covered in this chapter, no modern market-based financial system would exist in a usable form. This is because the formation and operation of contracts and financial instruments rely on these building blocks, as do organized exchanges in providing a hub for financial trading and intermediaries when they contemplate credit contracts. This chapter discusses those variables that influence the formation and performance of contracts, and can sometimes lead to their failure.

The conditions for financial sector development rest on three principles that are institutional, legal or policy related (Arner 2007). First, a market economy and any market-based financial system cannot exist if appropriate institutional and legal supports are not in place. These are a governance mechanism that establishes property rights and provides for the consistent enforcement of contracts and the resolution of commercial disputes. The setting must also provide for human capital development, which as we saw in Section 1.1 is important in facilitating growth (Lucas 1988).

Second, with these institutional foundations, certain legal underpinnings must then be available for the financial system to function effectively. These include the availability of enforceable collateral to support secured transactions, a system of law for the establishment and dissolution of corporate bodies, and transparent systems of taxation and funding for government. The system's effectiveness will require national and subnational governance to provide more broadly for the rule of law, which is taken to be transparent and non-discriminatory.

Third, a financial sector functions effectively in the context of appropriate macroeconomic policies. These policies operate best in the context of an appropriately designed and transparent institutional framework.

No sophisticated market economy or market-based financial system can function without these prerequisites, regardless of indigenous or acquired national characteristics or the form manifested by that system. Four main sections follow, beginning with an explanation of the importance of viewing governance, legal systems and economic development as a cohesive whole. We then consider theories of property rights, collateral, creditor rights and insolvency, and their practical results (especially in transaction formation and lending by banks and other intermediaries), and review Asia's current legal and customary treatment of collateral, creditor rights and insolvency. How does Asia rank in these respects, given that its regimes for creditor rights are a mix of global and national practice? One long research seam explored since the 1997 regional crisis has been the micro-level obstacles, impediments, oddities and omissions within and between states that appear to prevent Asian financial markets from either growing, performing effectively or becoming integrated with each other (Lejot, Arner & Liu 2006b; Arner, Lejot & Rhee 2006; Bhattacharyay 2010). We conclude with a discussion of enforcement of contracts – a subject that is central to finance. Overall, this chapter's institutional platform should be seen as foundational for the remainder of the book, regardless of regulation or ephemeral market behaviour.

5.2 Governance, legal systems and economic development

State governance and the appropriateness of political and economic structure have been of interest for more than 10,000 years, since the time that specialized human activity first allowed agricultural settlement. This in turn encouraged the development of writing systems necessary to sustain the continuing administration of such settlements. Building a 'perfect society' and creating governance systems to encourage its development has been a focus of thinkers from Confucius, Plato and Aquinas to Locke and Marx. All political and economic systems function in parallel, even though the interplay may not always be acknowledged by theorists. Certainly the relationship between politics or governance and economics was of central interest to Smith and Marx, and more recently to Keynes, Hayek and Friedman. Although politics and economics became distinct disciplines in the twentieth century, the new millennium saw a reviving interaction between governance and economics, partly encouraged by a new market orientation shared by many former command economies, and from the failure of other economic development models that had neglected institutional issues of governance.

The functions and development of financial intermediaries have become a focus of attention only recently in law, policy and economics, although each discipline is directly concerned with both the problem and its explanations. Similarly, the conditions influencing financial structure have begun to interest scholars and policymakers. Until the 1970s, few economic or finance theorists gave attention to the nature of financial systems or how they affect economic development. The importance and influence of the characteristics of financial markets and intermediaries has been accepted only since the 1980s, with the recognition of law and finance scholarship, and of institutional economics. Financial intermediation is now recognized as vital to many aspects of economic development, and what determines the nature of financial intermediaries and financial infrastructure is susceptible to both quantitative analysis and the tools of legal and economic theory.

By the 1990s the two polar alternatives of state-directed planning and laissez faire capitalism had been subsumed into a consensus as to the superiority of a market economy, functioning under the framework of an appropriate and transparent regulatory system. Government would take a benign but active role in addressing the interests of society through the provision of public goods that were agreed by consensus within each state, setting systems to limit or ameliorate market failure, and imposing sanctions to deter market manipulation or abuse, whether arising from monopolies or from cases where 'insider' or asymmetric information was held by privileged participants. Nonetheless, many differences remain among contemporary economic and governance models (Djankov, Glaeser, La Porta, Lopez-de-Silanes & Shleifer 2003). What then represent the best choices among available alternatives, and to what extent do those choices disadvantage certain interests?

For institutional scholars such as North and those in the law and economics school of governance, systems must provide two elements to support a market economy, regardless of its ideological preferences or resulting form:

- The system must provide for clear and usable property rights; and
- It must facilitate practical and fair contract enforcement.

Both literatures agree that these conditions are essential where there exist imperfect markets with discernable transaction costs, known sometimes as 'market friction'. While there appears to be agreement as to these basic points, the governance structure that best supports a market economy is less apparent, and may change in relation to the relative development of the economy.

Many scholars argue further that democratic models of governance are optimal in protecting property rights and enforcing contracts, although this was often the result they sought to prove. Olson has presented a convincing counter-argument: that more than one governance structure can provide these necessary features. An autocrat with a long-term time horizon has a strong incentive to support property rights and contract enforcement in order chiefly to maximize revenue from taxation (Olson 2000). Conversely, any democracy, while supposedly providing for property rights and the enforcement of contracts, may nevertheless become subject to inefficient outcomes due to its responsiveness to representative but factional interests. The autocracy is effective while the democracy in deficient. Neither autocracy nor democracy is of itself superior in providing beneficial support for a market economy. What is needed is a 'market augmenting government' (Cadwell 2000).

Contemporary anecdotal evidence lends support to Olson's theory, as perhaps with China and Singapore, compared to India or the Philippines. More formal empirical research suggests that policies are more important than democratic institutions, that human capital is more instrumental to growth than democratic institutions, and that poor states can alleviate poverty through sound policies even under dictatorships and democratic institutions become effective in the post-development phases (Djankov, Glaeser, La Porta, Lopez-de-Silanes & Shleifer 2003).

North sums up the interaction between the political system and property rights:

Broadly speaking, political rules in place lead to economic rules, though the causality runs both ways. That is, property rights and hence individual contracts are specified and enforced by political decision-making, but the structure of economic interests will also influence the political structure. In equilibrium, a given structure of property rights (and their enforcement) will be consistent with a particular set of political rules (and their enforcement). Changes in one will induce changes in the other.

(North 1990: 48)

This means that a national governance structure is important and must provide for property rights, the enforcement of contracts and human capital development. However, while some governance structures are clearly not conducive to liberty (any state run by Olson's myopic autocrat-bandit), a market economy can be supported by both autocratic and democratic governance systems. Each can also provide for institutional choices that fail to result in efficient, wealth-maximizing outcomes in a given economy.

The central issue therefore is property rights.

5.3 The significance of property rights

Property rights were first a concern for Aristotle (Robbins 1998: 29–30), and in due course for Hume, Smith, Marx and Weber. Despite this intellectual heritage the societal and economic value associated with property rights received little attention from economists for generations. Until becoming subject to intensive research in the late 1970s, the nature and institutional needs of finance were ignored or assumed away by generations of economists and finance specialists, and only maverick opinion took a differing view.

Marx's labour theory of value led radicals and revolutionaries to condemn personal property as class based and evidence of theft, especially the private ownership of land. Alternatives such as rights of land use and collective ownership varied between the legal and the informal in the Soviet Union and China, respectively, and still influence China and other Asian jurisdictions (Chen 2010; Glenn 2007). The importance of property rights began to receive significant contemporary attention when the disintegration of the Soviet bloc brought about a need to transform command economies into market systems. Development specialist Hernando de Soto also deserves credit for increasing awareness of the importance of property rights in poor communities, especially in relation to the potential impact of formally endowing individuals with such rights.

Classically, personal property is treated as a bundle of rights. It endows the owner with certain distinct rights, including the right to hold, use, manage, modify, transfer, or destroy a real or intangible asset. Questions of degree and time relate to all such rights, and the extent to which a property owner may exploit such rights may be constrained by the conflicting rights of others within a legal system, or as part of public policy when a regulator limits the free disposition of property by its owner. One may have outright ownership of a house, but if it was once the home of a celebrated author or civic leader, or was designed by a renowned architect, then heritage rules may prevent the demolition of the house for commercial reasons or building an extra storey. Property can be real or personal, tangible or intangible. The more complex a system of property rights, the more effective is their potential use in the context of finance and the raising of capital. According to North:

> Property rights are the rights individuals appropriate over their own labour and the goods and services they possess. Appropriation is a function of legal rules, organizational forms, enforcement, and norms of behaviour – that is, the institutional framework.

(North 1990: 33)

De Soto sees capital as the engine of a market economy, with property rights as the mechanism that allows it to be deployed effectively (de Soto 2000). Relatively poor countries often fail to produce capital sufficient for economic development due to five main failings in property systems. First, such societies may have substantial capital, yet it represents a dead or unrealized resource in that it comprises assets or claims that cannot be freely used or mobilized, often for reasons of custom or the absence of suitable legal rules. Second, capital is intrinsically difficult to define or recognize. Third, many states have neglected the importance of the preceding two factors, an attitude that de Soto argues has only slowly started to change:

> The substantial increase of capital in the West over the past two centuries is the consequence of gradually improving property systems, which allowed economic agents to discover and realize the potential in their assets, and thus to be in a position to produce the non-inflationary money with which to finance and generate additional production.
>
> (de Soto 2000: 65)

Fourth, while de Soto's process of mobilizing property rights needed in emerging or transitional economies had occurred earlier elsewhere, it was often poorly understood or documented even in relatively sophisticated states. Finally, laws need to reflect national or local circumstances in order to allow the effective transformation of property rights into capital.

For de Soto:

> A well-integrated legal property system in essence does two things: First, it tremendously reduces the costs of knowing the economic qualities of assets by representing them in a way that our senses can pick up quickly; and second, it facilitates the capacity to agree on how to use assets to create further production and increase the division of labour.
>
> (de Soto 2000: 63)

De Soto concludes that formal property systems are required to produce six effects so as to allow individuals to generate usable capital. These are a mix of the specific and socially aspirational (de Soto 2000: 49–62):

- Making certain the economic potential of existing assets;
- Integrating dispersed information into a single dependable registration system;
- Making individuals accountable for their economic actions;
- Providing for the fungibility of assets;
- Marshalling individuals into valuable social networks; and
- Protecting the integrity of legitimate transactions.

The identification and protection of established and accepted property rights, including rights over intellectual property, are therefore essential in any market economy (Klapper, Laeven & Rajan 2004: 27–8). De Soto notes that such rights only evolved slowly in today's advanced economies, making it regretfully difficult even for historians to know how they function or become established. Without templates of this kind it may never be simple for emerging or transition economies to adapt those experiences or systems, even respecting the integrity of local culture. Finally, the recognition of property rights is not self-justifying – such rights must be available for use other than in self-liquidating non-executory transactions.

5.4 Collateral and creditor rights

The key to the effectiveness of property rights in supporting economic growth is thus the ability to use them to support finance: this is the realm of collateral, credit rights and insolvency. This section contains summaries of appraisals of the effectiveness of current law and practice as to collateral and creditor rights in 12 jurisdictions. They examine aspects of the creation and treatment of secured creditor interests, processes for insolvency, securitization and the functional relationships between these related aspects of law.

Collateral and legal systems

Many of the terms used here and in the chapters that follow are defined briefly in the glossary. One oddity is collateral, which in English law can mean a source of additional secondary security. This is always confusing. We use collateral to mean an asset with a known or calculable value that is pledged or charged by its owner to provide security for a loan or other credit. It can be real or intangible property, and may be owned by a third party who effectively makes a loan of collateral to the debtor, which is the story of Shakespearian credit told in Section 6.2.

Taking security for a loan means employing legal techniques such as mortgages, charges or pledges to specify when and how a creditor may enforce and take ownership of the collateral. If the debtor defaults then, subject to the terms of the credit agreement and the security documents, ownership of the collateral will pass to the creditor and usually be sold or auctioned to help liquidate the debt. In some jurisdictions, and with variations for local contractual practice, that is the end of the matter between debtor and creditor, but in jurisdictions that have followed provisions of the German commercial code the debt may last until being fully repaid or cancelled by a court. Differences in practice between the main families of law appear throughout this chapter, and we might see the results as tests of the law and finance school's assessments of comparative creditor and property rights.

As illustrations, we discuss some examples of large-scale secured lending in Chapter 6. We also introduce securitization – with a potentially confusing similarity in terminology. However, security and securitization are wholly different, for security refers to the process of taking collateral to protect a lender's interests and securitization is a generic form of transaction that is widely used by lenders for funding purposes or to assist their risk and balance sheet management. As a further point, 'securities' – as introduced in Chapter 3 – are freely transferable financial instruments, and not collateral, although they may in fact be collateralized or secured, for instance in securitization. Finally, as well as discussing the concepts underlying property and creditor rights and collateral, we also explain comparative aspects of law in more detail than non-lawyers may be used to seeing. Our aim is to show the formative importance of these issues to day-to-day finance. Institutions matter.

The effect of globalization on market practice and the harmonization of financial regulation means that the private law that governs international financial transactions differs less by virtue of where the parties are domiciled, or where a contract is executed, than by issues of judicial enforcement, including the willingness of courts to provide equitable and predictable judgments to creditors, both domestic and foreign. The quality of insolvency provisions also affects the willingness of lenders and investors to provide funds for capital investment. By contrast, legal frameworks for the taking or enforcement of collateral may be influenced by informal or traditional national or local commercial custom, although remaining subject to the prevailing form of law and the roots of national law.

Of our 12 jurisdictions, ten have undergone or intend to enact reforms in these areas, and the remaining two are common law jurisdictions that are among the more sophisticated in the region in commercial law and regulation. We do not suggest that either Hong Kong or Singapore is an institutional benchmark – indeed, reforms in Japan's civil code and statutes have guided changes among other civil jurisdictions, and China, South Korea and Taiwan have adapted to their own needs laws first found in the German commercial code (Chen 2010).

Legal systems based on English law are generally conducive to using all kinds of conventional collateral as security, including property and movable capital assets such as ships and aircraft. This helps explain why most large-scale transnational project finance transactions that involve a package of security contracts use the relatively effective English law form of security to safeguard the risk position of lenders, although the package will usually rely on mortgage or charge documents that are proscribed in the domicile of the collateral. Other forms of law can be equally effective but are more idiosyncratic or procedurally demanding, as we shall see below.

Several systems in Southeast Asia offer little protection to the lender or creditor. As a general rule, systems based on English law provide a simple platform for security except where the law conflicts with statutory provisions for insolvency. Asian legal systems based on German law can be effective but are often heavily rule-based. The concept of legal families (David & Brierley 1978) is used in Table 5.1 to show how our jurisdictions acquired their differing systems of law, but scholars often differ as to which family a jurisdiction belongs.

Issues of policy or principle that we raise in this chapter have been debated since Asia recovered from the 1997–98 financial crisis, so while commercial law and regulation is often lacking the matters addressed here have had attention for over a decade from policymakers and legal and commercial interests. In no case can the legal, regulatory or policy background be described as complete or fully integrated, even in Hong Kong or Singapore or where comprehensive reforms have been introduced, as with China's 2007 Property Law or Vietnam's 2005 Law on Enterprises.

A series of tables below appraise national legal frameworks for creditor rights, secured claims, the effectiveness of insolvency systems, and the compatibility of these systems

Table 5.1 Compatibility of creditor rights and insolvency systems

	Principal source & system of current law	*Form of legal transplant*
Cambodia	French civil	Imposition
China	Mixed (German civil, Socialist)	Adoption
Hong Kong	English common	Imposition
Indonesia	Dutch civil	Imposition
Japan	Mixed (German civil, US)	Imposition/adoption
South Korea	German civil	Imposition/adoption
Malaysia	English common, Shari'ah (commercial)	Imposition/adoption
Philippines	Mixed (Franco-Spanish civil, US)	Imposition
Singapore	English common	Imposition
Taiwan	German, Japanese civil	Imposition/adoption
Thailand	French civil	Adoption
Vietnam	Mixed (French civil, Socialist)	Imposition/adoption

Sources: Authors' analysis; David & Brierley (1978); Glenn (2007); Wood (2007a).

for enforcement. Two further tables examine Asia's legal provisions for securitization, that is, the institutional factors that make any transaction succeed or fail. We discuss securitization as used by commercial banks in Sections 6.2 and 6.4, and in more detail in Section 8.3 as part of a narrative on complex securities. In each case the appraisals acknowledge not only black-letter law and regulation but also qualifications to reflect enforcement issues, integration with related laws, and the stability of the overall regulatory setting. Commercial participants in Asia have often found that national laws suffer from uncertain application even though they appear to be clear. The results can become manifested in complex private financial transactions, where contractual drafting seeks to mitigate such legal risks.

It is now generally accepted that the form and practice of law influences economic behaviour, and that institutional quality is an important determinant of credit creation. Factors such as legal origin, the nature of the acquisition or founding of law, and details of its application and enforcement, are seen in features of governance, economic systems and structure, commercial culture, corporate behaviour and financing patterns. These conditions also affect broader variables such as national output and personal income. The tables in this chapter and the research upon which they are based adopt the viewpoint of users, that is, principals and agents that become subject to the law rather than those involved in its creation or administration.

At the same time, the operation of law will always be associated with institutional costs, so that no assessment can ignore issues of efficiency and consistency in the organization and management of legal systems. This is especially valid in the context of creditor claims and times of corporate distress. The objective of the reform of laws governing security and creditor rights will generally be to influence behaviour through changes in costs.

Collateral and creditor control

Collateral exists as part of national commercial practice and socio-economic constraints that vary among jurisdictions, even with globalization forcing integration in commercial practice and financial regulation. Periodic surveys of law, institutions and secured transactions show the reasons for taking security differing everywhere by intention, nature and degree (World Bank 1989, 2002; Keinan 2001). This affects whether the granting of collateral is an efficient choice for commercial or individual borrowers or for creditors at large. Analysis of 12 European transition economies suggests that the provision of collateral is important in inducing national development (Haselmann, Pistor & Vig 2010), and finds that a collateral regime is more important in stimulating bank lending to households and SMEs than the prevailing bankruptcy regime.

This result contrasts with prior LLSV studies in which variables related to collective enforcement and reorganization were used as proxies for creditor rights. The existence of a strong collateral regime is also critical to effective bankruptcy systems. At the same time, taking security is not generally a way to signal good credit quality but the reverse, as with non-recourse project finance. This is contrary to the findings of certain studies of domestic US practice, except where recourse to the principal debtor is non-existent or limited. Another view is that collateral provides incentives for lenders to monitor loan performance and is correlated with poor business conditions or the debtor's financial distress (Rajan & Winton 1995). The traditional reasons why borrowers are thought to grant security were also questioned by Schwartz (1981, 1984). Assuming that the value of an enterprise is unrelated to the composition of its capital (Modigliani & Miller 1958), how is giving security a cost effective practice, given that it may deter other potential lenders, and since the priorities it establishes interfere with the aims of the US bankruptcy code to support the enterprise in times of distress?

Historical turning points may not fit with today's observations. In the English Industrial Revolution, the existence of reliable non-possessory land mortgages failed to induce banks to lend in significant amounts to industrial capitalists. This allowed some historians to discount the importance of finance in development (Dobb 1947; Flinn 1966: 52–3). Similar inaction by banks was recorded in the US at the turn of the twentieth century (Lamoreaux, Levenstein & Sokoloff 2004: 27–30). A reliable non-possessory chattel mortgage appeared in England around 1850 but was arguably not trusted by lenders until the early twentieth century (Goode 2004: 586). England's earlier eighteenth century 'financial revolution' was long underestimated in its effect on later commercial development (Neal 1994: 151), and another narrative economic historian bemoans a similar lack of attention to private finance in economic growth studies, describing the service sector as the 'neglected variable' (Hartwell 1971).

Joseph Schumpeter's 1939 description of the working of capitalism draws on his earlier approach to interest and credit creation that came to be disputed by contemporary traditional classicists (Edwin Cannan), radicals (J.M. Keynes and Joan Robinson) and is still controversial today. It includes a generic description of the role of credit creation in banking not attempted by his contemporary critics. Schumpeter's approach includes a means by which a bank lender may overcome transaction obstacles and thus lessen the costs resulting from asymmetric information, which would otherwise often force the adoption of clearly incomplete lending contracts. In the same way, modern structured finance techniques such as non-recourse project finance or securitization hope to limit the incompleteness associated with all financing contracts. In these specific examples, structuring results in the debtor having no post-finance surplus value, so as to become theoretically constrained from engaging in activity outside the financed enterprise. The creditor has economic control of the enterprise.

By contrast, lending conducted under typical general loan agreements involves credit risks subject to unquantifiable Knightian uncertainty, since lenders can only be partially informed as to the activities of their borrowers. Even though lenders hope to mitigate the effects of incomplete contracts by incorporating performance covenants and assignments of actual or future revenues into contracts, the result will inevitably be subject to general practice and the comparative negotiating strength of the two parties. Even if a lender has full knowledge of an enterprise, the debtor's chosen actions may lead to default, which can be economically rational. This would be the case with home mortgage loans where the value of collateral falls below the amount outstanding, providing there are legal limits to creditor rights in bankruptcy.

Other mechanisms to encourage contract compliance (given that few non-fraudulent debtors in advanced economies now face the threat of prison) include socio-economic forces of the kind associated with unusual lending markets – for example, in the financing of the trade in diamonds or ship purchases (Section 6.4). By this view, control collateral is not related to information asymmetries but is a sanction to encourage compliance by the debtor. In terms of institutional analysis it will typically constitute a distortion, enabling credit substitution to become the means by which a bank lender avoids the moral hazard associated with asymmetric information. Our analysis suggests three purposes in collateral for those involved in financial bargaining, shown in Table 5.2.

An adequate institutional infrastructure provides banks with confidence as to the risk of repayment. This in turn enables banks to extend the duration of their loans and reduce their regulatory capital costs. Two aspects of lending infrastructure are especially important for risk management: an effective system for taking security, and sufficient information for

Table 5.2 Theoretical functions of collateral

Transformative	Informative	Incentive related
1. Mitigation or substitution in credit risk for a potential financier	1. Signal credit risk strengths or borrower status	1. Effect on costs and information for credit creation
2. Change in capital asset use to make financing available	2. Signal risk or bargaining weaknesses	2. Provide financiers with known credit risks
	3. Facilitate credit substitution	3. Encourage contractual compliance by collateral providers

security and credit appraisal through accounting standards, audit practices, credit rating methodology and oversight, and acceptable credit information systems.

As an institution of risk management, an effective collateral system allows lenders to reduce unwanted credit risk and have confidence that their security may be realized where necessary to permit the full or partial repayment of a loan. Effective security creation and registration thus provides two advantages for lenders. First, it allows the limiting of monitoring costs through partial or complete credit risk substitution, providing that no failure to monitor collateral leads to an erosion of security protection. Second, it increases simplicity in lending decisions, thereby raising the probability that credit approvals will be given. A contrary view is that over-reliance on collateral in lending to commercial business is inefficient and beset with moral hazard, because it disassociates the creditor from having an interest in the borrower's commercial prospects. Islamic finance transactions try to solve this problem by melding the interest of the contractual creditor into the general commercial success of the borrower (see Section 11.4).

If property rights are to create capital, they must be applied to procure funding so that the taking of security is the lender's simplest form of risk mitigation. Loans are disbursed when the lender is given a contingent claim to property of a proportionately equivalent or greater value. If the debt is not satisfied, the lender retains the property and need take little or no account of the credit risk of the borrower. In this simple case, the availability of collateral induces marginally greater lending. However, to prompt this simple transaction, the lender must be confident of retaining rights to the property given contractual non-payment by the debtor. Thus the borrower must have valid initial title to the property and the law must provide for certain and effective transfer of ownership in the event of the security being enforced. Finally, the lender will need a means to appraise supporting collateral. This has often been problematic for all economies in the context of loans secured by real property.

Complex collateral-based lending involves sophisticated distinctions between property rights and the certainty of contractual enforcement, derived from the prevailing legal and institutional framework. For example, in the simple transaction of the preceding paragraph, a borrower provides physical, recognizable collateral to secure its indebtedness, as in a common South Asian example of personal loans secured by quantities of gold or silver. This is collateral deployed in its most simple form. For the reasons we have outlined in this section, the use of collateral in secured transactions can become more complex only to the extent that it is supported by an adequate legal and institutional framework. If a borrower must deliver physical collateral to a lender then poorly capitalized enterprises will lack access to most secured lending, and excessive transaction costs render the exercise sub-optimal.

Institutional support may allow more advanced practices, so that a borrower is permitted possession of collateral that predates the creation of a new loan. Free use of its existing assets leaves the borrower able to manage the enterprise value of its land, buildings, plant or machinery. At a still more sophisticated legal level, a loan might be used to purchase real property or productive assets secured by those assets, with the borrower retaining their full use in ways that may be expected to assist in the servicing of the loan. This is simple to describe, but such purchase money security is not universally supported by security or bankruptcy law.

Whether national law allows or constrains these arrangements reflects an underlying view of the economic welfare associated with security and collateral. This is seen in the competing views of a commercial enterprise as being either revenue generating or a custodian of assets, and may result in the legal treatment of the purchase of money security as unfairly benefiting individual creditors at the expense of others. A third approach distinguishes between the common law view of the firm as a nexus of contractual bargains following Coase (1937), and the generic civil law approach that sees the firm as a commercial hub of rights and obligations.

Transaction complexity requires greater legal sophistication, and deploying movable property as collateral typically requires a more complex legal framework than with real property. Furthermore, while real or movable physical collateral is associated with the largest share of secured lending in emerging and developed economies, intangible property can also represent potential collateral. This may include intellectual property or trade receivables. The rights of a secured creditor could extend to defined classes of assets such as inventory or receivables, to a company's entire asset base in a whole business securitization transaction, or where debts are secured by floating charges as found in English law. They might also extend to the right to receive revenues rather than the actual receipt of revenues, providing in each case that the institutional system is sufficiently supportive.

Testing effectiveness

Our first appraisal deals with securitization. The technique emphasizes more intensive contracting than most forms of financing. It requires a transparent legal framework, clear accounting principles and regulatory support, although the same quality of conditions will also provide incentives for transactional regulatory arbitrage. Its success therefore depends upon how its governing system of law accommodates these institutions, and may help explain why securitization developed first in common law jurisdictions.

Modern common law systems regard the commercial contract as the result of economic bargaining, the primary aim of which is to bestow identified rights, the erosion of which may entail a penalty. Civil law jurisdictions have tended to view contracts as bundles of mutual obligations, which are thus intrinsically restricted and for which the courts are generally willing to require performance. The effect on lending contracts under civil law systems is generally to limit the potential for their unqualified sale, especially when the transferee is insubstantial. The same approach also tends to complicate the possible sale of future payment rights.

The essence of a supportive legal and regulatory framework is to ensure that neither law nor regulation lessens the structural integrity of legitimate securitized transactions, and that any transfer of assets is permanent and cannot be disturbed by external events, including subsequent actions by creditors of the originator. In the market for financial claims, securitization is a contractual alternative to intermediation managed within a financial organization, most commonly a bank or quasi-bank. It demands establishing contracts that are either simple – giving flexibility in operation and decision making, especially in relation to *ex post* events from which arise agency concerns as with traditional loan contracts – or more commonly complex arrangements among many parties (Scott 2006). The transaction cost view can be stated easily:

> When parties choose [contractual] forms that themselves ensure efficient investment and trade (such as a complete mechanism), they strongly prefer that these contracts not be renegotiated. Initial contracting costs can be high in relation to contractual gains, however, and then parties choose more simple contractual forms that require negotiation to ensure efficient investment and trade.
>
> (Schwartz and Watson 2004; 26)

Simple 'cash' securitized transactions vary by jurisdiction, but usually involve the irrevocable transfer of assets to an insubstantive special purpose vehicle (SPV) to which the asset seller has no ties of ownership or control. This often allows balance sheet defeasance for the seller, but this is a matter of regulatory and accounting practice.

Funding for the asset transfer is provided by the sale of securities to third-party investors. The transaction must withstand legal claims in bankruptcy against the asset seller. Its economics must withstand taxes and duties on transfer and in most cases securities issued by the transaction SPV must provide for the dependable subordination of claims. Cash deals use known or forecast revenues for debt service; synthetic deals are imitations of cash deals using credit default swaps, with periodic swap payments used for debt service. Cash securitization tends to be associated with funding, and synthetic deals with risk management or arbitrage.

Jurisdictions where securitization is well-established such as Hong Kong, South Korea and Malaysia are not necessarily alike in needs or objectives, and except in the common law jurisdictions of Hong Kong, Malaysia and Singapore, offshore transactions have usually been used to circumvent institutional weakness or obstacles in law or regulation. One way to consider Asian securitization is to look at three groups of jurisdictions: those that in principle freely allow cash transactions, that is, Hong Kong, South Korea, Malaysia and Singapore, those for which offshore cash transactions have been completed in significant volume, and those with obstacles to almost all deals. In all the review markets except Hong Kong, new domestic or offshore issues are subject to discretionary regulatory approval, but this is in no sense an obstacle unique to structured transactions.

Beginning with Table 5.3, our appraisal tables use a 1–5 rising scale to indicate the quality or effectiveness of certain specific factors. NA means that the law makes no provision in a specified matter, based upon our qualitative analysis. These tables use terms such as security and interest generically without referring to any particular system or jurisdiction.

The elements of law typically associated with securitized transactions in advanced markets are present in our three common law jurisdictions, especially those affecting existing or future claims originated by financial intermediaries. However, certain future claims that cannot be specified in ways expected by current law may be seen as hazardous source material by investors, as is often the case with credit card receivables. In some cases insolvency law has caused uncertainty as to the integrity of securitized transactions using cash receivables.

Where enacted, modern securitization legislation in civil law jurisdictions usually allows for the creation of SPVs or trusts, which would otherwise generally not be permitted under the provisions of national civil codes. Certain jurisdictions are affected by related issues

Table 5.3 Legal framework for cash securitization

Conditions	Sale, assignment or other conveyance of assets by originators to SPV				Creation, maintenance & operation of SPV		Other
	A	B	C	D	E	F	G
Cambodia	NA	NA	NA	NA	NA	NA	NA
China	1/2	1	1	1	1	1	1
Hong Kong	5	5	4	5	5	5	5
Indonesia	2	2	2	2	1	2	2
Japan	5	4	4	4	4	4	5
South Korea	5	4	3/4	4	5	5	5
Malaysia	5	4	4	3/4	4	4	5
Philippines	2/3	2/3	1/2	2/3	2/3	1/2	2/3
Singapore	5	5	5	4	5	5	5
Taiwan	4/5	4	3/4	4	4	2/3	4
Thailand	3/4	3	3/4	3/4	2/3	4/5	2/3
Vietnam	NA	NA	NA	NA	NA	NA	NA

A. Legal framework for creating, transferring, and perfecting ownership interests.

B. Restrictions on types or terms of financial assets that can be transferred.

C. Taxation and capital gain recognition issues by the SPV.

D. Default, foreclosure or repossession of source assets.

E. Legal and regulatory impediments, e.g., SPV bankruptcy remoteness.

F. Taxation or licensing requirements.

G. Restrictions on SPVs issuing multiple tranches with varying characteristics.

of law, tax or financial market rules, rather than pure securitization provisions. This adds to contractual uncertainty and applies in the Philippines, for example. Securitization transactions also require accepted commercial precepts that are not matters of legal policy, including for example, a lack of contractual restrictions to the transfer of financial claims. These exist throughout the review markets except generally for Singapore and Hong Kong. Table 5.4 summarizes the prevailing institutional background for securitization.

Legislation or decrees adopted in recent years remain largely untested in Indonesia and the Philippines. Those introduced in South Korea, Taiwan and Thailand appear to be sound, but have not yet been subjected to credit or valuation stress of the kind experienced after 1997. More generally, simple financial markets are greatly enhanced when the availability of collateral increases, even though there may be diminishing returns in the welfare created by collateralized lending.

As a minimum, functional markets require that real property used as security be left in the possession of the borrower, and that security over movable assets does not hinder their normal commercial use, as is often the case with traditional English common law mortgage or civil law possessory pledges. Developed financial markets typically operate with a wide range of feasible collateral assets, and sophisticated financial markets similarly require commensurate techniques for taking security, for example, in using future receipts and providing for securitization.

Anomalies nonetheless exist even in advanced financial markets. De Soto asserts that property must be allowed for use as collateral so as to encourage general development, but except in relation to the registration of ownership rights he conflates those legal and other institutional issues that limit or prevent the establishment of ownership rights (de Soto's

Table 5.4 Enabling legislation for securitization

	Year of enactment or proclamation
Cambodia	None
China	Bank sector securitisation legislation under preparation 2011–12. Trial deals permitted by CBRC and CSRC 2006–7 & 2012–13
Hong Kong	Permissive legal framework, except in conflict with bankruptcy laws that arise in transactions based on uncertain future cash flows
Indonesia	Pre-1997 securitization decrees. 2002–3 securities regulator guidelines
Japan	Perfection Law 1998. Asset Liquidation Law 1998/2000. Trust Business Law (Amendment) 2004
South Korea	1998 Asset-backed Securities Law. 1999 Mortgage-backed Securities Law. 2003 Korea Housing Finance Corporation Law
Malaysia	Generally permissive common law legal framework, except for future flow transactions. Well-established legal framework for Islamic securitized issues.
Philippines	2002 Special Purpose Vehicle Act, Republic Act No. 9182, enacted 2003. 2004 Securitisation Act, Republic Act No. 9567 (largely untested). Rules and Regulations (2005) over credit rating requirements and the use of SPVs
Singapore	Permissive legal framework, except for conflicts with bankruptcy laws arising in transactions based on uncertain future cash flows. Highly supportive REIT regulatory code 2001–5; Business Trust Act 2004
Thailand	1997 securitization decree. 2003 Asset-backed Securitisation Act. 2004 Special Purpose Vehicle Act
Vietnam	None

Source: Lejot, Arner & Schou-Zibell (2008).

'capitalization process') with the use of property as collateral. We believe that capital is created or released in most cases only if both aspects of the framework are in place, supporting the formal establishment of property rights, and the use of such rights as collateral for secured transactions. To refine de Soto's analysis, for a financial system to develop beyond a basic level:

- Property rights must exist and be verifiable; and
- Property must be freely usable within the law in support of funding.

Sophisticated financial transactions and state funding mechanisms exist in certain Asian states alongside relatively informal systems for finance and money transmission, including mutual credit organizations, microfinance and *hawala*.

Despite the importance of collateral and secured transactions, this area of law involves highly varied systems and is a technical matter in the most developed jurisdictions. Perhaps as a result, secured transactions tend to receive analytical attention at relatively advanced levels and involve emerging economies with legal systems that are developed sufficiently so as to sustain basic secured transactions.

When such transactions begin to be supported by a legal and institutional system, there is considerable development potential in using the result to allow more advanced secured transactions, especially in infrastructural financing where the credit risk given to investors is based on the project, rather than its sponsors or the state. Furthermore, sophisticated transactions may provide an interim financing solution for states with incomplete or emerging legal systems, subject always to the choices of the capricious investor.

Real property

Empirical research supports the view that systems of finance based upon property are highly influential in financial and economic development. In addition to de Soto's suggestions for energizing idle capital through legal reform, Rosenberg and Birdzell argue that prior Western economic development hinged partly on freedom of commercial innovation through trial and error, which was disallowed in centralized states elsewhere (Rosenberg & Birdzell 1986: 29–30). Torstensson (1994) analyzes property rights and economic growth to substantiate the findings of Rosenberg and Birdzell, and those of North and Thomas (1973) that favour efficient organization as being instrumental to growth (see our summary in Section 1.1). Byamugisha (1999) devised a theoretical framework to analyze the effects of property finance on the whole economy, arguing that the connection from real estate finance to financial development and economic growth has five features:

- Land tenure security and investment incentives;
- Land title, collateral and credit;
- Land liquidity, deposit mobilization and investment;
- Markets for land, transactions and efficiency; and
- Labour mobility and efficiency.

All must function effectively to facilitate real estate finance, and each demands the existence of an appropriate legal infrastructure. Given the significance of real estate finance for economic development, we might look to economies where the secondary refinancing of mortgage lending is prominent. Jaffee and Renaud (1996) analyzed factors hindering the development of home loan markets in the transition economies of Central and Eastern Europe, showing banks reluctant to make mortgage loans for house purchases because of the scale of risks they perceived in such lending: that is, the extent of credit, interest rate basis and liquidity risks. This is taken more assertively to suggest that a secondary mortgage market may help solve these problems by allowing banks to manage their loan books to meet preferences over risk concentration and duration.

A third study argues that successful land and real estate reforms must be 'comprehensive in design, even if implementation is phased in over time' (Galal & Razzaz 2001: 31). It contends that such reforms include three elements:

- Property rights, information, contracting and enforcement. Institutional reforms that better define property rights, reduce information asymmetries and improve contract performance;
- Finance and risk management. Capital market reforms making mortgage finance available at reasonable costs, especially for the poor; and
- Market regulation and fiscal policy. Reforms that reduce or eliminate distortions in the prices of goods and services, the production of which is enabled by land and real estate assets.

These conclusions tie effective mortgage markets to the broader concept of using real estate finance to encourage all aspects of financial and economic development. Jaffee and Renaud suggest that secondary mortgage markets confer two main benefits: to allow lenders to shed risks associated with holding mortgages, and in creating standards for credit evaluation and collateral procedures that lead to greater efficiency in new mortgage lending. They suggest that governments adopt catalytic policies in developing secondary mortgage market systems and institutions, which is the path followed by certain developed countries and several Asian jurisdictions. We should note that most of these prescriptions assign a welfare value to home ownership that may not be shared in all societies, whether affluent or otherwise and regardless of their legal systems.

Movable assets

Wide disparities exist in secured transactions law in developed economies, and are often central to distinctions between common and civil law traditions (Dahan 2000). As a result, there exist no internationally agreed standards or principles to govern secured financing (Goswami & Sharif 2000). Creating effective provisions for these transactions demands a mastery of many aspects of a legal system, including laws of property, obligations, insolvency and civil procedure, and of administrative procedures such as charge registration and enforcement. Nonetheless, research shows that the sound development of legal infrastructure underlies functioning collateral-based credit provision, and that inadequacies in such infrastructures hinder financial and economic development (Goswami & Sharif 2000).

A generic collateral and credit law devised by the BIS includes two main elements (BIS 2006). First are credit laws to govern commercial creditor–debtor relationships. These may be established by common law, contract law, civil codes or through specific legislation, for example, in usury laws, banking law or creditor protection laws. Second are pledges and collateral laws helping to create and enforce rights in collateral security, preferably through legislation rather than contract or common law. These establish priority rankings among secured and unsecured claims upon default or insolvency, requiring legislation of a specific or general application. Examples include:

- US Uniform Commercial Code (UCC) Article 9;
- EU Directive 2002/47/EC on financial collateral arrangements;
- OHADA (Organisation pour l'Harmonisation en Afrique du Droit des Affaires) Uniform Law on Security Rights 1997;
- EBRD (European Bank for Reconstruction and Development) Model Law on Secured Transactions 1997;
- United Nations Commission on International Trade Law (UNCITRAL) Legislative Guide on Secured Transactions;
- Cape Town Convention on International Interests in Mobile Equipment; and
- West African Economic and Monetary Union Regulation 15/2002/CM/UEMOA Regarding Payment Systems in the Member States.

The EBRD Model Law is one of the few international standards for secured transactions to have been applied successfully in collateral law reform, drawing upon the EBRD core principles and glossary (Simpson & Menze 2000). The ADB helped create new secured transaction frameworks, and the World Bank has addressed these issues in relation to insolvency. Other efforts have been made by the International Institute for the Unification of Private Law (UNIDROIT 1988; 2001) and in North America (ALI 1997), Asia (de la Peña, Fleisig & Wellons 2000) and Europe. Important harmonization efforts were made in respect of US UCC Article 9 and Canada's Personal Property Security Acts, both frameworks used as models in Asia. Section 5.4.6 looks at these matters as they now stand in the region.

Collateral in Asia

We have seen that effective provisions for secured lending can encourage the provision of credit and assist in the development of domestic financial markets. At the same time, any system involving widespread use of collateral may risk encouraging a monopolistic banking sector. Using secured lending as a proxy for informed corporate risk appraisal is arguably inefficient to the economy as a whole in that it encourages wasteful credit risk substitution and may be oppressive to trade creditors.

This has often been the position in Asia. Reliance by lenders on private and corporate real estate collateral in granting corporate credit may have contributed to the scale and suddenness of the 1997 financial crisis. Following the collapse of regional asset prices, this provoked a severe credit squeeze that affected otherwise healthy borrowers even in states least affected by the general drop in confidence. Collateral must be available as security to release the flow of capital but not so unreasonably as to protect the oppressive creditor and inefficient lender. These concerns prompt a series of questions applicable to any jurisdiction:

- To what extent is commercial secured lending or title finance possible?
- What legal provisions exist for home mortgages?
- What provisions are made for the transfer of secured claims?
- What are the principal effects of related legal reforms – for example, in civil jurisdictions that choose to enact wholesale securitization legislation?
- What is the position of secured claims vis-à-vis statutory priority – for example, in government or employee creditor claims?
- Is there simplicity of mortgage execution, perfection, notification, registration and enforcement?

Collateral and creditor rights

Table 5.5 synthesizes an analysis of these issues in the economies addressed by this study using our 1–5 scale. Split scores such as 2/3 represent an intermediate appraisal between two given levels. As with similar tables in this chapter, these are intended to reflect degrees of uncertainty as to commercial outcomes.

Granting security and making it effective is treated here as a form of property right, regardless of the nature of the legal system. Any appraisal will question how the law links the granting of security to the rights of general creditors in both normal and distressed circumstances. Table 5.5 shows how each system supports, undermines or confuses all aspects of secured transactions. No account is taken of informal systems even if they are commercially entrenched, but we acknowledge informal legal provisions peculiar to certain jurisdictions, for example in the Philippines and Taiwan, as we shall see in Tables 5.6 and 5.7. The law will ideally allow the cost-effective creation of security without affecting the debtor's day-to-day use of its collateral. It will be public, transparent, function without discrimination and be enforceable in ways compatible with declared public policy, especially in relation to insolvency, receivership and rearrangements following corporate distress.

We can see the effectiveness of these legal and administrative frameworks in several elements, not all of which are present in our sample. These include the ease and cost of creating reliable security interests, mechanisms for such interests to be disclosed, the costs and risks associated with enforcing charges, the relationship of security and collateral with insolvency

Table 5.5 Legal framework for creditor rights

	Enforcement of unsecured rights	Security interest Legislation	Registration and disclosure of secured rights	Enforcement of secured rights
Cambodia	1	1*	1*	1
China	2	2	2	2
Hong Kong	5	4	4	5
Indonesia	1	2	1/2	1
Japan	4	4	5	5
South Korea	3	1/2	1/2	2/3
Malaysia	5	4	4	5
Philippines	2	2/3	2/3	2
Singapore	5	4	4	5
Taiwan	3	4	3	3/4
Thailand	2	1/2	2	2
Vietnam	1	1	1	1

* When enacted, Cambodia's secured transactions law and other new provisions are expected to allow scores of 4.

and receivership practice, and the operation of creditor protection and stays to judicial enforcement. These are all contained in Table 5.5.

Civil and common law take different traditional approaches to security interests, so that reforms need to be sensitive to an existing contractual and legal setting. While the EBRD Model Law on Secured Transactions was intended to be adopted by any jurisdiction, the presence of developed legal systems in our sample makes any single benchmark impractical. A model might have value in other developing jurisdictions. Recent reforms elsewhere appear effective in supporting transaction creation, but are largely untested in prolonged economic stress. This applies to Indonesia, South Korea and Thailand, and to Cambodia's 2007 Secured Transactions Law and the registry for its implementation. In each case a further concern may arise for the integrity of new laws in relation to existing and succeeding legislation, given that measures are often introduced progressively. Legislation introduced in China since 2003 has required the rewriting of laws created in earlier days of reform. China's 2007 Property Law may come to be seen as having considerable impact on commercial activity (Chen 2010).

Asia's legal provisions for secured credit transactions were in 1997 as outdated and inefficient as its insolvency laws, but have since been subjected to far less reform. Attention after the recovery began in 1999 was directed to reforming corporate reorganization procedures and other features of insolvency law, even though such laws cannot work efficiently when secured creditors find it difficult to enforce rights in bankruptcy, and such delays had long been common (ADB 2000: 10–11, 70–5). Credit creation is similarly affected when either valid collateral must be held in possession by a secured creditor or limits exist as to the permissible categories of assets that may be used as collateral. These problems were also endemic before the Asian crisis (Vassiliou 2006: 21).

Real property

Each jurisdiction provides for real property to be used as collateral, but there is considerable divergence as how best to resolve many issues. These include the ease and efficiency with which charges or liens are created; requirements for registration and its usefulness to third parties; whether a mortgagor retains title to collateral while the advance that the charge secures is outstanding; and how secured creditors may enforce collateral rights. Differences also exist in the treatment of collateral arising from laws allowing ownership of real property by foreign interests.

The summary contained in Table 5.6 does not address the distribution of property rights which is a focus of de Soto's work on the relationship between state governance, property rights, and economic outcomes.

Table 5.6 Claims over real property

Cambodia	Mortgages are permitted over real property but enforcement of secured claims is problematic. Registration is efficient and effective. Foreign creditor may take a charge over but not own land.
China	Property Rights Law of the People's Republic of China 2007 covers both real property and movable assets, and for the first time in the PRC establishes rights in respect of both state and non-state interests. The law makes most real property ownership rights contingent upon registration (Art. 9–22). Art. 170–240 establish conditions for the granting of security interests by a property owner, including the right to mortgage real property and specified movable assets, and the right to pledge other assets, including certain defined intangibles. The creation of registry facilities throughout China will be a considerable task. Land may not be mortgaged, but mortgages over land-use rights are permitted. Transactions involving mortgages to be held by foreign entities are subject to prior approval and registration with the State Administration of Foreign Exchange (SAFE).
Indonesia	Security interests may be taken in land, but it may be difficult for creditors to enforce security interests. The process is inefficient; enforcement can take many years. Auction fees and taxes are high, and in practice, recourse to the courts is almost always necessary. Official registers are maintained manually causing delays for potential lenders searching for title or prior claims. Security rights may be impaired by the creation of parent company guarantees in respect of like debts.
Japan	Civil Code allows creation of mortgages over real property as well as fixtures and items attached to the mortgaged property (Art. 177). Recording is not required, but is necessary to determine priority (Art. 177). Mortgages may also be assigned to another creditor, but the principal debtor must provide consent or otherwise receive notice in order to foreclose (Art. 376, 377). Foreign ownership of land is permitted but must be reported to the Ministry of Finance and may be subject to approval that is influenced by transnational reciprocity.
South Korea	Most real estate rights must be registered. However, there are important exceptions, as for property acquired through inheritance or pursuant to a judgment auction.
Philippines	Real property may be mortgaged under provisions of the Civil Code. While both registration and notarization are necessary for creditor protection, the requirements are set out in a mix of statute and presidential decree. Ownership is retained by the mortgagor while a charge is outstanding. Delays in foreclosure can occur because the secured party must use the courts in the absence of any contractual agreement for extrajudicial foreclosure, so that mortgage contracts now explicitly address this problem. Contractual antichrists was a common form of commercial pledge, but it is becoming increasingly less used. Unless stated by agreement, mortgages over land will embrace subsequent buildings or improvements to the land, and may gain inadvertent priority over other subsequent charges. Foreign creditors may become mortgagees of land but not buildings, and may subsequently not take possession of land.

(Continued)

Table 5.6 (Continued)

Taiwan	Civil Code allows mortgages to be created over defined classes of real property and for possessory security or attachments. It has been customary for lenders to register a 'comprehensive mortgage' for an undefined amount prior to approving loans (practice elsewhere is to disburse funds subject to security conditions) but the practice struck down by the courts and reforms are pending. In addition, the right of 'dien' is allowed as a form of possessory pledge similar to a leasehold interest, created effectively over assets not specified in law. Registration in all cases is mandatory and efficient. Failure to register invalidates the charge. There is uncertainty as to whether notice or consent is required of a secured creditor for the creation of a subsequent mortgage. Foreign creditors are restricted as to the types of real property over which they may hold security interests.
Thailand	Real property may be mortgaged and registration is necessary to protect the secured creditor's rights, but foreclosure cannot occur unless loan interest or charges have been outstanding for five years, contributing to an inefficient enforcement process that can extend over many years. Separate charges are necessary in respect of plant or equipment contained in a mortgaged property, and may be subject to official inspection.
Vietnam	The 1992 constitution adopted the general recognition of private property rights but land ownership continues to be vested solely in the state. Nonetheless, rights of land use are clear and may be mortgaged under the Land Law of 1993.
Hong Kong, Malaysia & Singapore	All allow for charges over land, which must be registered to be effective in law. Hong Kong and Singapore also provide for mortgages to be taken over land, but in Hong Kong (since 1984) the mortgage must be created by a legal charge. Malaysian courts will generally recognize a charge that is executed but not yet registered. Each jurisdiction allows for the appointment of a receiver to protect a creditor's interest, and in each case a high level of predictability and efficiency exists as to the creditor's ability to enforce claims. Hong Kong land ownership is (with one unusual exception) held by the territory's government but this does not materially affect rights of land use nor the creation of security for finance. Land registration laws differ between Peninsular and East Malaysia. The taking of land and movable assets owned by Labuan companies as collateral is governed largely by the Offshore Companies Act 1990.

Sources: Authors' records; Blakemore & Mitsuki (2010: 16.01); Nurmansyah, Bakker, Rees & Adams (2006: 80); Ongkiko, Laforteza, Franciso & Canilao (2006: 135).

Movables and unencumbered property

The treatment of secured rights over movable property is still more varied. No jurisdiction has a comprehensive regime similar to the US code's Article 9, but the English-style law systems of Hong Kong, Malaysia and Singapore work effectively, although with certain specific omissions. Table 5.7 shows that delays and inefficiencies are common in the enforcement of secured rights. Limits to the assets that may be used as collateral is problematic almost everywhere in the region, including bars to taking security interests in chattel paper or accounts receivable, and a lack of provisions for charges over future property or the use of security to collateralize future loans.

5.5 Insolvency

At the formative stage of economic development, the risk and high incidence of defaults by debtors often prevent the efficient deployment of funds for investment. A framework of law

Table 5.7 Claims over movable assets

Cambodia	The Secured Transactions Law 2007 provides a modern legal framework for security, including support through an electronic registration system. However, enforcement is currently less certain, and the commercial effectiveness of the law may be coloured by other current omissions in law.
China	Property Rights Law of the People's Republic of China 2007 provides (Arts. 179–202) for the creation of mortgages over specified movable assets. Such mortgages will take effect only upon registration. Mortgages may not be granted over future property. Secured creditors must register their claims to protect all such non-possessory rights and may also protect themselves through possession in the form of a pledge. As with real property, foreign entities seeking security over movable property must comply with SAFE approval and registration procedures. The treatment of security interests in intangible assets such as bank accounts or receivables is less straightforward. Regulations have been issued allowing mortgages over such assets, but the effectiveness of these new forms of collateral is largely untested. Enforcement of unsecured claims can sometimes be resisted at local level; there have been reported instances in which banks and their clients have colluded to hide assets from the court.
Indonesia	Fiduciary Security Law provides that a debtor may transfer title in goods to a creditor and retain possession of the goods in the absence of any default. Pledges are also permitted. A fiduciary assignment may be taken for security purposes over intangible property and receivables. Enforcement of charges over movable property requires recourse to the courts, and both auction fees and taxes are punitive. Secured creditors seeking foreclosure against collateral must follow substantially the same court proceedings as unsecured creditors.
Japan	Movable assets may be 'mortgaged' under a title transfer system where legal title is transferred to the creditor and restored to the debtor following repayment.
South Korea	Rights in personal property may only be protected by possession. South Korean law does not recognize purchase money security interests or floating liens.
Philippines	Chattel mortgages and pledges are permitted over movable property and must be recorded. Philippine law does not recognize chattel mortgages over future property, but the courts have created exceptions for interests in inventories of raw materials, goods in process, and finished goods. Future obligations cannot be secured by chattel mortgages.
Taiwan	Non-possessory charges are possible under the Chattel Secured Transaction Act and by separate laws regarding ships and aircraft. Registration is mandatory in each case in order to protect priority. Enforcement is usually procedural and not judicially uncertain.
Thailand	Only certain forms of movable property may be mortgaged, including large ships, boats, floating houses, beasts of burden, and classes of machinery. Creditors holding rights of retention are also recognized as secured creditors. Other types of property may be pledged. Enforcement of secured rights requires either a court judgment or a public auction. Enforcement is slow and costly. Fixed and floating charges are not permitted at present, but would be allowed under draft secured transactions law. The enforcement of unsecured debts in Thailand can extend for many years.
Vietnam	Private property rights are constitutionally recognized and charges over movables permitted by the civil code. Improvements were made to Vietnam's secured transaction framework in 2005 amendments to the civil code, which took effect in January 2006. Further decrees are expected to assist with the implementation of these changes. A National Registration Agency for Secured Transactions has been established, with offices in Hanoi, Ho Chi Minh City, and Da Nang. However, enforcement of security interests remains difficult. Unless bankruptcy proceedings have been commenced, a court order is not necessary for the enforcement of a secured transaction.

(Continued)

Table 5.7 (Continued)

Hong Kong, Malaysia & Singapore	The laws in all three jurisdictions provide a variety of security over movable property (both tangible and intangible), including charges, liens, and pledges. Retention of title is also permitted. Security may be taken over future property. Fixed charges may be taken over tangible assets and floating charges may be taken over classes of variable assets such as inventory or book debts. The taking of fixed charges over book debts by secured creditors is more restrictive (guided by recent English case law). These English-origin systems require the registration of many types of charges, including charges over book debts and floating charges over the general undertaking of a company, but statutory rules are less clear and comprehensive than US UCC Art. 9. Usual practice in these three jurisdictions is for a debenture to provide a secured financial creditor with contractual remedies upon default, allowing appointment of a receiver or special manager. All have efficient debt collection procedures for unsecured creditors.

Sources: Authors' records; Bennett (2009: 464); Nurmansyah, Bakker, Rees & Adams (2006).

providing both for company incorporation and the orderly resolution of proceedings for recovery and insolvency is therefore crucial to development.

No commercial sector can function effectively without mechanisms to recognize and govern the exit of insolvent participants. The financial sector will abstain from lending to many companies and individuals if banks and consumer credit providers are uncertain of their ranking as secured creditors in a liquidation of their debtors, or whether a reliable means is available for the enforcement of properly constituted security. The general objectives of a system of corporate insolvency have been described as the reduction of uncertainty, promotion of efficiency, and fair and equitable treatment for all participants (BIS 2002). A functioning insolvency regime can thus help reduce and simplify the risks associated with lending, and the potential interest costs. If this is accurate, long-run credit availability and capital investment will increase, although we make no mention of the quality of the resulting investment (IMF 1999).

Functioning insolvency procedures are central to the legal and institutional environment of a market economy, regardless of whether public policy intends the law to favour debtors (as generally in the US), or creditors (as generally in jurisdictions influenced by German commercial law). Effective insolvency laws provide the means for the identification of uncompetitive participants and perhaps also for their controlled exit. It provides a penalty for the least competitive as well as a potential solution to the subsequent reallocation of resources. This view stresses the retroactive character of insolvency law, but also contains a preventive element by creating performance incentives for uncompetitive parties such that they avoid entering formal administration on behalf of creditors.

Several international organizations have assisted the development of standards for modern insolvency law and related systems. Many have focused on norms and standards for cross-border insolvency cases, such as the UNCITRAL Model Law on Cross-Border Insolvency (UNCITRAL 1997) and the EU Insolvency Regulation (EU 2000). A working group chaired by IMF lawyers created detailed principles for the development of workable, modern insolvency legislation (IMF 1999). While there is no international standard for insolvency law, the World Bank and UNCITRAL have worked for some years to develop a usable benchmark. The World Bank's Principles and Guidelines for Effective Insolvency and Creditor Rights Systems appeared in 2001 (World Bank 2001), since when revisions have taken account of national insolvency assessments conducted under the joint

IMF–World Bank Reports on Observance of Standards and Codes (ROSC) initiative. UNCITRAL issued a Legislative Guide on Insolvency Law (UNCITRAL 2005), a combination of model provisions and recommendations that builds upon the work of other international organizations including the ADB.

The World Bank sets nine objectives for effective corporate insolvency (World Bank 2001: 24):

- Integrate with broader national legal and commercial systems;
- Maximize the value of a firm's assets by providing an option to reorganize;
- Strike a careful balance between liquidation and reorganization;
- Provide for equitable treatment of similarly situated creditors, including foreign and domestic creditors;
- Provide for the timely, efficient and impartial resolution of insolvencies;
- Prevent the premature dismemberment of a debtor's assets by individual creditors seeking quick judgments;
- Provide a transparent procedure that contains incentives for gathering and dispensing information;
- Recognize existing creditor rights and respect the priority of claims with a predictable and established process; and
- Establish a framework for cross-border insolvencies, with recognition of foreign proceedings.

The principles that support these objectives cover five main areas:

- Principles 1–5. Legal framework for creditor rights. This section addresses collateral and secured transactions only in the context of insolvency.
- 6–16. Legal framework for corporate insolvency.
- 17–24. Corporate rehabilitation
- 25–26. Informal workouts and restructuring.
- 27–35. Institutional and regulatory frameworks for implementation of the insolvency system.

UNCITRAL's guide has two parts (UNCITRAL 2003), dealing with the design of the objectives and structure of an insolvency law, and core insolvency law provisions. It will be impossible to identify an international consensus in this area until the World Bank principles and final UNCITRAL guide are integrated and approved.

Insolvency and debtor–creditor rights

Debtor–creditor laws include systems for collecting debts, and insolvency systems for terminating the collection of unpaid debts. Collection systems include secured transactions, using movable property as collateral; mortgages, using fixed property as collateral, and unsecured lending, a system that employs no property or other rights over collateral. Banking practice in civil law jurisdictions often treats guarantees as providing security, which is not usual in common law systems regardless of any effect on mitigating credit risk. One view of the interaction between secured lending and insolvency law sees each as addressing distinct problems with separate solutions. A secured lending system determines how lenders are repaid, whereas an insolvency system establishes the appropriate treatment for defaulting borrowers.

Secured transactions and insolvency also overlap, and so the two segments of law must be compatible; neither can substitute for the other. Reforms of debtor–creditor laws must embrace secured lending and insolvency as well as other related areas of law. The need for drafting integration is far more widely accepted in Asia now than prior to the 1997–98 financial crisis. Regardless of underlying preferences in insolvency law, Asian economies are likely to gain by improving their respective laws on secured lending. This relies on the premise that access to credit and the terms on which it becomes available will improve for the borrower as the quality of collateral taking is raised, which as we have seen is not universally accepted. Effective secured transactions systems that allow for movable property to be used as collateral may allow distressed firms to gain access to credit and so avoid the final resort of insolvency. In such conditions, creditors may anticipate repayment without necessarily initiating insolvency.

All security interests must be properly publicized, whether through a public register or a declaration attached to a mortgaged property. This can be a charming practice that comes from traditions in maritime law, which often required a deed of charge to be displayed on the mast of a vessel, and it is common for commercial aircraft to have a metal plaque attached to a cabin wall, stating that the plane is subject to a mortgage. Publication puts existing and potential creditors on notice that a debtor has fewer unencumbered assets over which potential lenders might obtain meaningful interests. It may also disclose the order of priority for the distribution of assets if a debtor becomes insolvent. Registration is far more effective than systems that rely on possession as security since possession limits the economic use of the debtor's asset. Efficient enforcement of security interests is also essential and helps promote informal and judicial workouts, and can minimize the need for judicial involvement.

The essential need in the interaction between secured transactions and insolvency is for insolvency law to respect prior rights of secured creditors. If the law poses unequal or unfair threats to secured lending, banks will increase charges or restrict access to credit, especially to smaller borrowers. If a company has granted charges to a creditor in exchange for an identifiable value in credit then such charges ought not to be voided by any subsequent insolvency proceedings. Creditors should also be allowed to obtain collateral for unsecured claims, providing such transactions are completed before the commencement of any insolvency proceedings. The law may provide for the avoidance of security taken fraudulently or in materially unfair transactions. Interests obtained before insolvency proceedings begin should continue in post-petition proceeds, while post-petition grants of security should be permitted. Last, priorities in insolvency should generally be abolished. Most Asian economies would benefit from insolvency laws respecting the existing rights of secured creditors. However, in allowing exceptions and balancing the needs of secured transactions and insolvency, policymakers must first decide which approach is most appropriate.

Creditor rights and insolvency in Asia

Central banks and other financial regulators in these jurisdictions have encouraged informal out-of-court workout practices for multiple financial creditor cases similar to the well-established London Rules promoted in the 1970s by the Bank of England as a quick and consensual alternative to formal insolvency proceedings. The appraisals given in Table 5.8 take account of extra-legal guidance for collaborative multicreditor practice in Hong Kong, Indonesia, Malaysia and Thailand. This system presumes that financial creditors collaborate to block a single creditor advancing its position in ways that might provoke premature

Table 5.8 Development of effective insolvency systems

	Legal framework for corporate insolvency	Corporate insolvency implementation	Judicial decision-making and enforcement	Effective insolvency practitioners	Compatibility of creditor rights & insolvency systems
Cambodia	NA	NA	1	1	NA
China	2/3	1	1	1/2	1/2
Hong Kong	4	5	5	5	4/5
Indonesia	2/3	1	1	1/2	1/2
Japan	4	5	4	3	4/5
South Korea	4	3/4	3	3/4	3/4
Malaysia	4	4	4	4	3/4
Philippines	2/3	2/3	2	2/3	1/2
Singapore	4/5	5	5	5	4/5
Taiwan	3	3	3	3	3/4
Thailand	3	2/3	2/3	2/3	1/2
Vietnam	1/2	1/2	1	1	1/2

liquidation. Table 5.8 also gives our qualitative assessment of the compatibility of creditor rights and insolvency law.

Similar workout procedures were applied after the Asian financial crisis more frequently than formal reorganizations but with inconsistent results. Informal practice has tended to be successful where the courts have stood ready to support a consensus reached among creditors and debtors, and where debtors or their controlling owners have been unable to challenge the enforcement of foreign judgments. Most jurisdictions also set up public administrative agencies to assist with the restructuring of domestic financial intermediaries and the disposal of NPLs. Systems and practice are well-established and generally sophisticated in both Hong Kong and Singapore, but legislative reform has consistently lagged market practice and the willingness of the courts to intervene creatively in cases of corporate distress.

Pre-1997 weaknesses

Only Singapore had a pre-crisis insolvency regime adequate to deal with a high number of corporate failures. Other jurisdictions were hampered by antiquated or inadequate laws and procedures, many of which dated from colonial times. None maintained an effective formal corporate rescue procedure.

Hong Kong and Malaysian corporate insolvency procedures were modelled on mid-twentieth century English law. Thai law dating from 1940 was influenced by English personal bankruptcy laws, while Indonesian law was mainly Dutch in origin and dated from the late nineteenth century. South Korea's insolvency regime drew on 1920s and 1950s Japanese law, which itself derived from German and US laws and practice. Pre-1997 Philippines insolvency law dated from cumbersome Spanish procedures adopted in 1909 and from 1970s decrees that gave the Securities and Exchange Commission (SEC) limited authority over corporate rehabilitation. These measures were seldom used. Taiwan's laws were also derived from Japan's laws and then to a lesser extent from US law with the last pre-1997 amendments dating from the early 1980s, with most of the law on corporate insolvency contained in company law statutes. China's insolvency laws are more recent, with bankruptcy provisions for SOEs enacted in 1986 and those for NSEs in 1991. Vietnam's laws dated from 1995. All these regimes used liquidation-based procedures with the exception of Singapore. It is apparent that insolvency laws were widely ignored.

Hong Kong, Malaysia and Singapore share a structure of detailed liquidation or winding-up procedures and an abbreviated scheme of arrangement procedure for use in corporate rescue. These procedures are the region's most efficient, although in need of modernization, but the scheme of arrangement procedure is cumbersome and often costly. Hong Kong and Malaysia do not provide for an automatic stay on creditor claims in the absence of a winding-up order, while Singapore operates a stay only on unsecured creditors. In no case are there mechanisms to force recalcitrant secured creditors to cooperate constructively in a corporate rescue or reorganization. The result is that the procedure was rarely used before 1997–98, and far more often in Singapore than Hong Kong or Malaysia. Singapore also introduced judicial management procedures in 1987. These may be initiated either by a debtor company or its creditors and provide for an automatic stay of bankruptcy while a court-appointed manager assumes responsibility for the company and the preparation of reorganization plans for creditor approval (Lee 2003).

Post 1-1 2000 reforms

Two waves of reform took place after the crisis, first to insolvency laws in Indonesia, South Korea, Malaysia, the Philippines, Taiwan and Thailand, and later in Vietnam in 2004 and China in 2006. Reform is ongoing or pending in Cambodia, Hong Kong and Singapore. Thailand was severely affected by the 1997–98 crisis. Additions were made to the Bankruptcy Act in 1998 to facilitate corporate rescues, providing for the appointment of a bankruptcy planner to manage a debtor company and prepare plans of reorganization. Thailand also established a bankruptcy court with exclusive jurisdiction for larger corporate cases. Indonesia's Bankruptcy Ordinance was amended in 1998 by decree, creating a commercial court to hear bankruptcy cases, but its early life was 'beset by concerns of corruption and inconsistent application of the Bankruptcy Act' and '[t]he Indonesian Corruption Watch reports of corruption in the legal system is staggering' (Vassiliou 2003: 6–7). Further amendments were enacted in 2005.

South Korea made among the most significant changes to its formal insolvency laws, partly since high corporate sector leverage demanded immediate attention after the post-crisis withdrawal of credit. South Korea agreed with the IMF to amend its tripartite insolvency legislation covering liquidation, composition and reorganization. US bankruptcy law influenced the result, which included providing for creditor and management representation in composition proceedings and reorganizations, respectively. The time limit for reorganizations was halved to ten years. Amendments made in 2000–1 added a formal but non-judicial workout accord that included foreign creditors in reorganizations, and a Debtors Rehabilitation and Bankruptcy Act came into effect in 2006 to consolidate the three parallel insolvency laws. This further expedited corporate rescues, expanded the reorganization system and abolished archaic rules for workouts.

Modest changes to Philippine law were made in 2000, transferring authority for rehabilitation and suspension of payment cases from the SEC to the courts. Suspension of payment cases and corporate rehabilitation then became more common, but delays tended to block post-petition financing. A Corporate Recovery Act became law in 2010 after years of debate and is the first systemic statutory approach to insolvency. Reform of Taiwan's Company Law in 2001 cut the duration of the reorganization process and required that companies 'be capable of being revived through reorganisation' (Tsai, Yuan & Liu 2006: 156). Proposals to consolidate the bankruptcy and reorganization laws into a single Corporate Reorganization and Bankruptcy Act have been inconclusive since 2005.

China's enterprise insolvency law took effect in June 2007 and unifies a patchwork of existing bankruptcy laws, decrees and judicial interpretations. This improves both the liquidation and corporate rescue processes, introducing an office of the professional administrator and a detailed corporate rescue process that draws heavily on Chapter 11 of the US Bankruptcy Code. These procedures allow for reorganizations led either by an administrator or a debtor-in-possession under the supervision of the administrator. One controversy in the drafting process was whether SOEs should be made subject to the new law, and the act lessens the scope of State Council regulations in the bankruptcy of SOEs.

Vietnam's new Bankruptcy Law was enacted in 2005. This is a significant reform, and abolished the requirement that a debtor must exhaust 'all financial measures' to become eligible for bankruptcy relief, but may not be fully integrated with subsequent reforms in the 2005 Law on Enterprises and 2006 Investment Law. Cambodia enacted an insolvency law in 2007 to replace earlier incomplete rules.

Attempts at Hong Kong insolvency law reform pre-date the 1997 financial crisis. In 1996 the Hong Kong Law Reform Commission set out the framework for a new regime by which a qualified 'provisional supervisor' would take control of the company and be responsible for drafting proposals for creditor agreement. The first draft bill was gazetted in 2000, but was flawed by a provision for salaries to be paid in full or sufficient funds placed in trust for the purpose (Smart & Booth 2001). In advance of any legislative conclusion, the courts have creatively provided for reorganization in limited circumstances.

Singapore's insolvency regime is the most comprehensive and includes a scheme of arrangement provisions that have proven more popular than judicial management. A stay on unsecured creditor action gives a debtor time to propose such a scheme. The debtor can retain possession of assets and equipment, and avoid damaging publicity. As with Hong Kong and Malaysia, a weakness of Singapore's model is the split of corporate insolvency in company law and personal insolvency in bankruptcy law.

Legal insolvency reform is usually protracted. The practical needs of the 1997–98 crisis led to other commercial efforts beginning to rescue firms whose businesses could create value for creditors or other stakeholders. This produced two types of reform, the first of which were non-judicial workouts based on the London Approach, which surfaced in the Bangkok Approach, Malaysia's Corporate Debt Restructuring Committee (CDRC), the Hong Kong Approach, the Jakarta Initiative and the Workout Accord in South Korea. In contrast to the general experience in Europe, this semi-formal approach has been successful in cases where the parties involved are overwhelmingly of a single domicile, but only modestly helpful in most cross-border multicreditor restructurings. This approach and similar state-approved schemes have become complicated in the last decade by lenders engaging increasingly in credit risk transfer, from simple loan sales to the buying and selling of quasi-insurance protection through credit derivatives. These are important topics in Sections 8.1 and 8.3.

The second alternative established administrative AMCs as state-sponsored agencies to assist with the restructuring and disposal of bank NPLs. These included the Indonesian Bank Restructuring Agency (IBRA), Malaysia's Pengurusan Danaharta Nasional Bhd (Danaharta) and the Thai Asset Management Company (TAMC).

Danaharta had strong powers of enforcement and its results are viewed as important. Some AMCs concluded their work and were later closed. IBRA became substantial and was the largest national landowner before its dissolution in 2004 (Vassiliou 2006: 35). Its results were less effective than other AMCs due to its taking over distressed assets at balance sheet cost rather than market value, even though the payments made to the transferor banks were not necessarily of the same order. The forerunners to these agencies were the US Resolution Trust Corporation, which in 1989–95 acted as a conduit to acquire and recycle the financial assets of collapsed mortgage lenders, and the Korea Asset Management Company (KAMCO), formed in 1962.

China established AMCs to deal with NPLs accumulated by the four largest state commercial banks. China Xinda Asset Management Company (Cinda) was first in 1999 for the CCB and China Development Bank, followed by the China Huarong Asset Management Corporation for Industrial and Commercial Bank of China, Dongfang Asset Management Company (Oriental) for Bank of China, and China Great Wall Asset Management Company for Agricultural Bank of China. Regional AMCs were also established including the important Guangdong Guangye Asset Management Company.

Taiwan also successfully used the AMC model from 2001 and Vietnam established AMCs as a preliminary to banking sector reforms agreed with the WTO. Hanoi's finance ministry also created the Debts and Assets Trading Company to assist in commercializing state sector industry.

Creditor rights and insolvency

Effective regimes for insolvency go hand-in-hand with those for secured transactions, but this conjunction is generally weak in the region. Insolvency reform would benefit from improvements to secured transactions systems, for the toughest test of secured transactions and the rights of secured creditors is often within insolvency cases. The English system of company law adapted in Hong Kong, Malaysia and Singapore gives predictability to the rights of secured creditors, which customarily act outside a liquidation, are not subject to a general stay against creditors, and participate in informal schemes of arrangement only by consent. Only in judicial management cases in Singapore are secured creditors made subject to a general stay.

China, Indonesia, the Philippines and Vietnam adopt the US approach, by which secured creditors are subject to an automatic stay in both liquidations and reorganizations. South Korea, Singapore and Thailand make secured creditors subject to a moratorium in reorganizations but not in liquidations or compositions. Last, secured creditors of companies in Taiwan may act unilaterally outside both bankruptcy and reorganization. In jurisdictions where secured creditors are subject to an automatic stay, the courts have rarely applied principles of adequate protection when those creditors seek to be exempt. The Philippines system takes far less account of secured creditors in allowing reorganization plans, so that secured creditors have been known to rank with unsecured creditors.

5.6   Contract enforcement and dispute resolution

The most critical neglect in the region concerns enforcement and implementation, with the partial exceptions of Hong Kong and Singapore. This accords with an observation made of the law and finance school, that:

> The major function attributed to law is that it empowers creditors to enforce their contracts.... There is, however, scant attention paid to understanding the channel through

which changes in legal institutions get transmitted to the economy. How do improvements of creditor rights get transmitted to the economy? Which laws matter more? Do laws affect all market participants in the same manner? A good and thorough understanding of these questions is essential if one has to incorporate creditor rights into broader discussions on policy.

(Haselmann, Pistor & Vig 2010: 549–50)

This may suggest that the form or substance of law matters less than its enforcement. Half a century ago, Ronald Coase described the importance of the delineation and enforcement of commercial contracts, unusually using observations of industrial practice (Coase 1960). In a setting of imperfect markets with real transaction costs, such as the expense of enforcement, parties will tend to seek efficient results through bargaining rather than resort to law. This leaves a systemic gap, in that contracting cannot of itself eliminate market imperfections nor lead to stable long-term outcomes but only produce compensatory solutions to these problems.

The enforcement of contracts requires a system of governance to produce, apply and police effective solutions. Enforcement of contracts is not synonymous with the existence of the rule of law, but is one component of such a system. The rule of law is not a precondition for a market economy despite being frequently taken to be an important factor in economic growth and conducive to financial market development. Yet a governance system that enforces contracts and resolves commercial disputes in a credible and predictable manner is essential in a basic market economy, as well as allowing financial markets to develop beyond the simplest instantaneous transactions. This is important for institutional concerns such as the enforcement of financial contracts, insolvency and collateral systems, and dispute resolution procedures. Mechanisms for contractual enforcement and resolving commercial disputes may be considered more important than specific laws.

Our appraisal tables show that most jurisdictions have developed generally acceptable laws relating to creditor rights and insolvency, but have failed to reform their collateral and secured transaction regimes. When insolvency or collateral laws have been recently enacted, few jurisdictions have been effective in implementation or enforcement. This points to the essential links between effective governance, economic and legal systems, and property, collateral and creditor rights. It also helps our understanding of the institutional foundations of financial systems, including central banking, regulation and financial intermediary risk management. Its institutional foundations will be critical in the future of finance in Asia.

6 Credit risk and commercial banking

The global financial crisis of 2008 alerted the non-financial world to practices long-accepted within the industry but not previously examined by outsiders, raising popular concerns over principal–agent conflicts, false incentives given by regulation to financial behaviour, executive compensation, or breaches of assumed duties of fairness or disclosure that had never earlier been questioned. No industry is democratic, but the reaction to the crisis was the first mainstream questioning of global financialization to have occurred since it began in the mid-1970s.

This makes the chapters that follow something of a danger to the reader, for our plan is to describe financial intermediaries and markets rather as a surgeon begins work on a theatre patient. Chapters 6–12 deal with the mechanics underlying our analysis of Asia's intermediation and its institutional foundations in Chapters 1–5. Mechanics refers to the legal and regulatory basis for intermediation and the day-to-day practices and transactional activity of banks, professional investors, and users of the financial system among consumers, companies and governments.

The sequence starts in this chapter with credit-based commercial banks, which Chapter 3 showed to be prominent in the region's financial systems. We look first at the day-to-day utility banking and credit risk that is central to its operation, then examine a modern commercial bank, before explaining the important businesses of medium-term credit, project finance and cash securitization, both generically and in use in Asia.

6.1 Utility banking

A myth of long-standing is that commercial banking is prudent, conservative and spoiled only rarely by professional recklessness. This preconception is exemplified in a conceit of architecture. From the beginnings of commercial banking in the fifteenth-century Italian city-states of Florence, Genoa and Siena, banks expressed their stability with displays of built permanence that could be Spartan or opulent, but were always imposing. This sought to impress both the depositor and all competitors. It also had a practical purpose, for the more intimidating the outer wall the less likely was the theft of specie or bullion from the vault. Image is also important to support the deception inherent in most commercial banking that clients of the bank may expect to withdraw their deposits at any time given proper notice and according to contractual terms. The deceit is that it would ever be feasible for all deposits to be withdrawn at the same time.

The motives of the banker are logical: control of storage costs, lessened opportunity costs, and the promise of enhanced profitability through leverage. All this rests on the observation first made in Genoa that on any normal day few of its clients would visit the bank to withdraw a deposit. Providing the bank retained sufficient liquidity to meet that daily demand and assuming a similar number would enter the bank to make a deposit, then adjusting for seasonal factors such as agricultural loan demand or the expense of trade fairs, the bank need retain only a portion of its contractual needs for specie, gold or silver. It could thus base its lending on a *fractional reserve*, and create credit after making prudent allowance for late payments and defaults based upon historic and stable observations.

The veneer of prudence and probity discourages depositors from withdrawing funds that in aggregate are never available to all until a sharp loss of confidence occurs in a bank, whether for reasons of substance or rumour. Runs on bank deposits by panicked customers are not infrequent globally, and their self-fulfilling nature was seen most recently among Iceland's main banks in 2008 and in the context of Northern Rock in the United Kingdom in 2007. The bank that suffers a run that goes unstemmed is highly likely to collapse, and runs are often contagious, so that the risk-averse actions of individual depositors are rational even if systemically self-destructive.

Runs occur in spite of provisions for the state to provide or require deposit insurance schemes for retail or SME clients, the classes of depositor most susceptible to panic and vulnerable to loss. Deposit insurance is prevalent, although heterogeneous, among high- and middle-income economies (Barth, Caprio & Levine 2006: 132–6), but rare elsewhere due to its substantial contingent costs and the relatively high incidence of state ownership of banks in lower-income states. Even schemes in advanced economies can be so poorly understood as to impair their systemic value, as we saw in the run experienced by home mortgage lender Northern Rock in August–September 2007. Only Vietnam among our sample economies has no form of explicit deposit insurance; China's scheme is recently introduced and not fully implemented.

The deceit of fractional reserves was threatened by a collapse of confidence among individuals depositing with certain banks in Belgium, Iceland, Ireland, the Netherlands, the United Kingdom and the United States in 2007–8. This happened despite each state having well-established deposit insurance, in most cases with scale limits intended to lessen the moral hazard of consumers deliberately placing deposits with risky banks that might pay high rates of interest.

Ireland's response to threatened post-Lehman deposit runs was to guarantee the full amount of all Irish bank liabilities to third parties except those with no fixed maturity (Central Bank of Ireland 2008), which was to become in 2010 a cost that the state could not sustain without emergency loans from the ECB, Eurozone members, IMF, Sweden and the United Kingdom. As the global crisis deepened after September 2008 severe illiquidity in wholesale funding markets affected intermediaries throughout the world and was not confined to deposit-taking banks. Separate retail bank runs have occurred at intervals throughout Asia since 1980, often driven by rumour but usually powerful in effect. In China and India they have been confined to small regional banks; runs on large domestic and foreign banks have occurred in all other economies except Singapore and Vietnam.

If systemic confidence is maintained the fractional reserve formulation is acceptably prudent practice. The same statistical insight allows the transformation in duration that is inherent in utility banking, where retail deposit taking provides the resources for loans. This is exemplified in the risk of 'borrowing short and lending long', which helps explain why deposit runs are so corrosive (Diamond & Dybvig 1983). Utility banking always involves duration risk and some aspect of interest rate or interest basis risks, albeit that modern treasury management can use dynamic hedging techniques to offset or mitigate such exposures.

Since the creation of modern banking in the early Renaissance Italian states, and certainly since the invention of fractional reserve banking and credit creation, a preoccupation of banks has been to foster such confidence as to induce customers to deposit their cash. This was typified by the instruction, 'Spare no expense but dominate the Bund', given by the Hongkong & Shanghai Bank to the architects commissioned to build its opulent Shanghai head office, still standing on the waterfront Bund since 1923 (Yip 1983: 123). Respectability and dependability seemed to be embodied in the banks' major offices, formerly temples of sturdy design, nowadays high architecture. This chapter explains what happens within those walls.

The core functions associated with commercial banks in emerging and industrialized economies are as important as those provided by power or water utilities. Contracts entered by commercial or utility banks represent the most easily recognized forms of intermediation, including credit, loans and deposit taking, money transmission and trade finance. These simple tasks can be stubbornly challenging to manage and make the business of utility banking a good example of Coasian transaction-cost theory at work, something seldom acknowledged in the finance and banking literature.

Our analysis of credit risk and commercial banking covers all these topics, from the elemental question of what happens mechanically and institutionally when banks collect deposits and make loans, to the business configurations adopted by Asia's banks, which are among the world's largest by balance sheet capitalization and assets. We begin by explaining credit risk, then look at a generic model of commercial banking and its core activities, before examining more complex alternatives to simple lending, including the modern concepts of credit origination for redistribution and limited recourse financing for major assets or infrastructure. Many of the terms that we use in Chapters 6–11 are given a short definition in our glossary.

Credit risk

All new financial investment from the safest to the most precarious forms of lending involves a funds provider accepting credit risk. The process developed with medieval long-distance trade between North Africa and East Asia and the Champagne fairs of thirteenth-century France, and grew increasingly sophisticated in the Italian city states and Europe's northern coastal towns. It was aptly and accurately depicted by William Shakespeare as described in Box 6.1.

Even the simplest commercial banks manage several forms of risk in elemental deposit collection and lending, as we saw in Section 3.2. Credit is the most notable risk arising in that process, representing the capacity and willingness of a debtor to meet its obligations when due. This careful definition is not the full story of the risk of commercial lending, for it excludes cases where a debtor is unwillingly prevented from meeting its obligations, for example by the state imposing payment restrictions or quotas or a tax on debt service payments. In addition to credit risk, the act of funding and making a simple loan under a commercial debt contract may include:

- Basis and duration risk;
- Documentation risk;
- Legal and regulatory risks;
- Settlement and payment risk; and
- Sovereign and taxation risks.

Box 6.1 Shakespearean Credit Risk

The *Oxford English Dictionary* describes credit as 'belief, credence, faith [or] trust'. In a commercial setting it can be:

> trust or confidence in a buyer's ability and intention to pay at some future time, exhibited by entrusting him with goods, etc. without present payment...[or] reputation of solvency and probity in business, enabling a person or body to be trusted with goods or money in expectation of future payment.

The word suggests a process of extending credit based on any such judgment, a decision relying on both information and trust. William Shakespeare's characterization of credit decisions made under uncertainty takes place in Renaissance Venice, and includes a sketch of the risk mitigation and risk substitution qualities associated with collateral set out in Chapter 5.

Shakespeare introduces us to Antonio, a shipowner and trader who has lent generously to his feckless young friend Bassanio, who now asks for more. Antonio's ships are far away in pursuit of trade and he complains of being short of cash or other working capital:

> my fortunes are at sea;
> Neither have I money nor commodity
> To raise a present sum
> (Shakespeare, *The Merchant of Venice*, Act I:1)

Illiquid but solvent, Antonio still sees himself as an acceptable risk for a creditor:

> My ventures are not in one bottom trusted,
> Nor to one place; nor is my whole estate
> Upon the fortune of this present year
> (ibid)

This is risk aversion. Antonio diversifies his shipping exposure, as would any creditworthy merchant. With this self-assessment, friendship leads Antonio to allow Bassanio use of his name to raise funds elsewhere:

> therefore go forth;
> Try what my credit can in Venice do.
> (ibid)

Bassanio meets the banker, Shylock, asking that he lend Antonio 3,000 ducats (about US$300,000 today) so that Antonio can in turn pass the cash to Bassanio. Shakespeare's audience realizes that Shylock would not consider Bassanio a sound credit and requires risk substitution before making a loan. Shylock thinks aloud and concludes that Antonio is an acceptable risk given proper security:

Shylock: Three thousand ducats for three months and Antonio bound.
Bassanio: Your answer to that.

Shylock: Antonio is a good man.

Bassanio: Have you heard any imputation to the contrary?

Shylock: Oh, no, no, no, no: *my meaning in saying he is a good man is to have you understand me that he is sufficient.* Yet his means are in supposition: he hath an argosy bound to Tripolis, another to the Indies; I understand moreover, upon the Rialto, he hath a third at Mexico, a fourth for England, and other ventures he hath, squandered abroad. But ships are but boards, sailors but men: there be land-rats and water-rats, water-thieves and land-thieves, I mean pirates, and then there is the peril of waters, winds and rocks. The man is, notwithstanding, sufficient. Three thousand ducats; I think I may take his bond.

(Act I:3, emphasis added)

The scene began emotionally, but Shylock's analysis is pure credit assessment and as thorough as today's corporate rating agencies. Venice even had its equivalent of a Bloomberg terminal, with financiers and merchants swapping market gossip in the Rialto commercial district. Shylock tests his knowledge of Antonio's business affairs, assesses the risks of ships being lost or robbed at sea, and elects to make the loan providing he is given collateral.

The play turns on a separate aspect of contract law when the court decides that Shylock's collateral is flawed and unenforceable, but the pre-contractual analysis is faultless. Although Antonio's business faces real risks, he 'is sufficient' and therefore creditworthy. Shylock takes collateral to mitigate his credit risk because the judgment is probabilistic (Antonio's 'means are in supposition' rather than known for sure) but makes the loan due to his commercial belief in Antonio's capacity and willingness to repay the debt. This is the essence of credit risk.

At the end of the play, Shylock's skill in risk management is confirmed with Antonio's ships all returned profitably to Venice. The process of credit risk assessment is shown to be thorough, subjective and perceptive, even though Shakespeare's anti-Semitic treatment of Shylock might have his audience believe less in the moneylender.

More complex contracts will also entail forms of market, liquidity or exchange risks. In this chapter, we concentrate on credit arising in commercial banking transactions. We distinguish these risks that attach to any single transaction from the three forms of portfolio risk experienced by an intermediary as a whole, listed in Section 3.2 as credit risk, duration risk and value risk.

Commercial banks engage continually in assessing, providing, recovering and withdrawing credit from clients and counterparties. Making a loan means extending credit and thus acquiring funded exposure to credit risk. Transferring rights attached to the loan to a third party or collecting repayment in full signifies the reverse. The colloquialism 'credit creation' is taken from the process of fractional reserve banking, or the invention of money as if conjured from a black box.

The word credit derives from the Latin *credere*, to believe, so that the traditional meaning of credit risk in banking is to signify the banker's confidence in a borrower or user of trade finance, or conversely the depositor's confidence in the bank. Credit risk appraisal is essentially subjective, as *The Merchant of Venice* shows. It may have become subject to common practices, for example, in the similar approaches used for corporate analysis by the leading global credit rating agencies, and the price associated with credit risk is often well-informed by liquid financial instruments such as bonds, loans and credit derivatives, but it is neither homogeneous nor objectively determined.

Credit risk transfer is a recurring theme of the second half of our book, suggesting the importance of asset and capital management and the redistribution of risk to the modern global financial world. It is the means by which credit risk is acquired or shed to alter the risk–return profile of a portfolio of financial claims. Its techniques are used by borrowers, intermediaries or end investors, simple or sophisticated, and may or may not be funded. Funded credit risk transfer involves a real balance sheet transformation, as when a financial asset is bought or sold for a cash consideration. Examples of unfunded credit risk transfer include the sale or purchase of credit protection through insurance or credit default swaps (CDS) that we detail in Section 8.3. Buying or selling loans or securities are simple forms of funded credit risk transfer. Section 11.3 discusses infrastructural finance including whole business securitization (WBS) as an example of a non-traditional means to fund the sale of a complete business, thus representing a transfer of credit risk from corporate shareholders.

Common activities

Commercial banking has four core activities:

- Credit creation;
- Deposit taking;
- Money transmission; and
- Trade finance.

Some economies allow banks an indirect responsibility in corporate governance by holding semi-permanent stakes in client companies. This fifth function associated with the Rheinish model of capitalism is akin to private equity investment and discussed in Chapter 11.

The business streams that banks choose or are granted as concessions by national regulators have broadened over time, assisted by technical change and efficiencies derived from information technology. Investment fashion influences banks as much as it does industrial groups, so that financial conglomerates are favoured and their shares well-rated for certain periods, while at other times analysts prefer narrowly focused banks, reflecting cyclical preferences for banks either to diversify or make explicit their sources of income.

The permissible scope of banking varies from place to place, and several Asian and European states delineate the functional territory that banks may occupy. The trend of the last three decades has been for a softer national demarcation of permitted business streams, for example, banks may conduct insurance as principals in some states but such crossover functions are prohibited elsewhere for prudential or customary reasons.

Specialist lending is also common, especially in Rheinish capitalist states. The most durable case is Japan, where lending by certain banks provides long-term funds for industrial investment. Others have a shorter-term focus in consumer credit and SME loans, and a sizeable postal sub-sector engages in the simplest form of intermediation in collecting personal savings and investing the aggregate proceeds in Japanese government bonds (JGBs). Other states give fiscal support to specialist lenders, for example, Germany, South Korea, the Netherlands and Norway in ship finance. Many provide incentives to specialist housing lenders that can be organized either as banks or mutual associations.

These 'front office' commercial streams are supported by ancillary functions, known colloquially as the back and middle offices. In large organizations they typically include:

- Accounting and management information services;
- Brand management and communications;
- Compliance, internal audit and internal legal counsel;
- Human resource management;
- Information technology;
- Property resource management;
- Risk management;
- Transaction processing; and
- Treasury.

Some of these activities may be subject to external regulation, notably under the second pillar of Basel II. Many are now profit seeking, and assessed not as a central overhead but with an actual or assumed return on allocated capital.

Property management is a simple example. Not only can commercial divisions be charged market rents for space and resources, but more creative uses of the bank's physical and financial capacity can open additional banking opportunities. Construction expenses in property subsidiaries may generate accumulated tax losses, and these have been applied in jurisdictions such as Hong Kong or Japan to increase the bank's returns from major asset leasing, with the subsidiary becoming the primary lessor for airline or shipping clients.

It is especially common for treasury activities to be managed for profit as a corollary to the front-office businesses that they support, because their functions involve engaging with external counterparties in markets for credit, foreign exchange and derivatives, and are commercially identical to the bank's transactions with clients in these instruments. The bank's treasury manages the mechanics of all balance sheet and payment-related activity, and is both inextricably and constantly linked with the management of capital, risk and resources. Capital represents the bank's most scarce resource. This means that its allocation among front office and other functions both reflects the bank's business preferences and helps determine their results.

Some banks have devolved administrative functions to independent commercial settings, for example J.P. Morgan's approach to aspects of trading and credit risk management (explained in Box 4.1) was made into a profit centre called RiskMetrics and then sold in the late-1990s as a separate company. We will see shortly how these configurations of commercial banking are sensitive to the standard performance measures of external analysts, and has encouraged middle or back office functions to be increasingly treated as more than administrative cost centres.

Table 6.1 shows an array of common banking products and services allocated according to the needs of their retail and wholesale users, from payments and investment to credit-related instruments and advisory services, the more important of which we discuss in the sections that follow. Our discussion of commercial banking's fourth core activity of deposit taking is limited to the context of funding for loans in Section 6.3.

Table 6.1 Bank products and client needs

	Money transmission	Investment	Short-term finance	Insurance	Long-term finance	Advisory
1. Liquidity transactions	Debit cards Bank cards (ATM, POS) Cheques Foreign exchange Letters of credit Deposit & withdrawal Payment orders	Demand deposit Checking account Term deposit	Credit card Line of credit Trade finance Factoring			
2. Savings accumulation		Saving accounts Mutual funds Securities deposits Life insurance (single premium)		Endowment life insurance Pension funds		
3. Property				Life insurance	Mortgage lending	Brokerage
4. Consumer finance & working capital			Leasing Consumer loans Working capital lines	Property & casualty insurance		Cash management Treasury & risk management
5. Corporate finance					Securities issuance Term loans Partial recourse finance	Mergers, acquisitions & disposals

Trade finance

Trade finance and payment mechanisms are important in Asia's economy, as we described more broadly in Chapter 3. The core banking instrument in this field is the letter of credit or L/C, a form of *documentary credit* that links payment for goods with their delivery as specified in a supply contract.[1]

The L/C is a composite contingent undertaking issued by a bank in favour of a beneficiary or seller of goods in accordance with the instructions of a buyer, which is usually the bank's client. The bank scrutinizes documentary evidence of shipment and makes payment to the seller in one amount, or stages if it judges those documents to be authentic, and to conform with the supply contract. Banking scholars traditionally treat the L/C as a form of credit support for the seller, especially if it contracts with a remote or unknown buyer in a domicile whose courts may be unreliable in enforcing foreign claims, but there is empirical and anecdotal evidence that documentary errors and inconsistencies are only rarely enforced against the buyer (Mann 2000), notwithstanding that banking practice in this field is subject to protocols established by the International Chamber of Commerce's Uniform Customs and Practice for Documentary Credits (ICC 2007). This has legal status in some jurisdictions, notably the United States through its Uniform Commercial Code: Letters of Credit (5 U.C.C. §§101–18). The L/C may serve more as an indication of the authenticity of the trade sale and the good intentions of the buyer than as a guarantee of payment.

The documentary credit process has several generic steps:

- The buyer agrees to purchase goods at a predetermined price for delivery in a specified manner.
- Contract and settlement terms are provided to the buyer's bank, which issues an L/C to the seller's bank (the 'advisory' bank), electronically or in hard copy, that includes details of the supply contract.
- The advisory bank asks the seller to supply it with documents giving evidence of shipment. These may include bills of lading, airway bills, certificates of origin, customs declarations, inspection documents and insurance certificates.
- It is common for payments made under L/Cs to be evidenced by one or more bills of exchange. These are prepared by the seller, executed by the buyer to indicate its willingness to pay amounts stated on each bill to the seller when due, and endorsed by the buyer's bank as an indication of the validity of the buyer's promise, and in some cases to guarantee payment. This bank undertaking is traditionally known as an *aval*, and means that the bill may be presented when due at the buyer's bank for its face value without recourse to the buyer.
- Shipping documents are transmitted to the buyer's bank, and if conforming strictly with the terms of the L/C then the bank will instruct the advising bank to make payment to the seller in the manner specified in the L/C, and by implication in the supply contract.

This process can be made to cover 'sight' transactions, where payment is made as soon as the seller's documents are found to be complete, and term transactions involving L/Cs providing for payment in stages, which is common where the supply of goods involves several shipments. Supplier or export credit to buyers was important to the developmental state model, especially in Japan, South Korea and Taiwan, and often assisted with state subsidies. Trade finance is costly to use and operate, which helps explain why its scope extends to only a sizeable minority of commercial transactions. It may have been prevalent in Asia for other specific reasons:

- The region's export orientation;
- The importance of informal or indigenous practices in money transmission and cross-border trade finance;
- A weak institutional framework and poor credit analysis made trade finance more robust than other forms of financing;
- Commercial banks preferred self-liquidating short-term trade finance to forms of credit that are more difficult to appraise; and
- Trade finance for SMEs is typically provided on a secured basis, with collateral taken over the assets of both the company and its owners, which gives the bank considerable protection from competition.

The expense of establishing or maintaining trade finance resources represents a considerable barrier for non-Asian entrants, even though returns can be attractive in both absolute terms and in relation to risk. This means that the most successful trade finance banks are the larger local organizations that have significant market shares with SME clients, such as Bangkok Bank, Hang Seng Bank, Malayan Banking Bhd or OCBC Bank. Non-indigenous banks that are successful in Asian trade finance are those with a colonial positional legacy of the kind we describe in Section 3.3.

Cross-border money transmission

International trade finance and much of the world's transnational lending rely on systems to conduct payments and settlement, and deal in foreign exchange, all of which constitute an unglamorous and largely unseen feature of the global financial architecture. We notice its failings as individuals if a foreign cheque takes many weeks to clear or if a bank retains a payment for reimbursement for longer than warranted, but most payments are cleared and settled efficiently. The system generally has three elements:

- Networks of bank correspondents. Commercial banks act as agents for each other to facilitate settlement in domestic or foreign locations where the instructing bank has no physical presence. This was the seed of the international payments system, originating from the time that Edison's telegraph allowed remote communications. Correspondent banks keep accounts with each other for this purpose, known as *nostro* (my account with you) and *vostro* (yours with me) accounts.
- National state-controlled or supervised electronic clearing houses in the domicile of each tradable currency, which collect and distribute the net proceeds owed between banks as a result of all aspects of money transmission, trade finance and foreign exchange dealings, and in some cases dealings in securities. An umbrella system called TARGET2 (Trans-European Automated Real-time Gross Settlement Express Transfer System) operates in the Eurozone to settle transnational payments.
- Secure instructions for payment are made between banks through a global communications cooperative called SWIFT, or Society for Worldwide Interbank Financial Telecommunication.

If a Hong Kong company instructs its local bank to pay a sum in euros to a supplier in Cambodia, the payment (assuming it remains within the formal banking system) will be debited to the Hong Kong company's local-currency bank account, that amount sold 'at spot' for euros, and the sum credited electronically to the correspondent bank in France, for example, with which the Hong Kong bank keeps its euro nostro account. With it goes a SWIFT instruction to make payment to a second correspondent where the Cambodian supplier's local bank has its nostro, in Germany say, for the credit of that Cambodian bank in favour of the supplier. Payment between the correspondents is made either in France or Germany through a national settlement system, or if neither bank has an office in the other's domicile, through TARGET2, which connects all national Eurozone payment systems. Sophisticated settlement systems operate constantly in real time, as shown in Box 6.2, so that final settlement takes place between the two EU correspondents close to the moment of instruction, rather than as a close-of-day balancing exercise. Real-time payment processing exists in all our sample economies except Vietnam.

Box 6.2 Bankhaus Herstatt and Real-time Settlement

Financial incompetence or misdemeanours that bring down individual intermediaries have often led to major changes in global regulation. The collapses of the multinational commercial bank BCCI and the merchant bank Barings in the 1990s led to agreements on coordination between national regulators, giving banks less scope to avoid scrutiny.

The first modern transnational banking crisis began in an obscure German bank and was to impact global finance in several profound ways. Bankhaus Herstatt was a small Cologne private bank in which fraud led to insolvency, and in June 1974 was forced precipitately by its national banking regulator to cease business. Herstatt dealt actively in foreign exchange and the closure came during the New York trading day, which left payments in transit or suspense and many counterparties without funds to settle payment instructions with unconnected third parties. Some made remittances in expectation of receiving funds from Herstatt and suffered a settlement failure at the end of their trading day, and others found it difficult to recover funds paid to Herstatt before the closure became known. As with Lehman Brothers on a larger scale in 2008, the ripples of a single failure were systemically disturbing, and had two main effects:

- The beginnings in the BCBS of formal central bank cooperation and information sharing on the banks they supervise. After the failure of BCCI in 1992, this provided a workable setting for negotiation of a common formula for capital standards for internationally oriented banks, which resulted in the first Basel accord in 1988. Until Herstatt, central bank discussions on bank supervision were informal, guarded and damagingly self-protective.
- Recognition that settlement risks demand a means to prevent systemic failures resulting from modest payment or delivery defaults, especially when neither counterparties nor their regulators could know the volume of payments or securities in transit during any single day. The result were guidelines developed by the BCBS as to how the system could be made to function safely (BCBS 2000; CPSS 2001), and a gradual migration to allow transactions in all important currencies to be settled by real-time payment processing, on the principle that outward payments are contingent upon delivery.

Herstatt risk is unlikely ever to vanish, but its potential for systemic disturbances has been much lessened by this migration, albeit that it took '25 years of temporising with this recognised global exposure' to find a remedy (BIS 2001: 153).

Until recently the settlement of payment and securities transfers were generally made by a daily netting process little changed since the nineteenth century. Banks or securities dealers would aggregate the amounts they each owed or were due from the system at the end of the business day, and settled the net amount due through a central agency. The system was considered risk averse because netting reduced the need for excessive transfers, a principle that still applies in the markets for interest rate and currency swaps, as we explain in Section 8.2.

Herstatt showed how settlement by payment netting was flawed because it relied on discrete periods while trading was continuous, and led to the adoption of settlement by real-time continuous payment systems, and the abandonment of end-of-day netting traditions. TARGET2 is an example of a Real Time Gross Settlement (RTGS) system providing for Continuous Linked Settlement (CLS). This means that transactions are settled when instructed, so that if a delivery failure occurs its scale and location can be instantly known. Since 2002 a cooperative organization called CLS Group has had a similar function in eliminating FX settlement risk by connecting hubs in New York and London with electronic bridges to central banks and a clearing organization that processes OTC derivative trades. CLS is owned by 72 banks including 13 from Asia, and in 2010 settled 58 per cent of all FX trades in 17 active currencies, including the yen, won, and Hong King and Singapore dollars.

Foreign exchange

Most commercial banks buy and sell foreign exchange for their clients. Some trade currencies for their own account with banks and other professional counterparties in ways that may be informed by flows of client activity without directly facilitating those dealings. The most comprehensive survey of global FX activity is a triennial report prepared by the BIS thought to cover 97 per cent of all activity from which the data in this section are taken and which reflects average daily turnover in April 2010 (BIS 2010). Trades in seven major currencies account for 47 per cent of the total with the US dollar dominating as the leading currency for both trade and financial transaction settlement (ibid: 12), after which rank the euro, yen, Sterling, Australian and Canadian dollars and Swiss franc. The scope and depth of FX trading varies by currency so that the greatest variety of instruments and maturities exists among the most liquid major currencies that are free of national trading restrictions.

Pairs of currencies can be dealt in three ways:

- At spot, for immediate settlement. This accounted for 40 per cent of average daily FX market turnover in April 2010 and is closely related to the transnational trade in goods.
- Forward, or in trades executed today for future settlement (13 per cent of turnover), 54 per cent of which were settled within seven days in April 2010. Outright forward deals often arise through hedging foreign currency payments for goods.
- FX swaps, or combinations of spot and forward trades where one currency is sold for another at spot and simultaneously repurchased forward (47 per cent of turnover). FX swaps lasting seven days or less provided 75 per cent of such trades in April 2010,

and together with the overall scale of FX swaps indicates that much of this activity signals hedging or speculation with no direct connection to the trade in goods.

Trade execution takes place in several ways, including direct electronic dealing between counterparties, bargains conducted through an electronic platform operated by a bank or group of banks, and those executed through specialist money brokers either electronically or by voice communication. Minor currencies are somewhat less liquid and in some cases are quoted constantly only against the US dollar, euro and yen. They include those of Hong Kong, Sweden, New Zealand, South Korea and Singapore in declining volume of use (ibid). Exotic currencies are those for which trading is controlled, illiquid or dominated by few participants.

Activity in the major currencies is seen as the most efficient and liquid of all global financial markets but FX trading is concentrated in two ways:

- Five EU and US banks accounted for 61 per cent of 2008 global turnover. Their market share differed little between Asia, Europe and North America. Only one Asian bank was ranked among the most active 30 with a market share of less than 0.6 per cent (*Euromoney* 2008).
- The United Kingdom (37 per cent) and United States (18 per cent) are dominant locations for FX dealing based on average April 2010 turnover (BIS 2010: 19), which represents a consistent share over five triennial BIS surveys since 1998. Japan (6 per cent), Singapore, Switzerland and Hong Kong followed (each with 5 per cent shares).

Some aspects of the transnational settlement of payments and securities are subject to widely adopted treaties or conventions, but these functions are for the most part governed by national law and regulations. Organizations such as SWIFT, TARGET2 and national clearing and settlement operations are post-trade facilitators rather than regulatory bodies.

6.2 Core commercial banking

Our concept of a generic commercial bank has changed little over several centuries in spite of intense technological growth. Revenue is derived from an interest margin that accrues over the period of a loan and is positive in relation to the bank's cost of funding, and the claims created in this way by loans and deposits are treated as balance sheet assets and liabilities. This process is supported by shared administrative resources and a pool of capital intended to absorb losses incurred arising from NPLs and other distressed claims. Other activities can be seen as diversifications from this simple model, either to improve the bank's return on capital or to broaden the scope of revenue derived from core credit-based lending and deposit taking.

Banks generate revenue through the interaction of assets, liabilities and contingent and other off-balance sheet claims. Assets range from short-term credit, which the bank can usually withdraw at short notice, to medium-term loans, most of which have tenors of 3–8 years and are subject to complex credit agreements.

We make an important distinction between almost all assets and liabilities that appear on a bank's balance sheet from those of an industrial concern. While bank assets and liabilities are real and not fictional, they represent claims that have substance only in contract or quasi-contractual terms. Loans made by a commercial bank are recorded as short- or long-term assets in some part of its balance sheet. When funded these will involve enforceable rights to interest and repayment, but are not synonymous with real estate, plant and equipment or intellectual property that appear as assets on the balance sheet of a industrial group, even when secured against real property. Most bank assets and liabilities are claims only indirectly associated with real-world assets. One implication is that cross-sectoral comparisons are often purposeless, so that the scale or composition of the balance sheets of Toyota Motor Corp or Petroliam Nasional Bhd are wholly unalike those of Mizuho Bank or Malayan Banking Bhd.

Figure 6.1 shows the main components of the balance sheet of a commercial bank that we see as typical of many in East Asia. Our illustration is OCBC Bank, the main operating subsidiary of Singapore-listed Overseas Chinese Banking Corporation. We see OCBC Bank as both simple and sophisticated, in that it functions in relatively few business streams or geographical areas, but is based and regulated in an economy with an advanced and sizeable financial sector, has relatively strong A+/Aa1/AA credit ratings as we write, and conducts its Singapore and Malaysia banking businesses under the IRB approach of Basel II. OCBC Bank's operations outside Singapore, Indonesia and Malaysia are limited to 12 other economies, and are in most cases confined to single-branch operations. It ranked 11th by Tier 1 capital among Asian banks excluding those in China or Japan in *The Banker*'s mid-2010 survey and 96th among all global banks.

OCBC Bank organizes its commercial activities into consumer banking, corporate banking, transaction banking (payments, trade finance and custody), treasury, investment banking and investment management, with the first three dominating revenue and earnings. This is a typical modern former family-owned commercial bank that is effective but somewhat shielded by regulation from competition in its home market, and is thus not dissimilar to many medium-scale commercial lenders in East Asia or Europe. The group is unusual among its peers only by having taken control of a substantial Singaporean insurer and fund manager called Great Eastern Holdings in 2004, which accounted for around 20 per cent of the group's consolidated balance sheet and almost 25 per cent of non-interest income in 2010. Our analysis concentrates on the consolidated balance sheet, off-balance sheet items and income statement for the year ending in December 2010.

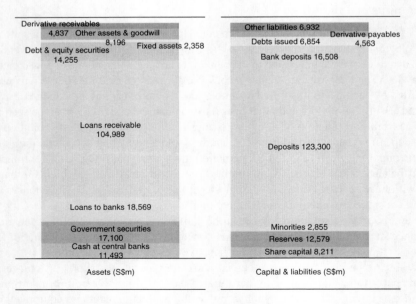

Figure 6.1　OCBC bank summary balance sheet, end-2010.
Source: OCBC (2010).

The balance sheet is a screen capture of the bank's financial configuration and condition, and its income statement depicts trading in a standardized period to the date of that capture. Bank balance sheets are generally less complete than those of industrial groups because off-balance sheet claims and other contingent liabilities tend to be relatively important for all but the simplest and underleveraged banks.

OCBC Bank's off-balance sheet items as at end-2010 are shown in Table 6.2B. Contingent liabilities are mainly guarantees and documentary credits, commitments that consist overwhelmingly of undrawn credit lines for clients, and financial derivatives shown by their gross nominal amount, rather than the bank's far smaller net exposure or credit risk, and largely represent foreign exchange and interest rate contracts (OCBC 2009: 101–2 & 148–50). In the normal course of business only a fraction of these off-balance sheet items would be expected to crystallize as assets or liabilities. The accounting treatment of off-balance sheet items is inconsistent but strongly influenced by Basel II provisions that banks provide capital

Table 6.2A OCBC Bank summary income statement, FY 2010

	FY 2010	*FY 2009*	*Change (%)*
Interest income	4,363	4,184	4
Interest expense	(1,416)	(1,359)	4
Net interest income	2,947	2,825	4
Profit from life assurance	437	727	−40
Fees & commissions (net)	994	730	36
Other income	947	533	78
Non-interest income	2,378	1,990	19
Total income	5,325	4,815	11
Staff costs	−1,283	−995	29
Other operating expenses	−971	−801	21
Total operating expenses	−2,254	−1,796	26
Operating profit before allowances & amortization	3,071	3,019	2
Amortization of intangible assets	−55	−47	17
Allowances for NPLs	−134	−429	−69
Operating profit after allowances & amortization	2,882	2,543	13
Share of results of associates & joint ventures	−2	0	–
Profit before income tax	2,880	2,543	13
Income tax expense	−433	−389	11
Profit for the period	2,447	2,154	14

Table 6.2B OCBC Bank off-balance sheet items

	As at end 2010 (S$ mm)	*Change from prior comparable period (%)*
Commitments	6,835	5.8
Contingent liabilities	40,143	15.8
Financial derivatives	391,147	15.5

Source: OCBC (2010).

against contractual but undrawn commitments using credit conversion factors that vary with the firmness of the commitment (BCBS 2006b: 26–7). The item stated by OCBC would therefore comprise undrawn credit lines, many of which might have a fixed maturity, but all of which could be readily cancelled by the bank.

Figure 6.1 shows the simplified composition of OCBC Bank's consolidated balance sheet, which we adjust to show investments of its ring-fenced life insurance fund on a net basis.

- Assets consist mainly of loans to consumers and corporate customers (58 per cent of total adjusted assets), interbank claims and other loans to banks (10 per cent), government bonds and notes (9 per cent), debt and equity securities (8 per cent) and cash and deposits with OCBC's supervising central banks (6 per cent).

- Of loans receivable, 52 per cent were denominated in Singapore dollars, and would represent claims domiciled in Singapore because of MAS restrictions on the offshore use of the currency. A further 32 per cent of loans receivable were claims in Malaysian ringgit or US dollars. Loans of more than three years' maturity were 48 per cent of the total, and short-term loans of up to 12 months accounted for 37 per cent of all loans. 43 per cent were loans related to construction or property. OCBC's gross level of NPLs was 1.2 per cent of loans receivable, against which the bank made specific provisions equivalent to 0.3 per cent of total loans. Over 64 per cent of NPLs were classed in the least troubling category of substandard, indicating some arrears of interest (see Box 3.3). This breakdown indicates a generally conservative credit policy albeit with a narrow geographical focus.

- OCBC held 15 per cent of assets in cash or government securities, chiefly for operating purposes and to meet statutory liquidity rules and reserve requirements, which contributes to the monetary policy interface between central and commercial banks. Some central banks control reserve requirements through disclosed formula, but their counterparts in China, India, Thailand and elsewhere are accustomed to controlling credit in a more direct and arbitrary way, as in PBOC's repeated increases in China's bank reserve requirements in 2010–11 to help restrain lending. We saw in Chapter 4 how Basel III will introduce a liquidity coverage ratio norm in 2015, affecting OCBC's management of this asset category.

- The bank's assets were allocated predominantly to corporate banking (30 per cent of the total), treasury (19 per cent) and consumer banking (14 per cent). OCBC's reliance on credit-related revenue meant that these three divisions contributed in similar proportions to operating profits.

- Liabilities largely comprise deposits made other than by banks (68 per cent of total net liabilities, capital and reserves), and bank deposits (9 per cent). Debts issued (4 per cent) consists mainly of commercial paper and subordinated debt that formerly qualified for regulatory purposes as part of Tier 2 capital.

- Deposits made by non-banks were largely term deposits (48 per cent of the total), and current and savings accounts (26 and 21 per cent respectively). The relatively high share of term deposits is valuable to OCBC's management of duration risk, even with its direct cost in higher contractual interest paid to depositors. Interbank and other deposits made by banks were around only 13 per cent of customer deposits. This liability composition is typical of conservatively funded and deposit-rich Asian commercial banks in the region's higher-income economies. Banks in Europe with a similar commercial focus would tend to rely more on bank funding and sustain a higher ratio of loans to deposits.

- The reasons for OCBC's deposit paradigm are several and reflect not only the commercial preferences of the bank but savings behaviour in its main markets, which we know from Section 1.3 to be high by global standards. The perception of OCBC Bank as a conservative intermediary may also improve the bank's market share of non-bank deposits, and it is not unusual for indigenous banks in Asia's main financial centres to be consistent placers of local currency in the interbank markets. Even well-established foreign banks fail to attract non-bank local currency deposits on the same scale and may lack the physical resources to do so. OCBC effectively collects far more deposits than it chooses to lend, or has the commercial acumen to make, so that its loan–deposit ratio at end-2010 was 85.1 per cent.

   We will see in Section 6.3 how the development of the global syndicated loan market relied partly on small- or medium-scale banks whose capacity to lend exceeds their capacity to develop business within conventional constraints on risk concentration. At the same time banks with low loan-deposit ratios were spared the cost or ignominy of seeking LLR funding during the global crisis.

   One example is HSBC, ranked fourth by total assets in 2009 by *The Banker*. HSBC's operations include commercial banking resources in Asia that share OCBC's low loan–deposit paradigm. As a result, the bank was among the least troubled by crisis illiquidity, even though its US mortgage subsidiary suffered substantial subprime loan losses in 2007–8. The Federal Reserve's Term Auction Facility (TAF) provided 28 and 84 day crisis loans to banks in the United States from December 2007 to April 2010, and was used by the substantial HSBC Bank USA in modest amounts five times between November 2008 and March 2009, far more sparingly than all its major competitors (Federal Reserve 2011).

   This aspect of utility banking was the most disrupted in the 2007–9 crisis, and unexpectedly illiquid interbank US dollar deposits had a material effect on banks in South Korea and Taiwan. OCBC's borrowing from the MAS, if any, is not disclosed but its 2010 balance sheet composition shows a relatively liquid and conservative lender, meaning that it would have needed little if any assistance during the crisis. US Federal Reserve and Treasury data show no use of their emergency liquidity lines by either Singapore banks or the Monetary Authority of Singapore on their behalf.

- Capital cushions losses in the value of assets and provides some safeguard against insolvency. Modern bank capital has two tiers of differing characteristics, Tier 1 of which is regarded as core capital and the most durable against loan losses. This comprises paid-up ordinary shares (common equity), perpetual non-cumulative preference shares with no fixed maturity or contractual put option for holders, and disclosed reserves resulting mainly from retained earnings.

   OCBC ended 2010 with Tier 1 capital amounting to 9.4 per cent of total net assets, and 16.3 per cent of total risk-weighted assets, which conforms comfortably with the forthcoming Basel III requirements shown in Table 4.4 as a further indication of OCBC's relatively low risk-profile. Ordinary and preference shares were 48 per cent of Tier 1 capital. This solid capitalization would lead banking analysts to ask whether OCBC's return on equity was correspondingly depressed relative to its peers. The result in 2010 was 12.1 per cent, slightly less than the previous year, consistent with levels achieved by Singaporean banks shown in Table 3.12 and indicative of the utility return to commercial banking that we described in Chapter 3.2.

- Tier 2 capital comprises claims that rank in liquidation ahead of shares and provide less protection against loan losses. They include hidden reserves where permitted by national regulators, asset revaluation reserves, provisions made for losses, as well as hybrid capital when allowed by national regulators, and subordinated debt instruments. Hybrid capital is, to date, permitted only for Swiss banks, but is conceptually a debt claim that in highly stressed conditions becomes subject to mandatory conversion to ordinary shares, as we explain in Box 6.3. Other forms of subordinated debt have long been popular among Asian banks and were issued regularly by OCBC, most recently in November 2010 as described in Box 6.3, but Basel III will strip the regulatory capital quality from such instruments and treat those outstanding from 2013 as simple liabilities. OCBC is relatively non-reliant on Tier 2 capital, which represents only 7 per cent of its total eligible capital.

Box 6.3 The Mystery of Contingent Capital

Basel's periodic revisions have often been welcomed by investment bankers who spend their time devising transactions to meet or circumvent its rules. The adoption of Basel III brought them two concurrent opportunities. The first was to deal efficiently, and at least cost, with a considerable outstanding volume of commercial bank subordinated debt issues that were to lose their status as components of Tier 2 capital and be treated purely as liabilities from 2013. OCBC Bank is one of many Asian banks that over two decades issued forms of subordinated debt with optional repayment provisions, all of which will become redundant as to their intended purpose (Table 4.4).

The FSB reasons that these instruments provided no protection against credit losses during the crisis. Although those losses may have been accelerated by fair-value accounting, the aim of new policies is to bolster capital to forestall any collapse in confidence that begins with unsustainable expected credit losses. Instruments designed to be loss absorbing under current regulations will thus lose their capital attributes as Basel III takes effect, and gradually constitute no more than costly funding. Many banks will redeem any outstanding issues or tender noteholders for their cancellation.

OCBC Bank issued US$500 million of callable subordinated 12 year notes only weeks before the publication of Basel III's capital guidelines, using a structure popular with Asian banks under current guidelines because it raises capital without forcing an equity dilution. The issue will rank fully as Tier 2 capital only until 2013, after which its regulatory capital value will amortize, making the notes increasingly costly for OCBC to maintain since the coupon paid to investors is far higher than the bank would expect to pay on its other conventional liabilities. This strongly incentivizes OCBC to exercise its call option after seven years, and limits reinvestment risk for noteholders.

The second opportunity provided by Basel III is a blank canvas on which investment banks are invited to produce their own designs. Basel will allow hybrid or contingent instruments to qualify as part of Tier 2 capital, but as we write has yet to indicate how those instruments are to be drawn. Contingent capital or 'Coco' issues are intended to be strongly loss absorbing, and contingent not as to early repayment options or coupon deferral but only in that they must convert automatically from debt to equity claims upon the occurrence of defined events associated with a significant deterioration in the issuer's financial condition, or a systemic threat with a similar impact.

Basel's intention is largely theoretical because the conditions for mandatory conversion have yet to be decided, although several banks and one national regulator have issued or approved Cocos in expectation of the rules being agreed. Three EU banks issued contingent capital in 2009–10 but only one did so with certainty that its regulator would treat the notes as Tier 2 capital. This was a US$2.0 billion issue that Crédit Suisse completed in February 2011 with the encouragement of the Swiss National Bank. This will convert to equity with no requirement for shareholder approval if the bank's Core Tier 1 CAR drops below 7 per cent.

The Swiss authorities transformed Basel's hypothetical opportunity into reality well before the BCBS could agree what might qualify towards Tier 2 capital. In the past, contingent capital referred to convertible bond issues arranged for distressed companies, but Basel III contemplates a rigorous instrument that removes any volition in use from both issuer and noteholders. BCBS first stated Cocos to be under consideration in July 2010:

> The Basel Committee has developed a proposal based on a requirement that the contractual terms of capital instruments will allow them at the option of the regulatory authority to be written off or converted to common shares in the event that a bank is unable to support itself in the private market in the absence of such conversions. At its July meeting, the Committee agreed to issue for consultation such a 'gone concern' proposal that requires capital to convert at the point of non-viability.
>
> (BCBS 2010e: Annex s. 5)

The later description of Basel III (BCBS 2010c) included no details of what might be allowed, and BCBS consultations continued well into 2011. This leaves the shape of future Cocos for speculation, although it is clear that suitable conditions must account for many uncertainties, such as:

- Whether conversion is a response to commercial or systemic stresses that may impact a bank's capital adequacy ratio (CAR) or the result of those stresses, for example in actual loan losses;
- Whether mandatory conversion needs to follow specific events that damage the bank's capacity to absorb loan losses;
- Whether those events are single occurrences or must persist for a period;
- Whether conversion takes place for an entire issue or may be triggered in stages;
- Whether conversion can be additionally required at the discretion of a regulator;
- Whether conversion is sensitive to the market price of the Cocos; and
- Whether conversion can result from specific trading strategies, for example, if short selling takes place in a bank's shares and depresses their prevailing price, which in turn triggers conversion of its contingent capital.

These and other dilemmas need solving in ways that promote systemic confidence, satisfy potential Coco investors, and make contingent capital cost effective for issuers. Crédit Suisse's initial issue was heavily oversubscribed and a conspicuous success, but at the time of issue the bank was well-rated and capitalized. Could Cocos be sold by less favoured banks that might have more need of Tier 2 capital?

Table 6.2A shows OCBC Bank's 2010 income statement. Interest income accrues on performing interest-earning assets, and net interest income results from deducting expenses that accrue on the bank's interest-bearing liabilities. This is the core source of commercial banking profits but is never entirely endogenous.

The margin between prevailing lending and funding rates in the financial sector at large is a measure of financial sophistication or depth as we outlined in Section 2.1, while the net interest margin of a single bank indicates its efficiency in relation to local conditions. High margins may indicate low efficiency in an unsophisticated financial system or one that is subject to bank cartels that fix loan or deposit rates. Low margins suggest either greater competition or a lack of skill in appropriate loan pricing. Mortgage lending in Hong Kong was conducted until the early 1990s at margins of several hundred basis points above the cost of bank deposits or interbank funds, despite being known for very low historic NPLs, but margins fell to more normal levels after deposit rates were made subject to competition in 2001 and home lending greatly encouraged by the creation of the Hong Kong Mortgage Corporation. The returns on local mortgage lending are currently unprofitable unless banks have access to very cheap deposits.

Figure 6.2 compares national interest rate margins in the latest year for which data are available, using the difference between the rate charged to prime borrowers and the average bank cost of retail funds. Prevailing interest margins are likely to be inversely related to GDP, but the picture is complicated by cyclical and local conditions. For example, in 2008 the respective interest margins of Germany and the UK were 7.04 per cent and 2.73 per cent.

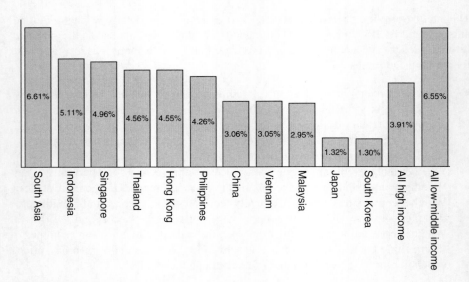

Figure 6.2 Interest rate margins, 2008.

We distinguish *margin* in this discussion from interest rate *spreads*, which in the general economy refer to the difference between specified prevailing short and long-term nominal rates, that is, the slope of the yield curve. South Asia is Bangladesh, India, Nepal, Pakistan and Sri Lanka. Data for Taiwan are unavailable.

Source: World Bank (undated b).

Performance assessment

Much of OCBC's 2010 non-interest income was based on extending credit, including loan fees and trade finance revenue, and the largest source of other revenue was profits derived from life assurance. Bank operating expenses are usually dominated by staff and IT costs, and OCBC's expense ratio is lower than banks that operate in more complex business streams that entail higher human resource costs. The bank's net income is stated after providing for NPLs, a relatively modest charge in absolute terms and compared to the prior year.

Table 6.3 shows a simple calculation of regulatory capital requirements according to prevailing Basel accord Standardized Approach guidelines. Our generic bank's assets total US$100, divided into eight categories with differing weightings for capital adequacy purposes, so that total risk-weighted assets are US$51.5 and require regulatory capital of US$4.12. Note that our bank still needs to maintain funding for US$100 of assets, even though its financial performance is assessed partly on the basis of risk-weighted assets of half that amount.

This gives a clue to the incentive that Basel creates for banks to manage the risk composition of their balance sheet assets, and when market conditions are favourable to use securitization and other forms of credit risk transfer to maximize returns on risk-weighted capital, both on the overall credit portfolio and components of its asset base. OCBC's approach is different, as with many conservative Asian commercial banks. Its risk-weighted assets at end-2010 were 58 per cent of total net assets, as shown in Figure 6.1, implying that the bank far exceeded its required minimum Tier 1 and total capital ratios. Excess capital can signify three characteristics that are not mutually exclusive:

- Safety for shareholders, in the form of low share-price volatility and regular dividends;
- Commercial risk aversion in credit creation and transaction seeking; and
- A constrained ability to create business opportunities.

If capital adequacy fails to meet required levels or is poor relative to the bank's peer group, then profits need to be retained and new equity raised from shareholders. Net profits are

Table 6.3 Simplified effect of risk–asset weighting (US$ mm)

	Nominal amount	Risk weighting (%)	Risk-weighted amount
Cash	1	0	0
Government securities rated AA− to AAA	10	0	0
Government securities rated A− to A+	5	20	1
Loans to banks rated AA− to AAA	10	20	2
Secured residential mortgage loans	20	35	7
Loans to companies rated A− to A+	20	50	10
Loans to companies rated below BB−	15	150	22.5
Consumer loans	10	75	7.5
Fixed assets	9	100	9
Total	**100**	**NA**	**51.5**
		Required capital (8% of risk-weighted assets)	**4.12**

Source: BCBS (2006b: 19–27).

otherwise available for distribution as dividends. Investment bank and rating agency analysts use a series of comparators to assess the performance and robustness of commercial banks. Attention given to these variables influences bank behaviour as in the way that Goodhart's Law predicts of monetary policy: for example, the ranking of salary expense ratios and cost-to-income variables of similar banks creates pressure for salaries to be reduced as a share of total employee compensation, and non-revenue functions to be commercially outsourced, in each case allowing banks to plead that their fixed production costs and headcounts are in check. OCBC's 2010 performance was poor in this regard. Staff numbers, compensation and total expenses adjusted for acquisitions rose and the overall cost–income ratio jumped by 500 basis points to 42.3 per cent compared to 2009. This is low by standards in high-income economies, but a deterioration that observers and shareholders would wish to see corrected.

Our final point on performance assessment concerns a moral hazard associated with depositors that was highlighted in the global crisis as banks being 'too big to fail'. Although commercial banks may engage in simple business streams, it is almost impossible for individuals to assess the credit risk of maintaining a deposit other than to rely on a third party credit rating or mandatory deposit insurance. OCBC Bank's 2009 annual report contained 170 pages of discussion on the bank's results, including financial and compliance information of considerable technical detail. The substantive part of HSBC's 2010 annual report covers 390 pages, including a nine-page financial glossary much like our own. Few individual depositors will read these reports; still fewer could assess the risk of depositing with one bank compared to its rivals. Even professional depositors that set deposit limits to restrict their exposure to any single bank may lack the resources to assess complex bank credit risk. Retail savers depend on the performance of supervisors, deposit insurance, rating agencies, and the perception of reputation to safeguard their funds. By this perspective there are no modern commercial banks unprotected by the state. All are too complex to fail.

6.3 Medium-term credit

In Chapter 5 we explained the spectrum of formality associated with bank lines. Medium-term credit is nearly always formal by being subject to non-trivial contracts with detailed provisions. The result can be simple or complex in use, so that revolving credits are a contractually dense form of a simple overdraft that allow a bank's credit commitment to be drawn, repaid and redrawn if the borrower meets commercial hurdles. Debt claims are defined obligations but incomplete contracts because information asymmetry is always present in their creation and operation, chiefly since the borrower knows more of its financial condition than its banker. The result is often detailed clauses and covenants in credit agreements, to protect and give negotiating leverage to the creditor.

Medium-term credit is a staple source of revenue for most commercial banks. OCBC is typical, with 64 per cent of loans at end-2010 being of more than 12 months maturity, that is, the dominant part of its largest balance sheet component. It also has a higher commercial profile than trade finance, can be quick and inexpensive to arrange, and above all is capable of providing positive interest margins with a degree of certainty as to future revenue accrual.

Here, we discuss the nature, terms and arrangement of two generic forms of credit: the syndicated loan and a more specialized form of facility for which the syndicated loan structure was first devised, that is, non-recourse financing for infrastructural projects and in particular object finance for major movable assets when the lender's principal credit risk is the project or the enterprise in which the asset is engaged. These models provide the greater part of medium-term credit granted by commercial banks in most Asian economies. Regulation and practice treat commitments of more than 12 months as medium-term, and most such transactions have a contractual life of 3–8 years. No rigid distinction exists between medium- and long-term loans but those with lives of at least ten years are taken as long term and usually associated with projects entailing lengthy payoff periods.

Syndicated lending

Syndicated loans are a style of credit transaction arranged by one or a small group of banks that are joined by others to make commitments and extend credit in concert and on identical terms. The scale and composition of syndicates follows conventions, risk preferences, market conditions and in some cases the borrower's preferences, with small-group transactions often known as 'club deals'.

Syndicate practice has existed in developed securities markets since the nineteenth century to help transaction arrangers defray the risks involved in raising funds (Baskin & Miranti 1997; Michie 2006), and was used extensively by New York banks to sell shares or bonds across the US through networks of brokers. Bank lenders adopted certain syndicate practices in the 1970s as a means of managing arrangement risks, even though some jurisdictions considered this collusive and anti-competitive until the 1980s. The hostility fell away and regulators began to value the model for two reasons:

- It allowed a dispersal of credit risk among a widening number of lenders that went unquestioned until the uncertainties of September 2008; and
- Cooperation among lenders and the adoption of standardized terms and documentation was conducive to dealing with large-scale non-judicial workouts, when distressed borrowers sought to renegotiate the terms of their debts. This feature of transnational lending began after Mexico declared a moratorium on foreign debt payments in mid-1982 and became entrenched by the Bank of England's London Approach, now widely adopted elsewhere.

The international syndicated loan market is now considerable, as we see from Table 6.4, which shows the volume of new loans completed in four sample years to 2010. Gross issuance is dominated by borrowers in developed economies, partly because the average size of their loans exceeds those of other groups. Asian borrowing is also sizeable and of a similar order to international debt securities issues from the same group. We must add a cautionary word: the table shows only disclosed international transactions, that is, deals notified to data publishers by their arrangers that have a cross-border element. Purely domestic loans and bonds are excluded, which reduces deal volumes in China, Japan, South Korea and elsewhere. The table illustrates the problem of incompleteness in transactional data referred to in Box 3.4, which is common to all financial markets except organized exchanges dealing in futures and option contracts.

Modern syndicated lending developed from simple supply and demand factors. US dollar liquidity in Europe led to the creation of Eurobonds as offshore debt securities in the early 1960s, but the supply of funds multiplied after 1973–74 after a fourfold jump in crude oil prices. Mounting OPEC revenues led to external payment imbalances, vast loan demand by

Table 6.4 Completed international syndicated loans (US$ bn)

	1995	2000	2005	2010	Net international debt securities 2010**
India	0.2	0.2	1.2	18.8	4.7
Hong Kong	2.8	3.7	6.2	10.4	7.8
China	4.9	1.3	2.8	8.6	25.9
Japan	0.2	4.1	5.0	6.8	0.3
Singapore	0.7	3.7	3.2	6.2	3.9
Taiwan	1.6	2.9	5.3	3.7	1.4
South Korea*	2.4	3.2	3.1	3.5	12.4
Indonesia	3.1	0.4	0.5	2.2	4.0
Thailand	2.0	1.0	1.0	1.6	1.2
Malaysia	1.1	0.6	1.7	1.1	5.8
Vietnam	0.2	0.0	0.1	1.0	0.0
Others	0.3	1.4	1.9	1.2	0.0
A. Total Asia	19.5	22.7	32.1	65.0	77.8
Developed countries	611.3	1,134.9	1,490.0	1,460.1	1,187.1
Offshore centres	16.9	37.4	40.5	53.2	13.8
All developing countries	75.1	101.2	194.0	263.6	212.6
International organizations	0.1	0.5	0.5	0.0	93.2
B. All transactions	703.3	1,274.0	1,725.1	1,776.8	1,506.7
Africa & Middle East	12.1	13.4	46.7	67.4	30.0
Europe	8.1	16.4	50.5	57.1	53.3
Latin America	8.0	31.7	27.2	25.0	63.5
Developing Asia	46.9	39.6	69.7	114.0	65.8
C. All developing countries	75.1	101.2	194.0	263.6	212.6

Asian (section A) economies listed in descending order of completed 2010 loans. Loan data cover disclosed transactions in which at least two lenders participate, at least one of which has a different nationality from the borrower. Developing Asia comprises the economies listed in section A except for Hong Kong, Japan and Singapore, plus Kazakhstan. Developed countries includes Japan. Offshore centres include Hong Kong and Singapore.

*2010 data are unavailable; the total shown is for 2009.

** Data are for international debt securities issuance net of redemptions in the same period.

Source: BIS database <http://www.bis.org/statistics/index.htm>

emerging states lacking energy resources, and a supply of ongoing liquidity to the international banking system.

The result was a new market to intermediate offshore Eurocurrency funds held outside their place of settlement, not least since certain OPEC states preferred their cash to remain in US dollars but outside the US because of advantageous deposit rates and the fear of sequestration. Higher oil prices favoured the economics of deep-water exploration and development, but this consumed capital beyond the capacity of any single financier, both for prudential reasons and due to national bank lending limits on single obligors and sectoral concentration. Costly offshore oil exploration, especially in the North Sea, required unprecedentedly large financing transactions that no single bank could bear and were considered too risky for debt capital market financing.

The banking system needed profitable new mechanics of intermediation to support sizeable lending transactions and to organize offshore liquidity as a source of durable funding and lessen the risk of it becoming flight capital. The solutions were syndicated credits to deal with excess loan demand, an international interbank market for deposits, and unlisted debt instruments to marshal the supply of funds.

Banks cooperated as lenders and funded their loans with short-term wholesale deposits, and by issuing large-denomination certificates of deposit (CDs) of 2–5 years maturity to extend the duration of their liabilities. Both instruments are now widely used in many developed financial systems. Fixed and floating rate CDs were adapted from traditional short-term promissory notes, and given a term structure by banks in London and Paris to capture large-scale liquidity from professional investors and cash-rich corporations. For banks lacking material foreign currency deposits these became the means by which they could participate in the burgeoning international syndicated loan market. By the 1980s, syndicated deals resulted in five apparent commercial advantages for banks resulting from separating transaction formation and lending:

- They lessened the commercial impact of prudential or regulatory lending limits, or capital scarcity;
- They introduced the flexibility of credit risk transfer to hitherto static loan markets;
- Larger loans become feasible, bringing additional revenue from arrangement fees;
- Returns to arrangers on their retained loan assets were improved by syndication; and
- Small banks gained access to far more diverse risks, including well-rated or physically remote borrowers.

The commercial impact was broader, in that large transactions not only became feasible but were arranged more rapidly than before, both for complex projects and in financing time-sensitive ventures such as contested acquisitions. Syndicated loans brought speed to deal formation, execution and any subsequent changes in terms, and these features crystallized over a period through to the late 1990s in two developments that are found in all major financial centres including Hong Kong, Singapore and Tokyo as Asia's transaction hubs:

- Standardized practice in syndicate formation, loan documentation and provision for banks to transfer their commitments; and
- Convergence with practice in the debt securities markets.

Modern loan and bond markets are interchangeable for many users and loans are a vehicle for acquiring funded credit risk for a variety of professional non-bank investors, especially in North America and Europe. Note that the participation in large loans of smaller banks and non-bank investors widens the incidence of information asymmetries, not only between lenders and unfamiliar borrowers but between arranging banks that know their borrowing clients well and those non-traditional lenders to which they syndicate risk that inevitably know less. The result is a commercial methodology in deal arrangement that has two related features:

- Intense contractual indemnification to absolve arranging banks of responsibility for providing information to syndicate members prior to the loan signing.[2] Lenders joining a transaction are deemed to have conducted their own credit appraisal, which is usually a convenient fiction but generally respected by the courts.
- Relatively narrow syndication or subsequent sale of loans to specialist borrowing sectors where the fiction would be too incredible to maintain.

These conventions evolved after disputes in the mid-1970s involving a New York bank that syndicated loans for Greek shipping group Colocotronis, which later became insolvent and defaulted. Several banks complained that they had been induced to participate by the arranger asserting itself as an expert in shipping risk, and sought remedies provided by US federal securities law. The cases were settled out of court but gave a lasting warning for all banks using English or New York law to document syndicated loans. Participating banks would be required to confirm the fiction that they chose to commit to the transaction solely after their own analysis and without relying on information distributed by the arranger. Practice also developed for transaction arrangers to confine syndication and any later 'secondary' loan sales to lenders with experience of specialist sectors. The case also showed that loans were generally distinct in law from securities, which has further consequences for investor protection.

The main elements of the generic transaction are:

- Syndicated deals are single loans made in concert. In law they are distinct or 'several' loans made on identical conditions as shown in Figure 6.3. It is rare for deals to comprise joint and several claims where the rights of lenders are mingled.
- An agent acts for the lenders to administer the loan after execution. This may be a transaction arranger or a specialist body such as an administrative trustee.
- The terms of the deal may be altered during its life by majority or supermajority consent of 66 per cent or 75 per cent respectively of outstanding commitments. Unanimous consent is sometimes needed to alter contentious terms but this is becoming archaic as an obstacle to efficient workout practice.
- Lenders are deemed to take a simplified contractual approach to funding their commitments that establishes how interest accrues and is paid by the borrower. These provisions include protection against interest rates becoming impossible to determine in times of stress or unexpectedly costly for one or more syndicate members. The 2007–9 crisis revealed weaknesses in this methodology, but changes to practice will take a long time to agree.
- Provision for payment sharing so that any payment delinquency is suffered proportionally by the lenders. If a payment of interest, principal or fees is only partly paid when due then the shortfall is borne by all the banks, and if the borrower deliberately or in error pays not the agent but a participant then the recipient passes the funds back to the agent for redistribution. Each bank is usually permitted to deal freely with the borrower in other businesses without their being affected by payment sharing.

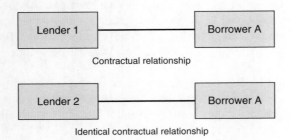

Figure 6.3 Claims under syndicated loans.

Deal formation and mechanics

The generic and legal structure is shown schematically in Figure 6.4.

Syndicated loan arrangement comprises two phases of contract formation and execution. The separation helps in mutually absolving the banks from responsibility for any pre-contractual work. Credit agreements commonly state that arrangers and other banks have no post-execution function in the deal and give strong protection for the agent in the conduct of its administrative duties. This is reflected in Figure 6.4. The transaction consists of parallel loans to a single obligor, all administered by an agent. The arranger is without rights or responsibilities under the deal, and is indemnified by each lender for any non-fraudulent actions that it took to advance the deal from conception to signing.

Deal formation differs from case to case, but a complex transaction would involve several steps. The prospective borrower issues a *request for proposals* (RFP) to banks that it knows or considers competent. One or more will respond with an outline *term sheet* stating the main conditions under which it will agree to arrange the loan, an indication of deal strategy, and the scale and nature of its proposed commitment to the process. That commitment may take several forms:

- Simple transaction management for a target amount with no firm commitment of funds, known as a *best efforts* deal.
- Transaction arrangement with an undertaking to deliver a specific amount of funds after signing, regardless of the success of the deal in syndication, generally known as an *underwritten* commitment. This arrangement is most common in Asia.
- An underwritten deal with a firm commitment as to the final cost of funds.

The borrower negotiates appropriately and gives a *mandate* to one or more arrangers to proceed with the deal, the parties signing pre-contractual heads of agreement stating the main terms and strategy of the deal including the *interest margin* or *spread* and the total arrangement or *front-end fee* as a percentage of the contracted loan amount. This is deducted from the loan proceeds after signing. Heads of agreement can become highly complex when supporting large-scale project or acquisition financing.

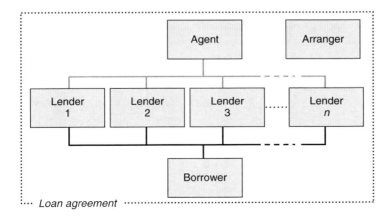

Figure 6.4   Generic syndicated loan.

The mandate sets rules for deal completion. It may allow commercial flexibility prior to signing, so that pricing is adjusted if conditions change and affect the deal's reception, a process known as *market flex* that points to convergence in loan and bond market practice. Unless the loan is small or a club deal, a period of *primary syndication* follows for the arranger to invite others to join the transaction and reduce its initial commitment. Those that join face lesser transaction or underwriting risks or provide lower commitments, which allows the arranger to keep a disproportionate share of the front-end fee, even if its *retention* or final lending commitment is small. Participants may never know the full cost of the loan, unlike bond issues where fees are typically standardized or disclosed. When the primary syndication ends the loan is *closed* and a credit agreement negotiated by the arranger and borrower executed by all transaction parties. With large deals the primary syndication may be followed by participants continuing to promote further sales of their commitments in a *secondary selldown*. This may be coordinated by the arranger for a short period but soon becomes competitive, and may subsist as a secondary market well into the life of the loan, especially if the borrower's financial conditions change.

Mandates are usually awarded competitively based on pricing and the reputational capital of the arranger, notably its success in completing past deals. The two variables are linked, for the correct price of a loan may not be a minimum total cost to the borrower but a clearing level that meets the borrower's objectives while attracting an appropriate number and quality of participants. These outcomes will affect both the borrower's later transactions and the arranger's reputation. We discuss reputational capital among competing banks in Chapter 7. Banks derive intangible branding value from having or appearing to have a part in deal arrangement. Leading banks began to widen this process in the 1980s, by creating a hierarchy of transaction titles for participants according to the scale of their initial commitment. These meaningless titles – lead or co-lead manager, manager, co-manager – have often been coveted as a sign of deal activity, but only arrangers have a real function before any loan is funded. Experienced arrangers take account of transaction titles in publicity and when deciding the order in which to invite potential participants into a deal.

Some of these practices are shown in the press report below of a simple loan signed in 2010, which we have deconstructed to identify its jargon. The heading suggests success, but remember that the arranger is the media's source. Only six participants joined the deal:

> SAN MIGUEL BOOST. The US$880m five-year loan for San Miguel has closed after an increase to US$1bn after receiving commitments from six other banks and not eight, as previously reported. The MLAs [mandated lead arrangers] were ANZ, Bank of Tokyo-Mitsubishi UFJ, Chinatrust Commercial Bank, Crédit Agricole, DBS Bank, HSBC, ING Bank, Maybank, Mizuho Corporate Bank, SMBC and Standard Chartered. All had bookrunner titles and active bookrunners were ANZ, BTMU, Crédit Agricole, DBS Bank, HSBC, Mizuho and StanChart.
>
> (*International Financing Review* 2010)

San Miguel Corporation mandated 11 banks to arrange a five-year US dollar loan. Seven became *bookrunners*, or those banks that manage the primary syndication on behalf of all lenders. The stated amount was increased after a limited syndication but this was planned in order to conjure success.

All of the bookrunners ended up with US$80m holds, except Maybank and HSBC, which took US$100m and US$95m. Banco de Oro committed US$40m, Bank of China joined with US$12m, Cathay United Bank and Export-Import Bank of the Republic of China took US$10m each, Bangkok Bank US$5m and Mega International Commercial Bank US$8m.

(ibid)

Six banks joined the deal with a total commitment of US$85 million, making this a large club transaction with no primary selldown for the MLAs, so that amounts raised from participants were used to increase the loan. This gives inventory for later *secondary* loan sales, for example allowing lenders to profit if the borrower's credit rating or general lending conditions improve.

> The facility pays a top-level all-in of 265bp over Libor – significantly inside the 450bp over Libor top-level all-in paid on a US$600m three-year facility signed in September 2009. The new loan refinances the September 2009 financing.

(ibid)

Bookrunners retain a higher percentage fee than the other banks. Interest accrues at a rate that is the sum of the Libor (London interbank offered rate) benchmark and a spread of 240 basis points. *Top-level all-in* refers to the effective interest rate received by the bookrunners amortizing a 125 basis-point front-end fee evenly over the five years of the loan. The new deal is priced *significantly inside* an earlier loan to San Miguel Corporation and will be used to repay that costlier funding.

A more complex example is a transaction arranged for mining group BHP Billiton in August 2010 that shows the potential of the structure for scale and speed of execution. BHP mandated several banks to arrange a US$45 billion loan facility divided into four *tranches* of varying *tenors* to support its hostile bid for Saskatchewan fertilizer group Potash. Six MLAs completed syndication in ten days and 24 banks executed the transaction in September 2010, but it lapsed unused when Canadian authorities vetoed the acquisition. The loan's size and speed of arrangement were bid-enabling in permitting BHP to make a cash offer to Potash shareholders, which no other form of financing could do. The borrower would have drawn the facility in full had its bid succeeded but refinanced the bulk of the loans within 12 months using longer duration bonds.

After signing the agent collects and makes payments between the banks and the borrower. Lending usually adopts Euromarket practice, by which advances are made for agreed *interest periods* commonly of between one and six months with the rate *fixed* at the start of the period, at the end of which the borrower pays accrued interest. Unless a repayment of principal is then due the loan is *rolled* for the next interest period at the then prevailing benchmark interest rate plus the spread. This *floating rate* arrangement is intended to allow banks to *match fund* their loans at the benchmark rate and be confident of earning the credit spread as a net interest margin. Figure 6.5 shows the timeline of wholesale funding mechanics for a three-year loan that has six successive six-monthly interest periods.

Libor is a prominent benchmark intended to represent a standard interbank cost of funds. It is determined daily for a variety of major currencies and periods, and has counterparts in Euros (Euribor) and several Asian currencies (Hong Kong's Hibor, Malaysia's KLibor, Singapore's Sibor, and others). These benchmarks provide operational standardization for a vast number of contracts for loans, floating rate securities and most interest rate derivatives. Syndicated credit agreements often include an informal fixing method should Libor be impossible to determine, and provision for banks to be compensated if the fixing underestimates

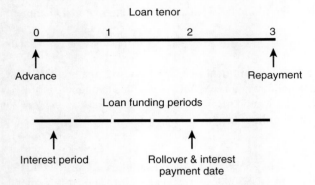

Figure 6.5 Interest rate determination and payment.

their true cost of funds, although these provisions are seldom used. Libor fixings are based on indications provided by panels of banks in response to the question: At what rate could you borrow funds, were you to do so by asking for and then accepting interbank offers in a reasonable market size just prior to 11 a.m.?

The method is long established, but the global crisis revealed Libor to be a poor measure of the true cost of funds. Many banks find wholesale deposits unavailable in a full range of periods during stressed times, but even in normal conditions bank practice may not reflect benchmark mechanics:

- Match funding is no longer standard practice. Banks tend not to borrow to support a single transaction but use pooled resources continually to fund their asset portfolios.
- Libor makes no provision for capital costs.
- Banks of all sizes and ratings were unable to access the interbank markets in 2008–9, although those markets were hitherto thought to be thoroughly reliable. This was a systemic problem, not merely one of credit differentiation by wholesale lenders resulting in certain classes or nationalities of banks being required to pay premiums for funds.
- Banks participating in rate-setting panels may choose to quote off-market rates for commercial reasons or to try to engineer a fixing distortion.

UK regulators proposed reforms to the Libor fixing process in 2012 (Wheatley 2012), and are likely to be followed by other leading jurisdictions. These changes involve regulatory supervision of the contributor panels, greater reliance on actual market rates instead of estimates, and post-fixing disclosure of each panel's submissions. The reforms will allow Libor to continue in use as a reference index in commercial contracts, although standardized loan agreements are certain to be modified over time to take into account the new rules.

Terms and conditions

No two credit agreements are identical, but contractual standardization has taken place over a long period and the principal terms of international syndicated loans are well known, not only because of legal factors but due to industry association pressure. North America's Loan Syndications and Trading Association, Europe's Loan Market Association, and the Asia

Pacific Loan Market Association (APLMA) each maintain standard documents intended to foster good practice and facilitate loan transfers. The APLMA's syndicated term loan and revolving credit facility agreement is one example, and contains terms and definitions of the kind summarized in Table 6.5.

Table 6.5 Syndicated loan model terms

Terms	Notes
Parties	Borrower(s), guarantor(s), lenders, agent. Other bank titles are included but explicitly given no function.
Amount(s)	Total aggregate commitment. The commitments of each lender will be stated in a schedule to the agreement or its execution pages.
Availability	Whether the loan amount is available in one or more tranches. Whether drawings may be repaid and reborrowed and subject to what conditions.
Conditions precedent	Events or actions that precede drawing(s), some procedural such as the delivery of borrower board approvals for the loan, and others substantive that relate to credit risk and ongoing disclosure.
Use of proceeds	Borrower's commitment to use the loan for an agreed purpose.
Interest benchmark, basis & spread	Calculation of periodic interest as a sum of Libor or another benchmark for permissible interest periods and a credit spread. When accrued interest is payable.Pricing may be a simple credit spread or a matrix that causes the spread to vary with the amount of lending outstanding, the credit rating of the borrower, or the duration of the loan.
Increased costs	Provision for compensation to lenders if their funding costs exceed the calculated interest rate.
Repayment	Schedule of reductions of the commitment.
Payments	How payments are made to the agent and how compensation is required for lenders if taxes or other deductions are incurred.How sharing provisions function among the lenders if a shortfall occurs in a scheduled payment.
Agent's duties	Schedule of what the agent does, may do if instructed, and may not do, and how it is held harmless by the banks against operational errors.
Representations & warranties	Statements by the borrower and any guarantor that collectively seek to narrow information asymmetries with lenders. They relate to its commercial and financial conditions, and the veracity of other statements. Breach of representations of warranties prevents any further drawings and gives the lenders rights of early repayment.
Events of default, cross-default & acceleration	Series of payment and non-payment defaults, that give automatic or conditional rights to the lenders to demand early repayment. May include a change of circumstances, by which an event of default occurs if there is a material and unremedied change in the borrower's conditions that threaten its obligations under the loan.Trivial or accidental defaults are usually ignored, not least because the events of default usually include cross-default provisions that allow acceleration of the loan if another transaction is declared in default or in some cases is capable of being so declared.
Covenants & financial covenants	Ongoing obligations, a continuing breach of which may constitute an event of default. These may include covenants as to leverage, liquidity, minimum net assets, limits to the sale of assets or businesses, any unapproved change of control, or unapproved distributions.

(continued)

Table 6.5 (continued)

Terms	Notes
Negative pledge	Undertaking not to give priority to subsequently created creditor claims. Exceptions are sometimes allowed for purchase money mortgages, where priority can be given over assets financed by a new loan.
Pari passu	Claim under the agreement must maintain their status with comparable debts of the borrower or guarantor in any reorganization or winding up.
Governing law	The form of law that governs how the agreement is interpreted. The courts of which state will have the right to hear actions brought under the agreement, and arrangements for filing complaints.
Majority voting & control	Changes to the agreement can be made by a majority or super majority, depending whether the change is commercially or legally substantive.
Transfer	Mechanics of transfer by lenders, restrictions on transfer, rules for disclosure of transfer.

Front-end arrangement fees are excluded by custom and specified in a side letter between the arranger and borrower. Well-rated borrowers will be able to negotiate fewer conditions or events of default that give additional or acceleration rights to lenders.

These model documents include commercial and administrative clauses that have evolved since the mid-1970s through many crises and reforms, but long-standing administrative provisions were shown in 2007–9 to be contractually incomplete. Practitioners will devise new reforms, but the problem may never be eradicated because contractual incompleteness is inevitable in documenting complex commercial practices:

> All contracts are incomplete. There are infinite states of the world and the capacities of contracting parties to condition their future performance on each possible state are finite.
>
> (Scott 2003: 1641–2)

Such incompleteness may take two forms. It is exogenous when the parties recognize that they lack the foresight to predict future events that may affect their contractual performance, and may be endogenous in that contracts are:

> deliberately incomplete, in the sense that parties decline to condition performance on available, verifiable measures that could be specified in the contract at relatively low cost ... suggesting that the parties had other reasons for leaving the terms in question unspecified.
>
> (ibid)

We suspect that those well-established clauses shown by the crisis to be unsatisfactory may be examples of endogenous contractual incompleteness. Any post-crisis revisions will simply be incomplete in other ways. The more subtle intention within these standard credit agreements is to encourage negotiation between borrowers and lenders when unexpected events occur.

One example is the material adverse change clause (MAC), which usually gives some right of action or redress to lenders if an event occurs that they reasonably believe will have a materially adverse effect on the borrower's operations or financial health, especially its capacity to meet the obligations of the credit agreement. The MAC is rarely invoked. Its use can damage bank reputations and future client relationships, so its main value is to bring parties to discussion ahead of trouble. MACs also appear in both simple loan mandates and detailed pre-contractual letters of commitment for complex financings, but are equally contentious and inimical to the concept of underwriting. Except in extreme cases, the parties are more likely to acknowledge a change of circumstances and quietly renegotiate the transaction's commercial terms.

Recourse, non-recourse and specialist lending

Recourse refers to the character of a credit risk. All sizeable enterprises have a commercial sponsor, but for reasons of cost, risk or to allow for exogenous institutional factors it may prefer to manage the venture with a degree of legal separation rather than administer it within an existing corporate organization. That choice affects the way that external finance is provided to the enterprise and whether the credit risk faced by lenders or investors is confined to the venture or has recourse to the sponsor.

We call *non-recourse finance* an arrangement where funds are provided to a project and are serviced and repaid solely by that enterprise, regardless of the condition of its sponsor. If the sponsor assists the transaction with credit support, such as a guarantee or agreement to provide conditional capital infusions to the project, then the credit risk is said to be *with recourse*. We can state the distinction in terms of claims:

- With recourse means that the financier holds a general claim against a substantive debtor, not merely the business stream that it funds.
- Non-recourse means that the financier has a priority claim against the business venture it funds, and no automatic claim against the sponsor.

Partial recourse transactions fitting within this credit spectrum are a common form of real project finance, where a sponsor provides credit support for a fixed period, while certain conditions prevail, or up to a cash ceiling. Basel II's internal ratings-based approach to quantifying credit risk identifies forms of specialist corporate lending covering finance for projects, objects, commodities and real estate, taking projects to be costly and complex installations such as power or chemical plants (BCBS 2006b: §§ 218–19). These risks share four qualities:

- Lenders are exposed to an SPV created purely to finance or operate physical assets;
- The SPV has no capacity to repay its obligations except from revenue derived from the assets being financed.
- Lenders have substantial contractual control over the SPV assets and the net revenue they generate; and
- Lenders are repaid solely from income generated by the SPV assets.

Our discussion concentrates on non-recourse object finance for major movable assets, covering ships, commercial aircraft, railway carriages and commercial satellites, because these examples best show how institutional factors affect transaction design. Institutional factors condition sponsors and financiers to favour a specific transaction structure that works to each party's advantage. Box 6.4 gives examples relating to movable assets such as ships and commercial aircraft. The generic non-recourse ship finance transaction is shown in Figure 6.6.

Box 6.4 Institutional Background to Object Finance

United Nations conventions provide that the high seas are commons belonging to no nation, and establish rules for their use under international law. Ships must have a nationality and stateless ships may not lawfully sail the high seas or call at a legitimate port. The Convention on the Law of the Sea states that:

> Every State shall fix the conditions for the grant of its nationality to ships, for the registration of ships in its territory, and for the right to fly its flag. Ships have the nationality of the State whose flag they are entitled to fly. There must exist a genuine link between the State and the ship.
>
> (Art. 91)

This was echoed in a decision of the US Supreme Court:

> Each state under international law may determine for itself the conditions on which it will grant its nationality to a merchant ship, thereby accepting responsibility for it and acquiring authority over it. Nationality is evidenced to the world by the ship's papers and its flag. The United States has firmly and successfully maintained that the regularity and validity of a registration can be questioned only by the registering state.
>
> (Lauritzen v. Larsen)

Open-registry states such as Liberia and Panama liberally allow foreign-owned vessels to fly their flags and together provide nationality for a large share of the world's merchant fleet. The convention further provides that:

> Every State shall (a) maintain a register of ships containing the names and particulars of ships flying its flag, except those which are excluded from generally accepted international regulations on account of their small size.... Every State shall take such measures for ships flying its flag as are necessary to ensure safety at sea with regard, inter alia, to: (a) the construction, equipment and seaworthiness of ships.... Such measures shall include those necessary to ensure (a) that each ship, before registration and thereafter at appropriate intervals, is surveyed by a qualified surveyor of ships.
>
> (Art. 94)

Such rules are typically adopted into national laws. The effect is to confer and record nationality on a ship and allow financiers to obtain and perfect ship mortgages as collateral for credit. 'Ship' is usually defined under national or territorial legislation for similar reasons and to allow the scope of a ship mortgage to be clear. For example, in Hong Kong:

> 'ship' (船舶) means every description of vessel capable of navigating in water not propelled by oars, and includes any ship, boat or craft and an air-cushion vehicle or similar craft used wholly or partly in navigation in water.
>
> (Merchant Shipping (Registration) Ordinance s. 2)

English case law provides guidance as to the property covered by a mortgage, stemming from a dispute involving a fishing boat where the court was asked to decide if a mortgage covered valuable nets found on board the vessel:

> A ship mortgage includes all articles on board at the mortgage date necessary to navigation, or the prosecution of the adventure without which no prudent person would sail.
>
> (Charles, J. in Coltman v. Chamberlain)

The importance for lenders of clearly drawn and enforceable mortgages is that ships regularly incur claims as part of their working lives, most of which can give rise to maritime liens:

> A maritime lien attaches to a vessel and can be enforced against the vessel despite a change of ownership, even if the writ is issued after the change of ownership. A maritime lien is an encumbrance on a vessel, not defeasible within a reasonable time by a change of ownership, unless that change is effected by a sale by a Court exercising Admiralty jurisdiction. While a maritime lien remains in existence the ship to which it is attached can be arrested at the suit of the person whose claim is protected by that lien in any Court exercising Admiralty jurisdiction.
>
> (Sheen J. in The 'Baranbels')

The risk for lenders is clear. Ships earn revenue from trade only when at sea, and the existence of a lien on a vessel will usually allow it to be arrested, that is, detained in port until the claim giving rise to the lien is settled or discharged. The UN-IMO Diplomatic Convention on the Arrest of Ships gives 22 expansive grounds for the existence of a maritime claim, including:

(a) loss or damage caused by the operation of the ship;
(b) loss of life or personal injury occurring, whether on land or on water, in direct connection with the operation of the ship;
(c) salvage operations or any salvage agreement, including, if applicable, special compensation relating to salvage operations in respect of a ship which by itself or its cargo threatened damage to the environment;
(d) damage or threat of damage caused by the ship to the environment, coastline or related interests; measures taken to prevent, minimize, or remove such damage; compensation for such damage; costs of reasonable measures of reinstatement of the environment actually undertaken or to be undertaken; loss incurred or likely to be incurred by third parties in connection with such damage; and damage, costs, or loss of a similar nature to those identified in this subparagraph (d);
(e) costs or expenses relating to the raising, removal, recovery, destruction or the rendering harmless of a ship which is sunk, wrecked, stranded or abandoned, including anything that is or has been on board such ship, and costs or expenses relating to the preservation of an abandoned ship and maintenance of its crew.
(Art. 1(1))

The UN Convention on International Interests in Mobile Equipment took effect in 2006 and will apply eventually to aircraft, railway rolling stock and commercial satellites or space assets. Its ancillary Aircraft Protocol deals separately with airframes, aircraft engines and helicopters, and so recognizes that ownership and creditor interests may vary as to aircraft bodies and their engines.

The convention establishes among the ratifying states a mutual recognition of ownership and security interests, and creates a system of international registration of ownership and security interests (Art. 16). A legitimate default entitles the holder of a security interest to take possession of the asset, and dispose of, lease or use it as they wish (Art. 8). Article 29 gives priority of claim to interests that are part of the international registry.

The beneficial owner of the vessel to be financed is assumed to control a fleet of ships. Both the ship's owner and its financiers are concerned to preserve the commercial freedom of this highly mobile and valuable property, and in particular to prevent maritime liens for claims against the vessel or its sister ships leading to spurious arrests. Separating the beneficial owner's fleet is a way to lessen those risks.

- The transaction begins with actual control of the ship channelled through a 'one ship' SPV domiciled in the state of registration, owning no other assets and having little or no administrative resources. That company contracts with charterers to employ the vessel, with the entire fleet managed by a separate ship-management company controlled by the beneficial owner that acts as agent for the SPV and owner.

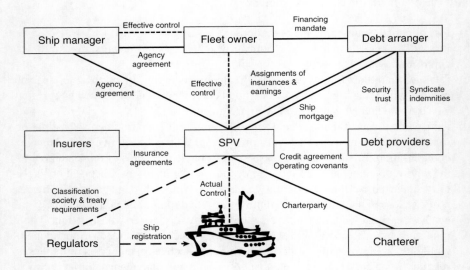

Figure 6.6 Non-recourse movable asset finance.

Contractual and ownership connections are shown respectively by solid and dotted lines. Broken lines indicate exogenous institutions that influence the transaction design.

- International law requires that the vessel be registered, properly insured and 'classed' or inspected periodically for seaworthiness by a ship classification society such as Lloyd's Register or Den Norske Veritas.

- Finance is provided to the SPV, enabling it to acquire the revenue generating ship. The terms of lending will require that the institutional requirements shown in the figure are maintained, so that the shipowner must ensure that until the loan is discharged the SPV engages in no other activity, and the vessel is properly mortgaged, employed, insured and maintained so as to meet regulatory requirements.

- Structural mismatches that make the loan riskier will require compensating credit support. If the term of a charterparty is less than the loan's remaining maturity, for example, the owner may be required to grant recourse in the form of a liquidity reserve or guarantee.

- We assume that the cost of the vessel is such that a syndicate provides finance. The loan arranger negotiates documentation which under English law would have three main parts: a credit agreement, statutory mortgage in the form stipulated by the ship registry, and either a deed of charge containing assignments of earnings and insurances over the vessel and commercial covenants matching those found in the credit agreement, or an assignment of a long-term charterparty or employment contract. The loan agent would also enter an agreement to share the value of the collateral and hold the security in trust for all lenders.

- The assignments require the owner to maintain the vessel and keep its operational payments current to avoid unnecessary maritime liens, in effect giving the lenders control of the vessel's net revenue stream and the proceeds of any insurance payments, for example to allow repayment of their claims in the event that the vessel is lost. The mortgage allows the lenders to take, seize and auction the vessel in the event of a loan default.

- If the ship is purchased secondhand the loan would be advanced in one amount and paid simultaneously with the transfer of ownership. Newbuildings ordered from shipyards can be financed in a similar way but with payment staged to match certain phases of construction. It is also common for shipyards to procure 'yard credit' for shipowners as a form of medium-term loan, with funds sourced from the shipyard's banks and with official support. Buyers also often require the yard to back its delivery commitment with a bank guarantee, and this would in turn be assigned to the shipowner's lenders while the ship was under construction.

The lender's objectives differ from those of the owner, although both wish to see the vessel sail safely and without arrest. It wants control over the proceeds of trading or a later sale of the vessel, an adequate commercial performance, and wishes to protect the enforceability of its collateral. This represents a desire for contractual completeness that supports the control theory of collateral. The owner wants to isolate this vessel from commercial risks and protect each member of its fleet against 'sister ship' claims and spurious arrests. The transaction is an attempt to devise a complete contract over the vessel's commercial operations, so that the loan's terms and covenants match the financial performance of the project for which it is made as closely as possible.

These core features exist in most successful transaction models involving movable assets regardless of the source of external finance, whether bank or non-bank lenders, equity investors, specialist shipping partnership funds as in Germany or Norway, or hedge funds as seen in 2006–8. They can be augmented by rights of recourse to corporate sponsors, or adapted

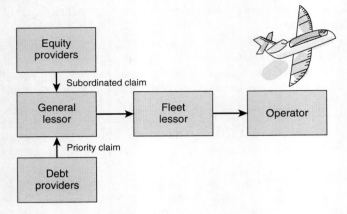

Figure 6.7 Basic aircraft lease.

into leasing structures, which for credit risk reasons is common in aviation finance. Asset values and revenues in the global shipping industry are highly volatile, but the commercial airline sector is notorious for unprofitable or failing operators, and the most common aircraft financing solution has been to rely on creditworthy financial lessors to intermediate between funds providers and equipment users, in the form shown in Figure 6.7.

The lessor acquires the aircraft and engines using an offshore SPV domiciled in a low-tax jurisdiction. Capital allowances accrue to the lessor and are usually not shared with the aircraft operator. The debt provider is given a priority claim over the aircraft and engines unless they are financed separately, while the lessor holds a subordinated claim against the aircraft. Residual ownership rights remain with the lessor when the financing transaction matures, as does the risk of a fall in aircraft values. The structure allows major leasing groups to demand substantial multiple order discounts from aircraft and engine makers that few airlines could negotiate. Engines are valuable, detachable from the aircraft and fungible, and are customarily financed separately from the airframe on which they fly.

Project finance sequencing

Complex fixed installations may require a succession of transactions, each predicated on the completion of identified stages and providing a repayment platform for its predecessor. The sequential concept is shown in Figure 6.8. A greenfield project might have five financing components with differing priorities of claim. Banks provide a revolving credit for the construction period, with the amount drawn adjusting to take account of progress, dispersals and receipts, and linking new advances to verifiable milestones. The revolving credit combines control of cash and debt management and defines the evolving credit risk for the lenders.

The project is commissioned when construction ends, and its outstanding accumulated debt and any accrued but unpaid interest is refinanced with a senior loan on terms sympathetic to cashflow potential, but without the earlier need to micromanage cash. This may combine with a longer-term mezzanine facility ranking junior to the senior debt, especially in highly leveraged cases. When the project's burden of debt peaks and the project is fully

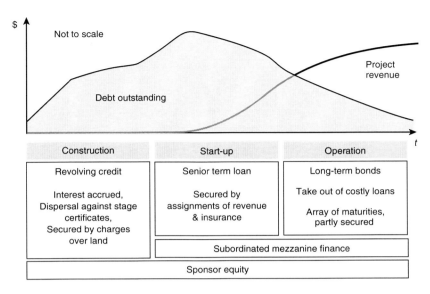

Figure 6.8 Project funding sequence.

operational, the outstanding senior loan is replaced by bonds of longer duration with redemption geared to the project's accumulating reserves. Throughout this timeline the sponsors will be required to provide and maintain an element of equity capital. All or part of post-construction financing may be provided by securitization, which isolates specified project revenues to meet the claims of bondholders.

Restrictive covenants are a device in debt contracts to constrain or compel an obligor's behaviour. They seek to give a degree of control to debtholders or a contractual community of creditors. They are usually negative in character, and provide a link to punitive or restorative actions such as default, acceleration and sharing of recovered proceeds, and so form an incentive for management of a borrower or project sponsor to meet its creditor's preferences. These covenants represent an attempt to deal with the agency problem that arises from the separation of borrower management from direct liability for any debtholder's claim. Covenants may be complex and comprehensive in non-recourse project finance, and help build the structure that makes the financing institutionally complete, which is impossible with general corporate borrowings.

Two traditions of credit risk management help explain the use of loan covenants. The most creditworthy corporate borrower may grant its lenders minimal financial or commercial covenants: for example, a negative pledge not to give precedence to subsequently created creditor claims (although some jurisdictions allow exceptions for 'new' funds), and to ensure that claims maintain their status in any reorganization or winding up (*pari passu* provisions).

Weaker corporate borrowers may be required to observe minimum credit ratings, a ceiling for leverage or total debt, prohibitions on new borrowings, minimum interest or dividend coverage, limits to distributions, the use of transaction proceeds, acquisitions, or on changes in activity. Other covenants stipulate how information is given to debtholders, and provide the means by which restrictive covenants are monitored.

A third non-traditional documentation solution became popular prior to the global crisis in the United States and Europe and was later criticized as inimical to sound lending, which involves documentation of a less restrictive kind. Known as 'cov-lite' transactions, these were negotiated not only with powerful and well-rated credit risks but with far less creditworthy companies in highly leveraged transactions. There is little doubt that cov-lite deals first appeared for competitive reasons as banks sought to arrange lucrative loans, but an argument is made that the concept is valuable in terms of avoiding the trigger of unwanted or unnecessary defaults that are difficult to remedy and leave no scope for discussion with creditors.

6.4 Cash securitization

Simple securitization of the kind used by many commercial lenders represents a further shift along a medium-term spectrum of deals, combining non-recourse finance with disintermediation from the conventional bank. While securitization now has connotations of complexity and regulatory arbitrage, its roots and commercial purposes are relatively simple and no more systemically threatening than other established forms of intermediation. That explains its place here; we leave discussion of more complex structures and uses to Chapter 8.

Central to our concept of cash securitization is an irrevocable removal from the lender's ownership of financial claims and their future cashflows, using those cashflows solely to generate distinct new funding resources. Non-bank enterprises may also separate and securitize distinct parts of their activities to reduce consolidated leverage or external financing costs, with the aim of obtaining a more favourable credit rating. They may also isolate businesses into trust arrangements for similar reasons or to alter aspects of corporate governance, most common with real estate investment trusts (REITs) or the business trust model created in Singapore. The result may be greater liquidity in certain business streams with other advantages in accounting, operating costs and credit standing, all motives best characterized as the commercial use of securitization (Schwarcz 2002).

Securitization can therefore be seen as the antithesis of the corporate framework for commercial activity. Securitization splits commercial activity from organizational or locational concerns and places it within a contractual setting. Its success depends upon the reliability of certain institutions, including property rights, contractual enforcement and actionable rights of transfer.

Cash securitization by banks is a form of intermediation outside the confines of a lending organization, and to be effective requires contractual completeness and the avoidance of distorting incentives. When properly practised it dispenses with the aggregation of claims within the intermediary and expressly avoids the mismatches inherent in bank lending. Credit intermediation entails three major transformations of duration, credit risk and value, as well as secondary effects prompted by risk management decisions that seek to offset those primary mismatches. All commercial banking intermediation thus involves opaque transformations, or what Section 6.1 called the 'black box' of banking, while cash securitization can be a transparent solution to these three elemental mismatches.

Empirical analysis suggests that securitization use varies as economies develop and financial markets become more sophisticated (Lejot, Arner & Schou-Zibell 2008). Not all advanced economies are prolific users, but it would be uncharacteristic for economies with effective and efficient financial systems not to support securitization. Certain Asian states have used cash securitization prolifically, but transaction volumes are far lighter than in North America or the EU.

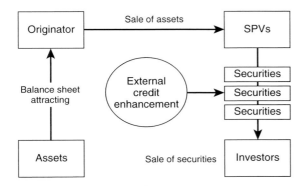

Figure 6.9 Generic cash transaction.

The generic transaction

Cash securitization is the irrevocable transfer of defined financial assets by their originator, funded by the simultaneous sale to third party investors of new securities issued by the asset buyer. The simplified generic model is shown in Figure 6.9. Neither the asset buyer nor any investor can claim transactional recourse to the originator. Ongoing aspects of the lending process will be replaced by contracts with administrative agents. Financial assets are sold by their originator to an insubstantive SPV in a tax-neutral domicile, with the purchase funded immediately or after a short period for asset accumulation with an array of new securities enjoying direct claims of varying seniority over all or part of the pool of assets. The sale allows the removal of assets from the originating lender's balance sheet.

Three mechanical features are common:

- Securities are issued by the SPV in tranches that carry different payment priorities, tenors and yields to their respective noteholders. Tranching manipulates cashflow from the securitized assets, meaning that the more conservative noteholders are provided with a claim ranking prior to all others with a lower compensating yield, and is more fully discussed in Chapter 8.
- Two SPVs are used sequentially in some jurisdictions to guard against a later attempt by a creditor of the originator to overturn the sale. This structure has often been used in civil law jurisdictions such as South Korea and Taiwan, in each case with the second SPV located offshore.
- Cashflow after expenses from the securitized assets is used mainly for payments due to the SPV noteholders, but a portion of receipts may be withheld as a form of credit enhancement to assist the operation of the transaction. Credit enhancement may be internal, as with a self-generated liquidity reserve, or external through a third party partial guarantee.

We distinguish this transaction from two others:

- Synthetic securitization involving CDOs that wholly or partly replicate the credit risk transfer involved in cash transactions using credit derivatives but no outright transfer of claims; and
- Covered bonds that share certain features of securitization and accomplish some of its objectives. Their transaction model is explained in Box 6.5.

Box 6.5 Covered Bonds

This form of secured finance is widely seen as a risk averse alternative to securitization, based on practice in civil law jurisdictions where the irrevocable transfer of claims can be difficult to uphold if the originator enters bankruptcy. It has long been used in Denmark, and in Germany where covered bonds are known as *pfandbriefe*.

The structure in its simple forms is popular in most European Union and European transition states because of investment incentives created by EU directives, as well as Iceland, Norway and Switzerland. South Korea began to allow covered bond issuance in 2009. Basel III will give a new value to covered bonds as an investment ranking before all other non-sovereign debt instruments for liquidity buffer purposes.

Covered bonds share two objectives of cash securitization, to assist in funding by intermediaries and provide homogeneous risks to investors. They are institutionally distinct in that unlike securitization they create a security interest for investors. Covered bondholders obtain preferential rights over pools of claims that remain funded assets on the balance sheet of the originating intermediary. Those assets 'cover' the new transaction as dedicated collateral without the irrevocable transfer of claims associated with securitization. Most jurisdictions require loan substitution within the pool so as to maintain a defined proportion of collateral 'cover'.

Markets in covered bonds at end-2009 were largest in Germany, Spain, Denmark, France, the UK and Sweden (ECBC 2010: 378–9), together accounting for over 85 per cent of a global market capitalization of €2.4tr (US$3.3tr; ibid). Few common law jurisdictions allow issuance, the notable exceptions being Ireland and the United Kingdom (Regulated Covered Bonds Regulations 2008, No. 3; Regulated Covered Bonds (Amendment) Regulations 2008, No. 1714). The concept has been studied in the United States since the federal housing agencies Fannie Mae and Freddie Mac became stricken by losses, but may conflict with federal bankruptcy law's hostility to the enhanced claims of covered bond creditors. *Structured covered* bonds can replicate the simple form by means of contractual provisions as an alternative for issuers in jurisdictions that lack enabling legislation, and this model was used successfully in the United Kingdom before 2008 and more modestly in Australia, Canada and the United States.

Covered bonds typically offer a funding cost advantage compared to securitized transactions, since bondholders retain rights of recourse to the originator. As a result they conventionally require less intensive structuring or credit enhancement. Covered bonds are associated with substantive intermediaries or their guaranteed subsidiaries but may involve the use of SPVs, usually due to quirks of national law. In contrast to cash securitizations, such vehicles will often be substantive in having dedicated management and administrative resources: for example, French covered bond law requires that pool assets subject to covered issuance be held and administered in a separate 'new' bank.

Covered bonds are primarily associated with European civil law jurisdictions. They resulted from legislation supporting development and social policy objectives begun in Denmark from 1850, in Germany from 1900, and more recently encouraged by the 1985 EU Directive on Undertakings for Collective Investment in Transferable Securities (UCITS) (85/611/EEC, OJ L 375 (1985)). Most create collateral pools from residential mortgages or loans made by specialist lenders for public infrastructure purposes. Since 2002 the market's growth has resulted largely from incentives created by further directives. Article 22(4) of UCITS requires that:

- The covered bond issuer must be a credit-providing organization;
- Covered bond issuance is to be governed by a special legal framework;
- Issuing organizations must be subject to special prudential public supervision;
- The set of eligible cover assets must be defined by law;
- The cover asset pool must provide sufficient collateral to cover bondholder claims throughout the whole term of the covered bond; and
- Bondholders must have a priority claim on the cover asset pool in case of a default by the issuer.

Covered bonds meeting these criteria are treated as suitable for EU fund managers and insurers to acquire with far greater freedom than usually allowed by risk concentration limits, and in some cases with a smaller cushion of regulatory capital.

The major distinction between covered bonds and securitization is conceptual, as a secured loan rather than the sale of future claims. Covered bonds require no transfer of pool assets to an SPV, although certain states stipulate that pool loans be housed in a dedicated subsidiary. In Europe, covered structures have assumed an importance and scale similar to the US RMBS market, but the concept is not entirely unknown elsewhere: secured loan transactions have been used elsewhere as funding tools, for example by the Federal Home Loan Banks in the United States. As an historical idea, the covered bond was first associated with the needs of public policy or public lending intermediaries, which have been common in different forms to most advanced economies.

The EU's Consolidated Banking Directive and Capital Requirements Directive (which introduced Basel II) encourages investment in covered bonds by allowing EU bank holders a 10 per cent risk asset weighting for qualifying bonds. Other rules permit covered mortgage bonds that conform with national laws to be used as central bank borrowing collateral in the same way as sovereign bonds. Others exempt covered issues from prudential limits to risk concentration.

Changes in investor preferences that began in the 2007–9 crisis, and the impact of Basel II's altering of securitization transaction economics, mean that the capital markets may find a greater prominence for the covered structure, with transactions that combine advantages from both securitized and covered issues. This has become a feature of the covered bond market in Spain, and after the return of generally normal conditions may be adopted more widely. Creating a covered tranche within a securitized transaction alleviates the need for aggressively tiered payment priorities among the classes of issue that make up the overall transaction. The covered tranche replaces all or part of a super-senior tranche, and thus allows more pool value to percolate down to more junior ranked notes.

The technique of securitization has been used with residential or commercial mortgage loans, impaired assets, corporate loans, credit card receivables and lease payments, all cases where lenders can demonstrate a high degree of payment predictability from similar but unconnected cashflows. All of these risks have been used in transactions in Asia in the last 15 years. A small number of securitizations of lease receivables and bank loans to SMEs have also been completed by banks in Japan, Malaysia, Singapore and Taiwan.

Post-securitization administration of the claims is often made functionally independent of the originator in order to remove its economic interest in their performance, although this practice has been questioned since the collapse of the US subprime mortgage market. Separation is necessary in order for the originating bank to defease the claims from its balance sheet, but it has been argued that a moral hazard arises due to the rational originator choosing to securitize its least valuable claims, and having no incentive to see their being repaid according to contract. By this argument the originator becomes feckless through the sale of claims from its balance sheet.

In 2010, legislators in the United States and European Union proposed that banks retain a 5–10 per cent portion of their securitized claims, a device known as having 'skin in the game', which some scholars believe will better condition behaviour. Others suggest either that aggressive lending practices were endemic in the subprime sector such that a more conservative model could never exist, or that retained interests are no guard against poor practices, since they were common until 2008 when banks arranged CDOs and other synthetic transactions. Large users of cash securitization also have a reputational incentive to make today's deal work for fear of making a succeeding transaction less feasible. It is common for securitizing originators to continue dealing commercially with any ultimate debtor client, except when securitizing NPLs, but they may not usually derive ongoing economic benefits from claims that become subject to sale.

Securitization's commercial benefits become manifest in one of five ways:

- As a means to make unacceptable risks satisfactory to an investor, assuming that a potential investor has known objectives for risk and return.
- Providing a credit rating higher than its respective sovereign ceiling or that of the originator. This may be especially attractive in the context of infrastructure financing in poorly rated economies.
- As the means to price pools of assets that are difficult to value, usually to make their sale feasible. This applies particularly to NPLs and other impaired claims.
- As a method to create capital market funding where none previously existed.
- As funding for asset originators where none was available at an acceptable cost, especially when lending becomes subject to quantitative regulatory constraints.

These applications represent tools to assist balance sheet management. In the 1990s securitization grew into a mechanism for both credit risk transfer and regulatory capital management, and must be assessed in the sense of allowing users to manage asset or liability portfolios, and also to move claims to or from the regulated banking sector and across borders (BIS 2005a).

Securitization expenses are typically high even if marginal transacting costs are reduced as a result of deal frequency, supportive legislation or regulatory change. This can be seen in expenses associated with data collection and verification, deal development, modelling, rating agency negotiation, marketing and contractual execution. US and UK RMBS and CLOs often use a master trust structure that became popular in the mid-1990s among banks wishing to arrange periodic deals. The master trust structure has scale advantages from being permanent in contrast to most transactions where the SPV is extinguished when the claims mature. The master trust's attraction is to allow new assets to be added to the collateral pool at any time. This has consequences for regulatory capital relief, but the main impact is to reduce the problem of adverse selection in four ways:

- A rating agency will rate the pool periodically;
- New collateral must meet criteria established at the start of the deal, so poor or unwanted risks cannot be legitimately added to the pool;
- The originator has an incentive to safeguard reputational capital or its costly investment in the structure is wasted; and
- The master trust usually leaves the originator with an intended ongoing economic interest in the collateral.

Legal and regulatory issues

Securitization places emphasis on intensive contracting as great as in any form of financing, requiring a transparent legal framework, clear accounting principles, and regulatory support. A deal's success therefore depends upon how its governing law accommodates these institutions, and may help explain why securitization first developed in common law jurisdictions.

Modern common law systems regard the commercial contract as the result of economic bargaining, the primary aim of which is to bestow identified rights, the erosion of which may entail a penalty. Civil law jurisdictions have tended to view contracts as bundles of mutual obligations, which are thus intrinsically restricted and for which the courts are generally willing to require performance. The effect on lending contracts under civil law systems is generally to limit the potential for their unqualified sale, especially when the transferee is insubstantive. The same approach also tends to complicate the possible sale of future payment rights. The essence of a supportive legal and regulatory framework is to ensure that neither law nor regulation lessens the structural integrity of legitimate transactions, and that any transfer of assets is permanent and cannot be disturbed by external events including actions by creditors of the originator.

It is essential to distinguish between cash securitization as a form of economic disintermediation and other forms that are substantially induced by regulation or accounting rules. Bank demand for securitization since the late 1980s was driven by increasingly harmonized capital regulation, creating transaction incentives among both bank originators and investors. This form of capital regulation created potential value and the enabling devices for securitization to reduce transaction costs.

Just as transaction costs are regarded by institutional economists as the catalyst for the transformation of firms as economic organizations, so regulation has a similar effect among financial intermediaries. Securitization by capital-regulated intermediaries was an intrinsic part of the Basel process. Not only did the introduction of the first capital accord cause banks to manage their credit portfolios to meet regulatory incentives, making securitization a commonly used tool, it also acquainted many investor classes with both securitized transactions and regulatory capital instruments.

Evolution and use in Asia

While the modern history of securitized transactions dates only from the late 1970s, the underlying concepts have been known for centuries. The sale of offices was a formal institution of the Byzantine Empire by the eleventh century, characterized as a form of prudent lending to the state made necessary by weak public finances (Andreas Andreades quoted in Laiou 2002: 7–8; Swart 1949: 99). Formal mechanisms provided incentives to tax collectors to overcome this weakness. Andreades argues further that tax farming through the sale of public offices was an institution of classical Greek city states and may represent the first examples of securitized transactions (Andreades 1933: 159–61).

Securitization became widely discussed in Asia after the 1997–98 crisis as a means to recycle impaired assets. Commercial interests had long argued that cash securitization had considerable potential for regional finance, yet its modest take up prompts the question as to whether this aspect of financial development lags other regions as a function of time, institutional conditions or as the result of economic conditions such as national savings and investment imbalances or relatively high private sector liquidity. Official support for securitization as a developmental tool later became a consistent feature of ASEAN+3 and ADB discussions on debt capital market reform after 2000, as we show in Chapter 12, but implementation was consistently slack. Conservative bank leverage limits the supply of loans for cash securitization even in Japan, where markets in structured securities have developed successfully.

Selective securitization activity increased in parts of Asia after 2000, notably Hong Kong, Japan, South Korea and Malaysia with RMBS deals, and in Singapore through CMBS issues. Securitization proved valuable in South Korea's substantial post-crisis restructuring when legislation allowed large volumes of NPLs and other impaired claims to be used as collateral for CDOs, a process of recycling instrumental in the recuperation of the economy. South Korea's KAMCO and Malaysia's Danamodal Nasional Bhd both sought clearing prices for NPLs from an assessment of the risk–return objectives of potential investors in securitized issues for the removal of assets from the balance sheets of collapsed banks.

Rating agency models of the behaviour and value of most asset pools under different conditions can generate price indications for the initiating asset sale more openly and less controversially than private sales negotiated between other AMCs and privileged investors. By contrast, sales of NPLs by AMC's in China and Indonesia to third-party investors were conducted under circumstances that precluded securitization with its underlying need for transparency. South Korea's process was regarded as successful but the completeness of what was involved is not always acknowledged:

> Securitization that uses lower-rated corporate paper as collateral ... only work[s] if there are also investors who are willing to hold ... the equity tranche which absorbs the first losses.
>
> (Gyntelberg & Remolona 2006: 72)

Deeply subordinated equity tranches accounted for up to 30 per cent of nominal issuance in KAMCO NPL securitizations, with KAMCO itself retaining much of those risks (ibid: 73; Fung, George, Hohl & Ma 2004). KAMCO's successful strategy relied heavily on state support for the credit risk transfer that it was able to engineer.

Completed securitization volumes in China, Indonesia, the Philippines and Thailand remain limited. Most jurisdictions now have adequate primary enabling legislation but minimal transactional usage. Securitization may be undeveloped or poorly used partly because factional interests favour the existing financial system, with its emphasis on bank credit creation serving closely held corporate sectors. Time dissipated China's need to instigate NPL recycling through structured finance, aided by its growth of international reserves and receptive IPO conditions for state banks. If long-debated securitization legislation is to produce substantial transaction volumes in China the driving motives may need to be different from elsewhere.

Housing loans have provided the most consistent source material for securitization based on non-distressed assets, in part due to official support (Gyntelberg & Remolona 2006: 65) and because reliable pool data for mortgages and consumer credit has been more often available than for heterogeneous corporate loans. New Asian securitization has accordingly focused more on liquidity and funding enhancement than the reallocation of credit risk by lenders, the main impetus to issuance in the United States until 2007.

Growing use of credit risk transfer was among the most profound developments in the post-Bretton Woods world of deregulated international finance. This relied on the two related innovations of credit derivatives and securitization, leading to a diffusion of risk geographically and by type of intermediary. Before 2007 it was widely believed that efficient credit risk transfer might help in crisis avoidance, but in 2007–9 it seemed instead to introduce profound uncertainties that grounded the interbank markets. If the location of credit risk threatened by valuation problems could not be identified then banks would be unable to determine with confidence the extent to which their counterparties might be exposed to credit losses problems. The conflicts associated with financial innovation are the subject of Chapter 10.

7 Investment banking and financial innovation

What connects the following names: Babcock & Brown, Bankers Trust Company, Barclays de Zoete Wedd, Baring & Co., Bear Stearns, Dean Witter & Co., Drexel, Burnham Lambert, Finance One, Hill Samuel, Kidder Peabody, Lehman Brothers, Merrill Lynch, Morgan Grenfell, Paine Webber, Peregrine Investments, Pierson, Heldring & Pierson, Robertson Stephens, Salomon Brothers, S.G. Warburg and Yamaichi Securities?

Historians may answer more quickly than lawyers or economists. These firms were all once prominent in investment banking. Most collapsed through unsustainable losses and were either liquidated or absorbed by rivals. Many had enjoyed high reputations, in some cases to the moment when their doors were shuttered. Joseph Schumpeter thought that financial innovation was a spur to development (Schumpeter 1934), but later considered 'creative destruction' of the kind that we might now associate with financial crises as a necessary feature of capitalism (Schumpeter 1976).

If collapses are inexorably linked to risk-taking then perhaps the proper aim of financial design is to open fire breaks to prevent systemic chaos and minimize losses in the real economy?[1] Even if we are not to worry about the loss of a Lehman or a Peregrine there remains a paradox of investment banking, that it delivers impressive commercial innovation alongside regularly abject business management. This is the focus of Chapter 7. We will also respond to an observation of three finance scholars that:

> There are many successful innovations that cannot be explained....Why do investment banks continue to invent and successfully sell complex new securities that outstrip our ability to value them? The truth is we don't understand why some innovations in markets succeed and others never get off the ground.
>
> (Brealey, Myers & Allen 2008: 973)

Our academic and practical experience suggests that much innovation is more imagined than real by virtue of being associated with rent seeking, and the need for banks to differentiate themselves before potential clients. Financial sector rents decay even with effective innovation of the type we describe in Section 7.4. Patent protection is uncommon for financial transactions and the ethic of competitive financial markets is to copy quickly any scheme that appears new and profitable, so transaction-focused investment banking needs to appear to innovate continually in order to generate revenue, impress clients and win business. Professional investors must deploy their available funds even in periods of extreme risk aversion, so transaction 'innovation' is self-reinforcing.

With due respect to Messrs Brealey, Myers and Allen, we feel that finance scholars err in treating many financial instruments as materially different from others. This chapter will discuss two influential financial innovations, but we are sceptical that these occur quite as often as the investment banking community wishes its clients to believe. Investment banking is both substance and veneer.

We propose a non-traditional distinction to explain the demarcation associated with commercial and investment banking, and then adapt a theory of reputational capital to explain our views as to the value and risks of investment banking (Lejot 2012). We use innovations in structured finance and derivatives to explain our case for investment banking's value, and go on to consider the societal, stability and welfare concerns prompted by the 2007–9 crisis. We end by looking at the future of investment banking in Asia and ask what has limited its success among indigenous banks?

Did a few prominent investment banks recklessly create unwarranted systemic risks before 2007 and what is the appropriate regulatory response? Our Stygian list is dominated by banks that were domiciled in English-style common law territories within an Anglo-American model of finance. This observation is far from statistically robust, but we search without success for examples of conspicuous failures in other systems. Regulatory policy in Germany long recoiled from financial innovation and preferred that it be tested in Anglo-American economies (Bernholtz 1999). If innovation is of conflicted value and potentially destabilizing then our casual observation has implications for financial system design and contractual liberty.

7.1 Origins

Modern investment banks have eclectic origins, among the great European merchant banking houses or *banques d'affaires* of the eighteenth and nineteenth centuries, in small trade-based finance and investment companies in many parts of Europe and North America, spreading in the eighteenth century to Asia and South America, and in the twentieth century US model of the broker–dealer, collecting fees and commissions by advising companies or selling their securities to investors.

Merchant banking came to be associated with immense political and financial power, notably with the pre-eminent European bankers of the early nineteenth century, Francis Baring and Nathan Rothschild, whose banking partnerships counselled and raised money for governments such that their influence ranked with kings and statesmen. '[The Rothschilds] are the brokers and counsellors of the kings of Europe and of the republican chiefs of America' (Niles Weekly Register 1835–36 quoted in Ferguson 1998: 267). Only large commercial banks tended to be incorporated until the twentieth century – a partnership ethic of innovation and teamwork persists in successful investment banking.

In 1810 Rothschild's bank became an affiliation of partnerships in five European states that was the world's largest and most powerful, and his death in 1836 led to a prolonged loss in market confidence (ibid: 276). Similar authority came to be associated with J. Pierpont Morgan, whose banks raised funds on a massive scale for governments and corporations, and whose advice was followed implacably in the largest US boardrooms. Morgan's legacy became a trio of powerful banks in New York and London. Morgan Stanley and JPMorgan Chase survive in the US in the twenty-first century, although appreciably altered by repeated mergers with the latter's New York Stock Exchange price history taken from the former Chemical Bank. Morgan Grenfell, the European arm of Pierpont Morgan's empire, was absorbed into Deutsche Bank in 1990 and the name discarded. Pierpont Morgan's second legacy was US antitrust legislation to deny his successors similar potential to control and consolidate American industry (Baskin & Miranti 1997; Burk 1989; Carosso 1970;

Hayes & Hubbard 1990; Kynaston 2002). Successful merchant banks and broker–dealers developed the core revenue-based activities practised by modern investment banks and contrasted in Table 7.1 with traditional commercial banking businesses.

For large investment banks from the United States, Australia, Europe or Japan this can comprise corporate finance and broking, transaction management and advice on mergers and acquisitions, corporate fundraising, stock exchange listings, credit rating advice, privatization schemes, the sale and trading of debt and equity securities, structured finance, venture capital and fund management. Most investment banks specialize to some degree, so Merrill Lynch was well-resourced in traditional broking or distributing securities to 'sell-side' clients while Lazard is predominantly an advisory house, especially in work in corporate mergers and acquisitions (M&A), and with governments. Banks also specialize within corporate finance categories, some focusing on privatization work (NM Rothschild), advising banks (Greenhill), acquisition targets or sponsors (Goldman Sachs, Morgan Stanley) or providing fairness opinions in contested takeovers (Houlihan Lokey, JPMorgan, UBS).

Almost all Asian firms lack a global or regional product capability and limit their transactional activities to their respective domicile, even though some have acquired significant minority shareholdings in non-Asian banks. Box 7.1 and Tables 7.2 and 7.3 highlight the main features of activity in 2010 and the sources of investment bank fees globally and in Asia. We show data for a single period because temporal comparisons disguise the impact on revenue of economic conditions and client demand. For example, 2009 revenues from new debt and equity issues were high because of post-crisis capital rebuilding and OECD quantitative easing, but new loan volumes and M&A transactions were meagre and well below their five year averages.

Modern investment banking differs in one crucial respect from the historic model, in that it acts not only for clients but assumes risk as principal, in some cases facilitated by transactions conducted for clients. Such proprietary trading involves the bank deploying capital in one of three ways:

- Dealing in securities or derivatives as arbitrage through the bank's trading book. This may include short selling, or holding securities as inventory for later sale.
- Investing in listed or unlisted companies or other non-financial assets.
- Investing in or sponsoring hedge funds or private equity funds.

Own-account dealing by banks in the United States will be restricted in scale from 2014 by the 'Volcker Rule' provisions of re-regulatory legislation (Dodd–Frank Act 2010: § 619). The motive for these limits came from losses incurred by banks engaged in creating and selling complex securities up to 2008, especially those holding substantial unsold inventories in

Table 7.1 Core business streams

Commercial banking	Investment banking
Credit creation and lending	Asset management
Deposit taking	Corporate finance
Money transmission	Securities underwriting
Trade finance	Sales & trading
Money market operation	Structured finance

Box 7.1 Investment Banking in 2010[2]

Gross investment banking fees are derived in this analysis from four business streams:

- M&A transaction advice, where banks are employed to advise clients primarily on corporate mergers, acquisitions, fairness of bids, sales or purchases of minority interests, balance sheet or debt restructurings, and privatizations.
- Arranging new issues of debt securities, including frequent issuer (MTN) programmes, and rating agency advisory.
- Arranging new issues of equity securities, including IPOs, secondary share issues, vendor placings and equity-linked securities.
- Arranging major syndicated loans, notably to support acquisitions and leveraged buyouts.

We take no account of transaction losses, for example where a new issue is sold at a loss, or of expenses associated with transaction arrangement. It is assumed that investment bank clients generally meet the out-of-pocket expense of completed transactions, and reimburse all or part of new issue stabilization costs but not any underwriting losses.

Fees paid to investment banks in 2010 totalled US$84.0 billion, an increase of 8.7 per cent from 2009 and the second consecutive annual rise. Total fees rose from US$49.3 billion in 2002 to US$116.9 billion in 2007, an average annual increase of 18.9 per cent, but collapsed by 35.2 per cent in 2008. We analyze fees in four ways:

- Arranging bank;
- Transaction type;
- Transaction domicile, customarily divided into four groups (the Americas; Japan; Asia-Pacific excluding Japan; and Europe, the Middle East and Africa); and
- Client industry sector.

The first three breakdowns are shown in Tables 7.2 and 7.3. These and other data show:

- The financial and energy sectors were the greatest sources of fees, together accounting for 37 per cent of the total (2009: 40 per cent). The same concentration applied in M&A and securities issuance but not in loans, where energy and industrial clients were dominant.
- US and EU firms dominate in fee-generation globally, in each regional grouping, and in each product grouping except for loans and equity issues, where Japanese and Chinese banks were respectively well-represented.
- No Asian bank appeared among the ten leading fee-earners, although Nomura replaced RBS in 10th place in the first quarter of 2011. Japanese banks were ranked 13th (Nomura), 16th and 20th in 2010.
- Asian transactions are dominated by large global banks in fee generation and numbers of completed deals, except in relation to debt and equity securities transactions in China and Japan, and in loans arranged across the region.

- There were 11 Asian banks in the top-20 ranked arrangers of IPOs, of which nine were Chinese, and one each were from Japan and Malaysia. With the exception of Nomura in tenth place, these rankings are based solely on domestic transactions due to considerable 2010 IPO volumes, mainly listings in Hong Kong and Shanghai. Asia-Pacific IPOs excluding Australia and Japan accounted for 58.9 per cent of the global total (2009: 61.7 per cent), and 35.9 per cent of all equity and equity-related issues (2009: 19.0 per cent).
- Except for JPMorgan Chase, the five-year share price performance of the investment banks shown in Table 7.2, plus Nomura, is poor in nominal terms and very poor relative to their respective home-market index. All the banks experienced sharp falls in share prices in 2008–9. Shares in JPMorgan Chase were little changed over the five-year period, and rose by 5.1 per cent compared to a 10.2 per cent rise in the Dow Jones Industrial Average. Nomura's share price fell by 84.6 per cent in the same period compared with a fall of 45.6 per cent in the Nikkei 225 index. None of these leading banks outperformed its home index over any extended period since 2006.
- Asia-Pacific and Japanese transactions accounted for 21 per cent of all fees (2009: 45.2 per cent), which is smaller than both North America (51 per cent) and Europe (25 per cent), but grew in cash terms by over 22 per cent. One qualification in inter-regional analysis is that fees in Asia-Pacific have been historically lower in relation to transaction amounts than in North America and Europe. This is usually attributed to competition in Asia being driven by expectations of future transactions, and to fees elsewhere being subject to well-established minima.

We show global and regional rankings for debt, equity and M&A transaction arrangers in Chapters 8–10.

Table 7.2 Investment bank global fee sources, 2010

	Total fees (US$ mn)	Year-on-year change (%)	Share of total fees (%)	Product contribution to fees (%)				5-year share price performance (%)
				M&A	Equity	Debt	Loans	
1. JPMorgan	5,372	−11.3	6.4	26	28	31	15	5.1
2. BofA Merrill Lynch	4,764	−1.8	5.7	20	25	34	21	−73.7
3. Goldman Sachs	4,388	1.5	5.2	45	29	22	4	−7.5
4. Morgan Stanley	4,232	12.8	5.0	35	36	25	4	−59.3
5. Crédit Suisse	3,462	12.4	4.1	31	27	33	8	−49.1
6. Deutsche Bank	3,370	12.3	4.0	25	25	38	12	−53.3
7. Citigroup	3,313	−15.2	3.9	23	26	40	11	−90.5
8. Barclays Capital	2,899	25.2	3.5	25	20	41	14	−54.9
9. UBS	2,794	8.6	3.3	32	37	26	5	−74.2
10. RBS	1,479	−17.1	1.8	10	13	57	20	−91.75
Others	34,087	NA	57.1	NA	NA	NA	NA	NA
Total	**83,998**	**8.7**	**100.0**	**36**	**27**	**25**	**13**	**NA**

Note: Price data as at 21 April 2011.

Sources: Thomson Reuters (2011); *Financial Times*.

Table 7.3 Investment bank fee sources, 2010

	Region (US$ mn)	*Share of total (%)*	*Year-on-year change (%)*
Americas	43,046	51	21.8
Europe	21,207	25	−13.5
Asia-Pacific	12,897	15	22.2
Japan	5,270	6	−2.7
Middle East & Africa	1,578	2	7.8
Total	**83,998**	**100**	**8.7**

Source: Thomson Reuters (2011).

a collapsing market, and the view of former Federal Reserve chairman Paul Volcker that systemic risks would be lessened by reinstituting a legal demarcation similar to Glass–Steagall. It would not restrict a fourth semi-proprietary activity, which is using capital to generate profits through facilitating client transactions. Banks arranging securities issues may choose to accrete securities into the market rather than maximize sales in as short a time as possible, and retain accruals or valuation gains prior to the position being eliminated. This is considerably more demanding in capital and hedging resources than undertakings to issuers to devote best efforts to distribute their bonds or shares, which we introduced in Chapter 6 as a minimal risk commitment by loan arrangers. Transacting in structured products has been highly profitable for similar reasons, but exposes banks to appreciable market risks. We saw how banks active in complex securities suffered profound accounting losses in the 2007–8 collapse of confidence, so that arranging and distributing securities is rarely the simple pass-through that was accepted practice until the 1970s.

Principal investment is not new. British, Dutch and French merchant banks, and German and other European universal banks, historically held shares in corporate clients, and banks in Japan and South Korea have long been engaged in large industrial groups through the closely woven *keiretsu* and *chaebol* described in Chapter 2.

Proprietary trading and private equity investment with a shorter time strategy developed in the United States in the 1980s, and until recently represented a significant part of activity for large investment banks. One approach involves a lengthy commitment, in which an early phase principal investment in shares or convertible securities is made well before an expected IPO. This is a common use of venture capital and securities market techniques for young companies, but after 2000 proved lucrative for investment banks dealing with substantial privatizations in Asia, with unusually well-rated start-up companies such as Google or Facebook, and with seasoned private companies such as commodity trader Glencore, which listed its shares in Hong Kong and London in 2011. The trend to principal dealing arose from three main factors:

- Worldwide deregulation of the financial sector;
- Technological growth leading to revolutions in trading and the use of financial derivatives; and
- Pressure from shareholders for banks to deliver favourable returns compared to utilities.

Engaging in proprietary activity, deploying costly technology and maximizing profits derived from fundraising for clients all require substantial capital, which helps explain an increasing concentration within investment banking since the early 1990s.

7.2 Investment and universal banking

A popular demarcation between commercial and investment banks grew during the intense financialization that began in the early 1980s. Its origins lay in nineteenth century English banking and mid-twentieth century financial regulation, which was especially restrictive in the United States after comprehensive reforms in federal law in the early 1930s, as we show in Box 7.2. At times similar restrictions have prevailed in other states such as Japan, as we described in Chapter 3.3.

Recent business and regulatory practice became less rigid but the suggestion of an administrative difference persists, especially in analyses of the global crisis. It reflects above all a more nuanced distinction of the perception of skills and resources that banks wish to imbue in their clients. Rather than use the traditional distinction that commercial banks extend credit to clients while investment banks create and trade in marketable securities such as bonds or shares, we approach the subject by treating investment banks as *innovators* of financial products and commercial banks as *users* of those products, regardless of the purpose for which they may be employed. We see the expansion of investment banking as central to the financialization trend from the late twentieth century.

Our analysis follows the most profound changes in the investment banking landscape since the late 1920s. Although this chapter charts the performance of well-known banks, it is more concerned with the process and functions of investment banking than any single organization or national group – indeed, two of the banks that feature in Chapter 10's M&A case study no longer exist as independent entities. Lehman Brothers entered bankruptcy proceedings in September 2008 while Merrill Lynch simultaneously sold itself to Bank of America to escape insolvency. Large parts of Lehman's operations in the US and elsewhere were acquired respectively by Barclays Capital and Nomura.

The credit collapse intensified in the final quarter of 2008 into a pervasive withdrawal of liquidity from banks of all types and in many countries. Access to wholesale funding is oxygen to all but the most conservative savings banks but was especially vital for the prominent, highly leveraged US investment banks, and in a matter of weeks they each lost their freewheeling independence, either collapsing into insolvency (Lehman Brothers), merging into deposit-rich banks (Merrill Lynch), or adopting a more conservative and closely supervised business model and raising capital from new strategic shareholders (Goldman Sachs and Morgan Stanley).

The split between commercial and investment banks is one that persists colloquially and often in academic analysis. It may also wrongly reflect an association with glamour or sophistication in business practices and resources. Commercial banks generate recurring revenue through the accrual of interest on credit extended to borrowers, while investment banks conjure strategies to exploit opportunities in markets and earn fees by being supposedly quick witted. In the real world, investment banks are rarely so gifted and commercial banks seldom so dull. Their core functions are seen differently according to the nature of the observer, which is important to our analysis and outlined in Table 7.4.

Our approach distinguishes between users and originators of financial instruments and services and emphasizes transactional innovation in the modern financial system. The Basel process and the regulatory arbitrage it induced among lenders is an example of influential innovation arising among national regulators and their client banks.

This portrayal is not wholly new. A theory of innovation by banks was published at the beginning of 'twenty-five years of capital market liberalization' (Eatwell & Taylor 2000: 36), but we extend the approach implied by the theory that 'new financial instruments or

Box 7.2 Dividing Banking

In US law the term 'securities' refers to a variety of financial instruments. It includes most tradable debt claims and all equity claims, according to SEC edicts made under provisions in the Securities Act of 1933. Defining securities and those intermediaries that might deal in securities were central principles in the distinction drawn between commercial and investment banks. This grew from federal laws that were specific in their aims: to limit share trading funded by banking sector credit, which the Roosevelt administration considered instrumental in the 1929 Great Crash.

The Glass–Steagall Act (Banking Act 1933) barred investment banks from taking deposits from almost all clients, and commercial banks from engaging or collaborating in many aspects of securities market activity, including the arranging or underwriting of new issues of shares and other securities, the sale of public securities to investors, and the holding of shares in non-banking companies. Similar legislation existed in Japan from the post-1945 occupation, until being substantially abolished by the Financial System Reforms Act 1992.

The results persisted in the United States until being eroded by regulatory arbitrage. US banks were active in the early growth of the Euromarkets, not least since they operated in Europe without the constraints that Glass–Steagall enforced at home. Euromarket trading and underwriting techniques inevitably migrated from Europe to the United States and, although challenged by litigation, were well-established by the mid-1980s in New York, Chicago and Los Angeles, with commercial banks arranging and distributing syndicated loans and trading in commercial paper with professional non-bank clients.

Glass–Steagall lost effectiveness when the courts found these activities to be permissible for commercial banks because the instruments involved were not 'securities', and the bar to commercial banks engaging domestically in many securities-related activities including underwriting and trading were finally abolished in 1999 by the Gramm–Leach–Bliley Act (Financial Services Modernization Act).

One provision of 1930s legislation left unchanged by Gramm–Leach–Bliley was a restriction preventing US banks or their parent companies from owning shares in non-financial sector companies (Bank Holding Company Act of 1956), which is unknown in other major jurisdictions in so broad a form, and has been thought to reflect long-standing support for anti-monopoly policies and cultural hostility to the banking sector's influence in the wider US economy (Roe 1994).

Gramm–Leach–Bliley allowed US banks to broaden their activities in a way similar to the European universal bank model by 'facilitating affiliation among banks, securities firms, and insurance companies' (Financial Services Modernization Act of 1999: Title I). In September 2008 the two remaining large independent investment banks, Goldman Sachs and Morgan Stanley, were granted licenses as bank holding companies, allowing each to accept deposits, obtain access to the Federal Reserve's discount window, and in consideration to submit to closer banking supervision.

Most economies in our sample restrict crossover banking activities, either with Glass–Steagall types of functional limits on directly transacting in securities or insurance (China, India, Thailand, Vietnam), or more commonly by restricting financial conglomerates or requiring functional subsidiaries to be separately capitalized (South Korea, Malaysia, Taiwan). Hong Kong, the Philippines and Singapore maintain the region's lightest functional restrictions (Barth, Caprio & Levine 2006).

Table 7.4 Concepts of commercial and investment banking

Focus	Commercial banks	Investment banks	
Permissible activities under law or regulation	Lending & deposit-taking	Securities underwriting and broking	
Credit risk focus	Lending & loan retention	Underwriting & distribution	
Dominant form of intermediation	Internal, based on private information	External, based on public information	
Use of capital	Large, ongoing	Small, temporary	
Revenue sources	Accruing interest; recurring & time dependent	Fees; non-recurring, trading dependent	Traditional categorizations
Role in national monetary policy	Critical	Negligible	
Access to lender of last resort facility	Yes	No	
Regulatory focus	Maintenance of capital	Market probity; investor protection	
Core function in national & global financial systems	Transaction users	Financial innovators	*Finance in Asia* approach

practices are innovated to lessen the financial constraints imposed on [client] firms' (Silber 1983: 89), and suggest that complex regulation tends to stimulate financial innovation (Desai & Low 1987: 113) to describe the wider practicalities of twenty-first century investment banking.

Financial innovation is also said to result from the imposition of regulation or taxes (Miller 1986), competitive supply or demand factors (Dufey & Giddy 1981), execution costs (Allen & Gale 1994: 36–41), agency concerns (Ross 1989), or regulatory arbitrage, as there is 'a strong incentive to innovate around prohibited or disadvantaged transactions' (Knoll 2008: 94). We see the innovatory behaviour of investment banks as driven by their need to distinguish themselves from existing competitors and deter new entrants. Product differentiation of this kind is made difficult in the financial sector because new ideas and instruments are rarely protected by copyright, and to some extent due to regulatory constraints. Investment banking's want of product differentiation helps explain the importance of reputational capital in capturing client business (Desai & Low 1987: 115).

We focus on innovation in financial instruments and intermediation practices, including those arising largely through technological growth, such as high-frequency share trading. A crude characterization is that commercial banks provide clients with credit using trade finance or loans, while investment banks sell advice and raise funds for clients by arranging issues of securities and distributing the results to third-party investors.

Risk management in commercial banks is associated primarily with asset and liability management of a lending portfolio and its funding base while investment bank risk management centres on allocating risk capital in underwriting, trading or hedging of securities and managing concomitant liabilities. Both forms of intermediation are reflective of techniques in portfolio management. Both also draw upon finance theory concepts that focus on balancing risk and reward, and the effects on the value of an asset or liability of marginal changes in economic conditions. Traditional risk management within lenders involves a longer time-horizon, with changes in exogenous variables such as interest rates or credit ratings reflected in marginal policy adjustments to accelerate loan reductions from one group of client borrowers, or to increase new lending to others. Risk management in investment banks takes a shorter time focus, and is concerned above all with the effects of exogenous changes on the day-to-day value of securities held or traded, and the valuation of other contingent commitments.

The result is less uniform when an investment bank arranges an issue of securities to raise funds for a client. The bank may sell the entire issue and be left with nothing that might count as a balance sheet item, in which case it will hope to collect arrangement or underwriting fees, and perhaps additional revenue by selling securities at improving prices into a rising market. This helps explain the objectives of block trading or many bought deals. The bank may alternatively hold a portion of the issue for its own account, partly for efficiency to help stabilize market prices or provide a trading inventory of securities, or it may be obliged by the terms of its underwriting agreement with the issuer to retain any residual portion of a new issue of securities that failed to attract third-party investors.

Innovation has blurred the division. The creation of securitization and liquid quickly-accessed money market funds in the 1980s gave US and other investment banks or broker–dealers the means to compete with commercial banks in collecting savings or making loans to consumers. Improving distribution techniques and the increasing acceptance of credit risk transfer gave commercial lenders the chance to manage both sides of their balance sheets to seek better returns with acceptable blends of risk. The growth of the syndicated loan markets in the 1980s gave many commercial banks access to a valuable product that could challenge the transactional advantage of investment banks.

7.3 Markets in information and reputational capital

A widely held theory of lending sees the bank intermediary performing a function associated with information, and especially the differences in information available to potential debtors and creditors. It focuses particularly on the extent to which information asymmetry creates behavioural incentives for creditors, debtors, intermediaries and depositors. Banks add value in the economy by intervening in the savings and investment channel to provide a vetting and monitoring function in lending decisions and administering loans that would be difficult or impossible for general creditors at large (Diamond 1984). They use skills and experience to price, make and monitor loans more effectively than others, and bridge asymmetries in information available to a borrower and potential creditors. Banks are taken to be relatively efficient providers of credit due to three attributes:

- Dedicated resources to collect and process information from borrowers;
- Professional systems and human resources in risk and transaction management; and
- Scale advantages in collating and reviewing credit information on debtors, for example, to compare the performance of a commercial debtor with those of its peer groups of direct and indirect competitors, or companies of similar size or domicile.

A similar theory has been articulated in relation to market-based intermediation, which is typically associated with investment banking (Morrison & Wilhelm 2007: 71–87). An investment bank creates a market in information through dealings and networking contacts with borrowers, investors and competitors, which in turn helps effective securities issuance and sales. Investment banks provide information on prospective transactions through the preparation and transmission of research to investors, that is, providing a market in information.

This suggests that the resources marshalled for financial intermediation by investment banks in transaction arrangement, credit research, and underwriting and distributing securities are of value to both investors and borrowers for similar, predominantly informational reasons. The bank adds credibility to information provided by a borrower by exploiting its accumulated reputational capital, or the perception of itself and others of skills, trustworthiness, confidence and competence in the resources it offers to clients or witnessed from completed deals. This can be regarded as a positional good, since it concerns not the absolute performance effectiveness of any single investment bank but the market's *perception* of that performance in relation to other competitor banks. Positional goods are valued partly for being scarce, regardless of price or income effects (Hirsch 1976). Not all banks can be market leaders.

A bank that is considered to be well resourced and trustworthy may be able to convince third-party investors that the opportunity it reveals to them is attractive and meets their preferences, whereas a less prominent or well-regarded bank would fail by the same test. This means that there are polar solutions to financial intermediation, one involving an internal process conducted within a bank lender, and the other organized externally in a public or private market by an investment bank. Whether a prospective borrower chooses one alternative or the other depends on their respective perceptions of transaction costs.

The same considerations face a potential saver, given the choice of depositing funds with a commercial bank or buying securities issued by that commercial bank through an investment bank. Assuming identical nominal yields on a deposit and a security, the transaction costs identified by the potential depositor–investor includes liquidity, or the ease of investment and withdrawal, and the ranking of a claim in any bankruptcy, including the limits of deposit insurance.

Reputational capital need not be associated with risky activities but depends in all cases on banks displaying to clients a high and consistent level of competence in engaging with the market. Penrose (1995) suggests that the growth of firms in general is attributable to their accumulated human and intangible resources. Intangible capital amassed in this way will be eroded by investment transactions that fail to match the market's performance expectations, by engaging in malpractice, or by misjudgement as to price or value. These considerations become well known among market participants so that an investment bank can develop a reputation for arranging expensive or poorly documented deals.

A second aspect of this problem occurs when many competing investment banks suffer comparable losses in reputational capital. Since reputational capital is intrinsically linked to comparisons among banks, there may be cases where the entire industry acts in a way that regulators or clients deplore and where the results lead to changes in practice, rather than a loss of transactional favour by a single investment bank. We have seen two notable examples of this herd behaviour since 2000:

- First, conflicts of interest within banks where sell-side research analysis is used habitually to obtain business mandates for buy-side clients. This was exposed among many US and European investment banks after a collapse in information technology shares in March 2000.

Investors were induced to buy securities by enthusiastic research reports prepared for and paid by issuers, and banks engaged in price manipulation of IPOs to reward or favour their leading clients. At least 12 prominent banks made payments in 2003 to forestall claims for fraud and market misconduct brought by the New York authorities and the SEC, prominent analysts were convicted of market manipulation and barred from securities activities, and the banking industry as a whole consented to a more rigorous separation of research from corporate finance (Augar 2005). One inadvertent result of regulating corporate and economic research was to confine its distribution to professional and HNW investor clients of investment banks and thereby limit analysis available to non-professional and non-aligned investors.

- Second, the collapse of the structured finance markets in the 2007–9 global financial crisis. A withdrawal of investors and liquidity from securitized and complex transactions was coupled with global disapproval of banks prominent in arranging and selling all forms of highly structured issues, whether to individual or professional investors.

What had been a strong source of revenue quickly became the cause of the most profound losses known by the modern banking industry. Few investment banks maintained their reputational capital in these circumstances, not least because the structured finance market has been seen as the result of financial innovation and as central to these banks' interests.

One case from this period exposed investment banking practices to the most intense scrutiny since 1929, involving Abacus CDOs, a series of structured securities created by Goldman Sachs. The firm sold notes issued by SPV Abacus to bank investors in 2007, but their synthetic nature entailed a hedge fund client of Goldman Sachs participating in the transaction in expectation of a decline in the value of the CDO's collateral, which was based on US RMBS. The SEC and a congressional investigation criticized Goldman Sachs as being conflicted in simultaneously arranging long and short positions for clients without full disclosure to both parties (SEC 2010; Senate Permanent Subcommittee on Investigations 2011).

The bank's view was that its actions were part of established market-making practice and that the existence of the hedge fund short position would have been known to any professional investor as being essential to the transaction mechanics. The controversy entered recent US re-regulation, which requires the SEC to consider whether US broker–dealers should be subject to a general duty of care when dealing in structured securities (Dodd–Frank Act 2010: § 913). This would resemble typical fiduciary responsibilities given to investment advisors and an EU requirement detailing how banks must act in the best interests of investor clients (EU Commission Directive 2006).

These examples of sudden scrutiny, of the kind we cited at the beginning of Chapter 6, suggest that the assessment of investment banking's reputational capital by their investor or issuer clients is sophisticated and segmented by business stream. This can allow a bank to err catastrophically in structured finance, but if it stays solvent to remain well regarded in corporate finance or asset management.

One difficulty in discussing reputational capital in the financial sector is that it may be easy to spot but impossible to measure reliably. Several analysts have sought to identify a causal relationship between the reputation of investment banks and the initial commercial terms or post-issue performance of the transactions they arrange, but the results are of limited value due to the difficulty of finding an acceptable variable to signify reputation.

From a sample of 501 US IPOs, Carter & Manaster (1990) found the perception of an underwriting bank's prestige to be linked to the arrangement of issues for low-risk corporate clients, which are taken to be demanding when awarding new issue mandates. This has intuitive support, but the study's main explanatory variable: (1) relies on one feature of a homogeneous segment of the US capital markets for investment banking products; (2) takes conditions in its sample period (1979–83) to be unvarying; (3) assumes that corporate reputation is exogenous; (4) takes no account of changes in practice over time; (5) neglects contributory aspects of syndicate practice among banks; and (6) assumes that the scale of capital and resources applied in each IPO is identical.

Reputation may be identifiable through surveys, for example gauging the views of corporate treasurers on banks in certain fields or geographical sectors. Material of this kind preoccupies the financial press during the slow seasons of December or mid-summer. Somewhat more rigorous are performance league tables, a marketing tool for all investment bankers showing the numbers or values of transactions of different types completed by or mandated to competing banks.

Financial league tables first appeared in the early Eurobond markets in the 1970s, published by the financial industry equivalent of celebrity magazines or websites, and were often studied more closely by bankers than their clients. Today they are collated by commercial data-providers over many sub-sectors with great attention to detail, and cover all transactions that can be aggregated, although banks know the art of inflating league table positions using a selective universe of data.

Tables can be generated for any period or comparison, and are ubiquitous in markets for new issues of shares, loans and bonds, as well as for merger or takeover transactions, measured by number and the headline value of the acquired company. Chapters 8–10 show examples of league tables for 2010 debt and equity new issues and M&A transactions. Industry journal *International Financing Review* currently publishes 81 weekly tables of completed debt and equity issues divided by all significant descriptive factors, including place or currency of issue, types of issuer, forms of transaction and place of execution. Other data collectors produce corporate finance league tables that rank banks by advisory fees and the value of transactions announced or completed.

Banks use league tables to assert their prowess to clients and build reputational capital, even though they are prone to manipulation, and are a proxy for reputational capital given a lack of plausible alternatives. League tables say nothing of the profitability of completed transactions or the risks incurred in deal execution, and at the year's end data compilers are watchful for deals completed for nil fees or friendly affiliates.

Historic and contemporary evidence suggests that reputational capital has real value to investment banks, although this has been tested rigorously in only limited circumstances. A study of American public companies for the period 1895–1913 found that the presence on a company's board of directors of a representative of J.P. Morgan & Co. had a significant positive effect on its share-price performance that could be attributed, not to Morgan's monopoly power, but to expectations that the director signified effective monitoring of the company by a trusted investment bank (DeLong 1991).

The study proposed that preservation of reputational capital was so important for Morgan that it inclined the bank to refrain from abusing its dominant position, by charging excessive new issue fees or broking commissions for example, which is an unconventional view of monopoly behaviour (ibid: 233). Morgan was more a universal bank in the modern European sense than a pure investment bank, in that it owned stakes in client companies and actively engaged in management decisions through board representatives, activities later prohibited to curb the bank's power.

The incentive- and cost-based solutions of these informational theories may not suit the views of earlier banking theorists who support an evolutionary view of financial sector development, reviewed in Section 2.1. Reputational capital depends on demonstrating a consistent competence in engaging with the market, and is easily eroded by mispriced or poorly received transactions. Capable investment banks add credibility to a client prospectus by applying accumulated reputational capital, which in effect represents the market's perception of its trustworthiness, confidence and competence in resources provided to clients or witnessed from completed deals. Yet post-crisis analysis argues that many banks were involved in controversial practices. If that reliance is so compelling, and investment banking requires competitive innovation and skills in transaction and risk management, then why are banks prone to poor management, erratic financial performance and periodic shocks?

7.4 Contracts and innovation

It is customary to describe the financial instruments available to borrowers or investors to reflect elemental legal differences. Our analysis adopts common practice in the world's leading markets to concentrate on three aspects of modern finance:

- Categorizing financial instruments as representing claims in the form of debt, equity or derivative contracts, or combinations of these elements;
- Emphasizing the convergence between instruments that has occurred since the late 1970s, and the central function of credit risk transfer in that process; and
- Stressing that borrowing and investing decisions are made for portfolio motives rather than as stand-alone transactions.

We also distinguish contracts from claims. Contracts are commercial agreements, financial instruments, or identifiable forms of transactions made under a similar framework of terms. Claims are rights owned by a party to a contract. This is a generic distinction drawn from no single jurisdiction. Claims may also exist for non-contractual reasons, for example, through non-judicial penalties or court awards for damages or restitution.

Contemporary capital

Traditional descriptions of financial claims and instruments arose from competing legal theories of contract. From this came the view that claims may be grouped into contracts or bundles of contracts with distinct features. Thus bank loans and bond issues are distinct forms of debt claims to which apply different market practices and regulation, while shares in companies are taken to be the most common form of equity claim. Hybrid instruments mix together characteristics of both debt and equity claims. Hybrids include equity-linked and convertible bonds, and perpetual callable issues by banks that rank as regulatory capital above equity capital but below senior debt. Basel III allows national regulators to sanction new hybrids called contingent convertible securities or Cocos, explained in Box 6.3 (BCBS 2010e). Most advanced jurisdictions recognize this elemental distinction, although public policy may choose to attribute differing rights or obligations in each case. This long-standing picture has been altered since the 1990s through innovation, including:

- The growing financialization and popular awareness of the financial industry in the global economy;

- The importance of information technology in the financial sector and its effect on the speed of instigating and executing multiple transactions;
- Widespread removal of controls on transnational movements of capital; and
- A general decline in inflation and nominal interest rates, increasing the incentive for investors to seek higher rewards from non-traditional financial claims.

Financial innovation and transactional creativity might be expected to thrive in this setting with two lasting results:

- A profusion of apparently new financial instruments, many of which will include simple variations in terms to meet the evolving preferences of investors, but more importantly including the emergence of derivatives as a separate class of capital and the use of embedded derivatives to create synthetic instruments.
- The behaviour of financial sector participants to be analyzed through their portfolio choices as to expected risk and return. This applies equally to banks, investors, savers, borrowers and the state as a user of finance.

These developments are not necessarily destabilizing or an indication that participants in the financial system are taking greater risks, but they do signal the importance for market practice, disclosure, regulation and supervision to keep pace with innovation. We will see shortly how the failure of rating agency practice to adapt to innovation in structured finance contributed to stressed conditions in 2007.

We treat derivatives such as swaps or options as a distinct category of financial instrument, rather than adjuncts to debt or equity claims. Others argue that financial derivatives are so important that they cannot be taken as subsidiary functions of real financial or physical claims (Bryan & Rafferty 2006). This view helps us highlight the importance of convergence in traditional markets or instruments, so that bonds and loans increasingly resemble one another, first in major currency markets and later elsewhere. The trend certainly applies to Asia's transnational credit and equity markets and in the more sophisticated ASEAN+3 financial systems.

Emphasizing the risk–return behaviour of investors, borrowers and intermediaries is similarly to stress the *functionality* of instruments, rather than their provenance or categorization in law. This means that we look at uses and effects, not motives or types of behaviour, and ask what each instrument can achieve in terms of adjusting the risk and return composition of portfolios of assets or liabilities.

Customary analysis treats financial instruments as distinct, using an approach historically adopted by English common law. Debt and equity are both forms of borrowing, except that the obligation to repay a debt is the result of contractual agreement. A borrowing evidenced by an equity share in a company is one that becomes due for repayment only in unusual circumstances, typically the voluntary winding up of a company when only a nominal amount would be returned to the claimant. At other times the holder of an equity claim relinquishes ordinary rights of repayment for an ownership interest in the company, and is thus a shareholder.

Debt and equity claims also represent ways to make marginal adjustments to asset or liability portfolios. A company making a new borrowing may shorten or lengthen the duration of its overall liabilities, or the same effect could result from decisions to buy or sell derivative contracts. Derivatives often become substitutes for more conventional debt or equity claims and may even carry de facto ownership rights, which can be controversial in contested takeovers where equity derivatives may be used to augment a predator's control over shares.

Debt and equity claims were commonly divided respectively into bank loans or tradable bonds, and ordinary or preferred shares. These elemental forms of claim were associated with longstanding market practices, which differed between economies of varying financial sophistication but were all conceptually similar.

While an equity claim due to a shareholder in Anglo-American common law jurisdictions represented a bundle of actual or contingent contract rights with historically limited interference from the state – for example, to assert the priority of tax claimants and certain others in a compulsory winding up – a similar claim existing under German federal law would be subject to broader public policy considerations, for example, making certain shareholder rights contingent upon the interests of employees and other stakeholders.

Above all, debt and equity claims could be separated for the purposes of institutional or regulatory analysis. Equity-linked claims include convertible bonds that behave as debt claims until an option is exercised, usually by the bondholder, that results in the conversion on pre-determined terms of the bond to shares – that is, the debt claim appears to transform into an equity claim. The economics of convertible bonds typically rely on bondholders buying a single call option over certain equity rights, the satisfaction of which is met through the redemption of their debt claim. Thus the traditional analysis split financial claims into debt and equity, and the law maintained a similar approach. We see this division as being unreliable in explaining the workings of today's investment banks and markets, and look instead at three elements of contemporary capital:

- Debt instruments. Borrowing contracts largely subject to intrinsic commercial terms.
- Derivative instruments. Contracts that alter prevailing risk–return qualities of portfolios of assets or liabilities.
- Equity instruments. Ownership contracts carrying shared rights of control over company management, and to ongoing income or repayment in a winding up, in each case subordinated to other contractual claims.

Debt and equity claims are products of innovation in the eighteenth and nineteenth centuries, respectively. All three were innovations of merchants or investment banks. Does this framework support innovation to come? Our definitions are not necessarily static – for example, much equity trading around the world has become indifferent to company ownership and the control features associated with equity claims. Between 35 and 50 per cent of 2010 turnover on major EU and US exchanges consisted of sizeable blocks of shares bought and sold purely to capture discrepancies between expected and prevailing prices, so corporate governance law is apparently out of step with market practice to the extent that it treats shareholders as enjoying collective ownership of a company.[3]

All financial instruments are formed from these three elements of capital. Investment bank revenue derived from creating or trading these claims varies according to the aims and commitments of capital and human resources, but can be attributed to five main sources:

- Underwriting fees. Commissions earned on committing to arrange and execute new securities issues.
- Dealing profits. Gains made from block trades, bought deals or underwritten trades in outstanding securities, plus inventory valuation gains and gross profits from market making.

- Broking commissions. Fees charged clients for transaction execution.
- Proprietary revenue. Income from deploying capital for principal risks.
- Treasury gains. Other funding or liability management revenue associated with securities activities.

We exclude revenue derived from unsold inventory and inadvertent risk positions.

Equities have undergone few changes since taking their modern form in the mid-nineteenth century (Baskin & Miranti 1997), as instruments carrying shared transferable ownership rights in companies. Transferable is not synonymous with freely tradable, since the sale or purchase of shares may be restricted by an issuing company, usually under provisions of law (Armour, Hansmann & Kraakman 2009: 11–12).

Investment bank innovation in equities is more concerned with the markets where they are listed and traded, rather than the contractual features of equity claims (as is the case with debt or derivatives). We describe high-frequency share trading as one such innovation. Questions of policy have influenced the rights and obligations associated with equities in most sophisticated jurisdictions far more than contractual innovation. Equity-related innovation has been associated with developing IPO and trading practice, stock exchange formation, demutualization and consolidation, transnational share issuance, and in benchmarking and fund management, where index and exchange traded funds are recent examples of transactional innovation.

One explanation is that many commercial terms of equities are found in the constitution of the issuing company or other corporate documents and are directly influenced by companies legislation or commercial codes. Section 9.1 discusses this in greater detail, especially the dilemma of ownership becoming disassociated from corporate control. Debt claims are usually self-contained contracts and expressed in an array of commercial terms, and trade in product or national markets that are subject to distinct practices, although these have converged in the last decade with cross-border cooperation and rule harmonization.

Standardized financial derivatives are a modern invention of merchants and bankers and have two distinct roots, the first developed as exchange traded futures and option contracts from practices originated in the 1850s Chicago commodity markets, which we outline in Section 8.2, and the second as OTC derivatives explained in Section 7.5, which are a product of 1980s corporate finance innovation. Both families of instruments exemplify the tradable and enforceable contract, based not on existing real assets of known value but on defined but intangible financial claims, where the contract is itself a 'thing' (Collins 1999: 202).

The commercial view of capital allows us to avoid legal uncertainties, notably where the courts are unaware of financial innovation, and against the express intention of the contracting parties seeking to recharacterize a new form of claim as something to which they are accustomed. Common law jurisdictions have been reluctant to enforce financial futures contracts (ibid: 211–12), and questioned whether interest rate swaps create payment obligations, given that contractual debts exist only because of an actual borrowing rather than mere exchanges of payment. Advanced civil law jurisdictions tend to avoid such doubts by relying on a general law of obligations. Legal uncertainties may be an inevitable result of true innovation (Henderson 2010: 416). They arise in the two examples of investment banking innovation that follow in this section on structured finance and in Section 7.5 with the creation of OTC derivatives.

Innovation in structured finance

Structured finance began as a 1970s offshoot of corporate finance that sought to broaden the competitive position of investment banks, especially to enable US broker–dealers to bypass Glass–Steagall restrictions. Since the early 1990s it has grown into a family of techniques used prolifically by intermediaries of all types and domiciles. We introduced securitization in Section 6.4 as a balance sheet and risk management tool of commercial banking, and here focus on innovations with which investment banks were most concerned in tranching and credit rating practice, which spawned the sizeable issuance of synthetic CDOs and other complex securities. The global financial crisis eliminated the more extreme leveraged transactions described here and in Chapter 8, but deal technology cannot be uninvented, and complex transactions can have defensive objectives for capital-conserving investors including pension funds, insurers, or HNW and family office investors.

A favourable view of structured finance, often associated with its use in Asia for financial and economic development, is typified by BIS analysis:

> Structured finance can have a positive influence on the financial system because it can transform ordinarily illiquid or risky assets into more liquid or less risky ones. It thus offers an alternative source of long-term funding in both domestic and cross-border markets, and can foster the development of domestic bond markets. In turn, this could promote greater bank and financial market efficiency, as it implies greater competition to meet customer financing needs.
>
> (Scatigna & Tover 2007: 71)

While acknowledging that proponents of securitization need to be cautioned as to its risks (ibid: 81–2), it is notable that such a constructive review was published in mid-2007 as the crisis brewed in the US structured finance markets. This seems to conform with a positive earlier BIS view of credit risk transfer (BIS 2005).

Two conjoined innovations helped structured finance to grow quickly in the 1990s: the development of tranching and the active involvement of credit rating agencies in transaction formation. Together, these allowed banks to create securities for a variety of investor preferences, including some that investors may not have previously recognized. Tranching sets payment priorities to create separate securities with distinct risk and return features, and generate an optimal use of both investor demand and the value over time of an asset pool. This mechanical innovation had two profound consequences:

- Securities created not for issuer needs, but fashioned according to the preferences of professional and other investors. This represents a broader application of the reverse enquiry principle explained in Section 8.1, by which sophisticated and HNW investors negotiate with frequent borrowers to issue securities to meet specific commercial demands.
- Increases in transaction volumes and systemic leverage based upon credit ratings becoming entrenched in regulation for banks and other investors with no discrimination between rating agency assessments of conventional corporate credit risk and in structured finance.

The concept is shown in Figure 7.1. Notes of different maturities and payment priorities are created using the economic value of the asset pool, and the credit rating of each tranche of notes is derived from the pool characteristics and the terms of the securitized notes.

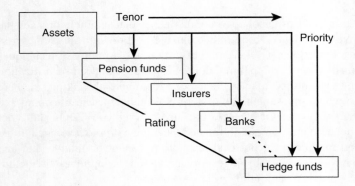

Figure 7.1 Simplified structured finance tranching.

Modern securitized transactions use pooled assets or income to create securities with combinations of credit ratings, yield and duration acceptable to different classes of investor. This has advantages for the asset originator in that it may allow for the sale of less viable risk, for example with NPLs or risk subject to legal or other contingencies, but the feasibility of any complex transaction depends on a bias in the use of proceeds to service the highest-ranking claims. It also demands the tiered subordination of claims, where the lowest priority tranches are so deeply subordinated as to be worthless in the event of payment problems, and thus acceptable to only a small number of risk-preferring investors.

Tranching seeks to extract the maximum value from the pool or reference assets over time. The payment *waterfall* created by tranching is contractually complex, even in transactions with few tranches. Figures 7.2A–7.2C show the contractual mechanics of a simplified cash CDO payment waterfall with five tranches, beginning in Figure 7.2A with the order of priority given to the main claims on payments from the asset pool.

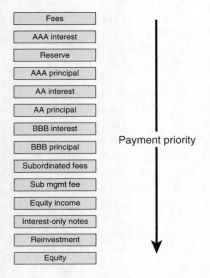

Figure 7.2A Cash CDO waterfall priority.

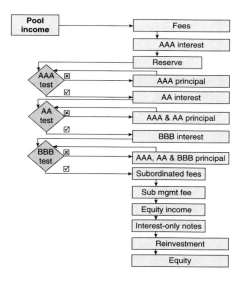

Figure 7.2B Waterfall treatment of interest payments.

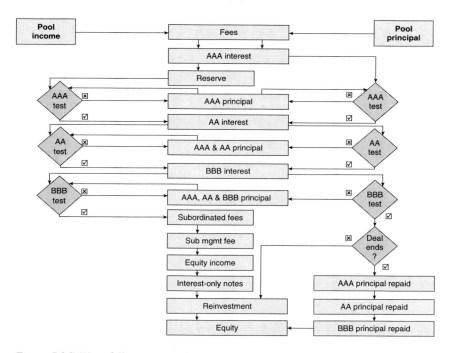

Figure 7.2C Waterfall treatment of principal payments.

At the top of the waterfall with the highest priority are transaction fees, trustee fees and expenses, payments to any hedging counterparty or swap provider, and fees due to the pool asset manager and administrative agent, all subject to an agreed cap. Interest due on AAA-rated notes follows in priority, then a liquidity reserve that helps smooth the timing of payments between the pool and all claims, and then notes with lesser ratings.

'Subordinated fees' refers to any amounts that arise in excess of the cap. 'Equity income' refers to an agreed maximum return on the most deeply subordinated investor claims, which can expect to be repaid, if funds allow, only when the entire transaction comes to an end. Reinvestment may be allowed in transactions where new assets are added to the pool as older components are repaid.

A recurring series of liquidity and solvency tests ensure that cash made available for distribution to noteholders pays interest and principal only at the most senior level until those claims are fully met, after which any surplus is allowed to flow down the waterfall to the next level of priority. This order applies iteratively to all payments from the asset pool. Each payment follows the waterfall's course, so that priority is absolute until a higher-ranking class of claim is exhausted or a test of condition is met. Figure 7.2B shows the treatment of interest generated by the pool, first meeting fees, then interest on AAA-rated notes, then a payment to the transaction reserve. Payments to the lower-ranking claims are then subject to a series of iterative tests, so that cashflow available after payments to the reserve are first applied to reduce any principal due on the AAA notes, only after which can the remainder be paid to service interest on the AA notes.

The tests are iterative, sequential and usually comprise minimum over-collateralization and interest cover relative to the outstanding claims under each set of notes. A similar procedure applies to payments of principal from the pool, shown in Figure 7.2C.

A failed AA test requires funds to be used to repay the AAA notes, after which the AA notes are repaid until the test is met. A failed BBB test requires repayment of AAA notes, then AA notes, and finally then BBB notes until the test is met. Even comparatively simple transactions require extensive modelling of pool performance, which demands that arrangers have adequate pool data, an understanding of the payment and default experience of sectoral risks comparable to the pool, and resources to forecast and test as complete a set of outcomes as is feasible. In all cases this function has been devolved to credit rating agencies with the tacit agreement and sanction of national regulators.

Investor preferences provide the starting objective in pricing and structuring, with transaction arrangers hoping to extract the greatest value from available pool resources. Such manipulation is central to all securitized issues and partly explains their relative complexity and expense. Structuring transactions has come to require active participation by credit rating agencies that model the waterfall treatment of payments under many conditions, and set terms for individual tranches to achieve target credit ratings. This involvement is materially different from corporate bond practice, but the rating agencies dispute the existence of a conflict and argue that their research is merely informative (Bell & Rose 2007), despite its quasi-regulatory function given by Basel II 2007.[4] Concern at the accountability of this involvement was voiced before the crisis by the BIS Committee on the Global Financial system, warning that:

> Tranching creates a layer of analytical complexity beyond that of estimating the loss distribution of the collateral pool. It requires detailed, deal-specific documentation... to ensure that the intended characteristics...are actually delivered under all plausible scenarios.
>
> (CGFS 2005: 11)

Intense interaction between investment banks and rating agencies became discredited in 2007–8, leading eventually to fresh consideration of the permissible roles of the agencies by the European Union, and in the United States under the Dodd–Frank Act.

Legal and empirical analyses see tranching as a means to extract advantage from segmenting investors. Institutional analysis would see tranching as creating payment priorities that in turn allow a high investment-grade credit rating to be given to as large as possible a portion of any single transaction. Experience suggests that tranching takes advantage of varying investor preferences, relying also upon the need for credit ratings by all institutional investors in structured transactions, given the infeasibility of their undertaking original analysis. Tranching helps meet the minimum criteria of the rating agencies, and hence minimizes the value of payments to be delivered to investors at a particular credit rating level in relation to the predicted present value of the asset pool. This helps explain why contractual completeness is vital to effective structured finance.

All but simple transactions employ internal and external credit enhancement to improve or stabilize the risk of any tranche. Internal enhancement usually takes the form of portfolio pool design, over-collateralization or the creation of a liquidity reserve; cash collateral, third-party insurance and guarantees are common types of external support. Such guarantees (or 'wraps') are provided by specialist 'monoline' insurers, which appeared in the 1970s US municipal bond markets, and became powerful facilitators of many structured and project finance transactions, but suffered a near-total collapse due to crisis credit losses, with their credit ratings being so hammered that insurance was no longer feasible.

Modern market crises unfailingly lead to criticisms of rating agency performance, since they appear so often blind to imminent credit problems, as in the Asian financial crisis and the collapse of the US subprime loan market. A moral hazard arises in the iterative process used to structure complex transactions. The 2005 CGFS analysis described the agencies' function in facilitating structured and synthetic transactions (CGFS 2005: 6), and the interactivity of this part of investment bank transaction formation. The report warned that:

> market participants, in using ratings, need to be aware of their limitations. This applies, in particular, to structured finance and the fact that the one-dimensional nature of credit ratings based on expected loss or probability of default is not an adequate metric to fully gauge the riskiness of these instruments.
>
> (ibid: 3)

It concluded:

> It is clear from this discussion that rating agencies are interactively involved in more than one dimension of structured finance issues such that they cannot be seen as independent external assessors of the results.
>
> (ibid: 23–4)

IOSCO's code of conduct for rating agencies introduced 'soft' regulatory attention to the problem, exhorting agencies to use 'rating methodologies that are rigorous, systematic, and, where possible, result in ratings that can be subjected to some form of objective validation based on historical experience' (IOSCO 2004: § 1.2). This was not the outcome with complex transactions before 2008. Rating agencies are criticized periodically for slow analytical reactions to worsening risks, sudden rating reappraisals, and an asymmetric approach to credit improvements and declines. Critics identify three potential conflicts of interest:

- Rating agencies are customarily paid by issuers whose securities they appraise. In structured transactions this will typically be the arranger's SPV;
- Many investors are permitted by law or regulation to buy securities only if they carry a minimum credit rating from a recognized agency, but lack rights of redress for faulty analysis; and
- Rating agency parents or affiliates may receive revenue or other commercial benefits from issuers or their bank advisors.

Concern over their structured finance activity is more fundamental, that actual conflicts are inherent in the creation of structured transactions. The issue arises from the quasi-origination function that the leading rating agencies undertake whenever complex transactions are formed.

Early in the 2007 crisis France's chief regulator and IOSCO head questioned the rating of structured finance transactions, noting that agencies have a participatory function in structured transactions (Prada 2007), and asked 'can a pure rating approach be an appropriate and sufficient answer to the investors' needs in terms of credit risk assessment on structured finance instruments?' (ibid: 7). The practice began to be reconsidered early in the global crisis, along with a new scepticism regarding quantitative risk modelling, notably by Taleb (2007), who argued that most models catastrophically discount the recurrence of unexpectedly large shocks.

A related concern exists in the United States, where rating agencies have acquired a quasi-legal position as arbiters of the contractual integrity of both corporate and structured issues. The agencies have won court approval for the assertion that their research opinions are subject to constitutional freedom-of-speech protection and are not actionable before the courts. Investors lack a contractual relationship with the agencies, and have no right to pursue claims for redress, for example if they bought securities that became subject to unexpected downgrades (Kettering 2007: 96–118). The paradox is that ratings are procedurally essential for investors and instrumental in risk-based regulation of banks in structured finance. Indeed, the conflict that arises from the rating agency being compensated by issuers is one that is essential to maintain in order to guard against litigation. This arrangement could not be sustained if agencies were paid by investors (ibid: 108). Solutions to these questions include:

- Requiring fees for structured finance ratings to be paid by investors or investor representatives. This would introduce wider concerns as to rating agency liability.
- Limits to permissible activities in terms of transaction types or the actions of intermediaries. The aim would be to encourage fuller disclosure of complex transactions, and restrict access to complex instruments (Corrigan 2008).

These type of restrictions may be criticized as denying contractual freedoms. They are also likely to spawn new forms of circumvention by encouraging a matching wave of transactional regulatory arbitrage, signifying a further cycle in investment banking innovation.

Structured finance is relatively underutilized in Asia and has yet to deliver wide-ranging results in terms of the systemic reforms or deal volumes predicted by its advocates, including official interests. Asian Securitisation and Infrastructure Assurance Pte Limited (ASIA Limited) was an Asian monoline insurer established in 1996 by the ADB and several commercial partners, but became dormant due to insufficient capital and to losses incurred in the Asian financial crisis (Lejot, Arner & Pretorius 2006b: 284–5). A new scheme called the Credit Guarantee Investment Facility (CGIF) came into being in May 2011 based on proposals of the ASEAN+3 Asian Bond Market Initiative. CGIF is a US$700 million credit substitution fund to wrap local currency debt issues by Asian companies and make them palatable to regional investors.

The main structured finance activity among Asian banks other than cash securitized deals has been outward investment in the CDO markets that collapsed in 2007–8, but not on an especially large scale. In Chapter 8 we discuss examples of Asian banks dealing for HNW private banking clients in small-scale CDOs issued under frequent-issuer debt programs, and with retail investors in Hong Kong, Singapore and Taiwan through complex credit and equity-linked notes, many of which became notorious in 2008.

7.5 Innovation in derivatives

Derivatives are known commercially as contracts, the value of which is a function of the price of an unrelated claim or asset. That *underlier* might be financial, a commodity, live-stock or metal, or an index or analogue signifying conditions such as price inflation or weather conditions. Derivatives can be based upon anything that may be contractually defined, however intangible, providing that the result has some commercial value for users.

Our generic approach is to class financial derivatives as contracts that allow users to acquire or discard the risks associated with a second claim without contractual engagement with that claim. This takes both today's derivative instruments and practices into account, as well as the nature of these contracts as a distinct class of capital, and where the price behaviour of the derivative instrument may influence the price of the underlying claim as much as vice-versa.

Derivatives include convertible bonds, options, futures or contracts for forward settle-ment and an array of contracts made between counterparties known generically as swaps. They may be used singly, in groups or embedded in more complex transactions. They began as adjuncts to borrowings or as devices to hedge against unforeseeable future changes in price, but are best seen today as contracts that stand alone and represent tradable financial claims. The essence of derivatives is their capacity to transform or augment other claims, and change the expected risks and returns of borrowers, investors, traders, hedgers and speculators.

The emergence of this third class of capital in the 1970s was the result of investment banking innovation, best shown by a landmark 1981 transaction devised by Salomon Brothers, later part of Citigroup, which gathered together new and outstanding bond issues for two prominent borrowers with a mechanism for the exchange of identified liabilities. This became the foundation of today's global OTC derivatives markets, by some measures the largest of all global financial sectors. Salomon constructed a form of transac-tional arbitrage based on debt capital markets that were then highly segmented, and became the progenitor of all contemporary bond issues, radically altering the pricing process for new issues.

IBM Corporation and the World Bank were highly rated AAA borrowers known to inves-tors in their respective preferred debt capital markets. IBM tended to raise external funds from the domestic and overseas capital markets in US dollars but had occasionally borrowed in foreign currencies, including outstanding deutschemark and Swiss franc bonds equivalent in mid-1981 to a total of US$290 million. These offered IBM an accounting profit due to post-issue exchange gains. The bonds were due for redemption in 1986. The World Bank preferred to borrow in currencies associated with low nominal interest rates, especially in deutschemarks and Swiss francs.[5] German and US 5-year government bonds yielded approximately 11 per cent and 15 per cent respectively in August 1981. Both the World Bank and IBM were substantial and regular borrowers that typically expected to command a liquidity premium for new issues, but in the early 1980s regular issuance began to tire the interest of both sets of investors, and the two issuers each experienced an erosion of demand and a hardening of new issue terms.

IBM wanted to crystallize the accounting gains in US dollar terms on its two foreign currency liabilities, but would need to ensure that it suffered no future currency losses before the bonds were redeemed. The World Bank wanted to continue to borrow in low interest rate currencies. The two organizations were rare issuers in each other's markets, creating a possibility for arbitrage to lessen the overall cost of simultaneous new issues. In real terms calculated over the life of the bonds, the total cost would be lowered by each borrower accessing the other's market. The proceeds of the borrowings would then be exchanged, leaving both IBM and the World Bank more favourably funded, and this was the arbitrage that Salomon presented to the two organizations.

What is now commonplace was a startling innovation in 1981 (Bock 1983; author recollection). Salomon estimated that new IBM bonds in deutschemarks or Swiss francs would be cheaper for the issuer by 20 bp than issues of identical duration from the World Bank, notwithstanding its identical credit rating. A saving of 5 bp favoured a World Bank issue in US dollars compared to IBM's prevailing terms. The rarity of each issue would improve the clearing price at which the bonds could be distributed. The problem solved by Salomon was that neither issuer had need for the other's preferred currency.

These conditions were not unusual. The major capital markets had been segmented since transnational capital controls were adopted in 1914, and the creation of the Euromarkets in the 1960s as a permissive innovation owed much to the design capacity of investment banks in evading national rules. IBM had debt outstanding, and so only the World Bank needed to raise funds to facilitate a collaborative transaction. It borrowed US$290 million through two issues, one with coupon and maturity dates matching those of IBM's outstanding deutschemark bond and the second matching dates on its Swiss franc issue. The US dollar net proceeds were sold at spot for deutschemarks and Swiss francs to fund future loans. Both parties now had liabilities outstanding on the payment date of the new US dollar issues. IBM and the World Bank agreed an irrevocable exchange of payments that matched the terms of the four bonds, including both principal and periodic coupon payments.

Each borrower had effectively accessed the more favourable market, exchanged the resulting liabilities, and shared the aggregate overall reduction in costs. Cashflows on the new World Bank US dollar issues were made to match in present-value terms payments due under IBM's deutschemark and Swiss franc bonds, taking into account ongoing exchanges of currencies.

The results are shown conceptually in Figures 7.3A–7.3D, and illustrate how the transactions became important in the creation of a new market. For simplicity we show payments on one matching pair of bonds in Swiss francs and US dollars, but the US dollar–deutschemark swap was conceptually identical. The diagrams show the periodic post-issue payment obligations. After the World Bank US dollar bonds were issued, two unconnected bonds existed in parallel, as shown in Figure 7.3A.

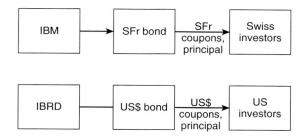

Figure 7.3A IBM–World Bank 1982 swaps.

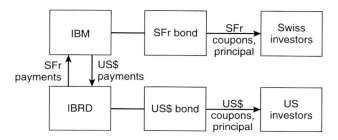

Figure 7.3B IBM–World Bank 1982 swaps.

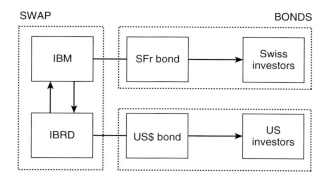

Figure 7.3C IBM–World Bank 1982 swaps.

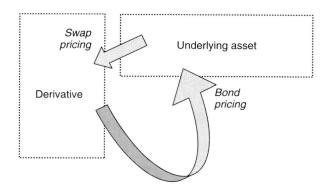

Figure 7.3D IBM–World Bank 1982 swaps.

The borrowers immediately exchanged responsibility for each other's payments as in Figure 7.3B, so for example US dollar investors were effectively to receive payments from IBM.

The bond obligations remained unchanged in law. The only new factor in the credit risks associated with the payments of the overall scheme were mutual obligations assumed by the two debtors. This treatment of counterparty credit risk is the only significant way in which these transactions differ from the thousands of swaps now executed daily. The IBM–World Bank deals led to the creation of highly liquid OTC swap markets, a transformation shown conceptually in Figure 7.3C.

Payments between the counterparties form the swap, which can be regarded commercially as separate from the underlying bonds. Each of the two swaps is a *derivative* of the bonds, and in modern terminology would be termed a cross-currency interest rate swap. Exchanges of interest payments in like currencies would form long-term interest rate swaps in a similar way.

The IBM–World Bank deal involved no exchange of principal at maturity in 1986, which would otherwise have made the transaction the equivalent of today's simple currency swaps. These transactions were subject to heavy negotiation that has long been redundant, with most such deals considered routine and capable of being arranged in minutes by many banks. Swaps can be transacted in seconds through electronic platforms such as Bloomberg.

Figure 7.3D illustrates our suggestion from the start of this section, that while the beginning of the OTC derivatives markets in the 1980s saw derivative contracts rely on the price behaviour of underlying assets, the two markets have developed symbiotically so that the price of each instrument influences the other. Many OTC interest rate and currency swap markets enjoy greater and more continuous liquidity than those in their corresponding underlying assets, and provide a reliable metric with which to price new issues.

7.6 Asian investment banking

Investment banking resources are widely used in Asia, and as we saw in Box 7.1 the region is an expanding transaction source for investment banks, both in intermediating savings and advising borrowing or acquisitive clients. New issue activity has been strong in China, India and elsewhere since 2009, with the demand for corporate advice being bolstered by outward Asian FDI.

Despite these favourable conditions, indigenous banks have failed to develop transnationally and are largely confined to national silos, either by choice or for lack of opportunity. Only Macquarie Bank and Nomura Securities have established regional transaction and product competence among investment banks domiciled in East Asia's time zone. Successful investment banks in Asia are either non-indigenous or confine activity to their home markets.

Is this transnational caution a function of effective foreign competition or a commercial or policy stance that prefers finance to be subservient to industry, as Section 2.2 saw in the Asian development model? We believe that the reasons reflect a mix of commercial preferences, institutional factors and questions of policy, and are common to all major Asian economies:

- Asian banks have a preference for transactional caution and capital conservation. Their tendency has been to follow client strategy rather than influence its direction.

- Much of the growth in revenue since 2000 is attributable to large transactions, including IPOs of Chinese and other state interests, all of which demand substantial capital and distribution resources that are found among few indigenous banks.
- The general national policy stance has been fearful since 1997–98 of innovatory or untrammelled finance, limiting domestic growth in investment banking and deterring banks with investment bank product skills for substantive foreign expansion.
- Commercial reasons include a bank lending orientation that we introduced in Section 2.2, and relatively low corporate demand for external finance.
- Demand for corporate finance advice and external funds are largely determined by location, in that outward FDI typically requires corporate advice and funding in the investee domicile. In any event, much of the growth in Asian FDI has been self-financed.
- Equity markets tend to be national silos. Investors have a pronounced home bias and investment banks involved in new issues may be unable to project their capabilities overseas. National barriers may also have deterred transnational cooperation between both investment banks and organized exchanges.
- Transaction expansion is constrained without relatively free access to domestic capital markets.

Such traditional obstacles take time to erode even in sophisticated financial systems such as Japan or South Korea. Activity is coveted by both indigenous and foreign banks, and although the volume of completed transactions is now growing it is less clear that deal volumes will develop so as to resemble those of other advanced economies. The result is often that completed securities and M&A deals involve transactional alliances combining product skills from non-Asian banks with client relationships of local firms, in some cases becoming semi-permanent joint ventures. This model also fits with widespread operational restrictions on foreign-controlled investment banks, and has been prevalent in China, Japan and South Korea.

Our characterization is simplistic, for successful non-Asian firms have effective dealings with Asian clients and Asian investment banks are not bereft of product skills, but three factors are clear:

- Most Asian investment banks lack effective resources beyond their home borders, both in buy-side product innovation and delivery, and in sell-side investor distribution.
- Asian banks suffer a lack of innovation, but when successful are entrenched in national commercial and political networks. Those with high product skills are domestic in focus, including CICC, CIMB, CITIC, Finansa and many smaller firms, especially in South Korea and Taiwan.
- Traditional indigenous professional investors adopt or are compelled by regulation to take a more conservative orientation than their OECD counterparts. This lessens the incentive for transactional innovation, although it may encourage alternative organizations to grow, as with the many private equity and hedge fund managers based in Hong Kong, Japan and Singapore, most of which were first established to manage Asian funds for non-Asian investors.

The most likely change to this pattern seems, as we write, to be an increase in national savings towards new investment territories or media. Investor caution may not vanish, but might ease enough to allow the larger securities markets to accept a far greater number of non-Asian listings and debt issues.

The long-term behaviour of Japanese investors would suggest that any such change may be slow. Structure and practice within Asia's financial sector most closely resemble a blend of the German model of deposit banking and corporate finance, with limited transactional innovation. Only CIMB, Macquarie and Nomura are repeated innovators on a material scale because each has sought to export its domestic product expertise. Other Asian banks have been constrained by national obstacles or shortages of competence or capital. Even Nomura has had limited success in two aspects of innovation that have beset Japan's policy-makers since 1997–98 and led them to sponsor several proposals to create a regional Asian currency, or instruments based on basket currencies similar to the former European Currency Unit, used in EU accounting and certain capital market issues until 1999. The aim would be twofold:

- Encourage risk-averse Japanese investors to deploy funds in Asia; and
- Encourage foreign borrowers to raise funds in the domestic markets of Japan.

Japanese officials have had minimal success in building support for a new currency to mitigate the risks involved in these two investment flows. Even though carry trade overseas lending financed in low-interest yen is often popular with Japanese banks and retail investors, the task of inducing Japan's professional investors to look to foreign risks appears to be treated as an official problem rather than one for investment banks to solve through innovation.

7.7 The end of innovation?

We argue that successful investment banks are associated with innovation in techniques, instruments or investment media. Chapter 10's case study of the 2007 sale of ABN Amro Bank shows a high order of transactional effectiveness. Merrill Lynch closed a landmark acquisition and received sizeable fees from deploying strong corporate finance and fundraising skills and taking appreciable underwriting risks in troubled conditions. The long-term result was less favourable. A deal was struck at a cyclical market peak with only limited due diligence on the target, and two of the three acquiring banks fell into state ownership. An observer might see this as great skill put to poor societal use, a view put in broader terms by leading regulators in Hong Kong (Sheng 2009), the UK (Turner 2009a) and US (Volcker, *Wall Street Journal* 2009).

Merrill Lynch itself disclosed in July 2008 a forced sale of CDO inventory, sizeable write-downs of investments and an emergency capital-raising. The bank sold a nominal US$30.6 billion in mortgage-related CDOs for US$$6.7 billion to a distressed investor, crystallizing a loss of 78 per cent of face value. The securities were created by the bank and valued at US$11.1 billion as at end-June 2008. The bank's overall first-half loss was US$6.6 billion, which followed net losses of US$8.6 billion in 2007 (Merrill Lynch 2008).

The bank was obliged to fund part of the CDO sale so that its net inflow was US$1.7 billion, or 5.5 per cent of the nominal amount. Merrill Lynch simultaneously announced a US$8.5 billion issue of new shares, but became forced to compensate the Singaporean SWF Temasek for losses sustained on its earlier purchases of shares in December 2007 and March 2008. The terms of those investments required Merrill Lynch to meet Temasek's mark-to-market losses were it to issue further shares within 12 months at a lower price.

A cautious head of the Korea Investment Corporation SWF was quoted in the *Wall Street Journal* as saying 'We have learned a lot from investing in Merrill Lynch and will take a more cautious approach in the future'.

In the year prior to these losses and fundraising, Merrill Lynch wrote down the balance sheet value of investments and securities by over US$45 billion, sold strategic assets and raised more than US$15 billion in new shares and regulatory capital. In the 12 months to end-July 2008 its share price fell by 68 per cent to US$24.33, during which time it offered highly effective advice and transaction resources to the consortium bidding for ABN Amro. Over the same period the S&P500 index, a broad measure of the performance of the New York stock market, fell by approximately 13.4 per cent, and its financial sector component by 36 per cent.

This is only one example of an enduring paradox. If investment banks are innovative, competitive and highly skilled in transaction and risk management, why is the sector prone to poor management and recurring losses? Even well-regarded banks have been involved in controversial or unethical practices, ignored conflicts of interest in acting for clients or in proprietary dealings. Many that were accepted as leaders in their fields no longer exist:

- Bankers Trust Company, once prolific structured debt arranger and derivative specialist. Acquired by Deutsche Bank after heavy losses.
- Barclays de Zoete Wedd (BZW), the first integrated UK investment bank and never profitable. Dismembered and parts sold to Crédit Suisse.
- Baring & Co., a venerable merchant bank. Destroyed by fraudulent trading and management incompetence.
- Bear Stearns & Co., at its 2008 collapse the fifth largest US investment bank, acquired by JPMorgan Chase under forcible US Treasury intervention following substantial losses on subprime securities.
- Dean Witter & Co., Kidder Peabody & Co., and Paine Webber & Co., substantial independent US broker–dealers acquired by competitors after poor results.
- Drexel, Burnham Lambert, leading leveraged finance specialist and high-yield bond underwriter, collapsed after persistent market manipulation and fraud.
- Lehman Brothers, Wall Street's fourth largest investment bank, suffered a debilitating withdrawal of credit lines leading to insolvency in 2008.
- Peregrine Investments Holdings, successful Asian corporate finance house made insolvent in 1997–98 by poor risk management of debt securities.
- Salomon Brothers, US debt securities specialist, fined in 1991 for market manipulation and sold to Citigroup, its reputational capital lost.
- Yamaichi Securities, a leading Japanese securities house, collapsed in 1997 from fraud and losses.

In each case the victim was broken up or forcibly acquired. Barings was sold in 1996 to ING for £1 after its capital was eliminated by catastrophic losses, incurred on a scale that might have been abated by competent risk management. The chief executive and senior figures were barred from holding directorships for several years after the courts found that Barings' managers had failed 'to make any proper or detailed examination of [a Singapore subsidiary's] reported profitability' and 'to pay any, or any sufficient, regard to [inter alia] the extraordinarily high reported profitability of [Baring Futures Singapore].' This small operation was the site of the fraud, which had generated false trading profits so large as to be infeasible given the low-risk nature of their source as described by per-petrator Nick Leeson. Barings' directors could only see profit (Re Barings plc and Others No. 5 1999).

Lehman Brothers was the landmark victim of the global financial crisis. It filed for bank-ruptcy protection in September 2008 after progressive share price falls and worsening access to short-term funding through the interbank or commercial paper markets made it impossible to sustain a highly leveraged balance sheet. Lehman's management had discussed the sale of a substantial interest to investors in China and South Korea but failed to agree terms, and despite frenzied talks with US officials and two potential bidders was allowed to collapse. Lehman's ingenuity and management hubris was unable to protect against a collapse of confidence. Rivals acquired Lehman's securities and corporate finance businesses within days. Lehman's winding up has been protracted, with immense and complex claims result-ing from its prolific activities in securities custody, structured finance and as a derivative counterparty.

Peregrine Investments was a successful Hong Kong corporate financier and equity broker, well regarded until 1997 as the region's first investment bank outside Australia and Japan. It broadened activities in 1994, believing that it could compete effectively with large non-Asian banks and remain independent only by engaging in fixed income and debt derivative businesses, but did so in a way that lacked both competence and capital. The firm collapsed in late 1997 from losses incurred on those new businesses.

Peregrine failed to recognize how its valuable core business was an inherent limit to expansion, and that diversification would end its independence. Peregrine's original corpo-rate finance arm was bought by BNP Paribas and recovered, although confined to clients in China and Hong Kong. Peregrine was unable to export its model while solvent. The frac-tured nature of Asia's financial markets meant that expansion required a large partner such as a regional bank or alliances with similar firms outside Hong Kong. Neither alternative attracted Peregrine's directors.

No indigenous Asian bank has overcome the twin obstacles of scale and national borders that led to Peregrine from diversification to collapse. A Hong Kong enquiry found no evidence of malfeasance by Peregrine directors, but stated that its businesses had 'broadened beyond the skills and experience of its founding management' (Farrant 2000: s. 2.179), that the Peregrine's fixed-income subsidiary had 'glaring holes in its arrangements for credit risk management' (ibid: s. 2.169), and that its key directors, despite being 'highly intelligent and ambitious', were poorly informed as to the risks to which Peregrine was exposed (ibid: s. 2.173). Peregrine's formative success was attributable to *guanxi*, as the preferred advisor of an influential Hong Kong investor.

A related example that suggests a link between the collapse of a large investment bank and systemic instability was the 1998 collapse from trading losses of US hedge fund Long Term Capital Management (LTCM). The fund's operations resembled a trading-focused investment bank and its principals were former Salomon traders. This link may be a clue to the inconsistent fortunes of the investment banking sector. Most enterprises are subject to cyclical variations in commercial activity and sentiment, and banks are especially vulnerable to changes in confidence. Commercial banks have endowments of accruing revenue, but the archetypal investment bank derives recurring revenue in a more limited way – for example, from asset management fees. The result is competitive pressure for ongoing innovation so as to sustain revenue and returns on capital. This risks prudential concerns receiving secondary weight in a bank's overall strategy. Goldman Sachs has reputedly the strongest and most independent risk management culture of today's large investment banks, but its historic performance is inconsistent since becoming incorporated in 1999.

Speculative trading is popularly associated with financial instability, but there may also be a theoretical link with which investment banking is also concerned. That systemic instability may be associated with financialization and financial speculation was suggested by Hyman Minsky in a theory both criticized and largely untested. This proposed that the behaviour of market participants during a bull-market phase grows less wary of risk and makes precipitant falls in values increasingly likely. When prices drop in value, traders are forced to liquidate their most valuable or conservative assets, which in turn intensifies the fall but appears to be sub-rational behaviour not predicted by traditional theory (Minsky 1982).

The proposition appeared in a period of general stability prior to the financialization that began in the mid-1980s, and was attacked by a distinguished scholar of financial development as ignoring then current conditions (Goldsmith 1982). The theory received warmer interest after later financial crises, the first being LTCM in 1998. A former IMF chief economist has also written of risks to stability associated with financial innovation, despite being generally supportive of modern financial market activity (Rajan 2005).

Poor management is the common feature of our examples. After research and sales malpractice were revealed among US investment banks in 2000–1, *The Economist* stated that 'Investment banks are among the worst-managed institutions on the planet because they are built on a loose confederation of franchises and outsize egos' (*The Economist* 2002). A narrative of the demise of BZW suggests that it was a bank staffed by 'clever people' engaged in 'clever transactions', but which failed in so doing to produce acceptable returns on capital at any stage in its life (Vander Weyer 2000: 6). A later head of the successor bank, Barclays Capital, stated in January 2011 that BZW '[i]n its entire history...never made any money outside of the UK or outside of its core UK business, and frankly, it was trampled by the US bulge bracket firms' (Treasury Select Committee 2011: Q618). This remark may be relevant to Asia's investment banks.

We shall only know in the long-term whether the 2007–9 global financial crisis was a cyclical phenomenon from which investment banking and financial innovation will recover, or the end of a generation of strong investment bank influence over global commerce. Regulatory reactions to the crisis involving restrictions on structured finance or credit risk transfer could have either positive or negative effects on investment banking prospects. Banks that find legitimate transactional arbitrage to avoid or lessen the impact of regulations for clients are likely to attract above average returns, but their shareholders may be less willing to provide capital for high balance sheet leverage. Large investment banks may be given less contractual freedom of action, which may lead to a bifurcation of investment banking activity and financial innovation generally. A limited number of global banks will engage in capital-intensive transactions and trading, and a larger number of smaller firms and hedge funds specialize in narrow business streams without the full degree of regulation to which commercial banks and universal investment banks submit. The investment bank sector may be incentivized to return to its nineteenth century merchant banking partnership roots.

Did the global crisis signal the death of investment banking? In the sense of lightly regulated financial innovation the answer may be yes, but it is difficult to uninvent transactions or practices that proved profitable for some users even if the broader welfare effects were more questionable. We do not foresee the death of investment banking in the sense of an abandonment of functional or product innovation, but it is likely for a time to be accompanied by closer supervision and will search for a profitable and sustainable archetype.

The crisis may well mark the end of the 1990s Anglo-American investment bank model of high balance sheet and credit risk leverage, and of the comparatively free manipulation of risk to and from the balance sheets of large intermediaries. It seems likely to have ended the standalone structured finance-oriented Wall Street investment bank that relied on wholesale market funding and unquestioning levels of general confidence.

8 Debt securities, derivatives and complex transactions

Many people begin their day seeing or hearing overnight news through television, radio or the web. Whenever finance is mentioned the narrative will focus on home or foreign stock markets: 'How did the Dow close?'; 'Where is the Nikkei?' Equity markets and prominent share prices form the universe of finance for many observers, at least outside personal concerns of consumer credit, pensions or bank deposits. Chapter 9 deals with this area of popular attention. Here we look at markets and instruments that are mysteries to many outside the financial sector, despite being subtly influential in their lives to a greater extent than equities or stock markets, and explain the operation of generic examples of these important transactions.

Almost every topic in this book is determined or influenced by the behaviour of debt capital markets. Tradable debt is central to all modern economies, regardless of their strain of capitalism, by virtue of facilitating markets in interest rates and credit risk. Capital allocation tends to be poorer when those price signals are unreliable, as in several Asian economies where interest rates are centrally managed or bond trading is curtailed. Well-functioning debt markets provide a price indicator for all financial and economic activities. They sit squarely at the heart of our book for these mechanical reasons and because they influence commercial conduct in more qualitative ways. States that lose the confidence of debt markets and investors will be pressured to adjust their economic policies, as Greece and Ireland found in 2010–11. These are only recent examples of the many sovereign debtors with similar experiences. Defaults or restructurings of domestic or external debt are far from uncommon, both historically and in the modern financialized era since 1970. The result are summarized in Box 8.1.

Confidence can recover and allow states or state agencies to renew commercial borrowing at home or abroad quickly, as South Korea and Iceland found respectively in 2001–2 and 2011, but the debt markets can remain sceptical of less credible states for long periods.[1] Large corporate debtors suffering a deteriorating financial performance will often experience signals from the debt markets well before a lack of confidence impacts their share price, and encourage a change in commercial strategy before any formal debt restructuring. Skilful and transparent borrowers may see their fundraising strategy rewarded with favourable savings in marginal debt service costs, which is the general experience of the World Bank and a few notable corporate issuers. Global debt markets are not necessarily correct in their judgements but have considerable influence on all commercial activity.

Nothing in our narrative is directly concerned with the morality of borrowing, traditional religious views of debt contracts or the residual association of borrowing with profligacy and exploitation common to many Asian, Islamic and Western cultures. We are agnostic as to the place of debt in society, while recognizing that both canon law and the Shari'ah have

Box 8.1 Sovereign Debt Defaults

A survey of sovereign debt defaults and restructurings to 2008 lists 77 incidents involving domestic obligations since 1740, and 239 involving external claims since either 1800 or the year of the debtor state's independence (whichever is later). Domestic debt comprises bonds or other claims denominated in the borrower's home currency but issued in any financial centre; external debt involves claims denominated in foreign currencies issued at home or in overseas markets.

- The external cases comprise 126 in Latin America, 73 in Europe, 26 in Africa and 14 in Asia, with the latter divided among China (twice), India (three times), Indonesia (four times), Japan, Myanmar and the Philippines (once each) and Sri Lanka (twice).
- 48 (62 per cent) of domestic debt cases occurred in 1970–2008.
- 75 (31 per cent) of external debt incidents occurred in 1970–2008.
- 11 external debt incidents occurred in Asia in 1949–2008. This excludes cases where a restructuring was agreed with commercial creditors with no prior overt or threatened payment moratorium, as with South Korea in late 1997.
- Many states experienced several separate incidents and some were unresolved for several years. A small number involved a new government permanently refuting the obligations of its predecessor, as with post-revolutionary Cuba and the Soviet Union.
- Latin American states defaulted most frequently and for the longest periods, especially in their foreign borrowings. Of 19 European states in the survey, including Russia and Turkey, only six experienced no external debt defaults or rescheduling between 1800 (or independence if later) and 2008, which are Belgium, Finland, the three Scandinavian states and the UK. Nine states underwent these incidents at least five times.

These results are useful for comparative reasons and to illustrate how common are hiatuses in the markets for sovereign debt, although the survey's definitions apply modern concepts of default and restructuring to historical periods and betray considerable subjectivity. Defaults are easily recognized if they involve a permanent refutation of contractual claims or non-trivial non-payment of interest or principal, but not when creditors anticipate defaults by volunteering to renegotiate the terms of their claims, as was unsuccessfully proposed by French bank creditors of Greece in June 2011 (Fédération Bancaire Française 2011).

Defaults on domestic debt include archaic examples where the state varied the terms of its debts by refusing payment in the form specified by contract or custom, such as ending a creditor's right to receive payments in bullion or forcing conversion of domestic foreign currency bank deposits into local currency. These uncertainties resemble those described in Box 3.3 in the treatment of NPLs by banks of different jurisdictions.

Modern practice in external debt rescheduling has developed since Mexico's 1982 foreign payment moratorium into a complex informal institution, shown in Section 5.4 as a set of collaborative rules that national regulators usually encourage banks and other financial creditors to follow. The aim of negotiations is typically for creditors to accept a payment standstill and refrain from enforcing their claims, providing that the debtor commits to a commercially realistic debt rescheduling. Such arrangements are always more difficult when the composition of creditors or claims is varied, or if a hard payment default is institutionalized by rating agency actions so as to remove any flexibility from creditors. It is impossible to implement when official and supranational creditors are hapless or refuse to align, as with Argentina in 2001–2, an episode in which the IMF admitted to being ineffectual (IMF 2004), or the Eurozone in 2010–11, when member states were unable to agree expeditiously how to assist distressed members such as Greece and Ireland.

We think it unlikely that a future case will be as extreme as that of Newfoundland in 1933, a self-governing colonial dominion and not part of Canada, with external debt of US$101 million (Amulree Commission 1934: § 192). A collapse in cod prices made its fishing industry insolvent and left the government with no source of revenue. Unable to borrow or service its debts, Newfoundland traded financial support with London and ceded autonomy first to colonial Britain and later within federal Canada. An enquiry concluded that Newfoundland's 'present burden of public debt is wholly beyond the country's capacity, and it is essential that it should be lightened if the Island is to be saved from the imminent danger of financial collapse' (ibid: §195(1)), a conclusion that we believe applied equally to Greece in 2011. Newfoundland's choice was between 'between democracy and default' (Hale 2003: 60), a view that critics of post-1997 IMF policies in Southeast Asia have regularly made.

Sources: Reinhart & Rogoff 2009: 97–100, 112–16; authors' archives.

influenced the development of debt contracts and instruments, as we suggest in Section 1.1, just as many modern institutions created incentives for successful financial innovation. The innovations we discuss in this chapter have two main features:

- Most are recent; and
- All sprang from transaction solutions developed by investment banks, which is the theme of Chapter 7.

A mid-1970s conference agenda shows how, not long ago, financial innovation could be discussed with no mention of infrastructural finance, asset-backed securities, financial derivatives or Islamic finance (Jaffee 1975), all techniques that are now familiar. 'Derivative' appeared as a term in finance only in the early 1990s (Swan 2000: 5–18), before which it suggested differential calculus rather than a separate world of futures, options and swaps. A 1983 Bank of England symposium on the nature of financial innovation noted 'an acceleration in the development...of new financial instruments and techniques' (Bank of England 1983: 358) and 'the impact on financial activity of regulatory and supervisory structures' (ibid), but focused on competition for savings and how market volatility had caused a jump in demand for short-term securities and money market mutual funds, as if the 11 central banks present knew that innovation was coming without a notion of what form it might take.

We argue in Chapter 3 that Asia's post-1949 financial systems owed much to the preferences and policies of the state. We see little evidence of successful direct official involvement in global financial innovation – indeed, Section 12.5 shows the limits of recent attempts at Asian capital market reform where state-led innovation has lacked commercial force. Regulators may create rules such as the Basel capital regime that innovators then circumvent, but new transactions or techniques have flowed from the commercial sector since the 1980s with the incentive of deregulation but without direct prompting from the state. We sense that modern innovation in finance is meagre in Asia for this very reason, and discuss in Chapter 13 the implications for the region's future preferences and development. Global innovation may have accelerated in the late twentieth century as states lessened qualitative control of markets or intermediaries, even if that proves to be a passing phenomenon following the 2007–9 crisis.

This chapter introduces a spectrum of debt securities transactions, from the simple to the highly complex. The more intricate are concoctions of many contracts, including embedded options or other derivative elements. We describe the features of the international debt capital markets including the current state of the bond markets in Asia, looking at the nature and commercial terms of common debt securities, their legal form and structure, and the processes involved in new issues and transaction settlement. We also examine differences between bonds and syndicated loans of the kind explained in Section 6.3, and legal and regulatory concerns brought about by convergence between these generic instruments.

Our aim is not to describe every variation of debt securities, derivatives or markets, which quirks of history or local practice make impossible, but to offer an understanding of international deal formation and market operations to which most forms of issue can be compared. Section 8.2 looks at the nature and uses of our third class of capital in exchange-traded and OTC financial derivatives, and builds on the innovation narrative of Section 7.5. We then discusses the credit derivatives markets in their own right and as a link to complex forms of structured finance, including transactions and practices that were severely questioned by the global financial crisis. Synthetic securities and even simple CDS have been held responsible by observers for inducing or exacerbating the crisis, and have, since 2009, become the objectives of re-regulation in most leading jurisdictions.

Most of the instruments and transactions appearing throughout the chapter are *intrinsic* contracts, as explained in Section 7.4, in that their commercial terms are largely self-contained, unlike equity claims which are strongly influenced by statute and separately drawn rules for corporate governance. Most take a standard form resulting from commercial practice, although one result of the 2007–9 global crisis is closer regulatory attention in jurisdictions including Hong Kong, Singapore and the UK to the design of financial instruments, which reflects concerns over the mis-selling of complex products, as described in Box 8.6. A second theme of the chapter concerns the mechanics of credit risk transfer, which we reviewed in the context of the global crisis in Section 2.5. Table 8.1 shows the main forms that this transformation may take according to whether or not it is funded and the nature of the risks involved.

The debt and derivative markets are infected by jargon for reasons associated with rent seeking and the club behaviour of semi-public financial networks, and so we define many terms used in this chapter in our glossary.

8.1 Debt contracts, loans and bonds

Loans and bonds are popular terms for financial instruments representing current or future claims against a debtor. The creation of loans and bonds can be similar processes, although

Table 8.1 Credit risk transfer

	Funded	Unfunded
Single risk	Simple loan or securities assignments or sales	Credit default swaps, guarantees & standby letters of credit Insurance contracts
Multiple risks	Asset-backed securities Index credit-linked notes Cash CDOs Re-securitization (CDO-squared) Exchange traded funds	Multiple name, portfolio or basket CDS All synthetic CDO & CDOs-squared

most bonds are more quickly initiated, syndicated, distributed and closed. Bond issues for well-known or frequent borrowers may take only hours to prepare and execute, and no more than three days might elapse between an arranging bank receiving a new issue mandate and the payment date when the borrower receives the transaction's net proceeds, as with the example cited in Table 8.5. The corollary is that the bespoke nature of loans provides more flexibility in drawing and usage. Two commercial factors distinguish bonds from the generic syndicated loan explained in Chapter 6:

- Most bonds are repaid in a single amount. Bonds can use tranching to simulate the phased amortization common in loan contracts, but this will increase deal expenses and reduce overall liquidity.
- Bonds traditionally have longer feasible maturities than loans. Most are within a 2–12-year range, but many have far longer lives.

The distinction reflects historic funding behaviour among commercial banks and other inter-mediaries. While banks funded loan assets using deposits and other short-term borrowings, bond portfolios consumed the investor's own resources or funds committed to it for long periods, as with superannuation funds or life insurers. This implies that bond investors face uncertain reinvestment risk if they allow an issuer the option of early redemption. The inves-tor implicitly writes a call option for the borrower in such cases, and expects compensation in the form of a premium to the nominal value of the bonds in the event that the option is exercised. Compensation for reinvestment risk is rarely necessary with loans.

Loans and bonds were once easily distinguished in design, in use and in law. Bonds were simple contracts largely free of conditional clauses or covenants and were usually designed to facilitate post-execution secondary sales among holders. This explains the liquidity pre-mium that can attach to highly regarded and practised issuers such as the European Investment Bank, Hutchison Whampoa, KfW Bank or Toyota Motor and others listed in Tables 8.4A and 8.4B. Bonds of these borrowers often trade expensively,[2] in that prevailing secondary market prices generally result in low credit spreads compared to similar risks, despite their high issue-frequency.

Bond issuers were traditionally governments or state agencies of advanced economies, supranational organizations such as the Asian Development Bank or World Bank, or com-panies of high profile and credit standing. Loans were made by banks to a wider range of credit risks among public organizations, companies or projects, and included restrictions to the transfer of outstanding claims between lenders. The parties to loans would typically remain unaltered until the debt was discharged. The conventional view of finance scholars is that this allowed closer ongoing relationships between debtors and loan creditors compared to a more distant connection with bondholders – for example, in the disclosure of commercial information or compliance with operating covenants. Banks have an advantage from this asymmetry, regardless of the disclosure requirements that securities regulation imposes on bond issuers. The reality is more subtle. SMEs generally lack access to the debt capital markets, deal with only few bank lenders and rarely create inter-creditor information asymmetry concerns. Substantial borrowers that arrange both bonds and loans seldom discriminate between types of creditors, but share commercial confidences with a few trusted advisors, usually the investment banks that provide them with high-level advice. Disclosure asymmetries vary between lenders more than creditor types.

Transferability or potential liquidity was, until the mid-1980s, an indicator in sophisticated markets of whether a claim was evidenced as a bond or loan. The distinction is steadily becoming archaic. Loans trade as freely as bonds in Europe, North America and parts of Asia, bond issuers may be weaker credit risks, and all can be subject to equally intricate terms. These instruments can be near substitutes for some users, and while market practice still uses different contractual structures to execute loans and bonds, the commercial differences are now slender and associated mainly with credit risk. The trend results from several factors:

- A greater focus on returns to capital in bank lending. Banks look first to their own financial objectives rather than the presumed value of client relationships.
- Many insurers, hedge funds and other non-bank intermediaries are becoming willing to make or buy loans.
- Investors of all kinds wishing to manage their portfolios freely by buying or selling financial assets.

Any categorization of instruments is irrelevant to these choices. The classic features of loans and bonds can be itemized instead by type and effect:

- Loans are made by small groups of well-informed parties. Loan contracts are therefore adaptable and can include complex provisions for drawings and repayment, and covenants to give a degree of control to lenders. Loans are easy to amend unless a borrower has great negotiating leverage.
- Bond contracts need simple terms and credit risks to ensure transferability and liquidity. Bonds are quick to arrange and difficult to amend because contractual changes require the consent of a group of creditors that is diversified, shifting and often anonymous.
- Syndicated loan contracts provide for a facility agent to administer the transaction *for the lenders* as we saw in Section 6.3. Lenders decide where necessary on amending the terms of the loan, subject only to involuntary actions resulting from the triggering of cross-default provisions. Bond contracts usually appoint a fiscal and paying agent or its equivalent to administer the issue *on behalf of the obligor* and limit the agent's freedom to propose changes to the issue's terms.

These differences began to erode in the 1980s, although the uses of bonds and loans still vary. Project finance is one market segment in which loan transfer is modest and where loans and bonds remain distinct, but the contractual model of infrastructural finance developed by Macquarie Group that we describe in Section 11.3 has challenged that simple distinction. Free transfer of loans has been historically disfavoured by project sponsors who may be constrained from sharing commercial confidences with loan buyers with which they have no working relationship – for example, those resulting from covenants requiring disclosure of proprietary supply or sale contracts. This also creates conflicts for banks needing to make adequate disclosure to non-bank investors. Most loan-transfers associated with non-recourse finance occur after project completion or in distressed transactions where creditors sell their claims to specialist investors.

The transaction structure of a generic international bond is shown in Figure 8.1. A large number of investors buy bonds, the terms of which are set out in relatively simple form in a bond contract or indenture, in most cases lodged electronically as a *global note* with a clearing house or depositary.[3] The ownership entitlements of bondholders appear as book entries in the same registry or one with which it is electronically linked. Box 8.2 shows that bonds as physical instruments are virtually a curiosity of history, and the term *bearer* bond is now taken as an antonym for *registered* securities rather than a negotiable claim evidenced on paper.

The issuer's obligations to investors is contained within the bond contract. It also enters a separate subscription agreement for deal execution by a group of banks known as a syndicate and, depending on its governing law, either a trust deed or paying and fiscal agency agreement for the administration of the issue. The prospectus is a pre-execution document that helps channel information about the deal and the issuer to potential investors and is never contractually part of the issue. Market practice provides that investors are deemed to have independently assessed the transaction without relying on the issuer or bank arrangers, which is a convenient fiction to lessen potential liabilities for error.

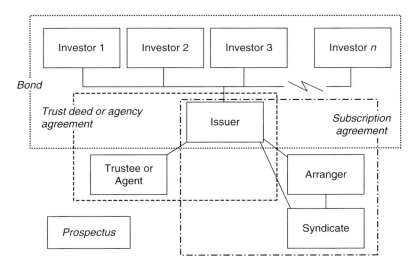

Figure 8.1 The generic bond issue.

The number of investors *n* shows the widespread distribution of the issue. Solid lines represent contractual relationships while the issue is outstanding. Broken lines indicate the parties to each element of documentation. The prospectus is specifically excluded from being a contractual part of the deal to minimize any post-execution liability for errors or mis-statements of fact.

Box 8.2 Bearer Bonds, Tax Evasion and Money Laundering

All bonds were once paper certificates issued to investors in bearer form. They were negotiable instruments that stated the commercial obligations of the issuer and provided a physical mechanism for the bondholder to collect payments, whether or not the holder was the rightful owner of the bond. Each time a coupon fell due, the holder would present the certificate at a bank appointed by the issuer where, in return for payment, the paper would be authenticated and a portion 'clipped' to avoid duplication.

The legal character of negotiability varies from one jurisdiction to another, but in accepted transnational practice means that a claim is transferable merely by delivery. A buyer obtains title to the bond without needing to register a claim or execute a separate document, and need not worry as to whether the seller had legitimate possession of the instrument. Domestic US practice is unusual because most bonds are registered and not strictly treated as negotiable instruments, with the mechanics of transfer governed by the Uniform Commercial Code (UCC Art. 8 §§ 301–7).

Bearer bonds in physical form have become unacceptable in most states in recent years, especially when September 2001 made terrorist financing and money laundering heightened concerns of the G7 and its Financial Action Task Force. Bearer bonds in this traditional sense have thus steadily fallen into disuse except in several idiosyncratic markets. The format is seen not only as susceptible to crime, but as a vector for criminal payments and tax evasion. There is little doubt that money laundering grew to a substantial scale by 2001, when the IMF estimated global flows of up to US\$1.5 trillion, or 4.5 per cent of global output (Dalhuisen 2010: 391), but it cannot be known whether bearer bonds were as important in those transfers as high-value banknotes or physical assets. Their modern function is likely to have been driven by motives associated with anonymity and taxation, sufficient to compensate investors for the risks of loss or theft.

Bonds in physical bearer form were popular in the early Eurobond markets and widely available outside the US until the early 1990s. Issuers then began questioning the expense of giving investors the right to request paper certificates. Most international bonds now exist as a unique global note delivered electronically at issue to a central securities depositary (CSD) such as Clearstream, DTCC or Euroclear, or a commercial custodian on its behalf. Bondholder claims are recorded as electronic entries in CSD accounts and bond sales executed by transfers between accounts or across an inter-CSD 'bridge'. This two-stage process is known formally as immobilization. Today's bearer bond is freely transferable without the holder being registered in the way that shareholders typically appear on a company registry.

Electronic settlement has become common for international bonds and money market instruments and in most OECD national debt markets. The transition from paper to digital entry may take two forms: immobilization or dematerialization. The latter is common for money market instruments and government bonds and involves no paper certificates or global notes whatsoever, so that both the debtor's overall obligation and the rights of each holder are recorded electronically. The transition has legal consequences in many jurisdictions for the nature of the bond or noteholder's rights, the most important of which concerns the treatment of claims in transit, or being transferred between CSDs or custodians.

Bondholder rights are generally not weakened by immobilization or dematerialization providing that the jurisdictional location of their property is known and reliable.

Any concerns would relate to transnational conflicts of law and the risk that a CSD or intermediary became insolvent while securities were in transit, matters addressed by international treaties. Electronic settlement is common in Asia for local currency government notes and bonds but available or mandatory for other debt securities only in Hong Kong, Japan, South Korea, Malaysia and Singapore.

US law made bearer bonds prohibitively expensive for domestic use in the early 1980s (Dalhuisen 2010: 591). They remained common in Europe and other international markets because coupon payments were made without deduction for withholding taxes, but this justification became less critical when issuers grew more willing to provide for 'grossing up' compensation payments in the event of a tax deduction, and through the EU Single Market in financial services, leading to withholding taxes becoming less widespread. These reforms also helped the demise of the mythical Belgian Dentist, the archetypal wealthy retail Eurobond investor of the 1980s, who bought bonds over the phone from a bank or broker and made a discreet annual journey from Brussels to Luxembourg to have the coupons clipped and funds paid anonymously into an offshore account.

Debt securities

Organized trading in short-term government loans probably began in sixteenth-century Antwerp, an innovation developed from the sale of public annuities that began in Europe in the late Middle Ages (van der Wee 1977). Adam Smith thought it inevitable that the rulers of states with developed trade and investment would be strongly tempted to spend freely and fail to accumulate a fiscal surplus. The final chapter of *The Wealth of Nations* notes that among seventeenth- and eighteenth-century European monarchs only Frederick the Great (1712–86) and his late father were not spendthrift, and that:

> The parsimony which leads to accumulation has become almost as rare in republican as in monarchical governments. The Italian republics, the United Provinces of the Netherlands, are all in debt. The canton of Berne is the single republic in Europe which has amassed any considerable treasure.
>
> (Smith 1776: 508)

The result was that borrowing became necessary to finance wars, since:

> An immediate and great expense must be incurred in that moment of immediate danger, which will not wait for the gradual and slow returns of the new taxes. In this exigency government can have no other resource but in borrowing.
>
> (ibid: 509)

Luckily for the borrower:

> The same commercial state of society which, by the operation of moral causes, brings government in this manner into the necessity of borrowing, produces in the subjects both an ability and an inclination to lend.
>
> (ibid)

Investors willing to buy securities to fund the state existed in many parts of the continent by the mid-seventeenth century, notably in the Dutch United Provinces (Kindleberger 1984: 156), making Amsterdam the leading financial centre of its day. Recognizable markets in debt securities only appeared after 1693, when Antwerp's innovation of negotiable trade bills became adapted in London to the sale of transferable long-term government bonds (Lejot, Arner & Pretorius 2006a). Two features were important to their success:

- Predictable, non-arbitrary taxation that provided continual revenue for the state and allowed investors to make a clear judgment as to credit risk; and
- Secure creditor rights in transfer to reconcile the time horizons of debtor and creditor.

Adam Smith cites both as necessary conditions for successful state borrowing. These innovations gave confidence to investors to deal with credit and liquidity risks and made large-scale public borrowing feasible. The states adopting these reforms soon became those most able to raise funds. England's 'financial revolution' from 1688 made possible a public bond market (Dickson 1967: 457), the absence of which 'would have effectively stopped [the state] from borrowing on the scale it needed' (ibid). Institutional scholar Douglass North calls the 1689 English Bill of Rights an essential change because '[a] capital market ... will simply not evolve where political rulers can arbitrarily seize assets or radically alter their value' (North 1990: 101). Similar problems persist today in parts of Asia (Arner, Lejot & Rhee 2006).

Western governments borrowed freely in the eighteenth and nineteenth centuries when preparing for war (Ferguson 2001), in amounts far greater than those available from banks or moneylenders. The need to finance military spending instigated the first public debt markets (Baskin 1988) which then opened access to commercial borrowers such as canal builders and railroads (Davis & Gallman 2001). Most sophisticated capital markets have a history of financing organized conflict, which was a considerable incentive to early financial development.

Bond market activity was first centred in London and Paris, migrated to New York after 1914, and eventually found a transnational setting that grew into today's global markets in major and secondary currency issues. Strict national regulation of issuance and capital flows under Bretton Woods led, in the 1960s and 1970s, to powerful Eurobond markets that were only partly associated with any single financial hub. These expanded in the 1980s to rival the leading national bond markets in scale, and resulted in innovations in issuance and trading practice that have since seeped into national markets, such that the global market in bonds is integrated across borders far more than the fragmented markets in equities.

Composition and scale

The world's debt markets are large in nominal terms and in relation to global output, but how large in relation to other forms of claim depends upon when the question is asked. This is due to cross-market valuation anomalies explained in Box 3.4, and because the *qualitative importance* of each financial market shifts according to general conditions, leading to *quantitative changes* in relative scale. At the end of 2010, the global debt capital markets were over 1.7 times the size of the global equity markets but no-one would expect the multiple to be the same in 2012 or 2020. In two decades the aggregate global equity market capitalization has approached the scale of the bond markets only twice, in 1998 and 2006, partly because of steadily increasing outstanding debt (as shown in Figure 8.2).

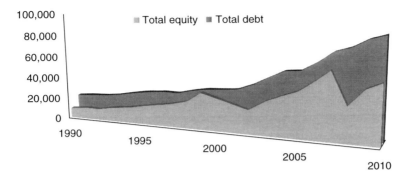

Figure 8.2 Aggregate bond and equity market capitalization, end-period 1990–2010 (US$ bn). Debt includes domestic and international bonds and short-term notes. Equity capitalization is taken from shares traded on the 51 member exchanges of WFE but any exchanges excluded are trivial in scale.
Sources: BIS (2011) WFE.

Nominal bond market issuance leaped in 2009–10 because:

- Many governments issued bonds prolifically as part of an accommodative monetary policy and to support a post-crisis recapitalization of banks;
- Bank credit was depressed, so larger companies raised money outside the banking sector; and
- Post-crisis demand for bonds was supported by investor risk aversion, implying a switch from equity to debt and a reduction in portfolio duration.

Even a broad explanation of the value and components of the debt markets needs qualifying by time, place and momentum, but an end-2010 sketch of sectoral capitalizations shows the following:

- Global debt capital markets significantly larger than global equity markets, at US$94.5 trillion and US$56.8 trillion respectively, as at end-2010 (BIS 2011; WFE).
- Domestic debt capital markets more than twice the size of the international markets, accounting for 70.8 per cent of the total.
- Government issues outstanding representing 58.0 per cent of all domestic notes and bonds. The financial sector accounted for 32.0 per cent of the total, and the aggregate of domestic corporate issues was comparatively small.
- Short-term instruments were 25.1 per cent of domestic debt but a trivial component of the international markets. The difference stems from money market instruments being functionally important in national monetary policy.
- All debt capital markets heavily skewed toward issuers in developed economies, measured both by current issuance and end-2010 market capitalization. This result is less pronounced if the size of markets is adjusted for GDP.
- The largest nominally capitalized segments of the domestic debt capital markets by residence of issuer were the US (37.7 per cent of the total), Japan (20.5 per cent), France

(4.7 per cent), China and Italy (each 4.5 per cent) and Germany (3.8 per cent). South Korea and India provided respectively 1.6 per cent and 1.1 per cent of the total.

- The largest nominally capitalized segments of the international debt capital markets by nationality of issuer were the US (26.0 per cent of the total), UK (11.3 per cent), Germany (9.9 per cent), France (7.2 per cent) and Spain (6.4 per cent). No other group exceeded 5 per cent of the total. Japan, South Korea and China accounted respectively for 1.5 per cent, 0.51 per cent and 0.27 per cent of total capitalization.

International bonds are sold and traded in all large financial centres not subject to cross-border capital controls, with 70–80 per cent of new issues made from the US and UK in 2009 and 2010. London is by far the largest hub for international bond trading, accounting for around 70 per cent of total volume in 2010.

Money market instruments

Debt contracts with maturities of less than 12 months are generally known as money market instruments. They vary in form and sales practice according to national customs, not least because they were the earliest form of traded negotiable instrument. Modern short-term claims have features of the kind shown in Table 8.2. Most accrue no interest and are sold at discounts to their nominal or *par* value, which is the amount due at redemption.

These characteristics are conducive to liquidity and inexpensive issuance, and make money market instruments important in the day-to-day operations of all banks in most financial systems, providing a mechanism linking national or regional monetary authorities with the banking sector, and in some cases indirectly to non-bank intermediaries.

Most uses of money market instruments arise from liquidity management, either in managing portfolio duration risk, short-term investment of surplus cash, or short-term borrowing. The state is the dominant issuer of short-term instruments throughout Asia, usually in the form of treasury bills or promissory notes, even when its fiscal balance is small or positive, so that some of the region's domestic currency money markets have been more liquid and better resourced than its long-term debt markets.

The global composition of claims against banks and governments is shown in Figure 2.4A, with money market instruments accounting for 9 per cent of the total in December 2006. Table 8.3 illustrates the growth of outstanding short-term claims in our sample economies

Table 8.2 Money market instruments

Characteristics	Notes
Examples	Government bills, bank certificates of deposit, corporate commercial paper
Liquidity	Generally high
Maturity	1–364 days. Shorter tenors of up to 90 days enjoy greater market depth
Coupon	Usually none. Claims are sold at discounts to nominal value
Transferability	Freely transferable, in some cases as bearer instruments
Eligible for discounting	Many claims of shorter tenors are acceptable as collateral for short-term advances by central banks, providing they meet minimum rating criteria
Repo market	Usually acceptable as collateral by commercial counterparties

Table 8.3 Outstanding short-term domestic local currency claims (US$ bn)

End period	1995	2000	2005	2010	Share attributable to issuer types (%, end-2010)		
					Banks	Govt	Corporates
China	1.8	11.1	387.0	975.6	11.5	76.4	12.1
Hong Kong	17.5	32.0	32.1	40.2	42.1	52.4	5.5
India	16.4	5.7	29.3	127.3	59.1	21.2	19.6
Indonesia	0.0	6.3	7.6	16.7	0.0	100.0	0.0
Japan	1,007.1	1,491.6	2,569.3	3,791.7	11.6	85.1	3.3
South Korea	104.8	133.7	303.3	391.4	42.1	33.5	24.4
Malaysia	28.9	14.9	24.9	24.8	82.2	5.7	12.1
Philippines	14.4	11.1	17.4	18.8	0.0	87.9	12.1
Singapore	10.5	18.4	31.2	59.3	8.5	89.9	1.6
Taiwan	53.9	56.6	42.2	50.4	16.4	36.8	46.8
Thailand	0.5	5.0	23.8	94.0	0.0	97.9	2.1
US	2,351.9	3,701.6	4,651.8	5,406.9	49.6	48.2	2.2
All countries	**6,013.0**	**7,790.6**	**11,798.6**	**16,881.1**	**36.8**	**58.8**	**4.4**

Data include both money market instruments and seasoned bonds of up to 12 months remaining life. True domestic money market instruments outstanding in all countries was US$12,563.1 bn at end-2010. No data are available for Vietnam.
Source: BIS Quarterly Review Tables 13A and 17A.

between 1995 and 2010, together with the shares contributed by bank, government and corporate issuers, and comparisons with US and global outstanding claims. The US and Japanese markets are comfortably larger than all others.

A pattern of innovation after the 1970s widened the features and uses of money market claims. Investment banks created new instruments and collective investment schemes to help fund their securities activities and compete with commercial banks in short-term lending and attracting savings. The results include:

- Commercial paper. Short-term, unsecured, unsubordinated promissory notes issued by non-bank borrowers, commonly for 30–180 days.
- Asset-backed commercial paper (ABCP). Holders share claims on pooled securitized assets. ABCP was a primary funding source for SIVs and bank conduits until mid-2007.
- Medium-term instruments, especially 1–5-year floating rate certificates of deposit (FRCD). FRCDs provide banks with some certainty of funding, especially in currencies for which they lack natural deposits, and were instrumental in the growth of the global credit markets described in Section 6.3.
- Money market mutual funds and exchange traded funds (ETFs). These are continuing arrangements rather than short-term instruments, but function as near-cash investment media for retail savers. ETFs typically have low dealing costs, which has also encouraged index fund managers and hedge funds to be prolific users. Money market mutual funds were created by US investment banks in the 1970s to assist their funding and compete with government Treasury bills and bank CDs. ETFs appeared in the 1990s and grew quickly in scale, as we explain in Box 8.3.

Box 8.3 Exchange Traded Funds

Financial crises do more than cause chaos and upset confidence. They cloud all financial instruments involving a degree of complexity, not always for rational reasons, but because investors and regulators fear the reputational risk of repeated gaffes. Exchange traded funds (ETFs) began as simple money market products but have grown in scale and complexity such that in 2010–11 they became subject to regulatory concern as to their possible impact on organized markets (FSB 2011). These centre on four issues of stability:

- The immense hedge fund use of ETFs for algorithmic securities trading or high-frequency trading (HFT). The risk of excessive sudden price volatility resulting from the rapid execution of many computer-generated trades was exemplified by the May 2010 'Flash Crash' dislocation to the New York Stock Exchange described in Section 9.5 when ETFs provided much of the day's trading volume (CFTC & SEC 2010: 39–40).
- Growth in transactional complexity through synthetic ETFs. These share certain characteristics of complex cash and synthetic CDOs and are thus intuitively linked to the collapse of the structured finance markets in 2007–8. Synthetic ETFs can create path-dependent or leveraged returns, or use complex hedging with non-conforming assets, to replicate the behaviour of simpler indexes. A simplified synthetic ETF is shown in Figure 8.3.

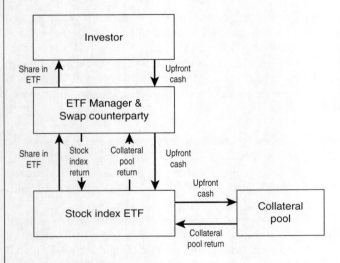

Figure 8.3 Simplified synthetic ETF.

The transformation conducted by the ETF manager and swap counterparty is shown here as an exchange of the collateral pool return for a stock index return. In practice this would be accomplished in two parts: first, an asset swap of the collateral pool return against an interest rate benchmark (Euriboror Libor); and second, a total return swap of that interest rate benchmark against the ETF's stock index return. ETF managers lacking a derivatives capability will enter swaps with external counterparties but in doing so will erode their returns from the transaction.

- Growth in capacity for securities lending, which may increase systemic leverage, and in periods of uncertainty may impact negatively on liquidity and the ability of shareholders to redeem their interest in ETFs. ETF fees and bid–offer dealing spreads are highly competitive, encouraging ETF managers to lend collateral securities to other market participants to increase their returns, but this might impede the liquidity of any single fund in times of stress.
- Banks relying for funding on the sale of synthetic ETFs, which European regulators suggest is 'a material source' in the EU (Bank of England 2011: 47).

In the simple cash model the investor purchases ETF shares and the proceeds are used by the fund's manager to acquire collateral. With physical or cash ETFs this will comprise a basket of securities that resembles in composition the index that the ETF will track. No material transaction risks then arise. The fund manager buys or sells collateral when necessary to match any index revisions or net flows of cash to or from the ETF, but will otherwise leave the collateral untouched. The basket is not an exact match for the index in most cases and basis risk is therefore inherent to the structure, which the manager will hedge using revenue obtained from conventional securities lending using the collateral (FSB 2011: 2).

In the more complex synthetic model of Figure 8.3 the collateral and index composition are unlike. The collateral pool is identified and managed for reasons of potential revenue and risk correlation with the index, and may be entirely different in nature from the index, so that a Paris CAC-40 equity benchmark index is collateralized by Asian or American securities. The ETF enters a total return swap with the ETF manager that provides the required index return to the shareholder in exchange for revenue earned on the collateral pool.

The concept is not dissimilar from the arrangement formerly used by Lehman Brothers to generate steady returns for its retail buyers of structured notes, described in Box 8.6. It also suggests risks that a failure of the swap counterparty would leave the synthetic ETF with assets that were different to the intended portfolio, or that a synthetic ETF manager might unreasonably include unsold assets from its securities inventory in a collateral pool.

ETFs began in the 1990s as index-tracking listed money market funds, which resembled mutual funds but provided greater ease of use to buyers through their exchange listing. The product was simple, inexpensive to buy or sell, and became popular with both retail and professional investors in North America and the EU that sought a broad exposure to market risk, such as the benchmark S&P500 index of US listed companies. The global ETF market was valued at approximately US$1.5 trillion in May 2011, of which most were simple physical funds. Around 85 per cent of ETFs in the US and Canada are simple and half of the EU total, with the rest using synthetic structures.

Two-thirds of ETFs by volume were listed on US exchanges at the end of 2010, with the remainder divided mainly between European (22 per cent) and Asian stock markets (7 per cent). The risk composition of those ETFs is shown in Figure 8.4. Assets held by ETFs at that time totalled US$1.2 trillion, of which around US$450 million were invested in North American equity funds, and around US$210 million equally in fixed income and emerging markets funds.

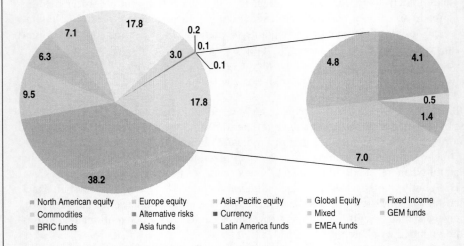

Figure 8.4 Asset composition of ETFs, end-2010.

Source: IMF (2011).

The left chart shows emerging market funds (17.8 per cent of total assets), which are broken into five types in the right chart where the data refer to the share of each risk category in the total. GEM means global emerging market funds. BRIC funds engage in risks in Brazil, Russia, India and China.

Sources: CFTC & SEC (2010: 39–40); FSB (2011); Ramaswamy (2011).

Conventional short-term debt contracts are homogeneous and of low value. They generate capital gains or losses only rarely, for example in the event of a default or recovery from distressed conditions, so traders hope to generate revenue either from dealing margins or the flow of large-scale activity with clients.

Bond basics

Bonds are tradable long-term debt instruments used by many intermediaries and investors. Most are commercially simple. *Principal* is collectively advanced by investors and remains outstanding until repaid in one amount at *maturity*. Over this period or *tenor* the bond accrues and periodically pays a pre-determined *coupon* to the holder. At any time the *yield to maturity* of the bond is an indication of its effective period rate of interest to redemption, usually calculated by discounting the bond's purchase price and contractual cashflows at the prevailing yield to maturity. For a bond with a tenor of n years, a fixed annual percentage coupon C, and a nominal redemption value of 100, the price is given by the formula:

$$P = \left(\frac{C}{(1+y)} \right) + \left(\frac{C}{(1+y)^2} \right) + \left(\frac{C}{(1+y)^3} \right) + \ldots + \left(\frac{C+100}{(1+y)^n} \right)$$

where y is the yield to maturity. Solving for yield to maturity given the bond's price is an iterative calculation that produces an approximate result, but this is unimportant providing practice is uniform because the results are used only for comparisons. Care is needed to compare yields on securities issued in different market segments to adjust for variations in calculating accruals between coupon payment dates, or where coupons are paid with differing frequencies.

Yields to maturity are the simplest and most durable of all bond comparators. This single variable y provides one of two important means of comparing debt securities, the other being a *credit spread* in relation to *risk-free* government bond yields, or interest rate swaps of the same tenor or *duration*. Unless unusual or small in volume, the bond may be freely bought and sold until some time before its final year, after which it behaves as an illiquid money market claim.

Many coupon styles have been devised to meet investor preferences, but the markets can be divided into three main types:

- Fixed rate bonds. A fixed coupon rate is applied to the nominal principal and usually paid once or twice annually.
- Floating rate notes (FRNs). The coupon varies periodically over the life of the bond, calculated as a spread above a short-term index such as Libor or Euribor as with syndicated loans, and usually paid quarterly or semi-annually.
- Complex issues known as structured notes. Periodic payments or principal are calculated and paid according to formulae set at the time of launch.

We also distinguish between domestic and international issues, albeit that the exact demarcation is blurred. Domestic bonds are made in the local currency of the issue domicile and generally sell predominantly to home investors, although many are open to all. International issues are less easily defined but are taken to be bonds denominated in a foreign currency for any issuer, or sold as global issues without distinguishing between investors at home or abroad. Other definitions dating from the early Eurobond markets are now archaic. Most of our discussion deals with international issues because of their pervasive influence on all markets, and we also consider the growth of local currency bonds in Asia.

Figure 8.5 shows the outstanding composition of the international bond markets by type of instrument, with fixed rate issues divided among government, corporate, bank and supranational issuers, and fixed rate bonds accounting for 69 per cent of the total. The volume of new issues in any period varies with interest rate expectations, for example a marginally higher proportion of FRNs would appear if rates were generally rising.

Fixed rate issues are the largest segment of the international bond markets, mainly because of their use by large, frequent borrowers, especially sovereign, supranational and agency (SSA) issuers. FRNs tend to be issued predominantly by banks to fund their floating rate loan books. Tables 8.4A and 8.4B show the most prolific overall issuers in 2010 in order of aggregate amounts raised. Many of these organizations appear regularly in the markets according to their needs and investor demand for risk.

The prevailing price of fixed rate bonds is a transparent link between interest rate determination and the valuation of capital assets and commercial enterprises, even though modern long-term yields are also influenced by the behaviour of interest rate and credit derivatives. Day-to-day changes in short-term and period interest rates alter the price of any fixed rate bond because its periodic coupon makes the bond's yield to maturity vary inversely with its

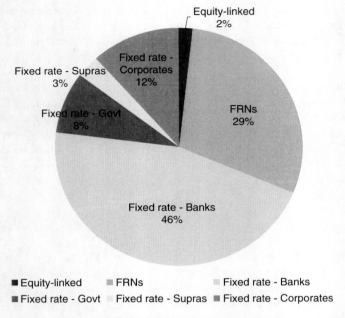

Figure 8.5 Composition of outstanding international bonds, end-2010.

The total outstanding was US$26,773 billion, compared to US$54,591 billion in domestic issues for which no breakdown is available.

Source: BIS Quarterly Review Table 13B.

market price, given that the bond is redeemed at par, that is, 100 per cent of the nominal principal.

If a five-year bond issued today has an annual coupon of 4.5 per cent and, assuming no credit rating changes, its prevailing price 12 months later would be an inverse function of the yield at that time of *four year* securities, that is, of period rates on debt contracts and derivatives of the same remaining tenor or duration as the bond. This comparison is made continually until the remaining life of the bond is short, and explains the effectiveness of price formation in the most liquid debt capital markets. Any change in prevailing interest rates has an immediate effect on the price of outstanding fixed rate bonds to compensate for the fixed coupon becoming either more or less valuable relative to the yield.

Other factors also influence this calculation:

- The *convexity* of the issue, a measure of the bond's sensitivity to changes in prevailing interest rates.
- *Investor preferences* for high or low coupons relative to current yields, together with a secondary consideration of the taxation of current revenue compared to capital gains or losses.
- Changes in *credit ratings* will impact spreads and produce a parallel shift in the prevailing yield curves of frequent issuers. A borrower with bonds outstanding in various tenors that experiences a rating decline will expect to see its yield curve move outward, signalling higher costs for future issues of all tenors.

Table 8.4A Most active global corporate bond issuers, 2010

Issuer	No. of deals	Nominal amount (US$ mn)
1. General Electric	37	31,697
2. Wal-Mart Stores	6	14,047
3. Porsche Automobil	23	12,747
4. BP	4	11,134
5. Toyota Motor	34	9,518
6. Peugeot	9	8,667
7. ArcelorMittal	5	7,709
8. Total	11	7,590
9. Renault	11	7,348
10. Microsoft	2	6,960

Five of these issuers were also the most active combined users of loans and bonds.
Source: Thomson Reuters (2011).

Table 8.4B Most active global bond issuers, 2010

Issuer	No. of deals	Nominal amount (US$ mn)
Fannie Mae	36	110,050
KfW Bankengruppe	157	94,585
European Investment Bank	222	83,943
Federal Home Loan Mortgage	30	79,320
Banco Santander	51	63,443
Lloyds Banking Group	53	57,681
Rabobank	111	34,020
Royal Bank of Scotland	30	33,767
Groupe BPCE	59	33,094
Federal Home Loan Banks	38	31,997
General Electric	37	31,697
Canada Mortgage and Housing	8	29,731
Crédit Agricole	46	28,608
World Bank	102	27,770
BNP Paribas	37	26,761
HSBC	46	24,717
ABN AMRO Bank	26	24,336
Italian Republic	9	22,879
ING	25	22,863
Intesa SanPaolo	19	22,498

Eleven issuers were banks, eight were SSAs and one was a corporate. Italy was the only sovereign issuer in this table of international transactions but others were equally prolific issuers in their home markets.

Two issuers were supranational bodies, four were North American and the remainder were EU-domiciled. Among frequent issuers in 2010 only two were Asian, Toyota Motor in 18th place (37 issues) and 25th-placed Export-Import Bank of Korea (30 issues). ABN Amro Bank is the domestic Dutch bank formed after the failure of the 2008 acquisition of its predecessor of the same name.

Source: Thomson Reuters (2011).

The nature of bond claims

All bonds are forms of claim, representing a defined entitlement for the holder even when that definition is given by a complex formula with unpredictable outcomes. Bonds are therefore incomplete contracts, and represent only a summary of the commercial relationship that a willing issuer and investor intend to enter. The terms of the bond are drawn to last until redemption through all expected circumstances, including significant changes in the disposition of the issuer, but can never fully anticipate all possible outcomes. The drama discussed in Box 6.1 has a bond carefully executed under seal to document the advance, but after an unexpected default Shylock is prevented from enforcing his claim because the court rules Antonio's unconditional guarantee unenforceable due to poor drafting.

Bonds are theoretically liquid, transferable and disclosed contracts. Regulation or customary practice mean that broad knowledge exists of the main terms of new issues and prevailing secondary prices of seasoned bonds in markets at large, rather than being confined to contractual participants. Commercial information providers, inter-dealer brokers and electronic dealing platforms are ubiquitous except in the least sophisticated domestic bond markets but tend to exclude non-professional parties, which helps explain the paradox of equity markets being clearer in the popular mind.

Bonds provide an open market for intermediation and, subject to contractual incompleteness, can provide an effective alternative to banks in the important temporal transformation that is central to intermediation. Their existence in an emerging economy can suggest a degree of financial sophistication, not only because effective capital markets demand financial infrastructure of some complexity, but because they may provide a plausible alternative to the banking system for funding and investment.

Debt transaction arrangement and trading can be both highly profitable and volatile. Banks earn upfront fees from most issues, but competition makes these highly rewarding only in cases involving complex risks or unusual features. Debt capital market returns tend to be associated with interest rate risks and managing new issue commitments. Banks compete to 'buy' or *underwrite* new issue mandates at a fixed cost to the issuer, intending to distribute to investors or *reoffer* the securities at a profit. Fees are not paid but deducted with transaction expenses from the proceeds delivered to the issuer, as Section 6.3 shows with syndicated loans.

Fees will be standardized in most sophisticated markets based on bond type, tenor and credit rating, but can be small, opaque and in many cases subject to fevered competition. This has often happened with coveted Asian issuers when arrangers knowingly commit to loss-making deals hoping for collateral benefits and league-table status. A US$500 million 10-year fixed rate bond launched for Indian Oil Corporation in July 2011 carried an upfront fee of US$1 (*International Financing Review* 2011b), for which the three joint arrangers perhaps tossed a coin? They also accepted a low expense cap, meaning that they would absorb around half of the issue's estimated US$500,000 legal and other costs. The prevailing upfront fee for a bond of this type and credit rating was 20–30 bp, or at least US$1 million.

The main terms of the generic transaction are listed in Table 8.5. Those above the divide are commercial conditions that allow participants to identify the bond, so that in the accepted jargon a US$750 million 10 year fixed rate bond issued by Kowloon-Canton Railway Corporation in May 2009, with a 5.125 per cent coupon paid semi-annually, would be known as *KCRC five and one-eighth of 19*.

From the issuer is derived the bond's credit risk and assigned rating, which can change from time-to-time, and thus its credit spread relative to risk-free rates and other issues of comparable duration. The tenor, periodic coupon, and issue price or prevailing secondary price taken together give two benchmark variables, the bond's yield and duration.

The terms below the line in Table 8.5 are known colloquially as the *boilerplate* and seen as administrative. Box 8.4 shows how contractual incompleteness makes this assumption hazardous.

Table 8.5 Core terms of generic bond issues

Term	Description	*IBM 7 5/8 % Notes due 2018*
Issuer	The borrower or primary obligor	International Business Machines Corp.
Guarantor	A third-party obligor providing direct secondary credit support	None
Type	Form of issue (e.g. fixed rate, FRN, or equity-linked)	Fixed rate
Amount	The gross nominal principal sum borrowed and due to be repaid	US$1,600 million
Maturity	Final redemption date	15 October 2018
Coupon	Nature of coupon, frequency of payment, accrual method	7 5/8 % pa, paid semi-annually (30/360)
Payment	Date on which the issuer receives the net proceeds	15 October 2008
Issue price	Price as a percentage of the nominal amount	99.628 %
Put/call options	Terms and permissible timing of early redemption options	US call option with make-whole mark up†
Fee	Upfront or front-end fee. May be split into several parts	0.4%
Rating	The bond's assigned credit rating	A+/A1+/A+ (S&P/Moody's/Fitch)
Credit spread	Margin over benchmark rate of same tenor or duration, based on credit quality	387.5 bp to 10 yr US Treasury yield
Launch yield	Sum of the benchmark rate and the credit spread	7.679% pa (semi-annual)
Form	Market segment (e.g. global, Euro or domestic issue)	Senior SEC registered global notes‡
Denominations	Minimum units in which the bond is issued and traded	US$100,000
Governing law	Form of law chosen for contract interpretation	New York
Status	The ranking of the bond vis-à-vis other claims against the issuer, usually including protective *pari passu* provisions	Senior unsubordinated unsecured notes ranking equally with other similar claims
Negative pledge	Issuer's undertaking not to create in future claims ranking ahead of the bond	Yes
Acceleration	Requirement for early repayment upon a default occurring	Upon agreement of 25% of bondholders
Cross default	Provision for the bond to be declared in default if the issuer defaults on other non-trivial financial claims	Yes, with limitations on amounts involved

(*continued*)

Table 8.5 (Continued)

Terms	Description	IBM 7 5/8 % Notes due 2018
Changes in terms	The minimum proportions of bondholders required to amend: (i) commercial terms; or (ii) other terms	(i) All bondholders (ii) Simple majority
Covenants	Commercial or disclosure undertakings by the issuer that continue while the bond is outstanding	Restrictions on change of ownership. Qualified maximum debt & secured debt
Listing	Details of stock exchange admission to the bonds	Not listed
Agent(s)	Appointment and duties of fiscal, paying or other administrative agents	Trustee appointed for the bondholders
Clearing, settlement	Provisions for transfer, payment and delivery	Three permitted depositaries
Selling restrictions	National restrictions on sales to retail or others investors at launch or later	None

† IBM's call option is US style, meaning that it is exercizable at any time, and at a price of par, providing that proper notice is given and that compensation is paid to 'make whole' bondholders in the event that the bond is trading at the call date at a premium to the nominal price.

‡ Global issues are sold simultaneously at the same price in several or many market segments, and thereafter traded within those market segments or from one to another. IBM's issue was sold initially in the US, Canada, EU, Hong Kong and Japan.

Source: IBM (2008).

Box 8.4 Hold-outs, Exit Consents and Collective Action Clauses

Bond provisions that were long neglected as purely administrative became contentious in the last decade due to anomalies in contracts written under New York law that were found to give unexpected negotiating leverage to recalcitrant borrowers.

The great majority of international bonds adopt English or New York law to govern their contractual form and enforcement. For the most part the results are little different, but English law documents generally support Euromarket practices providing for bondholders to be balloted over proposed changes in terms. These *collective action clauses* in fiscal and paying agency agreements or trust documents allow bondholders representing a majority of outstanding bonds to agree minor administrative changes, and a 66 per cent or 75 per cent super-majority to agree substantive commercial changes, which can include granting indulgence to a troubled debtor over the term or cost of a bond.

Such flexibility developed in the 1980s because of the increasing wish of bank lenders and the IMF to include bondholders in restructurings of international debts. In certain cases bondholders representing a small portion of creditors had held up agreements by threatening at the last moment to trigger formal defaults and chaotic insolvency, often to obtain better terms or be 'taken out' of the restructuring and repaid by more obliging creditors.

Bonds written under New York law were less flexible because domestic practice with corporate debtors was to refuse changes in commercial terms, mainly influenced by federal law (US Trust Indenture Act 1939). In the 1980s this practice was extended to international sovereign borrowers raising funds on Wall Street, many of them Latin American state and public sector issuers. It was gradually found that an outright ban on changes in terms was inconvenient, and many later New York issues provided for majority voting on boilerplate changes, so circumventing the statute (Wood 2007: 385).

A combative sovereign borrower might see this as an opportunity to buy its own issues in the open market to give it the minimum votes needed to bring about a change in terms, and to threaten hold out creditors with a procedural change that would indirectly impair the value of the bonds, a tactic known as seeking *exit consent*. In one case the threat was to change the bond's governing law from New York to Ecuador, a form thought less accommodating to foreign creditors, and in another to remove the bond listing, which would then bar some investors from holding the issue and force a distressed sale.

Simpler credit risk transfer and the blurring of distinctions between loans and bonds, or lenders and investors, have increased the need for all creditors to participate in prominent international debt restructurings. Each new sovereign debt crisis prompts academics and lawyers to propose a single mechanism for restructuring sovereign debts, but no consensus exists as to what that might be. Some important domestic bond markets continue not to favour collective action clauses.

New issues

We can best describe the new issue process with a deal narrative. The third column of Table 8.5 lists the main terms of bonds sold by IBM Corporation as one of three issues totalling US$4 billion announced on 9 October 2008. This was a conspicuous success despite the prevailing bleak sentiment, meaning that it was distributed quickly and the price of the bond tightened in relation to its launch benchmark. Initially sold at a semi-annual yield to maturity of 7.679 per cent, or 387.5 bp above that of the equivalent maturity US Treasury issue, the bond became marginally more expensive to buy in terms of its prevailing credit spread.

It was arranged by a *syndicate* of ten EU, US and Japanese banks, four of which (Bank of America, Barclays Capital, Crédit Suisse and Deutsche Bank) were *bookrunners* jointly responsible for coordinating distribution of the notes to buyers, and most at risk through their respective *underwriting commitments* to IBM to take up at a fixed price for their own account any part of the issue that failed to sell at launch. The four banks each underwrote 21.25 per cent of the entire US$4 billion transaction and US$340 million apiece in this 10 year issue, with the remaining 15 per cent committed equally by the six junior banks. Centralizing control of the syndicate books with one or very few banks usually helps distribution and *stabilizes* price formation. Some national markets use a formal bookbuilding system to coordinate and make transparent all investor orders, but this is more common with new share issues.

The three bonds together delivered US$3.96 billion in proceeds to IBM, taking account of discounted issue prices, fees and expenses. Transaction expenses totalled US$350,000, representing the costs of legal documentation and opinions, printing, SEC registration and obtaining credit ratings. Credit spreads and fees on the simultaneous five- and 30-year notes were each respectively lower and higher than this issue, in accordance with general practice. The three issues could be executed quickly, partly because IBM had registered with the SEC in 2007 a provisional umbrella prospectus to identify common terms and conditions of any forthcoming new issues, a device known more generally as a *debt issuance programme*.

The issue was announced and sold within several hours and settled three business days after the trade date, meaning that IBM received its proceeds two days after a long Columbus Day weekend. A contemporary report suggested that the deal's success 'endorsed the view that the bond market is open only for the strongest credits willing to go wide on spread' (*International Financing Review* 2008), implying that the credit spread was appreciably higher than IBM would have paid in normal conditions. The company showed transaction prowess at a difficult time, not least because the bonds were bought by risk averse investors seeking a liquid refuge for funds at a time of general stress. IBM issued in response to reverse enquiry, meaning that, unusually for very large transactions, it issued at the instigation of investors. All these factors add to the issuer's reputational capital and will often assist future fundraising.

IBM's deal narrative includes most aspects of the new issue process and the use of debt issuance programmes by frequent issuers. The pricing model for all new fixed rate issues is an array of comparisons made by the arranger that take account of any outstanding transactions that seem relevant, whether because of the nature, industry sector, borrowing reputation and credit risk of the issuer, the price performance of recent issues, secondary market credit spreads, or conditions in the interest rate and credit derivative markets. New issue yields are set as the sum of a market-determined credit spread and a benchmark interest rate, making benchmarking central to both new issue pricing and later valuations. Usable benchmarks include risk-free government bond yields, and interest rate swap rates and credit default swap premiums.

All these factors enter new transaction decisions. Pricing is compromised when benchmarks are unreliable or deficient, which is often the case with domestic emerging markets or in times of crisis. 'Risk free' is one of several accepted concepts displaced by the global financial crisis but yet to be superseded. It originated with the supposition that a sovereign issuer would always represent the best credit risk in the bond market of its own currency of issue, both for qualitative reasons and because the state could use monetary policy and print money to redeem any domestic claim, yet this is not a universal power and can always be debased.

Market practice takes the yield on German government bonds issued in euros as the risk-free Eurozone benchmark rate, but only because until now German yields have been the lowest among member states. Since Eurozone monetary policy is outside sovereign national control, the concept of 'risk free' is beyond all members, including Germany. The regularity of sovereign debt problems revealed in Box 8.1 makes 'risk free' doubly questionable, and adds to the controversy over the use of low or nil weightings of sovereign risks in the Basel capital accords.

New issues take three basic forms:

- Large syndicated issues such as our IBM illustration. These are liquid, usually sold globally or simultaneously in several markets, and are typically denominated in US dollars, euros or yen, or in lesser amounts in secondary currencies such as the Australian or Canadian dollar or Sterling.

- Smaller issues in minor currencies, initiated by reverse enquiry or targeted to specific buyers or investor classes.
- Heavily negotiated high-yield bonds, involving complex or lesser-quality credits or emerging market risks, usually including detailed performance covenants as found in term loans.

Bond types and investors are closely related within these categories. The style of commercial terms or coupons is ephemeral, devised by arrangers to match demand and whatever can be most efficiently sold. Fixed rate bonds include simple *straights*, with coupons set at prevailing levels at launch, longer-duration discount or zero coupon bonds with low or nil coupons and which are especially interest-rate sensitive, premium bonds with above-market coupons, and dual currency bonds where coupon and principal are differently denominated.

These and future variations have an ephemeral appeal to identified investor classes or preferences. FRNs include simple issues, with coupons periodically reset at prevailing rates, and others with option-based or leveraged coupons, including minimum or maximum rates, inverse coupons (a fixed rate less a floating rate), or coupons that switch between fixed and floating according to market conditions. Few of these examples are true innovations in the sense we explain in Section 7.4, although many are promoted as such by arrangers. They are instead time-sensitive responses to prevailing sentiment and investor demand, and the arranger's art to devise.

The new issue sequence for large transactions begins with deal negotiation and commitment, followed by pricing, syndicate formation, an electronic launch announcement, protection for syndicate members against inadvertent short selling, distribution where possible to investors at a fixed price, stabilization by the bookrunner to maintain the fixed price, the syndicate breaking and the issue declared *free to trade* – that is, to find a market-clearing price as the arranger withdraws from stabilization. Payment is made to the issuer on a settlement date between three and 14 days later. Underwriting by arrangers can entail commitments to deliver a specific sum to the issuer at an agreed spread above a benchmark, or more demandingly at a fixed overall cost. Small or complex deals may not be subject to overt competitive bidding.

All new issues are impacted both by national regulation and agreed practice among participants, especially in rules for investor protection and issuer disclosure. For most international bonds these take the form of *sales restrictions*, so that arrangers must ensure that global or other international issues conform to national or EU requirements, and are prevented from being sold at launch in ways that offend against local rules. US restrictions are the most intensive due to a long-standing presumption of securities law that non-exempt public issues be registered with the SEC. Looser rules exist in most advanced economies, including our regional sample. Two SEC rules made under the Securities Act of 1933 are especially influential in the international markets:

- SEC Regulation S (Reg. S) allows limited buying or selling of non-US issues within the US after 90 days from launch. This limits the entry of bonds into the registered domestic market but protects most transfers between home and overseas bondholders against later disputes, a device known as a *safe harbour*.
- SEC Rule 144A provides for securities issues to be sold in the US at any time without registration, providing they are *private placements* or are sold only to professional or *qualified investors*. One effect of Rule 144A on international issues is to stipulate minimum denominations of several hundred thousand units, supposedly to exclude interest from individuals.

The requirements of some jurisdictions can be demanding. Who is allowed to invest in securities varies according to custom from place-to-place. Chapter 9 shows how investor protection laws impact both on the duties of transaction arrangers and the operation of organized markets. EU member states share rules instigated by the directive on markets and financial instruments (MiFID) intended to promote a borderless single market in financial services and instruments – for example, setting common standards for prospectuses, issuer disclosure and in client dealing practices by intermediaries. Some of these rules have been re-examined since the global crisis, especially in relation to the duties of care expected of arrangers of complex or retail transactions, as we show in Section 8.3. Similar rules exist throughout Asia but are well developed only in Hong Kong, Malaysia and Singapore, and generally more burdensome in Japan and South Korea.

The practical side of new issues takes place in the fiscal agent or arranger's *back office*, with the organizing of payments, settlement, lodging bonds with one or more CSDs, and in many cases obtaining an exchange listing. The payment date marks a transition between primary and secondary dealing. The success of the international bond markets from the 1970s is inextricably tied to the efficiency of their provisions for settlement and clearing, especially in protecting counterparties against trading defaults where one party fails to deliver payment or securities.

Bonds tend to settle simultaneously *delivery against payment* with a standardized period of one or two days between trade and payment known as T+1 or T+2, and CSDs prevent an innocent party from delivering if its trade counterparty defaults. Similar practices have now migrated to most mature national bond markets. Listings are common but procedural. Few bonds are traded on stock exchanges, but listings have a marginal effect on investor access and in channelling issuer information.

Debt issuance programmes

IBM's October 2008 issues were guided by provisions in an enabling document filed earlier as a *shelf registration* with the SEC. In common with other frequent issuers, IBM's medium-term note (MTN) or debt issuance programme is a cost-effective way to gather the expected conditions of future issues and speed the process of issuance – for example, to avoid filing new information prior to launch. It can also encourage reverse enquiry by showing a willingness to issue quickly in order to capture demand or an opportunity for arbitrage. An enabling draft prospectus will be lodged with a stock exchange or regulator, with issuer information made public and renewed annually. Most programmes will give the issuer access to all feasible global or national markets through an outline of permissible commercial terms and sales restrictions, and the document will include the boilerplate clauses shown in Table 8.5.

With a programme in place, new issues are made using contractual *pricing supplements* listing the commercial terms specific to a deal, and giving effect to any single *trade* by incorporating the procedural terms, sales restrictions, issuer representations and disclosures contained in the programme document or prospectus. Pricing supplements can be brief if the commercial terms are simple, so that a traditional syndicated issue is described on one sheet of paper. Small structured trades initiated by reverse enquiry under an identical programme may require far lengthier pricing supplements.

The generic structure of debt issuance programmes under English or New York law is shown in Figure 8.6. The programme prospectus or memorandum sets out operational and procedural matters for all expected types of issue. It will usually name as dealers the banks

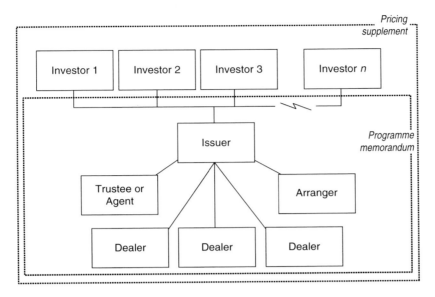

Figure 8.6 Generic debt issuance programme.

that will arrange the majority of future deals. These uncompensated posts are non-exclusive, and other banks will often lead proprietary issues or those in minor currencies in which they have distribution strength and reputational capital.

The World Bank is one such frequent borrower, issuing bonds of all kinds in any segment that delivers funding within its internal cost objectives. The aims of its Global Debt Issuance Facility are described in a prospectus published in May 2008 (IBRD 2008), with the bank's funding strategy allowing for three main types of issue (IBRD undated):

- Major currency benchmark or global bonds that are liquid investment vehicles.
- Minor currency issues intended for yield preferring investors or those with liabilities in the currency of issue.
- Structured notes aimed at risk-preferring investors, involving some form of embedded options, dual currency provisions, path-dependent coupons, or any 'unique structures as requested by an investor and designed together with the World Bank' (ibid), a statement intended to prompt reverse enquiry.

The programme also allows issues of commercial paper and notes intended for investors concerned with sustainable development. In the bank's 2010–11 fiscal year, 62 per cent of nominal issuance was made in US dollars, with Australian dollar and Sterling issues respectively accounting for 10 and 9 per cent of the total. Bonds were issued in 26 currencies, including those of China, India, Japan, Malaysia, Singapore and Thailand. None was made in Hong Kong dollars, Indonesian rupiah, South Korean won or Philippine pesos, suggesting that the prevailing terms of the relevant currency swaps failed to satisfy the World Bank's marginal cost targets in floating rate US dollars.[4]

Credit ratings

We discussed in Section 6.4 how credit rating agencies (CRAs) appraise asset-backed securities. The better known aspect of their work is simpler and longer established. Its origin is part of practice in the domestic US bond markets, and the growth in global CRA activity since the mid-1970s reflects a migration of that model without full acknowledgement of differences in practice and regulation elsewhere, a dilemma that became a concern in both the Asian financial crisis and the 2007–9 global financial crisis. It also highlighted long-standing conflicts of interest between:

- The respective aims of CRAs and investors, given that issuers pay for ratings specifically to assist the sale of securities;
- The commercial aims of CRAs and the regulatory status granted to their work under the Basel accords and by many national regulators of banks and insurers; and
- The information needs of investors and legitimate profit-seeking by CRAs, given that timely information of equal value to credit ratings may be available to investors from price trends in the credit and securities markets.

A further problem is that ratings have become almost ubiquitous for the financial markets, and their functions altered from simple information vectors to catalysts in formal commercial and regulatory practice in two particular contexts:

- The regulation of capital adequacy for banks and insurers, and rules as to the securities that professional investors may hold, all rely on credit ratings more than other external metrics; and
- Funding transactions that use a debtor's credit ratings as devices to prompt pre-payments or negotiations with creditors, as Section 6.3 explains of restrictive covenants.

G20 member states unsurprisingly found CRAs in April 2009 to be 'essential market participants' (G20 2009a: 6). This is despite the main CRAs having a poor predictive record in the modern era (Partnoy 2002), exemplified in sudden and sizeable downgradings of corporate, sovereign and structured finance ratings and a persistent backward-looking analytical focus.

One notorious example was Enron Corporation, a large US energy group that collapsed in 2001 having falsified its accounts for several years so as to disguise liabilities and create non-existent earnings. Enron announced a substantial third-quarter loss on 16 October 2001 and one month later catastrophically restated its financial results for the previous four years. It disclosed simultaneously to certain creditors that total debt shown as US$13.0 billion in its end-September balance sheet took no account of US$25.1 billion in claims classified in other ways or treated as off-balance sheet liabilities (Batson 2003: 15–16). One CRA lowered Enron's rating on 9 November, triggering a 27 November pre-payment option on a US$690 million borrowing that included a rating maintenance covenant (US Senate Committee on Governmental Affairs 2002: 114). A further credit rating cut would trigger acceleration under similar provisions of US$3.3 billion in two other transactions (ibid). Enron's senior debt ratings were reduced below investment grade by the leading CRAs on 28 November, and partly as a result the company lost all access to external funding. It filed for bankruptcy protection four days later.

A US senate committee investigation into Enron's collapse later concluded that the CRAs failed to exercise proper diligence, lacked appropriate inquisitiveness and accountability, and failed to meet the standards expected of organizations involved in monitoring corporate performance (US Senate Committee on Governmental Affairs 2002). It concluded that the CRAs approach:

> [F]ell short of what the public had a right to expect, having placed its trust in these firms to assess corporate creditworthiness for the purposes of federal and state standards. It is difficult not to wonder whether lack of accountability – the agencies' practical immunity to lawsuits and non-existent regulatory oversight – is a major problem.
>
> (ibid: 116)

The case illustrates the power of CRAs in precipitously forcing events, even though Enron was corruptly managed. One result of these controversies is that while the work of CRAs may be useful to market participants, many legislators and officials in the EU and US have grown steadily hostile to what they characterize as a protected oligopoly with quasi-regulatory status, suggesting that CRAs enjoy entrenched power without responsibility, as Rudyard Kipling once described a press magnate.

The term 'agency' is itself a misnomer. Most CRAs are profit-seeking enterprises without administrative, contractual or fiduciary obligations to users of their ratings or any direct regulatory authority, although some jurisdictions require that CRAs be licensed by securities regulators. Three US CRAs, Fitch Ratings, Moody's Investor Services and Standard and Poor's Corporation (S&P) dominate the marketplace,[5] analyzing securities and credit risks in most economies with a preponderance of their analysis focused on OECD risks. Moody's is thought to have the largest pure ratings coverage of the large CRAs and claimed 'ratings relationships' with around 11,000 corporate and 22,000 public finance issuers in 2010, and to have rated some 15,000 structured transactions (Moody's Corporation 2010: 8).

US issues accounted for the largest share in each category. Commercial or state-sponsored CRAs exist throughout our sample of Asian economies except Hong Kong and Singapore, in most cases focused on local credit risks. Their reputations are mixed and many suffer from analytical chauvinism. CRAs in India, Japan and Thailand are well established, and several others have associations with global CRAs.

Bond ratings began as subscription services for investors in the US securities markets of the early twentieth century, and remained a benign domestic business of corporate analysis and reporting until the 1970s (Sylla 2002: 32–8). A John Moody was the prime mover, devising a ranking system in 1909 that persists today among most CRAs. His reports on securities issued by railroad companies were entitled:

> Moody's Analyses of Railroad Investments Containing in Detailed Form; An Expert Comparative Analysis of Each of the Railroad Systems of the United States, With Careful Deductions, Enabling the Banker and Investor to Ascertain the True Values of Securities; By a Method Based on Scientific Principles Properly Applied to Facts.
>
> (Wilson 2011: 155–6)

Moody extended coverage over the following two decades to other issuers. The reports were sold to investors to enable the 'average holder of the stocks and bonds to have proper facilities for ascertaining the real values of investment holdings' (ibid: 156), but commercial and legal reasons eventually changed the orientation of Moody's and its competitors and the cost of ratings began to be borne by issuers. This introduced a moral hazard and severed any contractual nexus between investor and CRA, which in the absence of a legal or fiduciary duty of care made it impossible for US investors to claim against CRAs for faulty credit judgements. The agencies are effectively protected under US law as mere providers of opinions, even though their output has acquired a regulatory status. The heady claim of the title of John Moody's 1909 report is one that a modern CRA would never make for fear of reprisals.

John Moody categorized securities as higher or lower quality according to his judgment of whether or not credit risk was important to their price performance compared to shifts in interest rates. He also devised a descending classification by letter grade from AAA, AA and A through to BBB, BB and B and below that remains largely unchanged, indicating an issue's presumed probability of default. In most cases ratings are awarded at launch and reviewed periodically or after a development likely to affect credit quality. A majority of ratings given by the three global CRAs are investment grade, although the cyclical nature of credit risk means that only a small proportion of non-structured issues were rated AAA in 2010–11. Non-sovereign issuers pay initial and periodic maintenance fees to have their bonds or debt issuance programmes rated, while sovereign and certain bank ratings are unsolicited and not compensated. The established global CRAs are highly profitable.

The transition from BBB to BB is a significant inflexion between the lowest quality *investment grade* issues to the highest quality *speculative* securities, known also as high-yielding or junk bonds. Many investors set criteria to guide whether or to what extent they may hold securities of different ratings, and market practice or national regulators treat the investment grade qualification as an important distinction. Insurers and superannuation funds subject to prudential regulation may be prohibited from holding sub-investment grade bonds, or forced to sell any bonds that are downgraded to a BB rating.

This raises a further criticism of CRAs: that their actions can become self-fulfilling. A security downgraded below BBB will then fall further in price due to forced sales, making it more difficult for the issuer to raise funds and service its outstanding debts. Sudden downgradings characterized CRA behaviour in the 1997–98 regional financial crisis and may have contributed to the withdrawal of external finance, notably from South Korean borrowers.

Ratings typically distinguish between forms of claim rather than attaching to an issuer. Subordinated or secured bonds will usually carry respectively lower and higher ratings than the unsecured senior debt of the same issuer. Foreign currency bonds are often rated marginally lower than those in the issuer's currency of domicile, especially for securities ranked below AA. The ratings of sovereign bonds were treated as ceilings for all issues with the same domicile until the 2000s, practice then becoming less rigid with CRAs acknowledging the anomaly of highly creditworthy Asian corporate issues being constrained by low sovereign ratings. Similar logic allowed Johnson & Johnson to retain its AAA rating when S&P cut the sovereign rating of the US from AAA to AA+ in August 2011.

Since the 1970s, professional US investors other than specialist funds have been compelled by legislation to buy only securities with minimum credit ratings. Together with the use of ratings in the Basel accords' risk weightings described in Section 4.4, this gave CRAs a quasi-regulatory function. Those operating in the US were required to be licensed and to disclose certain of their operating practices, although with no formal appraisal of rating methods with either corporate or structured securities. More formal regulation of CRAs has been mooted since 2008 by the G20 forum and in the US and EU, in each case especially to address CRA involvement with structured transactions. The EU introduced regulations in 2009 based on IOSCO best-practice recommendations for CRAs and tightened its requirements in 2011 (EU 2011), making agencies operating in the EU subject to supervision by the European Securities and Market Authority (ESMA), a new regional securities regulator.

The reforms introduced by post-crisis US legislation are modest (Dodd–Frank Act 2010: §§ 931–9). They begin by noting that Congress recognizes that 'credit rating agencies are central to capital formation, investor confidence, and the efficient performance of the United States economy' (ibid: § 931), and require the SEC to monitor the performance of CRAs. The US agencies successfully lobbied against more radical reforms. The contrasting view of the EU Commission is less equivocal, that 'CRAs contributed significantly to the [then] current problems in the financial markets' (EU 2009).

Bonds in Asia

Adam Smith's description of European state profligacy has no modern application in East Asia. Section 1.3 shows how regular fiscal deficits are far from ubiquitous, and corporate and financial borrowers have until recently been modest issuers of debt securities. Large-scale central government borrowing through public debt issues is a new phenomenon except in Japan, associated more with monetary policy operations than the funding of public spending. The considerable expansion since 2000 in Asian debt issuance and market capitalization owes much to the need for central banks to sterilize their sales of foreign currency, as explained in Box 3.2. China and other states ceased currency intervention for periods in 2011 and issuance immediately shrank. A large share of sales of government bonds and notes in the 2000s was absorbed by commercial banks, with liquidity reserve requirements in many cases leaving no element of choice for the buyer.

As a result, Asia's local currency debt markets are a work in progress, or more accurately similar work in progress in separate national settings. The reasons are concerned with both supply and demand factors and with institutional conditions:

- A lack of scale itself deters investors from engaging in Asia's debt markets.
- A lack of committed indigenous or regional non-bank investors tends to deter consistent issuance.
- These two factors result, in many cases, in shallow, short lived or non-existent secondary liquidity, limiting the usefulness of bonds as treasury tools for both asset and liability managers, and making asset valuation uncertain for professional investors. Minimal trading increases new issue costs and makes investors fear being unable to buy or sell securities freely.
- Many non-specialist investors share an equity culture that militates against investing in debt securities.
- High bank liquidity and competition provide attractive costs for creditworthy borrowers. This leads to a lack of issuing consistency, both by central governments and regular commercial borrowers, increases the marginal cost of investor operations and hinders portfolio management.
- Relatively unsophisticated debt markets that lack liquidity, trading techniques or hedging instruments deter many non-bank investors, and increase the unhedgeable pricing and distribution risks for arrangers of new issues – for example, a lack of liquid money markets or adequate derivative contracts that allow or simulate short sales of government bonds or bills.

- Obstacles to transnational investment and trading contribute to a general lack of liquidity and functionality in local bond markets, often by directly restricting or discouraging through withholding taxes inflows from foreign non-bank investors. This makes regional investors more prone to buy or deal in G3 currency securities and non-Asian credit risks.

Japan's very sizeable domestic bond market is functionally sophisticated but illiquid in relation to its overall scale. It shares institutional features with Asia's developing markets that constrain issuance and investment by foreign counterparties. Investors in general may be discouraged from cross-border dealing in Asian bonds because of established practice, and the holdings of Asian equities by foreign investors inside and outside the region are far greater than in Asian bonds, although this may reflect a preference to hold equities as much as a bias towards 'home' issues.

In any event, a sizeable foreign involvement in Asia's capital markets is a comparatively recent phenomenon except in Japan, dating only from the mid-1990s. Excluding holdings of Japanese securities, end-2009 Asian cross-border investors are estimated to have held US$296.7 billion in equities in our core East and South Asian economies compared to US$102.4 billion in medium-term bonds, of which 42 per cent were South Korean bonds held largely by South Korean banks in Hong Kong, Japan or Singapore. Asian securities owned by UK and US investors totalled US$130.6 billion and US$511.9 billion respectively in equities, and only US$87.0 billion and US$32.7 billion respectively in bonds (21st Century Public Policy Institute 2011: 68–9).

Our focus is with medium-term debt issues. Asia's local currency money markets are far more fit for purpose due to prevailing bank liquidity, low ratios of bank loans to deposits, and the relatively simple needs of the state in conducting cash management and open market operations. Markets in government bills and other short-term instruments are well-developed and liquid in Hong Kong, Japan, Malaysia, Singapore and Taiwan. Those elsewhere are more modest in scale and functionality, with interest rate determination largely subject to central bank fiat, especially in China, India, Indonesia, the Philippines and Vietnam. Each differs qualitatively, but local currency interbank, CD and collateralized repurchase (repo) markets are undeveloped except in the foregoing five economies, in some cases for want of a reliable legal structure to protect counterparty claims or provide certainty of transfer (Loretan & Wooldridge 2008: 43). Sophisticated money markets typically use a range of instruments and techniques, including commercial paper, repo markets that accept a range of collateral securities, short-term FX and interest rate forward and option contracts, and short-term FX swaps, many of which are in their infancy elsewhere in the region (ibid: 45).

Most medium-term bond markets are now far larger in relative and absolute capitalization than after the Asian financial crisis. Many are operationally sophisticated, yet all remain incomplete as open alternatives to bank intermediation. They can be effective vectors for fundraising, especially by SSA issuers, but fail to provide the degrees of freedom for other users associated with developed debt capital markets. The main features of each national market are described in Table 8.6.

Poor credit quality often curtailed past activity, but this is no longer a widespread problem since most weaknesses result from institutional impediments. Behind the weak institutional setting are conflicted officials, with governments professing to favour financial development and be able to borrow freely at home while preferring not to allow markets to develop fully, a policy dilemma we return to in Chapter 13. A perverse result in the global financial crisis was that while 'the relative stability of the region's markets was clearly

Table 8.6 Features of domestic debt capital markets

China

- Substantial but fractured bond markets. These came into operation at intervals and involve different parties for different purposes. Important segments lack liquidity. Government issues spread evenly in maturities of 1–10 years.
- Substantial issuance by central government, PBOC, influential arms of central government (notably the Ministry of Railways), SOEs and state banks. Regular smaller-scale issuance by other banks. Minimal NSE issuance. Banks held 61 per cent of government bonds and arms of central government held 28 per cent of government bonds as at end-2010. Banks held 53 per cent of corporate bonds as at end-2010, with the remainder held mainly by insurers and general fund managers.
- Modest secondary liquidity except in bank issues in dealings between banks.
- Limited but developing interest rate and bond derivatives. Fractured and controlled markets means that new products are often available only to selected users.
- Very limited access to non-resident investors. Almost no access to foreign issuers.

Hong Kong

- Seasoned, sophisticated, narrowly exploited primary market. Limited government or corporate issuance. Significant issuance by banks, notably those without access to local currency deposits. Significant issuance by supranational agencies subject to favourable swap market conditions.
- Regular issuance of small local currency structured notes to HNW and private bank investors. Scope for growth limited by impact of US dollar currency peg on HK dollar interest rate determination. New corporate or foreign issues typically require favourable swap arbitrage. Few investors are willing to receive fixed-interest coupons.
- Well developed electronic central dealing platform and infrastructure for custody and settlement. Small retail investor demand component.
- Modest secondary liquidity except in highly sophisticated market in short-term government notes (EFNs).
- Regular feasible maturities of 10 years.
- Successful offshore market in Rmb new issues.

India

- State and bank primary issuance dominant. Substantial state-directed buying by banks and insurers.
- Highly restricted access for foreign investors.

Indonesia

- Underdeveloped government bill and bond markets, modest secondary liquidity. Sizeable issuance in central bank (SBI) notes and bills.
- Limited corporate issuance. Shari'ah compliant issues planned.

Japan

- Highly developed, very substantial markets for government, public sector, municipal and corporate debt.
- Domestic investor orientation. Foreign issuers in long-standing deep domestic Samurai yen bond issues, and Uridashi bonds in foreign currencies.
- Highly developed but parochial institutional investor base.

South Korea

- Very substantial market capitalization with relatively even contributions from public sector, bank and corporate issues.
- Domestic orientation with little foreign issuance or investment flows, partly due to capital gains and withholdings taxes and capital controls.

(continued)

Table 8.6 (Continued)

Malaysia

- Liquid and well-traded government bond sector.
- Successful, transparent and expanding hub for conventional state issues and Shari'ah compliant bonds, especially *sukuk* transactions.
- Small conventional corporate issuance.
- Large, sophisticated and expanding provident fund investment.

Philippines

- Limited medium-term issuance and minimal secondary liquidity.
- Traditional state and corporate borrower focus on foreign currency bonds.
- Limited professional investor base. Restricted access to foreign investors

---

Singapore

- Seasoned, highly sophisticated and well-used primary market, encouraged by government policy of over-funding state spending with regular and predictable issuance.
- Corporate issues well-traded and widely held.
- Significant issuance by banks, notably those without access to local currency deposits. Significant issuance by supranational agencies subject to favourable swap market conditions.
- Highly developed provident fund investment base.

Taiwan

- Large but functionally limited government and corporate bond markets.
- Large equity-oriented investor base.
- Substantially bank-led capital markets.

Thailand

- Regular government and state sector issuance but other users are modest.
- Liquidity low but improved since 2000 recovery.
- Restricted access to foreign investors.

Vietnam

- Very limited primary market in domestic instruments.
- Short-term investment profile. Limited liquidity.

Sources: Authors' archives; Chan, Chui, Packer & Remolona (2011); Goswami & Sharma (2011); Lejot, Arner & Liu (2006b).

welcome, it stemmed in part from structural weaknesses' (Munro & Wooldridge 2010: 161), which in turn constrained capital market development. Institutional obstacles and omissions prevent Asia's debt markets from realizing their potential, despite a decade of official attention, the regional aspects of which are discussed in Section 12.5.

The reasons for this lack of depth and maturity have bred a considerable literature, the themes and conclusions of which have changed little in a decade (Chan, Chui, Packer & Remolona 2011; Goswami & Sharma 2011). A consensus grew among scholars and policy-makers after 1997–98 that bond market development in Asia would improve the transparency of external financing, lessen cronyism and poor governance among banks and their corporate clients of the kind discussed in Section 3.3, and provide all savers with more choice. Even though reforms have been unquestionably positive since the regional crisis subsided, our earlier analysis holds true: that national settings contain common institutional obstacles or omissions to market development (Lejot, Arner & Liu 2006a), and these are important for reasons explained in Section 5.1. The problems are of four types (ibid: 319–21):

- Legal impediments, including qualified or uncertain property rights, parochial court behaviour towards foreign complainants or in enforcing foreign judgements, uncertain creditor rights in bankruptcy or debt reorganizations, and factors that impede securities transfer, lending or payment netting.
- Fiscal impediments, especially discrepancies in the treatment of claims, arbitrary or penal withholding taxes on foreign or non-bank holdings of securities, and duties and impositions on transfer.
- Regulatory factors, including restrictions on permissible issuers, the commercial terms of issues, cross-border investment in local currency securities, uncertainty arising from competition between regulatory agencies, and poor rules for disclosure by issuers or CRAs.
- Systemic issues, such as restrictions on settlement or custody, erratic general illiquidity, prohibitions on short sales, lack of reliable benchmark yield curves, uncoordinated state debt issuance, and variations in settlement practice. Systemic concerns are where post-2000 reforms have been most effective.

A former Federal Reserve chairman idealistically pictured the US bond markets as a financial spare tyre, complementing the banking system and able to substitute for dysfunctional lenders during times of stress (Greenspan 2000). Asia's markets are important but far from indispensable, which encapsulates the failure of reforms to achieve traction and of commercial transaction initiatives to become generic. Even popular new markets suffer limitations, as Box 8.5 shows of the offshore Renminbi bond sector that became highly visible in 2010–11.

Box 8.5 Dim Sum: A New Offshore Bond Market?

Marketing practice often provides financial instruments with perky names to attract attention and suggest originality. Seasoned examples include Yankee, Samurai and Bulldog bonds, which are respectively foreign issues arranged in the domestic US dollar, yen and Sterling markets.

The last of these is now dying, as did the Dragon bond after a brief life in Hong Kong and Singapore in the early 1990s. The Panda bond is rarer even than the creature whose name it shares, having been seen only seven times since 2005. These are yuan bonds sold in China by foreign issuers, to date the ADB, IFC and the China subsidiaries of HSBC and Bank of Tokyo – Mitsubishi UFJ. All but one were no larger than Rmb1 billion (US$147 million) and none is liquid. One issuer withdrew plans for an eighth Panda in 2010 and the species is likely to vanish with the appearance of a more attractive rival in Hong Kong, at least until such time as China removes all capital controls and gives full access to its markets to foreign issuers and investors.

The newcomer is the Dim Sum (點心) yuan bond, first issued in Hong Kong in 2007 but transformed into an important micro-market with the freeing of rules for issuance in February 2010 (HKMA 2010). The market is constrained by liquidity and risk concerns, but its status made it a competitive source of yuan funding in 2010–11. Investor interest in this early phase is based largely on expectations of a rising yuan exchange rate, and most issues made in 2010–11 have been expensive, both in relation to onshore yuan yields and to comparable credit spreads in other markets.

China maintains strict capital controls and restricted currency convertibility, but acknowledges that the yuan will eventually become more freely used at home and overseas. The process began in late 2003 when PBOC allowed a pool of yuan liquidity resulting from trade payments to remain outside the mainland in Hong Kong, in effect sanctioning a controlled offshore deposit market. Several mainland state borrowers issued retail bonds in Hong Kong to capture that liquidity from 2007, with ten issues made in substantially larger amounts than the Panda market. Settlement of wholesale trade payments in yuan outside China was allowed in 2009, causing Hong Kong's yuan pool to grow quickly, especially from early 2010. Yuan deposits were only 1.2 per cent of all deposits with banks in Hong Kong at end-2009, but 5.5 per cent of the total at end-2010 and over 9 per cent at end-May 2011, rising in only 17 months from Rmb62.7 billion (US$9.7 billion) to Rmb548.8 billion (US$84.8 billion). The Chinese currency now exists in three parallel markets:

- Onshore Renminbi, identified by the currency symbol CNY. Used in mainland China and restricted for use in funding and investment. Cross-border capital movements are strictly controlled but thought open to abuse through over-invoicing or disguised FDI, as we observe in Section 2.4;
- Offshore Renminbi (CNH) in Hong Kong. Freely used for issuance and investment but restricted and requiring prior permission for use in China; and
- Offshore synthetic Renminbi instruments created using non-deliverable forward (NDF) FX contracts by banks in Hong Kong and Singapore. Settled in US dollars.

This is the result of China's restrictions on capital movement. The build up of offshore liquidity resembles aspects of the early Eurocurrency markets, in this case to avoid a presumed loss from future currency appreciation, and the trial Dim Sum market a near mirror of the Eurobond markets under the Bretton Woods system, when UK regulators allowed banks in London to arrange offshore debt capital market issues of all kinds but seldom for locally domiciled issuers and never denominated in Sterling.

Early in 2010 the HKMA signified its willingness for Dim Sum bonds to be issued by borrowers of all kinds, and has assisted the market by helping with settlement architecture, so that offshore yuan bonds can be settled through the HKMA's real-time securities settlement system. It stated plainly that:

> With regard to the RMB funds that have flowed into Hong Kong, Participating [banks] can develop RMB businesses based on the regulatory requirements and market conditions in Hong Kong, as long as these businesses do not entail the flow of RMB funds back to the Mainland. ... Participating [banks] can conduct

RMB businesses in accordance with the prevailing banking practices applicable to the businesses conducted in other foreign currencies.... The range of eligible issuers, issue arrangements and target investors [for Rmb bonds] can be determined in accordance with the applicable regulations and market conditions in Hong Kong.

(HKMA 2010)

Onshore and offshore yuan CNY and CNH trade separately with different exchange rates and implied forward interest rates. Dim Sum bonds use the offshore yuan and to some extent compete for investor interest with synthetic CNY instruments in the NDF market, which are mainly intended as a yuan currency play. Issues have been made regularly, starting soon after the HKMA announcement with the market's capitalization reaching Rmb130 billion (US$20.0 billion) from over 100 issues in the first half of 2011. China and Hong Kong banks were the most numerous issuers, followed by several mainland agencies, China's finance ministry, and a handful of foreign multinationals including Caterpillar, McDonalds, Unilever and Volkswagen. China's later August 2011 composite deal was the largest to date at Rmb20 billion (US$3.1 billion) in four tranches of tenors ranged from two to ten years. The market soon became attractive to higher-risk local and mainland companies, albeit with investor interest sufficiently discriminating for several such issues to be withdrawn before launch.

Issuing offshore yuan bonds in Hong Kong is no more onerous than issuing in local currency or US dollars, but using the proceeds in the mainland entails a non-Chinese issuer obtaining permissions from SAFE, PBOC and, for bank issuers, the Commerce Ministry. Mainland issuers have a similar burden of needing permissions from CSRC, PBOC, and access to NDRC's foreign borrowing quota. These approvals may take several months to obtain and are not always granted. Funds raised in Hong Kong or elsewhere can be deployed for onshore equity infusions or shareholder loans, providing PBOC agrees the commercial terms. The usefulness of the market for borrowers is therefore currently limited, albeit that demand for yuan assets has made CNH borrowing costs lower than for onshore Rmb (CNY). The market is risky for users in several ways:

- Investors face liquidity risks and low yields;
- Borrowers face uncertainty as to being able to issue bonds and deploy funds usefully; and
- Prevailing tenors are shorter than with onshore CNY issues, leading respectively to reinvestment and refinancing risks for investors and borrowers.

We see the value of the Dim Sum market as a trial for increasing currency convertibility, and a measure to internationalize the use of the Renminbi without a significant domestic impact. Its scale will be limited unless a considerable rise occurs both in yuan-settled foreign trade and precautionary offshore yuan liquidity.

Sources: Chia, Li & Tan (2011); HKMA (2011); Hui & Bunning (2010); *International Financing Review* (2011a).

Asia's debt capital markets have domestic and global components, with sovereign and state-sector issues dominant in each case. The bifurcation is the result of history, especially since the region's credit prospects rose faster in the early 1990s than its indigenous capital market capacity. Issuers raised funds in foreign currency bonds for want of reliable domestic markets, and local and foreign investors welcomed the lower FX risks associated with holding major currency securities. Section 2.3 shows how that reliance on unhedged foreign currency borrowing was an important catalyst in the 1997–98 financial crisis.

Bonds denominated in G3 currencies dominate Asia's international issuance, although second-tier markets such as the Australian dollar are amenable to sound credit risks. Primary international issues are sold largely according to credit spreads and borrower recognition, so that well known or regular issuers have an appeal to investor classes in North America and Europe. These include prominent companies and state agencies from Hong Kong, Japan, South Korea and Singapore, but if we exclude Asian banks the list of non-Japanese frequent issuers is brief in all cases.

Issuance by low- or sub-investment grade companies is largely confined to US dollar bonds, and is a limited segment targeted towards specialist high-yield investors. There is little consistent regional new issue or trading activity in conventional Asian investment-grade bonds, so that G3 new issues tend to attract investors that share the issuer's domicile, which is an indictment of institutional weaknesses given the region's general reliance on the US dollar as an investment medium. An early 1990s trial of 'Dragon bonds' was more creative marketing by investment bankers than substantive market creation and quickly foundered. Table 8.7 gives a comparison of issuance in 2000 and 2010 for Asia and other important sources of issuance.

The largest share of all 2010 international issuance was of fixed rate bonds, at 83.0 per cent of the Asia total, 80.3 per cent for Europe 80.3 per cent, and 83.4 per cent for North America. FRN issuance mainly by banks was highest for Italian and Danish risks at 33 and 26 per cent of the respective totals, and 18–22 per cent of the national totals for Spain, Germany, the Netherlands, the UK and South Korea. Convertible bonds were more significant in Asia-Pacific than anywhere except Switzerland (16 per cent), notably in Taiwan and China (79 and 29 per cent, respectively). Most convertibles are fixed rate bonds with options for the issuer's obligations to be extinguished, in return for which the bondholder receives ordinary shares in the issuer. Convertibles often appeal to equity-oriented investors, and are favoured for governance reasons by closely held companies in Taiwan and China.

Foreign currency issuance has certain continuing features:

- A significant proportion of Hong Kong, Philippine and Singapore bonds is issued in foreign currencies, while such issuance is a small share of the total for China, Indonesia, India, Japan, South Korea, Malaysia and Thailand (Black & Munro 2010: 99).
- Nominal foreign debt outstanding is low except in China, Japan and South Korea. Debt outstanding is low in relation to GDP in Indonesia, the Philippines and Vietnam, higher in South Korea and Malaysia, and notably higher in Hong Kong, Singapore and Thailand.
- Nominal corporate debt is small except in China. Corporate debt is low in proportion to GDP in China, Indonesia, Japan, Thailand and Vietnam.
- Issuance in G3-currency international bonds is non-trivial in China, Hong Kong and Singapore, trivial in Indonesia, Malaysia, Thailand and Vietnam, but consistently higher in Japan and South Korea.

Table 8.7 Change in total international bond issuance, 2000 and 2010

	2010		2000	
	No. of issues	*Amount(US$ bn)*	*No. of issues*	*Amount(US$ bn)*
Japan	58	39.1	106	26.4
South Korea	145	24.7	25	6.2
Hong Kong	65	20.9	5	5.8
Philippines	42	17.4	3	1.7
China	37	13.9	2	1.0
India	22	9.3	–	–
Singapore	17	6.2	8	2.3
Indonesia	14	5.5	1	0.4
Malaysia	5	3.1	3	1.4
Taiwan	5	2.9	9	1.7
Thailand	5	2.0	–	–
Vietnam	1	0.9	–	–
Total Asia Pacific	**419**	**147.2**	**162**	**46.7**
Germany	646	307.1	894	298.1
UK	300	263.4	454	130.3
France	405	255.9	261	78.4
Spain	193	168.9	153	46.4
Netherlands	320	151.1	239	78.3
Luxembourg	253	110.3	16	3.1
Italy	127	105.0	174	60.2
Total Europe	**2,947**	**1,826.3**	**2,733**	**832.3**
US	1,157	880.6	1,198	605.4
Total North America	**1,318**	**999.6**	**1,246**	**618.7**
Global total	**5,125**	**3,182.6**	**4,642**	**1,625.0**

Data include all disclosed international and global issues. Asia-Pacific issuers were confined to the states and territories shown. European issuers included those from Central and Eastern European states, the Russian Federation and four other CIS states.
Source: *International Financing Review* <http://www.ifre.com/data/>

- Issuance in G3-currency international bonds in relation to GDP is non-trivial in Hong Kong, South Korea, Malaysia, the Philippines and Singapore.
- US dollar bonds are preferred throughout the region. Euro issuance is slight. More surprisingly there is little regional issuance in Hong Kong dollars or yen. Singapore limits the use of its currency for cross-border purposes.
- Short-term securities are high in relation to GDP in Malaysia, Japan, Taiwan and Hong Kong. Malaysia is highest at 50 per cent (ibid: 41), with the others in the mid-30 per cent range and similar to the US. Singapore's level is comparable to the UK in the low to mid-20 per cent range. All others are lower than the EU's 20 per cent.

What makes markets?

Asia's leading companies are generally able to issue debt securities at home and abroad, so weak markets are less a funding concern than one linked to to the interests of investors and a general loss of financial utility. In the light of this analysis we must ask: Do certain root conditions favour well-functioning debt markets? Finance scholars traditionally argue that the economy with no effective bond market lacks a price mechanism to benchmark capital costs, lacks hedging instruments to assist commercial risk management, restricts non-bank investment and offers few choices to savers. It is less clear that the corporate sector in a bondless economy necessarily faces a higher cost of funds, and governments are generally able to raise finance without an independently functioning bond market, by intervening in the banking and savings sectors, as we know from recent issuing experience.

One CRA argues that effective corporate debt markets require the following common foundations (Standard & Poor's 2003), although we know of few successful markets where these factors exist consistently:

- A strong, independent securities regulator that operates sound rules for issuance and trading;
- An extended period of macroeconomic stability. This may be the least common condition and provides no certainty of financial development or sophistication;
- A strong legal system and bankruptcy procedures. These factors are usually treated as conducive to all forms of financial activity, whether or not they involve open and effective markets;
- Coordinated advanced payment, settlement and custodial systems. These are infrastructural features now common to most Asian economies; and
- A developed base of natural buyers of long-dated securities such as pension funds and insurers. This is the feature most obviously missing from the region given that banks and offshore investors cannot be described as 'natural' buyers of bonds.

The list may be incomplete but fits the more successful and broadly used Asian markets, notably Japan, South Korea, Malaysia and Singapore. An alternative is to examine the completeness of Asia's debt markets and financial infrastructure:

- Does Asia's financial culture make mature bond markets infeasible and inevitably subordinate to banks? Section 2.2 suggests that this has some validity.
- Do immature or underused debt capital markets indicate an intermediate stage of evolutionary underdevelopment? We argue that this is incorrect and consider policy choices to provide a more pertinent explanation.
- Would new regional structures assist securities investment, trading and new issues? This has been the focus of national policy cooperation since 2000, especially under the ASEAN+3 Asian Bond Market Initiative (ABMI), as Section 12.5 explains. The results are more elaborate than successful bond markets in North America or Europe, involving state sponsorship, schemes to enhance credit risk with shared collateral or state guarantees, and plans for bonds denominated in composite currencies, all complexities that are more likely to encourage sophisticated analysis than active trading.

8.2 Financial derivatives

Global derivative markets have developed profoundly in scale and utility in the 30 years since the prototype IBM–World Bank cross-currency interest rate swaps. We focus on OTC contracts because of their primary functions in intermediation and as the most conspicuous result of that generation of innovation. We also review the longer-established classes of exchange traded futures and options whose main uses are as treasury products in hedging, speculation and trading by deal arrangers and asset and liability managers. In each case we look at the concepts associated with financial derivatives, their uses and users, and the traditional and post-crisis approaches to regulating derivative instruments and users. We also review Asia's more limited and idiosyncratic derivative markets.

Not all innovative intermediation is entirely new. The Osaka district of Dôjima was home from 1730 until 1938 to an organized rice market, with many sophisticated features of today's futures exchanges (Schaede 1989). Cuneiform contract tablets for the sale of goods and chattels for future delivery existed in the Middle East in the early second millennium BCE, and may closely resemble modern instruments (Swan 2000: 31–48). Aristotle describes a fourth century BCE option strategy involving forward purchases of olive-oil pressing capacity, in a narrative cautioning against amoral monopoly power using an early example of insider trading and market manipulation (Aristotle. Politics, Book I xi: 4 1259a 6–23).

Each historic example of successful derivatives has relied on standardization, particularly in contract design and the dissemination of price information, whether trading takes place through a central exchange or dealt directly between contracting parties. This was evident with forward contracts on the Chicago commodity and livestock exchanges from 1850, London's metals and 'soft' commodity markets in cereals and sugar from the late 1870s, modern markets in crude oil and precious metal futures, and all financial futures contracts since the 1970s. The most prolific OTC derivatives based on interest and currency rates share the same elemental quality.

The origins of Chicago's commodities and futures exchanges illustrate this facet of futures market development (Cronon 1991). Grain from the US Midwest was transported and sold by individual farmers at minor commercial hubs until the mid-nineteenth century, so that growers bore all the risks of falling prices or volatile demand. The development of railroads and canals revolutionized the transportation process, allowing farmers to deliver grain to new local storage elevators, from where it could be shipped in bulk to a single major city and sold in standard sizes and qualities. Grain became fungible upon being fed into the elevator, and farmers found they could use negotiable warehouse receipts as loan collateral prior to receiving the sale proceeds of their crop. The Chicago Board of Trade agreed dealing rules for grain contracts for future delivery in 1856, and its system of trading was written into Illinois state law in 1859, allowing for standard contracts and a separation of ownership rights from the physical good. That separation is said to create an 'abstract claim on a golden stream' (ibid: 120). The same features underlie today's derivative markets, involving the exchange of property rights over goods or intangible assets that may not exist when the exchange is made. The derivative contract itself becomes the object of the trade (Collins 1999: 211).

Derivative concepts

Section 7.4 introduced financial derivative contracts as:

- Transforming instruments intended to alter a user's mix of expected risks and returns; and
- Of such character and importance as to represent a third class of capital alongside debt and equity.

All financial, commodity and similar derivatives are evidenced by private law contracts. Most use standardized documentation that results from their either being traded on an exchange or conforming to the global practices promoted by the industry association, ISDA. Any single contract may be used by a borrower, investor, trader, speculator or government, whether they are ordinarily risk preferring, neutral or risk averse. Table 8.8 lists common examples according to whether they have historically been dealt directly over the counter or through an organized exchange, and between forward- or option-based contracts. Instruments such as FX and interest rate options are traded in both settings.

The two trading settings share certain features:

- Each may involve centralized clearing, settlement and price reporting.
- Approximately 69–99 per cent of OTC contracts were processed through electronic platforms as of June 2011, the share varying by underlying asset type (FSB 2011b: 25). Only equity derivatives, certain commodity derivatives and non-standard FX options fell far below this range.
- In 2009 the G20 agreed that standard form OTC derivatives should be executed on an exchange or through an approved electronic platform by end-2012, involving centralized clearing, settlement, reporting and maintaining collateral. Interest rate, currency and credit default swaps are profoundly affected by the change.
- Migrating OTC contracting increases competition among existing exchanges and new trading platforms. Partly as a result, exchange trading no longer implies a territorial or product monopoly.
- Settlement was once made by the physical delivery of underlying assets, but the trend since the early 1990s has been towards settling standard form derivatives in cash. This helps deter dominant participants from cornering a market or manipulating prices, and prevents contracts from becoming impossible to settle for lack of deliverable assets or willing sellers of such assets.

Table 8.8 Traditional derivative categorizations

	OTC	Exchange traded
Forward-based contracts	Amortizing swaps. Basis swaps. Carbon emission allowance swaps. Commodity forwards. Commodity swaps. Cross-currency interest rate and basis swaps. Currency swaps. Forward rate agreements. Forward swaps. FX forwards. FX swaps. Inflation swaps. Interest rate swaps. Non-deliverable FX forwards. OIS swaps. Total return swaps	Commodity futures. Energy futures. FX futures. Government bond futures. Interest rate futures. Interest rate spread futures. Interest rate swap futures. Metal futures. Shipping and freight futures. Stock futures. Stock index futures. Weather futures
Option-based contracts	Callable swaps. Credit default swaps. Differential swaps. Extendible swaps. Forward swaptions. FX options. Interest rate caps and floors. Interest rate options. Non-deliverable options. Swaptions	Covered warrants. Currency warrants. Debt warrants. Equity index options. Equity warrants. FX options. Government bond options. Interest rate options. Stock options

The differences between the two settings are in contract formation and the treatment of user counterparty risk. Exchanges set contract standards and maintain risk-neutral central counterparties (CCPs) for all trades, so losses resulting from a trading failure or default accrue to the CCP. Exchanges limit CCP risk by requiring participants to deposit a cash or liquid margin based on the prevailing value of the traded contract. OTC markets involve direct contracting between counterparties, with each assessing the other's capacity to perform its obligations, especially if the claim is long in duration, as is the case with many swaps. Market practice commonly requires collateral to be posted against the present value of the net position between counterparties, either singly or across an array of outstanding contracts.

Both forms of dealing can be effective in facilitating transparent price discovery, so that it is incorrect to see one as inherently open and transparent and the other opaque and prone to manipulation. Markets tend to be illiquid, cartelized or subject to price distortion more because of the contracts they trade or the nature of final demand than their basic design. Many professional counterparties use OTC derivatives, and the markets in interest rate and currency swaps are competitive and liquid except where price formation in the underlying FX or money market is poor. The market share of the leading OTC traders is concentrated in a similar way to the global FX markets, with scale economies and the positional value of handling large transaction flows meaning that between six and eight counterparties account for more than 50 per cent of deals. This is not typically distorting in the largest market segments, but can make the pricing of simple but illiquid instruments opaque to non-professional or occasional users, including non-specialist intermediaries. Organized exchanges are far less prone to this lack of transparency or price consistency but can be less efficient for large-scale users.

The size of the global derivative markets is difficult to convey meaningfully for three reasons:

- The common measure of swap activity by volume is a means to calculate periodic or termination cashflows, not an amount that is fully at risk, as with the outstanding principal of loans or bonds;
- Summing transaction volumes across a range of instruments that are dissimilar is no more helpful than adding apples to oranges; and
- Users regularly enter derivatives contracts to alter or reverse an existing derivative position. This swells the volume of outstanding contracts and counterparty credit risk but may overstate systemic risk, especially when contracts are collateralized.

Thus the aggregate *notional value* of all outstanding contracts is remarkably large and appears to signify an infeasible result of modern financialization – for example, in comparison to the volume of world trade or real output. It greatly exaggerates the true market or credit risks faced by OTC counterparties or CCPs while those contracts are outstanding.

Table 8.9 gives some perspective on the problem by comparing the notional amounts of derivatives as at end-2010 with their overall value or replacement cost, the capitalization of the international bond markets and national output of two leading economies. While the notional aggregate of OTC derivatives exceeded US$601 trillion and was thus 41 times the size of US national output in 2010, the value of the market was appreciably lower at US$21,148 billion, and the credit risk equivalent of those contracts a more reasonable US$3,342 billion.

Table 8.9 Scale and comparisons, global derivatives markets, end-2010

All notional OTC derivatives of which:	US$601,048 bn	100.0 %
Interest rate contracts	US$465,260 bn	77.4 %
Foreign exchange contracts	US$57,797 bn	9.6 %
Credit derivative contracts of which:	US$29,898 bn	5.0 %
Single-name CDS	US$18,145 bn	
Net OTC derivative market value	US$21,148 bn	
Gross outstanding credit risk on OTC derivatives	US$3,342 bn	
Notional principal, exchange traded derivatives	US$30,115 bn	
of which interest rate contracts	US$28,718 bn	
All O/S international bonds	US$27,688 bn	
China GDP 2010 est.	US$5,878 bn	
US GDP 2010 est.	US$14,660 bn	

Sources: BIS <http://www.bis.org/statistics/index.htm>; *CIA World Factbook* <https://www.cia.gov/library/publications/the-world-factbook/>; *Economist* <http://www.economist.com/markets-data>.

Forwards, futures, options and warrants

Forward contracts require users to buy or sell an underlying asset at a predetermined price on a later date when the contract matures. Futures are forward contracts traded in standardized form on an organized exchange. The contract price is determined by the prevailing cash transaction price and the net cost of carry, that is, the cost of providing for forward delivery. Carry costs are derived from accrued interest or storage fees depending on the nature of the underlier, and explain the phenomenon associated with many commodities markets known as *contango*, when in normal conditions spot prices are lower than futures prices.[6]

Stock futures contracts are typical of this type of financial derivative. These entail commitments to buy or sell the cash value of a given number of shares on a specific future date and at a predetermined contracted price. That number is known as the *contract multiplier*. Physical delivery of shares is not permitted in most cases, so that any profit or loss is paid to the buyer or seller at expiry in an amount based on the difference between the contract and settlement prices. Stock futures give users a simple inexpensive means to simulate creating or closing short positions on shares that is unaffected by the cost of borrowing those shares in the underlying cash market.

Options are similar to forwards but lack the same imperative for delivery, so that an option holder may choose whether or not to exercise its option rights. Forward and option contracts can theoretically be written for any period. Most exchange traded contracts have relatively short maturities of between one and three months, as a function both of user demand and contract standardization, while the average maturity of bespoke OTC option contracts is far longer, with a large share of FX and interest rate options written for periods of five years or more.

Forwards and options differ in three main ways:

- In the volition given to the option holder, that is, an entitlement in respect of an underlier rather than an obligation.
- In the mathematical relationship between each instrument and its underlier. Forward contracts are linear functions of an underlying asset so that a price change in the latter

causes a proportionately identical change in the prevailing price of the derivative. Option contracts are non-linear functions of their corresponding underlier, so that a change in an underlying asset's price may cause a far greater proportionate change in the derivative's value.

- Options are asymmetric functions of the value of the underlying asset or instrument, in that the magnitude of price gains and losses in the derivative are unalike, given price gains or losses of equal size in the underlying instrument.

Price asymmetry typically increases the *leverage* associated with the non-linearity of option contracts, leverage being a derivative's risk–return characteristics compared to those of its underlying asset. Contractual complexity, price volatility and leverage are all subjects of an extensive finance literature from which the Black–Scholes model and several other option valuation methods have been drawn.

Call options give the holder the right to buy a fixed quantity of an underlying asset at a fixed *exercise price* on or until a given date. Put options give the holder the right, but not the obligation, to sell a fixed quantity of an underlying asset at a fixed price before or on a given date. The call seller or *writer* has a corresponding obligation to deliver the underlying asset at a fixed price to the call buyer. A put writer or *seller* must buy the underlying asset at a fixed price from the put buyer. *American options* may be exercised at any time before expiry and *European options* only at expiry.

Both call and put options may be bought or sold. It is possible but unlikely that the seller of puts and the buyer of calls will acquire identical risk and return dynamics. Common option transactions or tactics involve combinations of calls and puts to produce a payoff in specified conditions – for example, if the price of an underlier remains within or outside a given path or above or below a given floor or ceiling, or to produce a return from an expected change in asset prices while limiting the holder's exposure to an unexpected and contrary price move. Simple options are used by banks to hedge the risks associated with creating tailored transactions for clients, including interest rate caps, floors and collars, all of which are intended to limit, increase or set boundaries for that client's exposure to changes in interest rates.

Simple share options are a typical example of a standardized option contract, and are specified through five main variables:

- The underlying asset. The share on which the option is written;
- The number of shares to which one option relates, usually the minimum dealing amount of shares, or *board lot*;
- The exercise or *strike price*. The price at which the underlying asset may be dealt. A call option is said to be *in the money* if the strike price is below the prevailing price, or *out of the money* if the strike price is above that prevailing price;
- The expiry or maturity date. The date when the option expires or the last date on which an American style option may be exercised; and
- The option premium. The price paid to acquire the rights contained in the option.

Share options are usually protected against major changes in capital to exclude the effect of rights issues, buybacks, bonus issues or unusual dividends.

Warrants are a form of tradable options issued by companies, banks or investors to generate revenue or lessen borrowing costs. They may stand alone or initially form part of a broader host transaction, during the life of which the warrants may be detached and traded separately. Warrants are usually listed on an exchange but may be less liquid than conventional options by virtue of being proprietary in nature, with dealings usually managed by a single market maker. They are issued either for cash or in part satisfaction of payment in a larger transaction.

Simple warrants convey the right but not the obligation to buy (call warrants) or sell (put warrants) an underlying asset or its cash equivalent at a predetermined price. Call warrants might subsidize an issuer's overall borrowing cost, or allow a significant shareholder to liquidate its position in a company without depressing the cash share price. Many warrants are sophisticated combinations of calls and puts intended to deliver a specific combination of risk and return. Most have lives ranging from months to several years. Any single warrant is cancelled upon being exercised.

Six main factors influence the prevailing prices of all options and warrants, in most cases in ways that differ according to whether the option contains a call or put:

- The price of the underlier and prevailing interest rates. Both are positively correlated with the value of calls, and negatively correlated with the value of puts;
- The strike price, remaining option life, and dividend or coupon payment on underlier. Each is negatively correlated with value of calls, and positively correlated with value of puts; and
- The price volatility of the underlier. This is positively correlated with the value of both calls and puts.

The directional impact of price volatility on the value of all options is central to pricing models such as Black–Scholes that rely on historic volatility data, and explains why VaR methodology is common in risk management.

Most exchanges require outstanding futures and options positions to be marked to market each day. Daily gains and losses on each contract type sum to nil, leaving CCPs free of counterparty settlement risk. Daily contract values determine the amounts of collateral that contract holders must post as margin with the CCP, a system requiring an initial margin when a position is opened and a maintenance margin that varies with the prevailing contract price. Exchanges may allow margins to be set off against the contract holder's settlement obligations and retained if it defaults or fails to respond to a demand for increased collateral. End users deal though exchange members and will be expected to provide the required collateral under separate dealing agreements. Many exchange rules will be considered enforceable against non-members, as we show in Section 9.3. Market makers customarily post dealing prices during trading hours within maximum bid-offer spreads set by the exchange but may be released from the obligation to make firm prices in especially volatile conditions.

Activity in exchange traded futures and options is measured by the notional principal or numbers of contracts outstanding, or by periodic turnover in either the number of contracts or volume of notional principal traded. The long-term trend since the mid-1980s has been of rising global activity in both futures and options, although growth has regularly stalled or reversed because of exogenous shocks, especially in 2008–10. During 2009 and 2010:

- Global option contract volumes were more than double those of futures;
- Interest rate contracts accounted for around 90 per cent of both option and futures volumes;
- Around half of both futures and options volume was transacted on North American exchanges, including trades executed by users from elsewhere. Trading on European exchanges accounted for around 40 per cent of option volume;

- 30 per cent and 15 per cent of futures volumes took place in Europe and Asia, respectively; and
- Options trading on Asian exchanges was negligible at less than 1 per cent of global volume, almost all of which was in equity contracts. Asian exchanges trade in interest rate futures to the same proportional scale as in Europe or North America, but option trading is constrained by Asia's relatively undeveloped debt capital markets.

Interest rate and currency swaps

The core families of swaps are contracts for the exchange of periodic payments and in some cases for initial and final payments. Swaps began as carefully negotiated deals for which the arranger's task was to find matching counterparties and acceptable pricing. They grew quickly in the 1980s into liquid markets populated by large banks or their dedicated financial product companies as qualified market makers, using bonds, futures and options to manage the risk of unmatched open swap positions, and *warehousing* swap risk in portfolio in expectation of executing later offsetting trades.

This transformation of standard form swaps into liquid instruments led to an erosion in dealing spreads, and the profitability of the early market was lost to competition and ease of execution through specialist brokers, electronic execution platforms or trading systems such as Bloomberg or Reuters. The swap markets now include many forms of obligations created according to standardized ISDA practice, some of which are listed in Table 8.8.

The commercial terms of swaps are conceptually tied to the price of legally unconnected assets such as loans, bonds or foreign currencies. Thus the pricing of a swap would reference or be *derived* from prevailing bond yields, market indexes, currency rates or some other specific benchmark. Until the 1980s those reference prices were determined in segmented markets, so that the cost of funds for a well-known creditworthy borrower to raise Swiss francs through a fixed rate bond was poorly correlated with the pricing of a domestic term loan in Australia. Swaps accelerated the globalization of the world's financial systems by helping to meld one market to another. If the Australian loan was conspicuously cheaper than the Swiss franc bond the borrower could enter the loan, draw the proceeds, and use swaps to exchange its Australian dollar interest and principal liabilities for obligations in Swiss francs. The borrower would acquire credit risk exposure to its swap counterparty as the commercial price of meeting its funding preferences, so the real savings of the transaction would need to account for the assumed cost of capital associated with that marginal risk.

Growth in swap sophistication and information technology lowered financial borders more than any other instruments, impacting even markets partly closed to foreign capital flows such as China or India by allowing the creation of offshore synthetic debt and currency markets using non-deliverable forward contracts. These settle in freely transferable currencies but are valued by reference to domestic rates and prices. Many swap markets are now so developed that price formation is more continuous than with the underlying assets or indexes. Swap counterparties share the Ricardian comparative advantages of transacting in favourable markets, and so lessen the frictional costs associated with a segmented financial system.

The generic contract is illustrated by the simple fixed–floating interest rate swap shown in Figure 8.7. An exchange of payments takes place periodically over five years between a fixed-rate payor, which commits to pay annually an amount calculated as a fixed percentage of 1.836 per cent per annum of the swap's notional amount, and a floating rate payor, which pays a quarterly amount calculated at a percentage of the notional amount equal to three-month

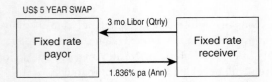

Figure 8.7 Simple interest rate swap.

By convention we show the flow of periodic payments due to each counterparty. Our example would be referred to as a five-year fixed-floating swap at 1.836 per cent with annual payments *against* three month US dollar Libor paid quarterly.

US dollar Libor. The fixed rate reflects conditions at the time of execution, and in this case would be determined chiefly by the yield to maturity of the benchmark 5 year US Treasury, prevailing credit spreads for 5 year risk associated with the fixed-rate payor, and supply and demand conditions in the market for swaps of similar duration.

The designation is a legal misnomer. Amounts due from each counterparty accrue on a daily basis and payments are made periodically, but none represents interest, or the cost associated with a debt. The generic interest rate swap involves no borrowing, although we shall see that this may not be true of more complex transactions.

Swap commitments are mutually contingent. In the standard format a payment default by one counterparty releases the other from its continuing obligations and leads to the termination of the contract. The value of the transaction at any time is determined by the net present value of its remaining cashflows, and represents the swap's *replacement cost* following a default, that is, a compensating payment that the non-defaulting counterparty would expect to make or receive in order to continue the swap with a replacement upon then prevailing terms.

This core transaction is the model for many variations, some involving complex payment formulae or contingent conditions. The most common variations are:

- *Interest basis swaps* for the exchange of floating rate obligations. These can involve opposing payments in two benchmarks such as US dollar Libor against US Treasury bill rates, two payment frequencies in the same benchmark such as one-month versus six-month Sterling Libor, or a combination of the two such as the three-month OIS rate against six-month US dollar Libor.
- *Currency basis swaps* involving payments based on floating interest rate benchmarks in two currencies, for example six-month Hibor against six-month Euribor.
- *Currency swaps* that allow the exchange in two currencies of periodic payments and a notional amount at both start and finish. FX rates used to calculate payments are usually set at inception, but the final exchange can also be made at the future spot rate. The swap is commonly designed to match payment obligations under two actual borrowings that may be outstanding seasoned loans or bonds, or new issues arranged simultaneously with the swap, and seeks to eliminate each counterparty's risk of currency appreciation or volatility. No initial exchange takes place if the swap is used to hedge payments due under existing liabilities.
- *Off-market interest rate swaps* where the periodic payment obligation of one counterparty is set well above or below prevailing market levels. The effect is a net transfer between the two counterparties that can be used to amortize an upfront payment or to

match the terms of a specific transaction, for example a zero coupon new issue or a seasoned fixed-rate bond with a coupon higher than prevailing rates. Off-market transactions involve significant credit risk and often resemble the process of lending.

Each of these models can be made subject to an option for one counterparty, a *swaption* being the right to execute a swap in a given period on pre-agreed terms, or to a delayed start in the form of a *forward swap*, with terms agreed today and payment accruals beginning on a later date. The 1981 IBM – World Bank US dollar–Swiss franc swaps would today be known as cross-currency interest rate swaps because they involved no exchange of notional principal, and in liquid markets would be executed using two fixed–floating interest rate swaps in US dollars and Swiss francs and a cross-currency basis swap involving US dollar and Swiss franc money market rates such as Libor.

The composition of the OTC markets is shown in Tables 8.10A and 8.10B. Interest rate and currency swaps dominate the markets for OTC derivatives by number and volume:

- Interest rate swaps form the largest component of all OTC derivatives, in 2008–10 amounting to around 60 per cent of the aggregate notional amount.
- Other OTC derivative activity is smaller in scale. This includes credit default swaps and currency swaps, as well as FX forwards, FX swaps,[7] forward interest rate agreements (FRAs), and OTC forward and option contracts on interest rates, equities and commodities.
- Interest rate swaps alone account for 85–90 per cent of the global swap markets. Activity within this segment varies according to prevailing conditions but is concentrated in swaps denominated in euros, US dollars, yen and Sterling.

Uses and users

We see derivatives as having distinct primary and secondary uses. Their primary use by professional intermediaries is in creating, amending or eliminating a risk position to alter

Table 8.10A Composition of global OTC derivatives markets (notional contract amounts, US$ bn, end-period)

	2008		2009		2010	
Currency swaps	14,941		16,509		19,271	
FX forwards & swaps	24,494		23,129		28,434	
FX options	10,608		9,543		10,092	
All FX contracts	**50,043**	**8.4%**	**49,181**	**8.1%**	**57,797**	**9.6%**
FRAs	41,561		51,779		51,587	
Swaps	341,128		349,288		364,378	
Options	49,968		48,808		49,295	
All interest rate contracts	**432,657**	**72.3%**	**449,875**	**74.5%**	**465,260**	**77.4%**
Equity-linked	6,471	1.1%	5,937	1.0%	5,635	0.9%
Commodity related	4,427	0.7%	2,944	0.5%	2,922	0.5%
Credit default swaps	41,883	7.0%	32,693	5.4%	29,898	5.0%
Other	62,667	10.5%	63,270	10.5%	39,536	6.6%
All OTC derivative contracts	**598,148**	**100.0%**	**603,900**	**100.0%**	**601,048**	**100.0%**

Source: BIS <http://www.bis.org/statistics/index.htm>

Table 8.10B Simplified composition of global OTC derivatives markets (replacement costs, US$ bn, end-period)

		2008		*2009*	*2010*
All FX contracts	4,084	11.6%	2,070	9.6%	2,483	11.7%
All interest rate contracts	20,087	56.9%	14,020	65.1%	14,608	69.1%
Credit default swaps	5,116	14.5%	1,801	8.4%	1,351	6.4%
Other contracts	5,994	17.0%	3,651	16.9%	2,706	12.8%
All OTC derivative contracts	**35,281**	**100.0%**	**21,542**	**100.0%**	**21,148**	**100.0%**

Source: BIS <http://www.bis.org/statistics/index.htm>

a portfolio of assets or liabilities. Users can enter or cancel trades in options, forwards or swaps as a substitute for dealing in underliers, but with smaller costs or capital commitments or with greater transactional leverage. In a simple risk-averse context they provide the means by which a borrowing or investment better meets the user's objectives.

Single transactions help align cashflows with the user's risk preferences or expectations – for example, to exchange revenue into a preferred currency, to lock into a fixed income stream if interest rates are expected to fall, to bridge from an Australian dollar liability to one in Swiss francs, or to hedge against rising costs. Secondary uses are those where derivatives equip intermediaries to construct or hedge other financial instruments – for example, using options to support sales to retail buyers of ETFs or warrants, or supply professional clients with interest rate caps or floors, bespoke options that respectively constrain exposure to rises and falls in interest rates.

Interest rate and currency swaps exist in three forms:

- Free-standing transactions with no involvement of principal except to indicate the notional amount from which payments are calculated;
- Free-standing off-market transactions documented as exchanges of payment obligations and that simulate a borrowing by one counterparty; and
- Contracts executed as embedded links in more complex transaction chains.

Swaps allow asset or liability managers to modify exposure to market risks or returns. If a company is given favourable terms for a US dollar borrowing, but later wishes to make interest or principal payments in euros, it can contract separately to exchange its liabilities over the remaining life of the debt to meet its risk or accounting preferences. The borrower's welfare gain is offset by an assumption of counterparty credit risk as with our Australian dollar–Swiss franc borrowing paradigm, meaning that it is obliged to service and repay the original contractual debt even if its counterparty defaults under the swap.

Banks are dominant swap market makers and users, which explains the high share of interest rate swaps in the total. Swaps help the bank's treasury hedge the continual mismatch between deposit taking and lending identified in Section 6.1. More generally, investors, borrowers, hedge funds and government organizations all use swaps for reasons associated with portfolio management, to alter the projected risk and returns of an array of assets or liabilities, or bring its expected performance closer to a benchmark or absolute objective. This applies in the case of a prominent borrower that frequently enters or terminates swaps to amend its aggregate interest, currency or credit risk liabilities, or a fund manager that decides that its investment income no longer matches its expectations of future interest rate movements and chooses to increase the proportion based on a floating-rate index such as Libor.

All derivatives augment other separate contracts so as to vary their overall commercial outcomes. Their use need not be risk preferring or speculative. The courts in leading jurisdictions such as England and New York have held swaps and other derivatives to be commercial and valid contracts rather than examples of gambling that might be unenforceable or illegal (Morgan Grenfell v Welwyn & Hatfield District Council; Korea Life Insurance Co. v Morgan Guaranty Trust Co. of New York), even if the cases involved plainly speculative uses.

A contrary view argues that many derivatives are aleatory, or gambling contracts, due to their uncertain outcomes, and would be unenforceable under US common law were it not for supervening legislation (Stout 2011). Most advanced jurisdictions remove any uncertainty through laws that exempt all financial contracts (or those when used by professional counterparties) from gambling restrictions, although states such Thailand allow enforcement in law only if the use is non-speculative (Henderson 2010: 536–9). A more subtle argument is that common law courts struggle to enforce certain derivatives because they lack an existing or material underlier and are wholly intangible (Collins 1999: 209–18). The result is that contract disputes are heard within organized markets where the participants know and obey the rules.

More generally, no observer can know a derivative user's disposition towards risk by analyzing any single contract because any transaction can be risk averse or speculative in its effect. Each of us could make identical contracts on a single day with three unconnected parties, Liu intending to be risk averse, Lejot risk preferring and Arner risk neutral, for each of us enters a marginal contract that can only be judged in risk–return terms in relation to the stance of an overall portfolio. Finance scholars properly calculate payoff scenarios on single contracts, but we cannot extrapolate that real contracts will always have a commercial winner and loser, because few users contemplate and enter a single contract to watch its isolated outcome. The derivative markets are not a zero sum game.

Box 8.3 showed how swaps facilitate the creation of synthetic ETFs. Here we look at three further derivative uses: covered warrants for retail investors, debt capital market new issues and asset swaps for sophisticated investors.

First, warrants became popular in Europe and Japan from the early 1980s through new issues known as *with warrant* bonds. Equity warrants gave the holder the right to buy a certain number of shares in the issuer at a predetermined strike price, and debt warrants the right to acquire additional bonds. The warrant's option value meant that the terms of the host bond could be tightened to lower the issuer's cost of funds. The warrants would later be detached from the host bonds and traded separately at low nominal prices to appeal to risk-preferring retail investors.

Demand for warrants tended to exceed supply, even though they were often costly in relation to their underlying shares or bonds. Supply vanished in falling markets since no issuer would contemplate warrants containing put options over their own debt or equity, making warrants one-dimensional compared to other instruments; useful in rising markets but otherwise worthless. The result was the creation of *covered warrants* as tradable option contracts, issued by banks with no connection to the underlying reference asset or risks. The concept was initially disliked by listed companies due to its suggestion of an external influence on their balance sheets, but the hostility faded in the 1990s and covered warrants became popular in certain markets of East Asia and Western Europe.

A product common in Hong Kong, South Korea, Singapore and Taiwan involves banks issuing inexpensive covered warrants that give the retail buyer a cash-settled option tied to the prevailing price of company shares, exchange rates, commodities or equity indexes. The upfront premium substitutes for the collateral margin that would be required by an exchange for a comparable futures or option position, and compensates for the issuer's hedging costs. A large proportion of covered warrants expire unexercized and worthless, with under-liers failing to meet strike prices (Lejot 2006), but warrant sales have been sustained by low entry-costs and local laws that limit legitimate channels for gambling.

Second, bond issuance was transformed in the 1980s by swaps eroding the segmentation of national markets, as with our Australian dollar–Swiss franc exchange. The launch terms of all issues are affected by swap market conditions, above all by the prevailing fixed rate of a standard interest rate swap of the same duration. Derivative pricing even affects unswapped transactions by providing a metric against which new issues are compared. New issue terms are continually influenced by interest rate, basis and currency swap prices, and swap yield curves give a pricing benchmark distinct from traditional risk-free rates. Figure 8.8 is an example of a typical swapped new issue. The borrower exchanges the bond proceeds and the equivalent of its coupon liabilities for payment obligations in its preferred currency, and commits to a final re-exchange of the notional amount when the transaction matures.

The issuer's effective funding cost is a floating rate based on three-month US dollar Libor and a margin that may be positive or negative but will usually be less than the issuer's conventional US dollar borrowing spread. The feasibility of the new issue in second tier markets depends on:

- The prevailing margin between the two floating interest rates, which in this case is largely driven by demand for Australian dollar funds by foreign entities and the demand for foreign currency funds by domestic users; and
- The availability at an appropriate cost of a fixed-rate payor, typically a domestic corporate liability manager.

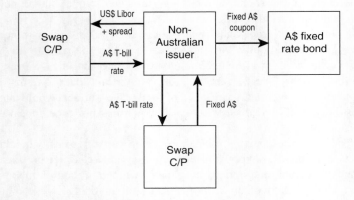

Figure 8.8 Simple swapped new issue.

The figure shows periodic payments over the life of the bond. The swap is a single transaction constructed from standardized components, in this case a fixed-floating Australian dollar interest rate swap and a US dollar–Australian dollar basis swap. The initial exchange and final re-exchange are not shown.

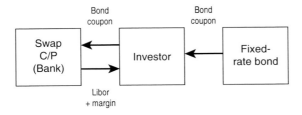

Figure 8.9 Generic asset swap.
The figure shows periodic payments over the life of the asset swap. The investor's counterparty receives the bond's fixed-rate coupon and returns a payment based on the investor's preferred floating rate. The swap counterparty has credit exposure to the investor rather than the bond.

These factors govern the volume of swapped new issues in the domestic bond markets of Australia, Hong Kong, New Zealand and Singapore, and occasionally in South Korea, Malaysia, the Philippines and Thailand, where foreign issuance is constrained. Frequent SSA issuers such as the EIB, KfW and IBRD are constant users of this simple arbitrage.

Third, investor packages known as asset swaps became widely used in the mid-1980s, and are now a staple instrument of all markets in which medium-term swaps are feasible. The examples shown in Figures 8.9 and 8.10 are models for many contemporary transactions.

The investor uses a swap to exchange the fixed coupon for a stream of payments that more closely suit its preferences, in this example a Libor-based flow. The transformation made with the swap can be complex, involving changes in currency, timing of payments or payments contingent upon defined exogenous events. There is no exchange of principal in the generic model, although a zero coupon asset swap can involve payment on the swap's fixed leg only at termination, so that an investor would receive periodic payments on the packaged asset swap despite the bond paying a nil coupon.

In the generic case, swap payments are contingent upon timely receipt of the coupon. Figure 8.10 shows a more complex example used since the 1990s in Asia and other emerging markets, notably by hedge funds, private banks and HNW buyers, with a minor currency bond held in custody for the investor and the swap counterparty exchanging payments into a major currency. Simple asset swap payments are fully matched by amount, interest basis,

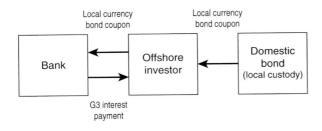

Figure 8.10 Cross-currency asset swap.
The figure shows periodic payments over the life of the asset swap. The counterparty receives the bond's fixed-rate coupon and returns payments to the investor denominated in a major currency. If the domestic currency is non-convertible then non-deliverable forward contracts can be used to make payments, commonly in US dollars or yen.

currency and frequency, but in these examples arrangers design mismatches between bond and swap payments to create option-related value and enhance their own transaction returns or those of their investor clients. Cross-currency instruments are packaged carry trades, some involving coupon-only swaps and others exposing the investor to principal currency risk.

Transactions such as these gave rise to structured and synthetic notes, providing artificial or cost-effective access to markets closed to foreign investors. Their design is explained in Section 8.3.

Documentation

ISDA is an industry lobbyist and a vector for the standardization of market practice. Its notable achievement is a family of documents developed since the mid-1980s and used globally in OTC derivative transactions, especially the core ISDA Master Agreement 2002 (ISDA Master). This commercial umbrella has encouraged harmonization in how counterparties enter, amend or terminate standard forms of derivative contracts, and facilitates bespoke trades for unusual needs – for example, in hedging interdependent funding, construction, environmental and output risks in a complex greenfield project.

The ISDA Master is a compact document of 14 sections and an eight-page schedule that together outline how two counterparties agree to transact. The schedule is a template for a transaction *confirmation*, which when executed will contain the commercial provisions of any single trade and incorporate the contents of the ISDA Master. Separate model documents exist for non-standard transactions and *credit support* through the taking of collateral. Most OTC derivatives are written under ISDA Masters and ancillary documents governed by English or New York law, although certain markets often apply local law in transactions between domestic counterparties, notably Japan and China. In 2010 ISDA released a model intended as a Shari'ah compliant master to be governed by English or New York law, and discussed further in Section 11.4.

ISDA's model documents encouraged four particular practices:

- Contract standardization;
- Collateral mechanisms to mitigate counterparty credit risk;
- Payment, regulatory and close-out netting; and
- Protocols for default and contract termination.

They also simplify operational administration by adapting long-standing FX market practice to allow a form of novation by repeated contract replacement, so that trades made over time between two counterparties may be treated as a single contract for netting and collateral purposes. All these factors produced transaction-cost savings that help explain the post-1990s growth in OTC derivative use, as well as the development of substantial leverage in relation to underliers in the decade preceding the global financial crisis.

Derivative netting takes four main forms:

- *Payment netting* within single transactions. On each payment date one counterparty makes a net payment that replaces two opposing gross payments. It may also take place among a number of swaps, with one party making a single payment to replace those due in all the designated contracts.
- *Close-out* or *termination netting* produces a single payment for the net amount due to one party when a swap or series of swaps ends prematurely. The 2002 ISDA Master

provides for an assessment of termination value that takes account of replacement costs and prevailing market conditions.

- *Cross-agreement* or *novation netting* extends across several agreements made by two counterparties. It reduces credit risk in an accumulation of transactions, and if successful will lower the collateral used in risk mitigation.
- *Regulatory netting* is a commercial objective rather than a discrete technique. It seeks to optimize regulatory capital relief by compensating for large or concentrated credit risk exposures.

Netting under OTC derivatives simulates the mechanics of payments and collateral margins of settlement within an organized exchange CCP. It also helps quantify the true risk of OTC derivatives and the difference shown in Table 8.9 between aggregate credit risk and contract value.

The ISDA Master is aspirational in these respects because the enforceability of cross-agreement netting varies between jurisdictions, and close-out netting prompted by default, bankruptcy or the restructuring of a counterparty is not universally accepted. This applies particularly in jurisdictions with origins in French civil law even if the confirmation uses English or New York law. Attempts to set off payments or enforce collateral may be blocked by the courts in the defaulting counterparty's domicile or challenged by third-party creditors due to the stance of its bankruptcy law, especially when reorganization is generally encouraged as a non-judicial solution to corporate distress.

ISDA lobbies for support of payment and close-out netting by pressing for the adoption of a model netting law, and by mid-2011 had identified 55 jurisdictions where the concept was accepted to varying degrees. These include at least 20 EU states, partly due to a directive intended to encourage the single market in financial services (Directive 2002/47/EC). Asia's bankruptcy laws are mixed in their tolerance of contractual provisions for netting, which affects the legal and credit risks associated with derivative contracts:

- Hong Kong and Singapore allow close-out netting without difficulty, based largely on their associations with English law.
- Malaysian law has a similar root, but its treatment of close-out netting was made uncertain by legislation passed after the 1997–98 financial crisis, allowing the state considerable scope to acquire failed banks.
- Japan, South Korea and India legislated in 1998, 2005 and 2006 respectively, to allow close-out netting according to ISDA suggestions (Japan Netting Law 1998; Debtor Rehabilitation and Bankruptcy Law 2005; Reserve Bank of India (Amendment) Bill 2006).
- Close-out netting is not permissible in China and Vietnam.
- Enforcement of close-out netting is unreliable in Indonesia, the Philippines, Taiwan and Thailand, although they each acknowledge its commercial value.

The treatment of close-out netting in the US has been an important exception to its Bankruptcy Code provisions (11 U.S.C. § 101 et. seq.). The code provides for a court-supervised moratorium or *automatic stay* on payments to specific creditor classes and on the termination of contracts (ibid: § 362), intended to give distressed companies time to negotiate a settlement with their creditors at large. ISDA lobbied for legal exemption from the stay for derivative netting, certain repo payments and the enforcement of collateral held against derivative credit exposure. It argued that the derivatives markets would function better if close-out payments, collateral, termination and preference disputes were treated as if the affected counterparty were not distressed and protected by the stay, and that exemption would lessen the risk that the collapse of a substantial swap counterparty would lead to Herstatt-style contagion of the kind described in Box 6.2. Congress accepted ISDA's assertion and wrote these exemptions into legislation (ibid: §§ 559–62). The result is controversial for some scholars, although their reasons vary. For example, it is seen as:

- Unfair to non-derivative creditors and a measure that is too broad in scope (Roe 2011);
- An inefficient solution that encourages excessive and wasteful financial activity (Edwards & Morrison 2005); and
- A populist view that derivative use was encouraged by the exemption to an extent that would inevitably be destabilizing (Bliss & Kaufman 2006).

Exemption certainly assisted the growth in activity, but no consensus exists as to whether the systemic results are destabilizing. Section 7.7 showed how the Federal Reserve initiated the 1998 rescue of LTCM with its sizeable derivative trading position for fear of exactly that risk, supporting the argument that the Bankruptcy Code in its present form encourages contagion. When Lehman Brothers collapsed ten years later the counterparties of its US subsidiaries made use of the exemption,[8] despite which the firm's failure led both to contagion and conflicts fought in several jurisdictions as to the enforceability of close-out payments and claims against collateral. Public funds were used to rescue AIG after Lehman fell to avoid contagion resulting from a rash of enforcement claims against guarantees and collateral provided by the US parent to support derivative positions taken by a UK subsidiary. There is no immediate prospect of a transnational resolution of these conflicts of law and opinion.

ISDA's second commercial achievement was to harmonize practice and minimize disputes over termination events and the results of defaults, although these questions remain contentious with respect to certain credit derivatives as we see in Section 8.3.

Regulation

By the mid-1990s the global approach to derivatives regulation had developed two intentions:

- Discourage and penalize mis-selling, unequal or unduly opaque transactions, market manipulation and other forms of misconduct; and
- Require that capital adequate to cover losses is held by regulated intermediaries or CCPs, with mechanisms to maintain collateral to mitigate counterparty credit risk.

The first objective differs in its treatment of professional and retail users. Most regulators hope to prevent mis-selling to the latter, leaving disputes among professional counterparties to be settled by negotiation or the courts. Post-crisis regulation in the US, EU and many other states and territories will increase product conduct supervision over retail instruments, a response to market failures of the kind found in Hong Kong and Singapore and explained in Box 8.6.

Disputes between professional users arose historically if eager but unsophisticated counterparties entered speculative or proprietary transactions that they could neither comprehend or value, or when derivative banks failed to disclose all aspects of complex deals. One egregious example involved a London municipal authority that entered 592 derivative contracts in the two years to March 1989 for its own account or as an intermediary with other public bodies. These included 183 swaps, 218 swaptions, 107 bond options and 69 interest rate caps, collars, floors and forwards (Hazell v. Hammersmith & Fulham LBC1989: 53). The aggregate notional amount of the contracts entered in 1987–89 was £6.1 billion (ibid), all intended solely for profit. We see this as a behavioural reaction to increasing financialization:

> [T]he treasury department [was] seduced by the apparently alchemic qualities of the financial markets. ... [Its] early success ... contributed to a sense that the local treasurers had become capable of reading the future more successfully than market-makers.
>
> (Tickell 1998: 877)

The treasurers were officials employed to manage public funds and provide for municipal services, the annual cost of which in 1988–89 was only £85.7m (Hazell v. Hammersmith & Fulham LBC 1989: 24). Outstanding borrowings totalled £390 million as at FYE 1989 (ibid: 54) and fair-value derivative losses were then 'well in excess' of £100 million (ibid: 23).

Misuse was common until the mid-1990s. Leading regulators then began to question the ease of sale of highly leveraged swap or option structures. In 1994 the Federal Reserve forced Bankers Trust Company to adopt more conservative and transparent sales practices with its non-bank clients. The bank was seen as technically proficient until a series of prominent mis-selling complaints led to a drop in reputational capital, earnings losses and ultimately acquisition by Deutsche Bank in 1999, a narrative amplified in Section 7.3. These and similar examples involved large non-bank counterparties or public bodies. Most began dealing conservatively before progressing to speculative trades that resulted in leveraged exposure to unexpected changes in interest or exchange rates. The complainants rarely succeeded in litigation. Three issues were involved, two of which have reappeared in disputes since 2007–8:

- Capacity of the buyer, for example when legislation forbids certain commercial dealings by public bodies. *Hazell* resulted in all derivative contracts entered by UK municipalities being held void and unenforceable, leading to considerable uncertainty in the capital markets as to the relationship between English law and financial innovation. The courts later accepted the offended banks' claims for restitution of amounts paid under derivatives with the local authorities due to mistakes of law (WestLB v. Islington LBC 1996; Kleinwort Benson v. Lincoln CC 1998). History was repeated in more recent cases involving Norwegian municipalities. Each borrowed through zero coupon off-market swaps, using the funds to buy complex notes or CDOs that promptly collapsed in value and induced defaults under the swaps (Haugesund & Narvik v. Depfa Bank 2009–10). The authorities were found to lack capacity under Norwegian law to borrow except in circumstances limited to clearly civic purposes, the swaps were commercially indistinguishable from loans and the contracts were declared void.
- Technical disputes on the ISDA Master – for example, in the calculation of post-default sums due between counterparties (Peregrine v. Robinson Department Stores 2000), or whether termination costs include hedging expenses prior to settlement (ANZ Bank v. Société Générale 2000). New conditions regularly lead to other such examples and refinements in standard contracts.
- Problems of mis-selling and disclosure, and the issue of whether banks or their clients have a duty of care in entering complex trades. Examples include Bankers Trust's 1993–96 disputes with Gibson's Greetings Co., Proctor & Gamble and PT Dharmala

Sakti Sejahtara. They show that complaints for mis-selling are traditionally difficult for professional buyers to establish, although potential litigants were probably encouraged when Bankers Trust settled with Gibson and Proctor & Gamble (Henderson 2010: 713).

- Gibson was a long-standing client of the bank that suffered losses on complex leveraged swaps. It complained that the contracts were unsuitable for its purposes, that Bankers Trust was not only favoured by information asymmetry in the transactions but knew of Gibson's conservative approach to finance and failed to show a duty of care in its dealings (Gibson v. Bankers Trust 1994).
- Proctor & Gamble made substantial losses on path dependent swaps and claimed Bankers Trust to have concealed the full terms of the transactions. It agreed to a settlement after the court refused its assertion that the bank owed the company a fiduciary duty of care when making the sale (Procter & Gamble v. Bankers Trust Co. 1996).
- Indonesian conglomerate Dharmala entered three increasingly complex swap transactions in 1994 that became loss-making, and was sued by the bank to recover defaulted payments (Bankers Trust International v. PT Dharmala 1996). Dharmala claimed that the bank had profited unreasonably from information asymmetry, had provided the company with economic forecasts prior to execution that led it to see the bank as a trusted advisor rather than a commercial transaction arranger, and that Bankers Trust had misrepresented the terms of the swaps and their suitability for Dharmala. An English court found that Dharmala was not owed a fiduciary duty of care but was entitled to a fair and complete explanation of a proposed trade, without which the seller might be liable for mis-selling, a warning that encouraged closer regulatory attention.

So many Asian counterparties suffered similarly through complex contracts prior to 1997 that a contemporary report saw an 'unending trickle of disaster stories' (*International Financing Review* 1995). Prominent examples were spread throughout the region, including companies from China, Indonesia, Japan, Malaysia, Singapore and Thailand, each featuring a shift from cautious to speculative investment, or the carefree use of options to lower ostensible borrowing costs. However, we stress that these cases constitute an incomplete sample. Derivative losses have never been ubiquitous and little attention focuses on counterparties that use financial derivatives cautiously or profitably.

The Federal Reserve's 1994 code of conduct required Bankers Trust to act responsibly in dealing in derivatives with non-professional clients by selling only appropriate products, to understand the client's needs and capabilities, to disclose all risks associated with a transaction and to price the deal transparently, precepts adopted in 1995 as a code of conduct by all major derivatives dealers.

This had two main elements. A principle for risk disclosure, suggesting that:

> A professional intermediary should consider providing new non-professional counterparties with disclosure statements generally identifying the principal risks associated with OTC derivatives transactions and clarifying the nature of the relationship between the professional intermediary and its counterparties.
>
> (Derivatives Policy Group 1995: V.II)

And a more specific principle:

> [W]here a non-professional counterparty has expressly requested assistance in evaluating an OTC derivative transaction in which the payment formula is particularly complex

or which includes a significant leverage component, the professional intermediary should offer to provide additional information, such as scenario, sensitivity or other analyses, to the nonprofessional counterparty or should recommend that the counterparty obtain independent professional assistance.

(ibid)

These were admirable principles written in weak terms. They also provided banks with exculpatory protection against claims for mis-selling, since the counterparty was made to acknowledge, when entering a transaction, that the seller had behaved satisfactorily. The code may have reduced the number of publicized disputes until 2007–9, but subsequent examples of mis-selling involving complex securities suggest that it failed to instil fully appropriate practices.

Other controversies linked to derivatives involve not mis-selling but fraud or failures in governance or risk management, notably with Allied Irish Bank (2002), hedge fund Amaranth Advisors (2006), Baring & Co. (1995), China Aviation Oil (Singapore) Corporation (2004), Enron Corporation (2001), Orange County Investment Pool (1994), Société Générale (2008) and Sumitomo Corporation (1996), spanning exchange traded and OTC contracts and a range of sophisticated jurisdictions.

They also appear consensually when a commercial or state body transacts in order to disguise leverage or another financial statistic. The concern is for accurate disclosure and an appropriate institutional setting, for derivatives have no inherently suspect qualities and need incomplete accounting rules to become window-dressing tools. Italy and Greece used derivatives to comply with a 3 per cent fiscal deficit-to-GDP ceiling set by convergence rules for states wishing to join the Eurozone (Dunbar 2003; Piga 2001), each executing off-market swaps to postpone central government debt payments. These were large transactions involving their respective arrangers in substantial counterparty credit risk that was hedged using credit derivatives, in the case of Greece by a German public sector bank (Dunbar 2003: 21).

The second regulatory goal developed from recommendations of the consultative Group of Thirty (G30 1993), which categorized risks associated with derivatives and outlined how they might be monitored and mitigated. This methodology became accepted practice among banks whose internal risk systems were endorsed by regulators, and was later codified by the BCBS. The first report cited seven risk categories:

- Credit;
- Market, or changes in the value of an underlier or collateral;
- Liquidity;
- Operational;
- Legal;
- Regulatory, including the failure to meet regulatory or legal requirements, and supervisory errors and omissions; and
- Reputational risk, resulting from an abrupt loss of confidence in a counterparty or system.

Some risks are addressed systemically – for example, by exchange rules in respect of trading, listing, selling and margins – and others by regulation or practice standards. The conventional approach to assess the risk exposure of OTC derivatives for capital adequacy purposes treats derivatives as extensions of credit, an assessment that is challenging for many unsophisticated users. It calculates a risk equivalent amount for a derivative portfolio comprising a general mark-to-market value and an estimate of future changes in value due to specific factors over the life of its components. Four problems arose in the 2007–9 crisis that exposed the framework as being too narrow and lacking specificity:

- Banks and CCPs are traditionally subject to different capital rules, supervised in many jurisdictions by separate agencies. In 2009 the FSB called for an alignment in the collateral and margin requirements of exchange traded and OTC contracts.
- Capital adequacy rules neglected shadow banking system users, including hedge funds, ETFs, SIVs, bank conduits, money market funds and vehicles based in lightly regulated offshore centres. All depend on credit and repo lines or prime brokerage funding provided by capital regulated banks, but this indirect supervision through the banking sector was tenuous.
- Capital regulation failed to anticipate the potential for instability caused by network effects such as concentration risks and systemic connectedness that derivatives may facilitate.
- Margins are calculated using historic default data, and correlations epitomized in the black swan paradox (Taleb 2007) – that unlikely shocks occur more often than predicted by conventional modelling.

Basel III adds two elements to the existing capital adequacy charge for counterparty default purposes (BCBS 2010c: 29–51):

- A *credit valuation adjustment* (CVA) for sovereign counterparties when transactions involve their own risk; and
- A charge for *wrong way risk*, where a negative correlation exists between counterparty credit risk and either the risk of the transaction or the value of collateral posted by the counterparty.

The FSB proposed separate rules to address systemic risk (FSB 2009):

- Standardized OTC derivatives should be traded on exchanges or electronic trading platforms and cleared through central counterparties;
- OTC derivatives contracts must be reported to trade repositories such as the Depository Trust & Clearing Corporation (DTCC); and
- Higher capital shall be required for those bespoke contracts that cannot be centrally cleared.

Simple objectives can require demanding implementation. Contract migration requires complex legal and operational reforms in many jurisdictions and may be incomplete by the FSB's 2013 target, even though a majority of most classes of OTC contracts are, or can be, processed electronically. Contract standardization is advanced in terms of total activity but more difficult to engineer for the remaining share, which includes simple contracts with trivial but unusual features such as delayed starts or irregular payment dates. The result is likely to be increased hedging costs for non-professional users and little curbing of trading activity.

Migration is a favoured solution because it encourages netting across a range of counterparties. This is taken to lower systemic risk, whether or not the result involves higher overall collateral or improved price transparency. The untested aspect of these reforms concerns risk concentration within CCPs. The FSB and IMF assume that shifting potential systemic risk from large banks is desirable, not least because it appears to lessen the 'too big to fail' hazard (Singh 2011). We are unclear whether the second-order effects of the move are fully known. CCPs have failed in the past when organized as non-profit utilities, and competition among today's far larger number of profit-seeking CCPs may become a concern in a future crisis.

Contract standardization, trade reporting, central clearing, counterparty capital measures and rules for CCPs and trade repositories appear in enabling legislation such as the Dodd–Frank Act and the European Market Infrastructure Regulation (EMIR). US regulation of derivatives has long been fractured and prone to supervisory competition, with OTC contracts and dealers exempted from the statutory regulation by the Commodities Futures Trading Commission CFTC to which exchange traded contracts and organized exchanges are subject. Dodd–Frank brings all contracts, dealers and markets under CFTC or SEC supervision, albeit through a complex division of responsibilities.

The Act also requires deposit-taking banks to isolate most derivative activities in ring-fenced subsidiaries from 2013 (Dodd–Frank Act 2010 § 716), replicating the financial product company model of 20 years earlier, when OTC derivative trading was based more on high credit ratings than collateral. These were well-capitalized subsidiaries of banks or insurers, protected from claims against their parents. Dodd–Frank seeks conversely to isolate the parent from unexpected losses in its ring-fenced subsidiary.

Among Asia's FSB participants, Hong Kong, South Korea, Japan and Singapore intend to adopt these reforms (FSB 2011b: Appendix VIII) while China, India and Indonesia will follow the precepts more guardedly for reasons of cost, complexity and a lack of indigenous trading activity.

Derivatives activities in Asia

Trading in OTC derivatives is substantial in both major and local currency products only in the financial hubs of Hong Kong and Singapore, and to a lesser extent in Japan and South Korea. Activity elsewhere is constrained by thin, illiquid or managed underlying debt markets and poor operational infrastructure (Goswami & Sharma 2011). Functional domestic interest rate swap and forward markets exist in India and Malaysia, but are limited or centrally controlled elsewhere. Effective offshore markets in non-deliverable forward foreign exchange contracts settled in G3 currencies exist where market access is otherwise controlled. Exchange-based interest rate, FX and equity futures and option trading is substantial in Hong Kong, Japan, South Korea, Malaysia and Singapore. Exchange traded bond contracts are important mainly in Japan and South Korea due to the scale of their respective government bond markets.

A distinguishing feature of the region's derivative markets is their high volume of exotic exchange traded and OTC options and structured retail or HNW option and warrant products. Structured is synonymous with proprietary, since each transaction is the creation of a single arranger. Market making, as practised in bond trading, is virtually impossible with complex transactions. Banks in Hong Kong, South Korea, Singapore and Taiwan became active arrangers of such transactions in 2000–2, some of which suffered material losses after 2007. This proliferation of path-dependent instruments takes various forms according to demand and underlying volatility, and has included rolling equity option contracts or *accumulators*, barrier, binary and ladder options, and credit, FX or equity-linked notes and short-term options for retail buyers.

8.3 Credit derivatives and complex transactions

Debt and equity claims represent comingled bundles of commercial rights and obligations. Most financial claims thus comprise several forms of risk, as Section 6.1 explains. Credit derivatives were devised in the 1990s as a solution to increasing demand for credit risk transfer and hedging instruments, and conceptually are contracts that isolate defined risks embedded in debt claims, allowing users to trade, hold or sell the credit risk of a debtor. The prevailing price of these contracts may affect that of the underlying debt instrument but no formal connection exists between the two. All the contracts described in this section are customarily taken as derivatives despite having no formal mathematical relationship with underlying reference assets.

In their simplest form, credit derivatives are contracts allowing the unfunded transfer of pure credit risk, free of other obligations or claims that may give rise to that risk. They provide the means to acquire, avoid or amend credit risk exposure without the prior agreement of the credit risk subject or reference entities. The reference may be the single obligation of a borrower or an asset class represented by a published tracking index – for example, for generic European or US corporate risks within a defined credit rating band.

Global contract volumes and trading grew rapidly until 2009, making credit derivatives the third-largest notional constituent of all OTC contracts. Credit derivatives have also acquired a prominence, despite the value of the market being relatively small and trading concentrated among comparatively few dealers. Post-crisis commentary has questioned contract specification and settlement, the morality of dealing in credit risk with no other direct interest in the underlying reference, and the systemic and general welfare impact of the sector as a link between conventional intermediation and a highly financialized world.

Concept and uses

Credit derivatives were created as hedging tools for banks wishing to manage regulatory capital and balance sheet risk, and grew in use because of their commercial adaptability and utility in regulatory arbitrage. The impetus for their development from one-off to standardized contracts were two transaction objectives:

- Cost effective changes in general loan portfolios; and
- Hedging carry trade instruments such as cross-currency asset swaps or credit-linked notes.

The first was possible through securitizing collateralized loan obligations (CLOs) involving an outright sale of pooled loans or participations (Lejot, Arner & Schou-Zibell 2008: 11). These were executed only at considerable expense that could not be recovered if the loans were prepaid and the CLO pool could not be replenished. In 1997 JPMorgan devised Broad Index Trust Offering (Bistro), a synthetic alternative that was simpler to arrange and distribute, in which participants and investors wrote indemnities for Morgan so as to simulate a credit sale. A conventional SPV sold US$700 million in securities that funded indemnity fees and provided a loss reserve for US$9.8 billion in loans, with this leverage based on the expected loss performance of the portfolio (*International Financing Review* 1997). Several banks had previously arranged bespoke credit derivatives, but this was the first wholesale use of such instruments outside the insurance sector. Bistro was the prototype of the synthetic securitization illustrated in Figure 8.13.

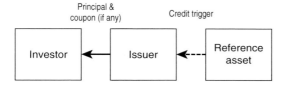

Figure 8.11 Credit-linked note.

Payments to the investor are contingent upon defined credit events related to the reference entity. The note is redeemed in full at maturity if the reference entity is not then in default.

The second objective was to hedge exotic asset swaps or credit-linked notes (CLN) and is shown conceptually in Figure 8.11. Simple asset swaps evolved in the 1990s into more complex transactions that kept the investor and its target credit risk legally separate. A bank would issue a security, payments on which were contingent on the performance of a reference entity or obligation, with the buyer's claim confined to the issuer with no subrogation rights against the reference entity.

This is a common way for buyers to acquire risks that are otherwise hard to access – for example, to gain exposure to a bond market closed to offshore buyers. The investor's rights against the issuer are tied to the default performance of the reference entity, equivalent to a stream of credit-based options written over the life of the note. The model proved popular with small banks and hedge fund buyers, but left arrangers needing to hedge the risk associated with the reference asset. One solution is to hold a debt obligation of the reference entity and use forwards or options to hedge any currency, interest rate or basis risk, but the economic result will be unprofitable to the issuer and unattractive to the investor. More cost-effective is to embed an indemnity in the note, making the investor liable for credit events impacting the reference entity in exchange for a higher compensating return. The investor receives an enhanced return on the note in exchange for writing a credit option for the benefit of the issuer.

That option is a credit default swap (CDS), the core contract of today's markets in credit derivatives. Most CDSs are written using the ISDA Master and incorporating ISDA's standard 2003 Credit Definitions document, although a small number are executed with specifically drafted documents. Figure 8.12 shows the simple CDS model.

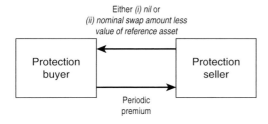

Figure 8.12 Credit default swap.

In exchange for a periodic premium, or *spread*, the protection buyer is held harmless if the reference asset experiences a defined credit event. If the CDS is triggered in this way the protection seller is liable for the notional amount of the swap less the prevailing value of the defaulted reference asset.

CDS spreads are distinct from the credit spreads associated with bonds described in Section 8.1, although both are functions of the market's perception of credit risk. The spread is also linked to the prevailing implied probability of default on the reference asset, shown here in simplified form for a one-period transaction:

$$p = \left(\frac{s}{(1-R)} \right)$$

where p is the implied probability of default, R is the recovery rate on the reference asset, and s is the spread.

We use CDSs to buy or sell *protection* against single or multiple credit risks. Selling protection in isolation implies taking a long credit risk position. The protection buyer effectively sells credit risk, whether or not it holds an existing portfolio position, and so the trade is analogous to a sale by a bond investor. The contract can be entered singly, in arrays or embedded in more complex instruments, as with all derivatives. It represents an unfunded form of credit risk transfer, and the premium due to protection sellers has historically attracted a lower capital charge than would an outright purchase of a debt claim. Simple generic uses are to:

- Acquire exposure to credit risks that may be otherwise unavailable, or not available at a preferred price;
- Acquire exposure to credit risks without liquidating other assets to fund the purchase;
- Reduce exposure to certain risks where the underlying cash market price is poor or liquidity non-existent;
- Create long or short credit risk positions without dealing in the equivalent cash markets; and
- Hedge the sovereign risk component of a cross-border corporate credit.

Table 8.11 gives a sample of typical applications and their most common users, and Table 8.12 shows the composition of notional outstanding CDS contracts as they stood at 2010–11. Many corporate CDSs can be more liquid in the sense of price continuity than their underlying debt obligations, so that prevailing CDS premiums provide a further metric for bond valuations and new issue pricing.

Multiple-name CDSs are based on baskets of credit or indexes of many similar classes of risks. They first developed as part of a solution to shortages of liquid underlying bonds, together with a transition for CDSs to be settled in cash rather than by delivery of the referenced asset. Data providers such as Markit and Standard & Poor's compile a large range of indexes based on combinations of credit quality, national or regional domicile, industry sector and volatility, all of which have both risk-averse and speculative uses. Complex credit derivatives include contracts based on CDOs, forward CDSs and CDS swaptions, while the most common embedded forms are:

- Total return swaps. Two counterparties exchange a variable return for one that is defined – for example, the overall performance of a reference asset is swapped for a periodic US dollar Libor payment. The total return payor is buying protection and so eliminates the market risk on its securities portfolio. Any mark-to-market losses are absorbed by the total return receiver. The reference asset may include equity or debt

Table 8.11 Simple CDS uses

Users	Objectives
Banks or securities dealers, long-risk assets	Lessen credit risk Lessen capital costs
Small banks with nil credit exposure	Obtain otherwise unavailable credit risk
Investors long or flat of portfolio credit risk Hedge funds, long, short or flat of single or portfolio credit risk	Change positions without cash dealing; arbitrage between cash and derivative contracts
Risk-preferring speculators Distressed creditors	Profit or lessen losses from single events – takeovers, mergers, bankruptcy

claims – for example, a total return swap involving a bond can be compared to an interest rate swap with a mark-to-market adjustment. Total return swaps also resemble the *sukuk* transaction explained in Section 11.4 without necessarily being Shari'ah compliant.

- Synthetic securitization. In the generic form shown in Figure 8.13, CDSs replace the sale of assets in the model cash transaction of Figure 6.9. The CDSs together share the risk characteristics of the originator's asset portfolio. The proceeds of notes sold by the SPV to third-party investors are held to fund the purchase of CDSs. This model has timing, disclosure and expense advantages over traditional securitization, and can be capital efficient, but will not usually achieve balance sheet relief. The model is also the foundation of highly complex synthetic instruments that were largely discontinued after 2007–8.
- Synthetic funding. A bank hedges the funding risks of a foreign operation using CLNs referenced to the local currency sovereign debt performance of that location.

Assuming identical regulatory treatment, the significant difference in transaction economics between cash and synthetic deals is that the proceeds of the sale of securities remain within

Table 8.12 CDS composition, end-2010

Total notional outstanding	US$29,898 bn
Of which:	
Single-name contracts	61%
Multi-name contracts	39%
Of all single-name contracts:	
Maturity of 1–5 years	70%
Investment grade credit risks, rated BBB – or higher	70%
Of all single-name contracts (end-Jun 2011):	
Sovereign credit risks	15%
Financial company credit risks	29%
Non-financial company credit risks	56%

The total notional outstanding fell by 17.1 per cent compared to 2009 and was 48.7 per cent below its peak as at end-2007. Contracts outstanding rose in the first half of 2011 for the first time since the global financial crisis.

Source: BIS <http://www.bis.org/statistics/index.htm>

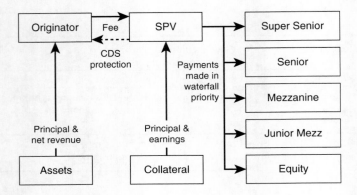

Figure 8.13 Synthetic securitization.

Synthetic transactions achieve one aspect of cash deals by providing originators with credit risk support through CDS. This alters the risk composition of the source balance sheet and if successful allows regulatory capital relief. Investors' claims differ from those in a cash securitization but replicate their risk–return qualities.

synthetic transactions and can assist in servicing the claims of investors, for example by maintaining a cash reserve for scheduled payments. Transaction economics dictate whether the SPV issues notes in fewer tranches than shown generically in Figure 8.13.

Mechanics

A single trade shows the mechanics of using CDS:

- Value 13 February 2012. Bank A buys credit protection against Company B, rated A+. Notional amount = US$10 million; maturity = five years; CDS premium = 250 bp per annum, payable quarterly. The contract is referenced to B's outstanding senior unsecured debt claims and provides for settlement by cash rather than physical delivery of the underlier if a credit event occurs.
- On 31 August 2012 Company B fails to pay interest on its senior unsecured debt. A credit event is declared. Days elapsed = 200; market value of reference asset = 35 per cent of nominal value; senior unsecured creditors suffer a 65 per cent loss.

Three payments are made:

- 90-day payment to CDS seller value 13 May (paid on Monday 14 May), 10mm × 0.025 × (90/360) = US$62,500.
- 180-day payment to CDS seller value 11 August (paid on the following Monday), 10mm × 0.025 × (90/360) = US$62,500.
- Final payment value 31 August, after a credit event is declared and the CDS expires, 10mm × 65 per cent = US$6.5mm, less pro rata premium 10mm × 0.025 × (20/360) = US$13,889. Net payment to Bank A = US$6,486,111.

Settlement must also address contractual completeness and legal risks:

- How are deliverable assets specified? Does the protection buyer choose the deliverable asset? Payment defaults on two classes of debt issued by a single obligor may be unalike and the claims valued differently.
- Settling CDSs for cash lowers the risks both of failure and market manipulation, for cornering becomes more likely if underliers are actually or artificially scarce. Vulture investors have been known to buy the cheapest-to-deliver claims of a troubled issuer in expectation of a credit event so as to force a price squeeze on the underlying claims.
- Dealing in protection without disclosure can be seen by corporate reference entities as an abuse of credit risk transfer, for example, that might alter a debt holder's willingness to negotiate in good faith during a debt restructuring.

ISDA has sought to deal with such concerns by harmonizing accepted credit events, establishing settlement protocols that counterparties incorporate into swap confirmations, and by encouraging cash settlement. Credit events must be specific and unambiguous to be effective, actionable and to avoid controversy or disputes. ISDA's 2003 Credit Definitions document specifies these events for both commercial and sovereign risks. ISDA also manages a process for settlement, involving standing *determination committees* that adjudicate whether a credit event is declared, and protocols to which counterparties are asked to adhere. The Credit Definitions 2003 includes a model CDS confirmation and is incorporated along with the ISDA Master into most contracts. ISDA specifies six standard credit events:

> Bankruptcy, failure to pay, obligation acceleration, obligation default, repudiation or moratorium, and restructuring.
>
> (ISDA Credit Definitions 2003: § 4.1)

Only the second, fifth and sixth usually apply to sovereign references. Each event is amplified in the document – for example, bankruptcy is defined in eight more specific ways intended to be inclusive in terms of contractual obligations and national practice. These events are unaffected by problems with any underlying obligations, such as a lack of capacity in the reference entity or contractual unenforceability, or others beyond its control such as a change in law or the imposition of capital controls that block payments on foreign debts.

ISDA maintains five regional committees for the Americas, Australia and New Zealand, Japan, non-Japan Asia, and Europe, the Middle East and Africa (EMEA), each comprising virtually the same 17–18 banks and investors. The committees respond to requests from market participants and decide when a credit event occurs, with provision for independent assessment if a committee is tied. The formal credit event triggers ISDA's settlement protocols and an *auction* to fix the value of reference obligations and thus the CDS settlement amounts. Japan Airlines filed for bankruptcy in early 2010 and a typical press release soon followed:

> ISDA announced today that its Japan Credit Derivatives Determinations Committee resolved that a bankruptcy credit event has occurred in respect of Japan Airlines Corporation (JAL). The Committee also voted to hold an auction for JAL.
>
> (ISDA 2010)

Committee membership is based on technical resources and derivative activity rather than relational choices but may be self-serving, with banks largely in charge of decisions that directly affect their own counterparties. Some non-bank holders of protection on Greek entities were critical of ISDA's failure to declare a credit event in 2011 after Greece negotiated a write-down of sovereign claims with representatives of the banking sector. ISDA responded that the proposal was consensual rather than a repudiation of claims as specified in its Credit Definitions (ibid: § 4.6(a)).

Politics and special interests make sovereign credit events subject to greater uncertainty than corporate risks, except where underlying claims are unusually structured. ISDA's defenders answer that CDSs are event-sensitive hedges, so that a decline in the prevailing price of Greek sovereign CDS in 2011 due to functional uncertainty would have been offset by an improvement in the price of underlying claims signalled by the terms of the voluntary write-down.

Concerns

Many concerns over the use and effect of credit derivatives are technical, for example:

- CDS trading is more concentrated than with other derivatives. This may impact price formation and lead to network effects carrying systemic risks. No more than 15 dealers are active as both sellers and buyers of protection. All are large banks since few other organizations have appropriate risk management or operational resources. Small banks and other financial groups are substantial users but protection buyers historically outnumber sellers.
- AIG was thus unusual and in great demand as a highly-rated non-bank protection seller, especially for banks involved in regulatory capital arbitrage. Its FYE 2007 accounts show outstanding sales of notional CDS protection of US$527 billion, of which around 72 per cent was largely to European banks, 'providing them with regulatory capital relief rather than risk mitigation' on corporate and prime residential mortgage loans (AIG 2007: 164). The protection sold was vast by any measure, unhedged (ibid: 163) and contributed to the later abrupt loss of confidence in the group.
- CDSs alter the behaviour of creditors in corporate restructurings, or create schisms between equally ranked creditors, in each case making an equitable solution difficult to conclude. A related complaint is that credit derivatives facilitate the economic transfer of creditor claims without notification to debtors, leading to conflicts of interest when a legal creditor holds no economic interest in a distressed company. These arguments are reasonable in isolation, yet the same asymmetries arise for other reasons within creditor groups. CDSs may also promote efficient reorganizations by offering an economic exit to recalcitrant creditors.
- CDSs reference specific debt claims or indexes and are thus an imperfect hedge for an obligor's general credit risk or other distinct claims. This *basis risk* may trouble unsophisticated users or when underlying claims are illiquid or heterogeneous.
- Contractual netting is less prevalent than with other OTC swaps, given that many single-name CDSs reference non-standard obligations. Multiple-name contracts are more conducive to netting because trades in any class of risks share an identical generic underlier. CDS netting may also be unwanted by users, for example among event-driven hedge funds that prefer to conceal their trading stance. This factor and general illiquidity make OTC counterparties intending portfolio shifts disinclined to novate or terminate CDSs.

- Contract migration to CCPs makes CDS netting more feasible, but savings are offset by a need for greater collateral to support OTC trading given that it becomes mandatory rather than discretionary (Singh, M. 2010).

CDSs also provoke broader issues of principle and calls for trading to be circumscribed. Political critics have claimed that CDSs facilitate undue leverage, promote undesirable credit risk transfer, create systemic risks through a lack of transparency, and help users to conceal their trading intentions unwarrantedly. A US enquiry found, unequivocally, that OTC 'derivatives contributed significantly to [the 2007–9] crisis' and 'without any oversight ... rapidly spiralled out of control and out of sight' (FCIC 2011: xxiv), such that 'the existence of millions of derivatives contracts of all types between systemically important financial institutions – unseen and unknown in this unregulated market – added to uncertainty and escalated panic' (ibid: xxv). Senior regulators in the EU, UK and US have questioned whether credit derivatives may harm general welfare (for example, Turner 2009a), with others condemning the free use of CDSs on quasi-moral grounds, claiming it to be unprincipled gambling (for example, Stout 2011).

The intellectual root of the moral concern is the resemblance of CDSs to insurance contracts, which many jurisdictions treat distinctively in law and regulation. Recall the Venetian merchant in Box 6.1. Insurance originated in shipping, probably in Genoa in the fourteenth century (Holdsworth 1917: 88), so two centuries later Antonio's voyages could only have been funded if his ships were insured. Two concepts survive from maritime insurance of that time, and continue to influence our cultural view of all insurance contracts:

- The insured needs a viable interest in the contract subject for its actions not to be regarded as gambling. Requiring an *insurable interest* means that the contract is a surety rather than a guarantee. The insured owns or controls the reference asset and insurance provides compensation for an actual loss. Credit derivatives provide fixed compensation rather than an indemnity against loss, have different protocols for settlement and make no demand for the protection buyer to hold an insurable interest.
- The enforceability of insurance contracts historically depends on the doctrine of *utmost good faith*, reflecting the technology available to Renaissance Italian city states. The condition of Antonio's fleet while at sea would be a mystery to the lender or insurer once the ships crossed the horizon. Without GPS, radar or radio the state of each vessel would be known only to her master and crew, so a duty of good faith in contract execution was intended as a representation or warranty to mitigate that information asymmetry. Such pre-contractual screening is absent from credit derivatives, for it is unlikely that a protection seller would ask its counterparty's motives and even less likely that it would expect a reply.

Antonio could not know the fate of his ships after they sailed beyond sight but he was aware of their condition beforehand and the competence and honesty of his crews. To contract for hull or cargo insurance without disclosing such information is one moral hazard to which insurance is always subject, the others being that a crew might take less care of their cargo knowing that it was insured, or that Antonio might insure a ship for more than its true value (Arrow 1963; Pauly 1968). Unfettered insurance reduces the incentive to behave cautiously.

By analogy, access to credit protection has a similar effect. Thus, to buy a CDS without holding its underlier is, to critics, to wish for a default and must always be speculative.

The argument is not new. Insurance was itself once seen as a 'contract upon speculation' (Carter v. Boehm 1766), a view that led to statutory limits to its use. If we see insurance and CDSs as economically similar, then the case for identical treatment is understandable, but neglects to consider:

- How modern insurance law is often unusual;
- Why advanced states tend to regulate insurance separately from other financial activities; and
- That dealing in credit protection is a portfolio operation and not necessarily speculative, as we see from Section 8.2, even when a protection buyer has no other interest in the reference asset.

The fear that credit derivatives might be challenged on these grounds led ISDA to obtain the opinion of leading English counsel, whose conclusion was clear (Potts 1997): that dealing in credit derivatives was not an insurance business under the then-prevailing UK law, and that CDSs and related instruments were neither contracts of insurance nor unenforceable as gambling contracts or bets. The opinion was narrow, relying on an argument similar to our discussion that credit derivatives and insurance are distinct due to the commercial and regulatory unusualness of insurance. It did not seek to characterize credit derivatives in any other way, which suited ISDA's case for continuing self-regulation.

Before 2007–9 the accepted regulatory view of efficient credit risk transfer was favourable (BIS 2005), based on its assisting liquidity in all forms of intermediation and providing for a broader dispersal of risk. The behaviour of CDS and debt investors in several notable cases confirmed this benign view. Global credit markets remained calm in mid-2006 as several large US auto groups approached bankruptcy and the ratings of substantial volumes of their outstanding bonds were sharply downgraded. CDS hedging helped stabilize bond prices and forestalled heavy selling by investors and sizeable losses. One study of the behaviour of banks in conditions of freely available credit risk transfer using credit derivatives and synthetic securitization concluded that the BCBS correctly identified the benefits of risk dispersal, and attributed efficiency gains to such techniques (Goderis, Marsh, Vall Castello & Wagner 2007).

A Federal Reserve Board chairman earlier gave a US congressional committee a confident view of OTC derivatives and argued against significant regulatory changes.

> [T]he array of derivative products that has been developed in recent years has enhanced economic efficiency. The economic function of these contracts is to allow risks that formerly had been combined to be unbundled and transferred to those most willing to assume and manage each risk component.... The Board recognizes that some derivatives are complex instruments that if not properly understood and managed can pose risks to individual users and possibly also to the overall stability of the financial system.
>
> (Greenspan 1994: 1–2)

At the same time it was:

> [I]mportant to recognize that significant advances in the management of market and credit risks including improvements both in financial methodology and in the design of management information systems lie behind the recent surge in derivatives activity.
>
> (ibid: 7)

The market's disciplinary effect was robust:

> A bank active in OTC derivatives contracts has a particularly strong self-interest in creating and maintaining counterparty relationships, because it has a continuing exposure to the non-performance of its counterparty for the duration of the contract.
>
> (ibid)

> [W]e expect senior management and the board of directors to have a good understanding of the risks in derivatives transactions.
>
> (ibid: 16)

Such confidence in the efficient market draws on the reputational capital concept introduced in Section 7.3. It clearly failed in 2007, and prevailing regulatory views are now very different. Raghuram Rajan is the only scholar we know of who addressed these concerns presciently, at a symposium entitled The Greenspan Era: Lessons for the Future (Rajan 2005), only to be admonished by a fellow Federal Reserve Board governor (Kohn 2005). The latter recanted and regretted participating in regulatory failure in evidence to a UK parliamentary committee in May 2011 (Kohn 2011).

Complex finance

Chapters 5–8 describe a progressive complexity in debt and derivative instruments, from simple credit lines, to syndicated loans and project finance, cash securitization, cash CDOs and OTC swaps, debt issuance programmes and credit default swaps. Before the global financial crisis, these steps in post-Bretton Woods financialization culminated with complex synthetic transactions. Most fell into default and desuetude after 2008, but contractual technology persists in sustainable cases, including structures adapted by governments to rescue banks or the Eurozone, and ABMI's mission to promote Asian SME lending and bond issuance. Figure 8.14 shows a further example in resecuritization or *CDO-squared*. Bundles of

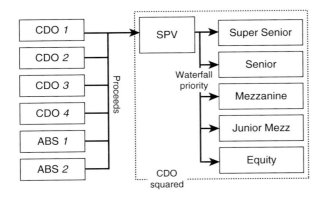

Figure 8.14 Generic resecuritization or CDO-squared.

In most cases the unrated super senior tranche is retained by the arranger but often hedged with credit derivatives or third party guarantees. It is presumed to be of relatively high credit quality. Not all CDO-squared use as many tranches as shown.

cash CDOs or ABS become source material for a new transaction using the waterfall structure shown in Figures 7.1 and 7.2.

Its original use was in banks repackaging, upgrading and distributing their unwanted securities inventory, perhaps a malign exercise but indistinguishable from NPL recycling described in Section 3.3. The structure relies on intense modelling and is susceptible to a lack of transparency.

This generic example is a template for more intricate synthetic deals, where proceeds from the sale of securities are used to buy credit protection structured to meet the expected risk performance of a risk pool. Box 8.6 explains how this model first became popular as a retail instrument in several Asian centres, and then notorious after the collapse of Lehman Brothers.

Box 8.6 Lehman's Minibond Transactions

The results of Lehman Brothers' failure was controversial in Hong Kong, Singapore and Taiwan because the firm's sales to retail buyers were prolific, especially through CLNs known as Minibonds. These were arranged by Lehman in 2003–8 and sold through 21 bank and securities dealer distributors in Hong Kong and nine in Singapore, all of which were paid substantial sales fees. Several Lehman competitors arranged similar structured notes but none suffered the transactional catastrophe that befell the Minibond programme.

Complex transactions can be legitimate instruments but present problems of completeness of disclosure that market regulators are usually expected to monitor, especially in contract formation at the point of sale to deter or penalize mis-selling. Complex instruments must either carry warnings that make clear their speculative nature, or be supported by information that is sufficiently complete and well-presented so as to allow the decision of a reasonable buyer to be fairly informed.

CLNs are one example. These are debt obligations where a holder's right to income or principal is tied to the performance of financial or other assets that are contractually and administratively unconnected to the notes. Any single issue will specify one or more reference variables whose uncertain outcomes dictate the return on the instrument. They first appeared in the late 1980s and are now bought by many professional and HNW investors, so that frequent borrowers will issue structured notes through reverse enquiry at the instigation of leading investors, and banks arrange new issues to match the expectations of their HNW clients as to the behaviour of interest rates, financial indexes or commodity prices.

Structured notes can target retail users, typically by using well-known companies or popular share issues as reference entities. Some are transparently speculative, but others are made to seem conservative in their headline terms, as with Minibonds. Contractual intricacy and probability based returns make structured notes exacting to value, as with all proprietary instruments based on subjective financial modelling. This makes product comparisons almost impossible.

At its pre-crisis peak, the market in retail structured notes in Hong Kong approached US$5 billion in claims. Lehman was by far the most successful arranger, with a 35 per cent Hong Kong market share and over 33,000 buyers, and a further 7,800 in Singapore. Minibonds were targeted solely to retail with a low nominal purchase price of around US$5,000 and accompanying gifts or supermarket coupons. When Lehman failed, 29 issues were outstanding in Hong Kong with claims exceeding US$1.6 billion, and nine in Singapore totalling US$400 million.

Most Minibonds were referenced to credit risks, so that the return on each issue was tied to the standing of well-known Chinese or international companies or banks. The last Hong Kong issue was completed in May 2008, paying quarterly coupons of 5–5.5 per cent, providing that during the three-year term of the notes none of seven reference entities entered bankruptcy or an involuntary reorganization or defaulted on its borrowings, in which case the notes would be redeemed immediately at a discount to their face value linked to the settlement value of credit derivatives for the reference entities. Those price data would be neither easily available nor helpful to most retail buyers. Lehman could also exercise a free call option to redeem the notes early without compensating the holder for reinvestment losses.

These features mean that a non-retail investor would see Minibonds as inherently costly and useless as investments or in hedging. Professional investors seeking similar speculative exposure will negotiate with an arranger or issuer and never accept uncompensated credit risk or incomplete disclosure of terms. A purchase might lead to losses but would result from balanced negotiation. Retail buyers have no such leverage.

The Minibond transaction is shown graphically in Figures 8.15 and 8.16.

Four commercial elements were involved:

- An advance by noteholders to the SPV, in return for which they received rights to a contingent periodic coupon and redemption proceeds;
- The purchase by the SPV of securities as collateral to support noteholder claims;
- An array of swap contracts between the collateral pool and Lehman; and
- The sale of credit default protection by the collateral pool to Lehman.

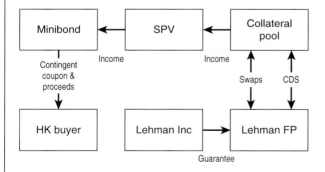

Figure 8.15 Simplified Minibond structure.
Sources: Lehman documentation held with the SFC; Lejot (2008).

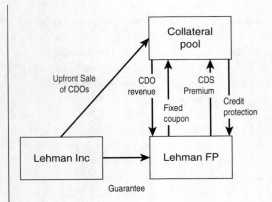

Figure 8.16 Collateral pool and Lehman relationships.
Sources: Lehman documentation held with the SFC; Lejot (2008).

Noteholders acquired claims against an insubstantive Cayman Islands SPV formed for Lehman's use. Each issue's proceeds were used to buy CDOs from Lehman with credit risks matching the reference entities. These provided security for noteholder claims and, at inception, equalled the Minibond issue amount. Lehman then entered interest rate or basis swaps with the SPV to concoct a single revenue stream matching the Minibond coupon dates. Finally, the SPV leveraged its collateral by selling credit protection to Lehman, entering CDS and receiving fees to enhance the revenue available to service the notes. Any CDS payment due to Lehman would have priority as a claim on SPV collateral.

Lehman thus created a buyer for CDOs and obtained credit protection to hedge its massive securities inventory, two purposes for which selling CLNs to retail was a lucrative by-product. The commercial bargain for noteholders is an enhanced return contingent upon there being no profound credit deterioration in a reference entity, whereupon their claims would be extinguished at a material discount, free of subrogation rights as with most CLNs.

These arrangements are not inherently unfair, and may be attractive to an informed buyer by reason of bounded rationality. Minibonds competed with conventional financial instruments but, notwithstanding their statutory treatment, may be better regarded as purely speculative and economically similar to gambling in Macau casinos or with the Hong Kong Jockey Club.

Less noticeable was a supervening condition requiring Lehman's parent to remain solvent. ISDA convention allows swaps contracts to be terminated upon the bankruptcy of a counterparty or its guarantor, and Lehman's bankruptcy filing was such an event. If the SPV were to terminate its swaps, the Minibonds would become subject to mandatory redemption even though no credit event had occurred among the many reference entities. This leaves a theoretical choice for the SPV, supervision of which devolves to the Minibond trustees: to terminate the swap contracts or seek replacement counterparties. Termination forces a sale of collateral, leaving minimal proceeds for distribution to noteholders net of SPV payments due to Lehman and noteholder trustees. The SPV is unable to withstand a collapse of the arranger since the trustees cannot reasonably become active managers. The model represents flawed structured finance resulting from Lehman's core purposes.

Prospectuses for debt and equity new issues customarily include information as to the use of proceeds, even in broad terms and with no covenant as to compliance. Lehman's core interest in its issues was not disclosed in Minibond prospectuses, which stated only that the SPV would receive a fee for its part in the transaction. No professional intermediary could have valued the notes using only the information provided to buyers in prospectuses and marketing material.

Securities law and regulation are not intended to prevent losses but to set standards for contractual behaviour. Regulators presume that a buyer will make a reasonable decision given fair and available information. No reasonable investor could have understood the terms of these complex notes and compared them with other available CLNs. The outcome of the Minibond saga in both centres was a series of agreements encouraged by Hong Kong and Singapore regulators by which the distributors repurchased most of the notes with generally modest discounts to the amounts invested, while admitting no culpability for wrongful practice.

Sources: HKMA (2008b); Lejot (2008); MAS (2009).

Pre-crisis professional buyers of similar deals included banks, bank conduits, SIVs, insurers and hedge funds. Hedge fund and bank buyers also leveraged long CDO positions by selling credit protection into CDO collateral pools. Others simply bought protection to short sell credit risk, as in the Abacus *synthetic CDO* transactions arranged by Goldman Sachs. The final Abacus deal in 2007 was a simpler version of Morgan's Bistro, referenced to a set of subprime RMBS chosen for its extreme riskiness. Hedge fund Paulson & Co. bought protection from the Abacus SPV against the reference pool, expecting its value to fall, while the Düsseldorf Landesbank IKB Deutsche Industriebank (IKB) took a long funded credit position by purchasing the SPV's notes (Abacus 2007; Dunbar 2004). The collapse in subprime mortgage values quickly made these worthless. IKB's feverish wish to buy high-yield assets took place long after RMBS prices had peaked. It collapsed five months after buying the notes with losses exceeding its capital by almost four times.

The arranger's conduct was questioned as conflicted by a Congressional committee in 2010, and the SEC filed a civil fraud complaint against Goldman Sachs, alleging that the bank sold opposing short and long credit positions and concealed from IKB the circumstances that led to the short position. This was settled out of court. All synthetic CDOs require both short and long interests. The cash note buyer acquired the credit risk that the hedge fund protection buyer was shorting, with the note proceeds used to pay the short seller when protection was triggered. This may not be an abuse of practice or breach an implied duty of care, but it clearly requires disclosure and ought not to be seen as comparable to the market-making process that characterizes liquid bond markets. Re-regulation has not yet considered a solution.

Over-complex transactions may have disguised the actual risk exposure for CDO investors. ISDA recently adopted a motto for its website banner, 'Safe Efficient Markets', which different readers may take as assertive, comforting or defensive. Concerns over derivatives or market practice lead to a broader question of how legal and regulatory environments deal with financial innovation, and whether they can accommodate both innovation and responsible financial activity without becoming unduly reactive or entangled in rules? We return to these issues in Chapter 9.

9 Equity securities, organized exchanges and corporate governance

> Since ownership now exists in the form of shares, its movement and transfer become simply the result of stock exchange dealings, where little fishes are gobbled up by the sharks, and sheep by the stock exchange wolves.
>
> (Marx 1894: 571)

As commonplace as debt and equity instruments are to developed financial systems, their respective narratives are remarkably different. One important result is that financial innovation since the Bretton Woods era varies considerably in form and impact between the two sectors, wherever it is observed and regardless of the transaction location's variety of capitalism. Innovation and financial development in loans and bonds centres on contracts, transaction types and commercial responses to regulation, and barriers between markets; similar factors influence equities to a far lesser extent. Innovation in share trading and issuance is focused overwhelmingly on the organized exchange as the forum for those activities, so that the setting rather than the transaction dictates commercial strategies and outcomes.

This is a double paradox. Share prices and interest rates in sophisticated economies can be correlated over protracted periods, and a constructional difference is hard to explain from a purely financial perspective given that corporate value is theoretically indifferent to the composition of capital (Modigliani & Miller 1958). We see an explanation in the distinct institutional origins of the two markets, especially in that the modern corporation and the shares it issues are products of early company law.

A further consequence is that while the nature of global equity claims is remarkably constant, the world's equity markets vary across states, between regions and more recently in their deployment of technological resources. National law also affects the communal rights of equity holders in providing differently for corporate governance, despite a post-1990s trend towards harmonized practice.

Equity markets are more idiosyncratic than their debt counterparts, although similarities are often seen in the short-term cross-sectional performance of share indexes, so that Monday's fall in New York induces selling in Tokyo or Singapore on Tuesday. This chapter therefore demands a more historical perspective than our analysis of debt instruments, despite the fact that recognizable debt claims preceded shares by several centuries. It also requires an explanation of how the law and practice of corporate governance impacts the nature of equity claims.

We are guided by two further observations. First, all transactional claims are influenced by regulation and comparative regulatory intensity, but we distinguish equities that typically function as the result of law from debt contracts that are largely self-contained. Second, while modern equity claims are recognizably similar to those first allowed in nineteenth-century

Europe, organized share exchanges are unrecognizably different, even though the most radical changes to the model date only from the 1980s. Accordingly, much of our focus is towards the development of the exchange, a narrative progressing from the Place Vendôme in Paris and City of London coffee houses, to electronic trading platforms known as dark pools and competition among new and established markets. Our analysis also highlights a persistent chauvinism that identifies the traditional stock market with its host economy, chiefly for four reasons:

- Most investors in both developed and emerging economies manage portfolios with a preponderance of securities and other assets of their own domicile, the *home bias* described in Box 9.1.
- Equity markets form a highly visible component of national financial systems and a sizeable majority of aggregate global claims against commercial enterprises (Figure 2.4B). Excluding Japan, Asia's aggregate equity market capitalization relative to GDP is higher than among most country groupings (Table 3.5), particularly with the newly industrialized economies of Hong Kong, South Korea, Singapore and Taiwan. Except for Japan, the capitalization of Asia's share markets comfortably exceeds the aggregate of its debt markets.
- Stock markets are culturally associated with national economic performance, even though the connotation may be flawed. It holds true for markets such as those in Mumbai or Shanghai that currently bar foreign listings, but most large exchanges see companies of many domiciles as eligible listing candidates and sources of revenue. Transnational share listings may provide issuers with a new source of funds, the reputational benefits of submitting to recognized standards of governance, or merely the commercial value of self-promotion. US travel-goods maker Samsonite's 2011 US$1.25 billion Hong Kong listing was as much concerned with luggage marketing as fundraising.
- The constitution, operations and regulation of the exchange had the same national connotation until the 1990s, when transnational alliances and mergers began among European and North American exchange owners. Chauvinism still attaches to most Asian exchanges, which tend to present themselves as commercial national champions, even if their revenue is protected by monopolies over listing services.

This chapter first discusses the nature of equity claims, before examining how they behave in terms of portfolio theory and asking why shares are issued, held and traded. Section 9.3 continues with the emergence of the equity marketplace represented by the exchange and its evolution from a self-managed private club. An historical paradox is that most of the world's exchanges were, until the end of the twentieth century, simultaneously private organizations owned, controlled and regulated by self-selecting members and viewed as national utilities or public goods, whether or not they were held in high popular regard.

We consider the development of the institutional framework of the modern exchange, rivalry between exchange owners and regulators, and the reforms that encouraged demutualization, profit seeking, competition and exchange consolidation, together with powerful new means of trading and challenges from alternative dealing platforms. Critics argue that automated high-frequency trading (HFT) can be systemically destabilizing or at odds with ordered and transparent share dealing, but we see a further distinct concern. Rules that govern share ownership and the nature of equity claims treat in an identical way the committed long-term shareholder and the programmed fund that owns vast blocks of shares for no more than several nanoseconds. Trading reality increasingly diverges from the institutional basis for share ownership and corporate governance, given that high-volume trading now contributes heavily to turnover on many share markets.

Section 9.4 looks at the performance and future of Asia's share markets, some of which are now sizeable and influential. Section 9.5 concludes by asking how corporate governance influences equity markets through national laws and standards of practice and in its relationships with company performance and ethical standards.

9.1 Equity claims and capital markets

The *Oxford English Dictionary* provides eight definitions of *equity*, with three further uses awaiting admission in December 2011. Not all relate to finance or commerce. It is no coincidence that actors unions in Canada, the UK and US are all named 'Equity' given that sixteenth-century English actors and playwrights were said to hold *shares* in a theatre *company* and divide the profits of performances. Closer to modern finance is the sense of equity taken from law and governance, including several uses that enter our discussion:

- A meaning in moral philosophy associated with fairness or equal treatment. Shares in a company are fungible and ranked equally among themselves.
- A sense of association with the rule of law, seen historically as important for the conduct of commerce.
- The underlying principle of justice, as well as a system of law that developed in England in the courts of Chancery that heard commercial disputes.
- A residual right, such as one remaining in property or an enterprise after the discharge of its debts. We speak of the equity that a homeowner has in real estate after accounting for a mortgage loan, or negative equity if the loan exceeds the prevailing price of the mortgaged house.

The last allusion gives a clue to the claim represented by a share, in the sense that the equity of redemption represents the net value of a company to its owners, when accounting arithmetic deducts from the gross value the total of debts and any preferred capital. Those net claims become *shares* when traded on an organized exchange in the case of public or *listed* companies, and in modern governance practice will *share* equally in that company's net value. The concept is universal and not associated with any specific form of law, although the mechanics of shared ownership and the rights attached to an equity claim differ from place to place.

Variations in the meaning of share or exchange show the hazards of financial jargon, as our introduction warned. Investment bankers advising on equity transactions refer to new issues as *primary* and *secondary*: the first being shares sold in an initial public offering (IPO) to inject funds into a company, and the second to allow the company's owners to raise funds by reducing their shareholdings. Section 8.1 shows the connotation of the terms in debt market practice to be very different.

Transatlantic confusion is found with *stock*, which was traditionally a bond in England and a share in the US, but *stock market* is ubiquitous since most exchanges historically dealt in both types of claim. Stock comes from medieval English accounting, which used a straight twig or *tally* to record borrowings. The tally was notched to show the size of the claim, then split in two, with one part (the stock) held until redemption by the creditor and the other (the stub) by the debtor (Innes 1913: 394). Share and equity are now interchangeable terms except with special categories of shares that carry preferential rights. Equities means ordinary shares or common stock, the foundation of corporate capital. We refer in this chapter to stock markets as that subset of organized exchanges where shares in public companies are listed, and treat 'share' and 'equity' as synonymous.

Finally, *bourse* is almost ubiquitous. Europe's legacy share markets include *die Börse* in Frankfurt, Oslo's *Børsen*, *la Bourse* in Paris and Madrid's *la Bolsa*, and the word is common among exchanges in other French- or Spanish-speaking states, several in North America, and *Bursa Malaysia* in Kuala Lumpur. Journalists use bourse in English to brighten their stock market analysis, perhaps unaware that its origins are disputed. To etymologists it derives from the Latin *bursa*, or bag, while several distinguished historians claim it to be taken from Beurse, a family of merchants associated with the centre of commerce in medieval Bruges. Urban myths begin with small truths, so for us the name suggests the place where merchants kept safe their credit slips.

Nature and entitlements

Shares are financial claims representing collective ownership interests. These are usually documented in the issuing company's constitution rather than prospectuses or listing documents. They vary little in form among companies of the same domicile, although the rules for incorporation in some jurisdictions distinguish between small or private companies and those that are publicly listed. Shares convey to the holder:

- Rights of ownership, implying participation in the company's activities through a claim over its net assets, and a share of net income through payment of any declared dividends;
- Ultimate rights of control, constrained by the delegation of day-to-day management and corporate strategy; and
- A lack of priority of claim in bankruptcy, effectively an obligation to sacrifice the capital commitment signified by the share. This is mitigated by being limited to a fixed amount, and by a right of disposal by transfer, which may itself be limited contractually by agreement between issuer and shareholder.

Ownership rights are subject to conditions. These are not contractually part of the equity claim because they exist as a matter of law or regulation, or are influenced by practice found in voluntary codes of governance. All differ between jurisdictions, so while non-shareholding stakeholders such as employees or local communities generally enjoy greater rights in developed economies in relation to the company than in the mid-twentieth century, those in Germany or Japan have more formal influence in its affairs than allowed by Anglo-American economic models.

Shares represent ownership claims in companies, many of which are *listed*, with their outstanding shares bought and sold on an organized exchange. With this comes a proportional entitlement to any declared profits through payment of a dividend, and a claim over the company's net assets after payment of all liabilities but enforceable only if the company is dissolved. These rights are described in a corporate constitution, the form of which is typically proscribed by statute or code. The arrangement allows companies to exist in perpetuity if they avoid commercial failure or a takeover predator, and be unthreatened by management succession risks or modest changes in ownership. Few public companies choose to wind themselves up and return capital to their owners for lack of appropriate investment opportunities, even when it may seem a sound choice. Voluntary cessation is virtually unknown except in fund management, so that companies such as film manufacturer Eastman Kodak that lose their core purpose tend to shrink, fail or be sold.

How this came about is a matter of economic and institutional history. Shared commercial interests were known in shipping ventures and merchant guilds throughout medieval Europe, as well as in trading communities of North Africa and the Middle East – indeed, the principle of the commercial Shari'ah is that the entrepreneur and financier share in the overall return and hazards of a commercial venture. Long ocean voyages demanded significant sums of speculative capital, so the sharing of interests allowed merchants to raise funds and investors to spread risks. These temporary specific ventures first developed into intricate partnerships in the Italian trading city states, and later in England and the Dutch provinces, into a single legal personality created by royal charter.

Shares were first issued in the sixteenth and seventeenth centuries under charters granted to colonial joint stock trading companies, notably the English and Dutch East India Companies in 1600 and 1602, respectively. Both became substantial enterprises, albeit assisted by delegated state authority (Michie 1999). The pace of company promotion accelerated in France and England in the early eighteenth century and produced an inevitable market bubble that burst in 1719–20, encouraging statutory restrictions on securities dealing in France and on company formation in England, that in each case lasted well into the nineteenth century.

Only when corporate need for capital grew beyond the capacity of the system to provide it was legislation enacted in England that allowed the creation of joint stock banks with individual subscribers for shares, and finally the early modern company. This limited the liability of owners for the company's obligations in the event of it failing, necessitating trading counterparties or creditors to be warned by the inclusion of 'Limited' in the company's name that their claims would be met only to the extent possible by the company alone.

The creation of a corporate legal personality thus gave the enterprise a commercial permanence and protection from the financial standing of the owners. Modern equity claims arose from a need for unprecedented funding for the transport infrastructure and capital goods of the Industrial Revolution, and the provisions of England's 1844 Companies Act (7 & 8 Vic. C. 110) and Joint Stock Companies Act 1856 (19 & 20 Vic. C. 47) proved sufficiently durable to facilitate long-term fixed asset formation (Morgan & Thomas 1969: 128, 131). Similar statutory provision was gradually made in much of Western Europe and North America. Today, shares traded throughout the world closely resemble those sanctioned in mid-nineteenth century England (Michie 2006), and the less reputable aspects of modern scandals and cronyism appear in Anthony Trollope's 1875 novel *The Way We Live Now*, a melodrama picturing notoriously sharp IPO practices.

Since the mid-nineteenth century, company shares have represented fractional rights of ownership that may be dispersed among many shareholders or concentrated in a small number of controlling interests, as with unlisted family or closely held companies. No real change has since occurred in the nature of equity claims, albeit that national reforms of rights favouring stakeholders or employees in a company will have diminished the share of a company due to the shareholder. Indeed, innovation in equities has generally lessened given that tiered classes of capital are now regarded as evidence of poor governance, although there are many examples of long-established companies with capital structures providing skewed voting rights. Differential structures are also popular for control reasons among technology companies, including Google and Facebook.

Ordinary shares are effectively perpetual, although in some jurisdictions tranches of shares can bought by the company from shareholders and cancelled. Partial share *buybacks* are conducted by auction, ballot, reverse tender, or spread proportionately among all ordinary shareholders. The share's general lack of a contractual maturity explains its need for transferability, and the connotation of shares in public companies with an organized exchange. The exchange is needed because the company can only redeem its shares at large and owners would otherwise be unable to alter their portfolios other than by using derivatives or securities lending.

The borrowing signified by a share in a company becomes due for repayment only in unique circumstances:

- A voluntary winding up of a company when only a nominal amount would be returned to the claimant; or
- A share buyback or cancellation, which may be an efficient way for a company to return capital or pay a dividend to its owners.

At other times the holder of an equity claim relinquishes ordinary rights of repayment for an ownership interest, and is thus a shareholder. Scholars first identified the dilemmas associated with this structure in the 1920s, just as it became common for large companies to be managed by professionals who typically lacked ownership interests, and owned collectively by many unconnected individual investors and intermediaries. The influential study of Berle and Means (1932) showed how the model created control and agency issues, making the participatory claims represented by shares largely illusory, and requiring mitigating rules of governance to prevent management acting in its own interest rather than that of the owners. The agency problem assumes that these goals are distinct or misaligned. It is universal and of especial concern in Asia where:

- Direct retail participation by small shareholders is relatively high, as a corollary of the relatively small scale of funds under professional management throughout the region;
- The *free float* or proportion of shares in Asian companies that is available to trade is relatively low. This is especially true of listed companies in which the state is a significant owner; and
- Governance practice is generally less protective of minority interests than in OECD states.

Legislation may also limit a company's freedom of action for reasons of public policy, commonly to protect stakeholders such as employees or certain creditors during a bankruptcy. This illustrates how aspects of the equity claim are impacted by being entrenched directly in company law or commercial codes, or indirectly through the requirements that the law places on a company's constitution. A long-established example is that companies in many jurisdictions are prohibited from distributing dividends to shareholders if the company is apparently insolvent, whatever the intention of the majority owners or company managers.

Issuance and trading

The behaviour of share prices is influential for three broad reasons:

- Sectoral or aggregate price changes are taken as economic indicators and measures of general confidence. This is partly justified by finance theory's approach to share valuation, deriving its price from the present value of the company's retained and future earnings, even though this may never be distributed to owners. The model is one of several used to compare companies in similar sectors. Valuations are made in practice according to both sectoral and general factors, and include the ratio of the prevailing share price to past or projected earnings (p/e ratios), net asset values, economic value added (EVA) and multiples of revenue to cashflow.

- The cost of issuing shares is a benchmark for corporate performance and in assessing the advisability of committing resources to new investment projects. Prevailing share prices give important clues as to the true attributed cost of capital, and are one means by which business projects can be externally assessed, as discussed in Box 3.1.
- Most exchanges have bellwether shares that are tracked for clues as to the market's aggregate performance – for example, Cheung Kong in Hong Kong, Samsung Electronics in Seoul, Singapore's SingTel, or General Electric and Microsoft in New York. These change over time, such that Apple or Google have displaced General Motors in popular US attention. Leading shares will be included in market, regional or sectoral indexes, which have a profound and universal effect on actual investment decisions.

That the price performance of leading shares or indexes is suggestive of national economic health becomes implausible when markets increasingly trade shares in foreign companies or their composition is skewed to certain sectors. The most conspicuous market indexes of the Hong Kong and London exchanges are respectively weighted towards the property and extractive sectors, while the US NASDAQ exchange has a preponderance of technology companies. Tables 9.1 and 9.2 show the number of listings on leading exchanges as at December 2010, together with the share of foreign listings of the most internationally oriented exchanges.

Two characteristics distinguish the markets for shares from other forms of intermediation. First, stock markets do not themselves raise money but provide a forum allowing changes in share ownership. Issuance takes place outside the exchange silo, in a process similar to that described in Section 8.1 for new debt issues, only more elaborate. Second, all models of intermediation do more than channel funds into investment, whether or not it is productive, but the overall effects may often be unclear.

Section 2.1 shows that, by convention, financial development is taken to be the ratio of bank credit and debt and equity market capitalization to GDP. Bank credit represents the outstanding stock of lending, and bond market capitalization measures the aggregate outstanding principal, in each case including claims against financial sector participants, whereas the measure of share market scale is distinct. Equity capitalization is not a measure of funds raised but a combination of new money from IPOs and the prevailing market value of existing listed companies. Finance theory holds that share prices are functions of expected economic value, which differ by sector and from one national exchange to another, and if the market is efficient reflect all known information concerning the issuer (Fama 1970). Aggregate capitalization may be high in a market where no new funds are raised. Equity capitalization is both different and more subjective than the two other factors contributing to financial development.

All companies with permanent paid in or subscribed capital have owners unless constituted as cooperatives, trusts or SPVs whose ownership is nominal or contractual. The dispersal of ownership varies, increasing as companies grow and become prone to list their shares, giving a progression of company types:

- Privately owned self-managed SMEs;
- Larger private, professionally managed SMEs with ownership confined to families, associates and employees or their representatives;
- Unlisted companies with outside strategic commercial or financial shareholders. This can be an ongoing arrangement in the German corporate model, where a bank may be both financier and leading external shareholder;

Table 9.1 Listed companies by exchange, end-2010

	Total	Domestic	Foreign	Total 2009
Bombay SE	5,034	5,034	Nil	4,955
Toronto (TSX Group)	3,741	3,654	87	3,700
BME Spanish Exchanges (1)	3,345	3,310	35	3,472
London SE	2,966	2,362	604	3,088
NASDAQ OMX	2,778	2,480	298	2,852
Tokyo SE	2,293	2,281	12	2,335
NYSE Euronext US (2)	2,238	1,787	451	2,327
Australian Securities Exchange	1,999	1,913	86	1,966
Korea Exchange	1,798	1,781	17	1,788
National Stock Exchange India	1,552	1,551	1	1,453
Hong Kong Exchanges	1,413	1,396	17	1,319
Osaka Securities Exchange	1,273	1,272	1	1,322
Shenzhen SE	1,169	1,169	Nil	830
NYSE Euronext Europe (3)	1,135	983	152	1,160
Bursa Malaysia	956	948	8	959
Shanghai SE	894	894	Nil	870
Taiwan SE	784	752	32	755
Singapore Exchange	778	461	317	773
Deutsche Börse	765	690	75	783
NASDAQ OMX Nordic Exchange	754	752	2	797
Tel Aviv SE	613	596	17	622
Warsaw SE	584	569	15	486
Thailand SE	541	541	Nil	535
Mexican Exchange	427	130	297	406
Indonesia SE	420	420	Nil	398
Johannesburg SE	397	352	45	396
BM&FBOVESPA (4)	381	373	8	386
Tehran SE	369	369	Nil	364
Istanbul SE	339	338	1	315
SIX Swiss Exchange	296	246	50	339
Luxembourg SE	290	30	260	267
Athens Exchange	280	277	3	288
Amman SE	277	277	Nil	272
Philippine SE	253	251	2	248
Lima SE	248	199	49	241
MICEX (5)	245	245	Nil	234
Colombo SE	241	241	Nil	231
Oslo Børs	239	195	44	238
Santiago SE	231	227	4	236
Egyptian Exchange	228	227	1	313

1. BME is the parent of the exchanges in Barcelona, Bilbao, Madrid and Valencia.

2. NYSE Euronext US is predominantly the New York Stock Exchange and its second market NYSE Arca.

3. NYSE Euronext (Europe) operates the Amsterdam, Brussels, Lisbon and Paris exchanges.

4. BM&FBOVESPA operates the São Paulo Stock Exchange.

5. MICEX is Russia's largest exchange.

Source: World Federation of Exchanges (WFE), a trade body of 52 mainly legacy exchanges, accounting for 45,508 aggregate listings as at end 2010. Data show the number of companies that have shares listed on each exchange, excluding investment funds and unit trusts. Foreign companies are those incorporated in a different state to the exchange's location. Exchanges in East and South Asia are shown in bold.

Table 9.2 Sizeable foreign listings, end-2010

Exchange	Total listings	Foreign listings as a share of the total (%)
Luxembourg SE	290	89.7
Mexican Exchange	427	69.6
Bermuda SE	45	68.9
Singapore Exchange	778	40.7
London SE Group	2,966	20.4
NYSE Euronext US	2,238	20.2
Lima SE	248	19.8
Wiener Börse	110	19.1
Oslo Børs	239	18.4
SIX Swiss Exchange	296	16.9
Irish SE	59	15.3
NYSE Euronext Europe	1,135	13.4
Johannesburg SE	397	11.3
NASDAQ OMX	2,778	10.7
Deutsche Börse	765	9.8

Bermuda, Mexico and Luxembourg are offshore listing centres and the only exchanges with more foreign than domestic listings.

Source: WFE.

- Pre-IPO companies with a significant minority of shares or share options held by one or more financial investors such as private equity or venture capital funds, introduced more fully in Section 11.2. Some states do not allow such companies to grow beyond a certain scale or dispersed ownership, so that a closely held company, such as Facebook at end-2011, is forced to choose between listing and shrinking; and
- Public listed companies, which may be closely controlled or have substantial share-holder registers. Control may stem from an outright majority shareholding, through constrictive cross-shareholdings as with the *chaebol* or *keiretsu* described in Section 2.2 and in conglomerates with multiple listings such as Samsung or Jardine Matheson, or through share classes carrying differential voting rights. Self-protective corporate structures are disfavoured in the US and UK as signifying poor governance, and users may be valued at discounts to their industry sector. The Murdoch family's control of News Corporation is one such example. Others are seen more benignly, notably Warren Buffet's Berkshire Hathaway holding company and the eponymous Swire group. Close control is common among large listed Asian companies.

Listed companies include specialized forms where legislation and listing rules allow, with REITS, business trusts and infrastructural companies as examples. Many jurisdictions provide several incorporation formats and designations for companies of different characteristics, so a typical German private company is a *Gesellschaft mit beschränkter Haftung* (GmbH, or company with limited liability) and a public listed company an *Aktiengesellschaft* (AG, from the terms for share and society).

Most EU states use similar models, as do China (有限公司 or *yǒu xiàn gōng sī*, and 股份有限公司 or *gǔ fèn yǒu xiàn gōng sī* for limited and publicly listed company respectively), Indonesia (*Perseroan Terbatas* or PT, and *Perseroan Terbuka* or PT Tbk), South Korea

(유한회사 or *yuhan hoesa*, and 주식회사 or *jusik hoesa*), Malaysia (*Sendirian Berhad* or Sdn Bhd, and *Berhad* or Bhd), Singapore (Private Limited or Pte Ltd, and Limited) and Thailand (บริษัทมหาชนจำกัด or bor-rí-sàt má-hăa chon jam-gàt, and บริษัทมหาชน จำกัด or bor-rí-sàt àyk-gà-chon jam-gàt, respectively for limited and public company limited).

Jurisdictions using 'Corp.', 'Inc.' or 'Ltd' for both private and public companies include all US states, Hong Kong (有限公司 or *yau han gung se*), Japan (株式会社 or *kabushiki-kaisha* (KK) for company with shares) and the Philippines. Some distinguish companies within the public sector, for example with Indonesia's designation *persero*. Japan has a myriad of public sector enterprise categories as a product of reforms introduced under the occupation administration in 1946–47 (see Box 2.3; Hadley 1949).

Shares in public companies are sold and become listed through several mechanisms, in some cases in a form prescribed by a listing authority or delegated by it to the exchange, as with Hong Kong. These include IPOs or introductions to the exchange, secondary listings of new shares or those of a strategic shareholder, and bonus issues, rights issues, vendor placements, private placements, and partly paid issues where the purchase price is paid in instalments or upon a call by the issuer.

Listing candidates range from a growing company seeking funds for expansion or an established company floating a minority interest, to a private financial investor taking a company public to realize profits from a phase of restructuring following either a leveraged or management buyout (LBO or MBO), privatization, or demutualization. A US$2.0 billion Hong Kong IPO by Chow Tai Fook Ltd in December 2011 is typical of the sale of a minority stake by the controlling owner of a substantial company, in this case 10.5 per cent of existing share capital. Samsonite is a long-established company, acquired, delisted, restructured, leveraged and sold through its IPO by private equity investors. The Appendix to this chapter explains the steps that form the process for a substantial generic IPO.

Privatization has two meanings: one where a controlling shareholder acquires the company's minority interests and delists its shares (that is, taking a company private), and the other derived from the sale of shares in public sector commercial or utility interests (creating a private sector enterprise). This began as a large-scale phenomenon in the 1980s, with the UK being first to corporatize and sell shares in its telecommunications and energy monopolies, a process that spread to many other states. Most examples in Asia have been partial privatizations, where government retains a controlling interest post-IPO.

All companies may restrict sales of shares through lock-up provisions that prevent influential shareholders from disposing of their holdings soon after a listing. It is common in Asia for private or closely held companies to sell shares to strategic *cornerstone* investors to influence wider demand in a later listing, imposing a lock-up period customarily of between six months and two years. The Appendix gives an example in a 2010 IPO of shares in Chongqing Rural Commercial Bank.

9.2 Portfolio theory and financial globalization

Why do we hold, trade or short sell equities? Shares carry the value of potential capital gains, recurring but uncertain dividend income, and long but unknown duration, together with risks that are simultaneously firm-specific, sectoral and general. Above all, shares provide risk exposure to defined market segments, an investment rationale discussed in Section 11.1. We examine here the theory underlying portfolio decisions in both its simple and modified forms.

Domestic CAPM

Traditional pricing models that examine asset allocations assume that an investor is concerned only with a portfolio's expected returns and risk, with the latter measured by the proxy of price volatility (Sharpe 1964; Lintner 1965). Investment decisions are made in a closed economy with no access to foreign assets, and the investor may not borrow securities or incur debt of any kind, which makes short selling impossible. The objective of diversification is to eliminate risks specific to any single firm, that is, the portfolio's *non-systematic* or diversifiable risk. What then remains is pure market risk, or *systematic* non-diversifiable risk. This cannot be altered within the parameters of the model. It is impossible for the portfolio holder to change its exposure to market risk, although efficient capital markets allow fair equilibrium pricing of such risk. CAPM's core concept is that a security's expected return is related to its contribution to the risk of the market portfolio (Stulz 1999).

Investors assessing the risk and return of a single security are assumed only to consider how it is expected to contribute to the risk of the portfolio (Sharpe 1964). All investors are taken to share identical expectations based on access to the same information, so that each holds a homogenous market portfolio. The contribution of the risk of a security is signified by beta (β), which is given by Equation 9.1:

$$\beta_i = Cov(r_{it},\ r_{mt})\ /\ Var(r_{mt}) \tag{9.1}$$

Where β_i is the coefficient for firm i; r_{it} is firm i's return in period t; and r_{mt} is the market return over that period. Beta thus equals the ratio of the covariance of the returns of the individual security and that of the market portfolio to the variance of the market portfolio's return.

Any security contributing greater than proportionately to the risk of the market portfolio has a higher beta, and in theory commands a higher risk premium. The general form of the CAPM is given by:

$$E[r_{it}] = r_{ft} + \beta_i[E(r_{mt} - r_{ft})] \tag{9.2}$$

Thus the expected return from firm i's share in period t equals the risk-free rate (r_{ft}) plus the firm's risk premium, determined by the product of beta and the market risk premium ($r_{mt} - r_{ft}$).

CAPM helps compute a security's expected return and cost of equity, and guide asset selection in the composition of an optimal investment portfolio. The model is widely used but its validity easily challenged. It cannot be tested because the composition of any true market portfolio is unknown, an observation known as Roll's critique (Roll 1977). Using proxies for the market portfolio leads to misspecification errors, and the usable market portfolio neither includes all assets nor faithfully reflects the contribution of each component to the universe of assets. Any conclusions or inferences are therefore difficult to interpret. The beta coefficient is not the sole influence on expected returns – for example, a firm's size and the ratio of its book value to market value are both important in determining expected equity returns, while beta may itself be of little impact (Fama and French 1992). Expected returns are influenced by historic share prices, structural market characteristics such as bid–offer spreads and prevailing liquidity, and information asymmetry.

Transnational asset pricing

The international finance literature extends from its domestic antecedents (Adler and Dumas 1983). A fully open economy allows foreign access to its capital markets and permits residents to hold assets abroad, so that the risks associated with the domestic economy are distributed among both home and overseas investors. The benefit to domestic investors of exposure to both classes of assets is that diversification leads to a degree of risk reduction, unless foreign and home risks are correlated. Unexpected good news in one economy may offset deleterious shocks elsewhere. This suggests that given access to global markets, portfolios may enjoy lower risks with an unchanged expected return, or a higher return for a constant variance (Harvey 1991; Stulz 1999). Six conditions must be met for CAPM to hold in an integrated global market, requiring that:

- Investors take account of no factors other than risk and return, and on that basis seek to hold efficient frontier portfolios;
- Investors share identical views of expected returns and risks of all assets.
- Investors base their objectives on nominal returns;
- Unlimited borrowing and lending are permitted at a risk-free rate;
- No transaction costs or taxes exist; and
- All investors are passive price takers.

In these conditions, all investors hold identical portfolios, with an optimal mix of risk and return coinciding with the envelope given by the efficient frontier. The risk premium of any single asset is proportional to the risk premium of this market portfolio and the beta of the asset. The market portfolio becomes the world market portfolio with its unrestricted universe of assets. CAPM thus holds for the integrated market, as shown in Equation 9.3:

$$E[r_{it}] = r_{ft} + \beta_{iw}[E(r_{wt} - r_{ft})]$$ (9.3)

Equations 9.2 and 9.3 differ in several ways. The market portfolio in (9.3) includes all risky assets in the integrated global market, and beta measures the extent to which returns on the risk asset *i* respond to the returns on the world market portfolio. Similarly, only systematic risk is rewarded and not risk specific to any single firm. The international CAPM in Equation (9.3) relies on two conditions:

- Each investor uses its domestic currency but at purchasing power parity, so that there exist no FX arbitrage opportunities or carry trade to enhance returns; and
- Investors share identical consumption preferences and consumption baskets.

It is clear that these assumptions make the international CAPM inherently imperfect in understanding portfolio choice in a globalized setting. Purchasing power parity is broadly accurate only in the very long term, so that FX risk is a real factor in cross-border portfolios in the absence of a shared currency or credible currency peg. Investors view exchange rate risk from the perspective of their respective domestic currency, and will dispute the risk–return characteristics of any single portfolio and compute differing efficient frontiers. Consumption preferences differ from one state to another and taxes, transaction costs and capital barriers may make it difficult or unattractive for investors to hold the world market portfolio.[1]

One study found that the sensitivity of 17 country returns to a world return, that is, beta in Equation (9.3), predicts some of the dynamic behaviour of country returns (Harvey 1991). It suggests that the explanation is incomplete because markets are not fully integrated, but neglects risks attributable to more than one factor. The world market portfolio is also impossible to define, making the predictive record of the international CAPM a victim of Roll's critique. MSCI, Markit and other data providers construct proprietary equity indexes as proxies for aggregate market portfolios to give investors benchmarks for performance.

A persistent home bias among most investors also weighs against the international CAPM. If the world capital market is seamlessly integrated, and investors seek only to maximize returns and minimize risk, their portfolios should be configured towards an optimal combination of return and risk, meaning that the weighting of specific assets should be determined by their risk and return dynamics rather than the domicile of their issuers or currencies of issue. In practice, most investors have a propensity to hold domestic assets and forego the full benefits of international diversification, because of path dependence, a sense of national obligation, or regulations that leave the investor no choice but to stay largely at home. Box 9.1 further explores the puzzle of the home bias and shows how new share issue structures try to mitigate its effects.

Box 9.1 The Puzzle of Home Bias

Home bias is the tendency of savers and asset managers to hold domestic securities despite the benefits of diversification offshore (French & Poterba 1991). Similar propensities arise in other aspects of economic activity, but portfolio home bias results from especially strong institutional forces and may be the most entrenched and universal example of its type.

We would expect national investment and savings to be highly correlated only when financial markets were poorly integrated. Greater integration would induce savings to behave non-discriminatively and select investment media from all those feasible markets with favourable risk and return characteristics. Domestic saving nonetheless explains over 90 per cent of national variations in capital investment (Feldstein & Horioka 1980), with significant correlations between domestic investment and savings in 25 high- and 32 low- and medium-income economies observed in 1990–97 (Obstfeld & Rogoff 2000).

Home bias also exists in international trade (ibid). All economies are more likely to conduct commerce domestically than with their foreign neighbours, even allowing for the disincentive effect of import tariffs (McCallum 1995). This is partly explained by many commercial activities being inherently local, and that trade barriers are formally or culturally associated with national borders. Manufacturers may refrain from selling overseas not only if it involves high transaction costs, but if they lack suitable human capital to do so. Logistics managers such as Li and Fung connect Asian OEM and ODM suppliers with OECD buyers in this way, compensating for transactional frictions just as the ADR does for recalcitrant US portfolio investors.

Our puzzle is to explain the persistence of the home bias when the benefits of portfolio diversification are generally accepted. Our question is to decide why this may be important? The equity portfolio home bias (H_i) for any State (i) is given by an index:

$$H_i = 1 - \left(\frac{Foreign\ equities\ held\ by\ State\,(i)\ as\ a\ share\ of\ all\ equities\ held}{Equity\ capitalization\ of\ all\ other\ states} \right)$$

A value of one indicates an economy holding no foreign securities.

One with a nil value has a portfolio of domestic securities aligned with the theoretically balanced global weightings. The average home bias weighted by market capitalization among the G20 economies excluding Saudi Arabia was 0.66 in 2007, as Table 9.3 shows, meaning that the average holding of foreign equities was one-third less than in the optimal weighted portfolio (Haldane 2011a: 23). The overall bias of OECD investors fell after the mid-1990s, especially when currency risk was eliminated within the Eurozone. It remained far higher in the emerging G20 group, for which it varied only marginally over the period from 1995.

Table 9.3 G20 home equity bias, 1995–2007

	1995	2000	2005	2007
Japan	0.93	0.92	0.84	0.84
Australia	0.81	0.83	0.79	0.74
Canada	0.67	0.69	0.67	0.68
France	0.80	0.78	0.59	0.62
US	0.72	0.76	0.61	0.56
UK	0.66	0.68	.058	0.56
Italy	0.71	0.65	0.54	0.54
Germany	0.65	0.58	0.45	0.48
Weighted average advanced states (8)	0.79	0.76	0.64	0.61
India	0.99	0.99	1.00	1.00
China	0.96	0.94	0.98	0.99
Russia	N/A	0.97	0.98	0.99
Turkey	0.95	0.98	0.97	0.98
Indonesia	0.99	0.98	0.99	0.98
Brazil	0.97	0.96	0.96	0.97
Mexico	0.94	0.98	0.86	0.91
South Korea	0.98	0.97	0.90	0.82
South Africa	0.94	0.70	0.72	0.79
Argentina	0.79	0.70	0.58	0.59
Weighted average (10) developing states	0.96	0.93	0.92	0.94
G 20 weighted average	0.80	0.77	0.66	0.66

Source: Haldane (2011a).

No data are available for the EU or Saudi Arabia. Weighted averages are calculated using each economy's aggregate equity market capitalization. Higher values indicate a greater domestic portfolio orientation.

Home bias in 2007 was complete or nearly complete in China, India and Russia. Outward capital restrictions might account for these results but the bias appears high even where controls are less extensive than in China or India. The data also contain unusual cases indicating that intrinsic or local factors contribute to lowering or maintaining the home bias, for example:

- Falls occurred in 1995–2007 in Argentina, South Africa and South Korea. This may suggest high domestic volatility, or evidence in Argentina of capital flight and a lack of relatively safe domestic assets.
- Home bias remained relatively high in Japan, Australia and Canada. An intuitive explanation is that each had well-developed financial markets with relatively little penetration by overseas intermediaries.
- Germany's home bias was low and fell over the period in question, although it steadied in 2005–7. Modest domestic cash equity markets may affect the propensity to invest overseas.

Identifying such factors from a small sample is empirically difficult even if we control for others that are ubiquitous and intuitively persuasive, including capital controls, domestic financial depth, comparative credit quality, per capita GDP, changes in external trade, or even a general lack of investible savings.

Capital is not fully mobile. Overt and hidden frictions and barriers impede transnational capital flows, meaning that funds for portfolio investment can be deterred from leaving the home economy or dissuaded from entering a second. Well-informed investors who believe themselves to be rational decision makers may have perceptions of foreign risk that are partial or subject to information asymmetries compared to domestic securities. Savers may require their asset managers to invest at home for chauvinistic reasons, whether or not this conforms with rational preferences, and protective regulation may constrain foreign diversification by insurers or other risk-averse asset managers.

Why might this matter? Capital flows resulting from falling home bias may be large in absolute terms and especially in relation to the overseas markets to which funds are drawn. Not all the economies in our sample are substantial or have significant disposable savings, and when their equity markets are illiquid because of small free floats the impact of a modest fall in home bias in a large OECD economy may be considerable, as if a big fish suddenly entered a small pond (Haldane 2011a: 5). For example, a 0.1 reduction in the weighted home bias for advanced G20 countries in 2007 would have been equivalent to a portfolio switch of around US$4.5 trillion towards foreign markets as a whole (ibid), or two-thirds of the end-2007 market capitalization of the emerging G20 economies.

The effects of reductions in home bias for any investee market are impossible to predict, however the results might be familiar if we consider the period immediately before the 1997–98 regional crisis when foreign banking and portfolio inflows rose throughout Southeast Asia and South Korea but began leaving in haste late in 1996. The problem has not disappeared, given Asia's post-2000 propensity to export capital to developed economies, part of the puzzle of capital flowing to OECD states from developing economies rather than the reverse (Prasad, Rajan & Subramanian 2007).

Scholars have considered other ways to capture the relationship between risk exposure and returns in a global context. Keppler (1991) and Keppler and Traub (1993) found that dividend yields and firm size affect equity returns across national markets. Erb, Harvey and Viskanta (1994) found that sovereign risk is a significant indicator of country returns, which in turn can guide global asset allocation. Ferson and Harvey (1994a; 1994b) examined a range of equity market indicators and found that many were significant only in relatively developed markets. These included the ratios of share price to book value, price to cashflow, price to earnings, and variables for national volatility, price momentum and reversal indicators, term interest rate structures, relative inflation and relative GDP. The result suggests two observations:

- Domestic investment in emerging market equities is less subject to formal portfolio selection than comparable flows within developed markets. This may itself reflect the proportionately higher share of activity in emerging markets attributable to direct retail investors.
- Foreign investment in emerging equity markets is a function of sovereign credit risk to a greater extent than in developed markets.

The finance literature establishes that cross-border investment can reduce overall portfolio risk, despite somewhat equivocal evidence, and that global markets provide natural hedges even for parochial investors. This increasingly influenced transnational portfolio accumulation,[2] and in the last 20 years contributed to profound changes in the functioning of organized exchanges, the subject of our next section.

9.3 Organized exchanges

Successful share exchanges fulfil two intermediation purposes, in allocating funds for portfolio investment and providing a medium for share trading.[3] For example, Bursa Malaysia identifies itself as facilitating:

- A central order-book, allowing trade negotiation, matching of buy and sell instructions or *orders*, and trade reporting;
- Data storage, and dissemination of price and trade information; and
- Market surveillance, that is, a regulatory tool for Malaysia's Securities Commission, and the means by which Bursa Malaysia polices trading activity.

Some exchanges also provide a forum for listings associated with defined standards of regulation, access and transparency. These activities generate revenue in the form of fees and commissions levied on exchange membership, trade execution, new listings and listing maintenance, and the sale of real-time and archival records to data providers such as Bloomberg or Thomson Reuters and index compilers such as MSCI and Markit. Vertically integrated exchanges with internal resources for clearing and settlement have a further source of revenue that is often lucrative. Each activity is also associated with the secondary functions of supervising trading on the exchange and in some cases the regulation of listed companies, either in collaboration with a public agency or through a form of delegated authority.

Exchange operations connect through the price mechanism, so corporate demand for listings is a function of the availability of investor funds, trading liquidity and the perceived quality of regulation. Liquidity relies on investor demand, whether securities lending is permissible to allow short selling, the market capitalization in relation to firm size and the float of shares available to trade, and flows generated by new share issues.

The availability of investment funds depends on the perceived quality of listings, and regulation in relation to prevailing prices as multiples of past and projected earnings. An exchange with adequately perceived regulation may sustain an overall earnings multiple less than that of one associated with a more rigorous regime, making shares cheaper to the investor but cutting demand for listings. A more intense regulatory setting gives confidence to investors, and encourages portfolio inflows and new listings at relatively higher multiples (Jackson & Roe 2009), although US evidence suggests that the severity of national enforcement of securities law deters both domestic and foreign listings (Coffee 2007).

None of these considerations is new. They affected seventeenth-century trading in Jonathan's Coffee House as London's first prominent place of exchange for securities, and the institutional framework for organized exchanges that developed after that time remained conceptually similar until relatively recently. A separate development was to transform modern share trading and is highlighted by an ambiguity that appeared in the late 1990s. While capitalization has always measured the value of shares listed on an exchange, it now also refers to the value of an exchange whose shares are listed on that exchange – almost as if the self-listed exchange wanted to disprove Russell's principle that no mathematical set can be a member of itself. The pursuit of profit by stock exchanges may be both rational and acceptable, but leads inevitably to concerns and conflicts, and can leave practice misaligned with national law.

Evolution

Our narrative includes developments in law, market practice, regulation and exchange competition. It divides into two periods, the first extending from the seventeenth century to the 1980s, and the second beginning with ostensibly simple reforms in New York and London in 1975 and 1986, respectively, to abolish fixed broking commissions that led to a near universal transformation of exchange configuration and behaviour.

Recent changes have taken place in several dimensions, including the nature of market making and trading, competition between traditional or *incumbent* exchanges and new exchange formats known generically as alternative trading platforms (ATPs), and consolidation among incumbent exchanges. Large share blocks are now bought and sold primarily on private platforms to avoid price disruption,[4] rather than on national legacy exchanges, although trades may settle through common CSDs.

Many leading stock markets became more open and competitive after the 1980s but are increasingly threatened by new platforms and new ways of trading, including HFT. Marx's view of a stock exchange run by sharks and wolves was far from revolutionary and is shared by critics of modern practice, although the concern has shifted from exchanges being cartels run for their members' interests to whether they give equal access to all classes of user or are conflicted by commercial objectives.

We identify four functional phases in exchange development. Reforms tended to be initiated in each case in the US or UK and then adapted elsewhere:

- From 1670, private or informal associations controlled by members but with relatively low barriers to entry. Membership became restricted and costly after 1914.

Dealing commissions are fixed throughout the period. From 1933–34, exchanges increasingly act as proxy securities regulators.

- From 1975, fixed commissions gradually abolished as being anti-competitive, resulting in expanded membership and trading volumes, and in demutualization, with exchanges increasingly owned by closely held private companies.
- Mid-1990s, the need to fund technological growth encourages broader ownership though an infusion of outside shareholders, profit seeking and competition. The regulatory balance alters with many exchanges no longer treated as public utilities and made to return certain proxy regulatory functions to the state.
- From 2000, further competition from quasi-OTC electronic platforms including private *dark pools*, many owned by banks or fund managers. This encouraged self-listing and consolidation among incumbent exchanges, and led several to establish or acquire dark pools to protect their overall trading liquidity.

Equity markets evolved in the final two phases technically, in pricing and distribution efficiency, and through the re-establishment of international equity offerings, which were rare between 1914 and the early 1980s, a period characterized by an historian of exchanges as one of control, suppression, regulation and evasion (Michie 2006).

Early exchanges were private clubs. They charged members an entry fee to buy and sell securities and bills of exchange, and gradually adopted rules to regulate dealings. The first, of no more than a sentence, was the Buttonwood Agreement made in 1792 by 24 Manhattan stockbrokers who, according to legend, traded in the shade of a Wall Street sycamore:

> We the Subscribers, Brokers for the Purchase and Sale of the Public Stock, do hereby solemnly promise and pledge ourselves to each other, that we will not buy or sell from this day for any person whatsoever, any kind of Public Stock, at least than one quarter of one percent Commission on the Specie value and that we will give preference to each other in our Negotiations.
> (Markham 1995: 134)

Dealing beneath a tree is a myth; the agreement is fact, and set a model of restrictive practice that was copied by exchanges in other centres and lasted for almost two centuries. The New York Stock Exchange (NYSE) would become 'one of the most powerful non-governmental bodies in the world' with the help of self-regulation through its 'miniature [internal] legal system' (Banner 1998: 114). This arrangement was not without its critics, one seeing the 'settled policy of the [New York Stock] Exchange to keep its affairs as secret as possible [as] an anomaly in law' (Emery 1896), but the cartel subsisted until 1975.

London's brokers created a Deed of Settlement in 1802 to similar effect as the Buttonwood Agreement. Their market developed largely without externally imposed regulation, until in 1986 the London Stock Exchange (LSE) was forced by threat of antitrust litigation to abandon the restrictive practices of fixed commissions and closed membership (Michie 1999: 543–53). These reforms, known as 'Big Bang', were thought politically essential if the exchange was to function efficiently in an integrated global financial system. The exchange could continue regulating its own activities, but other aspects of UK securities regulation and investor protection were for the first time assumed by the state. Big Bang was itself modest and a misnomer, but led to profound shifts in exchange and share trading behaviour.

While major Dutch, French and German exchanges operated under enabling legislation from the early nineteenth century, the first significant change to stock market management came in US reforms prompted by the 1929 Great Crash. The Securities Exchange Act of 1934 codified the rights, obligations and status of exchanges more comprehensively than in any civil jurisdiction, allowing US exchanges to retain their dealing monopolies and self-regulation, subject to registration with the newly created SEC, and in return for policing the securities markets on its behalf. The act was meant to forestall chaos and contagion:

> National emergencies, which produce widespread unemployment and the dislocation of trade, transportation, and industry, and which burden interstate commerce and adversely affect the general welfare, are precipitated, intensified, and prolonged by manipulation and sudden and unreasonable fluctuations of security prices and by excessive speculation on such exchanges and markets.
>
> (Securities Exchange Act of 1934, § 2)

It is easy to think of this complaint being heard in Congress in 2008–9 after several Wall Street firms received infusions of federal capital. We see the strong investor protection stance of the US as being path dependent, resulting from a cultural distrust of power in banking and the securities sector. It persists, notwithstanding a decline in the proportion of shares owned by retail investors who most need legislative support. A sizeable majority of US equities is now controlled by mutual funds and professional managers, whereas over 90 per cent were directly owned by individuals in the late 1950s (Markham 1995: 133). Federal securities regulation consumes resources that make the US a consistent outlier among OECD members in regulatory cost and intensity (Jackson & Roe 2009). Over time, the 1934 Act became influential in Australia, China, Japan and South Korea, and more recently in EU states including the UK, which maintained a looser principle-based regime until late 2007.

Stockholm's exchange began the trend of demutualization in 1993, followed in succeeding years by Helsinki, Copenhagen, Singapore (SGX), Sydney, Amsterdam and, in 2000, by Deutsche Börse, Hong Kong, LSE, Toronto and NASDAQ. Consolidation started consensually with the creation of Euronext in 2000–2 by the exchanges of Belgium, France, the Netherlands and Portugal,[5] since when NYSE and Euronext merged and LSE combined with Borsa Italiana. Other similar changes are noted in Table 9.4E. These agreements led to contested proposals, and more recently to regulators blocking several transactions as anti-competitive, as in 2012 with Deutsche Börse's proposed merger with NYSE Euronext, or for nationalistic reasons, as in that between SGX and the Australian Stock Exchange in 2011. Asia's few consolidations have involved exchanges of common domiciles such as Jakarta and Surabaya or Tokyo and Osaka, repeating patterns of consolidation among provincial exchanges that occurred from the 1960s in Europe and North America. Transnational changes of control among Asian exchanges are unlikely until competition from new trading platforms becomes as strong as elsewhere.

Operations and scale

Share dealing takes two forms, based either on market making or order matching. Market making was once common to traditional OECD exchanges that, as cartels, could cap for members the risks associated with quoting continual and actionable prices. Smaller and emerging exchanges are predominantly order-driven, including most in Asia, and market making for clients takes place off the exchange in the region's important centres. This means that brokers compete for orders from investors or others wishing to trade in shares, but that sales or purchases are executed only when the exchange or platform is able to match the appropriate volume of orders at an indicated price. Non-traditional electronic trading platforms and dark pools are order driven. Traditional exchanges may disclose outstanding unfulfilled orders to facilitate general price formation; dark pools and other ATPs do the converse, and withhold the scale of outstanding orders from participants. LSE, NYSE and other legacy exchanges now rely on limited market making, instead using electronic order matching for all shares that are heavily traded, and earning fees from users for the sale of order-book data.

Bargains made verbally or electronically on traditional exchanges are executed and reported instantly to the exchange CCP and settlement instructions given to a CSD. The reporting sequence can vary when trades are made through non-traditional platforms, although settlement is usually no different. In some cases the trade will be reported promptly to the listing exchange, but other platforms operate by *crossing* shares directly from seller to buyer with disclosure made only to the issuer's share registry.

Speed of settlement is both a function of technological resources and an objective of regulators to reduce systemic risk. Advanced exchanges operate or outsource to continuous real-time settlement systems, which usually means that equity trades settle one working day after the bargain is made, known as T+1. Settlement periods in Asia range from one to three days. Lengthy settlement periods of one or two weeks based on the physical delivery of share certificates also allowed unfunded short-term dealing and naked short selling within the account period but are now largely archaic. The same is increasingly true of the association of the exchange with a physical place. Most equity trading initiates between brokers' offices, even if transacted on exchanges that retain a central trading floor such as NYSE or the Stock Exchange of Hong Kong (SEHK). All such bargains are executed through the exchange and all contracts made with its CCP, allowing centralized settlement and collation of trading data. Settlement practice has been influenced by debt market innovations of the kind described in Section 8.1.

Tables 9.4A–9.4E illustrate the scale and listing characteristics of the leading 20 global equity markets and those others in Asia within our sample, excluding Vietnam, where activity is currently modest. They show the:

- Proceeds raised by new issues regionally and globally, including IPOs, *follow on* sales of ordinary shares and equity-linked transactions;
- Value of shares traded on the leading 20 exchanges and others in our sample;
- Average daily turnover on the leading 20 and other Asian exchanges;
- Average turnover velocity on the leading 20 and other Asian exchanges; and
- Total capitalization of companies listed on the largest global exchanges, arranged by region.

These data are provided to the World Federation of Exchanges by its 54 members, which are traditional exchanges. They exclude activity neither transacted on nor reported to those markets – for example, share trades that are privately crossed.

Table 9.4A Equity and equity-related new issues, 2009–10

	Proceeds 2010 (US$ bn)	No. of deals	Proceeds 2009 (US$ bn)	% Change in proceeds
All issues	854.1	4,439	872.7	−2.1
US & Canada	200.1	745	249.1	−19.4
Asia	306.6	1,836	165.7	+85.0
Australia	29.1	477	59.3	−5.05
EMEA	180.0	829	268.7	−33.0
Japan	58.3	107	64.3	−9.4
Latin America	51.6	66	30.5	69.2
Ordinary shares	765.8	4,156	777.3	−1.5
US & Canada	166.4	666	215.3	−22.7
Asia	290.0	1,771	155.1	+86.9
Australia	27.2	486	53.9	−49.5
EMEA	156.0	770	232.4	−32.9
Japan	53.6	94	60.2	−11.1
Latin America	50.9	65	29.2	+74.1
Global IPOs	269.4	1,149	113.9	+136.5
US & Canada	37.0	123	16.7	+121.4
Asia	157.7	760	70.3	+125.9
Australia	7.3	43	2.2	+232.2
EMEA	42.1	162	9.2	+359.3
Japan	11.6	22	0.6	+1,750.6
Latin America	8.1	20	13.4	−39.7
Global secondary issues*	496.3	3,007	663.4	−25.2
US & Canada	129.4	543	198.6	−34.9
Asia	131.2	1,011	84.9	+54.6
Australia	19.9	423	51.7	−61.4
EMEA	113.9	608	223.2	−49.0
Japan	42.0	72	59.6	−29.6
Latin America	42.9	45	15.9	+169.7
Global convertible issues	88.4	283	95.4	−7.3
US & Canada	34.5	79	33.8	+2.1
Asia	16.7	65	10.6	+57.6
Australia	1.9	11	5.1	−61.9
EMEA	24.0	59	36.3	−33.9
Japan	4.7	13	4.1	+16.7
Latin America	0.7	1	1.3	−43.6

* Secondary issues in this table are sales of shares in existing listed companies, not as defined in section 9.1.

Source: Thomson Reuters (2011).

Table 9.4B Value of shares traded, 2009–10

	2010 (US$ bn)	2009 (US$ bn)	Annual change (US$, %)	Annual change (local currency, %)
NYSE Euronext (US)	17,795.6	17,521.1	1.6	1.6
NASDAQ OMX	12,659.2	13,608.1	−7.0	−7.0
Shanghai SE	4,486.5	5,055.3	−11.3	−12.2
Tokyo SE Group	3,792.7	3,707.6	2.3	−4.8
Shenzhen SE	3,563.8	2,771.7	28.6	27.2
London SE Group	2,749.5	2,554.1	7.7	7.3
NYSE Euronext (Europe)	2,022.2	1,819.4	11.1	10.8
Deutsche Börse	1,632.1	1,426.4	14.4	14.
Korea Exchange	1,604.6	1,552.8	3.3	−5.6
Hong Kong Exchanges	1,496.2	1,416.4	5.6	5.9
TSX Group	1,366.3	1,239.9	10.2	0.4
BME Spanish Exchanges	1,360.8	1,181.1	15.2	14.9
Australian Securities Exchange	1,062.0	770.8	37.8	18.0
Taiwan SE	899.7	900.0	0.0	−4.7
BM&FBOVESPA	867.1	626.2	38.5	23.0
National Stock Exchange India	798.6	786.7	1.5	−4.2
SIX Swiss Exchange	790.2	709.7	11.3	2.5
NASDAQ OMX Nordic Exchange	749.5	656.5	14.2	13.8
Istanbul SE	410.6	301.1	36.4	32.5
MICEX	407.6	433.8	−6.0	−10.2
Singapore Exchange	288.4	245.4	17.5	9.9
Bombay SE	258.6	262.3	−1.4	−7.0
Thailand SE	211.7	123.1	72.0	58.8
Osaka Securities Exchange	179.7	170.5	5.4	−1.9
Bursa Malaysia	111.8	79.9	40.0	27.7
Indonesia SE	103.7	78.2	32.5	16.4
Philippine SE	21.6	13.9	56.2	47.3
All American exchanges	32,896.4	33,139.2	−0.7	NA
All EMEA exchanges	11,296.8	10,296.0	9.7	NA
All Asian exchanges	18,884.5	17,935.7	5.3	NA
All exchanges	63,077.8	61,370.9	2.8	NA

Total value of trading is the number of shares traded multiplied by their respective matching prices. A share sale and purchase is counted as one transaction. Exchanges in East and South Asia are shown in bold.
Source: WFE.

Table 9.4C Average daily turnover, 2009–10

	2010 (US$ bn)	2009 (US$ bn)	Annual change (%)
NYSE Euronext (US)	70,617.5	69,528.2	1.6
NASDAQ OMX	50,234.9	54,000.3	−7.0
Shanghai SE	18,539.2	20,718.6	−10.5
Tokyo SE	15,480.5	15,257.4	1.5
Shenzhen SE	14,726.4	11,359.6	29.6
London SE	10,782.5	10,095.1	6.8
NYSE Euronext (Europe)	7,838.0	7,107.0	10.3
Korea Exchange	6,392.6	6,137.4	4.2
Deutsche Börse	6,375.2	5,615.8	13.5
Hong Kong Exchanges	6,008.9	5,688.3	5.6
TSX Group	5,443.4	4,940.0	10.2
BME Spanish Exchanges	5,315.5	4,649.9	14.3

(*continued*)

Table 9.4C (Continued)

	2010 (US$ bn)	2009 (US$ bn)	Annual change (%)
Australian Securities Exchange	4,197.6	3,034.5	38.3
Taiwan SE	3,584.3	3,585.7	0.0
Sao Paulo SE	3,510.7	2,545.6	37.9
National Stock Exchange India	3,156.7	3,237.4	−2.5
SIX Swiss Exchange	3,110.8	2,827.6	10.0
NASDAQ OMX Nordic Exchange	2,939.2	2,584.5	13.7
MICEX	1,643.5	1,742.2	−5.7
Istanbul SE	1,642.4	1,194.9	37.5
Singapore Exchange	1,144.4	970.1	18.0
Bombay SE	1,022.0	1,079.5	−5.3
Thailand SE	874.7	506.4	72.7
Osaka Securities Exchange	733.5	701.5	4.6
Bursa Malaysia	450.9	319.5	41.1
Indonesia SE	423.2	324.7	30.3
Philippine SE	88.7	57.2	54.9

Average daily turnover is the annual value of share trading divided by the number of actual trading days. Exchanges in East and South Asia are shown emboldened.
Source: WFE.

Table 9.4D Average turnover velocity, 2009–10

	2010 (%)	2009 (%)
Shenzhen SE	344.3	445.5
NASDAQ OMX	340.4	492.3
Shanghai SE	178.5	228.8
Korea Exchange	176.3	241.6
Istanbul SE	150.6	178.7
Taiwan SE	135.3	177.1
NYSE Euronext (US)	130.2	158.7
Deutsche Börse	119.3	123.1
BME Spanish Exchanges	117.2	112.4
Tokyo SE Group	109.6	119.7
Thailand SE	94.5	87.6
Oslo Børs	94.1	114.1
Budapest SE	92.5	117.6
Australian Securities Exchange	82.3	81.2
NASDAQ OMX Nordic Exchange	79.7	99.4
NYSE Euronext (Europe)	76.5	83.9
London SE Group	76.1	91.1
TSX Group	74.1	95.4
Osaka Securities Exchange	71.2	98.5
Hong Kong Exchanges	62.2	79.0
National Stock Exchange India	57.3	87.8
Singapore Exchange	53.3	67.3
Indonesia SE	36.5	49.6
Bursa Malaysia	32.1	33.4
Philippine SE	19.2	19.7
Bombay SE	18.1	27.6

Turnover velocity is the annualized ratio of monthly turnover to end-month market capitalization. Foreign shares are excluded. Exchanges in East and South Asia are shown emboldened.
Source: WFE.

Table 9.4E Market capitalization by exchanges, US$ bn, year end 1990–2010

	1990	1995	2000	2005	2010
Total Americas	3,417.5	7,644.2	16,450.1	19,894.5	22,172.9
NYSE Euronext (US)	2,692.1	5,654.8	11,534.6	13,632.3	13,394.1
NASDAQ OMX	310.8	1,159.9	3,597.1	3,604.0	3,889.4
TSX Group	241.9	366.3	766.2	1,482.2	2,170.4
BM&FBOVESPA	11.2	147.6	226.2	474.6	1,545.6
Mexican Exchange	41.1	90.7	125.2	239.1	454.3
Santiago SE	13.6	72.9	60.4	136.5	341.8
Colombia SE	NA	NA	NA	50.5	208.5
Lima SE	0.8	10.9	9.7	24.1	103.3
Buenos Aires SE	3.6	37.8	45.8	47.6	63.9
Bermuda SE	NA	NA	2.2	2.1	1.5
American SE (1)	102.3	103.1	82.7	201.4	NA
Total Asia Pacific	3,456.5	5,121.3	4,918.5	10,018.1	19,303.4
Tokyo SE	2,928.5	3,545.3	3,157.2	4,572.9	3,827.8
Shanghai SE	NA	NA	NA	286.2	2,716.5
Hong Kong Exchanges	83.4	303.7	623.4	1,055.0	2,711.3
Bombay SE	NA	NA	NA	553.1	1,631.8
National SE India	NA	NA	NA	516.0	1,596.6
Australian SE	107.9	243.5	372.8	804.0	1,454.5
Shenzhen SE	NA	NA	NA	115.7	1,311.4
Korea Exchange (2)	110.3	182.0	148.4	718.0	1,091.9
Taiwan SE Corp.	98.9	187.2	247.6	476.0	818.5
Singapore Exchange (3)	34.3	151.0	155.1	257.3	647.2
Bursa Malaysia	47.9	213.8	113.2	180.5	408.7
Indonesia SE	8.1	66.5	26.8	81.4	360.4
Thailand SE	20.8	135.8	29.2	123.9	277.7
Osaka SE (4)	NA	NA	NA	192.0	271.8
Philippine SE	6.6	58.8	25.3	39.8	157.3
Colombo SE	0.9	2.0	1.1	5.7	19.9
New Zealand Exchange	8.8	31.9	18.5	40.6	NA
Total EMEA	2,019.4	4,358.1	9,598.9	13,183.7	15,345.8
London SE Group (4)	–	–	–	–	3,613.1
NYSE Euronext (Europe)	NA	906.5	2,271.7	2,706.8	2,930.1
Deutsche Börse	355.3	577.4	1,270.2	1,221.1	1,429.7
SIX Swiss Exchange	157.6	398.1	792.3	935.4	1,229.4
BME Spanish Exchanges	111.4	150.9	504.2	959.9	1,171.6
NASDAQ OMX Nordic Exchange (5)	NA	NA	NA	802.6	1,042.2
MICEX	NA	NA	NA	266.4	949.1
Johannesburg SE (6)	136.9	277.1	131.3	549.3	925.0
Saudi Stock Market Tadawul	NA	NA	NA	646.1	353.4
Istanbul SE	19.1	20.8	69.7	161.5	307.1
Oslo Børs	26.1	44.6	65.3	191.0	295.3
Tel Aviv SE	8.3	35.1	65.3	122.6	227.6
Warsaw SE	NA	4.6	31.4	93.6	190.2
Wiener Börse	26.3	32.5	29.9	126.3	126.0
Luxembourg SE	10.5	30.4	34.0	51.2	101.1
Tehran SE	NA	6.5	5.9	36.4	86.6
Egyptian Exchange	NA	NA	NA	79.5	84.3

(*continued*)

Table 9.4E (Continued)

	1990	1995	2000	2005	2010
Casablanca SE	NA	NA	10.9	27.2	69.2
Athens Exchange	15.3	16.5	107.5	145.1	67.6
Irish SE	NA	25.8	81.9	114.1	60.4
Amman SE	NA	NA	NA	37.6	30.9
Budapest SE	NA	NA	11.9	32.6	27.7
Ljubljana SE	NA	0.3	3.1	7.9	9.4
Mauritius SE	NA	NA	NA	2.3	7.8
Cyprus SE	NA	NA	NA	6.6	6.8
Malta SE	NA	0.4	2.0	4.1	4.3
Borsa Italiana (4)	148.8	209.5	768.4	798.1	–
London SE (4)	850.0	1,346.6	2,612.2	3,058.2	–
OMX Copenhagen SE (7)	39.1	57.7	107.7	–	–
OMX Helsinki SE (7)	22.7	44.1	293.6	–	–
OMX Stockholm SE (7)	92.0	172.6	328.3	–	–
Total	**8,893.3**	**17,123.6**	**30,967.5**	**43,096.3**	**56,822.1**

Market capitalization is the number of issued shares of domestic companies and foreign companies not listed elsewhere, multiplied by their respective end-period prices.

1. Capitalization calculation methodology changed when American SE data included in NYSE Euronext US after 2008 merger.
2. Includes KOSDAQ data following merger in 2005.
3. From 2004 includes foreign companies listed elsewhere if the majority of share trading occurs on SGX.
4. London SE and Borsa Italiana consolidated into London SE Group after 2008.
5. Copenhagen, Helsinki, Iceland, Riga, Stockholm, Tallinn and Vilnius exchanges.
6. JSE data include market capitalization of all listed companies from 2004.
7. Copenhagen, Helsinki and Stockholm exchanges became OMX in 2005.
Source: WFE.

The average trade size varies between exchanges with the extent of each market's free float and contribution from retail trading, It is also influenced by the composition of listings. Average trades in London and New York are historically greater by volume than on the incumbent exchanges of Germany, Hong Kong, Singapore or Toronto, for example, because they each list more large companies. Constituents of LSE's FTSE 100 share index must have at least 25 per cent of their shares tradable and at least 50 per cent of shares in listed foreign companies must be freely traded to be part of any LSE index, regardless of the company's size or prominence.

The trend since 2000 has been for average trade values to fall, especially on LSE, NYSE and NASDAQ, because an increasing number of professional investors that are responsible for large bargains no longer use the traditional exchange but prefer execution through dark pools and other ATPs. LSE's average share trade in 1999 exceeded US$100,000 but fell in 2009 to around US$11,000, and the NYSE's average dropped from US$52,000 to under US$7,000 in the same period (*Financial Times*; Dealogic). The average trade size among 15 large legacy exchanges fell from around US$28,000 in 1999 to around US$12,500 in 2009 (ibid). Alternative exchanges are a clear threat to the liquidity, efficiency and profitability of their traditional competitors.

The transformation of many incumbent exchanges since the 1990s to self-listed profit-seeking companies had consequences for internal regulation, external governance, rule enforcement, competition and consolidation, and created new conflicts of interest.

Profit-seeking companies that list their own shares have incentives to build revenue, which may jar with public policy goals or the regulation of other listed companies. In particular:

- The commercial exchange competes for new listings to generate revenue. In some cases this may have led to changes in the design or application of regulatory standards; and
- Changes in exchange ownership may concern regulators, especially if outside strategic shareholders are beyond their scrutiny or where a foreign interest is involved.

Laws of organized markets

Whether their institutional source is self-set rules or delegated authority from the state as in the US Securities Exchange Act, the market's rules or law must address:

- Contracting practice among members;
- Contracting practice between members and others, mainly issuers and those that buy or sell securities; and
- The commercial relationship of the exchange with non-members.

All activity is influenced by conventional commercial and contract law, but aspects of market practice also require internal rules for contractual effectiveness – for example, some contracts involving delayed settlement were unenforceable in Anglo-American common law until the mid-nineteenth century (Banner 1998), a variant of the problem with certain derivatives identified in Section 8.2:

> The origin and early growth of the New York Stock and Exchange Board ... can be attributed in large part to the brokers' success in formulating rules to govern the new securities market and to resolve disputes involving members. In particular, the brokers filled the regulatory vacuum created by the unenforceability in New York courts between 1792 and 1858 of a class of contracts common in the securities industry.
>
> (Banner 1998: 114)

Stock market rules thus provide examples of privately drawn informal institutions that relatively closed communities may prefer to the use of law in enforcement matters or dispute resolution (Bernstein 1992).

The laws affecting organized exchanges must cover the regulation of markets and participants in trading and settlement, issuer behaviour, reporting and compliance, day-to-day disputes and malpractice, as well as market abuse, manipulation and misconduct, and give the exchange rights of sanction for any breach. Trading on organized exchanges is more than a simple nexus of contracts made among users (Goode 1990), so exchange rules between members must be enforceable by the exchange, and extend into the enforceability of contracts made between members and outside users. This means that investors implicitly accept the rules of the exchange in their dealings with members. The scope of legal powers of the exchange effectively augments contracts made between users, so that contractual freedom is partly constrained, as an example of public policy infecting contract law for reasons of general stability or investor protection. English and New York case law tend to favour the exchange against complaints in this regard, and both have allowed the internal rules of exchanges to be enforceable vis-à-vis outsiders and in unusual instances to alter unilaterally the terms of exchange contracts so as to preserve orderly markets (Shearson Lehman Hutton v. Maclaine Watson & Co. 1989).

Exchange rules may also use delegated authority in sanctioning market abuse and misconduct. Market manipulation is taken to be any attempt to skew an organized market to the perpetrator's advantage, including squeezes, cornering, spreading false rumours or direct price fixing. If the law defines market manipulation, it tends to do so in terms of actions or consequences but not always intent. For example, Hong Kong's Securities and Futures Ordinance specifies six types of misconduct that may lead to legal or regulatory penalties (adapted from Cap. 571 s. 245):

- Insider dealing, when trades are made based on price-sensitive corporate information that is not generally known.
- False trading. Creating a misleading appearance of market activity – for example, by simultaneously buying and selling shares at identical prices.
- Price rigging. Real or fictitious trading intended to alter or disrupt prevailing prices.
- Disclosure of prohibited transactions, or using knowledge of misconduct to influence a market price.
- Disclosure of false or misleading information inducing transactions by a third party.
- Market manipulation, when two or more trades are made that are intended to alter how another trader buys or sells securities.

The subjective quality of these activities is clear, partly because regulators may hope to avoid giving the means of escape to a possible offender. It is unsurprising that advanced jurisdictions differ as to what constitutes misconduct and how severely it is treated, although IOSCO encourages its members to base their rules and enforcement policies on common principles. Some regulators favour detailed rules of permissible conduct and definitions of misconduct, in some cases responding to practices involving computer-driven trading. German law specifies ten non-exclusive examples of actions that may produce 'false or misleading [price] signals or artificial price levels' (BaFin 2008: § 3) and five additional forms of behaviour that constitute 'deceptive conduct' (ibid: § 4).

The permissibility of conduct alters over time with forms of electronic trading for example, or the creation of derivative instruments able to affect prices in formerly discrete markets. Manipulation by human intervention is more difficult to prevent in cash equity dealing than futures or commodity markets since the latter can set restrictive position limits, which are usually available to stock market regulators only in limited circumstances where increasing shareholdings may breach takeover rules.

The global financial crisis led regulators to question other established practices, including price stabilization for new issues, usage conflicts with sell- and buy-side research, and the effectiveness of regulations in demanding best practice from banks and brokers. MiFID and SEC Rule NMS (National Market System) have since 2006–7 required EU and US brokers to provide clients with best execution practice and pricing, including full disclosure of conditions such as prevailing prices, price discrepancies between market makers, and the volume of securities that are bid or offered at any time. These imperatives may protect or assist non-professional and retail investors but can prejudice conservative 'long only' fund managers wishing to transact in large blocks of shares, so increasing their incentives to use dark pools.

Not all these concerns are resolved by public policy. The EU prevented Deutsche Börse's merger with NYSE Euronext fearing it might leave the combined entity able to exploit dominant positions in European exchange-traded derivatives and clearing services. This represents accepted competition policy for many sectors, but exchange consolidation has efficiency advantages for users over fragmented markets when judged by the direct expense of dealing, by allowing some netting of collateral when assets held by exchanges as position margins are not correlated, and by reducing search costs for small investors. Competition in this example is threatened less by a product monopoly than because profit seeking has subjected exchanges to the market for corporate control.

Technological growth and the future of the exchange

Technological resources are both costly, and crucial to trade execution and settlement. This makes exchange management and post-trade resources important determinants of competition among stock markets. Technological growth has not only improved conventional dealing, information gathering and settlement efficiency, but introduced wholly new forms of share trading to which the traditional exchange was unsuited. It also exposes a misalignment between market activity and aspects of the law under which it takes place, especially in *algorithmic trading*, or programmed HFT involving fast large-scale dealing. Box 9.2 explains how these systems function.

Box 9.2.   Trading Algorithms and HFT

Algorithmic trading involves large-volume share dealing using programmed sequences. Some seek to exploit infinitesimal price anomalies that result from the operational architecture of the exchange and the way that it collects and processes orders and others through the program's own inception. HFT is a variant of one form of algorithmic trading and has its own distinct purposes. Algorithms in general may have traditional uses, for example allowing execution of large orders by long-only investors that formerly could acquire blocks of shares only in IPOs or placements. Our interest is less in the transformation in the exchange induced by algorithmic trading but to show how this implies behaviour increasingly separate from its institutional setting. Does HFT demand that we reconsider the nature of shareholdings and the rights associated with equity claims?

One helpful analysis identifies three classes of algorithms and two interactive derivatives (MacKenzie 2011):

- Execution algorithms divide orders to allow the execution of large trades at steady prices. They continually assess trading volumes and post orders that they judge can be borne by the exchange or ATP, assessments using methods that vary from one design to another.
- Market-making algorithms, of which HFT is one form. These are akin to conventional profit-seeking trading but conducted in high volume and at great speed.
- Statistical arbitrage algorithms, which in their simple form hope to capture price anomalies in single securities, and in more complex versions to exploit short-term correlations between unrelated assets.

The two derivative algorithms create and cancel orders by anticipating trades that might be made in certain conditions by their competitors, or do so in ways that induce orders by others, a tactic known as *spoofing* (ibid).

HFT accounts for around 70 per cent of US trading volumes and provides the bulk of liquidity on most OECD markets (Foresight 2011). The SEC characterizes HFT (SEC 2010b: 45) as:

- High-speed sophisticated programs for generating, routing and executing orders;
- Short timeframes between establishing and liquidating positions;
- Placing many thousands of orders that are frequently cancelled shortly after submission; and
- Few significant unhedged positions held for any material time and seldom overnight.

It also requires exchanges and ATPs to allow co-location and individual data feeds to users to lessen trading latencies that slow the order process beyond the algorithm's needs.

Critics associate electronic trading in securities with the sinister or destructive. One recent fictional algorithm is a dark character that uses unremitting predictive logic to threaten its creators with violence and ruin (Harris 2011), a Darwinian tactic reminiscent of *2001: A Space Odyssey*. Our analysis is not morally based and our view of HFT is as agnostic as the description of debt in Chapter 8, so the following points are not intended to be judgemental:

- The connection between HFT and intermediation is remote and indirect. Such trading at most adds liquidity to markets that in some cases can be of general value in price formation and to traditional users.
- No link exists between HFT and fundraising for capital investment.
- HFT is of no value to the great majority of long-only investors.
- To the extent that algorithmic trading purposefully creates and cancels orders or spoofs its competitors, it is indistinguishable from market manipulation and in certain jurisdictions will be defined as an example of misconduct, as Section 9.3 shows with Hong Kong practice.
- Co-location and specialized data feeds are lucrative for exchanges and allow users to game the less well-connected. This ironically recalls the ethic of exchanges as gentleman's clubs, when trading profits were closely linked to inside networks.

These factors show HFT to be as non-traditional a use of the exchange as covered warrants or synthetic ETFs. It has been encouraged by regulation, including MiFID and similar US rules that explicitly promote competition between exchanges (Ferrarini & Moloney 2011). The resulting fragmentation of activity leads not only to competition among all platforms but also to a lack of transparency, which would concern 'ordinary' exchange share traders if they still existed outside Asia as a significant class of user. HFT alters the balance of equity among market users.

It became especially controversial in May 2010's *flash crash*, when NYSE experienced violent price changes with no apparent external cause. Trading was halted, the only human intervention in this narrative (MacKenzie 2011). An investigation found that instability originated in one large and correctly intentioned sell order in stock index futures placed by a simple execution algorithm, to which other programs in the futures and cash markets responded (CFTC & SEC 2010). Shares of several large capitalization companies briefly lost almost all their value, and the narrow Dow Jones Industrial Average (DJIA) benchmark dropped by over 9 per cent in 20 minutes, its largest intra-day fall, although it recovered after trading resumed to end the day only 2.8 per cent lower.

The Flash Crash confirmed to critics that computer-driven trading is associated with instability, leads to unwarranted speculation that lacks value in general welfare terms (Section 7.7; Turner 2009b), and creates false markets in single shares. Systemic risks may result from deliberate or inadvertent interaction between algorithms and, although many instruments and trading systems can cause instability algorithms, may have second-order effects that cannot easily be gamed because of these interactions. Although there is no firm evidence that HFT has increased price volatility, regulators are increasingly of the view that instability is an inevitable result of this transformation of trading.

Human factors persist in influencing market behaviour, notwithstanding HFT's encroachment into legacy exchanges. Price formation and dealing activity on 15 exchanges during the 2010 World Cup soccer tournament were affected while matches were played, especially in the home market whose national team was taking part and at any time when goals were scored (Ehrmann & Jansen 2012). Activity was more normal during the half-time interval. The phenomenon has been observed in less unusual ways – for example, at the end of the trading day or week (Hirshleifer, Lim & Teoh 2009). It remains to be seen if Olympic or World Cup algorithms could profit from human preoccupations, or the results if an exchange abolished trading hours and processed orders '24/7'.

Speed of execution, or *latency*, is a valuable resource, particularly for market makers and other high-frequency traders wanting the exchange to allow rapid multiple order processing and execution. One result is a paradox of financial globalization. The speed at which packets of data travel via a fibre optic cable has an upper bound, so if all exchanges use equally efficient technology then trade times can be improved only by server co-location, where an exchange rents space to users within its own processing site and charges for the privilege of least distance (MacKenzie 2011). The migration of exchanges to clouds and cyberspace from the Greek *agora* or Jonathan's Coffee House may not therefore signal the predicted end of geography (*pace* O'Brien 1992; Cairncross 2001). Co-location is driven by user demand and expected returns for the exchange, and most technical advances are intended to allow the exchange to absorb and execute orders in high volume, and disseminate price information at great speed. HFT can seek to exploit price anomalies arising purely from the mechanics of price formation and deal execution.

Transactional arbitrage hopes to identify and exploit price discrepancies in and between markets, and is explored in Chapter 11 due to its importance to active investors and in the regulation of non-bank intermediaries. Arbitrageurs have also influenced exchange organization and behaviour, especially since 2000, by encouraging new ATPs specifically to facilitate advanced technology trading. Many legacy exchanges responded with shifts in trading rules and permissible membership, factors that have led to overt markets in securities regulation, by which exchanges compete to repel or attract dealing and listing activity and new investors. A further result is that computer-driven trading questions the traditional purposes of the exchanges, even if we have no concern as to how it may impact price formation and transparency, or whether it is compatible with investor protection and overall stability. These questions concern the equity of share ownership, and whether fractured markets provide fairly for all users.

Dark pools are electronic trading circles that typically conceal their substantial liquidity from some users and all non-users. Access is confined to professional counterparties wanting speed of execution, the ability to trade shares in large blocks with little or no price disruption, and anonymity at least until post-execution. A platform developed by Reuters called Instinet was an early example from the mid-1990s. It later became a Nomura Securities subsidiary and itself a shareholder in the prominent dark pool Chi-X, which as we write may be the world's largest. Most were founded after 2000 and especially when MiFID and Rule NMS began to favour exchanges oriented towards retail users, and with the growth of passive index-tracking investment funds and cash ETFs that of necessity deal in large volumes.

At least 50 dark pools were registered at the end of 2011 to operate in the US and more than 40 in Europe. Far fewer exist elsewhere because only the EU and US wholeheartedly encourage exchange competition. Asia-Pacific ATP activity is constrained except in Japan and since 2011 in Australia by monopolies granted to legacy exchanges, regulatory restrictions on off-exchange trading or insufficient liquidity. ATP rules for users were influenced by an IOSCO study of exchange evolution focused on how private platforms might function with adequate transparency (IOSCO 2006).

A later IOSCO report contains guidelines for national regulation of dark pools (IOSCO 2011), and shows the irony of ATPs operating in ways that so closely resemble the lapsed private practices of legacy exchanges. This would clearly be a regulatory concern were it not for competition between all forms of exchange, whether traditional, transnational or ATPs. Exchange diversification has been most profound to date in the US, and SEC data show share dealing on registered exchanges under Rule NMS to be distributed relatively evenly between NASDAQ, NYSE, their respective secondary exchanges, a large number of ATPs and more than 200 broker–dealers registered as market centres. These hubs compete for orders where, until recently, NYSE was a near monopoly.

Concern over the future of the organized exchange may represent fear of the unfamiliar. Between 50 and 70 per cent of US and EU market liquidity is supplied by algorithmic trading, and research has failed to show that the result is directly destabilizing in the sense of increasing price volatility (see Box 9.2 and Foresight 2011: 10–11), or is deleterious to the functionality of organized markets in terms of liquidity, price formation or the costs born by traditional price-taking exchange users (ibid: 30–6). This suggests two uncertainties, one practical and one of principle:

- It may be too soon to identify any malign effects of programmed trading or HFT given their brief history, even if we were certain of the background to a shock as prominent as that cited in Box 9.2 from May 2010.
- Is HFT beneficial to the economy at large if we exclude value accruing to participants, even if it has no malign impact on individual market segments?

Any concerns as to the direct results of electronic trading are separate to broader issues that are yet to be addressed by leading regulators. These are dilemmas that flow from four conflicting functions of exchanges:

- As national champions competing for listings and inward capital flows, partly through differences in regulatory intensity and fees;

- As public utilities for intermediation that give access for individual savers to securities dealing, whether directly or through professional fund managers;
- As competitive profit-seeking listed companies that, in other industry sectors, would be acquisition targets or aggressors, especially as prey to hostile commercial interests or as predators of other exchanges. This challenges a chauvinistic view of traditional legacy exchanges and may lead to differences between external shareholders and any national policy objectives; and
- As hosts for forms of conventional or computer-driven trading that are indifferent to traditional shareholder rights and the precepts of company law or commercial codes.

The fourth of these dilemmas is an unresolved problem of corporate governance and the alignment of law with prevailing practices. It may have material consequences if ownership of a company or minority interests are contested, and is important in jurisdictions where share borrowing is conducted through repos, involving the sale and subsequent repurchase of shares on terms agreed at the trade's inception.

Repo agreements can include terms requiring the initial purchaser to vote as directed by the initial seller in any ballot of shareholders occurring during the repo's life, on the basis that the latter is the long-term beneficial owner of shares. In other cases the outcome of a hostile acquisition may be influenced by short-term or chance holders or borrowers of shares.

Is it fair for those who borrow shares or are legal owners for less than a day to possess ownership rights identical in law to those of committed investors? If this is objectionable, for what period must ownership subsist to be considered fair and actionable? A rule change that altered the rights associated with legal ownership would be controversial, even if it simply slowed the process of share registration. The problem will become increasingly apparent as most advanced jurisdictions abolish physical share certificates, and company share registries record changes in ownership in real time, simultaneously or shortly after settlement.

9.4 Equity markets in Asia

No system of country ranking, credit rating or economic classification can always be correct or taken fully seriously. Sell-side analysts that rate shares as 'buy' or 'sell' are not instructing their clients, but ranking companies on a scale of expected value, albeit one that confuses observers. Ratings of all kinds are benchmarks for comparisons – points of reference to signify a shift or trend in creditworthiness or value, and to assist in portfolio decisions. Stock markets can similarly be classed as *emerging* while never gaining permanently in quality, capacity, value and composition or in sophistication of use. Think of 'emerging' as a stock rather than a flow, or a condition instead of a progression. Asia's share markets are greatly changed since the 1997–98 regional crisis when only Japan's was clearly developed, despite which their character differs from those in Europe or North America. We believe these differences will persist as the region's markets develop further, given that:

- Liquidity and price volatility remain generally at levels associated with emerging markets;
- Retail trading and specialist retail instruments account for a large share of aggregate turnover; and
- No functional connection exists between any Asian exchange and a market for corporate control.

Scale and orientation

The region's share markets are more prominent in both dealing and issuing activity than at any time since the post 1997–98 recovery, although Tables 9.4A and 9.4E show how the distribution of new listings is skewed towards Greater China, India and South Korea. This advance results from:

- Asia's economic performance and contribution to global growth in the last decade, and its relative credit standing since 2007–8;
- A shift in confidence among local and foreign portfolio managers, leading to a favourable reweighting of Asian risk;
- More non-Asian companies wishing to list in Singapore or, since 2007, in Hong Kong; and
- Portfolio inflows to equity markets in non-Japan Asia becoming less subject to flight risk than prior to 2000.

The combination of inward investment resulting from transnational portfolio diversification and increasingly numerous issues from China and elsewhere made the region the dominant global host to IPOs and other new issues for the first time in 2010, albeit when sentiment was poor in EU and US markets. Hong Kong accounted for the largest volume of all IPOs by sums raised in both 2010 and 2011, which was appreciably higher than London or New York, although the 2011 total fell by more than 40 per cent from the prior year. SEHK, SGX, Shanghai and Shenzhen all ranked among the ten leading exchanges associated with IPOs in 2011.

The success is qualified. New issue volume is a poor guide to subsequent share prices, even if IPOs are priced cheaply to encourage retail subscription. Listings in Hong Kong, Singapore, London and New York from recent years suggest that the proportion of a company's shares sold in an IPO has a material impact on post-issue price performance, regardless of the listing location, and that share prices are susceptible to underperformance when the amount floated is small, regardless of the company's prospects. This reflects two particular concerns:

- Poor liquidity lowers demand from conventional 'long only' fund managers; and
- An improving share price is vulnerable to future secondary sales that can be made with no loss of control by core shareholders.

Global investment banks were the most prolific arrangers of Asian IPOs, as Table 9.5 shows, but five firms based in the region were among the leading 20 in 2010, far more favourable a performance than in the bond and loan markets in the same period. We attribute the result to issuers nominating relationship banks as co-arrangers, and to prescriptive supervision in China and other issuer domiciles. The region has also produced technical innovations that later migrated to Europe and North America, especially pre-IPO *cornerstone investors* and convertible issues intended to bolster a subsequent issue price and retail support. Private pre-IPO equity dealing is insignificant elsewhere except on a small scale with US high-technology companies.

Five Asian exchanges were among the world's leading ten in 2009 and 2010 by the value of shares traded (Table 9.4B), and average daily turnover (Table 9.4C). Regional activity in 2010 measured by total value was 66.8 per cent greater than in EMEA markets and accounted

Table 9.5 Arrangers of equity and equity-related new issues, 2010

	Proceeds (US$ bn)	Market share %	No. of deals	Imputed gross fees (US$ bn)	Rank in 2009
1. Morgan Stanley	80.7	9.5	322	1.4	3
2. Goldman Sachs	66.4	7.8	240	1.2	2
3. JPMorgan	62.2	7.3	347	1.4	1
4. Bank of America Merrill Lynch	55.7	6.5	287	1.2	5
5. UBS	48.9	5.7	267	1.0	4
6. Crédit Suisse	42.4	5.0	261	0.9	6
7. Citigroup	40.4	4.7	231	0.8	8
8. Deutsche Bank	38.3	4.5	194	0.8	7
9. Nomura	25.7	3.0	78	0.7	9
10. Barclays Capital	25.6	3.0	135	0.6	12
11. China Int'l Capital	13.6	1.6	21	0.1	11
12. RBC Capital Mkts	10.0	1.2	88	0.3	17
13. CITIC	9.4	1.1	31	0.2	19
14. Well Fargo & Co.	8.2	1.0	103	0.3	24
15. HSBC	7.8	0.9	47	0.2	14
16. Bank of China	7.7	0.9	35	0.2	30
17. Macquarie Group	7.4	0.9	82	0.2	13
18. Santander	7.4	0.9	18	0.1	18
19. RBS	6.8	0.8	87	0.2	10
20. Mizuho Financial	6.5	0.8	15	0.4	60
Top 20 total	**570.9**	**67.1**	**NA**	**12.0**	**NA**
Grand total	**854.1**	**100.0**	**4,439**	**20.3**	**NA**

Number of deals is the transaction total of each bookrunner. Issues with more than one bookrunner are included in each bookrunner's totals. Equity-related deals include convertible bonds and warrants. Issues of ordinary shares accounted for approximately 90 per cent of total proceeds.
Source: Thomson Reuters (2011).

for 30 per cent of the global total. Other exchanges are smaller and idiosyncratic, with their user compositions and activity distinct from major markets, largely as a result of entrenched monopolies and the importance of retail trading. Many are illiquid in the sense of having small free share floats, high turnover velocity or catering to retail users.

These are all factors symbiotically linked with prevailing levels of liquidity and associated with information asymmetry, in particular the extent to which those that use the stock market have access to private or privileged price-sensitive information. Professional investors fearing that they are disadvantaged in this way, in any jurisdiction, are likely to withhold funds from its equity market, so that liquidity is inversely correlated with the quality of regulation and corporate governance. Liquidity is judged by several variables, including whether there is:

- Sufficient depth to facilitate trades of substantial size without a material effect on prevailing prices;
- Resilience to enable prices to recover quickly after a large trade; and
- A feasible speed of execution at the prevailing price.

Section 9.3 explained how trading algorithms divide orders to compensate for these factors and improve the probability of execution with minimal disturbance.

Liquidity may also be affected by the size of prevailing bid–offer spreads, especially if price formation relies on market making. Turnover velocity, or the value of turnover adjusted for market capitalization, is an imperfect but common proxy for prevailing liquidity, and varies appreciably among the 13 Asian exchanges appearing in Table 9.4D. It tends to increase when free floats are small, for example with China's exchanges where SOEs list a fraction of total equity, and in markets subject to significant day-trading by individuals.

A notable proportion of turnover for many exchanges derives from retail participants, especially in northeast Asia. It centres on listed equity options and covered warrants as well as shares with popular home-market name recognition such as China Mobile, Chunghwa Telecom, HSBC or Samsung Electronics. Regional turnover in covered warrants and similar instruments in 2011 was US$887 billion, or 77 per cent of the global total, compared to EMEA's US$262 billion and a trivial amount on American exchanges (source: World Federation of Exchanges, WFE). The Hong Kong and South Korea exchanges together accounted for 97.5 per cent of turnover in Asia. We know from Section 8.2 that most covered warrants are notes issued by banks that give the buyer synthetic exposure to defined risks, so that little or none of the issue proceeds of these retail instruments flows into the non-financial sector. This exemplifies the primary function of exchanges as a nexus for savings allocation rather than a source of funds for capital investment, even if that use is perceived as speculative.

The region's legacy exchanges can be categorized as:

- Large and globally accessed, in Hong Kong, Singapore and Tokyo–Osaka;
- Large with restricted access in Mumbai, Seoul, Shanghai and Shenzhen;
- Medium-scale in Bangkok, Kuala Lumpur and Taipei;
- Small-scale in Jakarta and Manila;
- Fledgling markets in Hanoi, Ho Chi Minh City, Phnom Penh and Vientiane, the last two opening in 2012 and 2011, respectively;
- The Bombay Stock Exchange, Bursa Malaysia, the National Stock Exchange of India, SEHK, SGX and Tokyo–Osaka are profit-seeking companies. Those in Hong Kong, Malaysia, Osaka and Singapore are self-listed. Tokyo and Osaka agreed in 2011 to merge, and Osaka will delist upon completion; and
- The exchanges in Bangkok, Manila, Shanghai, Shenzhen and Taipei are part of non-profit-seeking mutual associations.

Retail engagement in Asian stock markets is reinforced by the widespread financial repression or lack of choice in savings intermediaries. It may also reflect entrenched demand for gambling products, not necessarily for ethnographic reasons but because most economies in our sample restrict the permissible channels for gambling. Small capitalization companies and younger growth stocks have typically less appeal for retail investors, which helps explain the lack of success of alternative or *second markets* similar in purpose to NASDAQ in the US. All alternative exchanges in the region are underused and illiquid.

Market regulators and corporate owners share a strong control ethic and are cautious in allowing exchanges to function as freely as their European or North American counterparts. Dominant family or state company owners frequently list small fractions of total equity, resulting in restricted floats that tend to increase price volatility, especially when shares become subject to significant foreign interest. Jewellery retailer Chow Tai Fook is a typical example, its 2011 listing in Hong Kong raising approximately US$2 billion from the sale of only 10 per cent of total equity. Small floats in segmented national markets encourage not only price volatility but arbitrary constraints on trading.

The architecture of all organized markets is affected by the nature of their respective users. Asian exchanges thus rely on manual or electronic matching of orders with price formation, determined by actual bargains rather than market making. This has historically penalized professional investor activity, especially when coupled with practical or enforced limits on dealing size and permissible price movements, both of which are common. Inconsistent ease of entry and exit for overseas investors also dampens trading activity by those fearing unexpected or arbitrary rule changes. Malaysia's restrictions on the export of the proceeds of share sales were in effect for only 12 months from September 1998, but are a persistent source of caution for many foreign investors.

Regionalism and reforms

Intra-regional listings and portfolio flows are limited by home equity bias and because cross-border dealing is costly or obstructed by regulation, as Chapter 8 showed of regional bond market activity. Singapore and Tokyo have been relatively open to foreign listings for long periods, although almost all overseas companies have withdrawn from Tokyo in the last two decades. The Osaka and Tokyo exchanges proposed rule concessions in 1996 to attract foreign Asian listings, with implementation prevented by lack of issuer demand and indifference among local investors, albeit that risk aversion rose at the same time as the gathering 1997–98 regional crisis.

Table 9.2 shows that the only exchange other than SGX with a non-trivial number of foreign listings was Taiwan, but this represents offshore companies of Taiwanese beneficial ownership. Hong Kong traditionally restricted non-local listings to companies domiciled in China, Bermuda or the Cayman Islands, effectively barring listings without local or mainland beneficial ownership. Overseas listed China companies often issue shares through offshore vehicles for fiscal or regulatory reasons, while precautionary motives associated with the territory's change of sovereignty resulted in many Hong Kong companies incorporating in offshore centres. Hong Kong's regulators began designating new jurisdictions from which listing applications would be accepted in 2007, and by March 2012 had named 20, including three Canadian provinces and two US states.

National rivalry has made exchanges and regulators reluctant to encourage local cross-dealing in overseas shares. A 2009 ASEAN Capital Market Forum protocol envisages the transnational distribution of IPOs by allowing member states to operate common listing requirements and disclosure standards, leading to Malaysia, Singapore and Thailand agreeing to allow sales of qualifying new issues within each other's jurisdictions by late 2012. This would involve making an IPO tranche available specifically to buyers resident in the two other states. It is unclear how the participants will provide for subsequent share dealing.

Such reforms are far from mechanical. Opening selective transnational investor access to IPOs, as contemplated by ASEAN, represents a restricted form of cross-listing, where an issuer submits to foreign rules to obtain access to a discrete investor pool. The regulatory consequences would be profound if a scheme were to be effective and equitable among domestic and foreign shareholders. Even if new issues are distributed in several jurisdictions under common rules and a uniform prospectus model, the rights of post-IPO local and foreign shareholders are likely to differ in effectiveness, at least while exchanges are as separate and national markets as segmented as in the case of the relevant eight ASEAN states.

The concept of *substitute compliance* allows a simplified listing and supervisory process for a foreign issuer when its home regulatory regime is considered by the host state to be of an appropriate standard (Jackson 2007). EU *passporting* rules allow a new issue to be distributed in any member state of the internal European market if the issuer meets the disclosure and prospectus requirements of its home regulators (EU Prospectus Directive 2003).

A bilateral arrangement of mutual recognition of disclosure standards for new issues and substantive corporate transactions known as the Canada/US Multijurisdictional Disclosure System was established in 1991 but never extended as first intended to the EU or UK (Jenah 2007: 72). This allows a Canadian or US company to file disclosure documents in both markets in the form stipulated by its home jurisdiction. The SEC has also considered a less expansive arrangement to allow exemption from registration for non-US securities firms dealing in foreign securities with US clients if they operate at home under a regulatory and enforcement environment similar to the SEC's (Tafara & Peterson 2007), but any plans for its introduction appear to have been shelved, at least until the Dodd–Frank Act reforms are implemented or otherwise settled.[6]

Similar bilateral arrangements in Asia, or comprehensive regional liberalization of the kind suggested in Section 12.5, are more distant. Electronic bridges allowing Indonesian residents, for example, to deal in shares of companies listed in Malaysia through their local exchange are difficult to implement because of parochialism and differences in national practice, despite being technically feasible: SGX has similar links with several non-Asian exchanges. An alternative could be for national exchanges to permit dealings in a common form of depositary receipt, each representing beneficial ownership in a foreign share held by a custodian in the place of listing. American Depositary Receipts (ADRs) have long been used to give US investors simple local access to overseas shares, and global depositary receipts are integral to large-scale international IPOs. An Asian adaptation would paradoxically be most likely to succeed in Hong Kong or Singapore, where generally acceptable standards of disclosure and regulation suggest that it would be least needed.

9.5 Corporate governance

That equities represent collective ownership interests of equal standing is not to signify that shareholders face no enforcement or expropriation risks. A company free of any fraudulent practices that issues only one class of ordinary (common) shares may still become a locus of disagreement between owners and managers that is detrimental to its value, and which neither the equity claim nor the company's constitution can resolve. Corporate governance is a modern term for such perennial concerns. Marx wrote that the formation of joint stock companies involved:

> Transformation of the actual functioning capitalist into a mere manager, in charge of other people's capital, and of the capital owner into a mere owner, a mere money capitalist.
>
> (Marx 1894: 567)

'Mere' is ambiguous in translation. Marx's scorn was reserved for other matters and his aim was to highlight the results of the functional specialization introduced by incorporation. Adam Smith wrote earlier of risks associated with separating ownership and control, anticipating today's principal concern:

> The directors of [joint stock] companies, ... being the managers rather of other people's money than of their own, it cannot well be expected that they should watch over it with the same anxious vigilance with which the partners in a private copartnery frequently watch over their own.... Negligence and profusion, therefore must always prevail ... in the management of such companies.
>
> (Smith 1776: 330)

In the modern era 'negligence and profusion' caused by misaligned interests among owners and managers led the SEC to issue, in the mid-1970s, an informal code of conduct intended to improve accountability among listed US companies. Corporate governance then began to receive increasingly formal attention in the US, Europe and Australia from the 1980s, partly since so many companies failed to adopt best practices voluntarily.

A German governance scholar observes that it was known neither as a term nor a concept in France or Germany before the mid-1990s (Hopt 2007: 81), which is often attributed to a perception that equitable standards of governance and corporate ethics are either intrinsic to the Rheinish stakeholder system and its Japanese equivalent, or that conflicts are inherent in the Anglo-American model (Dore 2000). German practice was disturbed in the late 1990s by an infusion of Anglo-American takeover practice and a market for corporate control initiated by the hostile and totemic acquisition of Mannesmann in 2000, leaving scholars less able to assert where better governance could be expected.

Interest in governance solutions prompted the OECD to create a voluntary code of practice for listed companies in 1999, which has influenced regulations and listing rules in many jurisdictions including non-OECD members (OECD 2004), and can be seen as a successful example of transnational law. The ADB issued a similar set of ten principles in 2003, written jointly with a UK pension fund manager. It lacks any material specific to the region, but states that failures in corporate governance were important causal factors in the 1997–98 crisis (ADB & Hermes 2003: 1).

The assertion is common because the principles contained in codes such as these tend to draw on a substantially uniform assessment associated with globalization, or 'one-way thinking' (Ramonet 1995: 1), while national governance rules and sanctions are highly varied. Many prominent US and European investors also publish detailed governance expectations, notably the California Public Employees Retirement System (CalPERS), which is a sizeable pension fund and has considerable sway with investee companies.

Legislation or changes to listing rules in the US and elsewhere have usually followed egregious abuses of managerial power, notably the 2001–2 collapses of Enron and WorldCom, both involving complex expropriations from shareholders and company pension schemes. The result has been a ratcheting of rules on disclosure and managerial accountability, just as the shock of BCCI or Herstatt prompted reforms in financial regulation. Corporate governance developed in all these respects into a universal concern of markets, managers and the law.

Concepts

Corporate governance is most simply 'the system by which companies are directed and controlled' (Cadbury Committee 1992: s. 2.5). The underlying concept of governance is more subtle, as the word's Greek origin suggests. *Kubernetes* is a ship's helmsman, but also refers to the play between how the vessel is steered and the Newtonian response of the sea.

Effective corporate governance is to anticipate the second-order consequences of managerial inputs as well as their immediate effects. Encouraging or requiring for effective governance is to help protect ownership or stakeholder interests without incentivizing rule avoidance or deterring management from engaging with commercial risk – a result that critics suggest is not achieved by demanding legislation such as the post-Enron Sarbanes–Oxley Act of 2002. CalPERS regards corporate governance as the relationship of 'shareowners', management and directors in determining the direction and performance of companies (CalPERS 2009), with the choice of shareowner suggesting an inclination towards active investor engagement.

The contemporary sense of corporate governance refers to both internal and external issues. The latter includes social factors and corporate citizenship. Our focus is narrower, even though aspects of external governance can affect share prices, trading multiples and company valuations.

- *Internal governance* is primarily concerned with the agency conflict identified in the finance literature (Berle and Means 1932; Jensen & Meckling 1976). It arises where ownership is diversified and also in Asia's more limiting circumstances due to the propensity of managing owners to list only small proportions of total equity.
- *External governance* deals with the company's relationships with employees, customers and other stakeholders, as well as societal objectives and environmental concerns.

Those broader concepts were formerly aspirational for Anglo-American corporate law but expressly part of corporate duties in German and Japanese practice. Germany's system of company law is demanding in this respect, its *co-determination model* requiring managers to serve the interests of both shareholders and employees, and employee councils to be represented at supervisory board level in all companies above a certain size. The two-tier board framework of large German companies seeks to isolate agency concerns, with a managing board given a wholly executive function and a supervisory board responsible to all stakeholders. Labour is participatory rather than a pure economic resource in opposition to management or owners (Dore 2000). Two-tier boards exist also in Brazil, China, Denmark, Indonesia, Japan, the Netherlands, Russia and Switzerland, although some jurisdictions give limited powers to supervisory boards.

Legislation in Australia and the UK now requires corporate duties to recognize the interests of non-traditional stakeholders, suggesting some convergence between advanced civil and common law jurisdictions, although the provisions are less prescriptive than in Germany's model. This widening of obligations suggests that standards of external governance are increasingly price sensitive. Many fund managers avoid the reputational risk of investing in poor or politically insensitive corporate citizens, an approach formerly confined to explicitly ethical investors, and companies thought to practise poor governance in these respects can often be valued at discounts relative to their peers.

Finance theory regards company managers as agents of shareholders, an arrangement that creates potential behavioural and performance-related conflicts if we assume that the interests of each group are not naturally aligned. Legal treatment of the matter varies, and the results differ between national financial systems. Commercial and state-sector banks in the Rheinish model introduced in Section 2.2 have historically held sizeable ownership interests in large corporate clients and may be represented on their boards of directors, assuming a part supervisory, part fiduciary function and giving an informed position from which to advise and monitor managers. Advocates argue that the system lessens conventional agency problems and may be constructive during periods of corporate stress, as when an influential creditor encourages others to refrain from precipitant action. It also compensates for thin corporate securities markets that have limited impact on governance (Prigge 1998: 1020).

Critics suggest that the comprehensiveness of this relationship makes the German–Japanese model inherently conflicted – for example, where a bank is both a fiduciary and a conventional commercial shareholder, has privileged information unavailable to other investors, creditors or competitors, and transacts with third parties in loans or securities involving the company's credit risk. The results of governance associated with German banks holding permanent equity positions in client companies have been found empirically inconclusive in

German studies (Mülbert 1998: 484–9), although some US research suggests German cor-porate performance is positively associated with concentrated ownership, in particular where control rests with a bank (Gorton & Schmid 2000). Commercial pressures and the adoption of international accounting standards made the leading private sector banks reduce their discretionary shareholdings after the mid-1990s (Mülbert 1998). Some had been sizeable – for example, as at September 1996 Deutsche Bank owned 24.4 per cent of Daimler-Benz, and the former Dresdner Bank held 25.1 per cent of Bilfinger Berger and 5.0 per cent of Bayerische Motorenwerke (ibid). Germany's concentrated corporate ownership would be familiar to observers of China, Japan or South Korea.

Modern governance scholarship amplifies the traditional agency question and identifies additional conflicts. Berle and Means were concerned with companies owned by many thou-sands of individuals, few of whom would be equipped to monitor management. A shift to narrower ownership has since occurred in the advanced Anglo-American model economies, with many individual shareholders replaced by organized fund managers, creating a second governance problem. Large investors have the advantage of rights of audience with manage-ment but are themselves subject to agency conflicts, while some passive index-tracking funds are unwilling to exercise rights of ownership and are constrained from selling shares in an index constituent.[7]

The most commonly identified practical problem arising from the agency issue in listed non-financial companies is how best to hinder expropriation of minority shareholders (La Porta, Lopez-de-Silanes, Shleifer & Vishny 1998). This may occur insidiously through excessive compensation, transfer pricing or opaque credit support with related companies, or strategically through asset disposals or dilutive share issues. *Tunnelling* refers to any extrac-tion of resources by controlling interests (Johnson, La Porta, Lopez-de-Silanes & Shleifer 2000), and is prevalent in states where standards of governance or enforcement are poor. A common form of anti-expropriation law gives pre-emption rights to shareholders to limit the amount of shares that a company may place with chosen buyers without first making an offer as a rights issue to shareholders at large. These rules vary considerably between jurisdictions and can deal only with transactions facilitated by share issues.

Rules and mechanics

The complexity of these concepts makes governance mechanisms intricate, difficult to implement and varied in their application and effectiveness, whether statutory, voluntary or market based, as the examples in this section show. Our discussion involves bodies and functions that vary according to national practice and often overlap:

- *Directors*, who together make up the company's *board*, whose function is to appoint *managers* and scrutinize their performance. Some jurisdictions stipulate or allow sepa-rately composed two-tier boards, one to supervise and the second to manage.
- Some directors may be managers. Others are *non-executive* appointments, who are compensated but not employed by the company.
- Some non-executive directors are *independent* in that they have no formal or former ties to the company or any controlling shareholder.
- The *chief executive* (CEO) is a director and the leading manager, and is given the board's authority to administer the company from day-to-day.
- The *chair* of the board or *chairman*, who may be independent or a senior manager shar-ing executive functions with the CEO.

Any generic taxonomy is indifferent as to how managers and directors differ functionally from one company to another or between jurisdictions, and how assertive individuals may influence the behaviour of others for their own benefit. Non-executive board members may refrain from or be unable to question an insistent chief executive, and shareholders cede management to controlling owners or professional appointees for entirely practical reasons. This delegation may effectively extend to more strategic matters, contrary to the precepts of governance, given that even major shareholders typically lack the resources or willingness to scrutinize management decisions and prefer not to vote publicly against incumbent management in general shareholder meetings. There exists some justification for management autonomy in that commercial confidentiality may constrain a company from disclosing details of potential price-sensitive transactions, although a leading shareholder may be *brought inside*, given notice of the proposal and subjected to a confidentiality and 'no action' undertaking.

Collective action by shareholders is demanding to initiate and execute, and to succeed requires a purpose that is warranted and specific. Many shareholders are unwilling to challenge assertive managers even when a proposal is so transformational as to be subject to a mandatory ballot. Regulators found that the Royal Bank of Scotland (RBS) conducted such 'very limited due diligence' (FSA 2011: 160) when leading a contested bid for Dutch bank ABN Amro in 2007 that the deal could 'reasonably be criticised as a gamble' (ibid). Some of RBS's largest shareholders expressed 'common concerns' to management (ibid: 166); none later voted against the acquisition.[8] Assertive managers deterred any challenge to the transaction by either non-executive directors or shareholders, even though deteriorating conditions forced RBS to consider invoking material adverse change provisions in its offer to ABN Amro prior to the shareholder ballot (ibid: 422).

RBS's ensuing collapse ironically contributed to the rare example of conspicuous activism cited in Box 10.1. Shareholders in the UK insurer Prudential refused 18 months later to support its agreed acquisition of AIA, an outcome that with hindsight was commercially questionable. Box 9.3 cites the example of Apple, a company that has regularly breached several principles of governance, despite which its capitalization became the world's largest in early 2012. Major shareholders such as CalPERS may have a voice with managers but exert the positive control associated with ownership only when successfully initiating collective action, which tends to occur more seldom than changes in managerial control through acquisition or shareholder disinvestment. US financial sector investors that are sufficiently resourced and informed to monitor and influence assertive managers have been said to be disinclined to do so because of political pressures and a cultural aversion to financial sector power (Roe 1994), but the explanation seems to lack more general application (Cheffins 2008: 45).

Mechanisms of five types are commonly suggested to promote improved governance, either singly or together (Becht, Bolton & Roell 2003: 18). They represent incentives to encourage responsible behaviour by managers or controlling owners and compensate for shareholders failing to act collectively. They also have important second-order effects, as with the ship's helm:

- The open election of a board of directors to which senior management is accountable. Some jurisdictions require the board to include members who are independent of management or controlling owners, and given authority in board subcommittees to scrutinize auditing, compensation, board nominations and changes to governance practice. Terms limits for independent directors help prevent their capture by management with the loss of credible authority.

Box 9.3.   Other People's Money: Apple's Agency Issue

Apple's success in revenue generation helped make it the world's largest listed company measured by market capitalization, which exceeded US$500 billion in March 2012. Largest may not mean most valuable. Apple's share price has long traded at lower multiples of projected earnings than other companies in its sector or the technology sector as a whole. One explanation is investor reticence. The cash price of the shares is high, revenue growth may be unsustainable, Apple has rarely paid dividends, and consumer electronic sales are volatile even for a virtuoso of design and marketing. Another explanation is that Apple's governance standards are recognizably poor.

The company's share price as at end-January 2012 was 33.1 per cent and 423.9 per cent respectively higher than one and five years earlier. This performance was far superior to an index of US electronic share prices and easily better than the broad market S&P500 index of leading US-listed companies, which was 1.3 per cent higher than 12 months earlier and 7.4 per cent lower than its end-January 2007 level. Apple neither paid dividends nor undertook a share buyback over that five-year period, but did issue substantial share options as incentives to management.

Apple's 1Q FY2012 per-share cashflow and net income were high compared to its peers, but the group's hoarding produced a consolidate cash balance at the end of the period of US$97.6 billion, larger than the current account surpluses of Norway and Russia and almost certainly far in excess of the company's needs in prudent operations, in planned capital spending or to provide backup for its forward commitments to suppliers.

Apple's cashflow from operations in FY2011 was US$37.5 billion, including net income of US$25.9 billion. Full-year capital expenditure was US$7.4 billion, total assets increased to US$138.7 billion, and retained earnings to US$75.7 billion. Apple's cash hoard may not have been fully usable, but the entire amount generated poor returns and was arguably a hostage from the company's owners. This is not malfeasance, but it indicates weaknesses in governance given that Apple's business is neither that of a bank nor a fund manager, and its overhang of cash helps maintain its share price discount.

Apple's founder Steve Jobs ran a conservative financial policy that allowed the company to feel itself free of finance, and function in a crisis without fear. The end-2011 accumulated cash seems to be a response to the global financial crisis, to the risks of having little or no access to external funding, or a precaution against a world whose financial system is sclerotic and cannot fund new spending. Apple's perversity in the face of finance theory is prudence taken to an extreme degree.

Jobs may have been able to ignore complaints over poor governance. His successor chose to respond soon after the release of 1QFY2012 results:

- Agreeing to endorse one of several proposals made by CalPERS to Apple shareholders to introduce majority voting standards in elections for board members (Apple 2012: 49–52);

- Committing Apple to sizeable distributions through dividends and share buy-backs; and
- Undertaking closer management scrutiny of ethics in the company's supply chain.

Agency concerns are common among closely managed technology companies and it may not be in Apple's nature to change practice as much as CalPERS hopes. The cash mountain is arguably a defence against those who own the company's shares.

- An effective market for corporate control, enabling shareholders or potential acquirers to depose poorly performing incumbent management or force changes in business strategy, without necessarily leading to change in ownership. These are common practices in the US where shareholders are accustomed to *proxy battles* involving an activist shareholder enlisting support from others and voting on their behalf in a ballot.
- The traditional arrangement in the German model where a leading non-controlling shareholder assumes a fiduciary position of monitoring management on behalf of all shareholders with no formal appointment.
- Defined fiduciary duties for management, thus increasing the effectiveness of class actions or other litigation to prevent decisions contrary to investor interests, or seek compensation for deleterious actions. This type of remedy is available in few jurisdictions outside the US.
- Aligning the interests of managers with shareholders through performance-based compensation.

Measures of director independence include whether a CEO also chairs a company's board, and the number of independent directors as a share of the total.

Studies of US practice support the value of the first and second mechanisms. Independent directors can influence the behaviour of managers and help ensure that the company is run in the interests of shareholders at large (Hermalin & Weisbach 2003). CEO chairmen are widespread in US listed companies, but many leading investors now advocate separating the two functions. This would follow an earlier change to UK practice proposed by the semi-official Cadbury Committee on governance in 1992 and adopted as a non-mandatory element of UK listing rules. Cadbury's ethic is 'comply or explain', a market compliance mechanism to encourage companies to follow its principles or explain publicly why they choose to do otherwise, allowing investors to revalue any transgressor.

Cadbury also recommended that boards be chaired by independent directors, so preventing a CEO from acceding to the chair. A board dominated by management is likely to be ineffective in monitoring its own performance, while independent boards will be less tolerant of underperforming CEOs (Weisbach 1988), and less inclined to approve internal candidates as CEOs (Borokhovich, Parrino & Trapani 1996; Huson, Parrino & Starks 2001). Companies with relatively independent boards appear to make more favourable acquisitions if the immediate share price reaction to an announcement is a reliable guide (Byrd & Hickman 1992), and bargain more intensively when the company is subject to a takeover bid (Cotter, Shivdasani & Zenner 1997). Evidence from Chinese companies also indicates that valuations are negatively affected when one director is both chairman and CEO, further signifying how board independence helps enhance corporate performance (Bai, Liu, Lu, Song & Zhang 2004).

Developed markets for corporate control have come to be associated with efficient resource allocation because changes in ownership allow potentially able managers to depose the ineffectual or corrupt. An early idealized case for limiting anti-monopoly restrictions on takeovers or mergers goes further, asserting that these markets provide more effective shareholder protection against agency problems than the legal or regulatory system (Manne 1965: 113).

Contested takeovers occur more frequently in the US and UK than in Germany, France or throughout Asia, implying a persistent market orientation and fewer constraints on externally induced changes in corporate control. Mannesmann's acquisition may have been an Anglo-American shock for German practice (Beck 2000; Homann, Koslowski & Luetge 2007), but nonetheless left the consensual model of governance largely unaltered. Most EU M&A deals in the succeeding decade have been consensual and with no cross-border involvement (Buelens 2008). More generally, while most takeovers increase the realized value of the target the results for acquirers are usually negligible or negative when assessed by overall value-added in the combined concern. Why bidders persist with unrewarding hostile takeovers is partly metrical:

- Hostile bids usually involve a *takeover premium*, meaning that control of the target is more costly than the market's valuation prior to a bid becoming known. Accounting practice generally requires that goodwill arising in a combined entity as a result of the premium be written off over a period, which erodes income and EVA.
- Hostile bids may be made for defensive or opportunistic commercial reasons that are strategically sound but inherently difficult to value.

Takeover premiums can also indicate expectations of operational improvements (Shleifer & Vishny 1997) – for example, to reduce combined costs through economies of scale. This was largely RBS's proposition to shareholders based on its acquisitions prior to bidding for ABN Amro. A further market-related mechanism is that publicity can detect and discourage violations of good governance (Dyck, Morse & Zingales 2010; Dyck, Volchlova & Zingales 2008) although a state-controlled media may be less effective in these respects (Djankov, McLiesh, Nenova & Shleifer 2003).

The final mechanism in our list of five can be troublesome. Performance incentives intentionally affect management behaviour (Jensen & Murphy 1990; Murphy 1999), yet in some cases lead to outcomes that are deleterious to the enterprise or its shareholders. Consider a more detailed definition of governance, as those institutional and market mechanisms that induce self-interested managers and any controlling shareholders to make decisions that maximize the value of the company to its owners (Denis and McConnell 2003; Jensen & Meckling 1976). This sensible ethic ignores subjectivities inherent in measuring performance, whether through the company's share price, return on equity or EVA, in the period chosen for assessment, in the independence of board remuneration scrutiny, or in the documenting of incentives.

Since the 1990s, many OECD banks have based management incentives on target returns on equity (ROE) as a proxy for capital-adjusted returns on assets, which are more difficult to measure and attribute between business units. The choice of target encourages greater leverage and distorts both commercial and risk outcomes (Haldane 2011c). Aligning the interests

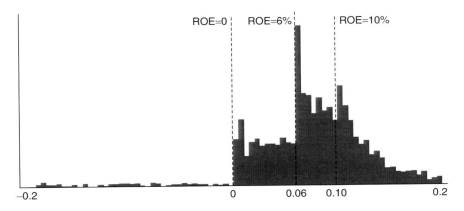

Figure 9.1 Distribution of ROE for listed Chinese companies, 1999–2005.
Source: Liu & Lu (2007).

of owners and managers through equity-linked compensation is an incomplete governance solution when managers can manipulate financial strategy to meet short-term targets for earnings per share or share prices – for example, with high leverage, by borrowing to fund share buybacks, or through delaying fixed asset formation crucial to the company's long-term prospects.

China's administrative approach to governance leads regulators to rely on published accounting data to monitor listed companies, and results in managers gaming detailed supervision rules (Liu 2006). For example, CSRC will approve a rights issue only if the issuer's ROE in three consecutive years is no less than 6 per cent and averages 10 per cent or more over the full period. A separate rule makes delisting mandatory if a company reports three consecutive years of net losses. Figure 9.1 shows how reported returns were distributed in a six-year period, with a disproportionate number of companies producing annual results marginally greater than 0, 6 or and 10 per cent (Liu & Lu 2007). Spikes in the histogram suggest that managers respond to the details of supervisory hurdles.

Governance in Asia

Governance practice is usually taken to be market- or control-based, drawing on the varieties of capitalism described in the literature's distinction between liberal market and coordinated economies (see Section 2.2; Hall & Soskice 2001). Market governance refers to a model in which the mechanisms used to mitigate agency problems are characterized by dispersed ownership, independent boards, effective disclosure, and externally by an active market for corporate control through mergers or takeovers, sophisticated investors and effective regulations to protect minority shareholders from expropriation. The model is exemplified by the CalPERS principles of 'accountable governance' described in Box 9.4.

Asian companies tend to employ control models of governance. Family or state interests use command mechanisms to deal either with agency concerns or more narrowly to pursue their own objectives. The model is characterized by concentrated ownership, boards selected from management or composed of directors who defer to managers, relatively incomplete

Box 9.4.   Principles of Accountable Governance

California's state pension scheme defines accountable corporate governance as the set of mechanisms that produce the most favourable long-term returns to shareowners, and are contained in the following principles:

- Governance practices should focus the board's attention on optimizing operating performance and returns to shareowners;
- Directors should be accountable to shareowners and management to directors. Directors must respond to shareowner enquiries on the decisions they make that affect the company's strategic direction;
- Corporate information must be readily transparent to permit accurate comparisons, and include disclosure and transparency based on globally accepted minimum accounting standards;
- Investors must be treated equitably and on the principle of one vote per share;
- Proxy materials should be prepared to provide shareowners with information needed to make informed decisions, and be distributed so as to encourage share-owner participation. Votes cast in person and by proxy should be formally counted and the outcomes of ballots formally announced;
- Every stock exchange should adopt a code of best practice, and listed companies should disclose to shareowners whether they are code compliant; and
- Directors and management should have a long-term strategic vision, the core of which emphasizes sustained shareowner value. Shareowners should encourage management to resist short-term behaviour by supporting and rewarding superior long-term returns, regardless of their investment strategies.

disclosure, and externally by inactive markets for corporate control, comparatively unsophisticated or pliable investors, little scope given to relationship banks or corporate financiers to counsel on governance matters, and weak enforcement of protection for minority interests. Although corporate governance has improved in several respects since 1997–98, we shall see that it remains often poor and consistently more variable than elsewhere, even in the developed economies of Japan, Hong Kong or Singapore. Survey evidence suggests that the culture and understanding of governance is most at fault (CLSA 2010).

Despite contrasts in the control and market models there is no unequivocal evidence as to which performs better in meeting governance or EVA objectives. Survey material in 2010 identified 40 Asian companies from a sample of 580 that practised high standards of governance, concentrated among highly capitalized, internationally oriented organizations in Japan, and to lesser extents in Singapore and Hong Kong (ibid: 28). Overall national rankings throughout the region are well below levels judged as 'world class' (ibid: 7) as we see in Table 9.7A, although this is an arbitrary benchmark.

The control model may have advantages in economies with repressed or undeveloped financial intermediation, when concentrated ownership enables a dominant shareholder to arrange substitute funding – for example, through cheap credit or cross-subsidies from related companies. Evidence of such arrangements contributing to EVA exists in India (Khanna & Palepu 2000) and Japan (Hoshi, Kashyap & Scharfstein 1991), and is resonant of the *chaebol* and *keiretsu* models cited in Section 2.2. Boards dominated by management can be nimble in responding to exogenous shocks, while incomplete financial disclosure may protect a company against capricious or threatening actions by government. Weaknesses are inherent in the control model however, and make it relatively ineffective in disciplining management or dominant shareholders, and in coping with succession planning. Above all, the model is susceptible to tunnelling and self dealing by controlling shareholders.

The quality of governance influences corporate behaviour and share price performance, both directly through the company's results and indirectly because good governance is rewarded by investors being willing to pay price premiums. Empirical support for these propositions can be seen in Figure 9.2, each section of which shows a metric of performance ranking according to S&P governance scores of a sample of 216 listed Asian companies. In each case the higher and lower thirds respectively represent the best and worst governed companies.

Complex and contrasting results appear in data from China and the US as to how ownership concentration and the value of listed companies are related. One analysis of Chinese companies (Bai, Liu, Lu, Song & Zhang 2004) found that:

- Concentrated ownership among large but not dominant shareholders is positive for valuations. This suggests that significant shareholders in this position are better disposed and able to monitor the largest shareholder and discourage tunnelling.
- Issuing shares to foreign investors helps improve valuations, by allowing monitoring by relatively demanding and sophisticated investors and because cross-border listings often entail high standards of transparency.
- Combining the CEO and chair positions harms valuations, indicating that an independent board generally enhances the company's performance.
- Valuations are lower when the dominant shareholder is the state.

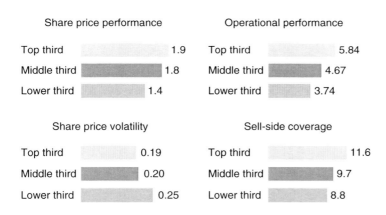

Figure 9.2 Corporate governance and performance.

Share price performance is measured by the market to book ratio, or the ratio of the sum of equity market capitalization and the balance sheet value of debt to total assets; operational performance by return on capital employed (ROCE); share price volatility as the ratio of the standard deviation of share price returns to average market returns; and coverage by the number of sell-side analysts issuing research on each company as a proxy for non-connected investor interest.

Sources: Authors' calculations. S&P governance scores 2001 (on file with authors).

Research using 1980 US data found a three-phase non-monotonic relationship between ownership concentration and company valuations. As concentration increases so the valuation first rises, then declines, and finally rises slightly for a second time, making an inverted-U shape (Morck, Shleifer and Vishny 1988). Changing incentives help explain these discontinuities:

- Increasing concentration from a low level has a positive impact on governance and valuations by dealing directly with agency issues. It lessens the free-rider monitoring problem arising from dispersed ownership, where no single shareholder has sufficient incentive to devote resources to scrutinize management. Investors with large stakes in a company are more likely to monitor a dominant shareholder and discourage tunnelling, as intended in the German governance model, so a concentration of shares among large non-dominant shareholders positively affects market valuations. This is consistent with findings for Chinese companies (Bai, Liu, Lu, Song & Zhang 2004) but to more pronounced extent.
- As concentration increases further in the second phase, these benefits are outweighed by the negative effect of potential tunnelling by the dominant owner. Tunnelling becomes easier to accomplish and more lucrative as concentration increases, causing valuations to tend to fall.
- When the dominant owner has full control of the company, tunnelling becomes self-expropriation and loses its purpose. Thus valuations increase modestly as ownership tends towards this limit.

Chinese data show the effect of the first phase of increasing concentration to be negligible on valuations. The second phase is far more pronounced and the third phase is similar to the US data, giving a U-shaped relationship between market valuations and the proportion of shares held by the largest shareholders (ibid: 604). Tunnelling persists even when the state is the dominant shareholder since its agents or functionaries retain personal incentives for expropriation.

The conditions that most differ between the two samples are a lack of diversified ownership among all listed Chinese companies, the relative functionality of internal governance, and the state being almost always the controlling owner whenever ownership is concentrated in Chinese companies. The results may be relevant elsewhere in Asia where similar conditions apply, for example in Indonesia, the Philippines or Vietnam.

Evidence from the 1997–98 regional crisis suggests that the adequacy of governance and minority shareholder protection better explain contemporary falls in local exchange rates and share prices than conventional macroeconomic data (Johnson, Boone, Breach & Friedman 2000). The conclusion is similar to one described in Section 2.3 and associated with Paul Krugman and Joseph Stiglitz, that cronyism and implied state credit support led to excessive unhedged foreign currency borrowing.

A related question is whether share prices were influenced during the crisis by control-based corporate structures and the behaviour of dominant owners. Pyramid ownership and share classes with differently weighted votes are common ways to separate control from ownership entitlements or 'cashflow rights'. One study of 800 companies in eight of our sample economies excluding China and Vietnam found that worsening general conditions and falling share prices increased the likelihood of tunnelling, for controlling owners understandably sought to ring fence their investment commitments (Lemmon and Lins 2003). A similar motivation is arguably less compelling when conditions are favourable.

Figure 9.3 Beneficial ownership of listed companies, FYE 1996.

Data taken from 2,980 listed companies, 41.6 per cent being Japanese, in our sample economies excluding Vietnam. The largest controlling shareholder is assumed to have at least 10 per cent of voting rights.

Source: Claessens, Djankov & Lang (2000).

The results also suggest a link between ownership structure, the scale of agency conflicts and company valuations. The share price performance between July 1997 and August 1998 of companies in the sample with pyramid structures separating cashflow and control rights was 12 per cent poorer than the remainder (ibid: 1466), while the extent of underperformance rose to 20 per cent when a pyramid structure was combined with strong managerial control (ibid).

Ownership structure may be both important in shaping governance outcomes and the weakest of governance mechanisms. Pyramids are common, not only among Asian companies (Claessens, Djankov & Lang 2000; Lemmon and Lins 2003), but to most high-income OECD states except the US and UK (La Porta, Lopez-de-Silanes & Shleifer 1999). The model uses one or more intermediate companies to give control greatly in excess of the owner's direct shareholding. Its impact is twofold because pyramids maximize economic rights and protect against hostile bidders.[9] Figure 9.3 illustrates one result: that most companies in the region have a single beneficial owner in the form of a family or the state.

Table 9.6 Ownership structures of listed companies in China, 2001–08

	2001	2002	2003	2004	2005	2006	2007	2008	Total
1. Central government controlled									
No. of companies	199	210	230	232	239	244	264	280	**1,898**
Control rights	0.484	0.489	0.476	0.472	0.461	0.431	0.434	0.435	**0.458**
Ownership	0.432	0.435	0.416	0.410	0.400	0.374	0.377	0.377	**0.400**
OC	0.883	0.871	0.852	0.846	0.850	0.859	0.861	0.855	**0.859**
Difference in control & ownership rights	0.052	0.054	0.060	0.062	0.060	0.058	0.057	0.059	**0.058**
2. Local government controlled									
No. of companies	660	662	640	644	619	571	568	569	**4,933**
Control rights	0.483	0.483	0.479	0.473	0.458	0.416	0.416	0.422	**0.455**
Ownership	0.463	0.459	0.451	0.441	0.424	0.380	0.378	0.381	**0.424**
OC	0.955	0.945	0.934	0.926	0.918	0.908	0.900	0.898	**0.924**
Difference in control & ownership rights	0.020	0.024	0.028	0.032	0.034	0.036	0.038	0.040	**0.031**
3. Non-state enterprises									
No. of companies	129	178	237	317	332	377	435	474	**2,479**
Control rights	0.355	0.341	0.347	0.353	0.346	0.343	0.360	0.370	**0.354**
Ownership	0.212	0.196	0.216	0.225	0.219	0.225	0.256	0.267	**0.234**
OC	0.579	0.567	0.603	0.623	0.621	0.642	0.699	0.709	**0.647**
Difference in control & ownership rights	0.142	0.144	0.132	0.128	0.127	0.118	0.104	0.103	**0.120**

Ownership is judged by the status of the controlling shareholder, which in this table implies control of at least 20 per cent of votes. Ownership is the proportion of shares owned by the controlling shareholder; control rights are the proportion of votes controlled by the controlling shareholder. OC is the ratio of ownership to control rights.

Source: Liu, Zheng & Zhu (2010).

Thus 52 per cent of 221 listed Singapore companies were family controlled, 23.6 per cent were state controlled, with 10.8 per cent and 12.2 per cent respectively controlled by widely held financial intermediaries and other companies.

In the same sample the average ratio of cashflow to voting rights weighted by the number of companies in each national grouping was 0.75, suggesting that the control rights associated with a hypothetical share were worth only three-quarters of their equitable entitlement. Japan's result was easily the lowest at 0.6, with voting rights exceeding cashflow rights by the greatest margin, followed by Indonesia (0.78) and Singapore (0.79). Companies in Thailand (0.94), the Philippines (0.91) and Hong Kong (0.88) showed the most equitable alignment in their respective average cashflow and voting rights.

Table 9.6 analyzes ownership structures of listed Chinese companies. Only those with controlling shareholders are included but the sample accounts for more than 90 per cent of the total.

The ratio (OC) of formal ownership to actual control by the dominant shareholder is a measure of the complexity of these structures. As with other similar studies, larger values of OC indicate greater alignment in the interests of controlling and other shareholders, and a value of one indicates parity between control and ownership rights in a structure that can be taken to be simple rather than complex. The eight year period averages OCs were 0.86, 0.92 and 0.65 respectively, in companies controlled by central and local government and listed non-state enterprises. The latter appear to have greater incentives to adopt pyramid structures than SOEs, perhaps due to recent improvements in corporate governance. Ownership structures of state companies become more complex over the period, shown by the decline in OC and rise in the difference between control and ownership rights. The sample also shows that:

- Most companies had dominant or controlling shareholders that on average held 34 per cent of total equity. That share fell between 2001 and 2008 from 39.8 per cent to marginally more than 30 per cent (Liu, Zheng & Zhu 2010: 2).
- More than 60 per cent of listed companies are controlled by central or local government.
- Deviations in control and ownership rights resulting from complex structures are most pronounced among non-state companies.
- Pyramid structures are widely used. An average of 3.4 tiers are needed to give control of a listed company (ibid), although private owners may use additional layers for tax management, succession planning or concealment. State owners have been encouraged to adopt pyramid structures by new regulatory restraints on split capital structures and non-tradable shares.
- Private controlling owners favour extensive pyramids more than state owners. Privately controlled companies also use more extensive pyramids when subject to lighter market and legal discipline and greater political discretion, but the converse is observed of state sector owners.

The quality of governance throughout Asia is shown in Tables 9.7A and 9.7B. These summarize findings from a 2010 regional survey, giving appraisals of the quality of general conditions in 11 markets and the rankings of companies in each of those markets in seven specific respects, including comparisons with the prior 2007 survey (CLSA 2010). Both tables show a variety of results.

Table 9.7A Market corporate governance ranking, 2010

	Total score 2010	CG rules & practices	Regulatory enforcement	Political & regulatory environment	Adoption of IGAAP	Institutional mechanisms & corporate governance culture	Total 2007 score (rank)
	67	**65**	**60**	**69**	**88**	**53**	65 (2)
Hong Kong	**65**	**59**	**63**	**67**	**80**	**54**	67 (1)
Japan	**57**	45	**53**	**62**	75	**53**	52 (5)
= 4 Taiwan	**55**	**50**	**47**	**56**	**78**	46	54 (4)
= 4 Thailand	**55**	**56**	**42**	**54**	73	**49**	47 (7)
Malaysia	**52**	**49**	38	**60**	**80**	32	49 (6)
= 7 India	49	46	36	**54**	63	**43**	56 (3)
= 7 China	49	47	36	**56**	75	30	45 (8)
South Korea	45	43	28	44	**78**	33	49 (6)
Indonesia	40	39	28	33	67	32	37 (10)
Philippines	37	35	15	37	75	25	41 (9)

The total score of an arbitrary 'world class' benchmark is 80. Bold type indicates scores greater than the simple average of national scores for each respective category. Results are based on survey data received from 580 companies. The number of completed questionnaires varies by location. No data are available for Vietnam. The CG score (column 2) is based on seven categories characterized as the respondent's identification of corporate governance and financial discipline, transparency, board independence, accountability of management, responsibility in relation to correcting for mismanagement, fair treatment of minority interests, and corporate social responsibility. Sources: Asian Corporate Governance Association; CLSA (2010).

Governance standards in each national market shown in the first column of Table 9.7A were well below a theoretical benchmark score of 80, taken to signify world-class governance of the kind embodied in the OECD's code of practice. Singapore and Hong Kong approached the level of many developed economies but Japan scored poorly for an advanced economy. All markets received higher appraisals of their formal rules rather than enforcement quality or prevailing governance culture.

This has commercial implications for share valuations and is important in understanding why the number of Asian companies achieving high scores for governance is limited and narrowly distributed. Table 9.7B shows those results. The greatest number of poor performers were respondents from China and Hong Kong. The highest average scores were for companies in Thailand, Singapore and Hong Kong. Companies generally scored higher in relation to formal rules than less tangible factors such as board independence, management accountability and policies towards social responsibility. Investors generally regard these issues with more concern than the companies whose shares they hold, one topic that we explore in Chapter 11.

Appendix: the IPO process

Variations in national law, taxation, listing rules, corporate customs, investor behaviour and financial practice ensure that share issuance differs in complexity and cost from one jurisdiction to another. Our itemization of the IPO process is a generic example of a sizeable new listing involving transnational investor subscriptions. It comprises several tranches intended for discrete investor groups to maximize participation by professional, HNW and retail interests, and to comply with national or EU selling restrictions. Our listing is conducted in an advanced market exemplified by Hong Kong, London, New York or Singapore,

Table 9.7B Corporate governance scores for companies, 2010

	Discipline	Transparency	Independence	Accountability	Responsibility	Fairness	CSR	Overall CG 2010			Overall CG 2007 (Rank)
								Low	High	Average	
Thailand	54.2	94.1	51.4	69.4	46.4	72.4	35.0	45.8	84.9	61.7	56.7 (2)
Singapore	59.5	87.0	52.8	32.2	52.8	57.2	66.1	41.9	88.5	57.8	50.3 (7)
Hong Kong	58.2	75.3	23.1	62.2	62.7	64.8	40.4	22.0	81.9	56.0	56.2 (3)
Malaysia	63.6	92.2	43.6	27.9	55.7	50.2	45.5	26.5	71.3	54.5	51.4 (6)
Philippines	51.6	83.7	47.6	35.4	38.4	59.4	64.6	33.0	76.6	53.9	45.5 (9)
India	56.0	78.3	24.1	48.7	47.8	58.8	59.3	34.2	77.3	53.0	51.6 (5)
Japan	47.7	76.4	21.2	50.7	72.4	60.9	36.0	10.4	80.3	53.0	58.9 (1)
South Korea	51.9	79.4	30.9	30.9	44.0	67.7	47.9	21.1	77.6	52.4	49.7 (8)
Taiwan	57.2	64.1	12.9	32.4	63.3	57.5	58.5	6.4	78.9	49.0	54.3 (4)
China	45.1	70.8	29.0	59.5	32.1	49.0	43.3	21.9	70.3	47.2	42.3 (11)
Indonesia	48.9	50.8	34.7	26.1	40.6	28.6	68.2	16.2	69.1	41.3	38.9 (12)
Average	**54.0**	**77.4**	**33.8**	**43.2**	**50.6**	**56.9**	**51.3**	**NA**	**NA**	**52.7**	**(NA)**

Results are based on survey data received from 580 companies. The number of completed questionnaires varies by location. No data are available for Vietnam. CG scores (last four columns) are based on seven categories characterized as the respondent's public commitment to corporate governance and financial discipline, transparency, board independence, accountability of management, responsibility in relation to correcting for mismanagement, fair treatment of minority interests, and corporate social responsibility (CSR), including environmental consciousness.

Sources: Asian Corporate Governance Association; CLSA (2010).

and we highlight details of the process with examples taken from a 2010 IPO for Chongqing Rural Commercial Bank (CRCB), China's twenty-first largest bank by assets at the time of listing. CRCB was incorporated in 2008 from 39 rural credit cooperatives in Chongqing municipality.

The international equity offering is far from new a phenomenon. Foreign companies issued shares in the dominant markets of London and Paris in the late nineteenth century, yet the modern form differs in one important respect: by being driven by general investor preferences rather than the customs of a single financial centre. The London stock market of 1900 was a hub for issuers from the Americas and the British Empire because of the presence in the UK of surplus funds for investment. Today's international equity issues are more fully transnational, and major markets attract both domestic and foreign portfolio flows. Some markets are partly segmented because of capital controls, arcane investor protection rules or the entrenched behaviour of professional or retail investors, the most significant examples being Japan and the US. Global offerings use local currency depositary receipts to match such needs.

The global IPO process is the most arduous form of securities issuance for arrangers, issuers and regulators, resulting from an array of applicable listing rules, disclosure requirements, and investor protection law and associated selling restrictions. Most regulators also require arrangers to be specifically accredited in order to introduce or *sponsor* listing candidates, which allows the listing authority some reliance on the arranger's competence to conduct due diligence. International debt market practice is decentralized and far less stringent.

Work on certain of the tasks and compliance demands listed here is conducted in parallel, giving a critical path for new listings of between four and six months from inception, assuming the issuer has a significant commercial and management record, acceptable accounting and governance standards, and is well prepared to engage with professional investors. The process will take up to 12 months in other cases. Execution times from the moment that the issue is approved in principle and publicly announced by a listing authority usually vary from eight to 15 weeks (Espinasse 2011: 77). More time will be needed if the issue straddles late July and August or December, and Lunar New Year for most issues sold in East Asia. Our outline explains the most important steps in common practice.

Request for proposals and the appointment of advisors:

Bidding banks would be expected to propose an issuing, documentation and syndication strategy, outline their marketing and due diligence needs, provide a preliminary valuation, fee expectations, and justify their reputational capital in transactional and league table prowess as described in Section 7.3 and in their capacity to marshal influential investors.

Choice of venue:

Listing requirements include appropriate disclosure and accounting standards, financial scale and performance tests, aspects of corporate governance, and the terms and free float of the proposed IPO. Tests of financial performance commonly include a minimum capitalization, and some exchanges require listing candidates to meet cumulative hurdles for net income, revenue or free cashflow. European exchanges generally set less specific financial tests than Hong Kong, Singapore, Tokyo or NASDAQ and NYSE but are more demanding as to a consistent operational history. These conditions are influenced by regulatory and exchange competition, and factored into the prospectus submitted for listing authority approval.

Some markets favour or restrict listings from certain jurisdictions or industry sectors, for example, London, Sydney and Toronto are more accommodating than other venues towards resource extraction companies. Such differences affect the feasible listing price and trading multiples.

The choice of venue largely reflects the advisor's appraisal of the host jurisdiction's initial and ongoing regulatory burden, prevailing trading multiples for comparable issuers, and the likelihood of the issuer being admitted to a prominent national index, such as the Hang Seng in Hong Kong or France's CAC40. Entry to a national index enhances local retail interest and demand from passive or index-tracking investors.

Choice of venue is important when issuers target specific investor types or nationalities, the resources of which vary from one market to another. Similar considerations apply to the strategic or financial benefits of simultaneous listings in more than one market.

Decisions on deal structure:

Most offerings are standalone public sales of ordinary shares. Large global issues may have separate tranches intended for local and foreign asset managers and configured to meet national selling restrictions, as described of debt issues in Section 8.1. For example, a Singapore IPO might comprise a local tranche for non-retail investors, one complying with SEC Reg. S for non-US domiciled asset managers, and a third under SEC Rule 144A targeted to qualifying US investors, as well as a small portion of shares reserved for local retail buyers.

Tactics may dictate more intricate structures. It is common in Asia to engage strategic investors prior to an IPO through a private share sale, or with convertible bonds that are extinguished some time after listing in favour of equity claims.

Shares in a new offering may also be reserved for cornerstone investors. CRCB's H-share IPO raised HK$11.5 billion (US$1.48 billion), split between a global tranche of 2.2 billion shares and one of 164 million shares targeted at Hong Kong retail buyers. Four cornerstone investors took part, HNW interests in Abu Dhabi and Hong Kong, a Taiwanese insurer and a local mutual fund, all contracting to buy and hold for at least six months a total of 16.2 per cent of the global tranche. Cornerstone contributions can be sizeable if conditions demand, so that 45.4 per cent of a June 2010 US$12 billion global IPO by Agricultural Bank of China was provided by 11 such buyers, including 31.7 per cent by Gulf and Singaporean SWFs. All agreed lock up periods of between six and 12 months.

CRCB's IPO was partly a secondary sale. Three Chongqing SOEs and one NSE together held 34.4 per cent of the issuer's equity before the IPO. They sold into the offer shares representing 8.5 per cent of the total to be issued, and options to allow the arranger to acquire a further 15 per cent, a tactic to help meet a 25 per cent minimum free float required by Hong Kong's listing rules. Exercising the options implied a 40 per cent dilution of the leading shareholders, which although significant was insufficient to constitute a change in control.

Other options include multiple listings, a reverse acquisition into an existing listed company, or issuing depositary receipts, which are tradable local currency claims on overseas shares held by a depositary and effectively a proxy security common to markets with entrenched practices or a significant home bias. ADRs are the best-known example.

Scale of offering, including the proportion of the company to be floated, the number of new shares to be issued, the size of any secondary sale, how shares are allocated between tranches, and whether to include an option to raise the number of shares offered to provide liquidity for price stabilization after trading begins, known as over-allotment or a *greenshoe*. CRCB's arranger provided for a 15 per cent over-allotment with its call option over shares held by the issuer's four leading owners. This was exercised in full 13 working days after trading in the shares began.

Due diligence and valuation is the lengthiest phase for most successful IPOs. The arranger conducts due diligence as part of an implicit bargain by which it lends reputational capital to the issuer to help complete the transaction, notwithstanding that the final documents presented to investors will contain no warranties as to the accuracy or completeness of marketing or prospectus information, nor an endorsement of the company's quality or prospects. Due diligence comprises several overlapping tasks:

- Assess the company's operations, prospects, financial performance, management and internal governance;
- Prepare a prospectus as an information resource for investors and to satisfy listing authority requirements. This also provides input to be filleted for sell-side research prepared as part of pre-issue marketing; and
- Value the company to provide guidance to investors, collect feedback and form an indicative IPO price-range.

On completing due diligence:

The arranger negotiates letters of comfort with auditors and any specialist appraisers such as engineering, environmental, real estate or resource consultants. It will also generate legal opinions as to the company's internal procedures, the legality of its operations and any known commercial disputes likely to be outstanding during the IPO process or that may affect the later share price performance and the capacity of the company to execute the issue. CRCB published opinions given by its China lawyers and independent real estate assessors. None of these letters or opinions will typically be actionable, for example by an aggrieved investor. They effectively substitute for a forensic examination of the issuer, and are the company's limited warranty to the arranger and implicitly to investors as to its resources and standing.

US practice for registered securities issues and those made under Rule 144A requires legal advisors to both issuers and arrangers to give written opinions as to the completeness and accuracy of information provided in a prospectus and any associated documents. These are intended to provide defences to breaches of SEC Rule 10b-5 under the Securities Exchange Act of 1934, which penalizes offering documents carrying material omissions or false information. Rule 10b-5 opinions are either qualified or costly. Opinion providers wish to avoid or compensate for any culpability, so that a tightly worded opinion necessitates intense and protracted due diligence.

Completion of due diligence triggers:

- The listing authority's in principle approval to the IPO, allowing the arranger to discuss the issuer's plans and prospects with leading investors.
- The arranger forming an underwriting syndicate to defray its risk, assist with marketing and distribution and help reciprocate past syndicate cooperation, as with many debt issues. It is common for issuers and some emerging market regulators to seek the inclusion of favoured banks, which the arranger may welcome for marketing reasons providing it involves no loss of distributional control or league table credit. CRCB's arrangers and

joint bookrunners were Morgan Stanley and Nomura; subsidiaries of Bank of Communications and DBS Hong Kong became junior underwriters.

- Preparation of syndicate agreements among the underwriters of each tranche, dealing with bookrunning rules, the sale and allotment processes, allocation of transaction fees and brokerage commissions, how shares are reallocated if necessary between tranches, and stabilization and other post-execution events.
- Preparation of a sale and purchase agreement between the issuer, arranger and underwriters. The company agrees to issue shares net of all arrangement and underwriting fees and deal expenses within a defined price range or at a fixed price, and the banks undertake to buy those shares subject to the listing receiving final approval and the representations and warranties agreed in due diligence.

Agreements will also be needed with cornerstone investors, including *lock up* provisions preventing disorderly sales of shares. Underwriting commitments are subject to extensive MAC clauses to protect against severe and unexpected price-sensitive events. CRCB's agreement with its underwriters included standard MAC provisions allowing Morgan Stanley and Nomura to revoke their commitments and withdraw the issue in the event of any form of *force majeure* affecting China, Hong Kong, the EU, Japan, the UK or the US, a suspension of share trading in Hong Kong, London, Tokyo or by NYSE or NASDAQ, or malfeasance or breach of obligations specific to CRCB. MAC provisions for equity issues are customarily more extensive than with debt issues, and are rarely invoked.

Selling the issue:

- Most IPOs conduct an investor roadshow using sell-side research and information collected during due diligence, usually in the form of a preliminary prospectus proscribed by the listing authority. CRCB's prospectus occupied a customary A4 sized 861 pages.
- The process involves meetings between company management and leading investors and large-scale presentations attended by smaller investors and the financial media. The outcome depends on discussions with influential investors, whether they are fund managers or well-resourced HNW interests.
- Roadshow stops are tied to the size and ambition of the issue. Substantial global offerings visit all first-tier financial centres and specialist hubs with agglomerations of likely investors – for example Boston, Edinburgh, Zurich and the Gulf states. They would avoid large-scale meetings in centres from which initial feedback was poor (Espinasse 2011: 155).

Bookbuilding:

- Marketing quickly becomes bookbuilding, intended to give the arranger a reliable idea of demand and to assist in price discovery within the publicly indicated range. The arranger's *book* records conditional expressions of investor interest, including numbers of shares and pricing tolerance. The range indicated for CRCB's IPO was HK$4.50–HK$6.00, equivalent to p/e ratios of 9.2–12.2 times contemporary prospective 2011 earnings. An indicative range must protect against uncertainty without losing value as guidance.
- The roadshow is partly a substitute for due diligence, in that all but the largest and most influential investors will be asked to commit to the issue having been given

information that they can test only by their own judgment of price, risk and the arranger's reputation.

- Bookbuilding is constrained by insider trading rules. A conflict exists between price discovery through sounding leading investors and evenhanded disclosure for all. The offer period for retail tranches is accordingly brief, beginning after subscriptions are obtained from fund managers, and in CRCB's case lasted for one day. Retail subscribers pay for shares at the top of the price range without knowing the final issue price or the size of their allotment of shares. Their cheques are cashed and excess payments returned only after the transaction closes.
- Collecting syndicate orders is centralized with the arranger or shared only with its close associates. The book for CRCB was closed with a decided final price of HK$5.25 per share.

Completion:

- Share allotment is followed by settlement and the delivery of net proceeds to the issuer. The listing authority grants permission to deal in the shares, dealing begins on the exchange or through ATPs. The issuer is permitted to celebrate.
- The arranger deducts from the gross sale proceeds the fees agreed in the underwriting agreement, and transaction expenses other than those met directly by the issuer include listing and regulatory fees, the cost of legal and other advisors, printing costs and road-show expenses. CRCB's IPO cost HK$372 million (US$48.0 million) or 3.2 per cent of the gross amount raised, including an underwriting fee of around 2.5 per cent, the major source of compensation for the arrangers. Fees are relatively standardized within each market, and tend to be highest in the US.
- The arranger will buy and sell shares where necessary to *stabilize* the early trading price and protect against short sales, profit taking into a rising share price, or the dumping by syndicate members of unwanted allotments. CRCB's arrangers bought and sold 156 million shares over three working days at prices between HK$5.07 and HK$5.25, and exercised their greenshoe option to assist in settlement. Major markets prohibit stabilization trades above the issue price but stabilization is generally exempt from rules covering market manipulation.
- Lock up periods for cornerstone investors are the result of commercial negotiation and may last as long as two years.

Private placements or vendor placements involve strategic transfers of substantial blocks of shares and can be as complex to distribute as IPOs, albeit meeting fewer regulatory hurdles and being executed in no more than one or two days. Blocks are usually bought by one or more underwriters at a discount to the prevailing price, marketed and sold to substantial investors, during which time normal share trading is suspended.

A notable example was the disposal by AIG in March 2012 of 1.72 billion shares in its former Asian subsidiary AIA, cutting AIG's shareholding from 32.9 per cent to 18.6 per cent. The sale was oversubscribed by 50 per cent and in two days raised HK$46.7 billion (US$6.0 billion) from nearly 300 investors, a 7 per cent discount to the prevailing level prior to the suspension of trading and at the bottom of the range indicated in bookbuilding. AIG undertook to sell no further AIA shares for at least six months. Such transactions are common in Europe and North America but were rare in Asia until the global crisis, when a number of OECD banks raised capital by selling blocks of shares in Chinese, Japanese and

South Korean banks that they had acquired as cornerstone IPO investors or in post-1997 restructurings.

Deal strategies are adjusted to suit prevailing conditions. CRCB closed its successful H-share issue in late 2010, but 14 months later the better known and more substantial Bank of Communications was forced by capital requirements to sell 20 per cent of additional equity in far less propitious conditions. The bank placed new shares with 12 strategic investors, raising six times more than CRCB's IPO from the sale of Rmb29.8 billion (US$4.7 billion) A shares in Shanghai and HK$32.9 billion (US$4.2 billion) H shares in Hong Kong.

Sources: Agricultural Bank of China Ltd., Global Offering Prospectus (30 June 2010); Bank of Communications Co. Ltd., Hong Kong Circular (23 March 2012); Chongqing Rural Commercial Bank Co. Ltd., Global Offering Prospectus (3 December 2010); Espinasse (2011); International Financing Review; SEHK.

10 Mergers, acquisitions and corporate control

The reasons for this chapter's inclusion in our book are so varied as to make it almost unreasonable to ask 'Why discuss M&A?' The topic is controversial, important in Asia as never before, and contains many facets of finance that are worthy of analysis, as well as the intensely human factors of ambition and hubris. The problem is that M&A is also subject to narrow anti-competitive nationalism, to corporate behaviour that is often irrational, and confounds scholars of finance and governance as to its post-execution value-added, if any. Corporate change clearly seems to benefit acquired companies and their former shareholders, directors, financiers and advisors, but we struggle to assess its value to successful bidding companies and their shareholders, to stakeholders such as employees and customers, and to the economy at large. M&A must have some other purpose, if not one that can be gauged objectively, perhaps as part of Schumpeter's myth of creative destruction?

No inviolable rules apply to this dilemma. Many acquisitions of listed companies are thought to destroy shareholder value in the acquiring or merged entity, but the measures of this apparently simple judgment are ambiguous and subjective. A company's share price may be depressed relative to a general stock market index or its peer group after an acquisition is announced or closed, but the outcome varies according to the period from which data are chosen. How can any result be compared with the counterfactual of what would transpire had a merger never occurred?

Directors of UK insurer Prudential Group agreed with its US competitor AIG in February 2010 to acquire AIA, a holding company for AIG's Asian interests widely thought to be a valuable asset in a growing market. The deal required funding which Prudential proposed to raise though a US$20 billion share issue, an amount somewhat greater than the company's pre-announcement market capitalization, as we show in Box 10.1. Prudential's shareholders baulked at the proposal's cost, structure and implications, as well as the audaciousness of their directors, and vetoed the deal and rights issue after three unhappy months of discussion, the company having failed to persuade AIG to negotiate a lower price. AIG changed plans and hurriedly listed 58 per cent of AIA's shares in Hong Kong in October 2010, leading to Prudential becoming vulnerable to a future hostile approach from AIA. Such demonstrable corporate failures are unusual and not always attributable to hubristic M&A ambitions, but the proposal was poorly handled by Prudential directors, notwithstanding its many complications such as:

- Needing many national regulatory approvals in Asia, where AIA's insurance licenses were long-held legacies that might be withdrawn or their transfer refused;
- Needing the loyalty of shareholders and many thousands of semi-independent AIA salespeople but failing to explain the mechanics of combining two disparate and complex businesses;

Box 10.1 Share Price Effects in the Prudential–AIA Proposed Merger

On 28 February 2010 Prudential announced an agreement with American International Group (AIG) to buy substantially all the insurance operations of AIG's Asian subsidiary, AIA. Opposition from Prudential shareholders forced the deal's abandonment in early June. The negotiated price was US$35.5 billion, with US$25 billion payable in cash and the remainder in Prudential shares. The cash portion required funding from a substantial US$20 billion rights issue similar in scale to Prudential's market capitalization before the purchase was announced, but 5.7 per cent greater than the company's value two days thereafter.

Shares in Prudential closed in London at £6.02 (US$9.16 at prevailing exchange rates) on 26 February, the day before the company confirmed its talks with AIG. Prudential had 2.55 billion ordinary shares in issue, valuing the company at £15.6 billion (US$23.8 billion). The share price fell by 19.8 per cent within two trading days, signalling alarm at the deal's magnitude and the dilution effect of the rights issue on the holdings of existing investors. It is not unusual for a bidder company's share price to fall when a proposed transaction becomes known, but this was an alarming drop in value that indicated a sizeable dilution of shareholder interests without clear prospects of recovery through a successful consolidation. Prudential needed to convince its investors that the deal had true merit and was more than a directors' vanity project.

The transaction process was protracted, which for agreed mergers is often unnecessary and costly. Prudential fostered uncertainty by failing to publish a prospectus for the rights issue quickly, with thorough information as to the group's strategic plans, and was embarrassed in mid-May by being temporarily blocked from doing so by the Financial Services Authority (FSA). If its financial regulator was unconvinced that the merged entity would be robust then how ready would shareholders be to provide a large cash infusion?

Throughout the process, Prudential's share price was depressed not only by the impending issue of new shares but by hedge funds taking arbitrage positions by selling Prudential shares, buying shares in AIG, or creating opposing option positions in the two stocks. This trading strategy relies on the broad findings of finance scholars that most mergers destroy value for the buyer even if they reward the target company's shareholders. Prudential tried to endear itself to Asian investors by listing its shares in Hong Kong and Singapore ahead of the planned rights issue, but the market's initial reception of the issue was poor and local trading in the shares (which continue to be listed despite the failed merger) has since been moribund.

Prudential's share price unsurprisingly jumped by 7 per cent on 2 June when the company confirmed the cancellation of the deal with AIG. Since its low of £4.87 on 2 March, and especially after the cancellation of the merger and rights issue, Prudential's share price has comfortably outperformed the main London FTSE 100 index, and by 3 May 2011 had risen by over 35 per cent to £7.77. Over the five years to May 2011 the shares rose by 14.6 per cent while the FTSE 100 index fell by 1.4 per cent. Prudential's share price has yet to reach its August 2001 historic high of £8.35, but these 2010–11 prices make it seem as if the merger had never been conceived.

With the merger abandoned, AIG revived its earlier plan to list AIA shares in Hong Kong. This successfully raised US$17.8 billion in November 2010. The shares traded six months later more than 30 per cent above the IPO price and comfortably outperformed the Hong Kong exchange's Hang Seng Index in the same period, valuing the company at over US$40 billion, or a 13.5 per cent premium to the sale price agreed between Prudential and AIG. This result looks superficially like an opportunity lost to Prudential, but in such complex circumstances it is impossible to know whether Prudential or its conservative core shareholders were correct in their thinking.

AIG proceeds from AIA's IPO were depleted by the common Asian practice of giving substantial pre-IPO share allotments to cornerstone investors, a tactic we describe in Section 9.3 that is intended to influence general retail investor sentiment and provide a measure of price certainty for large new issues. The cost of Prudential's flirtation with AIA was over US$625 million in payments to banks and other advisors, as well as fees to compensate AIG for the broken deal.

Source of price data *Financial Times*.

- Lacking support from the FSA as Prudential's lead regulator, which initially blocked the rights issue for political reasons and for fear that the merged entity would lack sufficient capital; and
- Needing to satisfy shareholders suffering from intense post-crisis conservativism, having included a substantial and highly dilutive rights issue without prior soundings with leading investors.

Shareholder concern at director hubris may be cyclical. Few concerns were voiced two years earlier at the sale of Dutch universal bank ABN Amro, a vast transaction successfully executed prior to the crisis becoming so debilitating to confidence. Not only are questions about the value of M&A hazardous to answer, they vary with cycles in business confidence, and with interests of some parties at variance with others. We note in Section 10.4 that the contest for control of ABN Amro was a unique transaction requiring many resource skills, in spite of which it was massively destroying of value soon after closing and made two of the successful bidders effectively insolvent. The only infallible answer to 'Why discuss M&A?' is 'To watch the drama'. M&A is a notable function of finance, its scale has become noteworthy in Asia, and it involves continual controversy.

We begin by considering corporate change from the perspectives of strategists and shareholders and then look at the functions undertaken by banks in promoting and facilitating corporate transactions. We discuss the factors leading to increases in Asian transaction volumes and explore their implications for finance and governance, closing the chapter with a case study showing the scope of investment banking resources deployed in the landmark acquisition of ABN Amro, and the controversies stirred by investment banks in such processes. One commentary following the failure of Prudential's bid for AIA suggested that the company's directors ought in future to listen more to their shareholders than their bankers, and noted that:

> Tying up 30 banks in the [Prudential rights issue] underwriting syndicate, meanwhile, meant that very few houses were free to produce research on the merits, or otherwise, of the deal. Pru, in effect, bought their silence. The banks, of course – knowing they stood to gain millions in fees, whatever the outcome and however shambolic the campaign – were happy to play along.

(Lex 2010)

This asks that the transaction skills of bankers be subjected to fairer rules, although it neglects the fact that there are few legal sanctions open in any advanced jurisdiction to shareholders who suffer losses due to the commercial misjudgement of managers.

10.1 Corporate change

Our analysis looks at several aspects of M&A and corporate change, but the topic is dominated by finance and organizational scholarship. One textbook avoids controversy over valuations by looking instead at 'sensible' and 'dubious' motives for acquisitions (Brealey, Myers & Allen 2008: 882–91). Sensible motives include efficiency gains, reducing inefficiencies and creating scale economies, while dubious motives include diversification and earnings enhancement. The former seem more strategic and the latter more financial, although corporate fashion can influence strategic decisions, so that shares in diversified conglomerates have been well rated at intervals and penalized by investors for lack of focus at other times.

Corporate finance activity in relatively free economies is itself usually cyclical, with M&A volumes concentrated in certain phases. This is especially true in the US, reflecting its long-established acceptance of corporate change and the scale and homogeneity of the domestic economy. One leading M&A practitioner has argued that the US experienced five transaction waves in the twentieth century (Lipton 2006):

- Horizontal consolidation in 1893–1904, driven by corporate scale and efficiency objectives, lax enforcement of the Clayton and Sherman antitrust acts, and a westward continental migration of economic activity.
- A 1919–29 wave of vertical integration driven by a post-war economic and credit boom, and powerful alliances between banks and industrial holding companies or trusts that ended abruptly in 1929's market crash. The iconic integration by General Motors of its principal supplier Fisher Body was typical of deals of this period.
- A conglomerate wave in 1955–73, characterized by many companies diversifying into unrelated businesses. Major groups were created by merger in this period but few survived intact after investors began to reappraise the value of conglomerate structures after 1969.
- Corporate retrenchment and takeovers in 1974–89 initiated by hostile leveraged transactions managed by colourful 'corporate raiders', many using LBO structures funded by readily available high-yield finance or 'junk' bonds. Japanese and other foreign buyers were also prominent in this period in acquiring US companies. The wave ended when the credit markets abruptly contracted.
- Large-scale mergers in 1993–2000, many involving share exchanges and consolidations including Exxon-Mobil, AOL-Time Warner and Citigroup-Travellers. Some transactions became the first large cross-border mergers, notably Daimler Benz-Chrysler and Vodafone-Mannesmann. A cyclical merger peak also occurred in Europe in 2000, measured both by the number and value of deals, although most transactions were made by companies of like nationality (Buelens 2008).

The author of this wave analysis ironically devised an infamous defence mechanism for bid targets known as the poison pill, a spoiling transaction to be triggered by events related to the hostile bid and intended to crush the value of the target. This helped reduce completed deals in the mid-1980s at the end of the fourth US merger wave. An unsuccessful poison pill appears in our Section 10.4 case study.

Lipton's wave characterization is less pronounced outside North America, largely because the contested takeover is exceptionally rare in Asia and became known only in the 1960s in the UK, remaining unusual in other large EU economies, including France and Germany. The corporate sectors in France, Italy and Spain have undergone prolific restructuring and consolidation through mergers in the last three decades, but most involved companies transitioning from close state or family control and few were contested or hostile transactions. Similar conditions favouring consolidation existed in Asia after the 1997–98 financial crisis.

Vodafone's 2000 acquisition of Mannesmann was viewed in Germany both unpopularly and by many scholars as an unwanted aassault, as though UK aggression would pollute the consensual governance of the Rheinish model. The transaction led to the prosecution of Mannesmann directors, who were said to have received excessive post-acquisition compensation, something common in Anglo-American M&A practice. Germany's Federal Supreme Court ordered a retrial after the directors were initially acquitted, and the case ending inconclusively in 2006.

UK practice changed because investment banks began to devise and solicit transactions and the outcome by the 1990s was similar to the US, with the difference that self-regulation of takeover practice tended to assist deal execution compared to the prescriptive US statutory framework. This has been described as 'family capitalism [being] largely sidelined in major public companies' (Cheffins 2008: 336), a transformation yet to occur in most Asian economies. Other common law jurisdictions are far more reserved, and the federal governments of Australia and Canada are known to block combinations with foreign interests for nationalist reasons.

The twenty-first century's first merger wave began in 2002 as share prices and economic conditions recovered from the bursting of the technology asset bubble in March 2000. It lasted until being halted by the onset of the global financial crisis in mid-2007. Figure 10.1 shows the number and values of announced transactions in 1995–2008. The volume of announced M&A deals peaked in 2000 and then fell, until 2007 when it reached a new high of US$4.2 trillion, before collapsing again due to evaporating confidence and credit availability.

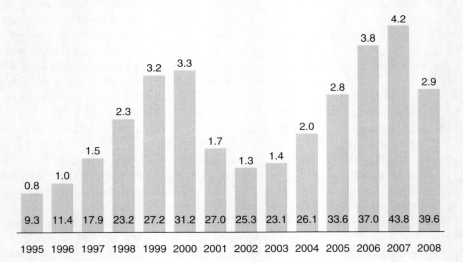

Figure 10.1 Announced global transactions, 1995–2008 (US$'000bn).
The number of deals is shown at the base of each bar ('000s).
Source: Thomson Reuters (2011).

Conditions began to stabilize in 2010 but with an unusually large gap between the number of announced and completed deals, not least due to the failure of several sizeable transactions for regulatory or nationalist reasons, including the Canadian government blocking BHP Billiton's bid for Potash Corporation, and Australia preventing Aluminium Corporation of China (Chinalco) from raising its minority holding in RTZ Corporation. The crisis also made shareholders understandably reluctant to support demanding acquisitions, as with Prudential and AIA. Box 10.2 and Tables 10.1A–10.1C give a summary of M&A conditions and outcomes in 2010 globally, in Asia and for those involving Chinese and Japanese interests. The largest number and most valuable deals in all regions clustered in energy, power, materials and resource companies for four main reasons:

Box 10.2 Global and Asia-Pacific M&A in 2010

Our focus in describing recent conditions and activity is with deal volumes and totals globally, in East Asia and specifically for China and Japan. We also look at the growth of all emerging market activity and the sectoral composition of target companies in announced transactions. The highlights in 2010 were:

- A 22 per cent general recovery in the global aggregate deal volume from a crisis slump in 2008–9;
- A modest rise in the number of announced global deals of 3 per cent to 40,660, of which 73.5 per cent were completed by end-December;
- A jump in activity to its highest level to date in Asia excluding Japan, accounting for 13.9 per cent of the global announced deal volume and 17.4 per cent including Japan;
- Deals involving emerging market parties were 33.1 per cent of the announced global volume, its highest share to date;
- US and EU banks dominated global advisory activity in their home markets and across all regions. Chinese and Japanese banks were ranked successfully in their respective home markets but not elsewhere;
- Transactions in the energy and power, resources and materials, and finance sectors provided 40–50 per cent of total M&A globally and in most regions. Government privatization activity was exceptionally low;
- A majority by volume of announced Japanese transactions since 2005 have involved outward acquisitions. A similar pattern began with China deals in 2007, and outward M&A involving China parties in 2010 was double the volume of inward transactions;
- Northeast Asian markets were the largest source of regional activity, with Japan, China, Hong Kong and South Korea in decreasing order of deal volumes; and
- Most Asia M&A currently involves no change in control. This is the converse of all OECD activity excluding Japan and South Korea.

The transactions included in Tables 10.1 and 10.2 are mergers, acquisitions, share repurchases, asset or business spin-offs, self-tenders, purchases of minority interests, and debt restructurings, which is broader than the M&A focus of Chapter 10 as a whole.

M&A transaction data for any specified period distinguish between deals *completed* in the sense of being formally executed (or 'closed'), those *announced* but pending and yet to close at the end of the period, and those announced and *withdrawn* within the period. Pending deals may complete or be withdrawn, and may result in double counting in the case of some contested takeovers. The number and scale of withdrawn deals as a share of completed deals is volatile and influenced both by factors that are endogenous to any single transaction and to general conditions. The latter include many that vary from time to time, by industry sector and by transaction domiciles, as well as the supply of credit and overall levels of confidence.

In the five years to end-2010, withdrawn deals averaged 21 per cent per quarter as a share of the value of global completed deals and were relatively high when overall M&A activity was also high. Withdrawn deals peaked at 59.3 per cent of global completed deals in the final quarter of 2008, unsurprisingly given the abnormal collapse of credit availability and confidence that followed Lehman Brothers' failure. In the same period withdrawn deals were also positively correlated with global unsolicited bids.

Table 10.1A shows fees paid by global M&A users in 2010 as a proxy for deal activity by industry sector. The leading sectors were numerous and involved large transactions. The composition of users varies over time and with economic conditions, so that energy and resource transactions have become more prominent in the last two to three years, not only as companies in those sectors became more valuable to bidders but due to notable corporate change having occurred earlier in other sectors, as we know of telecommunications, retailing and property. Deal fees are often subject to standard rates in OECD economies but are driven down by aggressive competition in Asia and elsewhere. Aggregate fees shown in Table 10.1A are chiefly functions of transaction values, sectors, bid multiples and deal numbers.

The geographical composition of completed 2010 global M&A activity is shown in Table 10.1B. North American and European transactions have long been dominant by scale and number but the distribution is increasingly diverse, both in overall activity and in landmark transactions taking place in non-traditional jurisdictions. Very large deals were completed in Brazil, South Korea, Mexico and Central Asia. China was the most active source of deals in Asia.

The shares of announced deals attributable to industry sector and identified regions is summarized in Table 10.1C, and illustrates the relative maturity of activity globally, in emerging markets, and in China. Sectoral concentration is higher in new M&A locations. Other data indicate that transactions involving at least one party from an emerging market have risen annually in number since 2002. Announced deals in all global markets were one third of the 2010 total, for a projected consideration of US$806.3 billion, an annual increase of 76.2 per cent. Deals involving Chinese companies accounted for the largest number and were valued at US$131.1 billion, followed by Brazil (US$104.2 billion) and Russia (US$66.5 billion). The largest single completed deal in 2010 was a US$27.5 billion sector merger of two Mexican telecommunications companies.

Table 10.2A shows the leading banks advising on all announced deals and the dominance of large US and EU banks in the global market. Most are banks involved in many business streams. Lazard and Rothschild are banks focused on corporate finance, and Evercore, Blackstone, Greenhill and Perella Weinstein are specialist corporate finance advisers, some associated with private equity fund managers. Aggregate activity is concentrated among relatively few large firms. Nomura is the sole Asian firm ranked in the leading 20.

Table 10.2B shows comparable results for Asia excluding Japan. Five Asian banks appear among the leading 20, including three Malaysian banks, Nomura, and CICC ranked strongly in eighth place. Transaction target industries were skewed towards materials (22 per cent of announced deals) and energy and power (19 per cent). In other data (not shown in Table 10.2) only Nomura and CICC, in fourteenth and twentieth place respectively, were Asian firms ranked as leading arrangers of all global emerging market transactions.

Table 10.2C shows a similar result for announced deals involving one or more Chinese principals. Those ranked include six mainland Chinese and two Hong Kong firms. Advisors for deals involving a Japanese acquirer or target are shown in Table 10.2D. Only four Japanese banks and one Japan–US joint venture were ranked in the leading 20, although Japanese banks advised on a far greater number of deals than their foreign competitors. Financial sector transactions accounted for 24 per cent of Japan's total by value, far more than elsewhere. Six non-bank specialists appear in the lower half of the table. Activity with Japanese parties was far more concentrated than deals conducted for parties in China. A home bias can be seen in the selection of advisors in emerging markets, but this is insufficient to prevent global banks from being successful in all regions. Rankings of providers of fairness opinions (not shown in Tables 10.1 and 10.2) are more favourable to local advisors.

Source: Thomson Reuters (2011).

- Companies in these four sectors are comparatively large;
- These sectors were subject to less consolidation in the prior decade;
- Prospects for companies in these sectors became attractive to investors and financiers due to cyclically high commodity and energy prices; and
- The average value of deals in these sectors compared favourably with average sectoral values, measured by the extent of the share premium of bids above prevailing prices prior to the bid announcement, and the ratio of deal value to the prior year's operating earnings before interests, taxes, depreciation and amortization (EBITDA).

By comparison the emphasis in deals struck a decade earlier in 2000 was with telecommunications, finance and electronics, both globally and in Asia.

Table 10.1A Leading global sectoral M&A users, 2010

	Industry sector	Fees paid 2010 (US$ mm)	Market share (%)	No of deals	Fees paid 2009 (US$ mm)	% Change in fees
1	Energy & power	4,923	16	2,605	3,914	+26
2	Financials	3,757	12	3,941	3,261	+15
3	High technology	3,206	10	3,799	2,048	+57
4	Materials	3,066	10	3,524	2,005	+53
5	Industrials	3,011	10	6,659	2,766	+9
6	Healthcare	2,604	9	1,841	1,912	+36
7	Property	2,043	7	1,754	1,562	+31
8	Staple consumer goods	1,978	6	2,165	1,427	+39

(*continued*)

Table 10.1A (Continued)

	Industry sector	Fees paid 2010 (US$ mm)	Market share (%)	No of deals	Fees paid 2009 (US$ mm)	% Change in fees
9	Consumer products & services	1,784	6	3,186	991	+80
10	Media & entertainment	1,714	6	2,264	1,088	+58
11	Telecommunications	1,292	4	684	1,112	+16
12	Retail	1,153	4	1,519	686	+68
13	Governments & agencies	16	NA	36	8	+109
	Grand total	**30,548**	**NA**	**31,968**	**22,780**	**+34**

In Tables 10.1 and 10.2 fees generated by transactions are either actual disclosed gross fees or those imputed by commercial data providers based on comparable transactions and prevailing practice. Bank advisors are given full credit for each deal they manage, unless they only act for minority interests or advise on part of any transaction. Other advisors are allocated a share of fees based on the number of advisors and their respective functions.
Source: Thomson Reuters (2011).

Table 10.1B Global M&A activity, 2010

	Deal value (US$ bn)	No. of deals	Average deal size (US$ mm)	Year on year change in value (%)
Canada	77.0	1,482	52.0	−9.1
US	687.2	6,496	105.8	−6.1
Brazil	67.1	420	159.9	−15.0
Other South America	27.8	522	53.3	NA
Mexico	44.8	145	309.3	NA
Other Central Americas	12.5	176	71.1	NA
Total Americas	916.5	9,241	99.2	−1.1
Africa & Middle East	57.5	668	86.1	51.8
France	45.6	1,214	37.5	22.2
Germany	46.7	1,052	44.4	−36.9
UK	146.4	1,950	75.1	−17.8
Other Europe	244.9	8,009	30.6	NA
Total Europe	483.6	12,225	39.6	−17.7
Australasia	77.4	1,494	51.8	46.1
Singapore	12.9	282	45.6	2.4
Thailand	9.7	495	19.6	93.2
Other SE Asia	17.8	860	20.7	NA
Total SE Asia	40.4	1,637	24.7	−1.6
China	55.4	912	60.7	15.1
Hong Kong	31.0	717	43.3	28.3
Other NE Asia	47.9	492	97.3	NA
NE Asia	134.3	2,121	63.3	47.0
South Asia	21.4	732	29.2	15.1
Central Asia	8.1	35	232.1	−10.7
All Asia ex-Japan	204.1	4,525	45.1	NA
Japan	108.1	1,778	60.8	61.8
All Asia	312.2	6,303	49.5	NA
Asia & Australasia	389.6	7,797	50.0	34.1
Total	**1847.3**	**29,931**	**61.7**	**0.9**

Data based on completed deals.
Source: Thomson Reuters (2011).

Table 10.1C Announced transactions by industry sector & region 2010 (%)

	Global	All emerging markets	Asia-Pacific emerging markets	China
Energy & power	20	19	19	20
Financials	15	14	14	17
Materials	11	18	22	24
Industrials	9	10	13	10
Healthcare	8	4	4	2
Telecommunications	8	15	5	NA
Property	7	6	7	10
High technology	7	2	2	2
Staple consumer goods	5	6	6	7
Media & entertainment	4	3	3	3
Consumer products & services	3	1	2	2
Retail	2	2	3	3
Government & agencies	1	NA	NA	NA
	100	100	100	100

'All emerging markets' comprise 21 economies in Central and South America, 70 in Africa and the Middle East, 20 in Eastern Europe, eight in Central Asia, seven in South Asia, 20 in Australasia, three in North Asia (China, Mongolia and North Korea) and nine in Southeast Asia (Brunei, Cambodia, Indonesia, Laos, Malaysia, the Philippines, Thailand, Timor-Leste and Vietnam). Asia-Pacific emerging markets comprise all economies in Northeast, South and Southeast Asia and Australasia excluding Australia, Hong Kong, Japan, South Korea, Myanmar, New Zealand, Singapore, Taiwan and Western Samoa.
Source: Thomson Reuters (2011).

Transaction types

The abbreviation M&A stands for five transaction types. Our analysis focuses on the first two:

- Mergers;
- Acquisitions;
- Privatization, meaning the disposal or corporate transformation of commercial interests by the state sector, and may include IPOs and strategic sales to private interests;
- Buyouts, chiefly delisting transactions by existing management, sponsored by private equity interests. It is common in Asia for controlling shareholders to tender for minority interests and delist their company's shares, a process often known as privatization but not associated with the state sector; and
- Consolidation or restructuring, notably non-core divestitures or subsidiary IPOs, in some cases prompted by distressed financial conditions or activist shareholder agitation, or to meet valuation and financing objectives as with REIT transactions.

Each category involves corporate change that affects ownership, not merely the allocation of capital.[1] They may be conducted voluntarily or because of commercial pressures, and may be contested by one or more rivals. The principals may be mutually amicable or hostile, and may change positions if their shareholders or financiers allow.

Mergers are commonly consensual and voluntary combinations of businesses. They involve an exchange of shares or cash payment to the smaller company, followed by a consolidation of share capital or the creation of a new holding company. *Acquisitions* refer to a larger company's purchase of one that is smaller, or a reverse takeover where a smaller company acquires control of a larger, longer-established or well-branded company, intending to retain its name and share listing.

M&A refers broadly to any capital market transaction resulting in a change in ownership or control. Mergers, acquisitions, formal joint ventures, private asset sales or proxy fights can all be classed as M&A if such changes take place. Proxy contests are part of US corporate practice and securities regulation as formal disputes over corporate strategy or control. A hostile bidder or minority interest will seek support (the proxy votes) of shareholders to elect sympathetic directors who will approve the bid or change of strategy upon joining the board. Statements made to garner proxies are regulated by the SEC in the same way as IPO prospectuses.

We can also classify transactions by the type of intended combination they represent:

- Horizontal combinations, where merging companies operate in the same commercial sector and produce broadly similar products. Economies of scale and scope are the usual motives, with the combined entity intending to improve operating income, reduce costs or increase its products, services or scope of distribution so as to improve competitiveness and market share. Horizontal mergers may also have defensive motives – that is, to capture a target to prevent it being absorbed by a competitor.
- Vertical combinations are mergers between firms that operate within one sector at different stages of the product cycle, and typically aim to secure a supply chain or complete a product chain. A well-known example in the finance literature is the 1926 merger of car panel manufacturer Fisher Body with General Motors (GM), although the case is controversial among economists. This was a symbiotic relationship between a dominant customer and monopoly supplier, with GM also owning 60 per cent of Fisher shares prior to the merger.

  The accepted view of finance scholars until 2000 was that Fisher deliberately ran inefficient factories located far from GM's assembly plants with profits protected by it being GM's sole source of panels under a ten-year fixed-margin supply contract (Klein, Crawford & Alchian 1978). This meant that Fisher had no incentive to improve efficiency. GM's performance suffered and by 1924 the company saw its contractual relationship with Fisher as 'intolerable' (ibid: 310).

  GM's solution was to merge with Fisher and consolidate the two operations in order to secure and improve the supply of car bodies, making this an example of vertical integration intended for reasons of *control*. This account was disputed by Nobel economics laureate Ronald Coase, who showed that Fisher was neither deliberately or inadvertently inefficient, nor its plants remote from GM, making the earlier analysis 'completely false' (Coase 2000: 21), or a finance scholarship myth. The two companies were cooperative rather than confrontational, and the merger was made to improve input and manufacturing logistics, give supply certainty to the manufacturing chain, and augment GM's existing management (Coase 2006: 268; Casadesus-Masanell & Spulber 2000: 99). This alters the accepted motive of the integration from control to *cooperation*, or from market failure in Fisher's apparent exploitation of its contract with GM to efficiency enhancement. It also supports Coase's earlier theory of transaction costs driving vertical integration (Coase 1937).
- Conglomeration refers to combinations of companies in different industries. Diversification may seek to reduce risk, and enable the combined entity to achieve financial synergies, lower capital costs and raise its financing capacity. The 2000 acquisition by American Online (AOL) of Time Warner was typical, as their respective

industry sectors were then regarded as distinct, although it is now common for telecom or internet service providers to integrate vertically with sources of media content.

The deal was vaunted as a merger of equal partners, but was made near the peak of AOL's value. Corporate synergies failed to develop, the value of the combined entity fell and AOL was finally sold in 2009. Earlier research found that a diversified company is worth less to a disinterested investor than a portfolio of comparable single-segment firms (Lang & Stulz 1994; Berger & Ofek 1995). This diversification discount has prompted much research that has consequences for corporate strategy, although the conglomerate structure is consistently popular in Asia. Asia's weak institutional setting and comparatively poor corporate governance leads to less general concern as to the impact of structure on corporate value.

Mergers may also be classified according to a value-chain framework, which is shown in simplified form in Figure 10.2. The dynamics of an industry are characterized by the path connecting opportunities for value creation, beginning in this case with inbound logistics in the purchase of raw materials, to manufacturing and assembly, marketing, product distribution and post-sale client support. Firms tend to operate in one or two value-creating segments. An inbound logistics firm acquiring a company engaged in distribution and sales results in a forward integration merger. If a technology infrastructure provider such as Cisco Systems acquires a network portal such as Facebook, the transaction is classed as forward integration. Backward integration occurs when a content provider such as Disney buys a designer such as Apple or an Apple component assembler such as Foxconn.

The value-chain framework is useful in understanding the M&A objectives of growing Asian companies. Many firms began as OEM or ODM suppliers positioned at the manufacturing and assembly segments of the value chain where operating margins are relatively low. Successful suppliers have an incentive to migrate to higher-margin segments of production by obtaining control of strategic intangible assets such as brands, or valuable technology and skilled human resources.

Corporate change can bring about these shifts more quickly than organic growth. Globalization has encouraged the drift of manufacturing and supporting services to regions of low labour costs, which alters the relative profitability of different phases in the value chain and increases the value of maintaining certain resource skills 'in house'. Substantial manufacturers use information technology to gain from early and later stages of the process, for example by improving input logistics and cutting inventory costs, an approach associated pre-eminently with Toyota's 'just-in-time' assembly model, or by capturing recurring revenue from customers through long-term post-sale service contracts, a business model that supports manufacturers of complex capital goods such as Boeing or Rolls-Royce.

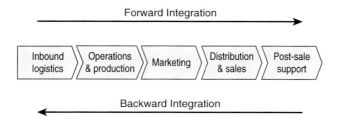

Figure 10.2 Generic corporate value chain.

Successful service arrangements formalize ongoing business relationships by extending the duration of a sale contract and increasing the probability of repeat sales.

Objectives

The most common motives for corporate change through M&A are:

- Synergy. This refers to additional value achieved through combining two firms, and applies to revenue streams, costs, finance and assets. The first two are operating synergies arising from improved operating efficiency through economies of scale or scope, and become effective through the acquisition of a customer, supplier or competitor. Financial synergies result from a lower cost of capital by smoothing cashflows, realizing financial economies of scale or better matching investment opportunities with internal cashflows. Asset synergies are created through the reconfiguration or redeployment of existing assets.
- Diversification. A firm uses M&A to position itself in higher-growth products or markets.
- Market power. Increasing market share improves the ability of companies to set or maintain prices above competitive levels.
- Strategic alignment. The acquisition of capabilities to help companies adapt to external conditions such as changes in technology, regulation or culture more rapidly than through organic change or experiment.
- Tax considerations. The motive to obtain unused net operating losses and tax credits, asset revaluations and to substitute capital gains for ordinary income. Many states now limit the scope for profitable companies to acquire loss-making companies which limits pure tax motives for acquisitions.
- Managerial hubris. Where an acquirer is more confident in its valuation of a target than the wider market. This is common in acquisitions and found especially among expanding companies that have undertaken small-scale transactions and begin to expect similar results from ambitious bids. Hubris leads acquirers to overpay by overestimating the gains from synergies (Roll 1986) and is central to our case study in Section 10.4. Empire building by managers is typical of the agency problem arising from the misalignment of shareholder and manager interests. Prudential's failed purchase of AIA is an example of managerial hubris, if not in the transformational nature of the proposal then in the behaviour of Prudential management towards its shareholders, the FSA and AIA's regulators in Asia. The hubris pervasive in our case study in Section 10.4 had calamitous results.
- Defence. A firm seeks an increase in scale through an acquisition intended to block or increase the cost of an unwanted hostile approach, that is, to make it less vulnerable to an unwanted takeover. Defensive mergers may also occur for consensual reasons if two companies combine or exchange shares to prevent one being acquired by a third party. This control tactic is common among Asian companies that lack widely dispersed shareholders.
- Regulatory arbitrage. An unlisted company acquires a listed company at home or overseas through a reverse takeover, with the intention of reducing the costs or disclosure requirements associated with initiating an IPO, or circumvent rules that demand a minimum period of profitable trading of companies seeking listings. The target is typically smaller than the acquirer, its shares may be only scarcely traded and the two companies' businesses may be entirely unrelated.

The motives for initiating a transaction may affect the eventual valuation of the target, for example, deals that are hostile or regarded as purely financial may be more costly to execute than those involving sectoral synergies or like-minded managers.

Objectives such as these were traditionally chosen by management and then recommended to shareholders, a process that raises agency questions as to misaligned shareholder interests and the rewards or motives of management, especially in the case of acquirer companies. The choice of objectives was subjected to two additional influences from the late 1980s, first with investment banks becoming more able to influence or manipulate managers, and more recently due to activist investors that compel managers to increase value for shareholders, both in public companies and with non-listed firms controlled by private equity funds.

The threat of a takeover may encourage managers of target companies to respond to shareholder interests by realigning their objectives and improving the company's performance, making corporate change through M&A a control device that can lessen the agency problem (Cheffins 2008: 361). These tactics need careful monitoring. It is often simple for managers to use delegated administrative powers to engineer higher returns, for example through buying shares from investors and shrinking the capital base when the company is liquid but not expanding (see Note 1).

Cyclical activity

Changes in the business environment tend to be both industry and time specific, which leads to clustering in M&A activity. Michael Jensen provides one explanation based on the suggestion that modern technological, political, regulatory and economic forces altered the world's advanced economies in ways that resemble changes experienced during the Industrial Revolution (Jensen 1993).

The spread of steam-driven transport and labour-saving machinery in the nineteenth century altered production processes so as to make many earlier systems and organizations redundant and in need of scrapping. Advanced economies in the late twentieth century experienced declining costs, increasing average but decreasing marginal labour productivity, reduced growth rates in income from employment, and excess capacity, leading to a 'modern industrial revolution' (ibid: 831) that is similar in impact to its forerunner, and so requires a plausible 'exit' for older excess capacity or redundant firms.

Jensen argued that corporate control systems, that is, internal rules of governance, often fail to fully deal with slow growth, excess capacity and similar changes, that competition in product or factor markets is too slow to be an effective control, and that the institutional influence of legal, political or regulatory systems is often conflicted and unable to deal with excess capacity and redundant capital. Firms needing to resolve overcapacity problems and improve efficiency require both internal and external control systems, and in these circumstances the market for corporate control through M&A may be an effective means to encourage companies to adapt to changing conditions.

Jensen's arguments may be more persuasive to Anglo-American capitalists than in continental Europe, or in Asia where large companies are often unlisted or closely controlled by family or state interests, and the influence of M&A is therefore constrained. They also fail to acknowledge the limits to M&A as a control mechanism when transaction origination is dominated by investment banks rather than principals. This was often the norm with post-1980 US M&A, with much activity propelled by external finance and prone to overpayment (Black 1989). The largely accepted 1980s view of hostile change in ownership leading to increased corporate efficiency and benefiting shareholders was less convincing after many costly failed takeovers. A more sceptical view developed in the mid-1990s, of M&A representing a shuffling of resources rather than the creation of new value (Deakin & Slinger 1997), so that the Anglo-American practice of freely encouraging corporate change was not always in the interests of other stakeholders, which the Rheinish corporate model is usually happier to recognize. For these reasons we see M&A as a *partial* solution to the accepted need for corporate change, because notably:

- It functions more effectively in some economies than others due to differences in corporate governance and the nature of equity market culture; and
- It favours some parties and stakeholders more than others.

Mitchell and Mulherin (1996) studied 51 US industry sectors in 1982–89, finding significant differences in sectoral takeover activity and a time clustering of those activities. Sectoral differences in takeovers and restructuring were directly related to the exogenous shocks borne by each industry, which fell into three main categories:

- Deregulation, notably in air transport, broadcasting and entertainment, natural gas extraction and transmission, haulage and transport leasing;
- Foreign manufacturing competition in clothes, textiles, car production and older heavy industries such as mass steel production; and
- Financial innovation providing ready access to credit to fund large transactions, especially in the buyout wave of the 1980s and the infusion of capital through private equity funds to support leveraged acquisitions.

These findings are also relevant in Asia where takeover and restructuring demonstrate cross-industry patterns and time clustering, driven partly by sectoral shocks or economic events that impact differently on distinct business sectors.

Governance and regulation

Takeover practice in advanced economies is generally regulated as part of company, securities and employment law so as to account for general concerns of fairness and transparency, prevent any single shareholder or controlling block from gaining unreasonably, exploiting a minority or significantly disadvantaging employees. Practice can vary greatly and in some cases is opaque, as in Germany and Japan where, since 2000, several takeovers involving substantial shareholders have been controversial. Other national obstacles will often allow states and territories to block domestic or transnational transactions for one or more reasons:

- Monopoly. Practice in North America, Australia and the UK is long established, and EU law affects both national and transnational concentrations. Anti-monopoly laws are far less transparent or effective throughout East Asia and have been successfully resisted by business lobbies even in competitive economies such as Hong Kong, South Korea or Singapore.
- Strategic concerns. National law customarily allows an investee state to block share or asset acquisitions by foreign buyers for specific reasons of strategic interest, as with defence contractors, resource extraction companies or electricity and water utilities. The US created an administrative Committee on Foreign Investment (CFIUS) in 1975 to

subject such purchases to review, and this arrangement has blocked several prominent deals involving non-OECD buyers, including CNOOC's purchase of Unocal in 2005 and Dubai World Ports acquiring the US port terminal interests of P&O Group in 2006.

- Economic nationalism. The same powers may also allow a foreign purchase to be blocked by administrative order for more arbitrary reasons. In 2010 Canada barred the takeover of Potash Corporation by BHP Billiton Ltd, and in early 2011 Australia blocked an agreed merger between the Australian and Singapore stock exchanges, each government stating simply that the deal was not in the national interest. Populist economic nationalism encouraged the French government in 2005 to prevent yoghurt maker Danone being acquired by Pepsico, with the prime minister avowing to 'defend the interests of France' (*Economist* 2005). Most states in Asia share the policy, and there are no sectors in the region where foreign ownership has been freely allowed, even if the state is known to encourage inward FDI.

- Other specific rules may allow the state to set limits for inward direct investment by SWFs or investors deemed to be part of a foreign state. This may have been a factor in Australia's preventing its stock exchange from merging because Singapore's SWF Temasek holds large interests in the Singapore exchange.

All these consideration make M&A a complex matter. It can be used strategically, or for defensive, predatory or spoiling motives; it may be voted through by shareholders for reasons of market share, efficiency, competition and anti-competition; it may be value and employment destroying or a central part of the efficiency of capitalism, providing discipline in the form of a market for corporate control; and it is likely to be guided by rules on fairness, governance, monopoly and haphazard perceptions of national interests. These complications provide scope for corporate financiers to earn substantial advisory fees.

10.2 Finance and deal mechanics

Questions of regulation and governance help explain why banks are involved in M&A transactions except in small or unusual cases, regardless of whether they require external finance. Advanced economies usually demand that banks provide a delegated or proxy supervisory function in M&A, which is feasible because banks are themselves subject to continued regulation. This implies that banks would become involved in transaction design and take on advisory roles even without fee or financing incentives.

The instigation and success of merger transactions are affected by factors either within the control of principals and advisors or ones to which the parties can only react (Lipton 2006). Some factors evolve or vanish over time, often as regulations are changed to remove arbitrage incentives, and so we have adapted the factors cited by M&A practitioner Martin Lipton to remove the impact of business fashion. In our view, the main exogenous M&A drivers are:

- Accounting, which affects the actual cost of deals and the method by which they involve external finance, mainly through rules for the post-transaction treatment of goodwill and those dealing with projected cost savings.

- Activism among long-term shareholders and other investors. This is important in our Section 10.4 case study.

- Credit availability through banks and capital markets, without which hostile transactions would be far fewer in number and investment banks would have less incentive to instigate deals.

- Legislation, especially monopoly laws, which signify a cultural acceptance or rejection of corporate change and combinations.
- National regulation, deregulation and economic protectionism that make cross-border transactions feasible for some parties and impossible for others. The consortium structure in our case study was devised by Merrill Lynch for reasons of cost and to remove certain national objections to the transaction.

Each of these factors impacts on the transaction behaviour of the principals and their advisors and condition deal design and tactics. In most cases they create a need for professional advice. What causes banks to be involved in M&A? This simple question hides three further questions: what attracts banks to M&A? What do banks do? And why do bidders, merger partners and targets involve banks in their affairs? We see three motives for bank participation in M&A:

- Regulation. Banks organize and monitor the conduct of transactions and can be made accountable for transgressions in takeover practice by virtue of being intensively regulated. They also bring impartiality to aspects of deal execution, for example in advising shareholders as to the value of competing choices.
- Professional input. Banks provide transaction skills and resources that are otherwise unavailable to principals. Companies such as Berkshire Hathaway or Hutchison Whampoa that are large and well-practised at inorganic growth by merger recognize the limits of their expertise and employ banks as deal managers and advisors. This has the further benefit of encouraging banks to share unsolicited M&A ideas, and prevents an unwarranted diversion of management time. M&A is highly labour-intensive.
- Self-selection. Banks choose to be involved in M&A because of direct and indirect rewards.

Our third factor needs amplification. Banks find M&A rewarding for overlapping reasons:

- Compensation. Transaction fees may be attractive, although fees paid in certain markets are notoriously competitive and difficult to assess or collect, as is often the case in China, South Korea and Southeast Asia.
- Reputational capital. M&A is demanding, so that successful deals immediately enhance reputational capital, which improves the prospect of capturing future deals.
- Spin-off transactions. Deals may involve other tasks, including fundraising and asset sales.
- Corporate intimacy and relationship control. The most valuable resource supporting investment bank product distribution is knowledge of client preferences and wants, which improves the probability of transaction completion. A successful M&A relationship signifies client contact at important levels.

These motives conceal a conceit of corporate finance. When a paper manufacturer decides to acquire a competitor, how likely is it that a bank will know as much about industry practice or papermaking economics as the protagonists? Bank involvement in M&A is due partly to convention, partly to regulatory and investor protection requirements, but largely explained by M&A itself being an intrinsic business. The papermaker knows more than the banker about turning pulp and waste into paper, but far less about mergers or the risks that transactions may fail or be trumped by a third party. Competent firms know their WACC but need valuation skills to judge a target. The papermaker might consider a deal infeasible for cost or antitrust reasons until shown otherwise. Banks are needed even when deals are simple and consensual.

Financial sector transactions also need specialist advice, a degree of independence, and protection for investors against agency issues, so the first step for a bank seeking to buy another is to hire a separate bank advisor.

The presence in a transaction of an established M&A bank may also raise investor confidence in the bidder or a target defending its independence. Well-regarded investment banks provide information resources to investors through reputational capital, as we saw in Chapter 7. Banks of high reputation can augment that resource with an implicit recommendation of deals merely by being present, effectively to bridge or interpret gaps in information or understanding. Reputational capital can be ephemeral or product specific. Merrill Lynch raised its M&A reputational capital in 2007 by managing the purchase of ABN Amro while simultaneously having to make accounting provision for vast structured finance losses. Competence rarely extends to all business streams.

Deal mechanics

Banks typically take one or more of several roles in large multi-party corporate transactions, and a bank may:

- Propose its own deal concept to a client but would otherwise be hired as an advisor and mandated to undertake specific duties by the executive directors (the managing board in the Dutch–German governance system), or by non-executive directors (the supervisory board) on behalf of minority shareholders;
- Provide strategic and tactical transaction advice. This includes appraising the deal's commercial prospects, and planning for regulatory considerations and potential competitive threats;
- Provide a target's shareholders or minority interests with fairness opinions as to the value of a bid;
- Persuade shareholders or regulators to support or block a deal;
- Provide execution and administrative support for bidders. This may include acquiring shares or equity derivatives in the target;
- Develop defence and alternative strategies for targets. This may include placing volatile shareholdings with supportive investors, or devising poison pills;
- Conduct fundraising, which may include debt or equity, or something more complex such as a whole business securitization to redeem short-term debt, a vendor placing of shares given to the target company owners as consideration for a merger and intended by them for sale, or a planned sequencing of funding transactions;
- Manage publicity, to bring media interests into play for support and to assist in marshalling investors; and
- Manage compliance issues, particularly for listing, legal or regulatory disclosure requirements, judicial concerns, transaction stage timing, and safeguarding information, the burdens of which vary considerably by jurisdiction.

Each factor appears in our Section 10.4 case study. Some are addressed by including specialist consultants in deal teams but all are managed by the leading bank advisor. The greatest technical task devolved to investment banks is one of persuasion, especially in hostile deals – to develop material with the principals that will according to need:

- Persuade bidder shareholders that an immediate dilution of their interests is likely to be compensated by the value added over time from a completed deal;

- Persuade target shareholders of the value of independence. The converse need to convince target shareholders of the value of selling the company is needed far less often because they customarily receive a windfall by selling their shares to the bidder; and
- Convince national regulators of bidders and targets of the justification for their clients' case.

The results for banks

The outcome of this labour in 2010 is illustrated by Tables 10.2A–10.2E, which show the ranking by gross transaction fees (before deal expenses) of the leading banks involved in M&A globally, in Asia-Pacific excluding Japan, in all global emerging economies, and in China and India, together with the rankings of providers of fairness opinions, and the overall ranking of banks in order of gross fees earned. The deals from which these data are collated are announced mergers, acquisitions, repurchases, major asset or business sales or spin-offs, tenders for share buybacks, purchases of minority interests and debt restructurings, which is broader in scope than the focus of this Chapter. We use announced rather than completed deals in these illustrations (except for Table 10.2E showing fees collected in completed deals) because announced deals that fail to complete represent substantive activity in terms of the market for corporate control and in the reputational capital of corporate financiers.[2]

Indigenous banks are important providers of corporate finance for M&A in China, India and Japan, but the most common observation from these tables is the transactional dominance of US and EU banks. This has persisted since records began and signifies a significant body of experience, reputational capital, and a barrier to entry for cross-border transactions. Local Asian banks may be successfully active in advising clients in their home markets but none has yet developed a transnational M&A franchise.

Table 10.2A Leading advisors in announced global M&A deals, 2010

		Deal value (US$ bn)	Market share (%)	No. of deals	Rank 2009
1	Goldman Sachs	554.6	22.8	370	2
2	Morgan Stanley	538.1	22.1	394	1
3	JPMorgan Chase	440.1	18.1	320	3
4	Crédit Suisse	412.8	17.0	318	6
5	Deutsche Bank	341.8	14.0	259	7
6	UBS	329.5	13.5	288	8
7	BofA Merrill Lynch	293.1	12.0	241	5
8	Citigroup	279.6	11.5	204	4
9	Lazard	275.8	11.3	277	10
10	Barclays Capital	257.8	10.6	159	9
11	Rothschild	155.6	6.4	261	11
12	BNP Paribas	128.6	5.3	125	20
13	Nomura	120.4	4.9	171	16
14	Société Générale	98.8	4.1	46	28
15	HSBC	81.4	3.3	80	17
16	Evercore	80.6	3.3	38	12
17	Macquarie	75.9	3.1	139	35
18	Blackstone	75.3	3.1	44	19
19	Greenhill	72.7	3.0	61	31
20	Perella Weinstein	64.5	2.7	25	30
	Grand total	**2,434.2**	**100.0**	**40,660**	**NA**

Source: Thomson Reuters (2011).

Table 10.2B Leading advisors in announced M&A deals, Asia-Pacific excluding Japan, 2010

		Deal value (US$ bn)	Market share (%)	No. of deals	Rank 2009
1	Morgan Stanley	58.3	12.5	57	1
2	Goldman Sachs	51.0	10.8	54	5
3	UBS	46.8	9.9	59	2
4	Crédit Suisse	42.0	8.9	79	3
5	Deutsche Bank	35.2	7.4	43	9
6	BNP Paribas	26.3	5.5	22	16
7	Barclays Capital	25.8	5.4	17	34
8	China International Capital	25.7	5.4	30	8
9	JPMorgan Chase	25.4	5.4	37	10
10	BofA Merrill Lynch	25.2	5.3	26	6
11	Citigroup	23.1	4.9	38	4
12	Standard Chartered	22.2	4.7	29	19
13	Rothschild	21.0	4.4	37	41
14	RHB	18.7	3.9	24	80
15	RBS	18.2	3.8	14	29
16	HSBC	17.9	3.8	24	13
17	CIMB	16.7	3.5	56	27
18	Nomura	15.6	3.3	23	7
19	AMMB	13.2	2.8	38	51
20	Macquarie	12.1	2.6	32	38
	Grand total	**474.6**	**100.0**	**9,573**	**NA**

Source: Thomson Reuters (2011).

Table 10.2C Leading advisors in announced M&A deals, China, 2010

		Deal value (US$ bn)	Market share (%)	No. of deals	Rank 2009
1	China International Capital	25.3	13.3	28	2
2	Crédit Suisse	14.7	7.7	24	3
3	CITIC	10.5	5.6	14	11
4	JPMorgan Chase	10.4	5.5	7	15
5	Goldman Sachs	9.3	4.9	13	10
6	UBS	7.3	3.8	11	12
7	Bank of Nova Scotia	7.1	3.8	1	32
8	Deutsche Bank	6.7	3.5	17	9
9	Morgan Stanley	6.4	3.4	11	1
10	Rothschild	6.0	3.2	7	63
11	Somerley	5.7	3.0	15	23
12	Guotai Junan Securities	5.7	3.0	10	64
13	Jefferies	4.2	2.2	4	71
14	Southwest Securities	4.0	2.1	6	20
15	Huatai Securities	3.9	2.1	18	31
16	Haitong Securities	3.8	2.0	8	14
17	Anglo Chinese Corporate Finance	3.5	1.9	9	46
18	Macquarie	3.4	1.8	4	39
19	BNP Paribas	3.4	1.8	9	13
20	Nomura	3.0	1.6	6	16
	Grand total	**189.7**	**NA**	**3,483**	**NA**

Data are based on transactions with any involvement of a China domiciled party.

Source: Thomson Reuters (2011).

Table 10.2D Announced M&A deals, Japan, 2010

		Deal value (US$ bn)	Market share (%)	No. of deals	Rank 2009
1	Nomura	55.3	44.9	114	1
2	JPMorgan Chase	29.5	24.0	18	5
3	Mitsubishi UFJ Morgan Stanley	21.2	17.2	49	NA
4	Daiwa	19.3	15.6	57	3
5	BofA Merrill Lynch	18.7	15.2	20	9
6	Citigroup	14.0	11.4	19	8
7	UBS	13.6	11.1	7	6
8	Mizuho	12.0	9.7	104	2
9	Deutsche Bank	10.5	8.5	20	11
10	Goldman Sachs	9.9	8.0	15	4
11	Sumitomo Mitsui	9.7	7.9	101	16
12	KPMG	6.6	5.4	32	21
13	ABeam M&A	5.7	4.6	9	35
14	Barclays Capital	5.5	4.5	8	15
15	Perella Weinstein	4.8	3.9	2	34
16	Lazard	4.2	3.4	6	18
17	Centerview	3.8	3.1	1	–
18	Rothschild	3.0	2.5	7	58
19	GCA Savvian	2.6	2.1	27	25
20	Greenhill	1.8	1.5	6	13
	Grand total	**123.2**	**100.0**	**2,786**	**NA**

Data are based on transactions with any involvement of a Japan domiciled party.
Source: Thomson Reuters (2011).

Table 10.2E Leading global M&A fee earners, 2010

		Fees paid (US$ mm)	Year on year change in fees (%)	Regional contributions to total fees (%)				
				Americas	Europe	Asia Pacific	Japan	Africa, Middle East & Central Asia
1	Goldman Sachs	1,964	+47	64	23	11	2	1
2	Morgan Stanley	1,413	+33	54	26	12	6	2
3	JPMorgan Chase	1,392	+19	60	25	7	3	5
4	Crédit Suisse	1,034	+42	57	31	11	1	0
5	BofA Merrill Lynch	909	+9	75	11	10	2	2
6	UBS	851	+26	42	32	20	1	5
7	Lazard	844	+35	44	41	5	1	10
8	Deutsche Bank	834	+41	49	35	10	5	1
9	Rothschild	744	+21	26	63	9	0	1
10	Citigroup	731	+10	57	24	13	5	2
	Total	**30,545**	**+34**	**51**	**29**	**14**	**4**	**3**

Data based on completed transactions.
Source: Thomson Reuters (2011).

How can the value of corporate finance be assessed, even if these banks appear to profit from their work? M&A provide the most interesting and challenging transactions for banks and can be highly rewarding, but it is less clear that value is consistently produced by such deals, either for the principals, their shareholders or at a societal level. In terms of the exit provision or transformational value of M&A transactions identified by Jensen, a positive effect on incumbent managers may arise equally from expectations of deals that are threatened but fail to materialize or deals that are announced but fail to proceed to execution.

10.3 Activity in Asia

Any regional assessment must be prefaced by the historical limits placed on M&A. A large share of deals involve no change in control, which is often blocked by dominant shareholders or economic nationalism. We doubt that a transformational deal involving external interests such as the one described in Section 10.4 would be permitted in any economy except Hong Kong or Japan, and it is more likely in all cases that corporate change would be more modest than elsewhere and conducted consensually by domestic interests. An increase in corporate restructuring did occur after 1999 and involved several large acquisitions by non-Asian interests, but as the region's economy recovered the need for corporate and bank balance-sheet repair lessened. This meant that M&A would focus on creative rather than recuperative corporate change, allowing companies to migrate to new business models and enhance their operating performance and internal governance.

The region has developed as a source of deals of all kinds, although the balance of completed transactions is skewed towards transfers of partial ownership and consensual arrangements. Figure 10.3 shows that M&A activity in Asia over 1997-2008. Prior to the Asian financial crisis M&A activity was negligible in scale and sophistication, accounting for no more than 5 per cent of global deals. Volumes increased significantly after 1998, and in 2010 Asian M&A accounted for over 22 per cent of all activity, as Box 10.2 shows. The total value of announced Asian transactions (excluding Japan) peaked in 2007 at US$460 billion, fell during 2008–9 and then recovered to a new high in 2010 of US$474.1 billion. The flow of M&A funds has altered at the same time, with more Asian firms and direct investors engaging in outward M&A. We see six factors as characterizing Asia's distinct and growing

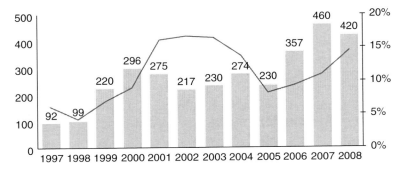

Figure 10.3 Aggregate Asia M&A and its share of global activity, 1997–2008.

Japan is excluded from Asia deal totals. Left scale shows the volume of announced disclosed deals (US$ bn). Right scale shows Asian deal volumes as a share of the global total.

Source: Thomson Reuters (2011).

market, which the following sections consider, expanding an earlier McKinsey & Co. analysis (Anandan, Kumar, Kumara & Padhi 1998):

Overcapacity

We saw in Section 1.3 how fixed asset formation has driven the region's economy since the early 1970s, but excessive investment and resource misallocation due to weak intermediation tends to produce overcapacity in many sectors. Excess capacity requires mechanisms for effective withdrawal, and as suggested by Jensen M&A may become important in dealing with unwanted capacity.

Corporate consolidation

Geographical diversity and trade barriers have tended to limit the development of large national companies, leaving many industries fragmented and prone to diseconomies of scale, and unable or unwilling to engage in new product or brand development. This contributes to overcapacity and provides additional potential for consolidation.

Deregulation

Several states relaxed their statutory limits on foreign shareholdings after 1999, including South Korea, the Philippines, Singapore, Taiwan and Thailand. China's ceiling remains at 25 per cent generally, but Beijing is more tolerant of the scope of permissible foreign direct investment. The State Development and Planning Commission indicated, in its 1995 Catalogue Guiding Foreign Investment in Industry, those sectors and investment projects that would be allowed or prohibited from receiving foreign involvement, and a 2002 revision was less limiting in scope.

Restructuring for efficiency

East and Southeast Asia have historically been home to many SOEs and closely controlled conglomerates whose activities rely on political patronage. This aspect of the region's corporate culture is widespread, notwithstanding institutional improvements made to transparency and governance since the 1997–98 financial crisis. The resulting operating inefficiencies have been notable over long periods among South Korea's *chaebols* (as we saw in Box 2.5), with many Chinese SOEs (examined in Section 3.1) and among groups favoured by patronage in most ASEAN states. A recognition has developed in the last decade that corporate change through asset or whole business spin-offs or privatization may assist in reducing such entrenched inefficiencies, providing long-term scope for M&A. Our transaction predictions are nonetheless cautious, since growth in activity is likely to be constrained by the comparative concentration in regional corporate ownership.

Migration to competitive models

One consequence of Asia's export orientation is that many firms act as ODM or OEM suppliers, and suffer low operating margins by being confined to assembly functions. A more profitable model can result either from organic growth or by manufacturers using M&A to obtain control of brands, and the qualitative resources associated with marketing, client service and product development. An early and conspicuous example of this strategy was the transformation and expansion of computer assembly company Lenovo through its acquisition of IBM's personal-computer interests in 2005.

Table 10.3 shows the possibilities that corporate change can introduce to the production value chain. Most Asian firms lack strong intellectual capital and distinct brands that have value outside their home markets by comparison with more established multinationals, and both M&A and organic development will contribute to the development of more mature corporate sectors.

Outward FDI

Major companies in Japan and South Korea have engaged in outward cross-border investment for some years, both to deploy excess cash resources profitably and to expand their foreign production capacity. This trend to diversify the location of capital has spread since the mid-2000s to private sector companies in China, India and Malaysia, in some cases through high-profile acquisitions of seasoned OECD manufacturing companies, especially in automotive production, electronics, telecommunications and steel manufacturing.

A further distinct form of outward FDI now exists through state-owned investment. Asian sovereign wealth fund (SWF) resources are small compared to the aggregate of funds under commercial management by professional investors, but they have helped introduce new investment practices, particularly with the acquisition of foreign natural resources and

Table 10.3 M&A options along the production value chain

	Product → development	Sourcing → & tooling	Production →	Client sales & services
Typical Asian challenges	Weak intellectual capital and brands	Shortage of domestic natural resources to meet core domestic and export demand	Emerging competition with lower labour and other input costs	Highly competitive domestic markets
	Domestic competition from foreign multinationals	High input prices for energy and other extractive resources	Erosion of low-cost domestic capacity	Eroding market share and operating margins
Possible solutions	Develop or obtain strategic assets including technology, human resources, brands	Secure or acquire access to natural resources	Improve productivity on a global scale	Enter new developing markets (relatively easy) and developed markets (large but complex)
Expansionist solution involving M&A strategy	Predominantly oriented to M&A Mainly outward M&A transactions in open developed markets	Predominantly oriented towards M&A	Predominantly organic expansion	Combined M&A strategy and organic expansion

resource-based companies. These developments may provide a significant source of future M&A activity to the extent that the trend is allowed to continue by investee states.

10.4 Case study: ABN Amro Holding NV

A prominent European universal bank was acquired in 2007 and promptly dismembered, following a protracted and controversial €72 billion (US$101 billion) contested takeover. This was the first break-up of a large universal bank into its constituent businesses. ABN Amro Bank, the main component of Amsterdam-listed ABN Amro Holding NV, was ranked eighth by total assets at end-2006 among EU banks, controlled banking and finance affiliates in 56 countries and within the previous decade was among the largest 12 global banks ranked by market capitalization. We use this section to describe how modern corporate finance created this unprecedented outcome, and ask whether the case is exceptional and what prospects exist for it to be repeated in Asia.

Corporate finance is central to investment banking, with emphases that vary between banks of different type and nationality. It can be capital intensive or focused on advisory engagements, and in each case requires the use of varying skills and appetites for risk. It includes:

- Advice on corporate strategy, high-level dealings with leading shareholders (known in Europe as corporate broking), negotiations with other corporate stakeholders,[3] and liaison with financial or industry regulators and other state agencies.
- Client coverage, tactical input and transaction management in corporate acquisitions and disposals, reorganizations and rescues, M&A strategy in defence or attack, valuations and coordinating fundraising.
- Share flotation through IPOs or secondary offerings, block trades and vendor placings.
- Privatization advice and transaction management for governments, which became a substantial revenue source in the 1980s, applying traditional corporate finance resources to a new setting. This extended after 2000 to strategic and transaction advice to assist direct investment by SWFs.

We analyze the ABN Amro sale narrative because it contains many of these threads and demonstrates the breadth of investment bank transactional activity, skills and treatment of risks. Our account has insights into national banking supervision and competition policy and is as complete as any picture of contemporary practice, especially when set against a clouded market background as in 2007. Table 10.4 shows the landmarks that led to the deal closing in late 2007 (RBS Consortium 2007a). We refer to *closing* as the acquisition's approval by ABN Amro shareholders and becoming unconditional. *Completion* is the consolidation process that began with the closing.

Our narrative is limited to the highlights and results of corporate finance strategy. It involves drastically weakening financial markets and diminishing confidence as a setting for sizeable fundraising and the most valuable hostile acquisition made to date of a financial enterprise.

What transpired in the acquisition proved very different from the hopes of the bidders. One of the functions of M&A advisors is to provide principals with valuation input, but an early result of the US subprime crisis from mid-2007 was to make all bank share valuations hazardous. The acquisition developed such momentum that the winning bidders became locked into an inflated price with no means to avoid paying far more than warranted for a wasting asset.

Table 10.4 Landmarks in ABN Amro Holding break-up

2004–6	Negligible growth in ABN Amro group earnings and declining return on equity
To November 2006	Static ABN Amro share price performance
31 January 2007	ABN Amro share price €24.50
21 February	TCI letter to ABN Amro demanding that a vote be held at an annual general meeting of shareholders in April on a sale or break-up of the bank
March	Barclays and ABN Amro disclose merger talks
April	Barclays and ABN Amro announce terms of an agreed merger. Barclays would acquire ABN Amro for an all-share consideration. ABN Amro simultaneously announces the sale of its US subsidiary LaSalle Bank to Bank of America
5 May	Indicative counter-proposal from RBS, Fortis and Santander, including LaSalle
May–July	ABN Amro shareholder meetings, litigation over sale of LaSalle
	Revised Barclays bid with cash component
	Revised RBS consortium bid
	Subprime crisis begins to break with trading losses announced by major French bank Société Générale S.A.
	ABN Amro board withdraws support from Barclays bid but refuses to guide shareholder decision
13 July	Dutch supreme court permits the sale of LaSalle
	Final RBS consortium bid of €38.40 per share
10 August	ABN Amro shareholders vote to accept RBS consortium bid
September	Barclays bid lapses with minimal acceptance from ABN Amro shareholders
	Fortis announced €13.4 billion share issue. Santander announces €7.0 billion convertible bond issue
	Dutch finance ministry approval for the takeover
October	RBS consortium bid accepted by almost all ABN Amro shareholders
	Fortis agrees with EU competition authorities to make major disposals from ABN Amro's Dutch commercial banking businesses, valued at €0.7 billion
November	Santander announces €6.6 billion sale of Banco Antonveneto to Banco Monte dei Paschi di Siena, a profit of 57 per cent obtained in less than four weeks
December	Fortis and RBS announce intended split in ABN Amro Dutch non-retail clients
March 2008	De Nederlandsche Bank gives approval to the break-up of ABN Amro's core businesses, to be divided between RBS, Fortis and Santander
April	Fortis acquires ABN Amro asset management businesses
June	RBS rights issue raises £12 billion in emergency share capital
July	Fortis chief executive forced to resign
October	Fortis taken into part state ownership in Belgium and Luxembourg. All Dutch banking and insurance assets of Fortis (including ABN Amro Bank) acquired by the state
	RBS chief executive and chairman resign. RBS joins UK state-led recapitalization scheme to raise £20 billion in new Tier I capital

Sources: RBS Consortium (2007a); Authors' records.

Contemporary and post-crisis analysis have criticized the bidders for pursuing a cripplingly expensive transaction when market sentiment was collapsing and the credit crisis was inflating ABN Amro's fair value losses and eroding the value of the target. This may suggest that the market for corporate control is faulty, or at least subject to irrational or hubristic management. The case study involves a controversial outcome, tests the universal bank model in both rising and falling markets, and examines the effectiveness of investment banking.

The transaction was iconic in several ways:

- It was the world's costliest financial sector acquisition and the second most valuable purchase to date of any European company;
- Contested bidding for major public companies is seldom seen outside Anglo-American business circles;
- It was the first example of a sizeable international bank becoming a break-up target in a hostile takeover;
- It was the first transnational acquisition of a major bank by a bidding consortium of banks from several domiciles;
- It was the first acquisition of a major intermediary opposed by its leading national regulator, with the future regulation of the target company uncertain but central to the transaction's outcome, and that regulator then trumped by disgruntled shareholders and EU competition authorities;
- A minor but influential hedge fund shareholder in ABN Amro induced the sale and helped thwart a rival friendly merger agreed between the directors of two major EU banks;
- One investment bank initiated the transaction, and provided the bulk of acquisition advice and underwriting commitments to the successful bidders; and
- In the post-crisis environment, the disaster and destruction of value caused by the later collapse of two members of the consortium introduced a precautionary aggressiveness among institutional shareholders, which was later responsible for the rejection of Prudential's bid for AIA in 2010.

Not only was the deal unprecedented in scope, scale and transaction milestones, it revealed aspects of takeover and universal banking practice rarely seen by outsiders. The winning consortium of three banks revealed its break-up plan at the outset, and its revised bid was approved by shareholders before the final collapse of the US subprime loan market broke global confidence, raised loan loss provisions, and led to sharp falls in bank share prices everywhere. ABN Amro also introduced a poison pill to deter the hostile bidders, but the tactic was conditional upon their reaction and proved ineffective. It may even have made the deal easier to execute.

Payment of the sale consideration took place three months after general sentiment had begun to deteriorate. This fall in confidence intensified in early 2008 and eroded the market value and regulatory capital ratios of the winning banks so severely as to require two members, Royal Bank of Scotland (RBS) and Fortis, to raise substantial amounts of emergency capital within nine months of formally taking over ABN Amro in October 2007. This was less than six months after the break-up had begun.

Modern M&A practice

The sale of ABN Amro Holding involved three investment banking and advisory components, with the first two central to M&A practice:

- Valuation, corporate advisory resources, disclosure preparation, and acquisition transaction management provided to six public companies in five jurisdictions. Belgium, Delaware, the Netherlands, Spain and the UK.

- Transaction management and strategy in matters relating to compliance, regulatory negotiations, statutory disclosure, and liaison with leading investors.
- Underwriting, arranging, distributing and executing a series of public securities issues for three banks over six months, in amounts exceeding €66 billion, including stabilization, hedging and other risk management activities customary for new issues.

If our narrative included the aftermath of ABN Amro's sale, that array of transactions would include locating potential buyers for unwanted non-core businesses, corporate valuations, sale prospectus preparation and disposal transaction management for three major public companies, and further substantial fundraising transactions for at least two of the latter, one such deal becoming Europe's largest ever fundraising through an issue of shares in June 2008. Some of these secondary deals became distressed sales after two members of the consortium collapsed. Unwanted portions of ABN Amro continued to be owned by RBS as of June 2011.

The sale of ABN Amro shows the transactional scope of modern investment banking practice. It involved virtually all senior European and US corporate finance specialists in advising the protagonists:

- Merrill Lynch for the RBS consortium.
- Barclays Capital, Citigroup, Crédit Suisse, Deutsche Bank, JPMorgan Cazenove and Lazard for Barclays, which was ABN Amro's preferred partner.
- ABN Amro hired Goldman Sachs, Lehman Brothers, Morgan Stanley, NM Rothschild and UBS, two finance sector advisors in Greenhill and Fox-Pitt, Kelton, and its UK corporate broker, ABN Amro Hoare Govett.

The only notable investment bank absent from the ABN Amro case was Bear Stearns, which had no material M&A practice. Among banks ranked as global or regional M&A market leaders in 2007, only Macquarie Bank advised none of the six main ABN Amro takeover parties. Macquarie then ranked fourth among M&A specialists in non-Japan Asia by aggregate deal value and first by completed transactions. The principals also employed many non-bank advisors, including lawyers, accountants and public relations specialists, all of whom have become essential to large transactions.

One reason for bidders or targets to seek such comprehensive advisory coverage is to deny later deal access to a new third party, which was one of Prudential's tactics noted in Box 10.1. As we suggested in Section 10.2, large acquisitions are impossible without external corporate finance advice because the bank advisor can be judged by regulators and investors to conform with legal and customary takeover practice, or be held to account by the law, financial regulators or market sentiment for breaches of practice or warranty, or failures to disclose material events or changes in the condition of the principals.

In July 2008 an underwriter of a large rights issue by UK commercial bank HBOS was criticized by its peers for unusually aggressive trading tactics. Morgan Stanley sold short substantial volumes of existing HBOS shares to hedge the risk associated with an unsold position of the new issue that investors had rejected. Despite Morgan Stanley making the FSA aware of its intention, the bank experienced a reputational loss that damaged its standing with other clients. Short-selling in this example was seen as conflicted, unfair to other underwriters, favouring the short seller at the expense of the issuer, and representing a dilution of the bank's underwriting commitment.

The target

As at end-2006, ABN Amro was among the world's largest 30 banks measured by market capitalization and ranked in the top 15 by total assets. It was the product of 1991 mergers between Dutch banks of long-standing, and occupied a totemic position in Dutch corporate life. A hostile acquisition of such a national icon would have been controversial anywhere in continental Europe or Asia even a decade earlier, and a sale to foreign interests inconceivable in many jurisdictions, as we know from examples in France and South Korea. New Zealand's banks have been largely foreign owned since the 1980s mainly for reasons of scale. HSBC was permitted in 1992 to acquire Midland Bank, then Britain's fourth largest commercial bank, only upon agreeing to move its domicile and main listing from Hong Kong to London.

ABN Amro's managing board held separate informal strategic discussions in 2005–6 with RBS and Barclays, both large UK banks.[4] Barclays is not a classic European universal bank but is diversified in functional and geographical sources of revenue, and has major investment bank and credit card operations. The first tangible public move came in March 2007, when ABN Amro and Barclays announced their intention to negotiate a merger. The spur had been a vocal campaign and petitions to ABN Amro's boards by a London hedge fund, The Children's Investment Fund (TCI), owner of under 2 per cent of ABN Amro shares. TCI was known as an active investor that agitated for corporate change. In a letter sent on 21 February to ABN Amro's directors it drew attention to the bank's poor performance over the previous five years, and suggested that shareholders would gain materially from the bank being sold or dismembered, with its non-European and non-core businesses auctioned to third parties. TCI stated that because of 'management failures' and risks associated with the bank's current strategy:

> [W]e believe that ABN Amro's current market capitalization stands at a significant discount to the fair value of ABN Amro's underlying assets. The 'sum of the parts' analysis conducted by most sell-side analysts [bank research staff who prepare company analyses for investors] show [sic] that the aggregate value of ABN AMRO's businesses would justify a price significantly in excess of €30 per share [compared to €24.50 on 31 January 2007].
>
> (TCI 2007)

And as a result:

> We believe that it would be in the best interests of all shareholders, other stakeholders and ABN Amro for the Managing Board of ABN Amro to actively pursue the potential break up, spin-off, sale or merger of its various businesses (or as a whole).
>
> (ibid)

We can best illustrate TCI's argument with ABN Amro's own material. Figure 10.4 shows its commercial structure in the form eventually sold.

Revenue-seeking activities comprised seven 'client business units' shown in the top half of the image, two 'cross-business unit segments' known as Consumer Clients and Commercial Clients, each sharing management of activity found in the first group of seven, and three 'product business units' shown [sic] in the bottom three rows. The three product units would also seek transactions from larger clients of the other units.

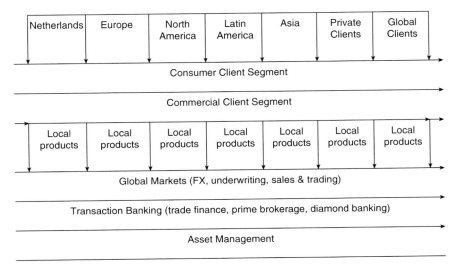

Figure 10.4 ABN Amro Holding structure, end-2006.
Administrative functions are excluded.
Source: ABN Amro Annual Report (2006).

This cross matrix arrangement is common among financial conglomerates but often engenders management and operating conflicts and a lack of strategic clarity. Both clients and staff rarely know the scope of the bank's resources, making it difficult to distribute the broadest range of products or identify the greatest number of transaction opportunities. ABN Amro's board sought to justify a strategy that appeared to many outsiders to lack focus, direction or acceptable returns. This characterization is one facet of traditional hostility to conglomerate corporate structures that we cited in Section 10.1, and is self-destructive for universal banks given their supposed countercyclical value. ABN Amro's global operations were hampered by these opaque objectives. The bank was well established in the Netherlands, Brazil, Italy and the US, but many overseas operations were small colonial legacies of the kind we described in Section 3.1 as pervasive in Asia. Their returns and prospects were poor, and forced ABN Amro to rely heavily on principal trading to meet its financial targets, a tactic never fully disclosed thanks to complaisant governance and poorly consolidated accounts.

Recurring underperformance meant that little of the bank's strategy was thought credible by sell-side researchers. Successful universal banks contain complementary activities where each has a competitive advantage, compared to conglomerates whose only strength is scale. A poor share-price history compared to its peers gradually restricted ABN Amro's scope to expand by acquisition. Its 2005 purchase of Italian commercial bank Banca Antoniana Popolare Veneta (Banca Antonveneta) was regarded as costly and a management distraction. Further acquisitions were not feasible.

Under such pressure, Barclays and ABN Amro released proposals for a €67 billion merger on 23 April 2007 comprising an offer of new Barclays shares for all the outstanding shares in ABN Amro Holding. The deal notably excluded LaSalle Bank, the substantive part of ABN Amro's US operations. ABN Amro's share price closed that day at €35.77,

46 per cent above its end-January level but below the stated value of Barclays' proposal, suggesting both that TCI's opinion had been perceptive but that observers were sceptical that Barclays' all-share offer would crystallize that break-up value for shareholders. A major task for Barclays and its advisors was to sustain shareholder support for the merger, maintain its own share price and preserve the value of the bid.

ABN Amro and Barclays would merge under a UK holding company headquartered in Amsterdam but supervised by the UK's FSA, for which approval was required from both sets of shareholders and Dutch and British regulators. ABN Amro directors also made a separate agreement that is best viewed as a poison pill to act as a disincentive to rival bidders. This was the US$21 billion cash sale of LaSalle, ABN Amro's Chicago subsidiary, a non-core asset in a Barclays merger but coveted by competing third-party interests. ABN Amro agreed to sell LaSalle immediately to Bank of America (BofA) with the proviso that if the sale were blocked by shareholders or regulators then ABN Amro would pay US$200 million in cash compensation to BofA. This would include circumstances where BofA chose not to match a higher counter-offer for LaSalle from a third party. Article 8.1(f) of the draft sale and purchase agreement of 22 April 2007 stated the termination fee to be 'an integral part of the transactions contemplated by this Agreement and that, without this Agreement, [Bank of America Corporation] would not enter into this Agreement.'

An indicative counter-bid was made on 5 May by an ad hoc consortium of three banks: RBS, Fortis and Banco Santander Central Hispano (Santander) – an unusual arrangement devised by Merrill Lynch, the investment bank that had successfully advised RBS in a transforming acquisition in 2000. Merrill Lynch acted as sole advisor to the trio and principal underwriter to each for a series of equity and regulatory capital issues to fund the bid. This represents a significant commitment of capital to support the underwriting and sale of new shares and hybrid securities and of corporate finance resources to manage a multifaceted M&A process. The contributions of the three banks to the transaction matched their respective interests in segments of the target, with RBS, Fortis and Santander holding shares of 38.3 per cent, 33.8 per cent and 27.9 per cent respectively in the acquisition vehicle (RBS Consortium 2007c: Sch. 1: Investor Commitments, 36).

Contested consortium bids are unusual because they introduce contingent risks into complex corporate settings, and were unknown in the financial sector or on the scale needed to secure ABN Amro. Consortium bids for financial intermediaries were successful after the Asian financial crisis in Indonesia and South Korea to allow partial foreign access to restricted targets. The structure allows national regulators to approve capital infusions for underperforming banks without loss of control to a single foreign bank or private equity investor.

The consortium's 29 May bid was initially valued at 8 per cent above Barclays' proposal. It contained a cash component of 70 per cent of the consideration to be paid to ABN Amro shareholders, with the remainder payable in RBS shares. TCI had insisted that greater value could be realized from an alternative to Barclays, welcomed the more favourable RBS proposal and opposed the uncontested sale of LaSalle. ABN Amro had stated LaSalle to be a core activity that it now seemed ready to cast away casually, perhaps to help conclude a deal with Barclays.

Contested takeovers are rare in the banking sector because the industry is both regulated and closely watched by governments due to its central position in national economies. This leaves advisors with few precedents to guide their deal tactics, and makes banks and conglomerates notoriously difficult to value. Most valuation models have greater relevance with commercial or manufacturing companies since the attributable value of banks relies heavily on human resources, reputational capital and volatile assets. The advising investment bank will examine as many comparisons as seem plausible or useful to investors, using current and future earnings multiples and discounted prospective cashflows. Earnings prediction is hazardous except with reference to sectoral performance, even with homogeneous specialist lenders.

The character of the target's shareholders altered completely during the protracted acquisition process. Small and institutional Dutch owners steadily sold their shares to M&A arbitrage funds that sought to profit from the transaction process. The merger with Barclays was insufficiently transforming to be rewarding for both traditional ABN Amro investors and TCI, but a credible alternative could have established competitive price tension and improved any final terms. The LaSalle sale agreement with BofA included a 'go shop' clause devised by Morgan Stanley, allowing ABN Amro to consider any a higher bid for LaSalle for a limited period. BofA could match the second bid but would collect the termination penalty by then abandoning its commitment. This made the disposal of LaSalle raise the cost of the purchase to a bidder other than Barclays.

Indeed, the first counteroffer by the RBS consortium was expressly conditional upon the LaSalle sale being revoked, as a precondition to the making of a formal offer and a condition that would form part of any such offer. The RBS team began its assault with an indicative offer for ABN Amro Holding and a firm offer of US$24.5 million for LaSalle's operations, with the former conditional upon ABN Amro accepting the latter. The Dutch supreme court later ratified a decision of ABN Amro shareholders to endorse the sale of LaSalle to BofA so that RBS's condition was never met. No other commercial precondition was included in the terms of the indicative proposal.

ABN Amro's directors were forced to defend the disposal against shareholder suits claiming breaches of fiduciary duties, and a claim by BofA in the New York courts coinciding with the consortium's first indicative proposal for contractual damages and an order restraining the sale of LaSalle to a third party. The Dutch supreme court finally sanctioned the LaSalle sale in July, and the RBS consortium quickly removed the condition from its final successful bid. The go shop provision had a secondary value in protecting ABN Amro's managing and supervisory board members from a shareholder claim for breach of fiduciary duty. Some observers suggested that the poison pill was created so close to the time of the agreement with Barclays that it would have been impermissible in other jurisdictions.

ABN Amro had granted Barclays access to its business records in March 2007 as part of preparatory due diligence conventional in any merger. The RBS trio's counter-proposal requested similar treatment but was from inception based upon wholly different due diligence objectives. The consortium members came together with expressly differing wishes to acquire, dismember and divide ABN Amro, something never attempted in the global banking industry. RBS was known to covet those of ABN Amro's US operations contained in LaSalle to merge with its more limited US banking business, so that the BofA poison pill appeared to be a deterrent for RBS, if not the other consortium members. The 5 May proposal specifically saw LaSalle as part of its overall plan, as we have seen.

The share prices of both Barclays and the consortium were pressured by the weight of the possible acquisition, doubts as to the ability of either to bring a transnational merger to effect, and a general deterioration in sentiment beginning in July. Leading RBS shareholders were indulgent to their directors because the bank successfully completed the hostile takeover and integration of NatWest Bank in 2000. This was critical to the eventual outcome, for Barclays was constrained in its ability or willingness to add a cash component to its bid. Although each rival increased the overall value of its final proposal, the greater cash element in the consortium bid began to seem unassailable by end-July. Barclays' shareholders feared that it might overpay for ABN Amro in a protracted fight, forcing down the bank's share price and eroding the market value of the Barclays bid.

RBS directors appeared determined to continue with the transaction in the final stages of the process despite having undertaken unusually limited due diligence, losing LaSalle, and with general conditions worsening as we saw in Table 2.4. It also became clear in August that if RBS was obstinate and largely indifferent to what was purchased, then the cash received from the sale of LaSalle would *facilitate* completion rather than its obstruction, because the acquirer would effectively receive the sale proceeds from BofA. Poison pills cannot game or be conditional upon the behaviour of a bidder. Release of the LaSalle proceeds was ironically later obstructed by Dutch regulators pending approval of RBS plans to apportion ABN Amro's domestic activities with Fortis, and the delay contributed to the collapse in RBS's post-acquisition financial condition.

Assailed by shareholders and stakeholders, the directors of ABN Amro withdrew support from the Barclays proposal and unusually made no recommendation to the shareholder general meeting. This may be the greatest irony of the case. A resourceful universal bank was unable to recommend its own destruction, even if that appeared to be in its shareholders' interests. The Dutch commercial code creates an obligation on public and other companies to recognize stakeholder interests beyond those of shareholders, extending to clients, employees and the wider community, and the conduct of ABN Amro directors in this context was fiercely debated at shareholder meetings. The consortium also needed to maintain the confidence of their respective shareholders. Was this too large a deal to absorb, or would the failure to capture LaSalle ruin RBS's opportunity? Merrill Lynch argued plausibly that RBS was among the few banks able to be judged in this respect, having won control of the far larger NatWest and successfully integrated its operations with sizeable cost savings.

After three months of antagonism, shareholder meetings, regulatory decisions and Dutch and US litigation, the consortium's final bid was accepted by the required majority of ABN Amro shareholders on 10 August, to take effect in October, by which time bank sector share prices had begun to fall. The shareholder vote followed one week after loss disclosures by BNP Paribas, IKB Deutsche Industriebank, Northern Rock and Sachsen Landesbank marked the true start of the 2007 credit crisis. BofA at once absorbed LaSalle and in March 2008 the three bidders were given approval by the Dutch central bank to break up ABN Amro's core Dutch businesses, the first such dissection of a major universal bank. The results are summarized in Table 10.4, although the process continued beyond 2010, long after the acquisition was sealed.

Dismemberment

ABN Amro's dissection was instrumental to the consortium proposal. An outline of its main elements appeared in its first letter to the ABN Amro board on 5 May:

> A business plan to be agreed by the [RBS consortium] Banks (for which the Banks expect to seek regulatory approval as part of the approvals for the transaction) will outline the approach to be taken to the continued running of the ABN Amro business, its orderly reorganisation into its continuing components and its operational and legal separation and distribution to the Banks. Whilst there may be selected asset disposals in due course, no element of the proposed offer will be conditional upon any such disposals, an agreement made by the three banks on 28 May. (Memorandum to the Supervisory and Managing Boards of ABN AMRO from the Banks regarding the Banks' commitment to make an offer for ABN AMRO subject to certain pre-conditions, 5 May 2007).

Merrill Lynch intended this benign passage to be read positively and without fear of disruption by ABN Amro management, shareholders, employees or Dutch regulators, and indicates the range of tasks that Merrill Lynch assumed. The same letter indicated how the core businesses would be absorbed into the consortium banks, largely in the manner shown in Table 10.5, except that no indication was given that Antonveneta would be sold after closing, and RBS assumed that it would win control of LaSalle.

Table 10.5 Disposal of ABN Amro Holding, 2007–8

Business	*Location*	*Post-execution (1) & any subsequent owners (2)*
ABN Amro consumer & corporate banking, asset management & private banking	Netherlands	1. Fortis, acquired in 2009 by the Dutch state 2. ABN Amro Bank reconstituted in 2010 and wholly owned by the Dutch state
Remainder of ABN Amro corporate banking & commercial businesses, incl. Hollandsche Bank-Unie	Netherlands	1. Fortis 2. Deutsche Bank. Sale by Fortis required by EU competition law
ABN Amro asset management, private banking	Global, except Brazil, India, Indonesia, Netherlands & US	1. Fortis 2. Sold or wound down
ABN Amro asset management, private banking	India & Indonesia	1. RBS 2. ANZ & HSBC. Distressed sale by RBS
Banco Antonveneta	Italy	1. Banco Santander 2. Banca Monte dei Paschi di Siena. Santander sold immediately on completion
ABN Amro Banco Real retail consumer banking, asset management, private banking; Latin American retail & commercial banking	Brazil	1. Banco Santander
LaSalle Bank	US	1. Bank of America
ABN Amro Bank wholesale & investment banking	Global, except Brazil & Italy	1. RBS 2. Distressed sale by RBS of many Asian & Middle Eastern operations.
AAC Capital Partners (ABN Amro's private equity interests)	Europe	1. RBS 2. Goldman Sachs & others
Consumer Finance	Global ex-Netherlands	1. Fortis 2. Sold or wound down
Shared assets (including Saudi Hollandi Bank, Prime Bank, & ABN Amro Private Equity).	Various	1. Retained by RBS pending unidentified future disposal

Sources: ABN Amro Holding NV Annual Report 2007; Authors' records.

ABN Amro saw itself as having three core retail and commercial markets in the Netherlands, Midwest US and Brazil, in each case where its footprint was substantial and well-ranked. Much of the bank's Asian operations were long established but poorly capitalized and resourced, although it claimed to have a '[s]trong corporate/mid-market footprint in [Greater] China, India and Pakistan' (ABN Amro 2006) and was growing in Australia, Malaysia, Singapore, Thailand and Vietnam. ABN Amro was a market leader in Eurozone fixed income underwriting and sales, and ranked strongly in non-American M&A advisory, albeit through a joint venture with NM Rothschild. It was well-ranked in league tables as an arranger of wholesale Asian debt and project finance transactions and was regarded respectably as a first- or second-tier securities dealer in regional debt and equity markets.

The bank's businesses were not market leaders outside the Netherlands but some were successful and ABN Amro lacked no important business component compared to other major universal banks such as Citigroup, Deutsche Bank or UBS. Banking was far more important as a source of revenue than insurance or asset management, compared to ING or UBS respectively, but Table 10.5 shows the comprehensiveness of assets that the consortium was able to dissect. The balance of business streams within universal banks will usually be a function of historical and regulatory factors:

- What operations were permitted under a single holding company at any time?
- Which activities were prominent at the time of corporate formation?
- Where are capital and human resources traditionally concentrated?

The 2007–8 configurations of Citigroup or ING derived proportionately high revenues from insurance because these were instrumental component businesses when each group came into being. No Asian-domiciled bank has the scope of activities associated with the major EU universal banks, and Citigroup was the sole US universal bank before revising its activities after being rescued by the US government in 2008–9.

The diversified model may have value in phases of market cycles but is at risk of attack when banking shares are historically undervalued relative to expected earnings as in the period from mid-2007. In one sense the hostile break-up of ABN Amro anticipated calls later made by activist investors for Citigroup and UBS to adopt a similar strategy when both began provisioning against subprime credit losses in 2007–8. Such investors suggest that the bank broken into discrete businesses would command higher stockmarket ratings than the diversified holding company, as a mirror of the common perception of conglomerates in many advanced economies.

Deal assessment

We preface our assessment with four statements of the obvious.

- Historicism has no place in the results of M&A. It is impossible to judge any outcome other than the RBS consortium taking control of its target for the price it paid and at the time of acquisition. We cannot know if an alternative would have been more or less effective or otherwise valuable for other companies or their investors. The actions taken by ABN Amro, Merrill Lynch and RBS irrevocably changed all feasible outcomes.

- Contested M&A deals have been consistently lucrative for investment banks since they became acceptable in the Anglo-American markets in the 1960s. Merrill Lynch's desire to complete a landmark deal was driven honourably by incentives for further prospects.
- Deals that appear to destroy shareholder value may have other unquantifiable benefits. Second-order results may appeal to company managers, if not to owners – for example, when a successful bidder overpays for its target but in doing so becomes temporarily too large itself to be acquired.
- The financial condition of RBS and Fortis quickly deteriorated after closing, when RBS was briefly the world's largest bank ranked by assets. Fortis became overextended and was taken into state ownership. The equity and credit markets began to doubt RBS's capacity to absorb its allotment of ABN Amro businesses sufficiently quickly to avoid a severe worsening of liquidity, capital adequacy and overall performance, and from early 2008 many commercial and financial counterparties cut the size and duration of deposits with RBS for fear of its insolvency. The bank became subject to majority state ownership in 2009.

One element common to large acquisitions was not part of the consortium's bid. In non-financial M&A deals, it is common for external finance in the form of transferable debt relying on the credit risk of the merged entity to be imported into the deal, and on which the eventual purchase would be contingent. This approach is commonly known as a leveraged acquisition, even though the scale of new debt taken on by the merged company is neither high nor aggressive, as with leveraged buyouts.

Leveraged acquisitions became lucrative transactions for investment banks in the US in the 1980s. Substantially the same investment banking skills were deployed in the ABN Amro case as any major leveraged acquisition, buyout or privatization. Each of the three banks funded its part of the acquisition with a large share-issue. RBS and Fortis issued new shares, and Fortis and Santander launched several regulatory capital and convertible issues. Merrill Lynch underwrote and arranged issues of shares and regulatory capital of €13.4 billion by Fortis, €22 billion by RBS, and €19 billion for Santander, not only to finance the bid but to provide evidence to regulators of the bid's feasibility.

This approach sought to exploit conditions when bank equity was still relatively well rated. A successful Barclays would have refrained from raising finance upon the merged entity given that it had no break-up plans for ABN Amro, and ABN Amro had itself assisted by planning to return capital to shareholders from the sale of LaSalle. The book value of ABN Amro's fixed assets was as modest as other large banks even, if undervalued (€6.3 billion as at end-2006). The consortium could in principle have linked financing to the acquisition, but this would have introduced three unwanted factors to the deal:

- Pledging ABN Amro assets to raise finance would have been regarded as hostile by Dutch shareholders and a prelude to a more radical break-up than initially disclosed.
- The introduction of additional leverage into the merged entity would have incurred regulatory disapproval.
- Unlike non-financial sector transactions, neither the consortium nor the merged entity could issue new debt on a material scale without breaching minimum capital requirements. New shares and hybrid issues both contributed to regulatory capital.

Accordingly, the consortium's formal proposal was not contingent upon financing. These factors show the importance of Merrill Lynch conducting the deal to win approval from four national regulators. This may be the most vital skill in managing financial sector mergers, especially across national borders. The majority of financial sector acquisitions involve parties from the same domicile, even within the EU where public policy has sought to foster a single market in financial services. Dierick (2004) found that over 60 per cent of EU financial sector M&A activity in 1990–2003 involved parties with shared domiciles and core businesses – for example, with banks buying banks and insurers buying insurers. The only significant exceptions were among Benelux parties, where a single market was pursued as common state policy.

The consortium agreement made by the three bidders on 28 May contained a more detailed treatment of the disposition of ABN Amro's businesses than earlier documents but still lacked precision given the size of the bid and the complexity of the target. ABN Amro was not an assembly of distinct businesses but an organizational web that would be difficult for any third party to value. The division of ABN Amro units in the consortium agreement referred to the section of ABN Amro's 2006 annual report entitled 'Results of operations by [Business Unit]' (ABN Amro 2006: 106–27), which is only an outline of scale and results (Consortium and Shareholders' Agreement (2007), Schedule 3 Part 2: The Acquired Businesses, pp. 53–4).

The consortium's letter of 5 May stated that due diligence would not be a condition of a formal proposal. Acquisitions contain surprises that appear only after closing, and in this case RBS and its partners acted from tactical considerations that included its competitor Barclays, and were relatively unconcerned as to the true value of the target. We see this as typical of a second-best acquisition strategy. Given that neither hostile nor friendly bidders are able to undertake a forensic audit of the target as part of due diligence except in cases involving distressed investment, it may be preferable to determine a bid in terms of the least costly level likely to succeed, rather than the true cost of the parts with a premium for goodwill and positional capital. The risk of this strategy is to produce less favourable outcomes when markets are in decline, as with this case.

The acquisition closed at a cyclical peak in OECD banking sector earnings and balance sheet multiples. When confidence began to ebb in mid-2007, so share prices in the winning banks quickly weakened. The result for RBS was a loss of market capitalization greater than its €28 billion commitment in cash and shares to ABN Amro shareholders. This catastrophic outcome led RBS to raise emergency share capital in mid-2008 of £12 billion (US$24 billion), then Europe's largest share issue of its kind. The chief executive of Fortis resigned in July, eight months after the ABN Amro deal closed. His successor followed almost immediately in September following a funding squeeze and collapse in the group's share price. Fortis's operations in Belgium and Luxembourg became subject to 49 per cent state control, and the Dutch government acquired Fortis's entire banking and insurance businesses in the Netherlands for only €16.8 billion. This included the Dutch arm of ABN Amro Bank designated for Fortis but then still held by the consortium's acquisition vehicle.

Nationalizing Fortis became imperative after the failure of a fire sale of its share of ABN Amro. Fortis had absorbed only the asset management businesses of ABN Amro before the tripartite state rescue since the remaining banking and insurance activities were being gradually divided between RBS and Fortis under Dutch regulatory supervision. The failure of Fortis led to a reconstituted ABN Amro Bank being formed in 2008–9 as a largely domestic entity with the support of the Dutch state. The remainder of Fortis was sold or liquidated.

The share price of each consortium member and of Barclays fell steadily in the 18 months after ABN Amro's first disclosure of merger talks in March 2007. This suggests superficially that the acquisition destroyed value for all those involved other than former ABN Amro shareholders, even with steep price falls in most OECD financial sector shares resulting from the 2007–8 global credit crisis.

In the six months prior to Barclays and ABN Amro agreeing merger terms in April 2007, ABN Amro Holding's share price outperformed the benchmark Dow Jones Euro Stoxx Bank sector index by around 60 per cent. One year after a frenzy of bidding, only Santander among the winning bidders appeared to gain from the outcome and its objectives. This resulted from the sale prior to completion of ABN Amro's Italian subsidiary, Banca Antonveneta, which recouped around 50 per cent of Santander's outlay and left it owning the sole objective of its participation, Banco Real, the core of ABN Amro's seasoned operations in Brazil. In the July offer memorandum to ABN Amro shareholders, Santander had outlined its views of Antonveneta without committing to its absorption (RBS Consortium 2007a: 56–7). We consider Santander and Merrill Lynch to be the only clear winners from ABN Amro. Merrill Lynch later lost its independence through matters unrelated to the transaction.

Barclays and ABN Amro sought to explain the business logic of universal banking in their April 2007 proposal, claiming that:

> The global financial services industry is fragmented. The sources of growth in demand are clear and compelling. The business model best equipped to benefit from these conditions is a universal bank. A successful universal banking strategy will align portfolio composition with sources of market growth and customer demand.
>
> Barclays Plc & ABN Amro Holding NV (2007b)

These claims are not synonymous with maximizing returns on risk-adjusted capital or shareholder equity, nor to achieving the share price performance sought by owners. Could the consortium have abandoned the deal in mid-2007 to save reputation and shareholder value? Its tactics made this unlikely, especially since Santander had an incentive to proceed in more extreme conditions than its partners, having pre-sold much of its interests to a competitor of Antonveneta. The bid accepted by ABN Amro shareholders included standard material adverse change (MAC) provisions that limited the consortium's degrees of freedom. These enabled the buyers to relinquish their obligation to proceed with the transaction in the event that worsening conditions impaired ABN Amro's value. The consortium's formal proposal of 20 July allowed the bid to be effectively cancelled upon:

(i) any event, events or circumstance that results or could reasonably be expected to result in a material adverse effect on the business, cashflow, financial or trading position, assets, profits, operational performance, capitalisation, prospects or activities of any of ABN Amro, [the consortium's acquisition SPV] RFS Holdings, Fortis, RBS or Santander ... [or]

(ii) a material adverse change ... national or international capital markets, ... financial, political or economic conditions or currency exchange rates or exchange controls (whether or not arising as a result of or in connection with any outbreak or escalation of hostilities or declaration of war or national emergency or act of terrorism or other national or international calamity); or

(iii) any suspension of or limitation in trading [in the shares of ABN Amro, RBS, Fortis or Santander]

(RBS Consortium 2007a)

MAC clauses are ubiquitous in large financial transactions but invoked in the rarest of circumstances, even when the requisite conditions are transparently met. Our view is that withdrawal would have been permissible given the unprecedented impact of the spreading credit market dislocation in August 2007, even if unpopular and the cause of litigation, were it not for a transaction structure that made the acquisition uniquely feasible.

Merrill Lynch's structure lowered ABN Amro's risk of the MAC clause being invoked by requiring each member of the consortium to be severally liable for a portion of the overall deal consideration. For the consortium to plead that the terms of the clause had been met due to a severe decline in market conditions was belied precisely by the success that each bank had enjoyed in raising its portion of funds, together over €66 billion (US$93 billion) in financing. The final terms accepted in September by almost all ABN Amro's shareholders consisted of 79 per cent cash raised from new issues, with the remainder paid in RBS shares. Barclays' final bid included only a 39 per cent cash element.

Since market conditions had not deteriorated so as to prevent these issues, how could the consortium revoke the acquisition without appearing capricious? By comparison, a single bidder might have abandoned more readily a deal that, by September, had radically changed for reasons beyond the bidders' control. Merrill Lynch had underwritten the banks' financial commitments to the merger, and therefore took and discharged considerable risks. Such risks can bring great reward and the promise of follow-on business, even where emergency funding is needed.

10.5 Prospects

What would be the outcome in a similar case in Asia? No indigenous bank has the global scale or breadth of businesses formerly controlled by ABN Amro, but a similar hypothetical example would be almost certainly infeasible unless it involved the acquisition of a bank by a competitor of the same domicile. A post-merger break-up of the target bank is still likely to be seen unfavourably by almost all national authorities, except to a limited extent in Hong Kong where foreign banks have acquired locally incorporated banks and where the three leading commercial banks are domiciled elsewhere.

Development Bank of Singapore (DBS) took over a consumer and trade finance bank Dao Heng in 2001 for a price widely felt to be high, but DBS wanted a platform to expand its Hong Kong operations and give it leverage into mainland China. DBS may be among the few Asian banks outside Australia or Japan with potential to become a universal bank, although its investment banking resources are modest and its overall prospects in Singapore limited by scale. DBS has been constrained in efforts to expand elsewhere in Asia, for reasons that we associate with parochial investee states or regulators.

As at end-2010 the Singapore government SWF Temasek Holdings was the beneficial owner of 27.3 per cent of DBS shares, which may have led certain overseas authorities to attribute non-commercial motives to the bank. The result has been failed ambitions to acquire businesses in Indonesia, South Korea and Thailand. Other foreign buyers have been similarly thwarted in seeking controlling interests in banks in China, Japan and South Korea. Temasek's interest in the Singapore stock exchange operator SGX contributed to the Australian government rejecting its agreed merger with the Australian exchange ASX in early 2011.

While foreign bank expansion by acquisition has typically been resisted in the region, widespread consolidation in the banking sector occurred in some jurisdictions after the 1997–98 Asian financial crisis. Japanese regulators have repeatedly encouraged consolidation in the banking sector since the mid-1980s, with substantial mergers arranged to assist in the recovery from loan losses and remove excess capacity. Foreign interests made strategic investments in stricken local banks after the 1997–98 crisis in China, Indonesia, Japan, South Korea, Taiwan and Thailand, but few outright purchases were permitted and the targets were generally not market leaders except for a limited post-crisis period in South Korea. Bank supervision in Asia is generally parochial when dealing with most foreign interests, and no regional authority exists with supervening influence of the kind held by EU competition authorities that allowed the sale of ABN Amro.

The WTO's 1999 General Agreement on Trade in Services (GATS) provides for liberalization in financial services and has considerable scope of application in banking, insurance and the securities sector, but deals mainly with market access for non-residents and the extension to such parties of national treatment by signatory states, so as to grant a foreign bank rights of business and investment scope identical to those of its domestic counterparts. Many national exceptions have been tabled by Asian signatories. Similar provisions exist within bilateral agreements involving Asian states, for example in the 2007 South Korea–US free trade agreement.

Entry into national Asian banking markets by acquisition has been increasingly obstructed since 2003–4. The Indonesian government acquired interests in many failed banks in 1997–98 and thereafter adopted a downsizing and recapitalization policy using AMC Perusahaan Pengelola Aset to monitor the recovery of the banks. Its aim was to raise new capital through strategic sales and share listings, and eventually return all or part of each bank to the commercial sector. Foreign banks and investors with financial sector expertise were encouraged to participate in the process and several took sizeable shareholdings, which in some important cases gave control to the investor. The recovery in the banking sector was widely acknowledged by 2006 and the authorities adopted less liberal policies, so that acquiring or transferring a controlling transnational interest in a local bank was discouraged.

This approach seems to have been taken on by other ASEAN states, so that in 2008 Malayan Banking Bhd was dissuaded by both the Indonesian and Malaysian authorities from buying strategic shareholdings in Bank Internasional Indonesia held by South Korea and Singapore investors. Standard Chartered Bank's similar efforts were frustrated by local and official interests. An identically restrictive stance has been taken since 2005 in South Korea and Thailand. This reflects a defensive attitude that echoes the controlling stance of China's financial regulators since 1997–98. Openness to foreign strategic investment in banks is thus a function of reciprocity and not to be conceded without agreed rewards.

We suggest that no Asian state or national regulator would currently permit the acquisition of a leading bank by a foreign investor or competitor. State policy has tended to encourage consolidation among small-scale banks partly to obstruct foreign acquisitions, as in Indonesia, South Korea, Malaysia, Singapore and Thailand in the last decade. Even if a sale were permitted, it is likely that undertakings would be demanded to prevent a break-up or on-sale of the target. Scope for a more radical transaction might develop in Australia if strategic reciprocity were offered by the investor's home regulator – for example, to permit a similar degree of freedom to an Australian bank aggressor – but not elsewhere for the foreseeable future.

Investment banks seeking M&A activity must rely on unaggressive tactics and look outside the financial sector for opportunities. Nationalism is apparent in finance and is likely to restrict a market for corporate control from establishing in the region. M&A deals are increasing in number and value in Asia but are likely to involve mainly changes in minority interests for the foreseeable future. Transactions for targets in other regions may become more prolific but risk similar parochial restrictions.

11 Non-bank and non-traditional intermediation

The channels for intermediation introduced in Chapters 6–9 are mutually competitive and complementary, in theory and partly in practice. Chapter 4 saw banks and open markets as systemic alternatives, and we look here at fund management and non-traditional intermediation, to encompass organizations that engage with banks and in financial markets as transaction users, counterparties or competitors, and the product alternatives to banks available to savers, borrowers and other users of money. Non-bank intermediation functions throughout our sample economies and is significant in several. Its scale and influence rises:

- As financial systems mature;
- When professional and individual consumers demand greater choice in financial instruments and services; and
- If governments encourage systemic diversity or become willing to loosen their control over intermediation.

We know from Section 3.3 that commercial mutual funds, insurers and other common developed forms are less entrenched in the region than in OECD markets, except generally in Hong Kong, Japan, South Korea and Singapore. Non-bank intermediation is virtually non-existent in the low-income economies outside our sample. Certain examples have become selectively important, including SWFs for China and Singapore, indigenous and foreign hedge funds for Hong Kong and Singapore, funded superannuation schemes serving public sector or military retirees in South Korea, Malaysia, Taiwan and Thailand, and Shari'ah compliant transactions and organizations in Malaysia.

Conventional narratives focused on Europe or North America typically include descriptions of fund management sub-sectors and comparisons of market scale. Our focus is towards the organizations, practices and commonalities associated with the non-bank financial sector, together with the institutional conditions that cause it to flourish. We consider the influence of arbitrage on investment behaviour and organizations more broadly than the algorithmic trading concepts introduced earlier in the book, as well as the impact on such activities of law, regulation and investor protection.

The chapter deals only briefly with state-sponsored savings schemes and quasi-commercial banks such as public postal and savings organizations, which in several economies are immensely well-resourced and important in intermediating private savings to the state sector. Also beyond its scope are investment activities associated with physical commodities and precious metals,[1] the organized exchanges that host markets in those goods, and specialized exchanges with global reach such as the Lloyd's insurance and reinsurance market.

The behaviour of non-bank intermediaries raises several continuing questions:

- What happens when financial activity is disintermediated from the regulated banking sector? Does this favour individual users, financial depth or access to financial products? Do the results vary from one economy to another as suggested in Section 2.2?
- Is bank and non-bank financial regulation sufficiently consistent so as not to induce regulatory arbitrage and inadvertently influence the transactional behaviour of one or both groups? For example, the Basel capital accords have led many banks to hold financial assets with favourable risk weightings, which tends to penalize pension funds as natural holders of long-term sovereign debt.
- Do certain non-bank intermediaries behave less transparently than banks or with less attention to risk management, such that their activities represent a form of regulatory evasion that justifies enhanced supervision?
- Are the agency and corporate governance problems identified in Section 9.5 of a different or heightened character in organized investment management?
- Is a large non-bank financial sector likely to assist general welfare, financial efficiency or systemic stability?

There are no consistent answers to these points. Non-bank intermediaries can be adept risk managers, empowering for individual savers and able to mobilize long-term capital investment with greater certainty than banks. They can also be highly leveraged, risk preferring, non-transparent, and regulated in compartmentalized silos so as to neglect systemic risks. Some form part of the shadow banking system, established partly to avoid oversight or compliance costs.

The impact on economic or financial market development of the depth and sophistication of non-bank intermediaries is variable and difficult to quantify. Case studies of Australian and Chilean pension reforms from the 1980s suggest a positive impact on growth, resulting from increased savings, investment and productivity providing that the scheme is mandatory. Narratives from elsewhere are inconclusive. Empirical studies of 38 OECD and emerging economies, including Indonesia, Japan, South Korea, Malaysia, the Philippines and Singapore indicate a generally positive association between increasing pension fund assets and per capita output growth (Davis & Hu 2008), and between selected pension fund assets and capital market development in a more limited sample of ten Asian and Australasian economies (Hu 2012).

Such evidence broadly accords with the view explained in Sections 2.1 and 4.2 as to the causal impact of finance in economic development, although the influence of growth in non-bank intermediation is likely to depend upon other conditions – for example, on pension funds and insurers having access to suitable investment assets through liquid and reliable debt capital markets (CGFS 2011; Davis 2005).

The overall thinness of Asia's bond markets has regularly been associated by academics and policymakers with a lack of scale in the region's non-bank intermediaries (21st Century Public Policy Institute 2011; Arner, Lejot & Rhee 2006; BIS 2006b; Chan, Chui, Packer & Remolona 2011; Eichengreen & Luengnaruemitchai 2006). Our view is eclectic, in that the causal association between market depth and the prominence of non-bank intermediaries is neither unidirectional nor sufficient to explain the market's underdevelopment. Pension fund and insurance investment are staples of certain OECD debt markets (CGFS 2011), but Section 11.2 shows that asset allocation by pension funds and insurers is subject to significant national variation.

In this chapter we distinguish between the *investor* as the ultimate owner or source of funds, and *fund managers* that become contractual agents or fiduciaries constructing and overseeing *asset portfolios* from segregated investor funds, or sell listed shares or private claims to raise an endowment of pooled liquidity. Portfolio supervision is known generically as *asset management*, whether it takes place as a primary or internal activity. Fund management takes place on behalf of or within several settings:

- Sovereign wealth funds (SWF), for example China Investment Corporation (CIC) or Temasek Holding, and state-endowed single-purpose bodies such as Hong Kong's Hospital Authority.
- Funded state sector superannuation organizations, which include Japan's Local Government Officials and Pension Fund Association and Malaysia's Employee Provident Fund, state-led provident schemes such as South Korea's semi-funded National Pension Service or Singapore's Central Provident Fund, and employer-sponsored private sector pension funds. Pension funds of all types devolve the management of designated asset classes or tranches of investible funds to commercial intermediaries, and are distinguished from *unfunded* pension schemes, which intermediate cash from workers to retirees.
- Well-capitalized commercial insurers such as AIA or Allianz, mutual or quasi-mutual insurers such as New York Life or Nippon Life, and reinsurers such as Munich Reinsurance or Swiss Re, for all of which asset management is secondary to a core purpose.
- Commercial managers of *collective investment schemes*, especially mutual funds. *Active* fund managers such as Fidelity or Wellington Management follow investment allocation and asset selection guidelines agreed with or promoted to investors. BlackRock and State Street Global Advisors are primarily examples of index tracking or *passive* fund managers.
- Hedge funds, especially long/short funds and including quantitative, event-driven and algorithmic traders. Nearly all hedge fund managers are closely held privately companies or limited partnerships, and range widely in their available fixed capital and human resources.
- Non-state foundations and endowments, for example those associated with educational, philanthropic or religious purposes, and private *family offices* that manage HNW resources directly and through private banks, conventional fund managers and fund of funds managers, many located in *offshore centres* such as Hong Kong, Monaco, Singapore or Switzerland.
- Private equity and venture capital fund managers direct investors in unlisted and young or expanding companies, respectively. LBO specialists such as KKR & Co. and Texas Pacific Group deploy substantial leverage when making large acquisitions, but private equity is also populated by many far smaller fund managers engaged primarily with SMEs. Most are closely held companies or limited partnerships.
- Managers of unlisted or listed infrastructural funds, including Macquarie Group, UBS and a number of large private equity firms. Fund managers in private equity, venture capital and infrastructural investment obtain resources for investment from the intermediaries identified in the foregoing categories.

We are less interested in how these organizations are administered or devise and sell their products than in similarities in their asset allocation and management and how institutional factors encourage patterns of behaviour. The focus is with those considered important in Asia and associated with the developments in its economic and demographic structure explained in Section 3.1. Our approach is to look first at important factors that influence fund managers, and then examine non-bank intermediation in two categories. *Traditional* fund managers means insurers, mutual funds, funded pension schemes, private equity and venture capital; those that are *non-traditional* means SWFs, specialist infrastructural investment, and hedge funds.

The traditional and non-traditional commonly differ in investment strategy. Non-traditional fund managers are more commercially independent, less constrained by market practice or regulation in their asset allocation and tactics, and far more consistent users of leverage, derivatives, short selling and asset lending to improve or defend their returns. All share administrative and operational practices, as with their use of custodians, although non-traditional fund managers often deal symbiotically with banks and securities firms, the clearest example being the relationship between hedge funds and the prime brokerage functions of banks, which tie the fund manager client to execute transactions with the prime broker in return for data, research and administration services.

We first examine contractual behaviour by investors and the effect of incentives on the portfolio choices of fund managers. Dividing the traditional and non-traditional helps identify:

- Forms of non-bank intermediation that are ubiquitous, albeit on scales varying from place-to-place;
- Specialist fund management peculiar to certain economies or varieties of capitalism;
- Those for which intermediation or the deployment of investible funds is essential but secondary to a core purpose, as with insurance or funded pension schemes; and
- Organizations and practices unique to Asia, excluding informal finance as outlined in Section 3.3.

The chapter ends with a description of Islamic finance, which has both traditional and non-traditional qualities. This highlights the contemporary growth in Shari'ah compliant financing and investment, its institutional basis and contractual outcomes, and how it compares with conventional finance, asking whether Islamic finance may be a more intrinsically stable form of intermediation conducive to general welfare.

The brevity of this chapter belies its importance and is explained by Asia's financial repression and lack of comprehensiveness in non-bank intermediation. Activity is restrained by variations in national rules and barriers to foreign entry, especially in traditional fund management. Established regional operations tend to be non-indigenous legacy license holders such as AIA or HSBC, as Section 3.1 identifies. Foreign entry is more marked in non-traditional sectors in the financial hubs of Hong Kong and Singapore.

How might Asian non-bank intermediation develop further in the coming decade? Three drivers may influence the result:

- Greater regional financial integration will reduce entry barriers and transnational transaction costs, and explained in Section 12.3.
- Maturing economies facing significant demographic changes will alter and increase demand for non-bank savings products, as suggested by household surveys in China (Seade & Wei 2010).

- An increasing governmental commitment to encourage deployment of savings within the region.

Such trends may not favour indigenous intermediaries. Some are certain to remain protected by formal or customary barriers to foreign intermediaries, even as national markets become increasingly sophisticated.

11.1 Investor behaviour

Professional investment choices are rarely the result of free will or the unwavering application of finance theory. Even when fund managers use first principles to design a model asset portfolio the results after implementation will be influenced by institutional constraints, transaction costs and the 'animal spirits' that Keynes associates with confidence and unpredictability in financial markets (Moggridge 1973: 165). Asset managers may plan to construct and administer portfolios using conventional finance theories, but their behaviour will be conditioned by other factors:

- Regulation and governance. Traditional asset managers are constrained as to permissible portfolio liquidity, solvency, credit risk, domicile and concentration. Many choose to be subject to rules prescribing ethical or social responsible investment.
- Benchmarking. All fund managers nominate or receive benchmarks against which their performance is appraised, except the few declared as *unconstrained investors* pursuing *absolute returns*. The nature of the benchmark can inadvertently impact portfolio selection and performance, a problem especially associated with equity funds.

Institutional factors influence both asset management structures and practice – for example, encouraging evasive formats such as SIVs, conduits and informal intermediaries as described in Sections 2.5 and 8.2, as well as forms of transactional and regulatory arbitrage. Practice is constrained by investor protection laws that encourage or prevent specific activities or confine their use to certain investors. The behaviour of fund managers as actual or implicit agents for investors is also subject to rules of governance, often written more narrowly than in corporate settings between shareholders and managers. Agency problems specific to fund management include performance incentive structures and their impact on portfolio management, and whether fund providers or owners can influence decisions in investee companies chosen by the fund manager. Others result from the fungibility of money complicating the tracing or recovery of funds in cases of distress or malpractice.

Regulation of asset management within traditional non-bank intermediaries is less granular and internationally uniform than the regulation of banks. Law and regulation tend to set reporting requirements and minimum standards of solvency and prudential conduct without stipulating how investment portfolios are managed, although EU directives on collective investment schemes set limits for mutual funds in terms of risk concentration and holdings of unlisted securities (UCITS Directives 1985 & 2001).

The International Association of Insurance Supervisors (IAIS) represents local and national regulators from over 130 states, including all but Indonesia from our sample, and seeks to encourage harmonized standards through a code of regulatory principles. These are detailed as to business conduct and capital adequacy but provide only a sensible overview of rule- or principle-based approaches to asset management and solvency, notwithstanding that the insurance sector's commercial model relies on fund management to generate profits and retained earnings.

For example, the regulator 'requires the insurer to invest in a manner that is appropriate to the nature of its liabilities' (IAIS 2011: 148), and 'only in assets whose risks it can properly assess and manage' (ibid. 149): Regulators should require that investments be 'secure' in terms of risk, liquid in relation to the insurer's liabilities, held in an 'appropriate location' and be 'sufficiently diversified' (ibid: 142). Derivatives can unsurprisingly 'be useful tools in the management of portfolio risk of insurers and in efficient portfolio management', but 'should preferably be used as a risk management mechanism rather than for speculative investment' (IAIS 2011: 152).

Insurance and pension fund regulators may have authority to intervene if concerned as to the value or choice of invested assets, providing they can require sufficiently detailed reporting. Hong Kong is typical in empowering the sector's regulator to prevent an insurer from writing or renewing policy contracts (Insurance Companies Ordinance s. 27), or making investments 'of a specified class or description' (ibid: s. 28), to require it to liquidate any investment assets, not hold assets outside Hong Kong and place those assets with a designated custodian (ibid: ss. 29–30), and prescribe a minimum asset to liability ratio (ibid: s. 35AA). When the results are opaque insurance users are forced to be guided by regulatory reputation.

The EU's insurance regime will become considerably more prescriptive of capital requirements and permissible investments from 2014 (Directive Solvency II 2009), while the FSB and IAIS began planning common regulatory and capital requirements in 2010 for those insurers deemed systemically important, a reaction to AIG's unwitting debacle. Insurers and pension fund asset managers incur occasional losses but most examples involve malfeasance or fraud: traditional fund management practices are generally conservative. The scale of risk accumulated by AIG's derivatives subsidiary was a notable exception, and partly the product of compartmentalized 'silo' regulation.

Benchmarking

The asset manager's benchmark is far more than a simple metric, having become the most important practical influence on the investor's choice of fund manager and portfolio design. It conditions asset class allocation, performance and individual asset selection, and how asset managers assess portfolio risk as a deviation from the benchmark, known as *tracking error*. Fund managers report periodic results in relation to benchmarks, which encourages their setting internal objectives rather than revenue generation or capital preservation goals that might often be more relevant to the investor. Unconstrained or *absolute performance* investment is unusual – few asset managers seek merely to maximize returns.

Benchmarking's primary advantage is in providing a means to compare disparate investment results, yet it cannot be treated as a dispassionate or risk-neutral tool. Benchmarking encourages active fund managers to target their performance relative to competitors, and the average performance of fund managers in relation to any class of assets will itself influence the benchmark outcome for that asset class.[2] A notable example is the widespread benchmarking of equity fund managers by indexes such as the TOPIX, S&P500 or FTSE100 that are weighted by market capitalization. Share prices may rise to an extent not supported by an issuer's prospects, an overvaluation that induces the fund manager to increase its weighting in the expensive share, and resulting in greater risk and poor overall performance for the investor. The fund manager encourages a price bubble despite supposedly behaving in a risk-neutral fashion (Fidelity 2012). The problem is exacerbated in Asia's relatively volatile stock markets where small free share floats are common.

Finance scholarship, as discussed in Section 9.2, asserts that portfolio diversification is favourable to performance, and that market-determined asset prices take account of all known relevant information. By implication, no investor can consistently outperform the market as a whole by active trading, or holding certain securities and rejecting others. These conclusions drew many investors to the view that over a sustained period nearly all active fund managers will fail to produce positive alpha results, that is, a performance bettering the behaviour of a market or asset class at large. Passive management or index tracking is preferable by this view if the investor's objectives are expressed in relation to a benchmark, especially one weighted by market capitalization. Fund managers may be successful and appropriately well regarded, but they cannot as a group consistently outperform an efficient market.

What followed has been a trend since the 1980s towards a growing share of invested resources subjected to index tracking, especially through sectoral mutual funds and cash ETFs. The investor specifies a class of assets bounded by the index or benchmark and accepts the return produced by that market at large. Passive funds have the further advantage of comparatively low dealing expenses, which appeals to all investors when alpha performance is unobtainable. Among the world's largest commercial fund managers as at end-2010, the compounded annual rate of growth in assets under passive fund management over ten years was 13.2 per cent compared to 6.3 per cent for the entire sample (Towers Watson 2011b: 18).

Assets subject to passive commercial management may account for 10–20 per cent of the global total, extrapolating from data showing assets under management (AUM) with the six largest index trackers (ibid: 20). It is far higher in the US and UK than in other advanced economies at 25–30 per cent (CGFS 2003), partly resulting from agglomeration among fund managers in London and the US Eastern Seaboard where large index trackers tend to locate. The share of passive funds in total AUM is impossible to assess reliably because:

- The universe of investment assets is itself difficult to quantify. National estimates vary in method, many investors conceal their resources for privacy or nefarious reasons, and while AUM data can be reliable in jurisdictions with substantial fund management activity they are not susceptible to aggregation across intermediary sub-sectors or national borders. The data shown in Figures 11.1A and 11.1B represent the substantial part of all known commercially managed global assets;
- Many managers of large funds manage both passive and active portfolios and are required to disclose portfolio composition only periodically and in disaggregated form to their respective investors. Detailed aggregated disclosure is usually voluntary; and
- Active fund management can be a guise for passive index tracking and thus an agency concern, either because a fund manager sees few opportunities to generate alpha positive results or reduces administrative expenses to improve its performance.

Usable benchmarks are without limit. Fund managers may adopt any index for which price determination is impartial and regular, including asset classes that span specific markets (for example the CAC40 or Hang Seng Index); regional (Asian or Latin American share or bond prices); sectoral (shares or credit risks of European or global car makers, SMEs); identified asset classes (spot prices of crude oil, copper or gold, or a commercial property index); or financial (a specified Libor, risk-free bill rate or bond yield, prevailing price inflation,

FX rates). Three of MSCI's widely used equity benchmarks focused on national investment classes are explained in Table 11.1.

Commercial data providers regularly add or remove individual index components. Changes to constituent states are infrequent, not least because any rebalancing has implications for both the reference states and existing invested funds. South Korea has for several years been considered likely to transition between MSCI's emerging and developed state indexes, with two implications for index tracking funds. Not only would the switch require investors to buy or sell the Korean components of the index they follow, either through dealing in securities or ETFs, but the change would require other compensating action given that Korea's weighting is larger in the emerging market index than it would represent among developed markets. Forced dealing and reinvestment risks are typical index composition

Table 11.1 MSCI global equity indexes, 31 May 2012

Index	*Markets*	*Components*
Emerging markets	21 markets. China, India, Indonesia, South Korea, Malaysia, Philippines, Taiwan, Thailand (8); Brazil, Chile, Colombia, Mexico, Peru (5); Czech Republic, Hungary, Poland, Russia (5); Egypt, Morocco, South Africa (3); Turkey.	2,700+ securities
Frontier markets	25 markets. Bangladesh, Pakistan, Sri Lanka, Vietnam (4); Argentina, Bulgaria, Croatia, Estonia, Kazakhstan, Lithuania, Romania, Serbia, Slovenia, Ukraine (10); Kenya, Mauritius, Nigeria, Tunisia (4); Bahrain, Jordan, Kuwait, Lebanon, Oman, Qatar, UAE (7). May in future include Bosnia Herzegovina, Botswana, Ghana, Jamaica, Trinidad and Tobago, and Zimbabwe.	9,000+ securities
Developed markets	24 markets. Hong Kong, Japan, Singapore (3); Australia, New Zealand (2); Austria, Belgium, Finland, France, Germany, Greece, Ireland, Italy, Luxembourg, Netherlands, Norway, Portugal, Spain, Sweden, Switzerland, UK (16); Canada, US (2); Israel.	6,000+ securities. Issuers of all sizes.
All country, all capitalization	45 markets, combining MSCI's developed and emerging markets.	14,000 securities, excluding very small emerging market issuers.

Source: MSCI (http://www.msci.com/products/indices/).

problems, although compilers can produce sub-indexes to help smooth transition adjustments and lessen precipitant selling. In this example, MSCI might publish pairs of indexes for both sectors, one including and the other excluding South Korea.

Equity index trackers can be seen as very long-term investors, for they hold shares until the issuer fails or is dropped from its index, and are in theory required to trade in the index components only after changes in composition or weighting. This arguably reinforces destabilizing herd behaviour. BP's share price dropped by 50 per cent in 2010 when the costs of its Gulf of Mexico catastrophe were unknown. The lower share price appeared cheap to some analysts in discounting too large a penalty for the disaster, but investors benchmarked to market capitalization indexes sold BP shares rather than average down their cash investment cost by buying the cheaper shares, thus crystallizing an irrecoverable loss.

Custom, law and regulation

Regulatory and behavioural institutions are profound influences on the organization and choice of domicile of fund managers, as well as their activities in portfolio management and transaction execution. *Contractual saving* is common in developed economies, meaning that investment flows accumulate with fund managers through pension contributions, stage payments, insurance premiums and savings plans, even in uncertain times when risk-averse investors might prefer to hide their cash away. Inflows continue when asset values are falling, partly offsetting outflows to investors who choose to redeem their claims. Credit lines limit the amounts that professional investors can deposit with banks or hold in government bills or notes, so that absolute disinvestment is impossible even when risk concerns are heightened.

The fund manager's reaction to outflows also contributes to weakened conditions, especially if it finances redemptions by disposing of assets that are less troubled and more liquid. Falling prices lead ordinary fund managers to sell their most valuable or lowest-risk assets since these are liquid and priced at the least discount. These sales intensify the market's overall fall, however irrational it appears to traditional finance scholars. Hyman Minsky saw the behaviour of market participants during the formation of asset bubbles as increasingly disregarding of risk (Minsky 1980).

Law and regulation influence conditions for arbitrage transactions and the ways that fund managers are permitted to interact with investors. The investor's objectives also affect its fund manager's performance. Arbitrage is defined in a narrow sense as the action of buying and selling identical assets or claims through one or more exchanges or markets to take advantage of price discrepancies or transaction cost differences. *Transactional arbitrage* means single or repeated deals, the gains from which are typically eliminated by transaction execution. Systemic or *regulatory arbitrage* arises from a trend or continuing opportunity that vanishes only upon the removal of trading barriers, segmentation or institutional changes. Regulatory conditions were important catalysts in the modern growth of hedge funds and shadow banking intermediaries.

Investor protection law impacts fund management practice by design and through inadvertent second-order effects. Most advanced jurisdictions distinguish professional and retail investors to facilitate regulatory support and a degree of contractual empowerment for small investors, for example to guard against unequal bargains of the kind described in Box 8.6. The origins of today's investor protection law are found in the ethic of post-1929 US legislation after the Great Crash and more broadly in a supervening requirement for contractual good faith contained in the German Civil Code (BGB § 242).

US securities law stipulates registration for most securities, intermediaries and fund managers; EU directives draw on both German and English law in separating the treatment accorded to professional and retail participants. The US exempts defined actors and transactions from certain protective rules, so that supposedly sophisticated or *accredited* investors may hold unregistered securities that are presumed to be of heightened risk. Those given exemption will be investors with professional capabilities or the means to survive a significant loss, that is, investors with a minimum annual income or net worth or demonstrable knowledge and experience in financial matters. MiFID initially allowed EU investors to forego elements of statutory protection, for example, in 'execution only' transactions with intermediaries or by declaring themselves fit to scrutinize complex investments (MiFID 2004: Art. 19(6) & Annex II). Reforms suggested in October 2011 would lessen that flexibility.

Statutory constraints on contractual freedom are widespread. After 2008–9 several jurisdictions prepared or introduced detailed product conduct rules to police the design and sale of financial instruments, ranging from insurance contracts to savings plans and complex securities. The result for our analysis is a surge over three decades in the scale and ubiquity of shadow banking, with asset managers adopting hedge fund and other non-traditional structures explicitly to avoid regulatory costs, and conservative 'long only' investors willing to place funds with the non-traditional sector in order to increase returns. Accredited professionals may invest with hedge funds but investor protection denies access to others. The results may be well-intentioned without necessarily encouraging fair opportunity or contractual freedom.

11.2 Traditional asset management

Our notion of traditional asset management includes primary users such as collective investment schemes and private equity, and funded pension schemes and insurers for which it represents a secondary activity. The former promote themselves to investors to establish reputational capital as Section 7.3 shows of investment banks, although non-bank intermediaries do so with greater specificity because benchmarked asset management results are now directly comparable and less readily manipulated than transaction league tables. The main differences between sub-categories of fund managers relate to investment objectives, the degree of external regulation on sales, solvency and portfolio choice, internal governance, and the investor's ease and cost of withdrawal, that is, the liquidity of its investment.

Mutual funds, pension funds and insurers

Most independent fund managers administer segmented real or financial assets for single investors, or collect pools of resources against which investors have proportionate claims. Their compensation usually comprises fixed fees based on AUM, and a variable share of profits on each fund subject to its benchmarked performance. Most are profit-seeking companies or limited partnerships where allowed by national law, and a small number of the larger examples are listed. Many life and specialist insurers such as marine protection and indemnity associations (P&I clubs) have historically used corporate or cooperative mutual structures and distributed their net income to policyholders, but the need for capital to protect against unexpected claims now encourages full or operational demutualization, especially among life insurers. Pension fund managers use many forms of commercial or non-profit structures.

Most *mutual fund* managers collect flows from investors by continual or periodic sales of redeemable units or tradable shares. The funds may be *open* or *closed ended*, meaning respectively that investors may commit new resources direct to the fund at any time or at designated intervals, as with ETFs, or only at launch or a time chosen by the fund manager for a *reopening*. Shares in most closed-end funds therefore trade on organized exchanges or platforms. Their price fluctuates in a similar way to conventional listed companies, and may trade at persistent discounts or premiums to their net asset value (NAV), the mark-to-market value of the fund attributable to each share. The price of shares or units in open-ended funds will deviate only exceptionally from their NAV. Both open- and closed-ended funds may be permanent or have fixed lives, the latter returning their accumulated net resources to investors when that period ends.

Mutual funds include money market funds that hold low-risk liquid debt instruments, index tracking funds, and others specializing in sectoral, geographical or industry risks, and funds intended to meet risk and return targets for capital growth or income, for example by investing in the technology sector, SMEs or companies recovering from distress. Just as investment banks use expected investor demand to shape the terms of new issues, so asset managers will create funds of any kind that can be costed, measured and successfully marketed, knowing that good investment performance will encourage retentions and assist future fundraising.

Money market mutual funds developed in the US from the 1970s to compete for retail deposits. They also provide a liquidity tool for professional investors by being easily traded and having relatively stable NAVs. Successful money market funds rely on depth and liquidity in the bills, notes and derivatives that form their investment universe, making it infeasible for traditional money market funds to develop in Asian currencies except in Japan and to modest extents in Hong Kong and Singapore, or in Shari'ah compliant form in any currency.

Discussing commercial fund management in Asia requires that we distinguish the source of investible funds from the domicile of the fund manager. A comparison between macroeconomic and market survey data shows considerable differences in the scale of funds available for investment in Asia and the amounts managed locally. Financial repression limits access to indigenous non-bank intermediation despite well-established demand, for example shown in household surveys in China (Seade & Wei 2010). The result is that investors direct resources to non-Asian fund managers except in economies that control foreign capital flows and entry by foreign fund managers, and in Japan where product supply and demand are balanced and home bias is strong.

Assets managed by the world's largest 500 fund managers at end-2010 totalled US$ 63.7 trillion, as shown in Figure 11.1A and 11.1B, and was considerably less than its nominal peak in 2008.

This group controlled 63.2 per cent of total AUM, a rise from 59.4 per cent over ten years. Concentration also exists within the sample, with 40.6 per cent of AUM attributable to the leading 20 fund managers, nine of which were bank subsidiaries, eight were independent and three were insurers. Large fund managers are overwhelmingly North American, European or Japanese (Towers Watson 2011b). Only five of the largest 100 were domiciled elsewhere, comprising two from Brazil ranked 82 and 93, and one each from Australia (69), South Africa (34) and South Korea (68). The full 500 include 27 domiciled in China with the highest ranked at 196, seven in South Korea, three in India and one in Hong Kong, but no other states from our sample. Around 40 per cent of the 100 largest fund managers were part of banking groups, with the extent of functional integration varying according to national law.

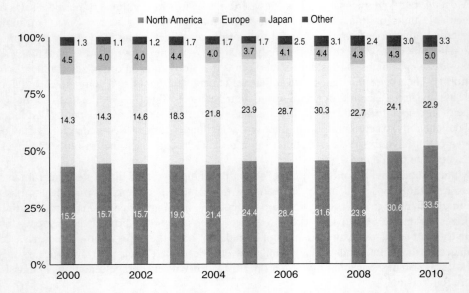

Figure 11.1A Composition of AUM, largest 500 commercial fund managers.

Composition of AUM shown by fund manager domicile. Figures in the chart area indicate AUM by region (US$ tn).

Source: Towers Watson (2011b).

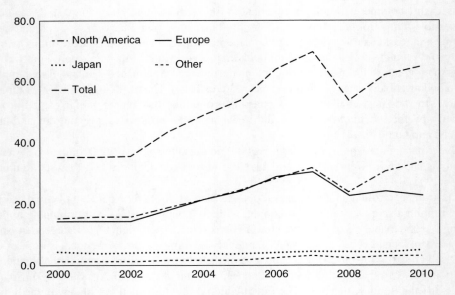

Figure 11.1B AUM, largest 500 commercial fund managers.

Scale of AUM shown by fund manager domicile.

Source: Towers Watson (2011b).

A third of the top 100 were independent fund managers and the remainder either insurers or specialist public sector organizations. The Basel III Capital Accord will require a legal separation in adopting states between banks and their fund management arms.

The scale and activities of *pension funds* and *insurers* vary considerably according to national practice, regardless of the size and sophistication of the host economy. Investment assets held by OECD life insurers and pension funds as a share of total national financial assets ranged as at end-2009 from 5 per cent or less in Greece, Spain, Austria, Turkey, Belgium, Italy, Luxembourg and France in ascending order, to over 20 per cent in Switzerland, Finland and the Netherlands and nearly 30 per cent in the UK (CGFS 2011: 6). The relative importance of life insurance and pension funds by the same measure also lacks a common explanation. Pension funds are of negligible scale in France, Greece and Luxembourg, small in Germany, Italy, South Korea, Spain and Sweden, but high in Australia, Finland, the Netherlands and the US; life insurance is trivial in scale in Australia, Austria, Mexico and the US but important in Denmark, Germany, Japan, Norway, Sweden and the UK (ibid).

These variations influence the functioning of national bond, equity and property markets, and illustrate how regulation and customary savings behaviour guide the configuration of intermediary groups. Banks, insurers and pension funds sell overlapping savings products, in some cases under mandatory direction, and the results differ for institutional reasons even among economies of similar output or savings rates. The results are also unexplained by the legal origins scholarship described in Section 4.1, at least among OECD members.

Employer-sponsored private sector pension funds are typically managed for single companies or industry sectors, and categorized as either providing *defined benefits* as a single amount or annuity based on the retiree's former salary, or requiring a stream of *defined contributions* that generate a lump sum or annuity as a function of fund management performance.

Public and private pension schemes often devolve management of designated asset classes or tranches of investible funds to commercial intermediaries. Seven Asian sovereign pension funds were among the world's largest 20 at end-2010 (Towers Watson 2011a), comprising three from Japan and, in descending order, one each from South Korea, Malaysia, Singapore and China. Within the same group, 39 per cent measured by AUM were public sector funds, 29 per cent were sovereign funds controlled directly by the state, 19 per cent were funds sponsored by private companies and the remainder were private industry sector funds. These outline rankings reflect not only the scale of fund commitments but more directly the results of asset allocation, since funds weighted towards fixed income outperformed equity oriented investors in 2008–10.

Pension fund AUM in the US and Japan accounted for 52 per cent of the total. Asia's total was larger than in Europe, even though pension coverage in our sample is limited as a share of population. Mandatory pension provisions are increasingly common in Asia, although commercial pension schemes are underdeveloped. Hong Kong, South Korea, Malaysia and Singapore have defined contribution systems, requiring companies and employees to pay into independently managed pension funds.

The Malaysian and Singaporean schemes are especially embedded in the wider economy, encouraging saving and permitting pre-retirement drawing, for example to finance home ownership or higher education. Most smaller economies in our sample operate defined benefit schemes with modest population coverage. Japan's population of 127 million is nearly twice that of Thailand, for example, while OECD data for their respective end-2011 pension fund AUM are US$1,388 and US$15 billion. Hong Kong and Singapore funds' AUM are each larger than the comparable aggregates for China and India, with respective combined populations of 12.2 million and 2.6 billion. These comparisons may be unreasonable results of scale or relative development, but show that the growth of formal funded pension provisions will eventually have profound results for the future of regional finance, given that unfunded schemes cannot cope with increasingly unfavourable demographics.

Most pension funds are generally conservative investors that use asset management to meet inter-temporal claims. Conservative investment implies a generally 'long only' stance focused on the duration and return of the portfolio, although many funds will engage in securities lending and other trading techniques to increase their returns and allow a similar freedom to designee fund managers. Pension fund portfolios can be heavily committed to equities, fixed income or property, and in many cases to direct investment through private equity or infrastructural funds, as described in Section 11.3. They use derivatives largely for hedging purposes, although some transact with banks in innovative inflation and longevity swaps, the typical aim of which is to exchange a variable or uncertain payment for one that is even and regular in a way similar to total return swaps and described in Section 8.2.

Insurance contracts are a savings alternative to bank deposits or money market mutual funds. The insured pays a premium to mitigate or transfer risk to an insurer, which in return makes a conditional undertaking to compensate the insured against loss, or provide a predetermined amount, making a commercial assessment of risk similar to that discussed in Box 6.1. Insurers use asset management as a transformational mechanism comparable to those undertaken within the commercial bank, and a means to generate revenue and build capital as a buffer against unforeseen liabilities.

Most property, goods and liability insurance are *indemnities*, or contracts that safeguard the insured against an actual loss, often in some form of owned property or commercial interest. *Non-indemnity insurance* includes life, personal accident and critical illness cover, which pays a predetermined sum or annuity upon the occurrence of a defined event. It can also include policies for fixed amounts to cover property, goods and marine insurance. Most advanced jurisdictions set strict rules on the use of non-indemnity insurance, partly for historic reasons to discourage gambling and because, unlike indemnity insurance, the exact nature of the insured subject cannot always be certain when the contract begins.[3]

Insurance developed in a recognizable modern form in the fifteenth-century Italian city states such as Genoa (Holdsworth 1917; Van Niekerk 1998), before becoming established in Spain and more formally in England, which provided the beginnings of insurance law and regulation. We would think of primitive insurance contracts less as compensation for loss or forms of contractual saving than as transactions designed to avoid restrictions in canon or Islamic law, for example by allowing a financier effectively to lend at interest to a commercial venture. In this form insurance is conceptually similar to merchant banking or private equity. The sharing of commercial risk and profit is an important precept of Shari'ah compliant finance.

Reinsurers function with higher balance sheet leverage than their insurer counterparties, mainly because the commitments they acquire are taken to be less subject to Knightian uncertainty or information asymmetry, and have less need for supportive capital.[4] Reinsurance is analogous to bank lenders buying or selling credit protection, that is, a form of balance sheet management characterized as unfunded credit risk transfer, but is considerably older in use.

Reinsurers provide indemnities that match single or multiple risks to which the insurer is exposed without altering the terms or parties to any underlying insurance contracts, which explains why regulators customarily require providers to be registered to guard against insurers claiming regulatory relief for inadequate transfers.

Most large reinsurers have European, US or Japanese domiciles. Lloyd's of London operates as an organized exchange in both insurance and reinsurance, and a substantial OTC reinsurance market operates in Bermuda for reasons related to its favourable legal and tax systems. Global reinsurance is a well-integrated OTC market comparable to that in major currency foreign exchange. Both are large in scale, liquid and quick in execution through networks of specialist brokers.

Non-life insurers are especially likely to use reinsurance to protect against concentrations of risk or reduce earnings volatility, since actuarial predictions of life insurance liabilities are usually more accurate than forecasts of crime, catastrophe or harsh weather. Reinsurance companies in turn use similar methods with other counterparties to match or redistribute risk, a process known as retrocession. Reinsurance also facilitates *captive insurance*, used by large companies to lower transaction costs or increase tax efficiency, in most cases involving a wholly owned Bermudan subsidiary providing insurance cover to its parent while hedging its entire risk exposure with unconnected reinsurers.

Private equity

We see private equity as a modern term for the merchant banking practice of long-standing mentioned in Chapter 7.1. Its foundation is that the financier's potential return from supporting a venture is greater if it becomes an equity participant rather than merely provide interest-bearing debt. This is especially true of early stage financing by venture capital funds, for which the risks associated with debt and equity claims are commercially similar when not subject to information asymmetries. Private equity refers to transactions or processes involving *direct investment* in companies by financial interests, often with leveraged third-party funds, and contrasts with direct investment by non-financial or *trade* interests, for example when a manufacturer acquires shares in a competitor.

Prominent protagonists include those firms associated with the first US LBOs in the 1980s, including Blackstone, KKR (Kohlberg, Kravis & Roberts) and Texas Pacific. Their transaction model is transformational, a process of acquiring mainly public companies by augmenting the third-party funds they control through substantial leverage, delisting the target and reforming its financial and operating performance, replacing or bolstering management, selling unwanted businesses, and planning an *exit* through a private trade sale or relisting IPO. Samsonite is cited in Section 9.1 as one example.

Private equity funds hold portfolios of investments but differ from collective investment schemes since all their assets are acquired for subsequent sale. Most funds will have a ten-year life with a period allowed for running down. Realizing profits is a core concern for the private equity manager, not least in Asia where changes in corporate control are infrequent. Fund managers unable to obtain full control are forced to take minority positions, and become dependent on a secondary IPO to realize any gains. Facebook's 2012 IPO was partly driven by this need among the company's early stage backers, a collection of individual HNW *angel investors* and specialist venture capital fund managers. There is a well developed market in *secondaries*, or asset transfers between private equity funds, but confined mainly to developed economies.

Most resources are committed to private equity funds by professional or HNW investors. They now include many pension funds and other conservative investors, some committing to funds with a sectoral focus such as property or technology to meet income or growth objectives. Investors hold restricted claims on the fund similar to differential voting rights or 'B' shares given to minority shareholders in closely controlled companies. Figure 11.2 shows

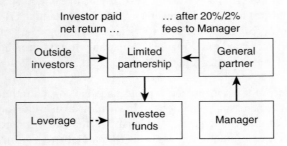

Figure 11.2 Generic private equity fund structure.

a common structure based on the US limited partnership model and adapted by other juris-dictions. The fund manager and investors respectively become the *general partner* and *limited partners*, skewing control rights and performance compensation towards the fund manager. Many hedge funds use a similar model.

The structure raises agency concerns given that investor funds will exceed the manager's commitment but typically be far less well rewarded. The general partner typically collects fees of 1.5–2 per cent per annum on AUM plus a performance-based component known as *carried interest*, payable if the fund's results exceed certain parameters but only upon the reduction or liquidation of the fund. This means that the manager's reward is contingent on investors recovering their initial capital infusion and an agreed yield, and in the example of Figure 11.2 is based on realized profits divided in the proportion 20/80 between the manager and limited partners, a split that may be more balanced when fundraising conditions are unfavourable or if a manager's transaction record is brief. Carried interest is favoured since it supposedly aligns the interests of investor and manager. It has also allowed private equity profits to be widely treated as capital gains for tax purposes.

Large LBOs rely on mutually contingent promises between fund manager, lenders and the target. This *private equity contract* facilitated many substantial transactions in the two decades to 2000 but later became subject to inter-party disputes. For speed of execution, the fund manager proposes to acquire the target through an SPV, typically called NewCo, lever-aging its capital infusion with as much debt as commercially feasible. NewCo has no resources, so the fund manager cannot assure the target's shareholders of its seriousness without demonstrating the support of lenders. Bank arrangers will not commit freely to fund a project that may take months to execute in changing conditions, while being unable to syndicate the debt or otherwise hedge their credit, market and event risks without knowing the deal's final terms and likelihood of acceptance by the target's owners.

Private equity contracts are detailed preliminary documents that allow the parties to nego-tiate in good faith with confidence that a transaction will proceed to completion. They con-tain protective clauses to permit banks to withdraw upon a MAC event, as explained in Section 6.3, and may provide the target with a break fee to compensate against an unforeseen withdrawal of interest. One reason for the volume of large private equity transaction to drop since 2007–8 is that lenders lack confidence to continue with this practice, not least after MAC clauses were invoked in several prominent cases in 2005–7 as lenders sought to avoid or lessen their commitments and were challenged by LBO arrangers or target shareholders.

Private equity has a substantial footprint in Asia measured by the number of operating fund managers, AUM and the amounts raised for new ventures, and especially since 2008 in the amount of *dry powder* they have available, or committed or vested but unallocated funds. Surveys suggest that India, China, Hong Kong and Singapore are popular locations for fund managers (Taylor 2011), and the amounts raised by Asian private equity funds have become substantial, signalling an improving perception of regional risk. Most operations are relatively small and manage no more than one or two discrete funds. Global activity tends to be volatile in scale, often secretive and, except for US-based funds, reliably quantified only by amounts publicly raised or completed transactions, although 'completed' is arguably more fitting with a transaction from which investors have crystallized profits through an exit rather than on the day of funding.

Returns on private equity appear to be variable. Data for invested funds and achieved performance are only partly available, not least because disclosure is usually voluntary, and successful managers who favour transparency will distort the overall results towards a self-justifying positive alpha. A study of 7,587 investments made by 417 investors in 1,398 US funds in the decade to end-2001 found differences in private equity returns obtained by different classes of investor (Lerner, Schoar & Wongsunwai 2007), notably with US university endowments achieving annual returns nearly 14 per cent above the sample average. Such endowment funds can be both sizeable and able to engage in non-traditional investment, and are always courted by private equity. If an investor's returns are correlated with its choice of fund manager then the more influential will be best informed in making their selection, given that they enjoy preferred access to information about a fund's plans and past performance.

Venture capital returns have been shown as only marginally better, and LBO funds to underperform broad benchmarks such as the S&P500 (Kaplan and Schoar 2005). Managers who outperform their investment sector through one fund are likely to outperform their competitors with any successor funds, and *vice versa* (ibid). Venture capital inflows are positively related to past performance, and outperforming managers are unsurprisingly more successful in raising funds. A further study of 419 US venture capital funds found no relationship between fund performance and the disclosed terms of compensation of general partners, although those found in well-established funds tended to be more performance dependent (Gompers & Lerner 1999). Investors seem able to restrict the rewards paid to promising but lesser-known fund managers.

11.3 Non-traditional intermediation

Our classification includes hedge funds, SWFs and infrastructural funds. All are generally less concerned with benchmarking than traditional asset managers, instead targeting absolute performance, capital or income preservation or specific strategic results. Some have real or perceived influence that exceeds their resources or AUM, as with many SWFs and certain infrastructural funds; some are transient, for example the SIVs and conduits managed or sponsored until recently by banks as *alternative investment vehicles* and described in Box 11.1.

Hedge funds

The hedge fund sector may be the most notorious in popular opinion of all modern classes of intermediary: LTCM's 1998 collapse haunts financial regulators; currency trading by George Soros's Quantum Funds was demonized in 1997 by a Malaysian prime minister as unnecessary, unproductive and immoral – five years earlier Quantum currency selling helped force the exit of Sterling from the European Exchange Rate Mechanism (ERM); and an

Box 11.1 Shadow Banking Arbitrage Vehicles

SIVs and conduits grew over two decades from simple and conservative investment vehicles to a substantial position in structured finance and regulatory capital arbitrage. What had seemed reliable proved suddenly vulnerable. They became immediately illiquid in the first days of the global financial crisis, then insolvent, and were either wound up or absorbed into the balance sheets of their bank sponsors or managers, in several cases leading to litigation in London or New York with investors complaining over poorly drafted contractual payment priorities and inadequate risk management. The fall in confidence that began in mid-2007 was fatal for the mismatched funding model that underpinned SIV and conduit profits. The collapse was rapid, not least because many vehicles were established expressly to invest in subprime RMBS not long before their prices peaked.

The foundational SIV was devised by Citigroup in the 1980s as a profitable means to defease and house low-risk, low-yielding financial assets and economize on regulatory capital. These were lightly capitalized companies, some private and others listed in London or Luxembourg, relying on borrowed short-term funds sourced from third-party investors, much of it using ABCP. The model SIV was financially independent while the generic conduit's sponsor bank provided it with committed standby credit lines. In each case short-term borrowing financed portfolios of highly rated long-term bonds, giving attractive returns on equity assuming a positive-sloping yield curve and small resources of capital. Both structures were classed as *alternative investment vehicles* but might equally have been the world's first virtual banks.

The sector expanded in size and number with the post-2000 growth in structured securities. While SIVs and conduits were initially associated with prominent US, EU and Japanese investment banks, the attraction of regulatory arbitrage led to their creating others for clients, most of which were smaller or under-resourced commercial or savings banks, including several from Hong Kong, Japan and Singapore. Individual vehicles ranged in AUM from around US$500 million to over US$50 billion. Over 30 were in existence by 2007. Aggregate SIV and conduit AUM reached US$1,850 billion at the structured finance market's peak, which they were then effectively helping to support. SIV assets were allocated 25 per cent and 10 per cent respectively to RMBS and CDOs in 2007 (Bank of England 2007: 19–21).

Confidence rapidly left the US dollar ABCP market in mid-2007. Several SIVs immediately defaulted on maturing notes that holders refused to renew. Funding became impossible despite several large SIVs protesting their solvency, but the gathering crisis left the sector unable to value or realize its ABS and CDO portfolios, and widespread liquidations followed. Financial innovation is hard to disinvent however, and the core model was soon adopted by central banks and governments as policy vehicles and crisis shelters. The Federal Reserve's three Maiden Lane SIVs have housed AIG assets prior to their sale; the Eurozone' funding vehicle the European Financial Stability Facility (EFSF) uses a conduit structure relying on contingent commitments from member states; and the Asian Bond Fund explained in Section 12.5 is a vehicle intended to promote issues of local-currency bonds.

eponymous fund managed by John Paulson created in 2006–7 a vast short position in synthetic US subprime mortgage risk that became both highly profitable and controversial in execution. Political views of hedge fund activity are frequently hostile, especially in Denmark, France and Germany, and an influential 2009 study for the EU Commission concluded that hedge fund trading can be destabilizing and required firmer supervision, although it was not a primary cause of the global crisis (De Larosière Group 2009). The 2011 Alternative Investment Fund Management Directive will intensify EU members' existing rules from 2013–14:

- Increasing transparency in hedge funds and others not subject to UCITS rules;
- Enabling national and EU regulators to monitor and respond to systemic risks resulting from AIFM activity;
- Introducing common rules for investor protection and choice, and competition among fund managers; and
- Increasing private equity's corporate social responsibility towards employees and others.

The sector is best characterized as comprising autonomous, mainly private, asset managers that allow access to their open-ended funds to a limited number and range of professional and HNW investors. A small number is listed and somewhat less restricted in accepting subscriptions, notably Man Group and Och-Ziff Capital Management. Hedge funds may follow complex investment strategies, charge high performance fees and deploy a wide range of tactics and instruments, in some cases with considerable secrecy, as Box 9.2 shows of HFT funds. A common objective is to generate returns uncorrelated with those of the broader equity or credit markets. Common tactics include the use of programmed trades, short selling and high leverage, although uncollateralized funding became generally unavailable to hedge funds after the collapse of LTCM due to credit concerns of lenders and their regulators. Some funds take consistent short positions as part of non-traditional *macro* or *event-based strategies*, typified by the examples of Paulson, Quantum, or the activist fund TCI cited in Section 10.4. Hedge fund leverage is now less concerned with the use of borrowed funds to maximize returns as with aggregate funded and synthetic risk exposure in relation to AUM.

Hedge fund managers have historically located in jurisdictions where regulation is informed but light, providing they restrict investor access. The first long/short equity fund was opened in New York in 1949 as a 'hedged' fund by a former diplomat, social scientist and spy named Alfred Winslow Jones (Mallaby 2010). Jones's operational model is still widely used. It sought to avoid US licensing requirements within the Investment Company Act 1940 by accepting no more than 100 accredited investors, and used the 1933 Securities Act's safe harbour provisions described in Section 8.1 allowing registration exemption when securities are sold only to those investors. Short selling was also deemed acceptable only for accredited investors. The SEC introduced closer regulation of the sector in 2004, but this was struck down by the courts as inconsistent with the earlier statutes (Goldstein v. SEC). Post-crisis US regulation intensifies hedge fund registration and disclosure but its main concern is to limit bank ownership or engagement in hedge funds as part of its Volcker Rule provisions (Dodd–Frank Act 2010). Small and restrictive funds will continue to carry a light supervisory burden.

Most funds use the general and limited partnership structure shown in Figure 11.2 for similar control reasons to private equity. Compensation and performance hurdles are also similar, with management fees frequently limited by *high water marks*, requiring NAV to ratchet upwards each year or exceed specified minimum returns. Managers tend to agglomerate in the US, UK and Switzerland, and more modestly in Japan, the Gulf, Hong Kong and Singapore, with AUM usually held offshore in tax-neutral jurisdictions. Two-thirds of a global total of around 9,500 hedge funds were managed from the US as at end-2010, with Europe and Asia respectively hosting 22 per cent and 6 per cent of the remainder (Maslakovic 2011).

The size and number of active funds alters continually, especially as many fail or are wound up if their objectives are met or become infeasible. Most lack extensive resources. The archetypal Hong Kong or Singapore hedge fund comprises two partners and a shared Bloomberg terminal, a characterization we owe to a well-known Asian hedge fund manager. The sector certainly relies on prime brokers as service providers for trade execution and clearing, custody, short-term loans, and above all securities lending, without which it could not hold non-synthetic short positions.

Hedge funds are best defined by objective, some of which are shown in Table 11.2. Most common is the long/short equity fund. These operate in liquid share markets that

Table 11.2 Illustrative hedge fund strategies

Type of fund	Strategy	Examples
Arbitrage	Convergence trades, algorithms or continuing programmes	Exploit deviations in prices or correlations between assets or asset classes
Event-based	Long, short or long/short securities and derivatives	Discretionary or automated trades to exploit price discontinuities resulting from anticipated or poorly discounted events, including transactional arbitrage in distressed debt and with changes in corporate control
Global macro	Leveraged portfolios and trading algorithms	Discretionary or automated trades in any financial or commodity markets to exploit price reactions to unexpected events, or generally anticipated but mis-priced economic trends or changes
Managed funds	All securities in any designated class	Discretionary or automated trades generally confined to single sectors, including equities, fixed income, emerging market debt or equity, SMEs, technology companies, or to specific market variables – for example, price volatility, credit rating anomalies, price and volume momentum
Market neutral & relative value	Long/short securities	Combined long and short positions in single risks classes in cash or synthetic securities, including equities, convertible bonds, fixed income, loans, ABS, and regulatory capital issues
Short only	Short securities, derivatives or other tradable claims	Sell cash or synthetic claims or asset classes perceived by the fund manager or calculated as overvalued

permit short selling, and are able to limit exposure either to the overall market in periods of weakness without fully disinvesting, or trade on perceived relative value, increasing potential returns by holding one share while short selling a second. The intention is often to take non-directional positions, creating positive alpha returns regardless of the market's results or volatility in the spirit of Mr Jones's appellation. LTCM's collapse was largely unconnected to hedging, arising from unhedged directional positioning in Russian and other emerging market debt. Long/short equity funds are thought to control 30–40 per cent of hedge fund AUM, followed in scale by global macro and event based funds (Bensted 2011), which follow strategies relying on the manager's insight, interests and technical resources.

Estimated aggregate AUM rose steadily from around US$400 billion in 2000 to a peak of US$2.15 trillion at end-2007, fell by 30 per cent within 12 months, then recovered to US$1.92 trillion at end-2010 (Maslakovic 2011). AUM with fund of funds managers that allocate resources to several single-purpose hedge funds fell over the same period to US$550 million, or 30 per cent of the total (ibid). Many such funds were loss-making in 2007–8, recalling the importance of informed selection of managers shown in studies of private equity (Lerner, Schoar & Wongsunwai 2007).

Over 60 per cent of end-2010 accumulated inflows were drawn from professional sources (Bensted 2011). Ten years earlier individuals provided 54 per cent of funds (Maslakovic 2011). These shifts resulted from professional investors growing increasingly comfortable in allocating assets to non-traditional management, while the sector's performance in 2007–8 led to sizeable HNW withdrawals hastened by the Madoff Ponzi fraud becoming known in late 2008, a scheme partly disguised as a fund of funds manager.[5] The largest share of non-HNW investment in 2010 was provided by funds of funds, endowments, public and private pension funds, and foundations, together accounting for 75 per cent of accumulated inflows (ibid), although some organizations simultaneously allocate resources directly and through funds of funds. Professional investors were largely North American or European, with 12 per cent drawn from elsewhere.

Hedge fund performance in 2009–12 was comprehensively erratic, 'the longest stretch of disappointment the industry has ever suffered' (Jones 2012), and seen in volatile or sub-standard returns and recurring losses, falling AUM and investor withdrawals. It illustrates agency concerns that affect all classes of asset management but are magnified when managers are especially well-compensated and autonomous. The size and crowdedness of the hedge fund sector means that only a handful of funds can outperform the broad financial markets or the sector as a whole with any consistency, which may encourage investors to question differences in standards of governance between the hedge fund sector and traditional asset managers. The hedge fund concept gives investors a means to protect capital values in a falling market and can contribute positively to overall stability, despite the fears of EU and other regulators, but it is less clear that these qualities are found only within this sector. George Soros's evidence to a US congressional committee two months after Lehman's collapse encapsulates this dilemma:

> During the current financial crisis, many hedge fund managers forgot the cardinal rule of hedge fund investing which is to protect investor capital during down markets. It is unfortunate that much of the money raised by hedge funds in recent years has come from the typically staid pension funds and endowment funds in their pursuit of alpha.
>
> (Soros 2008)

Sovereign wealth funds

Few public sector intermediaries excite scholarly interest. State pension funds in Japan, the Netherlands, California and Quebec control total AUM exceeding US$2.1 trillion and are suitably scrutinized by markets and investee companies, yet their operations are indistinct from many private sector counterparts. That assessment does not suit sovereign wealth funds, a separate category of state investment managers. SWFs have associations that may be political, diplomatic, strategic and covert as well as fully commercial, and incite unusual reactions from academic observers and investee states. Our interest in SWFs is twofold:

- How do SWF investment activities, governance and disclosure compare with their non-state counterparts?
- Do investee states or direct investment targets discriminate against SWFs as a result of their status, governance or activities, and can such discrimination be reasonable or be mitigated by SWFs or their sponsors?

SWFs are endowments that intermediate state resources. They lack a single definition and vary considerably in asset allocation, objectives and autonomy. Their AUM derive mainly from accumulated foreign reserves, and convention distinguishes those associated with revenue from *resource extraction* and others with *diversified export earnings*. Most SWFs manage assets funded by reserves rather than holding a direct allocation, preserving autonomy and avoiding conflicts with monetary policy sterilization. Most are state agencies or SOEs. All at times have been controversial, especially with overseas direct investment targets and in popular opinion.

SWFs have been categorized as having either strategic or portfolio management objectives and in their relative openness or secrecy (Lyons 2007). Transparency is inevitably associated with political provenance as few large SWFs are based in representative democracies, although many funds have recently become more fluid in their aims and transparency for commercial reasons and to avoid unwanted losses. Secrecy offends foreign opinion, discourages cooperation by investee targets and states, and strains relationships with external investment advisors. A single-purpose focus lacks logic unless the state is wholly unconcerned with financial results, which is less common than a generation ago – SWF losses often have political ramifications.

The sector is small measured by aggregate AUM, probably holding less than 3 per cent of global financial assets. SWFs nonetheless project disproportionate influence, especially those located in the Middle East and East Asia. State and provincial pension funds are long established in parts of North America and Europe but lack the political resonance of these newer non-OECD funds, and generally function under internationally agreed standards of governance. Growth in the scale and number of Asian SWFs is a recent product of finance in Asia, that is, an outcome of the policy orientation followed after the 1997–98 regional crisis and fully explained in Sections 2.2–2.3:

- Export orientation, managed FX rates and monetary sterilization;
- Relatively unsophisticated domestic financial systems; and
- Risk aversion, including a protective accumulation of foreign reserves.

Asia's new SWFs share two features, despite their differing commercial and policy objectives. First, they owe their endowments to diversified export earnings and currency management, and second, all were influenced by the experience of well-established peers, especially in Abu Dhabi, Kuwait, Norway and Singapore. Norway's Government Pension Fund – Global was founded in 1990 and has operated with consistently transparent governance, but most SWFs were secretive and limited in their public engagement until a more open phase began in 2000 with influential reforms at Temasek, coinciding with the expansion of other Asian SWFs.

Aggregate SWF AUM of US$4.8 trillion as at end-2011 was similar to the combined estimate for hedge funds and private equity, and thus far smaller than the respective totals for insurers, mutual funds or pension funds, which ranged from US$23.5 trillion to US$30.0 trillion (Maslakovic 2012). Table 11.3 lists the 20 largest SWFs ranked by their most recently disclosed AUM, eight being Asian or Australasian. Over 100 SWFs have been identified but fewer than ten are exceptionally well-resourced.

AUM may rise or fall. In 2011 Libya's SWF was found to have been plundered and subjected to poor external fund management, and many SWFs experienced losses on portfolio and direct investment after 2007–8, even though most were historically passive, risk averse and invested largely in OECD securities and real estate (Bortolotti, Fotak, Megginson & Miracky 2009). Irregular returns have encouraged several Asian SWFs to allocate part of AUM to more strategic investment policies, including consensual FDI and overseas acquisitions. That change in emphasis in asset allocation heightens the concerns of certain investee states, relating to:

- Secrecy and governance. Some SWFs provide scant information as to their resources and objectives.
- Relationship with government. SWFs may be subject to state direction in asset allocation and their behaviour as shareholders with investee companies and ventures.
- Unequal treatment. SWFs are often assumed to have valuable access to privileged state information.
- Financial stability. SWFs have little experience and unknown policies as creditors in cases of corporate or sovereign distress and multicreditor workouts. Many also represent unknown counterparty risks, which helps explain why Temasek obtained credit ratings in 2005.[6]

Legal or administrative restrictions often affect foreign investment in sectors deemed to be strategically important. Australia's government barred the national stock exchange's merger with SGX in 2011, and discouraged Rio Tinto Group from completing a strategic share exchange with Aluminum Corporation of China (Chalco) in 2009. Many states hold *golden shares* in privatized SOEs to block foreign control, as with Qantas, which is subject to statutory limits on foreign shareholdings (Qantas Sales Act 1992). US restrictions are comprehensive. A standing Committee on Foreign Investment (CFIUS) assesses inward investment proposals and can recommend that the federal government prohibit transactions under the Defense Production Act 1950 or Foreign Investment and National Security Act 2007. Similar provisions exist under specific legislation or reserved powers throughout our sample economies.

Recent US legislation specific to SWF investment requires that they observe minimum disclosure standards (Dodd–Frank Act 2010: § 1504), and provides for:

- Restrictions on direct or portfolio cross-border investment;
- Barriers to SWF involvement in identified sectors;

- Limits on controlling interests; and
- Differentiation or withholding of conventional voting rights.

The fourth provision conflicts with the principle of shareholders having equal claims, justified by the act's sponsors because SWF shareholders are not equal with others, a view disputed by funds such as Norway's whose standards of governance are acknowledged as high. This prompts the question of whether and to what extent OECD recipient states discriminate against direct or equity SWF investments compared to domestic or other foreign investors? The results are understandable, for all states constrain foreign participation in identified sectors or prevent inward investment for protectionist or political reasons. The OECD's investment policy principles aim to arbitrate in this dilemma by proposing that:

- Outright discrimination against any foreign investor is unreasonable;
- Transparent and predictable regulations are generally legitimate;
- New rules should not be made especially for SWFs; and
- Rules written for security motives must be proportionate to the need.

These precepts are recommended for investee states, providing that SWFs adopt the OECD's Santiago principles for SWF governance (OECD 2004), although it is clear that barriers to inward investment can be used capriciously or without differentiating between compliant and non-compliant SWFs. Table 11.3 shows SWF compliance scores with the principles. These can be read as proxies for comparative standards of governance, with an average score of 63 among the sample of 60 funds from which Table 11.2 is extracted (Truman 2011). The largest ten scored an average of 69. Four East Asian SWFs were ranked at or above the average, the highest being Timor-Leste's US$5.0 billion fund at 80. Most East Asian SWFs in the full sample occupied an intermediate range of 40–80, with only the Brunei Investment Agency far lower at 28.

The 30 Santiago principles are arguably aspirational and incomplete (ibid), but cover SWF structure, objectives, independence, transparency, internal governance and accountability, social responsibility, and competence and supervision in asset allocation, risk management and day-to-day activity.

Infrastructural finance

The third non-traditional intermediation channel is an adaptation of private equity that has raised the involvement of pension funds and other natural long-term investors in limited recourse financing for infrastructure, a form of risk that Section 6.3 distinguishes from more general claims. The financier in a non-recourse transaction has a priority claim and the benefit of operating covenants over the venture it funds, and either no claim or a limited claim against the sponsor. Funding, debt service and dividends are tied to the project's performance. The concept is difficult to introduce into public debt or equity issues, confining non-bank access to infrastructural risk to direct investment, which may represent an unwanted risk concentration for conservative asset managers.

One solution, associated in its most developed form with Macquarie Group, involves a hybrid private equity model of listed or unlisted specialist or sectoral funds. The model has been used by many fund managers but was taken to extremes of control and compensation by Macquarie, raising agency concerns over excessive profit-seeking and poor governance. The global crisis cut Macquarie's access to leverage, showed its model as unduly dependent

Table 11.3 Largest 20 SWFs, end-2010

	Main source of endowment	*Disclosed AUM (US$ bn)*	*Year founded*	*OECD Governance compliance*
Norway Government Pension Fund – Global	Resource extraction	561	1990	96
Abu Dhabi Investment Authority	Resource extraction	342	1976	71
China Investment Corp.	Diversified exports	332	2007	60
Kuwait Investment Authority	Resource extraction	296	1953	71
HKMA Investment Portfolio, Hong Kong	Diversified exports & fiscal surpluses	277	1993	74
Government of Singapore Investment Corp.	Diversified exports & fiscal surpluses	220	1981	78
Temasek Holding, Singapore	Diversified exports & fiscal surpluses	153	1974	82
National Welfare & Reserve Funds, Russia	Resource extraction	93	2008	52
Qatar Investment Authority	Resource extraction	80	2005	15
Australian Future Fund	Resource extraction & fiscal surpluses	77	2006	90
Investment Corp. of Dubai	Resource extraction	64	2006	22
Revenue Regulation Fund, Algeria	Resource extraction	57	2000	32
International Petroleum Investment Co., Abu Dhabi	Resource extraction	50	1984	26
Alaska Permanent Fund	Resource extraction	39	1976	96
National Fund, Kazakhstan	Resource extraction	44	2000	67
Brunei Investment Agency	Resource extraction	39	1983	28
Korea Investment Corp.	Diversified exports	38	2005	67
Khazanah Nasional Bhd., Malaysia	Fiscal surpluses	37	1993	48
National Pensions Reserve Funds, Ireland	Fiscal surpluses	33	2001	94
Mubadala Development Co., Abu Dhabi	Resource extraction	28	2002	66

AUM shown as at the latest available quarter end, December 2009–June 2011. OECD Governance compliance explained in main text. Libya was ranked 11th prior to catastrophic losses disclosed in 2011. Hong Kong's AUM include its Exchange Fund which represents the tied resources of its quasi-currency board. In our sample Indonesia, the Philippines, Taiwan and Thailand do not feature in the source data. State pension funds are excluded.
Sources: Monitor Group LP (2011); Truman (2011).

on bank credit, and forced operational reforms that may sustain the model and increase its appeal to investors.

Sectoral AUM in listed and unlisted infrastructural funds probably exceed US$2.0 trillion, the most prolific investors being state and commercial pension funds in Canada, the US, Australia, the Netherlands, the UK and South Korea. Macquarie had US$117 billion deployed in 118 self-managed businesses globally at the peak of its AUM in FYE 2008. Most were made by acquisition using the control structure illustrated in Figure 11.3.

This graphic adapts Figure 6.8 to show the completeness of control provided by the model. A substantially completed project has falling outstanding debt and operates in a regulated industry with predictable cashflows. The acquisition involves high initial leverage that would have been easily funded before 2008, given that lenders were confident in Macquarie's capability to refinance their loans with fixed-rate or securitized bonds. Macquarie's position is central, in:

- Using its capabilities in corporate finance to steer the acquisition;
- Coordinating syndicated loans and mezzanine finance to support the purchase;
- Taking operational control as project manager, having valued the target as a non-financial buyer;
- Negotiating and selling packaged or *stapled securities* to pension funds and other non-bank investors. Stapling refers to claims held in several commonly owned projects subject to a deed that prevents their separate sale;
- Arranging post-acquisition refinancing; and
- Scrutinizing each of these functions as risk manager.

Multiple roles provide Macquarie with both upfront and continuing revenue. A typical example is the 2006 purchase of UK utility Thames Water:

- Kemble Water, a vehicle controlled by Macquarie European Infrastructure Fund I, buys Thames Water for £8.0 billion (US$15.6 billion) in cash and assumed debt after contested bidding. Kemble sells its existing water and waste subsidiary to meet EU competition rules.
- Co-investors include the Alberta Pension Fund and Dutch civil service pension fund ABP. Macquarie Group's equity infusion of £250 million represents 3.125 per cent of the purchase price.

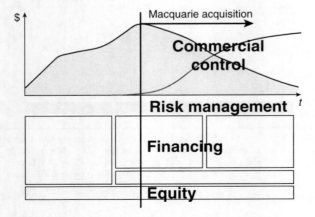

Figure 11.3 Macquarie's project control.

- Funding is completed with syndicated loans mandated by Macquarie totalling £4.0 billion, with tenors of 18 months and five and seven years.
- High initial leverage is mitigated with *accretion swaps*, or off-market interest rate or basis swaps between Kemble or Thames and Macquarie Bank that depress periodic liabilities and create a balloon payment that is eliminated upon refinancing.
- Kemble's debt is refinanced in August 2007 with a £4.1 billion whole business securitization arranged by Macquarie, using cashflows from Thames's regulated waste and water businesses. Some debt issues in this arrangement have index-linked coupons tied to Thames's revenue.
- In 2012 Kemble sells an 8.7 per cent shareholding in Thames to CIC.

Macquarie arranged a similarly funded €3.2 billion (US$4.1 billion) acquisition by its European Infrastructure Fund 4 of a gas distribution network owned by German utility E.ON in May 2012, with loans providing €2.7 billion of the price. Figure 11.4 gives a simplified impression of post-acquisition control in these examples, showing Macquarie vehicles in several revenue-generating positions.

The concept is more appropriate for acquisitions than development projects, which suits providers of long-term funds. Macquarie's cash contribution is usually limited. Infrastructural investment is not always innovative, yet this adaptation has been influential in aspects of governance, control and in eliciting resources from fund managers. The strategy is indebted to Australian pension law reforms that began in 1985, introducing tax-deductible employer contributions, leading to permanent increases in pension coverage and resources. This raised demand for long-duration financial assets, giving Macquarie and others a reliable resource for new funds.

The multiplicity of Macquarie's pre-crisis contractual involvement is shown in Figure 11.5, using the non-recourse structure of Figure 6.6.

Such close control elicited criticism over governance, transparency and sponsor compensation (Lawrence & Stapledon 2008), that we characterize as an indictment of contractual rather than traditional corporate governance similar to criticisms of securitization. Specific concerns included:

- The model being 'fraught with potential conflicts' (*Economist* 2008).
- Overpayment in acquisitions, fee structures encouraging large leveraged investments, and transaction economics requiring rising asset prices.

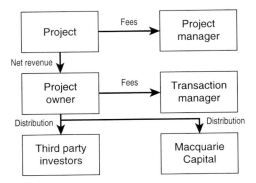

Figure 11.4 Post-acquisition revenue control.

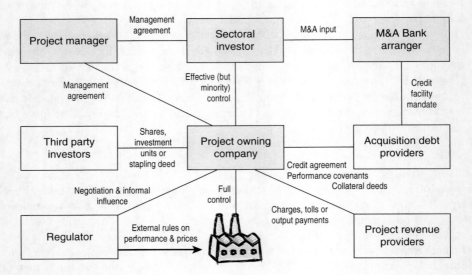

Figure 11.5 Macquarie's operational ubiquity.

Macquarie companies occupy the four shaded positions. These were reduced in the post-2008 revision to the central ownership functions, with those shown at the top left and right corners made subject to tender.

- Accounting policies overstating commercial performance, dividends declared from net fund revenues rather than net income, and fees not fully tied to project performance.
- Operational independence. Were Macquarie funds able to contract freely with third-party service providers? Were external investors disadvantaged if project requirements are supplied by Macquarie companies? Could the fund dismiss Macquarie as project manager?

Subsequent rating agency analysis acknowledges the model's contractual strengths. S&P has argued that creditors of Thames Water's securitization SPVs are protected by supportive regulation and ring-fenced cashflows that offset an 'aggressive [group] capital structure and dividend distribution' (Davidson 2011), a negative free operating cashflow and the risk of regulatory change (ibid). Contractual and collateral covenants give significant control to senior and subordinated creditors of the SPVs in the event that Thames Water experienced financial stress (ibid.).[7]

None of the critics' questions of principle were fully resolved when the post-Lehman credit squeeze necessitated changes to Macquarie's funding and operations. These reduced reliance on leverage, switched emphasis from listed to unlisted closed-end funds with fixed maturities, and allowed projects and funds to contract more freely with third parties. Macquarie lessened the comprehensiveness of its control and revenue sources, and in doing so caused its model to survive. Babcock and Brown, a smaller Australian infrastructural fund manager, collapsed from illiquidity in 2009, yet its funds were largely unaffected by the liquidation. Critics demanding more traditional corporate governance can instead be taken as implying a need for rejuvenated contractual governance and supervision.

Some 145 new, mainly unlisted, infrastructure funds were thought to be raising US$97 billion from global investors in mid-2012, with 25 focused on Asian risk (Preqin Ltd. 2012). The ten largest known investors in infrastructure had estimated commitments of US$71.1 billion, a group comprising five pension funds and four asset managers from Canada, Australia, the Netherlands and US, together with Venezuela's SWF (ibid). One index of infrastructural funds consistently outperformed MSCI's global equity index between July 2001 and April 2012. Using December 1998 as a base (100), the NMX30 Infrastructure Global Index and MSCI World Index respectively reached 140 and 340 at the end of the period (ibid), although this is a simplified comparison. If most infrastructural funds are unlisted with fixed maturities then this relative performance would be attributable largely to assumed reinvestment of stable infrastructural earnings.

11.4 Islamic finance

Our final section reflects on transaction techniques, organizational structures and supervision complying with Islamic principles and customs known as the *Shari'ah*. These provide full or partial alternatives to conventional intermediation, the extent varying with practice in the host jurisdiction. Those found in Iran and Saudi Arabia and certain other Gulf Co-operation Council (GCC) states are largely *traditional* in nature; others are recent and *adaptive* in replicating conventional instruments or practices in Shari'ah compliant forms. Islamic finance can be controversial, is rarely homogenous, and is important in four particular respects:

- Sizeable capital flows from Shari'ah compliant investors, especially in GCC states. Islamic and other financial hubs and certain non-Islamic issuers have responded by adapting structures to match investor demand, as Section 8.1 describes of conventional deal formation.
- Malaysia's and Dubai's growth as hubs for adaptive Islamic finance, and the ambitions of Hong Kong, Singapore and the UK to sanction transactions in Shari'ah compliant instruments written under local or English law.
- Uncertainty arising from conflicts between conventional and Shari'ah compliant deals and practices, especially in multicreditor workouts as in 2009–10 with the Nakheel Steel affiliate of the Dubai World group, and in disputes involving competing interpretations of the Shari'ah.
- Whether modern Shari'ah compliant finance can assist economic development in traditional Islamic states, which scholars see as long curtailed by restrictions such as those on permanent commercial organizations or the operational flexibility of Islamic banks (Kuran 2003, 2011; Vogel 1998; Warde 2012).

Our discussion concentrates on adaptive forms of Islamic finance, which are neither traditional nor entirely novel. Islamic commerce is ancient by contrast. The Prophet Muhammad and many of his early followers were merchants, and Islamic practices were followed throughout the extensive medieval trade routes between the Mediterranean and East and South Asia, and the risk-sharing principle that they embody was arguably institutionally important in fostering trade in testing environments (Greif 2006). Pilgrims undertaking the annual *hajj* incurred substantial costs that they could finance by engaging in trade along the route and in Mecca itself, making a sacred journey inextricably and acceptably associated with economic activity (Kuran 2011: 46). Finance in a conventional sense was wholly different, and two factors prevented it from becoming embedded in traditional Islamic culture:

- The Qur'an's prohibition on *riba*, or demanding excessive payments of a debtor. *Riba* is taken by traditional jurists to require a comprehensive ban on loans bearing interest, while scholars supporting adaptive practices may sanction transactions that use non-usurious proxies for interest, for example advance payment discounts, or sale and purchase agreements referencing Libor or other indexes.
- Restrictions on incorporation or permanent commercial organizations. Commerce could be undertaken by partnerships or a semi-permanent trust concept known as a *waqf*, but these were suboptimal for banking and inhibiting for economic development (ibid: 156).

The notion of corporate personality in modern civil and common law jurisdictions derives from Roman law and aims primarily to limit the liability of the principals to a commercial venture (Glenn 2007: 184). Traditional Islamic commerce is participatory, comprising activities in which the profits and risks of ventures are shared. The result is that the Shari'ah is generally hostile to those forms of finance capitalism that involve the external provision of funds without the financier bearing a proportionate share of like risk. Traditional thinking regards conventional insurance as similarly suspect. One result was that the banks established in the nineteenth-century Ottoman empire or wider Middle East were colonial and conventional in operation. The first truly Islamic bank opened only in 1975 (Warde 2012: 11). Limited banking systems and modest organized exchanges persist today even in high-income Islamic states.

Adaptive Islamic finance is thus modern, developing in phases since the 1970s as export surpluses encouraged GCC states to find acceptable ways to replicate or replace conventional financial transactions and organizations (ibid: 2). This led to the creation of national and transnational regulatory bodies, and a consensus among many states over the mechanisms needed to certify compliance, although with little interpretative uniformity.

Malaysia began creating institutional resources in the 1980s to support Shari'ah compliant transactions for domestic users, and especially as a hub for foreign investors and fundraisers, and now has complementary conventional and Shari'ah financial, regulatory and commercial judicial systems. Since 1997, its supervisory architecture has included a national Shari'ah Advisory Council within Bank Negara Malaysia that has exclusive certification and regulatory functions (Central Bank of Malaysia Act 2009: §§ 55–8). Other Islamic states devolve compliance certification to intermediaries or their representative bodies. Kuala Lumpur is an Islamic finance centre for many different users, especially in securities issuance, including those domiciled in GCC states with less liberal practices. Malaysia's relatively large pension fund sector has also helped facilitate growth in activity.

The estimated scale of financial activity considered Shari'ah compliant grew from US$509 billion in December 2006 to US$1.13 trillion at the end of 2010 and around US$1.3 trillion 12 months later (McKenzie 2012). This comprises assets of the banking, insurance (*takaful*) and fund management sectors, with banks accounting for 96 per cent of the 2010 total. Most banks hold a large proportion of assets as Islamic securities for liquidity purposes and to ameliorate treasury complexities inherent in fully compliant commercial intermediation. Around half of end-2010 assets were held in Iran (US$388 billion) and Saudi Arabia (US$151 billion), with smaller concentrations in Malaysia (US$133.4 billion) and the UAE

(US$94.1 billion). The only other states reporting assets exceeding US$50 billion were Kuwait, Bahrain and Qatar. The largest volumes in non-Islamic states were in the UK (US$19 billion) and Switzerland (US$6.6 billion). The share of Shari'ah compliant banking assets in national totals exceeded 40 per cent only in Iran, Bangladesh and Bahrain (ibid), and is negligible in Indonesia, the most populous Islamic state.

Principles and processes

Discussing Islamic finance from a conventional perspective is problematic because the two systems have such distinct objectives. One school suggests that weaknesses in the institutional foundations of Islamic commerce explain a relative decline in the economic performance of the Middle East compared to Europe or East Asia from around 1800 CE (Kuran 2003, 2011), in particular that laws and regulation failed to support permanent and commercially resilient enterprises or the extension of credit by the financial system.

Such conclusions are reached in their own terms even if accurate, that is, on the basis of a conventional appraisal of the value of economic success. The same view suggests more narrowly that Islamic finance will lack the utility and efficiency of conventional finance unless it develops intellectual support distinct from a traditional reading of Islamic texts (Kuran 1986: 159). This is arguably what has transpired over the last 20 years in Kuala Lumpur, and to a lesser extent in the acceptance of Shari'ah compliant transactions in non-Islamic centres such as London. We doubt that these examples would constitute acceptable domestic practice to scholars in traditional Islamic jurisdictions, but they may have a secondary developmental impact given that parties from restrictive states use adaptive transactions in other centres.

We distinguish *sources* of Islamic law from the *process* that conditions acceptable commercial activity. Both entail personal interpretation. The Shari'ah process varies between jurisdictions and because of subjectivity in compliance certification, involving opinions of scholarly individuals or panels that inevitably differ between and within jurisdictions. The functionality of compliant transactions is subject to exogeneities arising from competing doctrinal interpretations, and can represent a material legal risk.

The sources of law on which modern Shari'ah compliant finance relies are the Qur'an, or holy book of Islam; the *Sunnah* or trodden path, a manner of acting or a rule of conduct or practice associated with the life of the Prophet; the *Hadith*, or recorded aspects of the conduct or approval of the Prophet; and *ijma*, which refers to a consensus among scholars as to whether a practice is valid. The Shari'ah may involve *qiyas*, a method analogous to the doctrine of precedence to resolve cases not covered expressly by the Qur'an or *Sunnah*, but this is not universally accepted. Commerce is explicitly favoured over finance in the Qur'an (Ch. 2: 275–6):

> [T]hose who take usury will rise up on the Day of Resurrection like someone tormented by Satan's touch. That is because they say, 'Trade and usury are the same,' but God has allowed trade and forbidden usury.
>
> (Haleem 2005)

Islamic finance is distinguished by its character rather than a pure concern over profit or commercial ethics – indeed, the returns obtained by investors in commercial ventures can far exceed interest rates accruing to conventional lenders in similar schemes. Those characteristics seek to ensure that finance is lawful and non-exploitative, that it conforms with the Qur'an's prohibition of *riba*, and that it avoids *gharar*, or uncertainty associated with speculation. This implies that parties to a financial transaction must always be adequately informed as to its functionality, risks and potential costs, otherwise *gharar* is not fully excluded. The compliance of a financial instrument may therefore have a subjective quality, for example if a contractual price is given by a formula rather than stated simply. Other specific restrictions include prohibitions on financing activities regarded as socially detrimental, including gambling (*maysir*), or goods forbidden to followers of Islam. Financial activities require two further characteristics to be legitimate:

- An investor must share in the venture's or investee's risks and profits; and
- All transactions must be supported by identified tangible underlying assets.

Whether a financial contract or the conduct of an intermediary conforms with these precepts is the subject of an opinion or *fatwa*, given formally either by an independent jurist *(mufti)* or group of religious scholars designated by an intermediary as its Shari'ah board. *Fatwas* are usually non-actionable, but as much relied upon as legal opinions in conventional finance, with the distinction that it is not unknown for *fatwas* provided for a single transaction type to differ. Several international organizations exist in addition to national supervisory agencies to regulate or guide the development of the Shari'ah. Most are recently founded, the two most influential being:

- Accounting and Auditing Organization for Islamic Financial Institutions (AAOIFI) established in Bahrain in 1990, which issues standards covering accounting, audit practices, governance and models for compliance; and
- Islamic Financial Services Board (IFSB), founded in Kuala Lumpur in 2002, which prepares guidance for regulators of banks, securities dealers and other intermediaries engaged in Islamic finance, covering capital adequacy, risk management, governance and business conduct rules. IFSB also intercedes in standard setting for Islamic finance with the BCBS, IOSCO and ISDA.

Transactions and organizations

The requirements of compliance are embodied in two foundational instruments, *mushakara*, a generic form of partnership or equity participation that signifies cooperation in a commercial venture, and *mudaraba*, which is a more specific arrangement for investment based on profit sharing. Both can become contracts acceptable in all Islamic jurisdictions. They also facilitate other specific transactions and the conduct of intermediaries.

Each varies in its design and acceptability from state to state, for example in deposit taking and financing by banks. The first Islamic banks applied profit-sharing principles to simple commercial intermediation, using a 'double mudaraba' arrangement to collect deposits and make advances (Al-Omar & Abdel-Haq 1996: 3), so that a commercial partnership was drafted into the contracts between depositor and bank and between bank and borrower. These arrangements can be cumbersome in aggregate, and for treasury or risk management purposes, since the returns to the depositor and the bank cannot be fixed. The model is found mainly in traditional states. It is more common for *mudaraba* to be applied to other adaptive transactions, including sukuk and *takaful*, and for banks to ring fence Shari'ah compliant activity in an *Islamic window*, usually a segregated section or subsidiary of a conventional organization.

Transactions facilitated by *mushakara* and *mudaraba* include debt, equity and derivative instruments, leases and insurance:

- *Murabaha*, a sale of goods or other property with deferred payments. This may involve a bank buying a commodity for a client, and the client paying the bank at intervals or at maturity the cost of the commodity together with a charge or profit. *Murabaha* can be adapted for use in the interbank markets and syndicated loans.
- *Ijarah* is a lease structure used to finance a conventional asset purchase or in the provision of services in return for periodic payments of rent. A variation known as *ijara wa iqtina* is equivalent to a lease providing for transfer of ownership at maturity.
- *Istisna* is a sale contract by which a bank finances work in progress or construction of a building or installation by selling the assets to its debtor client with payments made in instalments.
- *Sukuk* (certificate) is the most widely used adaptive financing instrument, and taken to be the Islamic finance equivalent of a debt security. They exist in simple and complex forms, for example IFSB approved the issuance of securitized *sukuk* in 2005. The origins of *sukuk* are similar to medieval bills of exchange, a means by which financial obligations could be transferred (Hanif & Johansen 2012: 255), but they now have similar purposes to conventional debt securities, albeit with a structure representing a transferable ownership interest in specific underlying assets, rather than a claim against those assets or any income they might generate (ibid: 259). Shared ownership entitles *sukuk* holders to returns referenced to the underlying assets, but the simple form of *sukuk* is distinct from ABS (ibid: 260). *Sukuk* often provide for an exchange of payments that transforms the irregular gains from an asset sale and purchase into a regular income stream for the investor, a quality that suggests a comparison with total return swaps explained in Section 8.2.
- *Takaful* is compliant insurance based on cooperative principles that avoid *gharar*, and is similar in operation to conventional mutual insurance.
- *Tawarruq*, or commodity *murabaha*, is a structure involving the sale and purchase of a commodity so as to simulate a loan, and is generally unacceptable in GCC states.
- A *Tahawwut* (hedging) Master Agreement to be governed by English or New York law was released in 2010 by the ISDA and the International Islamic Financial Market, an industry lobby based in Dubai. It draws on existing derivative practice in civil jurisdictions by creating contracts of mutual obligations, and to exclude *gharar* is expressly for use in hedging. The document can be used wherever Shari'ah compliant derivatives are permitted and accommodates variations in jurisdictional practice by containing less detailed provisions than its conventional 2002 counterpart.
- Option contracts are classified either as *bay'urbun*, meaning a current sale with partial payment, or *khiyarat*, which refers to provisions in a contract allowing its terms to be altered.

Some jurisdictions dispute the acceptability of many of these models, and not all will be identical in practice given variations in scholarly views. A shortage of compliant instruments forces users in many states to rely on conventional instruments, the scarcity of short-term liquidity instruments being especially limiting for banks. The Shari'ah generally supports guarantee instruments but is inconsistent in its treatment of transfers of outstanding or defaulted claims.

Concerns and challenges

Widening use of Islamic finance has revealed several judicial or functional conflicts, notably involving distressed debtors. The logic of *riba* is that a creditor should participate in all the risks of the venture it funds, in particular to accept losses or waive a debtor's commitments in the event of its financial distress. Is this compatible with the consensual behaviour of conventional creditors exemplified by the London approach cited in Section 6.3? Workouts may entail creditors agreeing easier commercial terms or a partial reduction in principal, but their aim is usually to promote repayment rather than distribute the debtor's losses. The issue is relevant in cases such as Nakheel Steel which involved three forms of debt obligations:

- Conventional loans and bonds;
- Adaptive Shari'ah compliant claims written under English or New York law; and
- Other Shari'ah compliant claims written under the law of one of several Islamic jurisdictions.

Such conflicts of law are complicated by Islamic finance being unaccustomed to dealing with distressed debt and consensual workouts, and by bankruptcy itself being unfamiliar to the Shari'ah. The principle of loss-sharing may be a basis for non-judicial workouts but gives no guidance for negotiators, especially as the Qur'an requires the acceptance of loss (Ch. 2, 279–80):

> You shall have your capital if you repent, and without suffering loss or causing others to suffer loss. If the debtor is in difficulty, then delay things until matters become easier for him; still, if you were to write it off as an act of charity, that would be better for you.
>
> (Haleem 2005)

Disputes involving adaptive transactions governed by non-Islamic law create a further uncertainty as to whether the courts in non-Islamic jurisdictions may be willing to respect the intentions of contracting parties, despite not recognizing the Shari'ah as a form of law. Certain compliant transactions structures also require legislation to be viable in non-Islamic states – for example, asset sales integral to many models may otherwise produce unwanted tax liabilities.

A final uncertainty arises from competing certification. In 2011 Goldman Sachs established a US$2.0 billion *sukuk* issuance programme governed by English law for which its Shari'ah board issued a *fatwa* (Global Sukuk Co. Ltd. 2011). The prospectus warns investors to make their own determination of compliance, not only as associated with conventional legal risks but also:

- To provide for each investor's own standards of compliance; as
- Similar considerations will prevent *sukuk* being transferred to investors whose views of compliance are different.

Evidence of bank behaviour indicates little difference resulting from the conduct of conventional and Islamic intermediaries, except that Shari'ah compliant banking is more cautious (Beck, Demirgüç-Kunt & Merrouche 2010). A broader question prompted by the global crisis of whether it is ethical or advisable for finance to exist only for its own benefit may be one that Islamic finance may be more able than conventional finance to address, given its precept that finance and commerce should do no harm.

12 Regional financial integration

Our two final chapters look to the future of finance in Asia, a relatively positive topic at a time of considerable change and uncertainty. Not since July 1944 has the global community of nations tried to plan and integrate major changes to the prevailing international financial architecture. The earlier occasion was dominated by two industrialized economies; today's is the first when several Asian states are fully part of discussions, a contrast explained in Box 12.1. Redrawing the world's financial landscape after the first financial crisis of the twenty-first century focuses on regulation rather than currency stability and is subject to more diverse interests and influence, even if the process is far from fully representative.

This observation resounds with one aim of our book that was explained in the second section of the introduction, to examine global financial intermediation from a non-traditional perspective. A similar point has been made in relation to assessing Asia's regional security and international relations policies. It may often be useful to compare examples of regional integration as we do in the final section of this chapter, but theories of regionalism based on Western or European experiences struggle to explain the process in Asia (Acharya 2009: 26–7), and cannot provide a measure of its success or failure.

Another way to consider this subjective question is to take note of the hazard of seeing regional financial integration as a European or North American concept. This is a risk because almost all academic theory in this field is derived from Western norms and concepts that influenced the legally complex evolution of the EU, and differ intrinsically from those associated with practice in Asia. Much of this chapter is concerned with transnational financial integration and this is not a misleading term for the region, but a political analyst would be more likely to discuss regional cooperation or collaboration among Asian states, to reflect its deliberate institutional and legal character.

Regional integration among Asian states has varied functionally throughout the last 30 years. Progress in financial integration has almost always been incremental or unobservable, with policymakers unwilling to make demanding agreements that might erode sovereignty, or allow transactional integration to occur freely. The crisis of 1997–98 led to caution rather than reform in both these respects. We begin the chapter by assessing these circumstances and their results. Asian economic and financial integration may come to resemble certain aspects of European Community development from earlier generations, but could equally prove very different. We examine the tensions that have kept financial markets from interacting or opening to regional access, and describe cooperation to date in external monetary policy, which we contrast with the region's record in cross-border trade and manufacturing. Finally, we look at ASEAN+3's introduction in 2010 of the Multilaterized Chiang Mai Initiative (CMIM), which points to more radical future arrangements and gives us the chance to speculate further in our final chapter.

Box 12.1. Bretton Woods, the G20 and Asian Representation

We make the point in this chapter that assessing regional integration is inevitably a political exercise, and that the nature of integration within Asia is often judged to be weak, indecisive or conflicted, by virtue of its being read against a European or federalist state metric. The same is true of many historical financial events, where non-industrialized states had a minimal voice even when admitted to discussions. If the global crisis induced a shift in leverage towards leading Asian states in international negotiations, then questions arise as to its permanence, whether decision-making will reach different conclusions or involve a new process, and how those influences will affect the global financial architecture. How will finance in Asia affect twenty-first century finance in the world?

The agreements made in July 1944 for the creation of the IMF, the World Bank and the post-conflict currency system followed several years of preparatory work in the UK and US, culminating in three weeks of negotiations at Bretton Woods in New Hampshire. The talks were dominated by two states and influenced materially by few others. Contemporary American and British accounts are dismissive of the technical input of other states (Howson & Moggridge 1990: 181). The Soviet Union achieved its objectives of receiving credit from the US but then declined to participate in the IMF or World Bank throughout its existence (the Russian Federation became a member of each in 1992).

Bretton Woods began three days after a drafting conference in Atlantic City, called by the US to steer the main negotiations. The 15 states attending the drafting meeting were agreed among UK and US officials, principally John Maynard Keynes and Harry Dexter White, who became the leading discussants at Bretton Woods. Keynes wrote on 30 May (while the UK's negotiating stance for Bretton Woods was being agreed) that 24 of the 44 states 'clearly have nothing to contribute and will merely encumber the ground' (Moggridge 1980: 42). The diaries of Lionel Robbins, a leading member of Keynes's team, are still more scathing (Robbins was Eurocentric but not intolerant). The drafting meeting was a UK–US dialogue conducted among other attendees drawn mainly from occupied European and Commonwealth states.

The World Bank claims that 'the democratic process at Bretton Woods ensured that concerns of all countries were addressed' (World Bank undated). This is illusory. Representatives of 44 states attended but few had weight in discussions. 21 participants were from the Americas (the only continent not under occupation), although Argentina was absent, in common with neutral European states. Allied states including governments in exile numbered 20; 15 states were occupied, including Iceland, Iran and Iraq; parts of China and the Soviet Union were also under military occupation.

Bretton Woods had three Asian participants in China's nationalist government, the colonial administration of India, and the government in exile of the occupied Philippines. Australia, Canada, New Zealand and South Africa were British Commonwealth states and India a colony; all were substantial creditors of the UK and holders of Sterling-denominated financial assets. This represented two of several global imbalances resulting from military spending, post-1914 trade and constraints on capital flows that Bretton Woods hoped to solve when its agreements took effect from December 1945 and the IMF and World Bank came into being.

Finance ministers and central bank heads have met as the G20 since 1999, but the group became prominent during the 2007–9 global crisis as heads of government meetings. Those that met in October 2009 came from 21 states and the EU, with the Netherlands and Spain as observers. 12 of the 1944 Bretton Woods participants are G20 members and one is an observer. The group is more evenly sourced (five states each from the Americas and East and South Asia, eight from Europe including the European Commission), but this only approximates to the world's largest economies.

G20 members from East and South Asia consist of China, India, Indonesia, South Korea and Japan. In terms of the influence of members, nothing in the G20 approaches the concentration of power seen at Bretton Woods. Competing national views would make it difficult for the G20 to promote ambitious solutions – for example, to lessen systemic risks with radical reforms. Keynes left Bretton Woods for London to defend his negotiations in a parliamentary debate entitled Anglo–American Financial Arrangements, stating:

> Here is an attempt to use what we have learnt from modern experience and modern analysis, not to defeat, but to implement the wisdom of Adam Smith. It is a unique accomplishment … in the field of international discussion to have proceeded so far by common agreement along a newly-trod path, not yet pioneered, I agree, to a definite final destination, but a newly-trod path which points the right way. We are attempting a great step forward towards the goal of international economic order amidst national diversities of policies.
>
> (Keynes 1945: cc. 791–92)

The transition to the G20's more inclusive practice is not an isolated example. The 1985 Plaza Accord to engineer a fall in the value of the US dollar was made by five states. Seven Asian states out of 27 helped draft the Basel III capital reforms (BCBS 2010a). These changes will have effects not only on decisions of international groups but on the process of decision making.

The vocabulary of regionalism varies by scholarly discipline, so we need first to establish several definitions:

- Integration in commercial or economic policy refers to arrangements for the trade in goods and to FDI.
- Monetary integration refers to formal currency cooperation between states.
- Financial sector integration means lifting restrictions to cross-border transactions involving loan contracts, debt and equity securities, and access to intermediaries. It excludes FDI but not regional outward investment, which is almost always the product of financial transactions and advice.
- Political integration involves an elective sharing of national sovereignty, whether in commercial affairs, in trade-related cooperation, or in relation to security. This is our secondary concern, but political integration has an important impact on the first three conditions.

Integration associated with globalization has become especially notable in the transformation of China's economy because it relies on highly regionalized manufacturing and exporting, including FDI, assembly, functional outsourcing, and subcomponent supply. This web of connections is usually itself integrated, so that inward investment to China from Japan or Taiwan is contractually linked with component supply, design contracts and manufacturing subcontracts. China is a 'growing market for Asian exports' for these reasons (Gill & Kharas 2010: 6), which helps drives the integration process, albeit without necessarily encouraging financial integration.

Economic, commercial and financial regionalism in Asia have tended to be manifested in loose transnational organizations and institutions or through collaborative policies, especially towards regional trade, dispute resolution and monetary cooperation. We believe that issues of national and cooperative governance help explain why modest financial integration accompanies more complex economic integration in the region.

- Cultural norms and legal systems militate against innovation in financial markets and systems, insofar as reforms in transnational institutions or organizations would require sacrifices in state autonomy. This has been expressed consistently within regional groups and characterized as the quiescent 'ASEAN Way'. A preference for consensus encourages incremental regional reform.
- Other socio-economic institutions resist the adoption of market-based regional solutions, even when they might arise through state cooperation. In particular, financial integration is slowed by banking systems that dominate saving and credit creation and strong symbiotic relationships between the state and the banking sector. Entrenched interests will oppose losing their status in financial governance to regional institutions or organizations. We expect these factors to subsist for some time, notwithstanding the agreement of ASEAN members to create a legal personality for the organization through a charter that took effect in December 2008, and form an economic community of states by 2015 (ASEAN 2007: Art. 3; ASEAN 2009).

12.1 Concepts of integration

It may seem surprising in a globalized world that financial integration in Asia matches neither the rhetoric expended in its support after the 1997–98 crisis nor the degree of integration that exists in trade. By some measures it is exceeded by bilateral integration with Australia, New Zealand and most developed Western economies.

Cross-border trade flows, direct investment and cross-border investment in capital goods have long been greater and faster growing than other regional capital flows. Regional institutions and organizations concerned with finance are few and generally lack influence. The interplay between national and international finance is limited, even among states with sophisticated financial systems.

No existing market can be considered regional. Asian intermediaries freely participate in global transactions denominated in US dollars or euros while most regional markets remain underdeveloped and price opaque. This dichotomy persists despite increasing incentives since the 1990s for financial integration and notwithstanding the development of organizations such as ASEAN that might be expected to favour financial liberalization. It contrasts with EU financial integration, with Asia's enthusiasm for participation in the WTO, and with the sophistication of intermediation in several centres. Above all, it differs from a post-crisis consensus that integration would help guard against future shocks. As we saw in Sections 2.3, 2.4, 3.1 and 3.4, each economy instead took its own course after 1998, even though some of the results were alike.

Financial integration is associated with capital mobility (Machlup 1977: 71–2), although the term was not used in this sense before the mid-1950s (ibid: 13–16). True financial integration was known much earlier, for European equity markets were well-integrated by the mid-eighteenth century (Neal 1985: 221), although official control of capital flows began only in 1914. For us it represents the extent to which an economy's financial system is not shielded or made distinct from other national and international financial markets. It is the antithesis of the Bretton Woods international financial system that prevailed for almost 30 years after 1945.

Such integration is difficult to identify consistently because it can be measured only by proxy, and its use was very often conflated with other forms of integration (Gkoutzinis 2006). The concept has been closely analyzed since the 1990s, before which views as to what integration might mean were less developed and reflected the contemporary view that finance was generally subservient to trade or production. Financial integration tends to emphasize wholesale activity rather than retail intermediation for individuals. Legal or customary obstacles to transnational trade in retail financial services prevail even in the EU.

Financial integration is also taken to refer to the extent of correlations in price behaviour of two or more distinct markets, for example in equity securities or interest rates (Chi, Ke & Young 2006; Yeyati, Schmukler & van Horen 2006). This is not our approach, not least because 'price co-movements could reflect common factors and/or similarities in fundamentals, rather than the degree of integration' (Cowen & Salgado 2006). Common price-movements link to our subject only insofar as arbitrage undertaken on the strength of such correlations may involve capital movements of the kind obstructed by Asia's lack of integration. It implies 'mobility [of capital] and substitutability among comparable financial assets in terms of yields, maturities and risk in international financial markets' and the expectation of a 'full speedy adjustment of asset stocks in response to price changes' (Shepherd 1994: 77–9), but 'substitutability' today often includes synthetic transactions such as offshore non-deliverable derivative contracts or certain credit-linked notes, which exist because of, and to circumvent, capital controls or other barriers.

While true financial integration can be expected to lead to an international convergence of financial asset prices, the analysis in this chapter is more connected with the needs and preferences of market users. We see financial integration as distinct from integration in commerce, economic policy, monetary policy or political cooperation, however often such policies may be inter-related, and despite relying upon mechanisms commonly identified as political. It also differs from FDI even though such flows can be made through share purchases.

Shortly before the 1957 Treaty of Rome created the six-state European Economic Community (EEC), economic integration was said by a libertarian scholar to be 'the establishment of a condition which makes possible the free and reciprocal flow of trade between the various national economies' (Röpke 1954: 251), requiring both free trade in goods and free movement of capital. It is appropriate to assess Asia's contemporary integration with reference to the permissiveness of cross-border regional trade and capital flows and to look forward in the context of the global financial crisis to possible future directions. Röpke's description of the European Payments Union (1950–58) as an arrangement in functional cooperation, resembles the ASEAN+3 web of central bank payment lines explained in Section 12.5, and was one of 'two great international actions…to further Europe's economic integration' (ibid: 258), the second being the European Coal and Steel Community. Comparisons of Asian and European regionalism are useful for technical reasons but at no point in the chapter is EU experience taken as a model of principle. Indeed we are keen to avoid investigating Asian integration with a European prism or introducing a subjective assessment by using terms such as 'loose' or 'consensual'.

12.2 State cooperation and governance

Our premise is that Asian financial integration is unique and deliberately modest, even though cross-border acquisitions, joint ventures and other forms of regional cross-border investment are well-established and require substantial transfers of funding or capital goods. One IMF study found that:

> [t]otal financial liabilities in Asia (the combined stock of [FDI], foreign loans, and equity holdings) [are] typically lower than in other regions of the world. Moreover, intraregional financial integration – for example, measured directly by cross-border capital flows or indirectly by cross-border correlation of consumption growth – has been more limited than elsewhere. Consequently, Asian economies appear to have become more integrated with countries outside the region than within the region.
>
> (Cowen & Salgado 2006: 11)

A second analysis noted that while financial integration had increased after the Asian financial crisis, it had a 'troubled history' and remained 'patchy' (ADB 2008: 108), with markets being less mutually integrated than their global counterparts and less integrated in both respects than those in Europe.

Evidence of a direct relationship between financial integration and economic growth is inconclusive. Schularick & Steger (2006) suggest that developmental benefits associated with financial integration require prior domestic institutional reform, in particular the maintenance of adequate and enforceable property rights of the elemental kind we analyzed in Sections 5.2–5.4. The indeterminate result may signify empirical problems in measuring financial integration, which is most commonly observed in the ratio of capital flows, or holdings of foreign assets and liabilities, to national income, or represented by a binary indicator for transnational capital controls.

Lane & Milesi-Ferretti (2003) use an index based on the sum of foreign assets and liabilities to national income. This is contextually important in that if modest financial integration is linked to high national savings then the domestic disutility of foreign reserve accumulation is compounded by developmental effects (Lane & Schmukler 2006). That financial integration and economic growth cannot easily be linked empirically is significant in terms of state norms in Asia given that capital controls were anathema to the IMF between the 1980s and 1997–98. National capital controls have since been less disfavoured, partly because of their use by states such as China, India, Malaysia and Taiwan that were less affected by that crisis.

While governance has been taken to involve a proactive state 'sustaining coordination and coherence among a wide variety of actors' (Pierre 2000: 3) that might include transnational organizations, it may also represent the 'empirical manifestations of state adaptation to its external environment' or alternatively 'a theoretical representation of coordination of social systems' (ibid) by the state and others. Such conceptual inclusiveness allows a discussion of whatever governance is manifested through Asian regional financial integration, to include instances where none exists, that is, an absence of governance analogous to the view of Asian regionalism as a form of 'pre-governance' (Payne 2000: 214–15), and the actions of non-state commercial actors, especially from the financial sector. The most appropriate approach for this analysis may be to regard governance as '[t]he processes and institutions, both formal and informal, that guide and restrain the collective activities of a group' (Keohane & Nye 2000: 12). Weakness in these processes and institutions tend to reflect an absence of regional governance.

That Asia's financial integration lags its considerable economic integration may appear inconsistent with the sophistication of certain of its domestic financial systems. The explanation may result from cultural norms operating at state or sub-state level that influence behaviour within Asia's regional organizations, which we amplify in Sections 12.3 and 12.4. This influence is seen in an elective aspect of state governance, that is, the primacy of any national economic policies with which integration is deemed to be inconsistent. Such norms are clearly represented by the 'ASEAN Way' (ASEAN 1967), stemming from ASEAN's founding declaration and first treaty (ASEAN 1976), and involving consensual decision-making and commitments to mutual non-interference by members. It was characterized during the 1997–98 financial crisis by Singapore's foreign minister as stressing 'informality, organizational minimalism, inclusiveness, intensive consultations leading to consensus, and peaceful resolution, of disputes' (Acharya 2001; Jayakumar 1998).

The nature of financial governance in Asia, as revealed in the behaviour of its regional organizations and institutions, is thus the result of weak regional norms competing with paramount national policy. Today's level of financial integration may arguably be regarded as having been achieved in spite of those norms. Asia's economic integration was described in 1994 as having taken place 'spontaneously, through business decisions without an intergovernmental framework … indeed, in spite of some government hostility' (Cable 1994: 6). This remains an appropriate characterization of Asian financial integration. Most of the regional groupings formed up to 2005 in Asia are listed in Curley and Thomas (2007: 247–54). Financial integration appears to require certain enabling institutions which Asian states have chosen to avoid creating or allow to function freely. Note that the development of such institutions would not affect the rights of a state to obstruct or set conditions for inward foreign investment.

Since 1967 ASEAN has become the most conspicuous organization associated with Asian regionalism. This reflects both a growing disutility of APEC (Ravenhill 2001), and ASEAN's embracing China, Japan and South Korea through the ASEAN+3 mechanism. Throughout this chapter, ASEAN and ASEAN+3 are referred to as organizations or the products of institutional arrangements since their existence is real when measured by actions or norms. It is less clear in law that either body represents, at a non-trivial level, more than an association of states without legal personality.

The ASEAN Charter to which all members are party provides for ASEAN 'as an international organisation to be conferred a legal personality' (ASEAN 2007: Art. 3), following the recommendation of an ASEAN Eminent Persons' study convened as part of a 2005 initiative named 'Vision 2020'. When ASEAN chooses to make substantive agreements with third parties, for example in relation to trade with a non-ASEAN states, each member would enter a separate treaty. Until now, ASEAN has represented an expression of aims more than a substantive constitutional body. Furthermore, although an international body without formal legal personality may serve as a forum for its members to enter institutional arrangements (Ruggie 1992: 567), it will inevitably be weaker in action than organizations provided with autonomy and dedicated resources.

These qualities have together constituted a soft personality that intentionally constrains ASEAN's capacity in regional governance, and the ASEAN Way is an exemplar of 'collaboration without legalization' (Kahler 2000: 551). The region is an example of 'low legalization and possibly an explicit aversion to legalization', with 'codes of conduct ... favoured over precisely defined agreements' (ibid: 549). Legalization refers to a mix of rules, delegated authority and functional precision, in each of which ASEAN can be characterized as relatively weak (Abbott, Keohane, Moravcsik, Slaughter & Snidal 2000: 401–5).

ASEAN began discussing regional financial matters only in the mid-1990s. The step was influenced by the 1997–98 financial crisis, a consensual wish to distinguish the region from elsewhere, and a surge in the growth of trade with China and FDI to China from ASEAN members. The first venture in financial cooperation was a framework among national bodies for banking, capital markets, customs, insurance, taxation and related human resources, ironically made immediately prior to the onset of the Asian financial crisis in early 1997 (ASEAN 1997a). This protocol encouraged members to discuss macroeconomic and regulatory policies, improve policy and regulatory transparency, and promote links between the public and private sectors.

The agreement was made subject to ASEAN's consensual approach with the proviso that two or more members might engage in the implementation of programmes and projects at their chosen pace rather than be restrained by others. The qualification is less an advance in regionalism than acknowledgement that financially underdeveloped states may lack the means or wish to engage in joint policies.

Wholly new initiatives must be sanctioned by all members. The activities to which the states are urged to participate are stated briefly and without the 'functional specificity' that one theorist of regionalism considered as 'causally related to the intensity of integration' (Haas 1961: 372). The intention was rehearsed during the Asian financial crisis in December 1997 when, in a forward-looking statement, ASEAN heads of government undertook to:

> promote financial sector liberalization and closer cooperation in money and capital market [sic.], tax, insurance and customs matters as well as closer consultations in macroeconomic and financial policies.
>
> (ASEAN 1997b)

More generally, ASEAN and ASEAN+3 states have been unprepared to relinquish the degree of national policy control associated with weak or non-existent regional institutions and organizations. This is distinguished from an absence of regional governance inasmuch as it represents deliberate choice rather than a formative period that would lead to greater regional governance. It includes effective authority in governance given to certain non-state actors, especially in national banking sectors. Thus the extent of regional integration is consistent with shared norms, whether deliberately adopted as with the consensual ASEAN Way, the making paramount of other aspects of state policy, or indirectly managed as with the participation of commercial and banking interests in governance. Section 1.3 explained how the developmental state model was characterized by close directional relationships between the state and leading commercial interests. It has been asserted that:

> authority structures in the Asia Pacific serve the interests of dominant actors and state-business [sic.] coalitions, and that these actors are organized into informal networks of power, that is, particular informal modes of regional governance, serving private as well as public interests.
>
> (Soderbaum 2004: 419)

This institutional involvement of non-state actors in Asian governance is distinct from the more general proposition that international economic activities of all non-state participants may contribute to governance (Nye & Keohane 1971), as Chapter 4 showed with the engagement of leading banks in the creation of the first and second Basel capital accords.

The most dramatic result of subsuming regionalism to national policy objectives is seen in the accumulation of foreign reserves since 2000, largely as a consequence of the primacy of national exchange rate policies over financial integration or market development. The shared commitments and policies implicit in financial regionalism are constrained by national objectives, most clearly seen in the formation of the Chiang Mai Initiative scheme explained in Section 12.5.

The forcefulness of national policy has long been recognized in the context of regional integration, as '[o]rganizations with an economic mandate short of creating a common market or free trade area have great difficulty in influencing the policies of their members' (Haas 1970: 616). Yet most states adopted similar post-crisis policies, which would appear to be conducive to cooperation. While a modest degree of integration might impact on existing arrangements for governance, it seems that greater connectivity and interdependence among both Asian states and sub-state participants does not signify greater financial integration. Regional institutions and organizations require shared objectives among their founders, as well as mutual interdependence (Keohane 2002).

12.3 Integration drivers

Public initiatives for financial cooperation, integration and collaborative governance have been driven by four factors over the last two decades. These relate especially to the 1997–98 financial crisis, but also to growing economic integration, developmental issues, and political influences. The means by which these factors have encouraged integration are relevant to the policy formation processes used by Asia's regional bodies.

Crisis imperatives

The 1997–98 financial crisis had an enduring impact on national economies and policy formation. The economic and social dislocation provoked in South Korea and Southeast Asia by the dissipation of market confidence produced a concern among states that Asia lacked national and regional crisis remedies, since only non-Asian organizations such as the IMF were able to provide credit infusions sufficient to stem the draining of external resources. The view was most clearly voiced within ASEAN and by Japan, where it induced officials to propose certain new regional structures, including a monetary fund (Grimes 2009: 76–82; Hayashi 2006: 82–102; Lipscy 2003), which Section 2.3 characterized as an important part of the 1997 shock. The crisis also induced a lasting risk aversion among policymakers fearful of future instability and external interference in domestic governance. While this disposition helped induce limited financial reforms in individual economies, it also prevented the introduction of significant regional solutions that might involve financial integration, shown earlier in Section 3.1.

Controversy arose in mid-crisis in the international reaction to capital controls. China, Malaysia and Taiwan introduced or continued using barriers to the free movement of capital, contrary to the customary advice of transnational organizations. Each suffered less material falls in output and asset values in 1997–98, while the crisis was most severe in its impact on Indonesia, South Korea and Thailand which maintained minimal controls on inflows. This is not to imply simple causation from capital mobility to external vulnerability, but these examples were sufficient to encourage many others to see the policies of the Washington Consensus as deleterious to recovery (Demirgüç-Kunt & Detragiache 1998: 12), and gave weight to national norms at the expense of a regional orientation.

It is clear that financial integration as indicated by capital mobility is cemented for Asian policymakers as a condition that contributed to the crisis and the contagion that made it so severe. Such integration was inevitably to be a low priority for ASEAN+3. A chastened IMF is now less hostile to capital controls. After consultations with South Korea in August 2010, an official stated that rules introduced by Seoul two months earlier to restrict currency activities by domestic intermediaries were not capital controls 'but more ... prudential measures designed to insulate the banking system from rapid outflows of capital, so they're not, in our view, capital controls to begin with' (Lall 2010). South Korea's restrictions are narrower but otherwise similar to those introduced by Malaysia in 1998 and condemned at the time by the IMF and Washington Consensus proponents.

The crisis exposed a helplessness among Asia's regional organizations. In 1997 no Asian organization was able to provide support to any state, however temporarily, leading to the irony that Indonesia, South Korea and Thailand became tied to invasive IMF credit conditions quite contrary to ASEAN precepts. The Asian crisis not only revealed weaknesses in national financial systems, but in imperfect and entrenched regional economic and financial linkages that made each economy vulnerable to contagion from major shocks. Its aftermath produced discrete national reforms intended to bolster recovery and improve crisis avoidance. These sought to improve the effectiveness of national financial systems and alter the extent of state involvement in finance, but changes were modest except in China, South Korea and Malaysia, especially in legal and regulatory systems.

Finally, the crisis induced the first meaningful attempt to relax ASEAN's doctrine of mutual non-interference when, in 1997–98, Thailand proposed a policy of flexible engagement involving deliberate interaction among members. The requirements and implications were never developed but it was clear that the call recognized that ASEAN members faced an assault through collapsing currencies and the withdrawal of foreign credit that might be better resisted through more advanced cooperation than that contemplated by ASEAN consensus. The proposal received no support and was abandoned as unworkable.

Implicit in this narrative is that ASEAN will not engage in financial rule-making. With ASEAN+3 superseding ASEAN in policy formation, there is only a small chance that flexible engagement will be revived, given China's preference for the existing approach and a certain instability in ASEAN external relations, notwithstanding the common objectives expressed in ASEAN's Vision 2020. Nonetheless, regional initiatives prompted by the 1997–98 crisis but not carried into tangible financial regionalism now have a fresh incentive from the global financial crisis that began in August 2007. CMIM provides for credit decisions to be made by majority rather than consensus, although the mechanics are not fully disclosed, as we show in Section 12.5.

Economic influences

In the absence of national restrictions, expanding trade and investment might be expected to increase and broaden use of financial instruments – for example, in trade finance, funding for direct investment including acquisition finance and demand for credit, treasury or cash management products. While many Asian public and private sector users have access to sophisticated instruments and applications through international markets, the extent of activity within the region or denominated in local currencies is materially lower than suggested by flows of trade and investment. This is the most apparent systemic result of relatively undeveloped financial integration.

Unmet demand for financial instruments and systems associated with economic integration highlights impediments to regional and national financial activity – for example, restrictions on non-residents holding money market instruments (Arner, Lejot & Rhee 2006). Even though new issue activity has risen markedly in China, South Korea, Malaysia and Thailand in the last five years, many problems remain at national level for which a consensus on regional reform could be valuable.

Development issues

The precautionary accumulation of well-rated non-Asian securities may not have been an overt objective of policy but was closely connected to national currency and economic management. No single factor explains the growth in aggregate reserves (Cheung & Ito 2008).

Traditional motives include commercial trade demand, capital inflows through foreign direct investment, precautionary behaviour and mercantilist policies. We view the last two factors as indirectly important to integration. The scale of reserve accumulation prompts concern as to risk concentration, how external imbalances may have contributed to the global financial crisis (Arner 2009), and whether resources might be better allocated to finance social spending or infrastructural development.

One development imperative thus focuses on strengthening financial markets and focuses on giving more choice to savers so as to support investment. Other examples include using reserves to endow SWFs, introduced in Section 11.3. Singapore's Temasek Holdings is one of few Asian official funds heavily engaged in national strategic or infrastructural commitments and it would be a departure for Asia's SWFs to devote resources to regional development.

Political factors

Politics has a pervasive influence on regionalism. This is a major area of study that is beyond our book's direct scope, but several competing views are notable:

- First, we acknowledge that historic rivalries or antipathies among states are significant for regional integration. China's growing influence may have begun to encourage Japan and smaller states to favour mutual cooperation for reasons of economic security. This includes balancing China's influence by engaging with Australia, India and New Zealand in the ASEAN+6 or East Asian Summit (EAS) process.
- Similar post-colonial thinking helps explain the wish to counter the political–economic weight of the EU or US and excessive reliance on their currencies in trade and fundraising. At the same time such efforts can be diluted by a proliferation of bilateral trade agreements within the region, although it is argued that this 'noodle bowl' network of treaties may serve as building blocks for universal free trade (Baldwin 2006).
- Pressure from the EU and US prevented ASEAN from responding collectively to representations on its admission of Myanmar, and in responding to Japan's regional initiatives after the Asian financial crisis, although the latter was complicated by more controversial periods in Japan's modern history.
- An alternative view is that Japan has a domestic economic orientation and 'limited incentives to invest in regional cooperation' (Hamilton-Hart 2007: 132), but this

neglects the interest of Japan's commercial and political interests in advancing all forms of regional financial integration.

- An argument also dwelling on domestic Japanese concerns is that Tokyo's powerful bureaucracy favoured regional integration throughout the 1990s as a means to avoid socio-economic and political changes resulting from the collapse of asset prices after 1989 (Hatch 2010). Production was outsourced to lower-cost economies to avoid a material change of direction, but this view cannot easily account for Japan's relative indifference to financial regionalism.
- Broader security cooperation has been seen as one of 'three pillars' that might support more intense Asian political integration (Curley & Thomas 2007), and it has been argued that ASEAN 'has generated significant benefits in the form of security confidence building activities even though the gains from economic collaboration have been minimal' (Ravenhill 2001: 27), such benefits being most apparent in political and security matters (Goh & Acharya 2007).

Transmission mechanisms

Convergence in economic policy formation requires incentives and workable transmission channels. One characterization suggests four mechanisms through which convergence is made effective, namely policy emulation, harmonization, transnational penetration and the existence of elite policy groups with shared concerns (Bennett 1991). By this measure, Asia's regional channels may be seen as comparatively weak.

12.4 Integration and development

Financial integration has been subject to fluctuating attention, but Asia's transnational organizations are important for two reasons. First, they represent established bodies, and their limitations illustrate a lack of commitment to regional governance. Second, they have supported financial reform with funding and technical assistance. Initiatives to encourage financial integration have focused on the trade in financial services, cooperation in external monetary operations and capital market development, which we examine in turn in this section.

There is no single view as to whether Asian financial development is more appropriately directed at domestic or regional issues. The early Washington Consensus traditionally saw domestic development as contributing greater benefits in utility and crisis prevention, and treated regional development as being of secondary importance. Asian policymakers may be more malleable, but the result of these differences has been that any substantive reforms take place in the forum of least resistance.

Thus, ASEAN+3 has addressed development issues to which the US was opposed while APEC dealt with proposals that the US could endorse, including domestic market development. In the second case, post-crisis proposals were developed by APEC and the ADB to establish a regional financial guarantor to provide credit enhancement for structured transactions. This languished due to opposition from non-Asian APEC participants or ADB shareholders until May 2009 when ASEAN+3 agreed to capitalize a US$500 million fund for the purpose. A regional guarantor would formerly have competed with US commercial monoline insurers, but their lobbying influence slumped as their creditworthiness collapsed in 2007–8. Non-Asian interests were also concerned at the cost of capitalizing a commercial vehicle to provide regional credit enhancement (Lejot, Arner & Pretorius 2006b: 284–5). Our view is that domestic and regional approaches to reform may be mutually reinforcing, as we saw during the Eurozone sovereign debt crisis of 2009–10.

Trade in financial services

Limited growth has occurred in the regional trade in financial services and any improvement will occur only slowly. This has three aspects: in cooperation in financial services liberalization, the structure of the ASEAN Free Trade Area (AFTA) and APEC's interest in an international framework for financial services liberalization.

ASEAN's Framework Agreement on Services (AFAS) aims at reducing barriers to trade in services (ASEAN 1995b: Art. IV), by requiring members to negotiate to lift restrictions in market segments and expand their commitments under the GATS. The commitments are not confined to allowing transnational access to ASEAN members. ASEAN agreements and AFTA obligations are little different to WTO financial sector commitments, and any additional access granted to foreign interests is limited in most cases. A 2006 assessment of AFAS commissioned by ASEAN and Australia's official Regional Economic Policy Support Facility concluded that its performance was disappointing and unimpressive (Vo & Bartlett 2006: 6). APEC's contribution to tangible integration has been negligible due to its lack of institutional authority and political fragmentation.

12.5 Monetary and financial cooperation

Monetary and financial cooperation have been the only aspects of financial policymaking where states have taken substantive decisions to introduce regional arrangements, even if small in scale or imprecise in terms of use. These are CMIM and a series of capital market reforms under several banners, explained in detail in Sections 12.5.1 and 12.5.2.

The Chiang Mai Initiatives

The Multilateralized Chiang Mai Initiative announced in 2009 is an emergency credit agreement formed by the finance ministries and central banks of ASEAN+3 and Hong Kong (Bank of Thailand et al. 2010). These are highly practical counterparties as they often have day-to-day control of foreign currency reserves and domestic monetary policy, as explained in Section 4.3. It also has tactical value in allowing disclosure of no more than the headlines of the agreement.

Although rooted in Asia's experience of receiving IMF credit in the regional financial crisis of 1997–98, CMIM is not institutionally developed in consisting of rules of the detail associated with IMF practice for credit, surveillance or the obligations of members. It represents an advance in technical and policy collaboration but of a kind not customary among OECD central banks since 1999. An agreement to create CMIM was executed on or around 28 December 2009 and took effect on 24 March 2010. The document has 24 articles and 9 schedules but probably resembles a commercial heads of agreement, leaving the details of credit commitments and any single transaction to be agreed and executed later. This creates an institutional gap that we will discuss in the context of unforeseen systemic shocks. The gap is both essential to CMIM's functioning and makes the scheme inevitably transitional (Lejot 2011).

Little of the literature of Asian integration or post-Asian crisis policy deals with the use or utility of the region's evolving collaborative central bank credit lines. Scholars have tended to examine the political economy of the arrangements, citing their value in building confidence among participants or external observers, either as symbols of progress in integration, or an indication that a more demanding regional scheme might become feasible (Bergsten & Park 2002; Chey 2009; Grenville 2007; Grimes 2006; Nesadurai 2008; Pempel 2006; Soesastro 2006). One result is that the arrangements created by the 2000 Chiang Mai Initiative (CMI) are commonly accepted as stated by its sponsors, even when the scheme is viewed sceptically (Hamilton-Hart 2003). Less consideration has been given to the uses to which CMI's lines might be put, or their effectiveness in encouraging systemic stability, either in terms of central bank or market practice, or the institutional demands of shared commitments between members.

While many international financial arrangements are founded in law through overt agreements or adopted custom, Asia's regional financial integration has been less institutional, and CMIM shares that characteristic informality. Its effectiveness may in due course be tested, but some informality is necessary for three main reasons:

- CMIM relies on a non-constituent currency in its operations.
- The provision of credit within CMIM cannot be transparent without either the mechanics for appraisal, drawings, taking collateral, and repayments being revealed in detail, or conducted through a new organization that is appropriately capitalized.
- CMIM permits a participant to avoid contributing to a drawing (ASEAN+3 2010: Annex § 9).

There may also be doubts as to the uses for which CMIM is suited when they exclude crises that are not purely external liquidity shocks but are as debilitating as in 1997–98. CMIM's design can be questioned as to its suitability for acute solvency concerns, domestic crises that are instigated externally, and whether it can assist only with shocks resembling 1997–98.

While CMIM lacks formal elements and obligations of the kind associated with the Bretton Woods organizations, its semi-formal, semi-disclosed character is sufficiently robust for it to be regarded as substantive, as an example of regionalism with embedded national autonomy. Regional policy has long operated by consensus without legalization, while traditional thinking is that CMIM must be open and institutionally robust to be effective in the global financial system, both to avoid conflicts with general practice and due to its involvement in bilateral surveillance usually associated with the IMF. An alternative appraisal is that CMIM can succeed only by differing from other collaborations and thus requires a less formal foundation.

ASEAN+3 officials chose a subdued news day on 28 December 2009 to reveal:

the signing of the Chiang Mai Initiative Multilateralization Agreement following the conclusion on all the main components of the CMIM at the ASEAN+3 Finance Ministers' Meeting (AFMM+3) in May 2009. The core objectives of the CMIM are (i) to address balance-of-payments and short-term liquidity difficulties in the region and (ii) to supplement the existing international financial arrangements. The CMIM … will provide financial support through currency swap transactions to the CMIM participants facing balance of payments and short-term liquidity difficulties. Each CMIM participant is entitled, in accordance with procedures and conditions set out in the Agreement, to swap its local currency with US Dollars.

(ASEAN+3 2009c)

Most 'procedures and conditions' are withheld. An agreement was signed in December 2009 allowing CMIM to take effect with a 'step by step approach' (ASEAN+3 2007), which it duly did on 24 March 2010. Changes were then made in 2010 to equalize the commitments of the five large ASEAN members, and two years later to increase the scheme's scale and flexibility of use (ASEAN+3 2012). The earlier statement of principle reveals more of CMIM's design than December's press release: first, that the arrangement would be governed by a single contract; and second, that decisions on 'fundamental' CMIM issues would be decided by consensus and 'lending issues' by majority voting (ASEAN+3 2009a). The May 2009 statement suggested three interpretations of CMIM's possible principles and mechanics, depending upon whether the agreement creates several or partly joint obligations:

- That no volition is given to participants when swap requests are made and agreed by a majority, unlike an earlier ASEAN scheme that allowed members to decline participation.
- That members may refuse to join transactions and the shortfall compensated by the willing members.
- That such requests are only partly met.

These are practical questions. Similar strains appeared in Asia in 1997–98 and Europe in 2010 when certain states refused to participate in providing collaborative credit to others, as we shall see later in this section. The status of CMIM commitments and obligations was partly clarified in May 2010 with publication of an outline of the CMIM agreement. A participant may 'escape' from contributing to a drawing with the consent of a two-thirds majority of members, or unilaterally in 'exceptional cases such as an extraordinary event or …domestic legal circumstances' (ASEAN+3 2010: Annex § 9). This implies that participants in good standing could expect disbursal of funds to follow their making a swap request, that status being determined by prior 'review of [the requesting party's] economic and financial situation' and there being 'no events of default' (ibid: § 8). Event of default means a breach of terms on drawings under CMIM and would be determined by a two-thirds majority of members at sub-ministerial level. There is no indication that such events would include non-payment on other financial obligations. Each member 'is requested to comply with covenants such as submission of the periodic surveillance report and participation in the ASEAN+3 Economic Review and Policy Dialogue' (ERPD) (ibid), a regular non-binding information exchange of ministers and officials. Members are likely to issue drawing requests only if they are found not to be contentious during prior informal discussion. Neither the conditions for drawing nor the demands of surveillance have been fully explained. ASEAN+3 stated earlier that:

The regional surveillance mechanism should be further strengthened into a robust and credible system which will facilitate prompt activation of the CMIM. An independent regional surveillance unit will be established to promote objective economic monitoring [and when this] becomes fully effective in its function, the portion [of the facility not subject to IMF conditions for drawing] may be increased above the current limit of 20 percent.

(ASEAN+3 2009a)

That portion was increased to 30–40 per cent after the surveillance condition was agreed to have been met (ASEAN+3 2012). Institutional and operational matters associated with CMI and its predecessors were reviewed for ASEAN+3 in 2004 (Ravalo 2005). IMF conditionality is neither fixed nor unambiguous but evolves with the creditworthiness of debtors (Polak 1991).

Our discussion assumes that the IMF links access to its traditional standby facilities in the same fashion as during the Asian crisis, in effect demanding deflationary changes in domestic policy as consideration for access to credit (Buira 2003). This was seen in the region as intrusive and ill-founded, and IMF practice since 2009 for its Flexible Credit Line (FCL) scheme has been less demanding at the point of use, an arrangement that CMIM may come to resemble. We should note that IMF standby arrangements are commercially similar to credit lines but in law they represent decisions of the Fund rather than contracts with members (Gold 1979), made simultaneously with statements of policy by the recipient resulting from negotiations with the Fund. Such was the bitterly remembered IMF practice of 1997–98.

ASEAN+3 agreed in 2009 'to establish an advisory panel of experts to work closely with the ADB and the ASEAN Secretariat to enhance the current surveillance mechanism in order to lay the surveillance groundwork for the CMIM' (ASEAN+3 2009b). The outcome was an ASEAN+3 Macroeconomic Research Office (AMRO) separate from the ERPD and established in 2011 in Singapore 'to monitor and analyze regional economies' (ASEAN+3 2010: Annex § 8). CMIM became an objective in 2007 when ASEAN+3 finance ministers agreed 'that a self-managed reserve pooling arrangement governed by a single contractual agreement is an appropriate form of CMI multilateralization, proceeding with a step-by-step approach'(ASEAN+3 2007). Two years later, the global crisis had encouraged ASEAN+3 to adopt a more ambitious arrangement but one that lacks legal personality, as shown in Table 12.1. Participants receive borrowing limits based on fixed multiples of their respective contributions.

CMIM borrowing limits are smaller than support facilities created in the global financial crisis, and exceeded by the amounts provided in Asia in 1997–98 and explained in Section 2.3. Proponents of collaboration argued that reserve pooling in 1997 might have induced a recovery in regional confidence – for example, that had ASEAN+3 'established a cooperative mechanism in which they could pool their reserves to fend off speculative attacks, they could have managed the Thai crisis and minimized its contagion by supplying a small fraction of their total reserves' (Bergsten & Park 2002: 16; see also Pempel 2006: 249).

ASEAN+3 aggregate reserves exceeded US$700 billion in mid-1997, far greater than the credit extended to Indonesia, South Korea and Thailand. Although this hinted at a future CMIM it ignored the strain that any such exercise would have placed on regional monetary stability if intended for real use rather than as a contingent facility to reduce market volatility. It also stretches political credibility, for when the Thai baht collapsed, over 31 per cent of the region's reserves were held by Japan, making pooling irrelevant.

Purpose and history

If we ignore Asia's experience of the 1997–98 crisis, then an arrangement to collaborate in the use of international reserves would have two attractions:

- Assuming that holding excessive reserves has opportunity costs in domestic output, then collaboration could allow participants each to maintain lesser amounts. This argument

Table 12.1 Multilateralized Chiang Mai Initiative (US$ bn)

	Initial commitment	*Borrowing multiple*	*Borrowing limit*	*Borrowing limit/ST external liabilities (%) as at end-2009*
Japan	76.80	0.5	38.40	7.3
China	68.40	0.5	34.20	8.6
South Korea	38.40	1.0	38.40	27.5
Indonesia	9.104	2.5	22.76	46.2
Malaysia	9.104	2.5	22.76	63.3
Philippines	9.104	2.5	22.76	157.7
Singapore	9.104	2.5	22.76	14.7
Thailand	9.104	2.5	22.76	130.5
Hong Kong	8.40	2.5	6.30	3.4
Vietnam	2.00	5.0	10.00	97.5
Cambodia	0.24	5.0	1.20	784.3
Myanmar	0.12	5.0	0.60	294.1
Brunei	0.06	5.0	0.30	16.9
Laos	0.06	5.0	0.30	857.1
Totals	**240.0**	**NA**	**243.5**	**NA**

Short-term external liabilities means all cross-border bank claims of up to 12 months maturity (BIS Quarterly Review, Statistical annex, Table 9A). The commitments of Indonesia, Malaysia, the Philippines, Singapore and Thailand were made equal in May 2010, before which the Philippines' commitment was smaller than that of the others due to concern that its foreign reserves could not support a larger commitment.

Source: BIS, ASEAN+3 (2012).

has not formed part of headline CMIM discussions, and cannot be addressed without raising sacrosanct questions of currency policy. Without reform of national currency policies, reserve accumulation could continue even with a pooling scheme, indeed the accumulation of excess reserves may be destabilizing, since it is related to persistent external imbalances.

- The second motive is addressed directly by CMIM, that pooling reserves to help a member undergoing external trauma creates resources that would not otherwise be available. However, CMIM's design would allow it to deal with certain but not all such circumstances. Its effective purpose is to create contingent commitments that encourage or forestall market activity, without disclosing how those contingencies arise. Seeking to affect sentiment merely by disclosure resembles the original purpose of IMF standby arrangements (Gold 1979).

CMIM has two roots, a US$100 million network of bilateral FX swap lines created in 1977 by ASEAN's five founders, and a web of bilateral repo lines initiated by EMEAP in 1995–97. ASEAN's lines were used by Indonesia, Malaysia, the Philippines and Thailand in 1979–81 and by the Philippines in 1992 (Henning 2002: 14). Usage required the drawer to be in good standing with the IMF or have been granted standby lines by the Fund, a restriction that prevented use of the lines in 1997–98, although their scale was too modest to have been useful.

EMEAP's lines were similarly unused. In common with commercial repo lines, these allow a user with available collateral to raise US dollars for intervention or LLR purposes by discounting with a fellow member a portion of international reserves typically held as US or other sovereign securities. We assume that EMEAP repo lines exist among most of the group's members in amounts less than or of the same order as the US$5.7 billion nominal aggregate to which the HKMA was party at the end of 2008 (HKMA 2008a: 171). Their total is not disclosed. The lines may continue alongside CMIM for practical and confidentiality reasons.

ASEAN's lines evolved into CMI in 2000, supplemented by new commitments from China, Japan and South Korea:

> In order to strengthen our self-help and support mechanisms in East Asia [ASEAN+3] agreed to strengthen the existing cooperative frameworks among our monetary authorities through the 'Chiang Mai Initiative'... [which] involves an expanded ASEAN Swap Arrangement [ASA] ... and a network of bilateral swap and repurchase agreement facilities among ASEAN countries, China, Japan and the Republic of Korea.
>
> (ASEAN+3 2000: s. 6)

CMI's bilateral lines could be drawn for an initial 90 days and renewed up to seven times, with interest accruing at Libor plus an initial credit spread of 1.5 per cent, rising eventually to 3 per cent; that 1–7 day repos could be transacted under the same lines using as collateral US treasuries of up to 5 years' remaining life or the provider's local currency sovereign issues, with premiums of 2 per cent and 5 per cent, respectively; and that the ASA portion allowed for swaps of up to 180 days, renewable once (Ravalo 2005: 21–3).

China, Japan and South Korea accordingly created lines between 2001 and 2003 permitting FX swaps among themselves and with most of the five large ASEAN economies. ASA later grew to US$2 billion. All but ASA consisted of non-ASEAN lines with 49 per cent extended by Japan. Their terms adopt traditional IMF conditions for drawings in excess of 20 per cent of each line amount. Most are bilateral asymmetric commitments to swap US dollars for the beneficiary's currency. Of 17 lines in place in September 2010, the bilateral lines made in 2008 between China, Japan and South Korea use the provider's currency rather than US dollars; China opened a unilateral yuan line to the Philippines; Japan's made yen commitments to the Philippines, Singapore and Thailand; and South Korea's commitments to ASEAN participants are provided in won in undisclosed circumstances (Bank of Japan 2010). No line exists between South Korea and Singapore. In July 2010 China and Singapore established a bilateral yuan/Singapore dollar line of US$22 billion equivalent, the region's second largest continuing line after one of US$30 billion equivalent created in January 2009 between China and Hong Kong and available in their respective currencies.

CMI has remained undrawn since its creation, a period that includes occasions when members experienced demonstrable external instability, but certain ASA states may have refused support (Grimes 2009). For clarity, CMI comprises ASA and an arrangement of bilateral lines; CMIM is a new arrangement of commitments that are legally separate and may lead to the cancellation of some CMI lines. Lines provided by China, Japan and South Korea have a different utility and may not be dismantled even if ASA lapses. In January 2010 Bank of Japan and Bank of Korea renewed a crisis-related increase in their bilateral yen/won swap line for three months, and published an updated description of CMI only three weeks after the conclusion of the CMIM agreement (Bank of Japan 2010). When CMIM was announced in May 2009, CMI had grown to the equivalent of US$92 billion, excluding temporary increases made in 2007–9 (MAS 2008–9: 90). Regional lines probably remained unused during the global crisis.

Mechanics

We saw in Section 2.3 how Asia's regional crisis began in 1996 with capital flight that included portfolio shifts by Japanese and European banks. This exposed the fragility of Asia's financial systems in relying on foreign currency borrowings while lacking matching LLR resources, and further stimulated speculative sales of local currencies. Much of the flight capital had funded local banks that used the proceeds to finance domestic assets without hedging the resulting currency or interest basis risks.

The effect was doubly disruptive: a flight of capital pressured Asian exchange rates and led to exchange losses for cross-border borrowers. It also terminally removed their access to funding, and pre-CMI swap lines were ineffectual and never used in 1997–98. One significant difference between 1997–98 and later crises is that in the first, no material interbank run took place. Precautionary reasons led to the withdrawal of foreign currency lending, rather than the funding for that lending, which we regard as the core problem in the post-Lehman Brothers dislocation.

The workings of central bank FX swaps are simple. If a provider agrees to a swap request, it will sell or repo (that is, sell and repurchase forward) securities assumed to be held to a domestic reserve account and make the proceeds available in exchange for the recipient's currency in the spot transaction through simultaneous crediting of accounts. If the request is for a currency other than the provider's own, then the transaction generally includes a spot sale or repo of foreign securities held as part of the provider's international reserves, a transfer of US dollars to the account of the recipient at the BIS and of the swapped currency to the provider's account with the recipient or the BIS. This model represents CMIM's mechanics, with two rotating member central banks replacing the BIS (ASEAN+3 2010: Annex § 6). The agreement allows a member to decline to contribute to drawings in certain circumstances. It is likely that claims created for swap providers will be several in nature, created simultaneously on identical terms in varying amounts, so that CMIM involves like actions rather than a formal pooling of resources. It is not disclosed whether a participant may decline the renewal of an outstanding swap or what the consequences might be for full or partial liquidation of the amount outstanding, nor whether any provision is made for payment sharing in the event that a drawing is not fully repaid.

For the provider, this constitutes a credit risk choice. Deploying reserves involves a portfolio switch from foreign securities to a claim against the swap counterparty. When the swap is unwound at maturity the provider may reinvest in those securities or take delivery of its repo collateral. Each step in the process involves potential balance sheet effects for the two counterparties, with the provider facing a mark-to-market gain or loss on the securities sold or repurchased, and an FX gain or loss that may or may not be compensated by the recipient as part of the swap. Although these effects could be significant when markets are volatile, they are likely to be smaller than the translation of day-to-day balance sheet changes between the provider state's domestic liabilities and its US dollar reserves.

CMIM is contractual rather than substantive, so that in contrast with IMF practice or EFSF, a member's claim while a drawing is outstanding is recorded against its user. EFSF is a Luxembourg company owned by the 16 Eurozone states and was created in June 2010 by a framework agreement (EFSF 2010) to be a conduit for emergency loans to any Eurozone member, prior to the more substantive and permanent European Stability Mechanism becoming effective in October 2012. EFSF may borrow in the capital markets with its obligations guaranteed severally by the member states. It is essentially a captive vehicle: the conditions attached to its loans would be negotiated by the European Commission and administration of its borrowing outsourced to Germany's debt management office. The framework agreement resembles a complex credit agreement in terms of detail but in common with CMIM its pre-conditions for use are separate, and subject to decisions of all member states coordinated through the EU Commission, and 'in liaison' with the ECB and IMF (EFSF 2010: § 2(1)).

One effect of this subjectivity was observed shortly after EFSF's creation, when Slovakia at first declined to sign the framework agreement, and having relented under political pressure then refused absolutely to participate in a separate €110 billion EU–IMF emergency loan for Greece. Its decision was condemned by the head of the ECB and described by an EU Commissioner for economics and monetary affairs as 'a breach of the commitment undertaken by Slovakia in the Eurogroup [and a] breach of solidarity within the Euro Area' (Rehn 2010).

CMIM's use of a commercial agreement allows secrecy and is common among central banks. The Federal Reserve and the Bank of Japan have occasionally revealed specific terms of their lines to demonstrate conditionality, but these are exceptions. Establishing CMIM by treaty would create a body of legal standing similar to the IMF and necessitate detailed disclosure for which ASEAN+3 is unready. While the comprehensiveness of ASEAN+3 December 2009 agreement is undisclosed, certain provisions well-known in central bank practice may have been specified – for example, forms of drawing request and basic credit terms. The creation of AMRO allowed the permissible term of swaps to be expanded from an initial 90 days (ASEAN+3 2010: Annex § 5), to between six and 12 months depending upon whether or not credit was granted with IMF conditionality, with provision for lengthy renewals. ASEAN used a similar approach when creating its US$100 million swap arrangements in 1977, with basic agreement as to mechanics, swap size, maturities and renewals, priorities in disbursements, and appointment of an operational agent chosen by rotation among the members (ASEAN 1977). It also provided for willing members to replace any that were unwilling or unable to accede to swap requests. That members might opt out of swaps was made explicit in ASA's fifth revision (ASEAN 1992b). CMIM is less specific.

Members will commit to provide financial resources up to the amounts shown in Table 12.1, but the nature of their respective commitments is withheld. In the spectrum of lines described in Section 4.2, CMIM is an example of either the third or fourth type: facilities that are agreed but non-committed, or agreed and committed but not subject to specific preconditions. It may evolve into an example of the fifth variation where terms for advances are broadly pre-agreed, but without significant institutional augmentation this would impede external confidence building.

Central bank practice

CMIM's contingent permanence differs from general central bank practice of creating emergency liquidity resources in response to external shocks, most notably after 11 September 2001, the 2007 collapse of the US subprime mortgage market, and Lehman Brothers' failure in 2008. We saw in Section 4.3 that leading central banks feel that emergency lines can be created instantly, in most cases under standing authority, so that permanence had no real value given that FX rates were market determined. CMIM has a simpler purpose of deterrence, given that the IMF is not an unconditional international LLR. Its utility may result from it being a contingent arrangement, suited to caution or guide behaviour rather than meet any specific tasks. The desire among emerging economies to establish or maintain lines seems clear, so that CMIM reflects a persistent preference rather than a revival of outdated facilities.

Surveillance and competition

The global crisis had two effects relevant to this discussion:

- It advanced plans for CMIM so that its announcement in May 2009 was more ambitious than predicted; and
- As if to counter autonomous regional action, it led the G20 states to propose a broadening of member influence in the IMF.

In April 2009 the G20 recommended a shift in IMF quotas and votes to emerging and developing states from over-represented industrialized members. CMIM states had 14.44 and 14.28 per cent of IMF quotas and votes, respectively, when the G20 met in November 2010, compared to over 30 per cent in each case for the EU and 17.09 per cent and 16.74 per cent, respectively for the US. The IMF has responded to strictures of its performance by suggesting cooperation with regional arrangements such as CMIM (IMF 2010b, 2010c), confirming a view that IMF supremacy among international financial organizations may not be permanent (Henning 2006: 171). Credible regional bodies might usurp the IMF, notwithstanding its experience of bilateral surveillance and hierarchical standing in international law, for the IMF is unable to conduct open surveillance with members that wish not to be examined or have the results disclosed.

We see the IMF's traditional crisis support function as partly replaced by 'self-insurance', and its role in 'rule setting, coordination and surveillance ... marginalised by fora of a more "network" kind' (Wade 2007b: 137). This refers to functional regulatory groupings such as the BCBS, but might also include CMIM. The suggestion that the IMF co-exist with regional bodies may require the latter to obey rules to create no conflicts, be similarly transparent, lend for liquidity reasons only, and impose sound conditions (Henning 2006: 177). In this view, schemes such as CMIM would be formally notified to the IMF, would refrain from undercutting IMF conditionality, and adopt policies consistent with IMF stabilization (ibid: 178). At its most severe, this sees a competing CMIM as eroding IMF sovereignty, for example, by freely providing credit or forgiving defaults, but neglects CMIM's need to act so as to build external confidence. Similar considerations became clear for the Eurozone in 2009–10. Both CMIM and EFSF have the potential to alter IMF surveillance practice by virtue of its being referenced in their procedures in a qualitative way rather than with a formula of the kind that blighted CMI.

Without mutual CMIM–IMF surveillance it is unclear how detailed cooperation can be agreed. All CMIM states are IMF members and undertake to inform and collaborate mutually and with the IMF in macroeconomic policy (IMF Art. IV § 1) with Laos the sole CMIM non-signatory to Article IV, but these obligations are confined to exchange rate decisions and operations (Art. IV § 3) or reserve policy (Art. VIII § 7) and may be incapable of non-consensual enforcement by the IMF vis-à-vis non-debtor members (IMF 2006, 2010b). Moreover, Asia's participation in IMF standard-setting for economic performance and financial regulation is mixed. Table 12.2 shows the dates when members concluded IMF Financial Sector Assessment Programs (FSAPs) and four categories of its Reports on the Observance of Standards & Codes. These are examples of data sharing, economic monitoring, and technical and regulatory assessment.

The reluctance of CMIM members to engage in such processes suggests that its own mechanisms are a practical concern. The ADB Office of Regional Economic Integration was instructed in May 2009 to develop surveillance mechanisms for CMIM and investigate its

Table 12.2 FSAP and selected ROSC categories

	FSAP	Data dissemination	Monetary and financial policy transparency	Fiscal transparency	Banking supervision
Brunei	–	–	–	–	–
Cambodia	–	–	–	–	–
China	2011	–	–	–	–
Hong Kong	2003	1999	1999/2003	1999	1999/2003
Indonesia	2010	2005	2010	2006/2010	–
Japan	2003	2006	2003	2001/2004	2003
South Korea	2003	2003	2003	2001	2003
Lao PR	–	–	–	–	–
Malaysia[1]	–	–	–	–	–
Myanmar	–	–	–	–	–
Philippines	2010	2004	–	2002/2004	2004
Singapore	2004	–	2004	–	2004
Thailand	2009	2006	–	2009	–
Vietnam	–	–	–	–	–

Sources: IMF, Financial Sector Assessment Program. Online. Available HTTP: http://www.imf.org/external/np/fsap/fsap.asp> (accessed 1 October 2012); Reports on the Observance of Standards & Codes. Online. Available HTTP: http://www.imf.org/external/np/rosc/rosc.asp>; Fiscal Transparency. Online. Available HTTP: <http://www.imf.org/external/np/fad/trans/index.htm > (accessed 1 October 2012).

[1.] Malaysia underwent an FSAP examination in 2012.

resource needs, but AMRO is a limited resource that requires external intelligence coopera-tion, a point acknowledged by the IMF in July 2010.

ASEAN's Manila Framework for economic surveillance was dissolved in 2004, having been said by its sponsor to be losing momentum. Many observers echo finance minister statements that CMIM needs a full-functioning and independent arrangement (Aizenman, Jinjarak & Park 2010: 19). Surveillance is a function to gather and interpret data and issue stress warnings. It will fail as a credible appraisal process that assists confidence-building and decision-making if it lacks the means to require policy change. This demands opera-tional independence and a regional outlook so as to consider systemic risks that may induce contagion. An outsourced surveillance function would need explicit arrangements as to how its findings would impact national policies, while a dedicated resource within CMIM could only establish its credentials over time. Credible surveillance will, in time, lessen depend-ence on credit rating agency input for drawings and collateral, which became controversial in 2009–10 in the Eurozone because of its relationship with ECB collateral rules. ASEAN+3 acknowledged these concerns in 2012, and began to consider how AMRO might be made more substantive as an international treaty organization (ASEAN+3 2012: 3).

As an arrangement among states it is unclear that CMIM will challenge its members' adherence to IMF rules. However, it may be a device that increases regional autonomy and leverage for changes in IMF practice. The G20 asked the IMF in 2008 to engage in systemic surveillance in cooperation with the new Financial Standards Board. Having opposed the creation of an Asian monetary fund in 1999, the IMF was initially non-committal on CMI, and no senior IMF official commented publicly on CMI or CMIM between July 2007 and May 2009. A fuller reaction emerged only in late 2009, with a deputy managing director describing:

various ways to reduce [states' needs] for self-insurance.... At the regional level, bilateral and multilateral swap arrangements can diversify risks and the extension of the Chiang Mai reserve pool is a welcome development.... The largest degree of risk diversification could be achieved at the global level.

(Kato 2009)

This accords with G20 decisions that the IMF join the FSB in multilateral systemic surveillance (G20 2009b).

IMF interest in reserve demand is not academic but a path to a new function. In November 2009 the IMF managing director described CMIM as providing 'an important complement to IMF financing' (Strauss-Kahn 2009), and his deputy later stated that the IMF was investigating how to link with the Chiang Mai Initiative as an important complement to the IMF itself. The result is a more specific suggestion that cooperation might see the IMF as a backup to CMIM to reduce the global demand for reserves, a notion directed also at the Eurozone. The implication is that CMIM would replace certain reserves, and the IMF act as LLR to CMIM, given the assumption that CMIM has no permanent access to US dollar resources. The suggestion assumes that CMIM will not become self-sufficient by adopting one or more currencies of issue of its larger members, without which CMIM and national holdings of reserves are not perfect substitutes but are each dependent upon the other. One study states that '[a]n important issue which arises in connection with the swap deals is the extent to which they can mitigate the precautionary or self-insurance motive underlying the unprecedented reserve accumulation in developing countries' (Aizenman, Jinjarak & Park 2010: 17). We believe that this is far from the ASEAN+3 agenda.

The CMIM's future

Time may show CMIM either remaining a nexus of contracts or becoming an organization with operational autonomy. The outcome is dictated by and affects the nature of claims created under CMIM, the approach and actionability of CMIM surveillance, and whether pooling comes to involve a formal transfer of reserves. CMIM's agreement is likely to be a non-actionable contract creating obligations for state bodies to act in certain ways but without sanction, penalty, remedy or mitigation if any should default. CMIM's relationship with other organizations may also be unstated – for example, would CMIM remain open for use if it allows swaps free of conditions and IMF facilities are later withheld from the user? This depends partly on a softening of IMF conditionality, and the standing of any member with regard to FCL. The nature of IMF conditionality has begun to alter from the traditional standby facility practice of one-off negotiation of terms for credit, to one of continual surveillance and engagement with regional organizations.

As well as allowing members to avoid participating in drawings, CMIM is conditional in that it assumes an availability of US dollars through the application of reserves. There is little chance of US dollars becoming unavailable in general or among CMIM participants, some of which maintain colossal reserves, but this is not wholly impossible due to sudden scarcity, systemic dysfunction or Herstatt failure, compounding the shock against which CMIM hopes to guard. It is not unknown for major government bond markets to experience hiatuses in price formation, impeding the sale or repo of securities held as reserves. CMIM is contingent in that its long-term utility may be in deterrence of disruption or contagion rather than to alleviate the realized effects of an exogenous shock. It is substantive because of amassed reserves, but those reserves exist as a result of common exchange rate policies.

CMIM's use of the US dollar as its foundation lessens its effectiveness as a crisis facility while justifying an institutional vagueness. This resembles a characterization of certain states as suffering from 'original sin' due to an inability to borrow overseas in their respective domestic currencies (Eichengreen, Haussmann & Panizza 2003). CMIM is, by analogy, a constrained LLR arrangement. While Asia's reserves make exhaustion of use or non-availability unlikely, no conditional endowment can eliminate this institutional lacuna. CMIM has a purpose in crisis management but its capacity *in extremis* is limited.

The scheme's purpose is unspecified beyond catering for difficulties in 'balance of payments' or 'short-term liquidity'. This must include enabling a participant to obtain US dollars for external payment purposes, but liquidity has been shown by the global crisis to have both domestic and external manifestations, including interbank access to foreign currency funding. It is unknown whether CMIM would allow participants to obtain US dollars and then act as a domestic LLR, as did the Bank of Korea in 2008. To do so would be consistent with recent practice, but inevitably involves issues of credit risk and control for CMIM as a whole. For example, is the user central bank required to demand collateral for its domestic facilities as with LLR practice, or provide for an assignment to CMIM of the value of that collateral in more extreme circumstances? Such questions are linked inevitably to CMIM's appraisal and surveillance functions.

Unused central bank lines are usually treated as contingent items, becoming assets when drawn. CMIM thus represents a new contingent commitment for members. If a drawing occurs, the adopted treatment will depend upon whether the arrangement is substantive. As a nexus of contracts CMIM is analogous to ASA, so that drawings are made severally and channelled through an agent. If CMIM were a substantive organization managing pooled reserves, then it would create claims in favour of members that transfer reserves, as would EFSF.

The same treatment would apply if a substantive CMIM had access to US dollars from members only when meeting a swap request. A substantive CMIM would need to be capitalized or given contingent capital by members in order for the claims it issues to central banks to have value. True pooling could also be conducted through an organization such as the ADB, which could readily issue claims (currently rated AAA/Aaa) to members. CMIM will become effective by a nexus of contracts that uses agents for certain functions, even with the imperative for independent surveillance and assuming an ongoing access to US dollars. If it is to be given organizational substance and resources for integral self-management then it can function only with a capital infusion, or by evolving to use one or more currencies of issue of its members.

In principle, CMIM could assist in currency management but not with misalignments. It will not of itself protect against a run on domestic parties or credit, as would any LLR. Thailand's 2011 US$11.4 billion borrowing limit under CMIM was nominally little more than the reserves spent in buying baht on one May 1997 day, as we saw in Section 2.3. CMIM is of insufficient scale to fund similar tactics, even after its 2012 increase, but may be of an order to support intervention to prevent disorderly markets, which was always an incentive for emerging states to gather reserves. The central purpose of CMIM is to exist and to help avoid contagion, not to be used, a conclusion made without considering the politics of regionalism or autonomy. Analysts suggest that members might make 'greater use' of CMI or CMIM and neglect its lack of utility in all but trivial circumstances (Aizenman, Jinjarak & Park 2010: 19), and that institutionalization is unlikely to include automaticity in drawings.

CMIM hopes to provide a remedy to shocks remembered from 1997–98. Unknown threats are less well considered. A recent study isolates five forms of crisis: in external and domestic sovereign default, banking and currency crisis, and explosive price inflation, plus 'clustering' when an identified crisis alters into a second type (Reinhart & Rogoff 2009: 249), to which we might add securities, commodity and asset price bubbles and rapid deflation. The global crisis saw an interbank run not previously thought possible. CMI lines provided by China, Japan and South Korea allow for securities repos, but this was given little attention compared to their swap function, and derided for its lack of utility. A Bank of Korea official wrote in 2005 that the EMEAP repo system had then 'never been implemented', but this may refer to actual usage (Jung 2005: 124). The official added that '[u]nder the repo agreements, countries have been able to provide financial support in US dollars, with US Treasury bonds as collateral, during a very short period. Therefore, the agreements have not been so useful as a crisis resolution measure'. Even though repo lines proved essential in 2008–9 in funding LLR facilities, it has been asserted that swap lines 'can help maintain market confidence even during normal non-crisis periods' (Aizenman, Jinjarak & Park 2010: 20).

A CMIM agreement of the same detail as the EFSF framework agreement would consider requirements for at least six variables:

- Decision making in swap negotiation and operations;
- Accession and withdrawal of members;
- CMIM's standing, and relationship with other organizations;
- Permitted uses;
- Compliance and remedies; and
- Relationships with bank claims and other commercial interests, notably payment priority and whether CMIM activity is a credit event for ISDA protocol purposes.

More probable is that the only aspects of CMIM's functioning that may become subject to greater openness are its credit appraisal and surveillance mechanisms, which external confidence will demand and which will be impossible to conceal if they eventually involve new resources.

CMIM must choose whether swaps are allowed in requested amounts without the minority participating, or in proportionately reduced amounts, or whether a dissenting minority is compelled to participate in providing credit? This itself has credit risk implications, especially if participants regarded as sophisticated are thought to be in a dissenting minority. An alternative, assuming a surveillance system is seen to be established, would be for CMIM as a whole to make periodic declarations of the good standing of its members, so that outsiders would presume each member had access to funds. If the May 2009 statement is taken literally as to lending being subject to majority voting, then general confidence will rest upon significant non-disclosure, or more informally the willingness of well-resourced members to provide undisclosed credit support to recalcitrant lenders to induce their participation. CMIM may become known not as a precise and formal set of institutions, but a framework for 'commonly agreed action' (Cooper 2006: 2), which is not unknown among central banks.

Capital market reform

Post-Asian crisis attention to regional capital market development initially focused on national debt and money markets, but more recently considered wider securities reform and capital market development. Collaborative debt market development has comprised four efforts:

- ASEAN+3 Asian Bond Market Initiative (ABMI).
- APEC's efforts in developing securitization.
- More limited work by members of the Asia Cooperation Dialogue (ACD).
- EMEAP's contributions of reserves to two Asian Bond Funds in 2004–5.

Thailand initiated the ACD in 2002 among ASEAN+3, India and 14 other central Asian states, to explore regional cooperation to encourage capital market activity. The group's visibility fell after the end of Thailand's APEC chairmanship in 2004.

As with other regional concerns, success has been limited due to the reluctance of states to cede national governance and create regional policy capital. One uncontroversial example is that little effort has been made to allow non-bank intermediaries such as insurers or pension fund managers to hold foreign regional instruments, although they typically enjoy far greater freedom to acquire well-rated OECD investments. The result is that the only such organizations able to invest across the region are the very few that have long-standing operating licenses in several jurisdictions, AIA being the most notable. Reforms are needed but neglected or partial.

ASEAN+3, APEC and ACD

APEC's regional bond market initiative began in 2003 by exploring ways to encourage activity. ASEAN+3 later commissioned similar research as part of the ABMI, using working groups funded by the ADB. They investigated using securitization to increase the supply of debt instruments, improving credit risk by providing credit enhancement, improving clearing, custody and settlement systems, developing new credit rating agencies and encouraging information flows, harmonizing regulations to best practices, and removing legal and regulatory impediments to cross-border investment.

One group in 2008 commissioned advice from 26 commercial and public sector organizations on the future of cross-border clearing and settlement, which its ADB advisor disarmingly described as the first case of effective public and private sector dialogue for ASEAN+3. ASEAN and APEC have shown consistent sympathy for schemes to provide credit support for companies or infrastructural projects, and in 2009 ASEAN+3 elected to create a US$500m fund to guarantee local currency debt issues by Asian companies.

The final ASEAN+3 working group ended in conflict between national and regional interests. Charged to explore cross-border local currency bond issuance, the group's convener allowed it only to examine issuance by multilateral agencies. After encouraging inaugural issues in China and Thailand by the ADB and the World Bank's private direct investment vehicle, International Finance Corporation (IFC), the group declared its purpose fulfilled and was dissolved, leaving many omissions from its original agenda. Impediments to new issue and trading activity remain common but national limits to issuance is the most significant (Arner, Lejot & Rhee 2006). Most of these schemes lacked commercial vision, and provided a functional specificity 'so trivial as to remain outside the stream of human expectations and actions vital for integration' (Haas 1961: 372). ASEAN+3 renewed its objectives for ABMI in May 2012 (ASEAN+3 2012).

State sponsored bond funds

The non-Japanese Asian members of EMEAP endorsed ideas developed by Hong Kong and Thai officials in 2003–4 to create two Asian Bond Funds (ABF1 and ABF2), endowed by modest pooling of foreign reserves. The plan had two aims: to confront criticism of reserves being held in non-Asian securities, and assist a post-1997–98 belief that active capital markets could provide a stabilizing resource. Most commercial administrators of ABF1 and ABF2 have ironically been non-Asian organizations, reflecting the narrowness of regional intermediaries and a lack of plausible alternatives, problems we identified in Sections 3.4 and 11.2–11.3. Both funds are passive and index-based, and their size at launch was equivalent to less than 0.15 per cent of participants' aggregate reserves.

The funds are limited but innovative in two respects. Neither directly contributes to market liquidity but both departed from reserve management practice by including sub-investment-grade EMEAP sovereign securities as investible risks. ABF1 was initially a US$1 billion pooling of major currency bonds issued by Asian borrowers and held by EMEAP's Asian members. Many central banks deal in liquid foreign currency debt securities, but the assets held by ABF1 are illiquid and represent the fund's feasible investment universe. ABF2 was established as a US$2 billion fund for local currency issues, with families of single currency exchange-traded funds and regional index funds each holding sovereign and quasi-sovereign securities. The structural concept of ABF2 is shown in figure 12.1. Public information on the scheme has always been sparse, but not all the single currency funds were eventually established and the total amount under management is thought not to be significantly more than the original official infusion. ABF2s involves two regional vehicles, an index fund to invest in local currency securities for its own account, and a fund of funds exposed to a series of single currency funds.

The motive for this divided structure is to find a means for offshore investors to gain exposure to the most closed local markets. We see that result as a limited reform. Rather than each national authority resolving to dismantle investment obstacles, they chose instead a form of banking innovation to circumvent those problems. The result was inevitably modest. The scheme's supporters argue that it led to the creation of Asia's first exchange-traded bond fund and encouraged two jurisdictions to allow domestic exchange-traded funds; its regional index fund was the first non-bank intermediary to be granted access to China's domestic interbank bond market (EMEAP 2005).

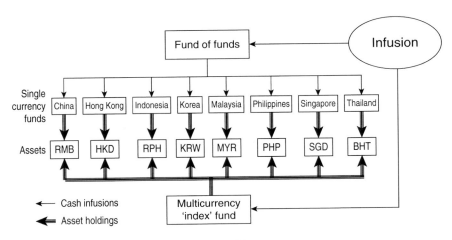

Figure 12.1 Construction of Asian Bond Fund 2.
Source: EMEAP <http://www.emeap.org/>

ABF2 theoretically circumvented obstacles that block foreign non-bank investors from buying local currency instruments, including problems of custody, enforcement, reliability of transfer and withholding taxes. Yet ABF2 is self-limiting. It denies securities custody to investors and relies on certain ETFs that are seldom bought by large investors, and index funds that are impossible to replicate or track. Its greatest impact was to raise awareness among officials of investment impediments, and to encourage the removal of some legal or regulatory constraints that made its objectives impossible to achieve more simply (Arner, Lejot & Rhee 2006). ABF2 is an interesting example of states devising a commercial solution to problems for which they are ultimately responsible.

Pre-establishment announcements in 2004 suggested this might be intentional, in that ABF2 would 'accelerate market and regulatory reform' (EMEAP 2004). Unsurprisingly, no such commitments were disclosed, even though they might have encouraged outside participation. The commercial test of ABF2 was whether it would generate liquidity or induce new participants to issue, invest or trade in local-currency securities, and this aspect of its performance has been poor. EMEAP members provided ABF2's launch infusion but no further resources, and the sums raised from commercial investors were limited in the five years after launch. EMEAP's 2006 review of the project characterized the funds as historic but describes ABF2 as merely useful, and lists the reasons for its limited commercial appeal (EMEAP 2006), a conclusion shared by a more recent BIS study (Chan, Chui, Packer & Remolona 2011).

Coordination among equity markets

National differences in corporate governance and share market practice are more path dependent than other forms of intermediation. Generations of brokers wrote rules rooted in history for their own markets, as we saw in Section 9.3, and stock markets in all common law jurisdictions except the US were relatively free of statutory intrusion until the 1980s. This means that we are less able to consider a global stock market than global banking or debt capital markets, even though we are accustomed to correlations in share prices: news reports almost every day will say that stock indexes in Tokyo or Sydney rose or fell in response to the previous day's trading in New York. It is no surprise therefore that integration in Asia's equity markets is limited, both in the number of transnational listings and the scale of cross-border portfolio investment. These factors exist in other regions but are compounded in Asia due to its retail and order-based orientation. Only recently has competition for new listings and from non-traditional equity trading platforms encouraged Hong Kong, Singapore and other established exchanges to seek listing prospects in new domiciles.

In the long term, regional integration may increase with the adoption of common standards by securities regulators, and with the encouragement of IOSCO, which guides their mutual cooperation, benchmarking and exchanges of information and provides a template for these matters (IOSCO 2002; Arner & Taylor 2009). The regulatory principles and standards devised by IOSCO include a prospectus template for cross-border share issues using IASB International Financial Reporting Standards (IFRS) (Arner 2002; Steinberg & Arner 2010), which became the model for the EU's 2003 Prospectus Directive.

Asian securities regulators formed a regional committee in 2007 to cooperate using IOSCO standards, and ASEAN's Capital Markets Forum (ACMF) adopted IOSCO's template in 2008 in a two-part scheme known as the ASEAN Standard and Plus Standard (ACMF 2008). This established a voluntary disclosure benchmark for conventional debt and equity new issues sold simultaneously in more than one jurisdiction. The first use of the plan was to facilitate easier transnational sales of securities through common disclosure standards, made in 2009 by exchanges and regulators in Malaysia, Singapore and Thailand. The arrangement would need to become more developed to allow multiple listings. ACMF's focus broadened and became more strategic with the publication of an ASEAN Capital Markets Integration Plan in 2009, which has six principles:

- Adopt international standards to the greatest possible extent possible;
- Progressive liberalization;
- Sequencing of reforms;
- Coordination;
- Consistent implementation with effective monitoring; and
- Communication and consultation to set priorities and build consensus.

ACMF seeks to create an enabling environment for regional integration, including a gradual liberalization of capital flows, improving market infrastructure and regional products and intermediaries, and strengthening implementation. The plan has a developmental focus at domestic and regional levels, with integration stemming from increasing mutual recognition of shared standards and an effective infrastructure and regulation. Whether this is as adequate a theoretical foundation after the global crisis is less certain, since transnational rule harmonization in banking regulation is widely thought to have failed to produce a robust and resilient system, or guide the conduct of national regulators during the recovery from crisis.

12.6 Global influences

We see three non-regional influences that may be relevant to Asian financial regionalism and its governance: the framework for international trade in financial services, international financial standards, and specific practices of European financial integration. None is a prototype for Asia, but all may have technical value in assisting ASEAN+3 discussions.

Financial standards reform

One response to financial crises in the 1990s was a series of standards and codes to deal with institutional weakness and contagion. The 1994–95 Mexican crisis caused industrial nations to seek mechanisms to protect against systemic instability induced by shocks of all kinds (Arner 1996). In 1996 G10 states concluded that robust systems are less susceptible to crisis and more resilient when they occur, citing three elements of robust financial systems:

- Creation of necessary underlying institutions and infrastructure;
- Promoting market discipline; and
- Creating regulatory and compliance arrangements to complement market discipline.

The IMF, World Bank and regional development banks were instructed by the G10 to provide technical assistance to strengthen national financial systems, and to cooperate in avoiding conflicting or disjunctive efforts. The system of international standards to encourage financial stability which emerged shortly after the 1997–98 crisis had four characteristics (Arner 2007; Weber & Arner 2008):

- International consensus as to elements necessary to sound financial and regulatory systems;
- International and national collaboration to formulate principles and practices including through the FSB, BCBS, IASB and IOSCO;
- National and regional implementation of standards into their respective legal and regulatory frameworks; and
- Promotion and monitoring of implementation by multilateral institutions.

The G20 subsequently chose to strengthen coordination and monitoring of implementation through the FSB and IMF. The burden of reform is nonetheless carried mainly by national governments. Both the WTO financial framework and evolving international financial standards are compatible with regional integration and may be mutually reinforcing.

EU integration

It is controversial to draw generic lessons from the EU approach as to prospects for regionalism elsewhere (Haas 1976: 173), and we have no reason to cross the boundary established at the start of the chapter. Europe's experience may help in discussing Asia's future if we isolate specific technical aspects of financial integration and avoid value judgements as to the merits or otherwise of the institutional setting that the EU adopted in the 1980s.

Europe's progression had three phases. Political leaders and officials first recognized the potential benefits of financial integration and the barriers to its taking place. An influential 1966 study addressed impediments to the functioning of Europe's national markets and their openness to foreign borrowers (Segré et al. 1966), identifying a home bias towards national governments and other domestic borrowers due to restrictions on permissible investment by banks and insurers. Few corporate securities were then listed outside their home markets. These conditions reflect how Asia's financial markets function over 40 years later, albeit with greater transactional sophistication. Financial integration among EU states is the result of ratcheting objectives adopted since the 1950s, leading to the creation of a single internal market in financial services and a common currency. Integration transformed markets among professional intermediaries but Europe's trade in retail financial services remains fragmented and not fully subject to cross-border competition. The EU's official view in 2005 was that:

> A long-anticipated surge in EU cross-border banking integration and consolidation has failed to materialize. This failure is striking in view of several apparently catalytic developments – notably the liberalization of capital movements and efforts to create an internal market in financial services.... However, cross-border integration have [sic.] not been major features of developments in EU retail banking in recent years and this latest disappointment suggests that obstacles – other than exchange rate risk – have yet to be addressed.
>
> (European Commission 2005)

A leading German banker agreed, that:

> a unified European financial market is still far from reality. One reason is that even where the [Financial Services Action Plan] has created a common legal basis, there are differences in actual implementation of the rules by the member states.... Another reason is that in some segments, Europe still lacks the necessary legal and institutional framework for truly integrated markets.... Even worse is the situation in retail markets.

[Furthermore] removing the remaining barriers to market integration will require what trade experts call 'deep integration', that is, addressing issues such as consumer protection regimes and mortgage collateral laws that have so far been the prerogative of individual member states.

(Ackermann 2007)

Academic analysis of the impediments to EU financial services harmonization concurs with these views (Gkoutzinis 2006: 51–63), and the same characterization applies to most Asian markets. They result from national socio-economic norms that reform and regulation find difficult to overturn, although the introduction of the euro may have induced similarities in national retail financial markets (Sørensen & Puigvert Gutiérrez 2006: 7–8).

Post-2009 re-regulation intended to reduce systemic risks and encourage deleveraging in Europe's banking sector may promote a home bias in risk-taking and capital allocation by banks and other intermediaries for the first time since the mid-1980s. That bias may extend beyond EU intermediaries. Precautionary ring-fencing of banks or insurers is a further post-crisis option, with national regulators requiring transnational intermediaries to capitalize separately their overseas located operations, a tactic that may be a relatively simple way to neutralize risks associated with the failure of highly complex banks (BCBS 2009: 16–19).

Regulatory ring-fencing was common in Asia before the global crisis and not obstructed by the GATS. It may have equivocal results for financial integration in raising global capital costs while discouraging the withdrawal of established foreign operations and the loss of legacy operating licenses. Ring-fencing can also be used for populist or protectionist reasons to discourage competition. It may even prove an unintended result if the Basel III bank capital requirements announced in September 2010 and outlined in Section 4.4 are adopted or enforced unevenly by certain states.

EU treaties provide for the free movement of goods, services, natural and legal persons, and capital. Investments may be made across borders without theoretical restriction, but these ideals had no real meaning until the mid-1980s when the second stage of financial integration began to focus on harmonization to common standards. Today's integration resulted partly from rulings of the European Court of Justice (ECJ). Markets are now considerably harmonized, and national legislation over most segments reflects common initiatives. States adhere to certain precepts so that decisions at EU level directly affect all within those states, while national governments may be penalized if they fail to legislate EU directives into law. No similar regional obligations exist elsewhere. EU experience shows more technically how collaboration and political integration may encourage the adoption of sound principles and practices, and the migration of commercial and regulatory practices from sophisticated to emerging states. The concept of mutual recognition and a system providing a single regulatory license for financial intermediaries now allow EU directives to set minimum norms without hindering competition.

The EU legislative framework for financial markets seeks equivalence among disparate regulatory and legal systems, so that regional initiatives recognize national legal and regulatory regimes (Steil 1996: 113). Full rule harmonization proved impossible for many activities and the European Commission adopted principles drawn from a 1985 white paper (European Commission 1985), that led to the Single European Act in 1987. This stipulated the framing of one seamless market based upon mutual recognition and common standards, specified by EU directives and brought into effect by domestic legislation. Member states would recognize each other's laws, regulations and agencies when they met accepted common standards, freeing the trade in goods and services without need for prior harmonization (Steil 1996).

The system uses minimum regional requirements to limit competitive deregulation by state actors and regulatory arbitrage by commercial parties. Regulatory arbitrage by the financial sector is now more common outside the EU or between the EU and other jurisdictions.

EU national financial regulation has intensified since the early 1990s with the needs of government and pressure from harmonization, access deregulation and prudential re-regulation inherent in the platform for unhindered capital mobility developed under the 1992 Maastricht Treaty. The framework for financial services provides minimum standards for intermediaries, securities and investor regulation, accounting and company law, with the premise that inter-mediation is unfettered by borders or restrictions and may function in an open internal market. Harmonization still leaves the framework incomplete, for it augments rather than replaces national laws. The result will be controversial in the post-crisis phase of re-regulation if it seeks to eliminate, reduce or simplify financial activities or certain forms of contracting, and may instead provide incentives for regulatory arbitrage. The EU's summer 2010 proposals to intensify regulation of hedge funds and other alternative investment managers may induce a migration of the more nimble operators to Switzerland or Asia.

Today's single market is manifested in passport directives, by which an authorized inter-mediary may generally be able to supply services overseas directly or through a foreign branch, without maintaining a permanent presence in its target market. Passport directives in financial services address banking, investment services, collective investment schemes, insurance and pension funds (Fraser & Mortimer-Lee 1993). The passport concept aims to promote competition and allow intermediaries to choose how they market products through-out the internal market. Passport directives define the intermediary to which they apply, its activities or operating segment, the conditions for functional authorization and the division of regulatory responsibility between home (domicile) and host (resident) states. Home states will be generally responsible for the supervision of intermediaries, their subsidiaries and branches and the fitness and propriety of their managers and major shareholders), and the hosts for transactional conduct within its jurisdiction. It also covers dealings with non-EU member states.

The creation of the single currency in 1999 had a further catalytic effect on market flows and transaction activity. EU members returned attention to regulatory convergence with MiFID, which stipulates rules for the conduct of financial activity. MiFID is a manifestation by treaty of common practice standards and is plainly conducive to financial integration. National implementation of MiFID since 2007 represents our third identified phase of EU development. Its recent post-crisis reforms include establishing four colleges of regulators to guide standards for national practice in banking, insurance and securities regulation and help identify and avoid systemic risks.

The interests of professional intermediaries may have been a force for financial integra-tion prior to the emergence of Europe's post-1980s political consensus. Until the 1990s introduced a common level of regulatory intensity, the Eurobond market was a permissive institution that developed as a lacuna, operating where no national market could function. It arose because of national legal and regulatory impediments to capital and investment flows. The market's scale came to rival national banking and securities markets, leading to nego-tiations in the early 1990s between industry representatives and regulators that resulted in offshore activity infiltrating national markets and subsuming many disparate local practices. Government bond markets are now less distinct or subject to archaic practices as a result, and heavily influenced by the efficient international practices described in Section 8.1.

The process became entrenched with the introduction of the euro. One contemporary source saw the early Eurobond market as a substitute for financial integration, given that capital mobility was only a secondary EU goal until the 1990s (Richebacher 1969). Others saw the Eurobond market as relying on an asymmetry between local and foreign targeted national capital controls (Genillard 1967), and a fine example of collaboration in a competitive setting. The Segré report was similarly prescient of the potential for financial integration, or how officially inspired integration might be confounded by commercial interests. If a capital market can be established anywhere, then what need is there for formal integration until monetary integration is also an objective?

Segré argued for the harmonization of non-retail financial markets in ways later encouraged by the success of the Eurobond market (Segré et al. 1966: 195, 202). There is little chance of Asia following this precedent until commercial interests are given a formal place in policymaking, regardless of whether the offshore European markets of the 1970s and 1980s were part of a trend towards financial integration or relied upon institutional barriers to be effective. ASEAN+3's initiative in securities clearing that we mentioned in Section 12.5 may be a small first step in this respect. A separate mid-2010 development explained in Box 8.5 may point to further long-term changes, with Beijing allowing an offshore market in yuan bonds to open in Hong Kong, albeit with restrictions on the use of proceeds in China. This resembles the Bank of England's cautious sanctioning of the early Euromarkets in the 1950s and 1960s, when a market in US dollar debt instruments opened in London to absorb the supply of offshore liquidity, notwithstanding prevailing capital controls (Schenk 1998). Then and now, the regulator's concern was that the new market would have only a marginal impact on domestic financial activity.

Integration's future

> From a 'bottom-up' perspective, the formation of a regional bloc is concerned with various dimensions of state-building. The rationale for regionalism is invariably that there are common goals which can best be pursued in concert with other states or actors.
>
> (Philips 2000: 386)

Even if a transnational model of regionalism has no application in Asia, the functionalism of this suggestion is a limited objective that ASEAN+3 members may be willing to accept in a period of global re-regulation and with changes occurring in prevailing IMF practices. CMIM fits this model because unlike ABF2 its effectiveness is not subject to commercial interests. This suggests that Asia can gain technical insight from EU experience:

> the principle of minimum harmonization together with mutual recognition principles underlines the potential for leaving integration to market forces once national legal and regulatory frameworks share common minimum standards.
>
> (Jordan & Majnoni 2002: 9–10)

The risks of this approach were made clear in 2007–9, for policies based on the adoption of common standards failed to anticipate a systemic breakdown. This is an important theme of Chapter 13. We are not suggesting abandoning financial integration through shared commitments to reform, harmonization to common standards, and mutual recognition through increasingly formal regional arrangements, but the preference of the EU for this style of progressive regionalism may not fit Asia's objectives, even if ASEAN or ASEAN+3 choose to become more substantive organizations rather than 'regional clubs' of states (Cable 1999: 61).

Economic and financial integration have lacked an institutional and legal framework designed within the region (Kahler 2000). Greater financial integration may require a new approach to take account of three aspects of policy:

- Recognition by states of their shared interest in protecting regional competitiveness. This might have political consequences, for example in considering whether mercantilism must be paramount in national economic policy. No Asian national economy has relinquished its export orientation since the model was adopted by Japan.
- Since regional organizations are constrained, financial development and integration depend on those involved in their instigation, whether they are state, commercial or other interests. The commercial sector has been included in financial integration only recently and has no clear function in governance. Financial integration may require 'multi-level governance' that involves many actors, rather than Asia's state-centric tradition (Payne 2000). Most financial development initiatives to date have been introduced by central banks or regulatory agencies without sustained input from potential users.
- It may be possible to liberalize the financial service sector through formal commitments and a revised AFAS. This would be a state initiative and would need to take account of regulatory responses to the 2007–9 crisis. The process would rely on progressive harmonization to regionally agreed prudential practice and market standards, as intended with the ACMF. Any such liberalization would begin with national reforms and continue through a process of mutual recognition. China may be influential in this respect if it encourages others to make liberalization commitments similar to those it negotiated as part of its accession to the WTO.

All these changes would augment convergence in financial activity and regulation. During the 1997–98 crisis, national authorities failed to find collaborative or regional solutions to isolated instability that quickly became contagious. Unless Asia devotes resources in governance to improve regional financial integration and support legal and regulatory reform, development will rely on a continuing export orientation to the detriment of general welfare and stability. Reserve accumulation and risk-averse national portfolio management may cease to be acceptable policy options in a less globalized world.

Crises and integration

Asia's global creditor position and the comparatively less severe impact that it suffered in the 2007–9 crisis led to an accrual of strategic influence, especially for China, Japan and South Korea, and altered the balance of regional authority between China and Japan. This contributed to practical reforms in 2009–10. First, the G20 committed itself to:

> a shift in [IMF] quota share to dynamic emerging markets and developing countries of at least 5% from over-represented countries to underrepresented countries using the current quota formula as the basis to work from.
>
> (G20 2009b: § 21)

The group also acknowledged that quota changes will alter IMF decision making and the composition of its executive board. Second, China questioned the US dollar's unrivalled reserve currency status, suggesting that reform might be included in a functional review of the IMF and the global financial architecture (Zhou 2009a). Finally, Asia's enhanced authority was applied in two regional contexts with the establishment of CMIM and an increase in the ADB's capital that had earlier been resisted by the US.

The global crisis was a seminal shock. Whether it proves conducive to financial integration given that enhanced leverage is not straightforward, but is affected by the following factors:

- Financial sector re-regulation may discourage transnational uses of risk capital and obstruct integration, at least until confidence is generally restored, even among well-integrated EU financial markets.
- Asia's prominence in a modified global financial system might lessen its incentive to introduce separate regional measures such as a semi-autonomous Asian monetary fund built upon CMIM.
- Pressure for financial integration may increase within ASEAN, a group without the leverage enjoyed within the G20 by China and Japan, and to a lesser extent to Indonesia and South Korea.

The themes in this chapter involve three tensions: between relatively free or restrained financial systems, between state autonomy and shared sovereignty, and between the financial preferences of the commercial sector and the state. We will seek some resolution of these issues in Chapter 13, which considers the future of finance in Asia.

13 The future of finance in Asia

Our final chapter turns from the present to a brief guess as to Asia's financial future. How might its possible outcomes compare in five or ten years with financial system architecture and operations in the rest of the world? Will finance in Asia continue to differ in style and structure both within the region and from other states, or undergo a convergence in its commercial behaviour, tolerance for risk, and the institutional basis of activity? How will future Asian finance compare with the Anglo-American model of financial capitalism that for a generation until 2007–8 dominated the growth of innovation and transaction volumes in global intermediation?

We began preparation for *Finance in Asia* in mid-2006, just as the US subprime mortgage loan market peaked in value, and 12 months before the coming crisis became manifest with BNP Paribas blocking withdrawals from three money market funds and stresses appearing in the interbank funding markets. Our starting precepts were that the nature and efficiency of finance are important for any host economy or region, and that finance in Asia has a character distinct from elsewhere. This also implies that its modern configuration is not merely a transitional phase in an evolution to an essentially universal model, indeed we are clear that there exists no such process or single model.

So severe was the impact of the global crisis on confidence and the public purse that business and product practices that had developed over a generation, insidiously and largely without controversy, became subject to attack, not only by traditional critics of financial capitalism among political economists or as exemplified in the 2011–12 *Occupy Wall Street* protests in a number of financial centres, but from establishment voices not typically associated with radical scholarship (De Larosière Group 2009; Prada 2007; Sheng 2009; Turner 2009a; *Wall Street Journal* 2009). Many attacks were visceral. They questioned the inherent stability of any leveraged financial system, the hubris of financiers, and whether modern finance had any positive value for development or the social good, in each case so fiercely as if to suggest financial repression as an alternative. Our original thesis as to the future of regional finance remains unchanged after six years, yet it became clear as the subprime-induced global crisis was succeeded by one involving stresses in Eurozone sovereign debt, that any future convergence will be far harder to articulate coherently.

The analytical premise of this book is that finance is demonstrably important for the pace and quality of development, even though the most effective finance carries unpredictable costs and systemic risks. For the purpose of future gazing we accept that effective finance is:

- Essential in some measure of sophistication in any modern society;
- Favourable for development at large, at least up to a certain point;

- Essential to avoid repression of disadvantaged societal groups; and
- Prone to instability that regulation cannot wholly remove.

These qualities make a conventional and frequently articulated case for the state to engage in appropriate regulation and informed supervision (Borio 2003; Crockett 2003), although a further consideration arises if we recognize that financialization of the economy generates negative externalities and commercial disputes. When dispute resolution and enforcement are not costless (compared to a Coasian solution free of transaction costs), demand dedicated resources, and may lead to unpredictable outcomes from litigation, then market failure may be more efficiently addressed through regulation than litigation (Shleifer 2012: 5–6).

Asia's economies chose to go further in this regard during their serial developmental phase for both political and cultural reasons, treating the state's function as not only regulatory or in providing formal institutions, but as an active participant in the financial system with its own preferences. After the experience of 1997–98, the region continued to hold closer control over the design and operation of finance than generally prevailing elsewhere, even in states where finance was prominent – for example, in the German model of the 1970s and 1980s which tended to withhold full commercial freedoms from the domestic operations of intermediaries.

Can Asia's approach now be taken as a doctrine of centrally influenced finance, as implicit in the developmental state model? Although we doubt that the region's features reveal a radically different economics, they do present a style of finance distinct from the archetypal Anglo-American or Rheinish systems. We are accordingly sceptical of the conclusion of a recent IMF study for example, that:

> [As] financial development has proceeded, Asian policymakers have come to appreciate the synergies and interrelationships between (i) creating capital and derivative markets, and (ii) modernizing bank and nonbank financial intermediaries.
>
> (Goswami & Sharma 2011: 3)

Reality is more complex, and for us this assessment has limited applicability.

Future outcomes also depend on a further question: whether the experience of global finance since 2007–8 marks a permanent change rather than a strong cyclical turn in activity, financial asset prices or regulatory conditions? Events since the start of the period appear to us not to constitute crises at all, but a discontinuity as significant as the crumbling of the Bretton Woods currency system in 1971–73. The dislocation was Anglo-American in origin and focus, and in the main it will be contemporary Anglo-American finance (conceptually rather than geographically) that undergoes the most profound changes, albeit with repercussions that are universal.

We anticipate a permanent change inasmuch as it involves the state reorienting its long-term funding, and through central banks becoming party to mass intermediation, that is, the state engaging as a central counterparty in the commercial funding of banks and acting as a holder of last resort for sovereign and certain financial sector claims. Post-Lehman mutual risk-aversion by banks, and the seizure of many money markets, will thus have consequences for the location of risk, regulatory intent, and post-recovery monetary policy. It can also be regarded as an involvement by the state in the functioning and direction of the financial sector similar to what has long prevailed in most of East Asia. As the Hong Kong government chose to acquire local shares in 1998, so OECD central banks did with government bonds in 2010–12. The shift is likely to include more aggressive and judgmental regulation, and encourage national competition in the application of regulation, representing a retreat from the universal acceptance of broad rules within most OECD states.

We have shown that weak institutions force intermediation in Asia to operate under many distortions. Banks are often poorly supervised and insulated from transnational competition, while ill-enforced requirements for corporate disclosure, lack of transparency among inter-mediaries, and unreliable bankruptcy laws and reconstruction procedures remain widespread throughout the region. Asia's financial system is insufficiently responsive to the consumer's increasingly sophisticated needs, and its banks fail to meet the logistical and funding require-ments of SMEs and other companies with which they are not linked through ties of owner-ship or kinship.

These weaknesses will grow in importance, for the five factors cited in Chapter 1 as accounting for the region's first phases of accelerated growth are no longer universally given. Savings rates will decline as the mean population age increases and with changes in the composition of overall activity; export-oriented policies will become less dependable due to uncontrollable external uncertainties. Other factors will turn less favourable or freely avail-able, including abundant and inexpensive labour, and easily achieved gains in productivity, increasing the possibility of less discipline in fiscal, monetary and exchange rate policies. Post-2000 reforms in supervision, governance and compliance have been real but selective, so that institutional flaws will continue to challenge Asia's real and financial economies, and make it less able to respond to demographical changes.

Economic policy is as subject to fashion as music or consumer culture. Western scholars once looked admiringly to 1960s Japan, and Anglo-American planners to 1970s Germany, only to favour the leveraged model of Anglo-American financial globalization. Certain of its features are now questioned if not discredited by the crisis, among them high leverage, the composition of capital, contractual complexity, semi-autonomous market practices, and regulatory design and supervisory quality. Financial development is shaped by both formal and informal conditions, implying that no single model can be successfully adopted without great care and significant national variation. Nor do we follow Charles Kindleberger's sug-gestion that a state imbued with financial complexity is likely to be in relative decline (Kindleberger 1984: 212–14).

Two factors suggest that Asian finance will continue to function in a more controlled manner than elsewhere. First, the region's governments strongly value stability, with the corollary reinforced since 2007–8 that financial activity cannot be allowed to determine its own path, a calculation quite separate from the universal acceptance of appropriate regula-tion. The second concern is less consistent. Growth is widely believed to require capital investment and a degree of state coercion in the direction and provision of credit, even in the more market-oriented economies in our sample. The result is to make a degree of financial repression desirable for policy reasons, leading to less choice in saving and an inadvertent second-order effect of promoting shadow banking and investment practices, which are espe-cially prolific in China, Indonesia, South Korea and Taiwan.

Such financial backwardness constitutes long-term folly. Underdeveloped financial systems make Asia unreasonably dependent on overseas financial markets and the accumu-lation of OECD assets, and so in recent years exposed it to risks associated with the sover-eign debt crisis and distortions to securities and commodity prices fed by quantitative easing. The paradox of capital flowing from poorer to richer states thus intensified largely as a result of the precautionary choices made in Asia after the regional crisis (Prasad, Rajan & Subramanian 2007). Flows to OCED states once signified risk aversion by Asia's interna-tional reserve or portfolio managers, yet the global crisis shows no asset is risk free. Both the paradox of capital and the Asian 'savings glut' (Bernanke 2005) may ultimately be explained by institutional distortions and an inadequate regional financial system rather than with standard economic theory, and are self-reinforcing in their impact on finance in Asia. The transactions and intermediaries described in Chapters 8–11 could all be improved or adapted for regional needs, whether local or transnational. Instead, the region relies too much on its banks, gives fewer choices to savers, and will not risk relinquishing state control. We therefore conclude that:

- Finance in Asia will remain distinct in its own way. Complexity in the real economy is less a determinant of the nature of finance than concern for overall stability, and so controlled financial development will still be evident in 2020.
- The impact of the global crisis will last well into the twenty-first century. This implies that Asia's model of finance will be adopted more widely and among certain OECD economies, and that financial sector liberalism is abandoned for at least a generation. Governments and central banks will become contentedly accustomed to acting as central counterparties for the banks they regulate and support in times of stress, and will be reluctant to withdraw from this position even if interbank funding markets regain their functional utility.
- Finance and financial instruments will continue to be used for non-traditional and non-social purposes such as high-frequency securities trading or gambling, but become steadily less freely available to retail users.
- The paradox of capital will persist until Asia finds a far stronger degree of countervailing financial independence, meaning that investors and reserve managers would then be more indifferent between local, regional and non-Asian risks of similar credit qualities. We expect no reduction in home bias among domestic equity investors for many years.
- Asia's commercial investors and SWFs will continue to trust FDI more than intermediated finance, partly because of inefficiencies in their domestic financial markets, and partly because they tend not to disfavour minority ownership positions.
- A degree of regional financial cooperation will continue, but will be constrained by national strategic rivalry and regulatory competition. Any form of Asian monetary union is now unlikely given the experience of the Eurozone and because of political differences in Northeast Asia.

Attempts to characterize future financial intermediation in Asia in a simple way will add little overall insight. We are sufficiently conventional to hold a consensus view of the benefits of financial development, yet we see Asian finance maintaining persistent differences from other regions. The outcome of the global financial crisis increases that conviction.

More generally, we expect new forms of systemic risks to result from unforeseen second-order effects of the current phase of re-regulation, for example in competition among organized exchanges, risks associated with network interconnectivity (rather than identified within intermediaries), concentration risks in CCPs, and legal risks associated with complex rules. Some regulatory changes will cause transactional activity to migrate to smaller, less transparent intermediaries such as closely controlled quasi-banks or fund managers. Financial sophistication is arguably a natural and valuable accompaniment to advanced forms of capitalism. Both finance and financial regulation must simultaneously be given incentives to strive to do no harm.

Notes

1 Asia's development model

1 Anoop Singh, Director, Asia and Pacific Department, International Monetary Fund (Singh 2010: 4).
2 Good records were kept of settler mortality among members of the clergy, judiciary and military.
3 Hong Kong was a sole exception as a consistently free port. In an era of strict controls it was also a convenient and discrete hub for international capital flows for both Britain and China (Schenk 1994).
4 Percentage quarterly changes in Singapore GDP at 2005 prices between 1Q-2008 and 1Q-2010 were +7.4, +2.7, 0.0,–2.5,–8.9,–1.7, +1.8, +3.8, +15.5. The greatest volatility occurred in the construction and manufacturing sectors (Singapore Ministry of Trade & Industry 2011).
5 World Bank per capita gross national income (GNI) data classify Macau, Japan, Singapore, Hong Kong and South Korea as high income economies (2009 GNI threshold US$12,196). No other member of our core group had a per capita income of more than twice the US$8,751 global average. Malaysia (GNI US$7,230) is ranked as upper middle income; Thailand, China, Indonesia, Philippines, India and Vietnam as low middle income; Laos and Cambodia as low income. Brunei and Taiwan are excluded. Macau is by far the highest-ranked East Asian economy, in a similar manner as very small outliers such as Monaco, Liechtenstein and the Cayman Islands (World Bank 2012)
6 Adapted from Lewis (2004).

2 Finance in Asia

1 We distinguish between transactional leverage in debt, which means the ratio of borrowing to supporting collateral or cashflow, and leverage in credit risk, which refers to complexity in asset-backed transactions, see Section 8.3.

3 Challenges to development and finance

1 Section 8.3 explains the 'shadow banking' network of lightly regulated intermediaries and complex transaction vehicles that flourished in the Anglo-American financial systems until 2008.
2 Bills are ubiquitous in Asia but commercial paper issuance is material only in China.
3 We exclude state-supported medium-term loans to importers of capital goods such as ships. Asia is both a provider and user of these 'buyer credits', as explained in Chapter 6.
4 Bank of China had a lengthy pre-revolutionary history but was effectively shuttered in 1950.

4 Financial systems and practice

1 National central banks in common currency zones may share their functions with a supranational central bank established by treaty, for example in the Eurozone and two African currency zones.

6 Credit risk and commercial banking

1 Federal law prohibits banks in the US from issuing financial guarantees and they rely instead on a synonymous instrument called a 'standby L/C'.
2 Most international syndicated loans and many others are governed by English or New York law which are both familiar with exculpatory provisions.

7 Investment banking and financial innovation

1 Schumpeter was unclear as to whether destruction is healthy at both firm and societal levels.
2 Data in this section are taken from Thomson Reuters (2011).
3 This simplification ignores price effects arising because conventional shareholders may attach value to the ownership attributes of shares.
4 Most credit ratings are produced by commercial organizations but 'agency' conveys an unwarranted disinterested and regulatory connotation.
5 The deutschemark was subsumed into the euro in 1999 and abolished in 2001.

8 Debt, derivatives and complex transactions

1 Iceland did not restructure or default on external debt but its entire banking system collapsed in October 2008 and was taken into public ownership, with the state dependent on IMF aid. Iceland issued US$1bn 5-year fixed rate bonds in June 2011 on fully commercial terms, 85 per cent of the issue reportedly being acquired by US fund managers.
2 It is customary to judge securities as cheap or expensive from the view of the holder, not the issuer.
3 A global note means a single certificate created to represent a complete securities issue, which may or not be global, that is, one sold simultaneously in many markets.
4 For example, if the IBRD were to issue in fixed-rate rupiah, regardless of how it planned to use the proceeds, it would simultaneously enter two simple currency and interest rate swaps, first to exchange its liabilities for rupiah principal and coupon payments for US dollar liabilities including a fixed rate of interest, and second to swap that fixed-rate liability for one based on a floating-rate US dollar Libor. The mechanics of swapped new issues are shown in Section 8.2.
5 Fitch is a US company owned since 1997 by French group Fimalac. Its sovereign and bank credit rating businesses were founded in the UK, acquired by Fimalac and merged with Fitch.
6 Future prices being lower than the spot price is known as *backwardation*. It indicates stress in the underlying asset market – for example, due to restricted supply of a commodity or financial asset, expectations of conditions that might depress future demand, or the result of unusual speculative or hedging tactics.
7 FX swaps are sale and repurchase transactions providing short-term funding in the currency purchased at spot (see Section 6.1), and are distinct from currency swaps.
8 Lehman was not a bank but a broker–dealer for regulatory purposes and US law provides separately for the reorganization of distressed banks.

9 Equities, exchanges and corporate governance

1 The model is faulty but unquestionably influential in supporting foreign diversification, a trend easily observable in the 1980s debt capital markets, where one of us was a young participant. US and European fixed-income fund managers, accustomed to holding a conservative mix of their respective domestic bonds and US Treasuries, used the international CAPM to justify migrating into British, French, German, Japanese, Canadian and Australian securities, a process that was conspicuous because it occurred far more quickly than the earlier diversification by equity investors.
2 Foreign portfolio diversification is subject to shocks and changes in sovereign risk, one example being Malaysia's 1998 imposition of controls on foreign disinvestment (see Sections 2.3 and 2.4).
3 Section 9.3 is taken largely from Lejot (2013).
4 Private refers here to user access rather than whether an exchange is operated by a listed company.
5 Together with the London International Financial Futures and Options Exchange (NYSE LIFFE).

6 Dodd–Frank arguably prescribes substitute compliance among several US agencies, for example in relation to derivative regulation.

7 ETFs can give synthetic exposure to companies in which a fund manager prefers not to hold shares, solving the tracking problem but not the governance issue.

8 The enquiry concluded that those shareholders 'must themselves share some of the responsibility for the problems at RBS' (FSA 2011: 167), which indicates an agency conflict without suggesting a remedy. Some scholars propose reducing the scope of limited liability to extend culpability to shareholders when a company is found to have done actual harm, citing general welfare or efficiency grounds (Hansmann & Kraakman 1991) or for ethical reasons (Crowe 2012). Commercial misjudgement does not of itself lead to sanctions in jurisdictions with adequate rule of law.

9 Pyramid ownership is usually stable. Pyramid investment schemes designed for embezzlement are inherently unstable.

10 Acquisitions, corporate finance & control

1 Cash-rich companies may legitimately return capital to shareholders through share buybacks if they believe that their WACC exceeds probable investment returns. The tactic can be controversial, as in 2007–10 when nominal interest rates were low and credit readily available to well-rated borrowers, who could borrow to finance a buyback and artificially improve their ROE.

2 Box 10.2 discusses the meaning of announced, completed, pending and cancelled deals.

3 But infrequently with employee representatives.

4 Dutch public companies are constituted with twin managing and supervisory boards, with the latter given fiduciary responsibility for shareholder and employee interests.

11 Non-bank and non-traditional intermediation

1 Physical dealing in soft commodities, raw materials and metals was confined until the late 1990s to specialist traders that bridged producers and end users. Low interest rates and rising demand for primary resources in East Asia then began to encourage hedge funds, investment banks, and ETF and other asset managers to buy and sell these asset classes, a trend reasserted after 2008 by concerns over financial sector instability and accommodative US and EU monetary policies.

2 One of us once worked in fixed-income sales. Visiting a substantial traditional UK asset manager immediately after the 1987 stock market crash, he was told by an angry chief investment officer that its performance for the year would be far better than planned and ahead of all competitors. At the time of the crash short-term considerations caused it to be underweight in shares but overweight in fixed-rate bonds whose value jumped when share prices collapsed. This positive alpha outcome was a deviation from declared strategy that would be seen as a tracking error and impossible to defend to investors.

3 Early life insurance was widely thought of as disreputable because a policy could be taken out against the death of an uninterested third party, such as a politician or celebrity. The preamble to the first English insurance statute refers to the need to legislate against 'a mischievous kind of gaming' (Life Insurance Act 1774), and so the act required the insured party to hold an *insurable interest* in the subject of the contract for it to be valid, a practice followed by many other jurisdictions. Section 8.3 examines a similar modern controversy over credit derivatives.

4 Severe losses among several specialist reinsurers of monoline insurance in 2007–9 (see Section 7.4), arose from risk concentrations arguably incompatible with traditional reinsurance capital standards.

5 Losses among Madoff investors are unknown but far less than a US$64 billion client account balance claimed as largely fictitious in the US Attorney's March 2009 complaint. An earlier article highlighted Madoff's secrecy ('Don't Ask, Don't Tell', *Barron's*, 7 May 2001), suggesting that its fund of hedge funds then had AUM of up to US$7.0 billion, making it 'among the world's three largest hedge funds'.

6 Temasek then began a borrowing programme for promotional reasons and to increase AUM leverage.

7 Claims of Thames Water securitized bondholders are distinct from those of investors in Macquarie funds or in the Thames parent, Kemble Water.

Glossary

A share 1. Class of listed share in China freely available only to domestic parties, *c.f.* B share, H share. 2. More generally, A shares were issued in many jurisdictions by those closely held companies maintaining several classes of equity with differing voting rights. This is increasingly regarded as poor governance and becoming archaic.

ABCP Asset-backed commercial paper. Promissory notes issued by SIVs and financial intermediaries to fund securities portfolios with noteholders sharing collateral rights over those securities.

ABF Asian Bond Funds. Two regional state-sponsored initiatives set up in 2003–4 to encourage investment in local currency debt securities.

ABMI Asian Bond Market Initiative. Post 1997–98 financial crisis umbrella for policy development associated with ASEAN+3 and the ADB intended to promote debt capital markets through infrastructural measures.

ABS Asset-backed security.

Acceleration Right of creditors to demand immediate payment following a defined event of default on a loan or bond.

Accounts receivable financing Secured short-term working capital facility, generally provided to companies with cashflow problems. A bank or specialist finance company makes loans against the discounted value of expected trade receipts.

Accrued interest Interest earned on a debt claim but not due for payment.

ADB Asian Development Bank.

ADR American depositary receipt. A security traded on a US exchange giving indirect rights associated with a foreign share issue, and the underlying shares held by a custodian.

Agent bank Bank or trustee that administers syndicated loans for their remaining life after signing.

Algorithmic trading Electronically driven large-scale trading seeking very short-term arbitrage opportunities, often involving negligible price anomalies.

All-in cost Annualized total cost of a borrowing expressed as a percentage of the nominal transaction amount, including fees and expenses.

Alpha The return on an investment in excess of the expected return associated with the risk of that investment. The aim of the active fund manager is often said to be that of maximizing alpha in its portfolio.

Alt-A US mortgage loans that are stronger credit risks than subprime loans but do not qualify for loan refinancing by the GSEs Fannie Mae or Freddie Mac.

American-style option Option contract that may be exercised at any time by the holder.

Amortization Repaying a loan or other debt claim in pre-determined instalments.

Annualize   Convert a periodic rate of interest to an annual rate to allow like-for-like comparisons of costs or yields.

Arbitrage   Transactions or trading strategies that exploit evident price inconsistencies, especially between separate markets or interfaces.

Arranger   Bank that instigates and executes a transaction.

ASA   ASEAN Swap Arrangement, a precursor to the Chiang Mai Initiative.

ASEAN, ASEAN+3   Association of Southeast Asian Nations. The most developed of several Asian economic policy groups. Its ten members form the ASEAN+3 grouping with China, Japan and South Korea.

Asset   In a financial context, a claim that appears on its owner's balance sheet such as a loan or contractual credit commitment.

Asset swap   Fixed-rate security held by an investor in conjunction with an interest rate or basis swap so that the coupon paid by the issuer is effectively transformed from fixed to floating rate, or to a different frequency of payment.

At the money   Option whose exercise price is identical to the prevailing market value of the underlier.

ATM   Automatic teller machine.

ATS   Alternative trading system. A non-traditional platform for share dealing, including dark pools.

Aval   Bank endorsement of a bill of exchange to provide a payment guarantee.

Average life   Period for which the average principal amount of a medium-term loan is outstanding, allowing for amortization, *c.f.* duration.

Axe   A trader with a long or short position or actual commercial interest in a market is said to have an axe.

B share   Class of listed share in China freely available only to recognized foreign controlled investors, *c.f.* A share, H share.

Backwardation   Condition in a futures or forward market where the prevailing spot price exceeds forward prices. Considered unusual compared to the more normal contango where the forward price reflects the expected cost of carry.

Basel I   The first Basel Capital Accord of 1988, a transnational agreement among national banking regulators implemented in 1992. Augmented in 1999 by the Market Risk Amendment, a protocol covering trading risks.

Basel II   The second Basel Capital Accord negotiated between 1999 and 2006 and implemented in 2007 in selected OECD states and Hong Kong.

Basel III   Revisions to the Basel Capital Accord published in December 2010 relating to bank liquidity, enhanced capital, capital composition and systemic risk, see capital buffer.

Basis swap   Interest rate swap involving two floating rate obligations or 'legs'.

BCBS   Basel Committee on Banking Supervision. Group comprising 27 mainly OECD central banks and financial regulators, and including those of China, Hong Kong, India, Indonesia, South Korea, Japan and Singapore.

Bear   Market participant whose outlook is negative, *c.f.* bull.

Bearer security   A claim, ownership of which passes by simple transfer as with a negotiable instrument. Increasingly archaic due to the risk of loss and usefulness in crime.

Bellwether   Large capitalization company whose shares are historically seen as emblematic of a stock market or market sector, for example, Cheung Kong or HSBC Holdings in Hong Kong, Sony or Toyota Motor in Japan, and City Developments, DBS Group or Singapore Telecommunications in Singapore.

Beta   Measurement of the risk of a single security relative to its entire market class.

Bibor   Bangkok interbank offered rate. Short-term baht interest rate benchmarks, *c.f.* Euribor, Libor.

Bid   Price a trader is willing to pay to buy a security or claim, *c.f.* offer.

Bill, or T-bill   Liquid sizeable short-term government promissory note with tenors of up to one year, *c.f.* note, bond.

Bill of exchange   Written demand for payment served on the buyer by a seller of goods or services, when signed by the buyer becoming a transferable financial instrument that may be presented for payment at the buyer's bank or negotiated for credit.

Black Scholes   Popular option pricing model using price volatility as the main input variable.

Block trading   Bought deal involving a large number of existing shares, *c.f.* vendor placing.

Bond   Long-term tradable debt claim, usually a form of negotiable security. In the US government securities markets, bonds have tenors of more than ten years.

Bought deal   Transaction in which a bank agrees to acquire an entire new issue of securities from an issuer at a fixed price or fixed spread to a benchmark intending to resell the holding at a profit.

bp   Basis point. A fraction equal to 0.01 per cent, commonly used to signify fees, commissions or spreads. 60 bp is thus 0.6 per cent.

Broad index   Market index with a wide composition, for example, the KOSPI is based on all Korean-listed shares.

Broker dealer   US term for a professional dealer in securities.

BSE   Bombay Stock Exchange. India's largest stock market by companies listed and market capitalization.

Bubble   Market phenomenon involving a fierce, unsustainable rise in asset prices drawing in many speculators, often preceding a crash.

Bull   Market participant whose outlook is positive, *c.f.* bear.

Business trust   Narrow purpose but substantive unincorporated organization, permitted as listing vehicles notably in Singapore, intended to allow higher leverage than conventional companies, attract interest from specialist investors through enhanced dividends, and permit control by minority owners, *c.f.* REIT.

Buy side   Investment bank resources in research, trading or broking directed to issuers and borrowers, *c.f.* sell side.

Call option   Right to buy an asset on a future date at a specified strike price.

Capital adequacy   The concept of banks holding equity capital, long-term subordinated liabilities and retained earnings to support their lending and other risk assets and provide a cushion against future loan write-offs.

Capital buffer   Basel III allows national regulators to impose a supervening capital requirement for banks, intended to provide a cushion against systemic risks.

CAPM   Capital asset pricing model. William Sharpe's method of measuring the volatility of expected returns as a proxy for risk, published in 1964, *c.f.* portfolio theory.

CAR   Capital adequacy ratio.

Carry trade   Unhedged cross-currency trade, using own or borrowed funds in a low interest rate currency to buy assets or securities denominated in a currency with higher prevailing interest rates, so that returns are contingent upon the strength of the bought currency.

Cash settlement   Execution of a derivative contract with cash payment rather than delivery of the underlier.

CCP   Central counterparty. Contractual hub of an organized exchange that acts as a legal party to all trades conducted by exchange members.

CD   Certificate of deposit, short- or medium-term negotiable promissory note issued by banks, *c.f.* FRCD.

CDO   Collateralized debt obligation.

CDS   Credit default swap.

Chaebol   (재벌) Generic term for South Korean conglomerates, often closely controlled.

Charge   Generic non-possessory security over real or movable property.

Cheque (check, US)   Negotiable instrument used to make payments to the debit of bank current (checking) accounts.

Chit fund   Informal savings groups often associated with Chinese diaspora communities.

CMI, CMIM   Chiang Mai Initiatives and the Chiang Mai Initiative Multilateralization, bilateral and multilateral central bank currency swap lines launched in 2000 at the ASEAN+3 finance ministers meeting in Chiang Mai.

Coco   Contingent capital debt issue contemplated by Basel III by a bank qualifying as Tier 2 capital, subject to mandatory conversion to equity upon a defined deterioration in solvency.

Collateral   Asset that is part of security for a loan or other provision of credit.

Commercial paper   Short-term tradable promissory notes issued by companies and SIVs, *c.f.* CD.

Commitment   An intermediary's formal willingness to provide credit or acquire risk.

Conduit   SIV used by a bank to defease balance sheet assets, but with the bank providing a standby credit line to fund the conduit if it becomes unable to borrow from third-party investors.

Consensus forecast   Average expected outcome of economic data or corporate performance taken from an informal panel of research analysts. Market prices will adjust to the consensus forecast prior to the release of data, and usually react if the outcome differs from the forecast.

Contango   Condition in a forward or futures market where the price of a contract exceeds the prevailing spot price. Contango is regarded as a normal market configuration resulting from financing costs between the spot and forward dates, *c.f.* backwardation.

Contingent capital   Hybrid bank debt issues that convert to ordinary shares upon the occurrence of defined events, such as a fall in capital adequacy.

Convertible bond   Corporate debt securities representing claims that may be redeemed by conversion to ordinary shares in the issuer, the terms of that conversion being set at the time of issue. Depending on the issue, conversion may be at the option of the issuer, the bondholder, or triggered by the issuer's share price or balance sheet leverage exceeding defined levels.

Coupon   Contractual periodic payment associated with a debt or hybrid security.

Cov-lite   Debt transaction for poorly rated issuers involving undemanding commercial covenants, intended to give negotiating flexibility to creditors and avoid unwanted acceleration following any trivial default.

Covenant   In credit agreements and other debt contracts, commercial undertakings made by debtors, breach of which allows creditors some restorative or compensatory action, such as increasing credit spreads or requiring additional disclosure.

CPF   Central Provident Fund. Singapore superannuation agency managing employee savings plans integrated with state-sponsored home loan schemes.

CSD Central securities depositary. Organization maintaining securities accounts for intermediaries that facilitates the transfer of ownership in securities and in some cases payment processing.

CLN Credit linked note. Usually an unlisted note or debt security issued by a bank, payments on which are contingent on one or more unrelated entities not becoming subject to a credit event.

CMBS Commercial mortgage backed security.

CRA Credit rating agency.

Credit default swap Elemental form of credit derivative, economically similar to an insurance contract, providing compensation or 'protection' against specified credit events including payment defaults by one or more borrowers.

Credit event Conditions or one-off events that affect the credit condition of a debtor or index of debtors, used as payment triggers in credit default swaps and in most cases defined in ISDA standard documents.

Credit rating Indication of the credit quality of a debt security published by a credit rating agency, usually at the instigation of the issuer.

Credit risk Likelihood that a debtor will choose or be forced not to service or repay a debt obligation according to its terms.

Credit spread Interest rate or yield margin that is the difference between the rate paid by a borrower and the risk-free benchmark rate for the same period.

Currency basket Two or more freely tradable currencies to which a state links its own currency's value by undertaking openly or otherwise to intervene to maintain its value within a narrow fixed range of the basket. The weighting of currencies in the basket usually reflects the composition of the state's external trade (*c.f.* currency peg).

Currency peg Open or perceived policy of a state to maintain the value of its currency within a narrow range of another freely tradable currency, most commonly the US dollar or a currency basket.

Dark pool Privately held, order-driven share dealing platform used by professional counterparties, with restrictions on trading access, designed to facilitate trades in large volumes without disturbing prevailing prices.

Day count Convention dictating the number of days in any month and year assumed for the purpose of calculating interest accruals, *e.g.* 30/360 or Actual days/365.

Defease To extinguish an asset and liability from a balance sheet by repayment, or a contractual accounting arrangement ('in substance defeasement'), for example, by pledging cash collateral to repay but not prepay a debt.

Delinquent Payment that is unpaid when due but not formally declared in default.

Depository receipt Tradable security usually representing synthetic rights over overseas listed shares, developed to counter limits on investors holding foreign securities.

Derivative Financial contract, the value of which is a function of an underlier, that is, an asset or index with which it has no contractual connection.

Discount rate Periodic rate of interest used in cashflow calculations.

Disintermediation Process by which flows of funds between savings and investments take place through open markets, rather than through banks or other organized intermediaries.

Distressed debt Claim against a borrower undergoing profound liquidity or solvency problems, usually valued at a large discount to its nominal price.

Distribution　1. Process of selling financial assets or securities to investors. 2. A qualitative measure of the capability of a bank or broker in distributing such claims.

Duration　Maturity of a debt security adjusted for periodic coupons. Bonds with high coupons have shorter durations than others of similar tenor, and will be less sensitive to changes in prevailing interest rates (*c.f.* portfolio duration, average life). Zero-coupon bonds have the longest duration of bonds with identical tenors.

DvP　Delivery against payment. Settlement arrangement by which securities are delivered simultaneously with and contingent upon the agreed payment.

Dynamic hedging　Risk management strategy using financial collateral or derivative contracts, commonly used by banks to protect against price movements in the value of ETFs, warrants, options or synthetic securities held as inventory or to which the bank is liable.

Earnings　Net income or after tax accounting profit.

EBRD　European Bank for Reconstruction and Development.

Economic rent　Surplus return or profit arising from a form of positional status or market monopoly.

EFB, EFN　Exchange fund bills and notes. Respectively short- and medium-term debt securities issued by the Hong Kong Exchange Fund to assist in the operation of domestic monetary policy, a proxy for Hong Kong government debt.

EMEAP　Executives' Meeting of East Asia Pacific Central Banks, a semi-formal gathering of 11 central banks.

EPF　Employees Pension Fund. Malaysian civil service superannuation fund, an influential investor.

Equity premium　For much of the twentieth century the prevailing dividend yield on shares listed in many OECD economies consistently exceeded the current yield on government bonds, a phenomenon known as the equity premium. The persistence of a premium is controversial among finance scholars but was instrumental from the 1950s in encouraging a strong equity orientation among general fund managers, especially in the UK and US.

ETF　Exchange traded fund.

Euribor　Benchmark euro interest rates of periods from one day to 12 months. Each is the modified average rate from those given by a panel of 44 banks (as at October 2011) and published daily at 11:00 hours CET. The panel includes banks from 12 Eurozone states and seven other large banks. For each period the rate submitted by the banks is that at which each would offer interbank term deposits to another bank of similar 'prime' quality.

European style option　Option exercisable at certain predetermined intervals.

EVA　Economic value added. Non-accounting assessment of company performance used in corporate finance valuations.

Exchange traded　Securities or other financial contracts that are traded on an organized exchange, for which the exchange itself acts as a central counterparty, see CCP.

External debt　Debt obligations denominated in foreign currencies.

External finance　Funds raised by companies from third parties.

Externality　Any result of commercial activity that fails to influence the market price of that activity. Often viewed as a form of market failure, externalities impose uncompensated costs or bestow windfall benefits on parties not directly involved in the causal activity. Poor air quality resulting from transport or manufacturing emissions and leading to health damage is often used as an example of a negative externality. Law and economics scholars follow Ronald Coase in arguing that market solutions can correct mispricing due to externalities, but states more commonly use regulation or tax policies to counter or compensate for externalities.

Fair-value accounting Form of mark-to-market accounting that values both assets and liabilities at their prevailing prices, contrasted with methods that use acquisition prices or 'book values'.

Fat tail Extreme events or observations that occur in the real world more often than predicted by normal statistical probability distributions are known as examples of 'fat tails', signifying the thick shape of the 'true' curve.

FDI Foreign direct investment. Cross-border capital investment in a whole business or commercial installation, contrasted with portfolio investment in equities.

Federal funds rate Market interest rate benchmark derived from the price of deposits held by banks at the US Federal Reserve, known as Fed Funds, manipulated from time-to-time following decisions of the Federal Reserve Open Market Committee to raise or lower US interest rates.

Flash crash One-day seizure in the US equity market occurring on 27 May 2010.

Flex pricing Syndicated loan market practice. A mandate is awarded with the arranger given latitude as to the final credit spread and other terms to provide for unforeseen changes in conditions or the credit standing of the borrower prior to closing.

Forward Contract made for future settlement.

FRCD Floating rate CD. Medium-term negotiable instrument that accrues interest at rates that are fixed periodically using Libor or another benchmark index.

FSB Financial Stability Board, organization created in 2009 by G20 members providing policy and research co-ordination among national agencies of 23 states and territories and several other international organizations and standard-setting bodies.

Future Standardized forward contract traded on an organized exchange and cleared by a CCP.

G3 Together the euro, US dollar and yen, the currencies most used in international financial transactions.

G7, G8 Group of Seven leading economies (Canada, France, Germany, Italy, Japan, the UK and the US), with Russia, the Group of Eight.

G10 Informal Group of Ten states historically influential in international economic organizations, notably the BCBS, IMF and World Bank, currently comprising Belgium, Canada, France, Germany, Italy, Japan, Luxembourg, the Netherlands, Spain, Sweden, Switzerland, the UK and the US as full or associate members.

G20 Group of Twenty leading economy finance ministries and central banks, comprising the G8, Argentina, Australia, Brazil, China, the EU, India, Indonesia, South Korea, Mexico, Saudi Arabia, South Africa and Turkey.

G30 Private research and lobby group drawn mainly from the academic, banking and regulatory sectors that was instrumental in winning acceptance of VaR methods, and in promoting rules for risk management of OTC derivatives.

GDR Global depositary receipt, *c.f.* ADR.

Gearing Leverage in UK English.

Glass–Steagall US federal legislation that from 1933 until its abolition in 1999 prevented commercial banks from dealing freely in securities, popularly associated with a formal separation of commercial and investment banking.

GSE US government sponsored enterprise, notably housing refinance lenders Fannie Mae (FNMA) and Freddie Mac (FHLC).

H share Shares in mainland China companies listed in Hong Kong, *c.f.* A share, B share.

Hang Seng Index Benchmark narrow Hong Kong stock market index.

Hawala   Semi-formal transnational money transmission network based in South Asia and a generic term for similar systems elsewhere. Remittances are made in large or small sums using a network of mutual contacts and compensating payments.

Hedge   To take risk positions intended to protect against price movements in an existing transaction or other components of a portfolio.

Hedge fund   1. Specialist fund manager that seeks to profit, not from directional price movements, but from the correction of specific market anomalies. 2. More generally the term is used to describe several types of non-traditional fund management models, many of which have absolute-return objectives rather than seeking to outperform a benchmark or index.

Hibor   Hong Kong interbank offered rate. Short-term Hong Kong dollar interest rate benchmarks, *c.f.* Euribor, Libor.

High-yield debt   Sub-investment grade borrowings with relatively high credit spreads.

HKEx   Hong Kong Exchanges and Clearing Limited, the self-listed owner of the Hong Kong stock exchange.

Hong Kong Exchange Fund   Investment fund managed by the Hong Kong Monetary authority to provide resources to maintain Hong Kong's currency peg to the US dollar.

Hundi   See Hawala.

Hybrid securities   Securities combining features of pure debt and equity securities (*c.f.* convertible bond).

IBRD   International Bank for Reconstruction and Development, the largest operating agency of the World Bank, with which it is often taken as synonymous.

IFC   International Finance Corporation, a World Bank direct investment vehicle.

Index   Synthetic price of an asset or group of assets such as share prices, used as a benchmark for performance measurement.

Intermediation   Process by which savings are channelled into investment or vice versa, or between sectors of the national economy.

Inventory   For a bank, unsold securities intended for distribution.

IPO   Initial public offering. First listing of a company's shares, compared with secondary, follow-on offerings or rights issues.

JGB   Japan government bond.

Jibor   Jakarta interbank offered rate. Short-term rupiah interest rate benchmarks, *c.f.* Euribor, Libor.

Junk bond   High-yield poorly rated debt security.

Keiretsu   Japanese industrial conglomerate with cross-ownership corporate structure.

Khazanah   Khazanah Nasional Bhd. Malaysian state investment agency instrumental in recycling distressed financial assets after the 1997–98 financial crisis.

KLibor   Kuala Lumpur interbank offered rate. Short-term ringgit interest rate benchmarks, *c.f.* Euribor, Libor.

Knightian uncertainty   Economist Frank Knight distinguished risky and uncertain events as respectively those to which a probability of occurrence could be attached and those that cannot be predicted. Uncertain events became popularly known as 'unknown unknowns' during the Iraq invasion from 2003.

KOSPI   Broad South Korean share benchmark index.

Labuan   Sabah island territory designated as Malaysia's offshore banking centre.

LBO   Leveraged buyout. Debt-funded acquisition of a listed company, usually by private equity interests.

Lease Rental contract for the use by a lessee of objects such as aircraft or ships, or fixed assets such as capital equipment or buildings, representing an alternative to medium-term borrowing by the lessee.

Leg Payment obligations of one party to an interest rate or similar OTC swap.

Leverage Proportion of debt due from a creditor in relation to its net worth. For banks the ratio of capitalization to total debt.

Liability Balance sheet claim against a debtor, including deposits held by a bank.

Libor London interbank offered rate. Benchmark interest rates collated in ten leading currencies by the British Bankers Association for periods from one day to 12 months, *c.f.* Euribor, OIS. Each is the modified average rate from those given by panels of between eight and 20 banks and published daily at 11:00 hours London time. For each period the rate submitted by the banks is that at which each would offer interbank term deposits to another bank of similar 'prime' quality. Libor is widely cited as a default benchmark in transaction documentation, and is calculated for Australian, Canadian, New Zealand and US dollars, Danish krone, euro, Sterling, Swedish krona, Swiss francs and yen.

LINK REIT Prominent listed Hong Kong real estate investment trust used to privatize municipal housing, retail and car parking assets.

Liquidity 1. The quality of market instruments being easily converted into cash or cash equivalents. 2. The depth and consistency of actionable prices in any financial market. 3. Balance sheet share of short-term highly rated money market instruments or cash.

Liquidity premium Large liquid bond issues that can be traded easily and quickly, and the issues of regular well-known borrowers may have marginally lower prevailing yields than identical bonds of the same credit rating.

Listing Shares in public companies trading on an organized exchange are said to be 'listed' and their issuers to maintain a listing, subject to regulatory and stock exchange rules.

LLR Lender of last resort. Emergency central bank liquidity function first articulated by Walter Bagehot, to lend funds freely against acceptable collateral to banks that are solvent but suffering scarce liquidity.

Loan to value In asset and real estate financing, the share of the purchase price funded by a lender. Maximum loan to value ratios have often been stated in the quantitative rules of East Asian regulators to help control credit growth and avoid asset price bubbles.

Long–short fund Long-standing hedge fund strategy, signifying funds that take long and short positions in assets or asset classes, usually to mitigate against directional market movements.

Long-term More than ten years.

M&A Mergers and acquisitions. Generic term for corporate transactional change.

Manager Courtesy title given to transaction syndicate members, usually signifying scale of initial underwriting commitment, as with co-lead manager or co-manager.

Mandate Arranger's transaction licence. Brief conditional limited life contract containing a client's exclusive instructions to its deal arranger.

Margin Percentage net operating revenue.

Margin call Rules of organized exchanges requiring counterparties with outstanding positions in derivatives to deposit cash or other liquid collateral with the exchange as a share of the initial contract value ('initial margin'), and to take account of subsequent daily price movements ('maintenance margin').

Market manipulation Malpractice usually involving the exploitation of a dominant position.

Markowitz model   See portfolio theory.

MBO   Management buyout. Debt-funded acquisition involving senior management taking control of a company, in some cases assisted by private equity interests.

Medium-term   1–10 years.

Microfinance   Commercial or concessionary lending to non-traditional, very small-scale creditors, usually individuals, cooperatives or village communities. Often gender based.

MLA   Mandated lead arranger. Bank that negotiates terms with a borrower, and then arranges and distributes the resulting syndicated loan.

Money market   National or transnational debt market in short-term debt instruments.

Monoline   Specialized insurers that issue guarantees for financial obligations, originally in the large US municipal bond market. Losses incurred after the monolines extended coverage to structured finance in 2007–9 caused many to lose their high credit ratings or become insolvent.

Monte Carlo method   Demanding probabilistic models used to study portfolio cashflows under complex changing conditions. The method allows for many correlated input variables and is often used when assets or liability portfolios have a significant option-based content.

Moral hazard   When rules or informal institutions induce behaviour contrary to the general good – for example, LLR facilities may encourage banks to make riskier loans for higher current revenues, knowing that their survival is not in doubt if the loans later fail.

Mortgage   Common form of legal instrument conferring rights over tangible property as collateral for credit.

MSCI   US listed compiler of securities indexes, widely used as benchmarks by professional investors, passive index funds and ETF managers, including Asian regional and emerging market debt and equity indexes.

MTN   Medium-term note. Promissory note or debt security issued under an umbrella debt programme.

Multiple   Arithmetical jargon. Share prices may be compared singly or in groups by reference to multiples of current or prospective earnings, and takeover bids are often stated as multiples of earnings or net assets.

NPL   Non-performing loan. Bank assets that are payment delinquent in scheduled interest or principle. Many regulators require banks to classify risk assets according to the lateness of payment, and make accounting provisions against potential loss.

NPV   Net present value.

Naked short   Short position in securities or derivatives when a seller has respectively not borrowed the securities or holds the underlier.

Narrow index   Any market index with a narrow composition, for example, the Hang Seng Index and Dow Jones Industrial Average are based on a small number of prominent shares in their respective markets.

Negotiable instrument   Instrument or claim, ownership of which passes freely by simple transfer or endorsement, such as a bill of exchange, cheque or promissory note – *c.f.* security, one for which transfer is usually more complex, excepting bearer securities.

New issue   Any debt or equity transaction while in the course of being arranged.

Nikkei 225   Broad benchmark Tokyo stock market index.

Nominal amount   Face value of a financial obligation.

Non-recourse   Form of financing when the credit risk and investor rights centre on a project, often owned by an insubstantive SPV, rather than a conventional corporate debtor.

Used in project and object finance to lessen potential claims against the project sponsor or beneficial owner, *c.f.* recourse, partial recourse.

Note   Generic term for debt securities with tenors of 1–10 years, *c.f.* bill, bond.

Novation   Substituting one party to a loan contract with the replacement assuming its entire rights and obligations, and considered the most effective form of loan transfer. Novation usually requires any security rights to be re-established.

Object finance   Form of project finance involving movable assets such as ships, aircraft or trains.

Offer   Price a trader is willing to accept to sell a security or claim, *c.f.* bid.

OHADA   Organisation pour l'Harmonisation en Afrique du Droit des Affaires (Organization for African Business Law Harmonization).

OIS   Overnight index swap. Fixed-floating interest rate swap for which payments on the floating-rate leg are calculated as an average of daily overnight rates, such as the Federal Funds rate rather than with reference to Libor or a similar index.

Open market operations   Central banks buy or sell short-term and other government securities to implement monetary policy, usually to influence interest rates directly, or indirectly via the exchange rate.

Option   Derivative contract giving the holder future rights to buy or sell an underlier on agreed terms.

OTC   Over the counter, Organized trading taking place not in a central exchange but among recognized participants, who contract with each other rather than each with a CCP.

Par   The full nominal amount of a claim.

Partial recourse   Form of finance where credit risk and investor rights consist of full claims against a project and secondary or partial claims against the project's sponsor or beneficial owner, *c.f.* recourse, non-recourse.

Payment date   Date when a new capital market issue is funded by investors.

Perpetual   Bond with no scheduled maturity date.

Physical settlement   Derivative contracts where settlement is made in the underlier rather than a cash equivalent, as in some commodity markets and certain CDSs.

Pledge   Semi-formal possessory collateral instrument, *c.f.* charge, mortgage.

Portfolio   Array of assets, liabilities or derivative claims.

Portfolio duration   Life of a portfolio adjusted for the timing of payments and receipts.

Portfolio theory   Notable element of finance scholarship published in 1952 by Harry Markowitz, that encourages investor diversification as a means to maximize a target overall combination of return and risk, the latter measured by the volatility of expected returns, *c.f.* CAPM.

PPP   Purchasing power parity, a measure of GDP that accounts for local costs.

Prepay   Repayment of a debt obligation before its due date, usually at the borrower's inception.

Price   1. Product of market making that involves a bid and an offer (a 'two way price'). 2. The cost of a new transaction proposed to a prospective issuer.

Price tension   Pre-issue discussions between deal arrangers and leading investors that may create a consensus after the suggestion of a price range.

Price/earnings (p/e)   Ratio of current share price to current of forecast earnings, used as a comparator between companies or market segments.

Priority   Order given to any ranking of secured claims. The holder of a second charge will normally be repaid only when the debt owed to a holder of a first charge is extinguished.

Private equity   Specialist fund managers that acquire or invest in non-listed companies or privatize listed companies, with a view to profiting from a later IPO.

Privatization   1. Sale to private investors or commercial interests of a public enterprise or utility controlled by a national or provincial authority. 2. Purchase by a controlling shareholder of the remaining shares in a listed company, allowing its shares to be delisted.

Promissory note   Short-term negotiable debt claim.

Prospectus   Information document provided to potential investors prior to a new securities issue, to explain the terms and risks of the transaction, usually subject to disclosure requirements by national regulators or market supervisors, and in some cases actionable by investors.

Put option   Right to sell an asset at a future date at a specified strike price.

Recourse   The nature of a debtor's commitment to financiers, *c.f.* non-recourse, partial recourse.

Red chip   Large capitalization, prominently listed, Chinese company, *c.f.* bellwether stock.

Regulatory arbitrage   Commercial behaviour decisively influenced by regulatory conditions or transnational regulatory differences.

Regulatory capital   Capital resources of a bank or insurer for regulatory purposes or to assess the resilience of the organization to losses.

REIT   Real estate investment trust. Single purpose but substantive listed unincorporated property owner and manager, popular in Singapore and used in Hong Kong, intended to allow higher leverage than conventional companies, attract interest from sectoral investors through enhanced dividends, and permit control by minority owners, *c.f.* business trust.

Reoffer   Underwritten new issues of securities are said to be bought by the arranger and reoffered to investors at a fixed reoffer price.

Repo   Repurchase agreement. Sale and repurchase of a security, usually spread over one or several days, effectively a loan of the security for a fee, used by investors to enhance portfolio returns, and by banks to obtain liquidity.

Repo rate   Effective interest rate derived from a repo transaction in government securities.

Retail   Buyers of financial instruments who are not professional investors or intermediaries and whose participation in any single issue is modest. They may be intelligent, clear-sighted and accustomed to buying and selling such instruments, but cannot fairly be seen as sophisticated.

RFP   Request for proposals, a communication given by prospective borrowers to elicit interest and indicative terms from potential transaction arrangers.

Rights issue   New issue of shares by a listed company, with existing shareholders given rights of first refusal to take up a portion of the issue proportionate to their holding, such rights often being separately tradable.

Risk   Probability of an event occurring.

Risk management   All techniques or organizational functions for measuring, monitoring and mitigating risks, reporting the results, and developing and managing compliance rules in relation to risk.

Risk-free   Benchmark government bonds denominated in the issuer's sovereign currency of domicile.

RMBS   Residential mortgage-backed security. A form of cash securitization.

ROIC   Return on investment capital, the ratio of post-tax income to total invested capital.

Rollover   Syndicated loan practice. A loan is advanced for a set interest period at the prevailing interest rate, at the end of which accrued interest is paid, the loan rolled, and the next interest period begins. The mechanism originates in generic Euromarket practice. Banks borrow in the interbank markets for periods matching loan interest periods, and borrowing and lending is based on Libor for that interest period.

Rule 144A   SEC guidance under the US Securities Act 1933, that allows securities to be marketed to US investors without the customary intensive procedure of registration, providing the securities are issued in relatively large denominations and made available only to professional investors.

S&P500   Widely-followed stock market index, a broad benchmark of the New York stock market.

Samurai bond   Yen bonds issued by foreign borrowers in Japan's domestic markets.

Sarbanes–Oxley   2002 US legislation intended to improve corporate governance after several high-profile bankruptcies, including weighty disclosure requirements and impositions on company directors and auditors.

SBI   Sertifikat Bank Indonesia. Short-term Indonesian central bank promissory notes.

Seasoned   Security or financial transaction beyond a defined period since being a new issue.

SEC   Securities and Exchange Commission. US regulatory agency.

Secured claim   Transaction where the rights of a creditor are supported by a charge over collateral of the creditor or guarantor.

Securitization   Sale of securities by an SPV to fund the purchase of assets or receivables from their originator and allow their defeasement from its balance sheet, or more generally a structured finance transaction that synthetically replicates the credit risk transfer of that process.

Security   Collateral taken to mitigate credit risks.

Seigniorage   Any value or profit that accrues to a central bank resulting from its monopoly in issuing notes and coins as currency.

Sell side   Investment bank resources in research, trading or broking directed to investors, *c.f.* buy side.

SEHK   Stock Exchange of Hong Kong, *c.f.* HKEx.

SET   Stock Exchange of Thailand.

Settlement   Execution by payment of financial transactions or new securities issues.

SGX   Singapore Exchange. Integrated stock market and derivatives exchange.

Shanghai Composite   Broad benchmark Shanghai stock exchange index.

Shareholder   A collective owner of a listed company.

Sharpe ratio   William Sharpe's measure of the success of a capital investment is the ratio of an investment's net return (above the risk-free rate) to its risk as indicated by the standard deviation (or volatility) of that return.

Short, sell short   To sell a claim or security without having ownership.

Short-term   Less than one year.

Sibor   Singapore interbank offered rate. Short-term Singapore dollar interest rate benchmarks, *c.f.* Euribor, Libor.

SIV   Structured investment vehicle. Certain large banks and other intermediaries created lightly capitalized, off-balance sheet SIVs from the early 1990s to acquire securities funded by sales of commercial paper or ABCP to third parties. SIVs generally held highly rated ABS and CDO tranches. This was successful until asset prices fell from 2007 and funding evaporated, leaving most SIVs to be wound up or consolidated by the arranging banks, *c.f.* conduit.

Sovereign risk The credit risk of the state as obligor.

Sponsor Instigator of a transaction or project, often its beneficial owner, but generally not the principal obligor.

Spot To deal at spot is to transact in a financial contract for immediate settlement, compared to forward dealing.

Spread 1 Difference between bid and offer prices. 2. Transaction margin or gross operating return.

SPV (SPE) Special purpose vehicle (entity). Insubstantive entity used as a contractual locus in securitization, project finance and complex financial transactions, usually in common law jurisdictions.

Stabilization Transaction arrangers buy or sell securities to stabilize prices and help maintain an orderly market during or immediately after the primary new issue process, with the cost of stabilization reimbursed by the issuer.

Straits Times Index Broad benchmark Singapore stock market index.

Subprime Generic name for home mortgage loans obtained by borrowers regarded as relatively poor credit risks, *c.f.* Alt-A.

Swap 1. Generic derivative contract. 2. Credit or FX lines between central banks. 3. Contracts for the spot sale and future repurchase of currency.

Swap curve Yield curve taken from the fixed-rate legs of fixed-floating interest rate swaps of increasing maturity, used as an alternative to traditional risk-free yield curves to price new bond issues.

Swaption An option to execute an interest rate or other swap.

SWF Sovereign wealth fund.

Syndicate Deal-specific group of banks assembled by an arranger or MLA to defray underwrite commitments, and in some cases to increase distribution capacity.

Systemic risk Risks resulting from financial sector interconnectedness, or from large intermediaries identified as potentially destabilizing.

Tankan Influential Bank of Japan survey on corporate confidence.

Temasek Prominent Singaporean SWF.

Tenor Contractual life of a claim.

Tier 1 Capital Basel Accord definition of highest-value bank regulatory capital, comprising equity, share premium reserves, accumulated retained earnings, and certain deeply subordinated perpetual debt securities.

Tier 2 Capital Basel Accord definition of secondary value bank regulatory capital, comprising certain subordinated debt securities of at least five years' tenor.

Tobin's q Ratio of market value to book value of a bank's equity capital.

Tombstone Post-transaction publicity notices usually listing the deal amount, purpose and participants ranked by size of initial commitment.

Total return swap An exchange contract involving the overall return on a security or asset paid against a benchmark such as Libor.

Trading Buying or selling securities or other financial claims. Trading can be risk-neutral, conservative or aggressive in either execution or results

Tranche Discrete portion of a debt or equity transaction subject to certain common terms – for example, a loan may be advanced in several tranches at different times.

Treasuries Colloquial name for US government issues of bills, notes or bonds.

Uncertainty Unquantifiable risk.

Underlier Reference asset, analogue or index from which a derivative is priced.

Underwriter   Transaction arrangers that commit to purchase securities or other claims at the time of issue, in many cases on fixed terms, so that the deal will be funded regardless of investor demand.

Value date   Date when a financial contract is settled by payment or exchange, usually following the execution or trade date.

VaR   Value at risk. Mark-to-market calculation of the portfolio or balance sheet impact of exogenous price changes.

Vendor placing   Block trade of shares integral to a corporate acquisition. Shares are issued to the seller to meet all or part of the acquisition cost, and are immediately bought at a fixed price by a bank and sold to third party investors.

Venture capital   Funds that provide equity finance for start-up or expanding young companies.

VIX   Index based on the implied volatility of the S&P500 index, used as a trading instrument and to predict short-term movements in the market followed by that index.

Volatility   Rate of change of price of a financial asset or index, and so a measure of price sensitivity associated with risk, and potential profit.

Vulture fund   Fund that buys deeply distressed corporate or other assets in expectation of their recovering in price, or profiting from a settlement or the threat of litigation with a debtor.

Waterfall   Contractual structured finance arrangement by which payments are made to noteholders in a strict descending sequence according to the priority of each tranche.

Withholding tax   Tax levied at source on interest, coupon and dividend payments, often to capture income paid to non-banks or non-residents, seen by financiers as deleterious to new transactions.

Yield   Return associated with a security or claim, commonly its yield to maturity.

Yield curve   Depiction of interest rates over a period for a homogeneous credit risk or single debt issuer. Traditionally the risk-free yield curve is taken from prevailing rates on sovereign debt in the issuer's currency of domicile.

Yield to maturity   Yield on a security or claim until its scheduled redemption, assuming reinvestment of periodic payments at a discount rate equal to the periodic payment expressed as a percentage of the nominal value.

Bibliography

21st Century Public Policy Institute. (2011) *Asian Bond Markets Development and Regional Financial Cooperation*, Keidanren, Tokyo. Online. Available HTTP: <http://www.21ppi.org/> (accessed 1 October 2012).

Abacus. (2007) ABACUS 2007-AC1, Ltd., *Offering Circular*, 26 April, on file with authors.

Abbott, K., Keohane, R., Moravcsik, A., Slaughter, A.M. and Snidal, D. (2000) The Concept of Legalization, 54 *International Organization* 3, 401.

ABN Amro Holding NV (2003–7) *Annual Reports*.

Acemoglu, D. (2008) *Introduction to Modern Economic Growth*, Princeton NJ, Princeton University Press.

Acemoglu, D., and Johnson, S. (2005) Unbundling Institutions, 113 *Journal of Political Economy* 5, 949.

Acemoglu, D. Johnson, S. and Robinson, J. (2001) The Colonial Origins of Comparative Development: An Empirical Investigator, 91 *American Economic Review* 5, 1369.

—— (2004) Institutions as the Fundamental Cause of Long-run Growth, National Bureau for Economic Research Working Paper No. 10481.

Acharya, A. (2001) The Evolution of ASEAN Norms and the Emergence of the ASEAN Way, 47 in A. Acharya (ed.) *Constructing a Security Community in Southeast Asia: ASEAN and the Problem of Regional Order*, Abingdon, Routledge.

—— (2004) How Ideas Spread: Whose Norms Matter? Norm Localization and Institutional Change in Asian Regionalism, 58 *International Organization* 2, 239.

—— (2009) *Whose Ideas Matter? Agency and Power in Asian Regionalism*, Ithaca NY, Cornell University Press.

Acharya, V., Franks, J. and Servaes, H. (2007) Private Equity: Boom and Bust? 19 *Journal of Applied Corporate Finance* 4, 1.

Ackermann, J. (2007) Europe Has to Storm Cross-border Financial Barriers, *Financial Times*, 25 January.

ACMF (ASEAN Capital Markets Forum). (2008) *ASEAN and Plus Standards, ASEAN Equity Securities Disclosure Standards and ASEAN Debt Securities Disclosure Standards*. Online. Available HTTP: <http://www.aseansec.org/acmf/introduction.htm> (accessed 1 October 2012).

ADB (Asian Development Bank). (2000) *Insolvency Law Reforms in the Asian and Pacific Region, Report of the Office of the General Counsel on TA 5795-Reg: Insolvency Law Reforms, Law and Policy Reform at the ADB*, Manila, ADB.

—— (2006) *Improving Governance and Fighting Corruption: Implementing the Governance and Anticorruption Policies of the Asian Development Bank*, Manila, ADB.

—— (2008) *Emerging Asian Regionalism: A Partnership for Shared Prosperity*, Manila, ADB.

—— (2010) *ADB to Contribute to ASEAN+3 Credit Guarantee Facility*, press release, 14 April. Online. Available HTTP: <http://www.adb.org/media/Articles/2010/13200-asian-credits-guarantees/> (accessed 1 October 2012).

—— (2011) *Asia Bond Monitor*, March. Online. Available HTTP: <http://asianbondsonline.adb.org/documents/abm_mar_2011.pdf?src = spotlight > (accessed 1 October 2012).

—— (undated) *Bond Market Indicators*, Asian Bonds Online. Online. Available HTTP: <http://asian-bondsonline.adb.org/regional/data.php#bond_market_indicators > (accessed 1 October 2012).

ADB (Asian Development Bank) and Hermes (Hermes Pension Management Ltd). (2003) *Corporate Governance Principles for Business Enterprises*, Manila. Online. Available HTTP: <http://www.adb.org/Publications> (accessed 1 October 2012).

Adler, M. and Dumas, B. (1983) International Portfolio Selection and Corporation Finance: A Synthesis, 38 *Journal of Finance*, 3, 925.

Aexlson, U., Jenkinson, T., Stromberg, P. and Weisbach, M. (2007) Leverage and Pricing in Buyouts: An Empirical Analysis, SIFR Working Paper, Stockholm.

Ahlers, J. (1946) Postwar Banking In Shanghai, 19 *Pacific Affairs*, 4, December, 384.

AIA Group Ltd. (2010) *Global Offering Prospectus*, 18 October.

AIG (American International Group, Inc.). (2007) *Annual Report* (SEC Form 10-K).

Aizenman, J., Jinjarak, Y. and Park, D. (2010) International Reserves and Swap Lines: Substitutes or Complements? National Bureau for Economic Research Working Paper No. 15804.

Akamatsu, K. (1961) A Theory of Unbalanced Growth in the World Economy, 86 *Weltwirtschaftliches Archiv*, 1, 196.

—— (1962) A Historical Pattern of Economic Growth in Developing Countries, 1 *The Developing Economies* 1, 3.

Akerlof, G. (1970) The Market For Lemons, 84 *Quarterly Journal of Economics* 3, 488.

Al-Omar, F. and Abdel-Haq, M. (1996) *Islamic Banking: Theory, Practice and Challenges*, Karachi, Oxford University Press.

Alesina, A. and Summers, L. (1993) Central Bank Independence and Macroeconomic Performance: Some Comparative Evidence, 25 *Journal of Money, Credit and Banking* 2, 151.

Alford, D. (2005) Core Principles for Effective Banking Supervision: An Enforceable International Financial Standard? 28 *Boston College International and Comparative Law Review*, 237.

ALI (American Law Institute). (1997) *International Secured Transactions Project*. Online. Available HTTP: <http://www.ali.org> (accessed 1 October 2012).

Allen, F. and Gale, G. (1994) *Financial Innovation and Risk Sharing*, Cambridge MA, MIT Press.

—— (1999) *Comparing Financial Systems*, Cambridge MA, MIT Press.

Allen, F., Qian, J. and Qian, M. (2005) Law, Finance, Economic Growth In China, 77 *Journal of Financial Economics* 1, 57.

Amulree Commission. (1934) Report of the Newfoundland Royal Commission 1933, London, His Majesty's Stationary Office, Cmd. 4480. Online. Available HTTP: <http://www.heritage.nf.ca/law/amulree/am_report.html> (accessed 1 October 2012).

Anandan, R., Kumar, A., Kumara, G. and Padhi, A. (1998) M&A in Asia, *McKinsey Quarterly* 2, 64.

Andenas, M., Arner, D. and Leung, M.W. (2009) The Future of the European Single Market for Financial Services, AIIFL Working Paper No. 8. Online. Available HTTP: <http://www.aiifl.com> (accessed 1 October 2012).

Anderson, J. (2006) *The Return of Asia, Part I: Investment Comes Home*, London, UBS Global Economics and Strategy Research.

—— (2009) The Myth of Chinese Savings, *Far Eastern Economic Review*, November.

Andreades, A. (1933) *A History of Greek Public Finance*, Vols. 1 & 2, Cambridge MA, Harvard University Press, 1992.

Angklomkliew, S., George, J. and Packer, F. (2009) Issues and Developments in Loan Loss Provisioning: The Case of Asia, *BIS Quarterly Review*, December, 69.

Aoki, M. and Patrick, H. (eds.) (1994) *The Japanese Main Bank System: Its Relevance for Developing and Transforming Economies*, Oxford, Oxford University Press.

Apple Inc. (2012) *Proxy Statement For 2012 Annual Meeting Of Shareholders*, Cupertino CA, 9 January.

Aristotle. *Politics, Book I*: xi 1259a 6–23.

Armour, J., Hansmann, H. and Kraakman, R. (2009) What is Corporate Law? 1 in R. Kraakman (ed.) *The Anatomy of Corporate Law: A Comparative and Functional Approach*, 2nd edn., Oxford, Oxford University Press.

Arner, D. (1996) The Mexican Peso Crisis of 1994–95: Implications for the Regulation of Financial Markets, *NAFTA Law and Business Review of the Americas*, 28.

—— (2002) Globalization of Financial Markets: An International Passport for Securities Offerings? 35 *International Lawyer*, 1543.

—— (2007) *Financial Stability, Economic Growth and the Role of Law*, Cambridge, Cambridge University Press.

—— (2009) The Global Credit Crisis: Causes, Consequences and Implications for International Financial Regulation, 43 *International Lawyer* 1, 91.

Arner, D., Booth, C., Hsu, B. and Lejot, P. (2006) Property Rights, Collateral, Creditor Rights and Financial Development, 17 *European Business Law Review* 5, 1215.

Arner, D., Booth, C., Hsu, B., Lejot, P., Liu, Q. and Pretorius, F. (2006) Property Rights, Collateral and Creditor Rights in East Asia, in I. Dalla (ed.) *East Asia Finance: Selected Issues*, Washington DC, World Bank.

Arner, D. and Buckley, R. (2009) Reforming the International Financial Architecture, AIIFL Working Paper No. 7. Online. Available HTTP: <http:www.aiifl.com> (accessed 1 October 2012).

Arner, D., Lejot, P. and Rhee, S.G. (2006) *Impediments to Cross-border Investments in Asian Bonds*, Singapore, Institute of Southeast Asian Studies and Pacific Economic Cooperation Council.

Arner, D., Lejot, P. and Schou-Zibell, L. (2008) The Global Credit Crisis and Securitisation in East Asia, 3 *Capital Markets Law Journal* 3, 291.

Arner, D., Lejot, P. and Wang, W. (2008) Assessing East Asian Financial Cooperation and Integration, 12 *Singapore Yearbook of International Law*, 1.

Arner, D. and Lin, J. (eds.) (2003) *Financial Regulation: A Guide To Structural Reform*, Hong Kong, Sweet and Maxwell Asia.

Arner, D. and Norton, J. (2009) Building a Framework to Address Failure of Complex Global Financial Institutions, 39 *Hong Kong Law Journal* 1, 95.

Arner, D. and Park, C.Y. (2010) Global Financial Regulatory Reforms: Implications for Developing Asia, Asian Development Bank Working Paper Series on Regional Economic Integration, Manila.

Arner, D. and Taylor, M. (2009) The Global Financial Crisis and the Financial Stability Board: Hardening the Soft Law of International Financial Regulation? 32 *University of New South Wales Law Journal* 2, 488.

Arora, V. and Vamvakidis, A. (2010) China's Economic Growth: International Spillovers, IMF Working Paper No. WP/10/165.

Arrow, K. (1963) Uncertainty and the Welfare Economics of Medical Care, 53 *American Economic Review* 5, 941.

ASEAN (Association of Southeast Asian Nations). (1967) *The ASEAN Declaration*, 8 August. Online. Available HTTP: <http://www.aseansec.org/1212.htm> (accessed 1 October 2012).

—— (1976) *Treaty of Amity and Cooperation in Southeast Asia*, 24 February. Online. Available HTTP: <http://www.aseansec.org/1217.htm> (accessed 1 October 2012).

—— (1977) *Memorandum of Understanding on the ASEAN Swap Arrangements*, 5 August. Online. Available HTTP: <http://www.aseansec.org/7914.htm> (accessed 1 October 2012).

—— (1992a) *Agreement on the Common Effective Preferential Tariff Scheme for the ASEAN Free Trade Area,* 28 January. Online. Available HTTP: <http://www.aseansec.org/12375.htm> (accessed 1 October 2012).

—— (1992b) *Fifth Supplementary Agreement to the Memorandum of Understanding on ASEAN Swap Arrangement*, 19 September. Online. Available HTTP: <http://www.aseansec.org/6305.htm> (accessed 1 October 2012).

—— (1995a) *The Bangkok Summit Declaration*, 15 December. Online. Available HTTP: <http://www.aseansec.org/5189.htm> (accessed 1 October 2012).

—— (1995b) *Framework Agreement on Services*, 15 December. Online. Available HTTP: <http://www.aseansec.org/6628.htm> (accessed 1 October 2012).

—— (1997a) *Ministerial Understanding on ASEAN Cooperation in Finance*, 1 March. Online. Available HTTP: <http://www.aseansec.org/1939.htm> (accessed 1 October 2012).

—— (1997b) *ASEAN Vision 2020*, 15 December. Online. Available HTTP: <http://www.aseansec.org/1814.htm> (accessed 1 October 2012).

—— (2007) *Charter of the Association of Southeast Asian Nations (ASEAN Charter)*, 20 November. Online. Available HTTP: <http://www.aseansec.org/21069.pdf> (accessed 1 October 2012).

—— (2009) *Declaration on the Roadmap for the ASEAN Community (2009–15)*, 1 March. Online. Available HTTP: <http://www.aseansec.org/22331.htm> (accessed 1 October 2012).

ASEAN+3 (Finance Ministers). (2000) Joint Ministerial Statement [The Chiang Mai Initiative], Chiang Mai, 6 May.

—— (2007) *Statement* [on the Chiang Mai Initiative], 5 May. Online. Available HTTP: <http://www.mof.go.jp/english/if/as3_070505.htm > (accessed 1 October 2012).

—— (2009a) *Statement* [on the Chiang Mai Initiative], 22 February. Online. Available HTTP: <http://www.aseansec.org/22159.htm> (accessed 1 October 2012).

—— (2009b) *Statement* [on the Chiang Mai Initiative Multilateralization], 3 May. Online. Available HTTP: <http://www.aseansec.org/22536.htm> (accessed 1 October 2012).

—— (2009c) *Establishment of the Chiang Mai Initiative Multilateralization*, 28 December. Online. Available HTTP: <http://www.info.gov.hk/hkma/eng/press/2009/20091228e3.htm> (accessed 1 October 2012).

—— (2010) *Statement, & Annex 1, Key Points of CMI Multilateralization Agreement*, Tashkent, 2 May. Online. Available HTTP: <http://www.aseansec.org/documents/JMS_13th_AFMM+3.pdf> (accessed 1 October 2012).

—— (2012) *Joint statement, & Annex 1, Key Points for Strengthening the CMIM*, Manila, 3 May. Online. Available HTTP: <http://www.aseansec.org/Joint%20Media%20Statement%20of%20the%2015th%20ASEAN+3%20Finance%20Ministers%20and%20Central%20Bank%20Governors'%20Meeting.pdf> (accessed 1 October 2012).

Asmundson, I., Dorsey, T., Khachatryan, A., Niculcea, I. and Saito, M. (2011) Trade and Trade Finance in the 2008–9 Financial Crisis, IMF Working Paper No. WP/11/16.

Augar, P. (2005) *The Greed Merchants: How the Investment Banks Played the Free Market Game*, London, Allen Lane.

Ayyagari, M., Demirgüç-Kunt, A. and Maksimovic, V. (2008) How Important Are Financing Constraints? The Role of Finance in the Business Environment, *World Bank Economic Review* 22, 483.

BaFin (Bundesanstalt für Finanzdienstleistungsaufsicht) (tr. BaFin). (2008) *Market Manipulation Definition Regulation: Regulation to Further Define the Prohibition against Market Manipulation (Market Abuse) 'MaKonV'*, 13 March. Online. Available HTTP: <http://www.bafin.de/nn_720786/SharedDocs/Aufsichtsrecht/EN/Verordnungen/makonv – en.html> (accessed 1 October 2012).

Bagehot, W. (1873) *Lombard Street: A Description of the Money Market*, London, Wiley 1999.

Bai, C., Liu, Q., Lu, J., Song, F. and Zhang, J. (2004) Corporate Governance and Market Valuation in China, 32 *Journal of Comparative Economics* 4, 599.

Bairoch, P. (1993) *Economics and World History: Myths and Paradoxes* Chicago IL, University of Chicago Press.

Baker, T. (1996) The Genealogy of Moral Hazard, 75 *Texas Law Review* 2, 237.

Balassa, B. (1964) The Purchasing Power Parity Doctrine: A Reappraisal, 72 *Journal of Political Economy* 6, 584.

Baldwin, R. (2006) Multilateralising Regionalism: Spaghetti Bowls as Building Blocs on the Path to Global Free Trade, National Bureau for Economic Research Working Paper No. 12545.

Bank of England. (1983) The Nature and Implications of Financial Innovation, *Bank of England Quarterly Bulletin*, London, September, 358.

—— (2007) *Financial Stability Report*, London, October.

—— (2008) *Financial Stability Report*, London, October.

—— (2010) *Financial Stability Report*, London, June.

—— (2011) *Financial Stability Report*, London, June.

Bank of Japan. (2010) *Agreement on the Swap Arrangement under the Chiang Mai Initiative*. Online. Available HTTP: <http://www.boj.or.jp/en/type/release/adhoc10/data/un1001a.pdf> (accessed 1 October 2012).

Bank of Korea. (2008) *Annual Report*, Seoul.

Bank of Thailand et al. (2010) *Joint Press Release* [of CMIM member central banks], *Chiang Mai Initiative Multilateralization Comes Into Effect*, 24 March. Online. Available HTTP: <http://www.bot.or.th/Thai/PressAndSpeeches/Press/News2553/n1053e.pdf> (accessed 1 October 2012).

Banker, The. (2010) China's Growth Story Shows No Sign of Relenting: Top 1000 World Banks 2010, July.

Banner, S. (1998) The Origin of the New York Stock Exchange 1791–1860, 27 *Journal of Legal Studies* 1, 113.

Barclays Plc and ABN Amro Holding NV. (2007a) Investor Presentation, Combination of Barclays and ABN Amro, 23 April.

—— (2007b) Press Release, ABN Amro and Barclays Announce Agreement On Terms of Merger, 23 April.

Barr, M. and Miller, G. (2006) Global Administrative Law: The View from Basel, 17 *European Journal of International Law* 1, 15.

Barro, R. (1991) Economic Growth in a Cross Section of Countries, 106 *Quarterly Journal of Economics* 2, 407.

—— (1997) *Determinants of Economic Growth: A Cross-Country Empirical Study*, Cambridge MA, MIT Press.

Barth, J., Caprio, G. and Levine, R. (2001) Bank Regulation and Supervision: What Works Best? World Bank Policy Research Working Paper No. 2725.

—— (2006) *Rethinking Bank Regulation: Till Angels Govern*, Cambridge, Cambridge University Press.

Barth, J., Lin, C., Ma, Y., Seade, J. and Song, F. (2010) Bank Regulation and Supervision: Boon or Hindrance for Efficiency? 201 in J. Seade (ed.) *Hong Kong as an International Financial Centre for China and for the World*, Hong Kong, Lingnan University Department of Economics.

Barth, J., Zhou, Z., Arner, D., Hsu, B. and Wang, W. (eds.) (2006) *Financial Restructuring and Reform in Post-WTO China*, London, Kluwer Law International.

Barton, D., Newell, R. and Wilson, G. (2003) *Dangerous Markets: Managing In Financial Crisis*, New York NY, John Wiley and Sons.

Baskin, J. (1988) The Development of Corporate Financial Markets In Britain and the United States, 1600–1914: Overcoming Asymmetric Information, 62 *Business History Review* 2, 199.

Baskin, J. and Miranti, P. (1997) *A History of Corporate Finance*, Cambridge, Cambridge University Press.

Batson, N. (2003) In Re Enron Corp. et al., Final Report of Court Appointed Examiner, US Bankruptcy Court, Southern District of New York, 4 November, Case No. 01–16034 (AJG).

Bayoumi, T., Tong, H. and Wei, S.J. (2010) The Chinese Corporate Savings Puzzle: A Firm-level Cross-country Perspective, IMF Working Paper No. 10/275.

BCBS (Basel Committee on Banking Supervision). (2000) *Supervisory Guidance for Managing Settlement Risk in Foreign Exchange Transactions*, Basel.

—— (2006a) *Core Principles for Effective Banking Supervision and Core Principles Methodology*, Basel, 5 October.

—— (2006b) *International Convergence of Capital Measurement and Capital Standards: A Revised Framework Comprehensive Version*, Basel, 29 June.

—— (2006c) *Results of the Fifth Quantitative Impact Study (QIS 5)*. Online. Available HTTP: <http://www.bis.org/bcbs/qis/qis5results.pdf> (accessed 1 October 2012).

—— (2009) *Report and Recommendations of the Cross-border Bank Resolution Group*, Basel, 17 September.

—— (2010a) *Group of Governors and Heads of Supervision Announces Higher Global Minimum Capital Standards (Basel III)*, press release, Basel, 12 September.

—— (2010b) *Proposal to Ensure the Loss Absorbency of Regulatory Capital at the Point of Non-viability, Consultative document*, Basel, 19 August.

—— (2010c) *Basel III: A Global Regulatory Framework for More Resilient Banks and Banking Systems*, Basel, 1 June.

—— (2010d) *Basel III: International Framework for Liquidity Risk Measurement, Standards and Monitoring*, Basel, 16 December.

—— (2010e) *Progress on Regulatory Reform Package*, press release and annex, Basel, 16 July.

Becht, M., Bolton, P. and Roell, R. (2003) Corporate Governance and Control, 1 in G. Constantinides, M. Harris and R. Stulz (eds.) *Handbook of the Economics of Finance*, Vol. 1A, Boston MA, Elsevier, North Holland.

Beck, T., Demirgüç-Kunt, A. and Levine, R. (2000) A New Database On Financial Development and Structure, World Bank Financial Sector Discussion Paper No. 2.

—— (2001) The Financial Structure Database, 17–80 in A. Demirgüç-Kunt and R. Levine (eds.) *Financial Structure and Economic Growth: A Cross-country Comparison of Banks, Markets and Development*, Cambridge MA, MIT Press.

—— (2003) Law, Endowments and Finance, 70 *Journal of Financial Economics* 2, 137.

—— (2006) Bank Supervision and Corruption in Lending, 53 *Journal of Monetary Economics* 8, 2131.

Beck, T., Demirgüç-Kunt, A. and Maksimovic, V. (2005) Financial and Legal Constraints To Growth: Does Firm Size Matter? 60 *Journal of Finance* 1, 137.

Beck, T., Demirgüç-Kunt, A. and Martinez Peria, M. (2007) Reaching Out: Access and Use of Banking Services Across Countries, 85 *Journal of Financial Economics* 1, 234.

Beck, T., Demirgüç-Kunt, A. and Merrouche, O. (2010) Islamic vs. Conventional Banking, Business Model, Efficiency and Stability, World Bank Policy Research Paper No. 5446.

Beck, T., Levine, R. and Loayza, N. (2000) Financial Intermediation and Growth: Causality and Causes, *Journal of Monetary Economics* 46, 31.

Beck, T. and Levine, R. (2002) Industry Growth and Capital Allocation: Does Having a Market- or Bank-based System Matter? 64 *Journal of Financial Economics* 2, 147.

Beck, T., Loayza, N. and Levine, R. (2000) Finance and the Sources of Growth, 58 *Journal of Financial Economics* 1–2, 261.

Beck, U. (2000) *What is Globalization?* Cambridge, Polity Press.

Bell, I. and Rose, J. (2007) *The Fundamentals of Structured Finance Ratings*, Structured Finance Commentary, New York NY, Standard and Poor's Corporation, 23 August.

Benmelech, E. and Dlugosz, J. (2009) The Alchemy of CDO Credit Ratings, 56 *Journal of Monetary Economics*, Carnegie-Rochester Conference, 5.

Bennett, C. (1991) What is Policy Convergence and What Causes it? 21 *British Journal of Political Science*, 2, 215.

Bennett, F. (2009) Getting Property Right: Informal Mortgages in the Japanese Court, 18 *Pacific Rim Law and Policy Journal*, 463.

Bensted, A. (2011) *Global Investor Report*, Hedge Funds, London, Preqin Ltd. April.

Berger, P. and Ofek, E. (1995) Diversification's Effect on Firm Value, 37 *Journal of Financial Economics* 1, 39.

Bergsten, F. and Park, Y.C. (2002) Toward Creating a Regional Monetary Arrangement in East Asia, Asian Development Bank Institute Research Paper Series No. 50.

Berle, A. and Means, G. (1932) *The Modern Corporation and Private Property*, New York NY, Macmillan.

Bernanke, B. (2005) *The Global Saving Glut and the US Current Account Deficit*, Homer Jones Lecture, St. Louis MI, 14 April. Online. Available HTTP: <http://www.federalreserve.gov/board-docs/speeches/2005/20050414/default.htm> (accessed 1 October 2012).

Bernard, M. and Ravenhill, J. (1995) Beyond Product Cycles and Flying Geese: Regionalization, Hierarchy and the Industrialization of East Asia, 47 *World Politics* 2, 171–209.

Bernholtz, P. (1999) The Bundesbank and the Process of European Monetary Integration, 731 in Deutsche Bundesbank (ed.) *Fifty Years of the Deutsche Mark: Central Bank and the Currency in Germany Since 1948*, Oxford, Oxford University Press.

Bernstein, L. (1992) Opting Out of the Legal System: Extralegal Contractual Relations in the Diamond Industry, 21 *Journal of Legal Studies* 1, 115.

Beta Finance Corporation. (2007) August Portfolio Commentary for Beta, 6 September. Online. Available HTTP: <http://www.londonstockexchange.com/LSECWS/IFSPages/MarketNews> (accessed 1 October 2012).

Bhattacharyay, B. (2010) Financing Asia's Infrastructure: Modes of Development and Integration of Asian Financial Markets, ADBI Working Paper Series No. 229.

BIS (Bank for International Settlements). (1997) *Annual Report*, Basel.

—— (2001) *Consolidation In the Financial Sector*, Basel, 29 January.

—— (2002) *Insolvency Arrangements and Contract Enforceability*, Report of the Contact Group on the Legal and Institutional Underpinnings of the International Financial System, Basel, 9 December.

—— (2005a) *Credit Risk Transfer*, Basel, 17 March.

—— (2005b) Foreign Exchange Market Intervention in Emerging Markets: Motives, Techniques and Implications, Basel, BIS Papers No. 24, 3 May.

—— (2006a) *General Guidance for National Payment System Development*, Committee on Payment and Settlement Systems, Basel, 8 January.

—— (2006b) Asian Bond Markets: Issues and Prospects, Basel, BIS Papers No. 30, 6 November.

—— (2009) *Annual Report*, Basel.

—— (2010) *Triennial Central Bank Survey: Report on Global Foreign Exchange Market Activity in 2010*, Basel, 1 December.

—— (2011) *BIS Quarterly Review*, Statistical Annex, Basel, June.

Black, B. (1989) Bidder Overpayment in Takeovers, 41 *Stanford Law Review* 3, 597.

Black, S. and Munro, A. (2010) Why Issue Bonds Offshore? 97 in BIS Papers No. 52, *The International Financial Crisis and Policy Challenges in Asia and the Pacific*, July.

Blakemore and Mitsuki. (2010) 1 *Japan Law Digest*.

Bliss, R. and Kaufman, G. (2006) Derivatives and Systemic Risk: Netting, Collateral, and Closeout, 2 *Journal of Financial Stability*, 55.

Bock, D. (1983) Exchanges of Borrowing, 135 in B. Antl (ed.) *Swap Financing Techniques*, London, Euromoney Publications.

Bordo, M. and Rousseau, P. (2006) Legal–Political Factors and the Historical Evolution of the Finance–Growth Link? 10 *European Review of Economic History* 3, 421.

Borio, C. (2003) Towards a Macroprudential Framework for Financial Supervision and Regulation?, Basel, BIS Working Papers No. 128, February.

Borokhovich, K., Parrino, R. and Trapani, T. (1996) Outside Directors and CEO Selection, 31 *Journal of Financial and Quantitative Analysis*, 337.

Bortolotti, B., Fotak, V., Megginson, W. and Miracky, W. (2009) Sovereign Wealth Fund Investment Patterns and Performance, Fondazione Eni Enrico Mattei Working Paper No. 22. Online. Available HTTP: <http://papers.ssrn.com/sol3/papers.cfm?abstract_id = 1108585 > (accessed 1 October 2012).

Bowtle, G. and McGuiness, K. (2001) *Law of Ship Mortgages*, London, LLP.

Boyreau-Debray, G. and Wei, S.J. (2005) Pitfalls of a State-Dominated Financial System: The Case of China. National Bureau for Economic Research Working Paper No. 11214.

Brandt, L. and Li, H. (2003) Bank Discrimination in Transition Economies: Ideology, Information, or Incentives? 31 *Journal of Comparative Economics*, 387.

Brealey, R., Myers, S. and Allen, F. (2008) *Principles of Corporate Finance*, New York NY, McGraw-Hill, 9th edn.

Brittan, S. (2010) Take Central Banks Down a Notch, *Financial Times*, 29 July.

Bryan, D. and Rafferty, M. (2006) *Capitalism with Derivatives: A Political Economy of Financial Derivatives, Capital and Class*, Basingstoke, Palgrave Macmillan.

Buckley, R. (2011) Beyond the Multilateralized Chiang Mai Initiative: An Asian Monetary Fund, in R. Buckley, R. Hu and D. Arner (eds.) *East Asian Economic Integration: Law, Trade and Finance*, London, Edward Elgar.

Buckley, R. and Arner, D. (2011) *From Crisis to Crisis: The Global Financial System and Regulatory Failure*, London, Kluwer.

Buelens, C. (2008) A Sectoral Perspective on Recent Trends in Mergers and Acquisitions, European Commission Directorate General for Economic and Financial Affairs. Online. Available HTTP: <http://www.worksproject.be/documents/Buelens.ppt> (accessed 1 October 2012).

Buira, A. (2003) *An Analysis of IMF Conditionality*, paper prepared for the XVI Technical Group Meeting of the Intergovernmental Group of 24, Port of Spain, February. Online. Available HTTP: <http://www.g24.org/buiratgm.pdf> (accessed 1 October 2012).

Burk, K. (1989) *Morgan Grenfell, 1838–1988: The Biography of a Merchant Bank*, Oxford, Oxford University Press.

Byamugisha, F. (1999) The Effects of Land Registration on Financial Development and Economic Growth: A Theoretical and Conceptual Framework, World Bank Policy Research Working Paper No. 2240.

Byrd, J. and Hickman, K. (1992) Do Outside Directors Monitor Managers? Evidence from Tender Offer Bids, 32 *Journal of Financial Economics* 2, 195.

Cable, V. (1994) Overview, in V. Cable and D. Henderson (eds.) *Trade Blocs? The Future of Regional Integration*, London, Royal Institute of International Affairs.

—— (1999) *Globalization and Global Governance*, London, Royal Institute of International Affairs.

Cadbury Committee (Committee on the Financial Aspects of Corporate Governance). (1992) *Final Report* Online. Available HTTP: <http://www.jbs.cam.ac.uk/cadbury/report/index.html> (accessed 1 October 2012).

Cadwell, C. (2000) Foreword, in M. Olson (ed.), *Power and Prosperity: Outgrowing Communist and Capitalist Dictatorships*, New York NY, Basic Books.

Cairncross, F. (2001) *The Death of Distance: How the Communications Revolution is Changing our Lives*, Boston MA, Harvard Business School Press.

CalPERS (California Public Employees' Retirement System). (2009) Core Principles of Accountable Corporate Governance, Online. Available HTTP: < http://www.calpers-governance.org/docs-sof/principles/2010-5-2-global-principles-of-accountable-corp-gov.pdf > (accessed 1 October 2012).

Campbell, J., Lettau, M., Malkiel, B. and Xu, Y. (2001) Have Individual Stocks Become More Volatile? An Empirical Exploration of Idiosyncratic Risk, 56 *Journal of Finance* 1, 1.

Capaldo, P., Härle, P. and Marrs, A. (2008) What's Next for Exchanges?, *McKinsey Quarterly*, March, 1.

Carosso, V. (1970) *Investment Banking in America: A History*, Cambridge MA, Harvard University Press.

—— (1980) *The Morgans: Private International Bankers, 1854–1913*, Cambridge MA, Harvard University Press.

Carter, R., Dark, F. and Singh, A. (1998) Underwriter Reputation, Initial Returns and the Long-run Performance of IPO Stocks, 53 *Journal of Finance* 1, 285.

Carter, R. and Manaster, S. (1990) Initial Public Offerings and Underwriter Reputation, 45 *Journal of Finance*, 4, 1045.

Casadesus-Masanell, R. and Spulber, D. (2000) The Fable of Fisher Body, 43 *Journal of Law and Economics* 1, 67.

Cecchetti, S. (2010) *Alternatives to Self-insurance*, remarks prepared for the Swiss National Bank–International Monetary Fund High-level Conference on the International Monetary System, Zurich 11 May. Online. Available HTTP: <http://www.bis.org/speeches/sp100512.pdf> (accessed 1 October 2012).

CEIC (undated) CEIC Macroeconomic, Industry and Financial Time-series Databases for Emerging Markets and Developed Markets.

Central Bank of Ireland. (2008) *Government Decision to Safeguard Irish Banking System*, Press release, 30 September. Online. Available HTTP: <http://www.financialregulator.ie/press-area/press-release

s%5CPages%5CGovernmentDecisiontoSafeguardIrishBankingSystem.aspx> (accessed 1 October 2012).

CFTC (Commodity Futures Trading Commission) and SEC (Securities and Exchange Commission). (2010) *Findings Regarding the Market Events of May 6, 2010: Report to the Joint Advisory Committee on Emerging Regulatory Issues*, Washington DC, September.

CGFS (Committee on the Global Financial System). (2003) *Incentive Structures in Institutional Asset Management and their Implications for Financial Markets*, Basel, 30 March.

—— (2005) *The Role of Ratings in Structured Finance: Issues and Implications*, Basel, 1 January.

—— (2010) The Functioning and Resilience of Cross-border Funding Markets, CGFS Publications No. 37, Basel, 24 March.

—— (2011) Fixed Income Strategies of Insurance Companies and Pension Funds, CGFS Papers, No. 44, Basel, 12 July.

Chan, E., Chui, M., Packer, F. and Remolona, E. (2011) *Local Currency Bond Markets and the Asian Bond Fund 2 Initiative*, Bank for International Settlements, 14 July.

Chang, H.J. (1999) The Economic Theory of the Developmental State, 182 in M. Woo-Cumings (ed.) *The Developmental State*, Ithaca NY, Cornell University Press.

Chang, S.J. (2003) *Financial Crisis and Transformation of Korean Business Groups: The Rise and Fall of Chaebols*, Cambridge, Cambridge University Press.

Chauffour, J.P. and Farole, T. (2009) Trade Finance in Crisis: Market Adjustment or Market Failure? World Bank Policy Research Working Paper 5003.

Cheffins, B. (2008) *Corporate Ownership and Control: British Business Transformed*, Oxford, Oxford University Press.

Chen, A. (1983) The Developing Legal System in China, 13 *Hong Kong Law Journal*, 291.

—— (2010) The Law of Property and the Evolving System of Property Rights in China, University of Hong Kong, Faculty of Law. Online. Available HTTP: <http://papers.ssrn.com/sol3/papers.cfm?abstract_id = 1615499 > (accessed 1 October 2012).

Cheung, Y.W. and Ito, H. (2008) Hoarding of International Reserves: A Comparison of the Asian and Latin American Experiences, Hong Kong Institute for Monetary Research Working Paper No.7.

Chey, H.K. (2009) The Changing Political Dynamics of East Asian Financial Cooperation, The Chiang Mai Initiative, 49 *Asian Survey*, 3.

Chi, J., Ke, L. and Young, M. (2006) Financial Integration in East Asian Equity Markets, 11 *Pacific Economic Review* 4, 513.

Chia, W.K., Li, K. and Tan, P.R. (2011) *CNH Market Guide: A Precursor to Internationalisation of the Chinese Renminbi*, Singapore, Royal Bank of Scotland Group, 10 March.

CIA (Central Intelligence Agency). (2010) The World Factbook. Online. Available HTTP: <https://www.cia.gov/library/publications/the-world-factbook/index.html> (accessed 1 October 2012).

Claessens, S. (2006) Access to Financial Services: A Review of the Issues and Public Policy Objectives, 21 *World Bank Research Observer*, 207.

Claessens, S., Djankov, S. and Lang, L. (2000) The Separation of Ownership and Control In East Asian Corporations, 58 *Journal of Financial Economics* 1–2, 81.

Claessens, S. and Laeven, L. (2002) Financial Development, Property Rights and Growth, 57 *Journal of Finance* 6, 2741.

Claessens, S., Underhill, G. and Zhang, X. (2006) The Political Economy of Global Financial Governance: The Costs of Basle II for Poor Countries, World Economy and Finance Programme Working Paper No. 0015. Online. Available HTTP: <http://papers.ssrn.com/sol3/papers.cfm?abstract_id = 944530&high = %20claessens> (accessed 1 October 2012).

Clarke, D., Murrell, P. and Whiting, S. (2008) The Role of Law in China's Economic Development, 375 in L. Brandt and T. Rawski (eds.) *China's Great Economic Transformation*, Cambridge, Cambridge University Press.

Coase, R. (1937) The Nature of the Firm, 4 *Economica* 16, 386.

—— (1960) The Problem of Social Cost, 3 *Journal of Law and Economics*, 1.

—— (1988) The Nature of the Firm (1. Origin; 2. Meaning; 3. Influence), 4 *Journal of Law and Economics*, 1, 3.

—— (2000) The Acquisition of Fisher Body by General Motors, 43 *Journal of Law and Economics* 1, 15.

—— (2006) The Conduct of Economics: The Example of Fisher Body and General Motors, 15 *Journal of Economics and Management Strategy* 2, 255.

Coffee, J. (2002) Racing Towards the Top? The Impact of Cross-listings & Stock Market Competition on International Corporate Governance, 102 *Columbia Law Review*, 1758.

—— (2007) Law and the Market: The Impact of Enforcement, 156 *University of Pennsylvania Law Review*, 229.

Collins, D., Morduch, J., Rutherford, S. and Ruthven, O. (2009) *Portfolios of the Poor: How the World's Poor Live on $2 a Day*, Princeton NJ, Princeton University Press.

Collins, H. (1999) *Regulating Contracts*, Oxford, Oxford University Press.

Collins, S., Bosworth, B. and Rodrik, R. (1996) Economic Growth in East Asia: Accumulation versus Assimilation, 2 *Brookings Papers on Economic Activity*, 135.

Commission On Growth and Development. (2008) *The Growth Report: Strategies For Sustained and Inclusive Development*, Washington DC, World Bank.

Cookson, R. (2010) Bolton bets on Chinese domestic consumption, Financial Times, 15 July.

Coombs, C. (1962) Treasury and Federal Reserve Foreign Exchange Operations, 48 *Federal Reserve Bulletin*, 1138.

—— (1976) *The Arena of International Finance*, New York NY, Wiley.

Cooper, R. (2006) Almost a Century of Central Bank Cooperation, BIS Working Papers No.198.

Corrigan, G. (2008) *Containing Systemic Risk: The Road To Reform*, Report of the CRMPG III, 6 August. Online. Available HTTP: <http://www.crmpolicygroup.org/docs/CRMPG-III.pdf> (accessed 1 October 2012).

Corsetti, G., Pesenti, P. and Roubini, N. (1998) What Caused the Asian Currency and Financial Crisis? Parts I and II, National Bureau of Economic Research Working Papers Nos. 6833 and 6834.

Cotter, J., Shivdasani, A. and Zenner, M. (1997) Do Independent Directors Enhance Target Shareholder Wealth During Tender Offers? 43 *Journal of Financial Economics* 2, 195.

Cowen, D. and Salgado, R. (2006) Globalization of Production and Financial Integration in Asia, in D. Cowen, R. Salgado, H. Shah, L. Teo and A. Zanello (eds.) *Financial Integration in Asia: Recent Developments and Next Steps*, IMF Working Paper No. 06/196.

CPSS (Committee on Payment and Settlement Systems). (2001) *Core Principles for Systemically Important Payment Systems*, CPSS Publications No. 43, Basel, 19 January.

—— (2000) The Hazard of Moral Hazard: Untangling the Asian Crisis, 28 *World Development*, 4, 775.

Crockett, A. (2003) International Standard Setting in Financial Supervision, lecture, Cass Business School, London, 5 February.

Cronon, W. (1991) *Nature's Metropolis: Chicago and the Great West*, New York NY, W.W. Norton.

Crowe, J. (2012) Does Control Make a Difference? The Moral Foundations of Shareholder Liability for Corporate Wrongs, 75 *Modern Law Review* 2, 159.

Cull, R. and Xu, L. (2003) Who Gets Credit? The Behaviour of Bureaucrats and State Banks in Allocating Credit to Chinese State-owned Enterprises, 71 *Journal of Development Economics* 2, 533.

Cumings, B. (1984) The Origins and Development of the Northeast Asian Political Economy: Industrial Sectors, Product Cycles and Political Consequences, 38 *International Organization* 1, 1.

Curley, M. and Thomas, N. (eds.) (2007) *Advancing East Asian Regionalism*, Abingdon, *Routledge*.

Dahan, F. (2000) Secured Transactions Law in Western Advanced Economies: Exposing Myths, in European Bank for Reconstruction and Development, 37 *Law in Transition*, London.

Dalhuisen, J. (2010) *Dalhuisen on Transnational Comparative, Commercial, Financial and Trade Law: Vol. 3, Financial Products, Financial Services and Financial Regulation*, Oxford, Hart.

Das, D. (2005) *Asian Economy and Finance: A Post-crisis Perspective*, New York NY, Springer.

David, R. and Brierley, J. (1978) *Major Legal Systems in the World Today: An Introduction to the Comparative Study of Law*, London, Stevens, 2nd edn.

Davidson, M. (2011) *Thames Water Utilities Cayman Finance Ltd.*, Standard & Poor's Global Credit Portal report, London, 26 January.

Davis, E.P. (2005) *The Role of Pension Funds as Institutional Investors in Emerging Markets*, Paper given to Korean Development Institute Conference, Population Aging in Korea: Economic Impacts and Policy Issues, Seoul, March.

Davis, E.P., and Hu, Y. (2008) Does Funding of Pensions Stimulate Economic Growth? 7 *Journal of Pension Economics and Finance* 2, 221.

Davis, L. and Gallman, R. (2001) *Evolving Financial Markets and International Capital Flows: Britain, the Americas and Australia 1865–1914*, Cambridge, Cambridge University Press.

De la Peña, N., Fleisig, H. and Wellons, P. (eds.) (2000) Secured Transactions Law Reform in Asia: Unleashing the Potential of Collateral, 2 *Law and Policy Reform at the Asian Development Bank*, 2.

De Larosière Group. (2009) *Report of the High Level Group on Financial Supervision in the EU*, Brussels, European Commission.

Deakin, S. and Slinger, G. (1997) Hostile Takeovers, Corporate Law, and the Theory of the Firm, 24 *Journal of Law and Society* 1, 124.

Degorce, P. (2007) TCI Letter to ABN Amro Holding N.V. Supervisory and Managing Boards, 21 February. Online. Available HTTP: <http://ftalphaville.ft.com/blog/2007/02/21/2666/tcis-letter-to-abn-amro/> (accessed 1 October 2012).

DeLong, B. (1991) Did J.P. Morgan's Men Add Value? An Economist's Perspective on Financial Capitalism, 205–36, in P. Temin (ed.) *Inside the Business Enterprise: Historical Perspectives on the Use of Information*, Chicago IL, University of Chicago Press.

Demirgüç-Kunt, A. (2006) Finance and Economic Development: Policy Choices for Developing Countries, World Bank Policy Research Working Paper No. 3955.

Demirgüç-Kunt, A. and Detragiache, E. (1998) Financial Liberalization and Financial Fragility, World Bank Working Paper No. 1917. Online. Available HTTP: <http://www.worldbank.org/html/dec/Publications/Workpapers/WPS1900series/wps1917/wps1917.pdf> (accessed 1 October 2012).

—— (2009) Basel Core Principles and Bank Soundness: Does Compliance Matter? World Bank Policy Research Working Paper No. 5129. Online. Available HTTP: <http://papers.ssrn.com/sol3/papers.cfm?abstract_id=iso9196> (accessed 1 October 2012).

Demirgüç-Kunt, A., Detragiache, E. and Tressel, T. (2008) Banking on the Principles: Compliance with Basel Core Principles and Bank Soundness, 17 *Journal of Financial Intermediation*, 511.

Demirgüç-Kunt, A. Feyen, E. and Levine, R. (2011) The Evolving Importance of Banks and Securities Markets, World Bank Policy Research Working Paper No. 5805.

Demirgüç-Kunt, A. and Levine, R. (2001) Bank-based and Market-based Financial Systems: Cross-country Comparisons, 81–140 in A. Demirgüç-Kunt and R. Levine (eds.) *Financial Structure and Economic Growth: A Cross-country Comparison of Banks, Markets and Development*, Cambridge MA, MIT Press.

Demirgüç-Kunt, A. and Maksimovic, V. (1998) Law, Finance and Firm Growth, 53 *Journal of Finance* 6, 2107.

Demsetz, R. (1999) Bank Loan Sales: A New Look At the Motivations For Secondary Market Activity, Federal Reserve Bank of New York Staff Report No. 69.

Denis, D. and McConnell, J. (2003) International Corporate Governance, 38 *Journal of Financial and Quantitative Analysis*, 1.

Derivatives Policy Group. (1995) *Framework for Voluntary Oversight*. Online. Available HTTP: <http://riskinstitute.ch/137860.htm> (accessed 1 October 2012).

Desai, M. and Low, W. (1987) Measuring the Opportunity for Product Innovation, in M. de Cecco (ed.) *Changing Money: Financial Innovation In Developed Countries*, Oxford, Blackwell.

De Soto, H. (2000) *The Mystery of Capital: Why Capitalism Triumphs in the West and Fails Everywhere Else*, New York NY, Basic Books.

Diamond, D. (1984) Financial Intermediation and Delegated Monitoring, 51 *Review of Economic Studies* 3, 393.

Diamond, D. and Dybvig, P. (1983) Bank Runs, Deposit Insurance, and Liquidity, 91 *Journal of Political Economy*, 3, 401.

Diamond, J. (1997) *Guns, Germs and Steel: the Fates of Human Societies*, New York NY, W.W. Norton.

Diamond, P. (1967) The Role of a Stock Market in a General Equilibrium Model with Technological Uncertainty, 57 *American Economic Review* 4, 759.

Dickson, P. (1967) *The Financial Revolution in England: A Study in the Development of Public Credit 1688–1756*, London, Macmillan.

Dierick, F. (2004) The Supervision of Mixed Financial Services Groups In Europe, European Central Bank Occasional Paper No. 20.

Djankov, S., Glaeser, E., La Porta, R., Lopez-de-Silanes, F. and Shleifer, A. (2003) The New Comparative Economics, 31 *Journal of Comparative Economics*, 595.

Djankov, S., McLiesh, C., Nenova, T. and Shleifer, A. (2003) Who Owns the Media? 46 *Journal of Law and Economics* 2, 341.

Djankov, S., McLiesh, C. and Shleifer, A. (2007) Private Credit in 129 Countries, *Journal of Financial Economics* 84, 299.

Dobb, M. (1947) *Studies in the Development of Capitalism*, London, Routledge.

Dore, R. (2000) *Stock Market Capitalism: Welfare Capitalism: Japan and Germany versus the Anglo-Saxons*, Oxford, Oxford University Press.

Drysdale, P. and Huang, Y. (1997) Technological Catch-up and Economic Growth in East Asia and the Pacific, 73 *Economic Record*, 222, 201.

Dufey, G. and Giddy, I. (1981) Innovation in the International Financial Markets, 12 *Journal of International Business Studies* 2, 33.

Dunbar, N. (2003) Revealed: Goldman Sachs' Mega-deal for Greece, 16 *Risk* 7, 20.

—— (2004) The Great German Structured Credit Experiment, 17 *Risk* 2, 17.

Dyck, A., Morse, A. and Zingales, L. (2010) Who Blows the Whistle on Corporate Fraud? 65 *Journal of Finance* 6, 2213.

Dyck, A., Volchkova, N. and Zingales, L. (2008). The Corporate Governance Role of the Media: Evidence from Russia, 63 *Journal of Finance* 3, 1093.

Easley, D., de Prado, M. and O'Hara, M. (2011) The Microstructure of the 'Flash Crash': Flow Toxicity, Liquidity Crashes, and the Probability of Informed Trading, 37 *Journal of Portfolio Management* 2, 118.

Easterly, W. and Levine, R. (2002) Tropics, Germs and Crops: How Endowments Influence Economic Development, National Bureau For Economic Research Working Paper No. 9106.

Eatwell, J. and Taylor, L. (2000) *Global Finance at Risk: The Case for International Regulation*, New York NY, New Press.

ECBC (European Covered Bond Council). (2010) *European Covered Bond Fact Book*. Online. Available HTTP: <http://ecbc.hypo.org/Content/Default.asp?PageID=501> (accessed 1 October 2012).

Economist, The. (1962) Survey, Consider Japan 1 and 2, 1 and 8 September.

—— (1999) The Business of Banking, 30 October.

—— (2002) Investment Banks: The Price of Atonement, 14 November.

—— (2005) French Business: Overreacting? Moi? 21 July.

—— (2007) European Bank Mergers: Revving Up for a Demolition Derby, 22 March.

—— (2008) Macquarie Group: For Whom the Tolls Swell, 17 April.

—— (2010) A Few Minutes of Mayhem, 15 May.

Edwards, F. and Morrison, E. (2005) Derivatives and the Bankruptcy Code, 22 *Yale Journal on Regulation*, 91.

EFSF (European Financial Stability Facility). (2010) *Framework Agreement*, 7 June. Online. Available HTTP: <http://www.efsf.europa.eu/attachment/efsf_framework_agreement_en.pdf> (accessed 1 October 2012).

Ehrmann, M. and Jansen, D.J. (2012) The Pitch Rather Than the Pit: Investor Inattention during FIFA World Cup Matches, Frankfurt, European Central Bank Working Paper No. 1424.

Eichengreen, B. (2009) Fostering Monetary and Exchange Rate Cooperation in East Asia, 11 in Chung Duck-koo and B. Eichengreen (eds.) *Fostering Monetary and Financial Cooperation in East Asia*, Singapore, World Scientific Publishing.

Eichengreen, B., Haussmann, R. and Panizza, U. (2003) Currency Mismatches, Debt Intolerance and Original Sin: Why They Are Not the Same and Why it Matters, National Bureau of Economic Research Working Paper No. 10036.

Eichengreen, B. and Luengnaruemitchai, P. (2006) Why Doesn't Asia Have Bigger Bond Markets? 40 in BIS, *Asian Bond Markets: Issues and Prospects*, BIS Papers No. 30, 2008.

El Qorchi, M., Maimbo, S. and Wilson, J. (2003) Informal Funds Transfer Systems: An Analysis of the Informal Hawala System, International Monetary Fund Occasional Paper No. 222, Washington DC.

EMEAP (Executives' Meeting of East Asia Pacific Central Banks). (2004) EMEAP Central Banks Announce the Launch of the Asian Bond Fund 2, Press statement, 16 December. Online. Available HTTP: <http://www.emeap.org/emeapdb/upload%5CPress%5C16dec04.pdf> (accessed 1 October 2012).

—— (2005) The Asian Bond Fund 2 Has Moved into Implementation Phase, Press statement, 12 May. Online. Available HTTP: <http://www.emeap.org/emeapdb/upload%5CPress%5C12may05.pdf> (accessed 1 October 2012).

—— (2006) Review of the Asian Bond Fund 2 Initiative, EMEAP Working Group on Financial Markets. Online. Available HTTP: <http://www.emeap.org/emeapdb/upload/WGMeeting/ABF2 ReviewReport.pdf> (accessed 1 October 2012).

—— (2010) Liquidity Management in EMEAP Money Markets: Possible Vulnerabilities and Scope for Cooperation, EMEAP Working Group on Financial Markets, July.

Emery, H. (1896) *Speculation on the Stock and Produce Markets of the United States, 1969*, New York NY, Greenwood Press, 13–21.

Erb, C., Harvey, C. and Viskanta, T. (1994) Forecasting International Equity Correlations, *Financial Analysts Journal*, November/December, 32–45.

Espinasse, P. (2011) *IPO: A Global Guide*, Hong Kong, Hong Kong University Press.

Euromoney. (2008) Foreign Exchange Poll, Vol. 39 No. 469, 196, May.

European Commission. (1985) Completing the Internal Market: White Paper from the European Commission to the European Council, Com(85) 310 final.

—— (2003) *The EU Economy: 2003 Review*, Brussels, Directorate-General for Economic and Financial Affairs. Online. Available HTTP: <http://ec.europa.eu/economy_finance/publications/ publication7694_en.pdf > (accessed 1 October 2012).

—— (2005) *The EU Economy: 2005 Review*, Brussels, Directorate-General for Economic and Financial Affairs. Online. Available HTTP: <http://ec.europa.eu/economy_finance/publications/ publication433_en.pdf> (accessed 1 October 2012).

Fama, E. (1970) Efficient Capital Markets: A Review of Theory and Empirical Work, 25 *Journal of Finance* 2, 383.

Fama, E. and French, K. (1992) The Cross Section of Expected Stock Returns, 47 *Journal of Finance* 2, 427.

Fan, J., Wong, T.J. and Zhang, T. (2005) *The Emergence of Corporate Pyramids in China*, Chinese University of Hong Kong.

Farrant, R. (2000) Peregrine Fixed Income Limited (in Liquidation), Peregrine Investments Holdings Limited (in Liquidation), Report Pursuant To the Appointment by the Financial Secretary of Richard Farrant as Inspector under Section 143(1)(A) of the Companies Ordinance (Cap. 32), Hong Kong Government.

Farrell, D., Ghai, S. and Shavers, T. (2005) *The Coming Demographic Deficit: How Aging Populations will Reduce Global Savings*, London, McKinsey Global Institute.

Farrell, D., Lund, S. and Puri, L. (2005) Reforming India's Financial System, *McKinsey Quarterly*.

Farrell, D., Marcheva, A. and Shavers, T. (2005) Mapping the Global Capital Markets, *McKinsey Quarterly*, March.

Farrell, D., Puron, A. and Remes, A. (2005) Beyond Cheap Labor: Lessons for Developing Economies, *McKinsey Quarterly*, 1.

Fay, S. (1996) *The Collapse of Barings*, London, Richard Cohen Books.

FCIC (Financial Crisis Inquiry Commission). (2011) *Final Report of the National Commission on the Causes of the Financial and Economic Crisis in the United States*. Online. Available HTTP: <http://fcic.gov/report> (accessed 1 October 2012).

Fearey, R. (1950) *The Occupation of Japan, Second Phase: 1948–50*, New York NY, Macmillan.

Federal Reserve (Board of Governors of the Federal Reserve System). (1999) *Annual Report*, Washington DC.

—— (2001) *Annual Report*, Washington DC.

—— (2011) *Regulatory Reform, Transaction Data: Term Auction Facility*. Online. Available HTTP: <http://www.federalreserve.gov/newsevents/reform_taf.htm > (accessed 1 October 2012).

Fédération Bancaire Française. (2011) Long-term Investor Initiative for Greece, 24 June, on file with authors.

Feldstein, M. (1998) Refocusing the IMF, 77 *Foreign Affairs*, 20.

Feldstein, M. and Horioka, C. (1980) Domestic Saving and International Capital Flows, 90 *Economic Journal* 358, 314.

Fell, R. (1992) *Crisis and Change: The Maturing of Hong Kong's Financial Markets*, Hong Kong, Longman.

Ferguson, N. (1998) *The House of Rothschild: Vol. 1, Money's Prophets, 1798–1848*, New York NY, Viking.

—— (2001) *The Cash Nexus: Money and Power in the Modern World 1700–2000*, London, Basic Books.

Ferrarini, G. and Moloney, N. (2011) *Equity Trading and the MiFID Review: Law, Market Change and Interest Groups in EU Financial Markets*. Online. Available HTTP: <http://ssrn.com/abstract=1989041> (accessed 1 October 2012).

Ferson, W. and Harvey, C. (1994a) Country Risk in Asset Pricing Tests, Duke University Working Paper.

—— (1994b) An Exploratory Investigation of the Fundamental Determinants of National Equity Returns, in Jeffrey Frankel (ed.) *The Internationalization of Equity Markets*, Chicago IL, University of Chicago Press.

Fidelity (Fidelity Worldwide Investment). (2012) Benchmarking & the Road to Unconstrained, April.

Fischer, S. (1996) Lessons from East Asia and the Pacific Rim, 2 *Brookings Papers on Economic Activity*, 345.

—— (1997) Maintaining Price Stability, *The Region*, June, Federal Reserve Bank of Minneapolis. Online. Available HTTP: <http://www.minneapolisfed.org/publications_papers/pub_display.cfm?id=3637> (accessed 1 October 2012).

—— (1999) On the Need for an International Lender of Last Resort, 13 *Journal of Economic Perspectives* 4, 85.

Flinn, M. (1966) *Origins of the Industrial Revolution*, London, Longman.

FOMC (US Federal Reserve Open Market Committee). (1997) Minutes. Online. Available HTTP: <http://www.federalreserve.gov/monetarypolicy/fomc_historical.htm > (accessed 1 October 2012).

Foresight. (2011) The Future of Computer Trading in Financial Markets, Working Paper, London, Government Office for Science.

Frame, S. and White, L. (2004) Empirical Studies of Financial Innovation: Lots of Talk, Little Action? 42 *Journal of Economic Literature* 1, 116.

Fraser, I. and Mortimer-Lee, P. (1993) The EC Single Market in Financial Services, 33 *Bank of England Quarterly Bulletin* 1, 92.

Freeman, M. (2001) *Lloyd's Introduction to Jurisprudence*, London, Sweet and Maxwell.

French, K. and Poterba, J. (1991) Investor Diversification and International Equity Markets, 81 *American Economic Review: Papers and Proceedings*, 222.

Froud, J., Haslam, C., Johal, S. and Williams, K. (2000) Shareholder Value and Financialization: Consultancy Promises, Management Moves, 29 *Economy and Society* 1, 80.

FSA (Financial Services Authority). (2011) The Failure of the Royal Bank of Scotland, Board Report, December. Online. Available HTTP: <http://www.fsa.gov.uk/rbs > (accessed 1 October 2012).

FSB (Financial Stability Board). (2011a) *Potential Financial Stability Issues Arising from Recent Trends in Exchange-Traded Funds*, Basel, 12 April.

—— (2011b) *OTC Derivatives Market Reforms: Progress Report on Implementation*, Basel, 11 October.

FSB (Financial Stability Board) and others. (2009) Guidance to Assess the Systemic Importance of Financial Institutions, Markets and Instruments: Initial Considerations, Basel, 28 October.

Fung, B., George, J., Hohl, S. and Ma, G. (2004) Public Asset Management Companies in East Asia, a Comparative Study, Basel, Financial Stability Institute Occasional Paper No. 3.

G10 (Group of Ten). (2001) *Consolidation in the Financial Sector*. Online. Available HTTP: <http://www.bis.org/publ/gten05.htm > (accessed 1 October 2012).

G20 (Group of Twenty). (2009a) *Declaration on Strengthening the Financial System*, London, 2 April, Online. Available HTTP: <http://www.g20.utoronto.ca/2009/2009ifi.pdf> (accessed 1 October 2012).

—— (2009b) *Leaders' Statement: The Pittsburgh Summit*, 25 September. Online. Available HTTP: <http://www.pittsburghsummit.gov/mediacenter/129639.htm> (accessed 1 October 2012).

G30 (Group of Thirty). (1993) *Derivatives: Practices and Principles*, Washington DC. Online. Available HTTP: <http://riskinstitute.ch/00007070.htm> (accessed 1 October 2012).

Galal, A. and Razzaz, O. (2001) Reforming Land and Real Estate Markets, World Bank Policy Research Working Paper No. 2616.

Genillard, R. (1967) The Eurobond Market, 23 *Financial Analysts Journal* 2, 144.

Gerschenkron, A. (1962) *Economic Backwardness in Historical Perspective*, Cambridge MA, Belknap Press.

Ghosh, S. (ed.) (2006) *East Asian Finance: The Road to Robust Markets*, Washington DC, World Bank.

Gill, A. Allen, J. and Powell, S. (2010) *CG Watch 2010: Corporate Governance in Asia*, Hong Kong, CLSA Ltd, 2 September.

Gill, I. and Kharas, H. (2010) *An East Asian Renaissance: Ideas for Economic Growth*, Washington DC, World Bank.

Gilson, R. and Roe, M. (1993) Understanding the Japanese Keiretsu: Overlaps between Corporate Governance and Industrial Organization, *Yale Law Journal* 102, 871.

Giovanoli, M. and Heinrich, G. (eds.) (1999) *International Bank Insolvencies: A Central Bank Perspective*, London, Kluwer.

Gkoutzinis, A. (2006a) How Far is Basel from Geneva? International Regulatory Convergence and the Elimination of Barriers to International Financial Integration. Online. Available HTTP: <http:// papers.ssrn.com/sol3/papers.cfm?abstract_id = 699781 > (accessed 1 October 2012).

—— (2006b) *Internet Banking and the Law in Europe: Regulation, Financial Integration and Electronic Commerce*, Cambridge, Cambridge University Press.

Glenn, P. (2007) *Legal Traditions of the World*, Oxford, Oxford University Press.

Global Sukuk Co. Ltd. (2011) *Base Prospectus*, 18 October. On file with authors.

Goderis, B., Marsh, I., Vall Castello, J. and Wagner, W. (2007) Bank Behaviour with Access to Credit Risk Transfer Markets, Bank of Finland Discussion Paper No. 4/2007.

Goh, E. and Acharya, A. (2007) The ASEAN Regional Forum and Security Regionalism: Comparing Chinese and American Positions, in M. Curley and N. Thomas, *Advancing East Asian Regionalism*, Abingdon, Routledge.

Gold, J. (1979) Stand-by Arrangements, 462 in J. Evensen and Oh Jai Keun (eds.) *Legal and Institutional Aspects of the International Monetary System: Selected Essays by Joseph Gold*, Washington DC, International Monetary Fund.

Goldberg, L., Kennedy, C. and Miu, J. (2010) Central Bank Dollar Swap Lines and Overseas Dollar Funding Costs, Federal Reserve Bank of New York Research Paper No. 429.

Goldsmith, R. (1969) *Financial Structure and Development*, New Haven CT, Yale University Press.

—— (1982) Comment on Minsky, 41 in C. Kindleberger and J.P. Laffargue (eds.) *Financial Crises: Theory, History and Policy*, Cambridge, Cambridge University Press.

Goldsmith, J. and Bradley, C. (1997) Customary International Law as Federal Common Law: A Critique of the Modern Position, 110 *Harvard Law Review* 4, 815.

Goldstein, M. and Turner, P. (1996) Banking Crises In Emerging Economies: Origins and Policy Options, BIS Economic Paper No. 46.

Gompers, P. and Lerner, J. (1999) An Analysis of Compensation in the US Venture Capital Partnership, 51 *Journal of Financial Economics* 1, 3.

Goode, R. (1990) The Concept and Implications of a Market in Commercial Law, 24 *Israel Law Review* 2, 185.

—— (1997) Usage and its Reception in Transnational Commercial Law, 46 *International and Comparative Law Quarterly* 1, 1.

—— (2004) *Commercial Law*, Harmondsworth, Penguin.

Goodhart, C. (1989) *Money, Information and Uncertainty*, Basingstoke, Macmillan.

—— (2010) Banks and Public Sector Authorities: The International Financial Crisis and Policy Challenges in Asia-Pacific, 307 in BIS Papers No. 52, *The International Financial Crisis and Policy Challenges in Asia and the Pacific*, July.

Goodhart, C., Hartmann, P., Llewellyn, D., Rojas-Suarez, L. and Weisbrod, S. (1998) *Financial Regulation: Why, How and Where Now?* London, Routledge.

Goodstadt, L. (2005) Crisis and Challenge: The Changing Role of the Hongkong & Shanghai Bank, 1950–2000, HKIMR Working Paper No.13/2005.

—— (2006) Painful Transitions: The Impact of Economic Growth and Government Policies on Hong Kong's 'Chinese' Banks, 1945–70, Hong Kong Institute for Monetary Research Working Paper No. 16.

Gorton, G. and Schmid, F. (2000) Universal Banking and the Performance of German Firms, 58 *Journal of Financial Economics* 1–2, 29.

Goswami, A. and Sharif, H. (2000) Preface, in N. de la Peña, H. Fleisig and P. Wellons (eds.), *Secured Transactions Law Reform in Asia: Unleashing the Potential of Collateral, 2 Law and Policy Reform at the Asian Development Bank 2*, Manila, Asian Development Bank.

Goswami, M. and Sharma, S. (2011) The Development of Local Debt Markets in Asia, IMF Working Paper No. WP/11/132.

Greenspan, A. (1994) Testimony Before the US House of Representatives Committee on Energy and Commerce, Subcommittee on Telecommunications and Finance, Washington DC, 25 May.

—— (2000) *Global Challenges*, speech to Financial Crisis Conference, Council on Foreign Relations, Washington DC. Online. Available: <http://www.cfr.org> (accessed 1 October 2012).

—— (2008) Testimony to US House of Representatives Committee of Government Oversight and Reform, Hearing on The Financial Crisis and the Role of Federal Regulators, Washington DC, 23 October.

Greif, A. (2006) *Institutions and the Path to the Modern Economy: Lessons from Medieval Trade*, Cambridge, Cambridge University Press.

Grenville, S. (2007) Regional and Global Responses to the Asian Crisis, *Asian Economic and Policy Review* 2, 54

Griffith-Jones, S., Segoviano, M. and Spratt, S. (2002) *Basel II and Developing Countries: Diversification and Portfolio Effects*, Institute of Development Studies. Online. Available HTTP: <http://www.ids.ac.uk/ids/global/pdfs/FINALBasel-diversification2.pdf> (accessed 1 October 2012).

Grimes, W. (2006) East Asian Financial Regionalism in Support of the Global Financial Architecture? The Political Economy of Regional Nesting, 6 *Journal of East Asian Studies*, 361.

—— (2009) *Currency and Contest in East Asia: The Great Power Politics of Financial Regionalism*, Ithaca NY, Cornell University Press.

Grossman, G. and Helpman, E. (1991) Quality Ladders in the Theory of Growth, 58 *Review of Economic Studies*, 43–61.

Gurley, J. and Shaw, E. (1955) Financial Aspects of Economic Development, 45 *American Economic Review* 4, 515.

Gyntelberg, J. and Remolona, J. (2006) Securitization in Asia and the Pacific: Implications for Liquidity and Credit Risks, Basel, *BIS Quarterly Review*, June, 65.

Haas, E. (1961) International Integration: The European and the Universal Process, 15 *International Organization* 3, 372.

—— (1970) The Study of Regional Integration: Reflections on the Joy and Anguish of Pretheorizing, 24 *International Organization* 4, 607.

—— (1976) Turbulent Fields and the Theory of Regional Integration, 30 *International Organization* 2, 173.

Hadjiemmanuil, C. (1996) Central Bankers' 'Club' Law and Transitional Economies: Banking Reform and the Reception of the Basle Standards of Prudential Supervision in Eastern Europe and the Former Soviet Union, 179 in J. Norton and M. Andenas (eds.) *Emerging Financial Markets and the Role of International Financial Organizations*, London, Kluwer Law International.

Hadley, E. (1948) Trust Busting in Japan, 26 *Harvard Business Review* 4, 425.

—— (1949) Japan: Competition or Private Collectivism? 18 *Far Eastern Survey* 25, 289.

—— (1970) *Antitrust in Japan*, Princeton NJ, Princeton University Press.

Haldane, A. (2010a) The Contribution of the Financial Sector: Miracle or Mirage? Speech to Future of Finance Conference, London, 14 July. Online. Available HTTP: <http://www.bankofengland.co.uk/publications/speeches/speaker.htm#haldane> (accessed 1 October 2012).

—— (2010b) Patience and Finance, paper given to Oxford China Business Forum, Beijing, 9 September. Online. Available: <http://www.bankofengland.co.uk/publications/speeches/2010/speech445.pdf> (accessed 1 October 2012).

—— (2011a) The Big Fish Small Pond Problem, speech to Institute for New Economic Thinking Annual Conference, Bretton Woods, 9 April. Online. Available: <http://www.bankofengland.co.uk/publications/speeches/2011/speech489.pdf> (accessed 1 October 2012).

—— (2011b) The Race to Zero, speech given to International Economic Association Sixteenth World Congress, Beijing, 8 July. Online. Available: <http://www.bankofengland.co.uk/publications/speeches/2011/speech509.pdf> (accessed 1 October 2012).

—— (2011c) Control Rights (and Wrongs), Wincott Annual Memorial Lecture, London, 24 October. Online. Available: <http://www.bankofengland.co.uk/publications/speeches/2011/speech525.pdf> (accessed 1 Octobe 2012).

Hale, D. (2003) The Newfoundland Lesson, 17 *International Economy* 3, 52.

Haleem, A. (tr.) (2005) *The Qur'an*, New York NY, Oxford University Press.

Hall, M. (2005) *Exchange Rate Crises in Developing Countries: The Political Role of the Banking Sector*, Aldershot, Ashgate.

Hall, P. and Soskice, D. (2001) Introduction, in P. Hall and D. Soskice (eds.) *Varieties of Capitalism*, Oxford, Oxford University Press.

Hamilton-Hart, N. (2003) Co-operation on Money and Finance: How Important? How Likely? 24 *Third World Quarterly* 2, 283.

—— (2007) 'Financial Cooperation and Political Economy' 116 in M. Curley and N. Thomas (eds.) *Advancing East Asian Regionalism*, Oxford, Routledge.

Hanif, A. and Johansen, J. (2012) Sukuk, 254 in C. Nethercott, and E. Eisenberg, (eds.) *Islamic Finance Law and Practice*, Oxford, Oxford University Press.

Hansmann, H. and Kraakman, R. (1991) Toward Unlimited Shareholder Liability for Corporate Torts, 100 *Yale Law Journal* 7, 1879.

Harris, R. (2011) *The Fear Index*, London, Hutchison.

Hartwell, M. (1971) *The Industrial Revolution and Economic Growth*, London, Methuen.

Harvey, C. (1991) The World Price of Covariance Risk, 46 *Journal of Finance* 1, 111.

Harvey, D. (2010) *The Enigma of Capital and the Crises of Capitalism*, London, Profile Books.

Haselmann, R., Pistor, K. and Vig, V. (2010) How Law Affects Lending, 23 *Review of Financial Studies* 2, 549.

Hatch, W. (2010) *Asia's Flying Geese: How Regionalization Shapes Japan*, Ithaca NY, Cornell University Press.

Hayashi, S. (2006) *Japan and East Asian Monetary Regionalism: Towards a Proactive Leadership Role*, Abingdon, Routledge.

Hayes, S. and Hubbard, P. (1990) *Investment Banking: A Tale of Three Cities*, Boston MA, Harvard Business School Press.

Henderson, S. (2010) *Henderson on Derivatives*, London, LexisNexis, 2nd edn.

Henisz, W. (2000) The Institutional Environment For Economic Growth, 12 *Economics and Politics*, 1.

Henning, R. (2002) *East Asian Financial Cooperation*, Washington DC, Institute for International Economics.

—— (2006) Regional Arrangements and the International Monetary Fund, in E. Truman (ed.) *Reforming the IMF for the 21st Century*, Washington DC, Institute for International Economics.

Hermalin, B. and Weisbach, M. (2003) Boards of Directors as an Endogenously Determined Institution: A Survey of the Economic Literature, 9 *Economic Policy Review* 1, 7.

Hirsch, F. (1976) *Social Limits to Growth*, Cambridge MA, Harvard University Press.

Hirshleifer, D., Lim, S.S. and Teoh, S.H. (2009) Driven to Distraction: Extraneous Events and Under-reaction to Earnings News, 64 *Journal of Finance* 5, 2289.

HKMA (Hong Kong Monetary Authority). (2008a) *Annual Report*, Hong Kong.

—— (2008b) Issues Concerning the Distribution of Structured Products Connected to Lehman Group Companies, Hong Kong, December.

—— (2010) *Elucidation of Supervisory Principles and Operational Arrangements Regarding Renminbi Business in Hong Kong*, 11 February. Online. Available <http://www.info.gov.hk/hkma/eng/guide/circu_date/20100211e1_index.htm > (accessed 1 October 2012).

—— (2011) *Hong Kong: The Premier Offshore Renminbi Business Centre*, Hong Kong, June.

Ho, C. and Michaud, F.L. (2008) Central Bank Measures to Alleviate Foreign Currency Funding Shortages, *BIS Quarterly Review*, December, 14.

Hobson, J. (1902) *Imperialism: A Study*, London, J. Nisbet.

Holdsworth, W. (1917) The Early History of the Contract of Insurance, 17 *Columbia Law Review* 2, 85.

—— (1937) *A History of English Law*, Vol. 8, London, Methuen, Sweet and Maxwell.

Homann, K., Koslowski, P. and Luetge, C. (2007) Introduction, ix in K. Homann, P.Koslowski, and C. Luetge, (eds.) *Globalisation and Business Ethics*, Aldershot, Ashgate.

Honohan, P. (2004) Financial Development, Growth and Poverty: How Close Are the Links? In Charles Goodhart (ed.) *Financial Development and Economic Growth: Explaining the Links*, London, Palgrave Macmillan.

Hopt, K. (2007) Globalisation of Corporate Governance: The Difficult Process of Bringing About European Union Internal and External Corporate Governance Principles, 81 in K. Homann, P. Koslowski, and C. Luetge, (eds.) *Globalisation and Business Ethics*, Aldershot, Ashgate.

Hopt, K. and Hippel, T. (2010). *Comparative Corporate Governance of Non-profit Organizations*, Cambridge, Cambridge University Press.

Hoshi, T., Kashyap, A. and Scharfstein, D. (1991) Corporate Structure, Liquidity, and Investment: Evidence from Japanese Groups, 106 *Quarterly Journal of Economics* 1, 33.

Hotz, C. (2005) China's Economic Growth 1978–2025: What We Know Today about China's Economic Growth Tomorrow, Working Paper, HKUST.

Howson, S. and Moggridge, D. (1990) *The Wartime Diaries of Lionel Robbins and James Meade, 1943–45*, London, Macmillan.

Hu, Y. (2012) Growth of Asian Pension Assets: Implications for Financial and Capital Markets, ADBI Working Paper Series No. 360.

Huang, Y. (2003) *Selling China: Foreign Direct Investment During the Reform Era*, Cambridge, Cambridge University Press.

—— (2009) China's Great Ascendancy and Structural Risks: Consequence of Asymmetric Market Liberalization, 24 *Asian-Pacific Economic Literature* 1, 65.

Hui, D. and Bunning, D. (2010) *The Offshore Renminbi: A Practical Primer on the CNH Market*, 1 December, Hong Kong, HSBC Global Markets.

Huson, M., Parrino, R. and Starks, L. (2001) Internal Monitoring Mechanisms and CEO Turnover: A Long-term Perspective, 56 *Journal of Finance* 6, 2265.

IAIS (International Association of Insurance Supervisors) (2011) Insurance Core Principles, Standards, Guidance and Assessment Methodology, 1 October. Online. Available HTTP: <http://www.iaisweb.org/> (accessed 1 October 2012).

IBM. (2008) Pricing Term Sheet and Preliminary Prospectus Supplement, US$4.0 billion New Issue, 9 October. On file with authors.

IBRD (International Bank for Reconstruction and Development). (2008) *Prospectus, Global Debt Issuance Facility for Issues of Notes with Maturities of One Day or Longer*, 28 May. Online. Available HTTP: <http://treasury.worldbank.org/cmd/pdf/GDIFprospectus2008.pdf> (accessed 1 October 2012).

—— (undated) *Bonds and Investment Products*. Online. Available HTTP: <http://treasury.worldbank.org/cmd/htm/worldbank_bonds.html > (accessed 1 October 2012).

ICC (International Chamber of Commerce). (2007) *Uniform Customs and Practice for Documentary Credits*, Paris, ICC Services Publishing.

IHS Global Insight. (2010) Country & Industry Forecasting. Online. Available HTTP: <http://www.ihsglobalinsight.com/> (accessed 1 October 2012).

IMF (International Monetary Fund). (1999) *Orderly and Effective Insolvency Procedures: Key Issues*, Legal Department, Washington DC. Online. Available HTTP: <http://www.imf.org/external/pubs/ft/fandd/2000/03/hagan.htm> (accessed 1 October 2012).

—— (2004) *The IMF and Argentina, 1991–2001*, Washington DC. Online. Available HTTP: <http://www.imf.org/external/np/ieo/2004/arg/eng/pdf/report.pdf> (accessed 1 October 2012).

—— (2006) *Article IV of the Fund's Articles of Agreement: An Overview of the Legal Framework*, Legal Department, Washington DC, June.

—— (2010a) *Regional Economic Outlook, Asia and Pacific: Leading the Global Recovery: Rebalancing for the Medium Term*, Washington DC, April.

—— (2010b) *The Fund's Mandate: An Overview*, Strategy, Policy and Review Department, Washington DC, January. Online. Available HTTP: <http://www.imf.org/external/np/pp/eng/2010/012210a.pdf> (accessed 1 October 2012).

—— (2010c) *The Fund's Mandate: The Legal Framework*, Strategy, Policy and Review Department, Washington DC, February. Online. Available HTTP: <http://www.imf.org/external/np/pp/eng/2010/022210.pdf> (accessed 1 October 2012).

—— (2010d) *Global Financial Stability Report*, October. Online. Available HTTP: <http://www.imf.org/external/pubs/ft/gfsr/2010/02/index.htm#c1figure> (accessed 1 October 2012).

—— (2011) *Global Financial Stability Report*, April. Online. Available HTTP: <http://www.imf.org/external/pubs/ft/gfsr/2011/01/index.htm#c1figure> (accessed 1 October 2012).

—— (undated a) *Commitments and Disbursements of the International Community in Response to the Asian Crisis*. Online. Available HTTP: <http://www.imf.org/external/np/exr/ib/2000/062300.htm#table> (accessed 1 October 2012).

—— (undated b) *Financial Access Survey*. Online. Available HTTP: <http://fas.imf.org/> (accessed 1 October 2012).

—— (undated c) IMF Data and Statistics. Online. Available HTTP: <http://www.imf.org/external/data.htm#data< (accessed 1 October 2012).

IOSCO (International Organization of Securities Commissions). (2002) *Multilateral Memorandum of Understanding Concerning Consultation and Cooperation and the Exchange of Information*. Online. Available HTTP: <http://www.iosco.org/library/index.cfm?section=mou_main> (accessed 1 October 2012).

—— (2004) *Fundamentals of a Code of Conduct for Credit Rating Agencies*. Online. Available HTTP: <http://www.iosco.org/news/pdf/IOSCONEWS78.pdf> (accessed 1 October 2012).

—— (2006) *Regulatory Issues Arising from Exchange Evolution*. Online. Available HTTP: <http://www.iosco.org/library/pubdocs/pdf/IOSCOPD225.pdf> (accessed 1 October 2012).

—— (2011) *Principles for Dark Liquidity*. Online. Available HTTP: <http://www.iosco.org/library/pubdocs/pdf/IOSCOPD353.pdf> (accessed 1 October 2012).

Innes, M. (1913) What is Money? 30 *Banking Law Journal*, 5, 377.

International Financing Review. (1995) Derivatives/Evolving through trauma, 29 April.

—— (1997) Bistro offers credit feast – Secondary first, 20 December.

—— (2007) SIV-lite downgrades highlight rating fragility, 25 August.

—— (2008) Big Blue's big bond, 11 October.

—— (2010) Philippines: San Miguel boost, 18 September.

—— (2011a) Investors warm to Dim Sum bonds, 21 May.

—— (2011b) How to win a mandate and lose a fortune, 30 July.

ISDA (International Swaps and Derivatives Association). (2010) ISDA to Publish Auction Terms for Japan Airlines Corporation, press release, 21 January.

Ito, T. (2007) Asian Currency Crisis and the International Monetary Fund, 10 Years Later: Overview, 2 *Asian Economic Policy Review*, 16.

Jackson, H. (2007) A System of Selective Substitute Compliance, 48 *Harvard International Law Journal* 1, 105.

Jackson, H. and Roe, M. (2009) Public and Private Enforcement of Securities Laws: Resource-based Evidence, 93 *Journal of Financial Economics* 2, 207.

Jaffee, D. (1975) Innovations in the Mortgage Market, 95 in W. Silber (ed.) *Financial Innovation*, Lexington MA, Lexington Books.

Jaffee, D. and Renaud, B. (1996) Strategies to Develop Mortgage Markets in Transition Economies, World Bank Policy Research Working Paper No. 1697.

James, H. (2009) *The Creation and Destruction of Value: The Globalization Cycle*, Cambridge MA, Harvard University Press.

Jayakumar, S. (1998) Stick to Basics, speech to ASEAN ministerial meeting, 24 July. Online. Available HTTP: <http://www.aseansec.org/3924.htm> (accessed 1 October 2012).

Jenah, S. (2007) Commentary on a Blueprint for Cross-border Access to U.S. Investors: A New International Framework, 48 *Harvard International Law Journal* 1, 69.

Jensen, M. (1993) The Modern Industrial Revolution: Exit and Failure of Internal Control Systems, 48 *Journal of Finance* 3, 831.

Jensen, M. and Meckling, W. (1976) Theory of the Firm: Managerial Behaviour, Agency Costs and Ownership Structure, 3 *Journal of Financial Economics* 4, 305.

Jensen, M. and Murphy, K. (1990) Performance Pay and Top-management Incentives, 98 *Journal of Political Economy*, 225.

Johnson, S., Boone, P., Breach, A. and Friedman, E. (2000) Corporate Governance in the Asian Financial Crisis, 58 *Journal of Financial Economics* 1–2, 141.

Johnson, S., La Porta, R., Lopez-de-Silanes, F. and Shleifer, A. (2000) Tunnelling, 40 *American Economic Review Papers and Proceedings*, 22.

Johnson, S., Macmillan, J. and Woodruff, C. (2002) Property Rights and Finance, 92 *American Economic Review* 5, 1335.

Joint Forum (2010). Review of the Differentiated Nature and Scope of Financial Regulation: Key Issues and Recommendations.

Jones, S. (2012) Hedge funds battered by euro crisis, *Financial Times*, 20 June.

Jordan, C. and Majnoni, G. (2002) Financial Regulatory Harmonization and the Globalization of Finance, World Bank Policy Research Working Paper No. 2919.

Jorion, P. (2001) *Value at Risk: The New Benchmark for Managing Financial Risk*, New York NY, McGraw Hill.

Jung, J. (2005) Regional Financial Cooperation in Asia: Challenges and Path to Development, *BIS Papers* No. 42.

Kahler, M. (2000) Legalization as Strategy: The Asia-Pacific Case, 54 *International Organization* 3, 549.

Kane, E. (2005) Basel II: A Contracting Perspective, National Bureau of Economic Research Working Paper No. 12705.

Kaplan, S. and Schoar, A. (2005) Private Equity Performance: Return, Persistence and Cash Flow, 60 *Journal of Finance* 4, 1791.

Kapstein, E. (2006) Architects of Stability? International Cooperation among Financial Supervisors, BIS Working Papers No. 199. Online. Available HTTP: <http://www.bis.org/publ/work199.pdf> (accessed 1 October 2012).

Kato, T. (2009) Impact of the Global Financial Crisis and its Implications for the East Asian Economy, speech, Seoul, 16 October. Online. Available HTTP: <http://www.imf.org/external/np/speeches/2009/101609.htm> (accessed 1 October 2012).

Kavanagh, B. (2003) The Uses and Abuses of Structured Finance, Cato Institute Policy Analysis No. 479. Online. Available HTTP: <http://www.cato.org/pub_display.php?pub_id = 1338> (accessed 1 October 2012).

Kawai, M. (2009) Global Financial Crisis and Japan–ASEAN Economic Cooperation, speech to Japan–ASEAN Dialogue, 11 September, Asian Development Bank Institute. Online. Available HTTP: <http://www.adbi.org/speeches/2009/09/15/3326.kawai.gfc.8th.japan.asean.dialogue/> (accessed 1 October 2012).

Keinan, Y. (2001) *The Evolution of Secured Transactions, Background Study for World Bank World Development Report*, Washington DC, World Bank.

Kennedy, S. and Benjamin, M. (2007) Central Banks Face Rising Pressures From Politicians, *Bloomberg News*, 19 February.

Keohane, R. (2002) From Interdependence and Institutions to Globalization and Governance, 1–23 in R. Keohane (ed.) *Power and Governance in a Partially Globalized World*, London, Routledge.

Keohane, R. and Nye, J. (1989) *Power and Interdependence*, New York NY, HarperCollins.

—— (2000) Introduction, 1 in J. Nye and J. Donahue (eds.) *Governance in a Globalizing World*, Washington DC, Brookings Institution Press.

Keppler, M. (1991) The Importance of Dividend Yields in Country Selection, 18 *Journal of Portfolio Management*, 24.

Keppler, M. and Traub, H. (1993) The Small Country Effect: Small Markets Beat Large Markets, 2 *Journal of Investing*, Fall, 3, 17.

Kettering, K. (2007) Securitisation and its Discontents: The Dynamics of Financial Product Development, New York Law School Public Law and Legal Theory Research Paper Series 07/08 #7. Online. Available HTTP: <http://ssrn.com/abstract=1012937> (accessed 1 October 2012).

Keynes, J.M. (1945) Anglo-American Financial Arrangements, 138 H.L. Debates, London, *Hansard*, 18 December.

Khanna, T. and Palepu, K. (2000) Is Group Affiliation Profitable in Emerging Markets? An Analysis of Diversified India Business Groups, 55 *Journal of Finance* 2, 867.

Kim, J.I. and Lau, L. (1994) The Sources of Economic Growth of the East Asian Newly Industrialized Economies, 8 *Journal of Japanese and International Economics* 3, 253.

Kindleberger, C. (1984) *A Financial History of Western Europe*, New York NY, Oxford University Press.

King, F. (ed.) (1983) *Eastern Banking: Essays in the History of the Hongkong and Shanghai Banking Corporation*, London, Athlone Press.

King, R. and Levine, R. (1993) Finance and Growth: Schumpeter Might be Right, 108 *Quarterly Journal of Economics*, 717.

Kingsbury, B., Krisch, N., Stewart, R. and Wiener, J. (2005) The Emergence of Global Administrative Law, 68 *Law and Contemporary Problems*, Summer–Autumn, 15.

Kiyotaki, N. and Moore, J. (1997) Credit Cycles, 105 *Journal of Political Economy* 2, 211.

Klapper, L. (2006) *A New Database On Foreign Borrowing and Risk Management of Firms Around the World*, Washington DC, World Bank.

Klapper, L., Laeven, L. and Rajan, R. (2004) Business Environment and Firm Entry: Evidence from International Data 27, World Bank Policy Research Working Paper No. 3232.

Klein, B., Crawford, R. and Alchian, A. (1978) Vertical Integration, Appropriable Rents, and the Competitive Contracting Process, 21 *Journal of Law and Economics*, 297.

Knoll, M. (2008) The Ancient Roots of Modern Financial Innovation: The Early History of Regulatory Arbitrage, 87 *Oregon Law Review*, 93.

Kohn, D. (2005) Comment on Rajan: Has Financial Development Made the World Riskier? Paper presented to Federal Reserve Bank of St. Louis symposium, 25–27 May. Online. Available HTTP: <http://www.kc.frb.org/publications/research/escp/escp-2005.cfm> (accessed 1 October 2012).

—— (2011) Evidence to House of Commons Treasury Committee, 17 May. Online. Available HTTP: <http://www.parliamentlive.tv/Main/MeetingDetails.aspx?meetingId=8411> (accessed 1 October 2012).

Krugman, P. (1994) The Myth of Asia's Miracle, 173 *Foreign Affairs* 6, 62.

Kuijs, L. (2006) *SOE Dividends: How Much and to Whom?* World Bank Policy Note, Beijing, 17 October.

Kuran, T. (1986) The Economic System in Contemporary Islamic Thought: Interpretation and Assessment, 18 *International Journal of Middle East Studies* 2, 135.

—— (2003) The Islamic Commercial Crisis: Institutional Roots of Economic Underdevelopment in the Middle East, 63 *Journal of Economic History* 2, 414.

—— (2011) *The Long Divergence: How Islamic Law Held Back the Middle East*, Princeton NJ, Princeton University Press.

Kynaston, D. (2002) *The City of London: A Club No More 1945–2000*, London, Chatto and Windus.

La Porta, R., Lopez-de-Silanes, F. and Shleifer, A. (1999) Corporate Ownership Around the World, 54 *Journal of Finance* 2, 471.

—— (2002) Government Ownership of Banks, 57 *Journal of Finance* 1, 265.

—— (2008) The Economic Consequences of Legal Origins, 46 *Journal of Economic Literature* 2, 285.

La Porta, R., Lopez-de-Silanes, F., Shleifer, A. and Vishny, R. (1997) The Legal Determinants of External Finance, 53 *Journal of Finance* 3, 1131.

—— (1998) Law and Finance, 106 *Journal of Political Economy* 6, 113.

—— (2000) Investor Protection and Corporate Governance, 58 *Journal of Financial Economics* 1–2, 3.

—— (2002) Investor Protection and Corporate Valuation, 57 *Journal of Finance* 3, 1147.

Laiou, A. (2002) *The Economic History of Byzantium: From the Seventh through the Fifteenth Century*, Washington DC, Dumbarton Oaks Studies No. 39.

Lall, S. (2010) Press briefing on 2010 IMF Article IV consultation with Korea, IMF Asia and Pacific Department, Washington DC, 1 September. Online. Available HTTP: <http://www.imf.org/external/np/tr/2010/tr090210.htm> (accessed 1 October 2012).

Lamoreaux, N., Levenstein, M. and Sokoloff, K. (2004) Financing Invention during the Second Industrial Revolution: Cleveland Ohio 1870–1920, National Bureau of Economic Research Working Paper No. 10923.

Landes, D. (1998) *The Wealth and Poverty of Nations: Why Some are So Rich and Some So Poor*, New York NY, W.W. Norton.

Lane, P. and Milesi-Ferretti, G. (2003) International Financial Integration, IMF Working Paper No. WP/03/86.

Lane, P. and Schmukler, S. (2006) The International Financial Integration of China and India, Institute for International Integration Studies Discussion Paper No. 174. Online. Available HTTP: <http://ssrn.com/abstract=925872> (accessed 1 October 2012).

Lang, L. and Stulz, R. (1994) Tobin's Q, Corporate Diversification and Firm Value. 102 *Journal of Political Economy*, 1248.

Larsen, P. (2008) Dutch approve break-up plan for ABN Amro, *Financial Times*, 11 March.

Lastra, R. (1996) *Central Banking and Banking Regulation*, London, London School of Economics Financial Markets Group.

—— (1999) Lender of Last Resort: An International Perspective, 48 *International Comparative Law Quarterly*, 339.

Lawrence, M. and Stapledon, G. (2008) Infrastructure Funds: Creative Use of Corporate Structure and Law – But in Whose Interests? University of Melbourne Department of Law Working Paper, February.

Lee, P. (2008) The Franchise: Why Goldman Sachs is in a League of its Own, *Euromoney*, July.

Lee, S.L. (2003) Is Singapore's Insolvency Regime Excessively Pro Creditor?, 12 *International Insolvency Review*, 37.

Lejot, P. (2006) Cover Up! Hong Kong's Treatment of Covered Warrants, 36 *Hong Kong Law Journal* 3, 266.

—— (2008) Dictum Non Meum Pactum, Lehman's Minibond Transactions, 38 *Hong Kong Law Journal* 3, 585.

—— (2011) Institutional Completeness in the Chiang Mai Initiatives, 248 in R. Buckley, R. Hu and D. Arner (eds.) *East Asian Economic Integration: Law, Trade and Finance*, London, Edward Elgar.

—— (2012) Investment Banks and Investment Banking, in G. Caprio, T. Beck, C. Calomiris, T. Hoshi, P. Montiel and G. Schinasi (eds.) *Encyclopaedia of Financial Globalization*, Oxford, Elsevier.

—— (2013) The Place of Law: Legal and Regulatory Influences on Financial Sector Agglomeration, University of Hong Kong PhD Dissertation (unpublished).

Lejot, P., Arner, D. and Liu, Q. (2006a) Policy Concerns and the Value of Regional Markets, 243 in D. Arner, Park Jae-Ha, P. Lejot and Liu Qiao (eds.) *Asia's Debt Capital Markets: Prospects and Strategies For Development*, New York NY, Springer.

—— (2006b) Missing Links: Regional Reforms for Asian Debt Capital Markets, 12 *Asia-Pacific Business Review*, 3, 309.

Lejot, P., Arner, D. and Pretorius, F. (2006a) Institutional Reform and Economic Development, 119 in D. Arner, Park Jae-Ha, P. Lejot and Liu Qiao (eds.) *Asia's Debt Capital Markets: Prospects and Strategies for Development*, New York NY, Springer.

—— (2006b) Promoting Market Development with Structured Finance and Regional Credit Enhancement, 284 in D. Arner, Park Jae-Ha, P. Lejot and Liu Qiao (eds.) *Asia's Debt Capital Markets: Prospects and Strategies for Development*, New York NY, Springer.

Lejot, P., Arner, D. and Schou-Zibell, L. (2008) Securitization in East Asia, Asian Development Bank Working Paper Series on Regional Economic Integration No. 12, Manila.

Lele, P. and Siems, M. (2007) Shareholder Protection: A Leximetric Approach, 7 *Journal of Corporate Law Studies*, 17.

Lemmon, M. and Lins, K. (2003) Ownership Structure, Corporate Governance and Firm Value: Evidence From the East Asian Financial Crisis, 58 *Journal of Finance* 4, 1445.

Lerner, J., Schoar, A. and Wongsunwai, W. (2007) Smart Institutions, Foolish Choices? The Limited Partner Performance Puzzle, 62 *Journal of Finance* 2, 731.

Levine, R. (1999) Law, Finance and Economic Growth, 8 *Journal of Financial Intermediation*, 36.

—— (2003) Bank-based or Market-based Financial Systems: Which is Better? 11 *Journal of Financial Intermediation*, 398.

—— (2004) Finance and Growth: Theory and Evidence, National Bureau for Economic Research Working Paper No. 10766.

Levine, R., Loayza, N. and Beck, T. (2000) Financial Intermediation and Growth: Causality and Causes, 46 *Journal of Monetary Economics*, 31.

Levine, R. and Zervos, S. (1998) Stock Markets, Banks and Economic Growth, 88 *American Economic Review* 3, 537.

Lewis, W.A. (1954) Development with Unlimited Supplies of Labour, 22 *The Manchester School* 2, 139.

Lewis, W.W. (2004) *The Power of Productivity*, Chicago IL, University of Chicago Press.

Lex. (2010) Pru's Fees, *Financial Times*, 2 June.

Liebig, T., Porath, D., Weder, B. and Wedow, M. (2007) Basel II and Bank Lending to Emerging Markets: Evidence from the German Banking Sector, 31 *Journal of Banking and Finance*, 401.

Lin, J.Y. and Monga, C. (2010) The Growth Report and New Structural Economics, World Bank Policy Research Working Paper 5336.

Lintner, J. (1965) The Valuation of Risk Assets and the Selection of Risky Investments in Stock Portfolios and Capital Budgets, 47 *Review of Economics and Statistics*, 13.

Lipscy, P. (2003) Japan's Asian Monetary Fund Proposal, 3 *Stanford Journal of East Asian Affairs* 1, 93.

Lipton, M. (2006) Merger Waves in the 19th, 20th and 21st Centuries, inaugural lecture, Osgoode Hall Law School, York University, 14 September. Online. Available HTTP: <http://osgoode.yorku.ca/media2.nsf/events/1E37719232517FD0852571EF00701385> (accessed 1 October 2012).

Litton, H. and Chang, D. (1971) Chinese Money-loan Associations 1, 1 *Hong Kong Law Journal*, 194.

Liu, Q. (2006) Corporate Governance in China: Current Practices, Economic Effects and Institutional Determinants, 52 *CESifo Economic Studies* 2, 415.

Liu, Q. and Lu, J. (2007) Corporate Governance and Earnings Management in China's Listed Companies: A Tunnelling Perspective, 13 *Journal of Corporate Finance* 881.

Liu, Q. and Siu, A. (2011) Institutions and Corporate Investment: Evidence from an Implied Return on Capital in China, 46 *Journal of Financial and Quantitative Analysis* 6, 1831.

Liu, Q., Zheng, Y. and Zhu, Y. (2010). The Evolution and Consequence of Chinese Pyramids, Peking University Guanghua School of Management and University of Hong Kong School of Economics and Finance Working Paper.

Loretan, M. and Wooldridge, P. (2008) The Development of Money Markets in Asia, *BIS Quarterly Review*, September.

Lucas, R. (1988) On the Mechanics of Economic Development, 22 *Journal of Monetary Economics* 1, 17.

Lyons, G. (2007) State Capitalism: The Rise of Sovereign Wealth Funds, submission to US Senate Committee on Banking, Housing, and Urban Affairs, Washington DC, 13 November. Online: Available HTTP: <http://banking.senate.gov/public/index.cfm?Fuseaction=Hearings.Detail&earingID=4c63b142-fd5c-4b82-aff9-75e254271056> (accessed 1 October 2012).

Ma, G. and Wang, Y. (2010) China's High Saving Rate: Myth and Reality, BIS Working Papers No. 312.

Macey, J. (1998) Regulation and Disaster: Some Observations in the Context of Systemic Risk, 405 in R. Litan and A. Santomero (eds.) *Brookings-Wharton Papers on Financial Services*. Washington DC, Brookings Institution Press.

MacKenzie, D. (2011) How to Make Money in Microseconds, 33 *London Review of Books* 10, 16.

MAS (Monetary Authority of Singapore). (2008–9) *Annual Report*, Singapore.

—— (2009) *Investigation Report on the Sale and Marketing of Structured Notes Linked to Lehman Brothers*, Singapore, July.

McCallum, J. (1995) National Borders Matter: Canada–US Regional Trade Patterns, 85 *American Economic Review* 3, 615.

McCauley, R. (2007) Comment on 'Regional and Global Responses to the Asian Crisis', 2 *Asian Economic Policy Review* 71.

McCulley, P. (2007) Remarks in General Discussion on Housing and Monetary Policy, Federal Reserve Bank of Kansas City symposium, Housing, Housing Finance, and Monetary Policy, Jackson Hole WY, 1 September. Online, Available HTTP: <http://www.kansascityfed.org/Publicat/Sympos/2007/PDF/GeneralDiscussion6_0415.pdf> (accessed 1 October 2012).

McGuire, P. and von Peter, G. (2009) The US Dollar Shortage in Global Banking and the International Policy Response, BIS Working Paper No. 291.

McKenzie, D. (2012) Islamic Finance, TheCityUK Research, March. Online. Available HTTP: <http://www.thecityuk.com> (accessed 1 October 2012).

McKinnon, R. (1973) *Money and Capital In Economic Development*, Washington DC, Brookings Institution.

Machlup, F. (1977) *A History of Thought on Economic Integration*, London, Macmillan.

Maddison, A. (2006) *The World Economy*, Vols. 1 and 2, Paris, OECD Development Centre.

Maimbo, S. (2003) *The Money Exchange Dealers of Kabul: A Study of the Hawala System in Afghanistan*, World Bank Finance and Private Sector Unit. Online. HTTP. Available <http://www1. worldbank.org/finance/html/amlcft/docs/(06.23.03)%20the%20hawala%20system%20in%20 aghanistan%20(maimbo).pdf > (accessed 1 October 2012).

Mallaby, S. (2010) *More Money than God: Hedge Funds and the Making of a New Elite*, New York NY, Penguin.

Mann, R. (2000) The Role of Letters of Credit in Payment Transactions, 98 *Michigan Law Review*, 2494.

Manne, H. (1965) Mergers and the Market for Corporate Control, 73 *Journal of Political* Economy 2, 110.

Markham, J. (1995) Guarding the Kraal: On the Trail of the Rogue Trader, 21 *Journal of Corporation Law*, 131.

Martin, M. (2008) Hundi-Hawala: The Problem of Definition, 43 *Modern Asian Studies* 4, 909.

Martin, W. (1967) Reciprocal Currency Arrangements, 53 *Federal Reserve Bulletin*, 958.

Marx, K. (1894) *Capital*, Vol. 3 tr. E. Mandel (1981), London, Penguin Books.

Maslakovic, M. (2011) *Hedge Funds*, TheCityUK Financial Market Series, London, May. Online. Available HTTP: <http://www.thecityuk.com> (accessed 1 October 2012).

—— (2012) *Sovereign Wealth Funds*, TheCityUK Financial Market Series, London, May. Online. Available HTTP: <http://www.thecityuk.com> (accessed 1 October 2012).

Merrill Lynch (& Co. Inc.). (2008) *Annual Report*. Online. Available HTTP: <http://ir.ml.com/> (accessed 1 October 2012).

Mersch, Y. (2010) Governor, Central Bank of Luxembourg, The Framework for Short-term Provision of International Reserve Currencies to Sovereign States and Central Banks, speech to East Asia-Pacific Region and the Euro Area Central Bank High-Level Seminar, 10 February, BIS Review 15/2010, 2. Online. Available HTTP: <http://www.bis.org/review/r071025d.pdf> (accessed 1 October 2012).

Michie, R. (1999) *The London Stock Exchange: A History*, Oxford, Oxford University Press.

—— (2006) *The Global Securities Market*, Oxford, Oxford University Press.

Miller, M. (1986) Financial Innovation: The Last Twenty Years and the Next, 21 *Journal of Financial and Quantitative Analysis* 4, 459.

Ministry of Finance (Japan). (1998) A New Initiative to Overcome the Asian Currency Crisis, 3 October. Online. Available HTTP: <http://www.mof.go.jp/english/if/e1e042.htm> (accessed 1 October 2012).

Ministry of Trade & Industry (Singapore). (2011) Key Economic Indicators. Online. Available HTTP: <http://www.mti.gov.sg/Researchroom/Pages/default.aspx> (accessed 1 October 2012).

Minsky, H. (1980) Capitalist Financial Processes and the Instability of Capitalism, 14 *Journal of Economics* 2, 505.

—— (1982) The Financial-instability Hypothesis: Capitalist Processes and the Behaviour of the Economy, 13–39, in C. Kindleberger and J.P. Laffargue (eds.) *Financial Crises: Theory, History and Policy*, Cambridge, Cambridge University Press.

Mishkin, F. (1997) The Causes and Propagation of Financial Instability: Lesson for Policymakers, paper presented at Federal Reserve Bank of Kansas City symposium, Maintaining Financial Stability in a Global Economy, Jackson Hole WY, 28 August. Online. Available HTTP: <http://www.kc.frb. org/publicat/sympos/1997/sym97prg.htm/> (accessed 1 October 2012).

Mitchell, M. and Mulherin, J. (1996) The Impact of Industrial Shocks on Takeover and Restructuring Activities, 41 *Journal of Financial Economics* 2, 193.

Modigliani, F. (1970) The Life Cycle Hypothesis of Saving and Inter-country Differences in the Savings Ratio, Introduction in W. Eltis, M. Scott and J. Wolfe (eds.) *Growth and Trade, Essays in Honour of Sir Roy Harrod*, Oxford, Oxford University Press.

Modigliani, F. and Miller, M. (1958) The Cost of Capital, Corporate Finance and the Theory of Investment, 48 *American Economic Review* 3, 261.

Moggridge, D. (ed.) (1973) *The Collected Writings of John Maynard Keynes, Vol. 7, The General Theory*, London, Macmillan.

—— (1980) *The Collected Writings of John Maynard Keynes, Vol. 26, Activities 1941–46 Shaping the Post-war World, Bretton Woods and Reparations*, London, Macmillan.

Mollenkamp, C. (2007) Index with odd name has Wall St. glued; morning ABX.HE dose, *Wall Street Journal*, 21 June.

Mollenkamp, C., Taylor, E. and Singer, J. (2007) Battle royal: Amid European fray, biggest bank deal ever, *Wall Street Journal*, 23 April.

Monitor Group LP. (2011) SWF Assets Under Management Table. Online. Available HTTP: <http://www.monitor.com/Portals/0/MonitorContent/imported/MonitorUnitedStates/Articles/PDFs/Monitor_SWF_AUM_Assets_Table_07_07_2011.pdf (accessed 1 October 2012).

Moody's Corporation. (2010) *Annual Report*, New York NY.

Morck, R., Shleifer, A. and Vishny, R. (1988) Management Ownership and Market Valuation: An Empirical Analysis, 20 *Journal of Financial Economics*, 293.

Morck, R., Yeung, B. and Yu, W. (2000) The Information Content of Stock Markets: Why Do Emerging Markets Have Synchronous Stock Price Movements? 58 *Journal of Financial Economics*, 1–2, 215.

Morgan, E.V. and Thomas, W. (1969) *The Stock Exchange: Its History and Functions*, London, Elek, 2nd edn.

Morris, I. (2010) *Why the West Rules – For Now: The Patterns of History, and What they Reveal about the Future*, New York NY, Farrar, Straus and Giroux.

Morrison, A. and Wilhelm, W. (2007) *Investment Banking Institutions, Politics and Law*, Oxford, Oxford University Press.

Mukherjee, A. (2004) Asian central banks should follow Korea's lead, *International Herald Tribune*, 19 October.

Mülbert, P. (1998) Bank Equity Holdings in Non-financial Firms and Corporate Governance: The Case of German Universal Banks, 445 in K. Hopt, H. Kanda, M. Roe, E. Wymeersch and S. Prigge, *Comparative Corporate Governance: The State of the Art and Emerging Research*, Oxford, Clarendon Press.

Munro, A. and Wooldridge, P. (2010) Motivations for Swap-covered Foreign Currency Borrowing, 145 in BIS Papers No. 52, *The International Financial Crisis and Policy Challenges in Asia and the Pacific*, July.

Murphy, K. (1999) Executive Compensation, in O. Ashenfelter and D. Card (eds.) *Handbook of Labour Economics*, Vol. 3, Amsterdam, North Holland.

Nabar, N. and Syed, M. (2010) Investment and Rebalancing in Asia, 57 in *IMF Regional Economic Outlook Asia and Pacific, Consolidating the Recovery and Building Sustainable Growth, Pt. III*, Washington DC, October.

National Bureau of Statistics of China. (2008) *China Statistical Yearbook*, Beijing, China Statistics Press.

Neal, L. (1985) Integration of International Capital Markets: Quantitative Evidence from the Eighteenth to Twentieth Centuries, 45 *Journal of Economic History* 2, 219.

—— (1994) The Finance of Business During the Industrial Revolution, 151 in R. Floud and D. McCloskey (eds.) *The Economic History of Britain Since 1700*, Cambridge, Cambridge University Press.

Nesadurai, H. (2008) The Association of Southeast Asian Nations, 13 *New Political Economy* 2, 225.

North, D. (1990) *Institutions, Institutional Change and Economic Performance*, Cambridge, Cambridge University Press.

North, D. and Thomas, R. (1973) *The Rise of the Western World: A New Economic History*, Cambridge, Cambridge University Press.

Nukul Commission. (1998) *Analysis and Evaluation on Facts Behind Thailand's Economic Crisis*, Nation Multimedia Group trans., Bangkok, Nation Multimedia Group.

Nurmansyah, E., Bakker, T., Rees, C. and Adams, D. (2006) Indonesia, at 79 in *Asian Development Bank, Asia-Pacific Restructuring and Insolvency Guide*, London, Globe White Page.

Nye, J. and Keohane, R. (1971) Transnational Relations and World Politics: An Introduction, 25 *International Organization* 3, 329.

O'Brien, R. (1992) *Global Financial Integration: The End of Geography*, New York NY, Council on Foreign Relations Press.

Obstfeld, M. and Rogoff, K. (2000) The Six Major Puzzles in International Macroeconomics: Is there a Common Cause? 339 in B. Bernanke and K. Rogoff (eds.) 15 *National Bureau for Economic Research Macroeconomics Annual*, Cambridge MA, MIT Press.

OCBC (Overseas-Chinese Banking Corporation). (2009) *Annual Report*, Singapore.

—— (2010) OCBC Group Achieves Record Full Year Net Profit of S\$2,253 million for 2010, Media release, Singapore, 18 February.

OECD (Organization for Economic Cooperation and Development). (2004) *Principles of Corporate Governance*. Online. Available HTTP: <http://www.oecd.org/daf/corporateaffairs/principles/text> (accessed 1 October 2012).

—— (2008) *Declaration on Sovereign Wealth Funds & Recipient Country Policies*. Online. Available HTTP: <http://www.oecd.org/document/29/0,3746,en_2649_34887_40790173_1_1_1_1,00.html > (accessed 1 October 2012).

Okazaki, T. (1993) The Evolution of the Financial System in Post-war Japan, 37 *Business History* 2, 89.

Olson, M. (2000) *Power and Prosperity: Outgrowing Communist and Capitalist Dictatorships*, New York NY, Basic Books.

Ongkiko, R., Laforteza, C., Franciso, C. and Canilao, C. (2006) Philippines, at 134 in *Asian Development Bank, Asia-Pacific Restructuring and Insolvency Guide*, London, Globe White Page.

Palan, R. (2002) Tax Havens and the Commercialization of State Sovereignty, 56 *International Organization* 1, 151.

Partnoy, F. (2002) The Paradox of Credit Ratings, 65 in R. Levich, G. Majnoni and C. Reinhart (eds.) *Ratings, Rating Agencies and the Global Financial System*, Boston MA, Kluwer Academic Publishers.

Patrick, H. (1966) Financial Development and Economic Growth in Underdeveloped Countries, 14 *Economic Development and Cultural Change* 2, 174.

Pauly, M. (1968) The Economics of Moral Hazard: Comment, 58 *American Economic Review* 3, 531.

Payne, A. (2000) Globalization and Regionalist Governance, in J. Pierre (ed.) *Debating Governance: Authority, Steering, and Democracy*, Oxford, Oxford University Press.

Pelkmans, J. (1997) ASEAN and APEC, A Triumph of the 'Asian Way'? in P. Demaret, J.-F. Bellis and G. Jimenez (eds.) *Regionalism and Multilateralism after the Uruguay Round: Convergence, Divergence and Interaction*, Brussels, European Inter-University Press.

Pempel, T. (2006) The Race to Connect East Asia: An Unending Steeplechase, 1 *Asian Economic and Policy Review*, 239.

Penrose, E. (1995) *The Theory of the Growth of the Firm*, Oxford, Oxford University Press, 3rd edn.

Philips, N. (2000) Governance after Financial Crisis: South American Perspectives on the Reformulation of Regionalism, 5 *New Political Economy* 3, 386.

Pierre, J. (2000) Introduction, in J. Pierre (ed.) *Debating Governance: Authority, Steering, and Democracy*, Oxford, Oxford University Press.

Piga, G. (2001) *Derivatives and Public Debt Management*, Zurich, International Securities Market Association.

Polak, J. (1991) *The Changing Nature of IMF Conditionality*, Princeton NJ, Princeton University Essays in International Finance No. 184.

Pomerleano, M. (1998) The East Asia Crisis and Corporate Finance: The Untold Microeconomic Story, *Emerging Market Quarterly*, Winter.

Popper, K. (1959) *The Logic of Scientific Discovery*, London, Hutchinson.

Porter, R. (1966) The Promotion of the 'Banking Habit' and Economic Development, 2 *Journal of Development Studies*, 346.

Potts, R. (1997) Opinion: Credit Derivatives, London, Erskine Chambers, 24 June, on file with authors.

Pozsar, Z., Adrian, T., Ashcraft, A. and Boesky, H. (2010) Shadow Banking, Federal Reserve Bank of New York Staff Report No. 458, July.

Prada, M. (2007) Address to European Securitisation Forum, European CDOs, Credit Derivatives and Structured Credit Products Summit, 7 September. Online. Available HTTP: <http://www.europe-ansecuritisation.com/mpradaseptspeech.pdf> (accessed 1 October 2012).

Prasad, E., Rajan, R. and Subramanian, A. (2007) The Paradox of Capital, 44 *Finance & Development*, 1, March.

Preqin Ltd. (2012) Infrastructure Spotlight, May. Online. Available HTTP: <http://www.preqin.com/reports> (accessed 1 October 2012).

President's Working Group on Financial Markets. (1999) Hedge Funds, Leverage, and the Lessons of Long-term Capital Management, Washington, DC Online. Available HTTP: <http://www.treasury.gov/resource-center/fin-mkts/Documents/hedgfund.pdf> (accessed 1 October 2012).

Prigge, S. (1998) A Survey of German Corporate Governance, 943 in K. Hopt, H. Kanda, M. Roe, E. Wymeersch and S. Prigge, *Comparative Corporate Governance: The State of the Art and Emerging Research*, Oxford, Clarendon Press.

Prystay, C. (2008) Rivals Microsoft and Google take top honors in Asia, *Wall Street Journal*, 26–28 September.

Quintyn, M. and Taylor, M. (2002) Regulatory and Supervisory Independence and Financial Stability, IMF Working Paper WP/02/46.

RBS Consortium. (2007a) Offer Memorandum and Listing Particulars, Public Offer by RFS Holdings BV for all the Issued and Outstanding Ordinary Shares, Nominal Value of €0.56 Per Share, in the Capital of ABN Amro Holding NV, 20 July.

—— (2007b) Consortium and Shareholders Agreement, 28 May. Online. Available HTTP: <http://www.investors.rbs.com/investor_relations/webcasts_abnpage.cfm> (accessed 1 October 2012).

—— (2007c) Proposed offer for ABN Amro of €38.40 per ABN Amro Share, press release, 29 May. Online. Available HTTP: <http://www.investors.rbs.com/investor_relations/webcasts_abnpage.cfm > (accessed 1 October 2012).

Rajan, R. (2005) Has Financial Development Made the World Riskier? Paper presented to Federal Reserve Bank of St. Louis symposium, The Greenspan Era: Lessons for the Future, Jackson Hole WY, 25–27 August. Online. Available HTTP: <http://www.kc.frb.org/publications/research/escp/escp-2005.cfm> (accessed 1 October 2012).

Rajan, R. and Winton, A. (1995) Covenants and Collateral as Incentives to Monitor, 50 *Journal of Finance* 4, 1113.

Rajan, R. and Zingales, L. (1998a) Financial Dependence and Growth, *American Economic Review* 3, 559.

—— (1998b) Which Capitalism? Lessons from the East Asian Crisis, 11 *Journal of Applied Corporate Finance*, 40.

—— (2003a) The Great Reversals: The Politics of Financial Development in the 20th Century, 69 *Journal of Financial Economics* 1, 5.

—— (2003b) *Saving Capitalism from the Capitalists*, New York NY, Crown Business Press.

Ramaswamy, S. (2011) Market Structures and Systemic Risks of Exchange-traded Funds, BIS Working Papers No. 343.

Ramonet, I. (1995) La pensée unique, *Le Monde Diplomatique*, January.

Ravalo, J. (2005) Enhancing the Chiang Mai Initiative to Address the Medium-term Needs and Vulnerabilities of the Region. Online. Available HTTP: <http://www.aseansec.org/17907.pdf> (accessed 1 October 2012).

Ravenhill, J. (2001) *APEC and the Construction of Pacific Rim Regionalism*, Cambridge, Cambridge University Press.

Ray, R. (1995) Asian Capital in the Age of European Domination: The Rise of the Bazaar, 1800–1914, 29 *Modern Asian Studies* 3, 449.

Raynes, S. and Rutledge, A. (2003) *The Analysis of Structured Securities: Precise Risk Measurement and Capital Allocation*, New York NY, Oxford University Press.

Redding, G. (1990) *The Spirit of Chinese Capitalism*, New York NY, W. de Gruyter.

Reed, H. (1980) The Ascent of Tokyo as an International Financial Center, 11 *Journal of International Business Studies* 3, 19.

Rehn, O. (2010) Statement by Commissioner Olli Rehn on Today's Vote by Slovakia's Parliament Rejecting the Participation in the Loan for Greece, MEMO/10/368, Brussels, 11 August. Online. Available HTTP: <http://europa.eu/rapid/pressReleasesAction.do?reference=MEMO/10/368&format=HTML&aged=0&language=EN&guiLanguage=en> (accessed 1 October 2012).

Reinhart, C. and Rogoff, K. (2009) *This Time is Different: Eight Centuries of Financial Folly*, Princeton NJ, Princeton University Press.

Reserve Bank of India. (2009) *Report on Trend and Progress of Banking in India* 2008–09, Mumbai.

Richebacher, K. (1969) The Problems and Prospects of Integrating European Capital Markets, 1 *Journal of Money, Credit and Banking* 3, 337.

Robbins, L. (1998) *A History of Economic Thought: The LSE lectures*, Princeton NJ, Princeton University Press.

Robinson, J. (1953) The Generalisation of the General Theory, 69–142 in J. Robinson *The Rate of Interest and Other Essays*, London, Macmillan.

—— (1965) *The Accumulation of Capital*, London, Macmillan, 2nd edn.

—— (1979) *Collected Economic Papers*, Vol. 5, Oxford, Blackwell.

Rodrik, D., Subramanian, A. and Trebbi, F. (2002) Institutions Rule: The Primacy of Institutions Over Integration and Geography in Economic Development, IMF Working Paper WP/02/189.

Roe, M. (1994) *Strong Managers, Weak Owners: The Political Roots of American Corporate Finance*, Princeton NJ, Princeton University Press.

—— (2011) The Derivatives Market's Payment Priorities as Financial Crisis Accelerator, 63 *Stanford Law Review*, 539.

Roe, M. and Seigel, J. (2009) Finance and Politics: A Review Essay Based on Kenneth Dam's Analysis of Legal Traditions in the Law-Growth Nexus, 47 *Journal of Economic Literature* 3, 781.

Roll, R. (1977) A Critique of the Asset Pricing Theory's Tests, 4 *Journal of Financial Economics* 4, 129.

——. (1986) The Hubris Hypothesis of Corporate Takeovers, 59 *Journal of Business* 59, 197.

Romer, P. (1986) Increasing Returns and Long Run Growth, 94 *Journal of Political Economy* 94, 1002.

——. (1990) Endogenous Technological Change, 98 *Journal of Political Economy* 5, S71.

—— (2010) Which Parts of Globalization Matter for Catch-up Growth? National Bureau for Economic Research Working Paper No. 15755.

Röpke, W. (1954) Economic Order and International Law, 86 *Recueil des Cours* II.

Rosenberg, N. and Birdzell, L. (1986) *How the West Grew Rich: The Economic Transformation of the Western World*, New York NY, Basic Books.

Ross, S. (1989) Institutional Markets, Financial Marketing and Financial Innovation, 44 *Journal of Finance* 3, 541.

Ruggie, J. (1982) International Regimes, Transactions and Change: Embedded Liberalism in the Post-war Economic Order, 36 *International Organization*, 379.

—— (1992) Multilateralism: The Anatomy of an Institution, 46 *International Organization* 2, 561.

Rybczynski, T. (1997) A New Look at the Evolution of the Financial System, 3 in J. Revell (ed.) *The Recent Evolution of Financial Systems*, London, Macmillan.

Sachs, J. (2001) Tropical Underdevelopment, NBER Working Paper 8119, February.

Sakakibara, E. (2009) Remarks to ADB Seminar on Regional Economic Integration, Manila, 14 May. Online. Available HTTP: <http://www.adb.org/Media/printer.asp?articleID=12896> (accessed 1 October 2012).

Samuelson, P. (1964) Theoretical Notes on Trade Problems, 46 *Review of Economics and Statistics* 2, 145.

Scatigna, M. and Tovar, C. (2007) Securitisation in Latin America, Basel, *BIS Quarterly Review*, September, 71.

Schaede, U. (1989) Forwards and Futures in Tokugawa-period Japan, 13 *Journal of Banking and Finance*, 487.

Schenk, C. (1994) Closing the Hong Kong Gap: The Hong Kong Free Dollar Market in the 1950s, 47 *Economic History Review* 2, 335.

—— (1998) The Origins of the Eurodollar Market in London: 1955–63, 35 *Explorations In Economic History*, 221.

—— (2000) Banking Groups in Hong Kong, 1945–65, 7 *Asia Pacific Business Review*, 2, 131, Winter.

—— (2002a) Banks and the Emergence of Hong Kong as an International Financial Center, 12 *Journal of International Financial Markets, Institutions and Money*, 321.

—— (2002b) *Hong Kong as an International Financial Centre: Emergence and Development 1945–65*, London, Routledge.

Schipper, K. (1989) Commentary on Earnings Management, 3 *Accounting Horizons* 4, 91.

Schularick, M. and Steger, T. (2006) Does Financial Integration Spur Economic Growth? New Evidence from the First Era of Financial Globalization, CESIFO Working Paper No. 1691. Online. Available: <http://www.ssrn.com/abstract=884434> (accessed 1 October 2012).

Schumpeter, J. (1934) *The Theory of Economic Development: An Inquiry Into Profits, Capital, Credit, Interest and the Business Cycle*, Cambridge MA, Harvard University Press.

—— (1939) *Business Cycles: A Theoretical, Historical and Statistical Analysis of the Capitalist Process*, New York NY, McGraw-Hill.

—— (1976) *Capitalism, Socialism and Democracy*, London, Allen and Unwin, 3rd edn.

Schwarcz, S. (2002) The Universal Language of International Securitization, 12 *Duke Journal of Comparative and International Law*, 309.

Schwartz, A. (1981) Security Interests and Bankruptcy Priorities: A Review of Current Theories, 10 *Journal of Legal Studies* 1, 1.

—— (1984) The Continuing Puzzle of Secured Debt, 37 *Vanderbilt Law Review*, 5, 1051.

Schwartz, A. and Watson, J. (2004) The Law and Economics of Costly Contracting, 20 *Journal of Law and Economic Organisation* 2, 2.

Schwartz, N. and Story, L. (2010) Surge of computer selling after apparent glitch sends stocks plunging, *New York Times*, 6 May.

Scott, R. (2003) A Theory Of Self-enforcing Indefinite Agreements, 103 *Columbia Law Review* 7, 1641.

—— (2006) The Law and Economics of Incomplete Contracts, 2 *Annual Review of Law and Social Sciences*, 2, 279

Seade, J. and Wei, X. (2010) The Demand for Financial Services in China: A Household Survey, 295 in J. Seade, P. Lin, Y. Ma, X. Wei and Y. Zhang (eds.) *Hong Kong as an International Financial Centre for China and for the World*, Hong Kong, Lingnan University Department of Economics.

SEC (Securities And Exchange Commission). (2010a) The SEC Charges Goldman Sachs With Fraud In Connection With The Structuring And Marketing of A Synthetic CDO, Litigation Release No. 21489, 16 April. Online. Available HTTP: <http://www.sec.gov/litigation/litreleases/2010/lr21489.htm> (accessed 1 October 2012).

—— (2010b) Concept Release on Equity Market Structure, Release No. 34–61358; File No. S7-02-10, 14 January. Online. Available HTTP: <http://www.sec.gov/rules/concept/2010/34–61358.pdf> (accessed 1 October 2012).

Segré, C. et al. (1966) *The Development of a European Capital Market: Report of a Group of Experts appointed by the EEC Commission*, Brussels, European Economic Community.

Senate Permanent Subcommittee on Investigations. (2011) *Wall Street and the Financial Crisis: Anatomy of a Financial Collapse*, Washington DC, 13 April.

Sharpe, W. (1964) Capital Asset Prices: A Theory of Market Equilibrium Under Conditions of Risk, 19 *Journal of Finance* 3, 425.

Shaw, E. (1973) *Financial Deepening in Economic Development*, Oxford, Oxford University Press.

Sheng, A. (2009) *From Asian to Global Financial Crisis: An Asian Regulator's View of Unfettered Finance in the* 1990s *and* 2000s, Cambridge, Cambridge University Press.

—— (2011) Central Banking in an Era of Quantitative Easing, Levy Economics Institute Working Paper No. 684. Online. Available HTTP: <http://ssrn.com/abstract=1924353> (accessed 1 October 2012).

Shepherd, W. (1994) *International Financial Integration: History, Theory and Applications in OECD Countries*, Aldershot, Avebury.

Shin Hyun Song. (2010) Financial Intermediation and the Post-crisis Financial System, BIS Working Papers No. 304.

Shleifer, A. and Vishny, R. (1997) A Survey of Corporate Governance, 52 *Journal of Finance* 2, 737.

Shleifer, A. (2012) *The Failure of Judges and the Rise of Regulation, Walras-Pareto Lectures*, Cambridge MA, MIT Press.

Silber, W. (1975) Towards A Theory of Financial Innovation, 53 in W. Silber (ed.) *Financial Innovation*, Lexington MA, Lexington Books.

—— (1983) The Process of Financial Innovation, 73 *American Economic Review* 2, 89.

Simpson, J. and Menze, J. (2000) Ten Years of Secured Transactions Reform, 20 in European Bank for Reconstruction and Development, *Law in Transition*, London.

Singh, A. (2010) Asia Leading the Way, 47 *IMF Finance and Development*, 2.

Singh, M. (2010) Collateral, Netting and Systemic Risk in the OTC Derivatives Market, IMF Working Paper No. WP/10/99.

—— (2011) Making OTC Derivatives Safe: A Fresh Look, IMF Working Paper No. WP/11/66.

Singh, S. (2010) Remarks on the Development of Financial Markets in Asia and the Pacific, 211 in BIS Papers No. 52, *The International Financial Crisis and Policy Challenges in Asia and the Pacific*, July.

Slaughter, A.M. (2004) *A New World Order*, Princeton NJ, Princeton University Press.

Smaghi, L. (2009) Developments and Prospects for the European Economy in 2009, speech to Conference Altagamma, Scenari 2009, Milan, 30 March. Online. Available: <http://www.ecb.int/press/key/date/2009/html/sp090330.en.html#> (accessed 1 October 2012).

Smart, P. and Booth, C. (2001) Reforming Corporate Rescue Procedures in Hong Kong, 1 *Journal of Corporate Legal Studies*, 485.

Smith, A. (1759) *The Theory of Moral Sentiments*, Oxford, Clarendon Press, 1976 edn.

—— (1776) *An Inquiry into the Nature and Causes of the Wealth of Nations*, Books IV–V, London, Penguin, 1999 edn.

Smith, C. and Stulz, R. (1985) The Determinants of Firms' Hedging Policies, 20 *Journal of Financial and Quantitative Analysis*, 391.

Soderbaum, F. (2004) Modes of Regional Governance in Africa: Neoliberalism, Sovereignty Boosting and Shadow Networks, 10 *Global Governance*, 419.

Soesastro, H. (2006) Regional Integration in East Asia: Achievements and Future Prospects, 1 *Asian Economic and Policy Review*, 215.

Solow, R. (1956) A Contribution to the Theory of Economic Growth, 70 *Quarterly Journal of Economics* 1, 65.

Sørensen, C. and Puigvert Gutiérrez, J. (2006) Euro Area Banking Sector Integration: Using Hierarchical Cluster Analysis Techniques, Frankfurt, European Central Bank Working Paper No. 627.

Soros, G. (2008) Statement Before US House of Representatives Committee on Oversight and Government Reform, Hedge Funds and the Financial Markets, Washington DC, 13 November, on file with authors.

Standard and Poor's Corporation. (2003) *How Domestic Capital Markets can Help Sovereign Creditworthiness*, New York NY.

Steil, B. (1996) *The European Equity Markets: The State of the Union and an Agenda for the Millennium*, Washington DC, Brookings Institution Press.

Steinberg, M. and Arner, D. (2010) *International Securities Law*, The Hague, Kluwer Law International, 2nd edn.

Stiglitz, J. (1996) Some Lessons from the East Asian Miracle, 11 *World Bank Research Observer* 2, 151.

—— (1998) The Role of International Financial Institutions in the Current Global Economy, address to the Chicago Council on Foreign Relations, Chicago IL, February 27.

—— (2010) *Freefall: America, Free Markets and the Sinking of the World Economy*, New York NY, W.W. Norton.

Stiglitz, J., Sen, A. and Fitoussi, J.P. (2009) Report by the Commission on the Measurement of Economic Performance and Social Progress. Online. Available HTTP: <http://www.stiglitz-sen-fitoussi.fr/documents/rapport_anglais.pdf> (accessed 1 October 2012).

Stokes, P. (1997) *Ship Finance*, London, LLP.

Stout, L. (2011) Derivatives and the Legal Origin of the 2008 Credit Crisis, 1 *Harvard Business Law Review* 1, 1.

Strauss-Kahn, D. (2009) The International Monetary System: Reforms to Enhance Stability and Governance, speech, Beijing, 16 November. Online. Available HTTP: <http://www.imf.org/external/np/speeches/2009/111609.htm> (accessed 1 October 2012).

Streeck, W. and Yamamura, K. (eds.) (2001) *The Origins of Nonliberal Capitalism: Germany and Japan in Comparison*, Ithaca NY, Cornell University Press.

Stulz, R. (1996). Rethinking Risk Management, 9 *Journal of Applied Corporate Finance*, 8.

—— (1999) The Globalization of Equity Markets and the Cost of Capital, NBER Working Paper No. 7021.

Swan, E. (2000) *Building the Global Market: A 4,000 Year History of Derivatives*, London, Kluwer.

Swart, K. (1949) *Sale of Offices in the Seventeenth Century*, 's-Gravenhage, Martinus Nijhoff.

Sylla, R. (2002) A Historical Primer on the Business of Credit Rating, 19 in R. Levich, G. Majnoni and C. Reinhart (eds.) *Ratings, Rating Agencies and the Global Financial System*, Boston MA, Kluwer Academic Publishers.

Tadesse, S. (2002) Financial Architecture and Economic Performance: International Evidence, 11 *Journal of Financial Intermediation*, 429.

Tafara, E. and Peterson, R. (2007) A Blueprint for Cross-border Access to U.S. Investors: A New International Framework, 48 *Harvard International Law Journal*, 31.

Taleb, N. (2007) *The Black Swan: The Impact of the Highly Improbable*, London, Allen Lane.

Taylor, S. (2011) *Asia-Pacific Private Equity*, London, Preqin Ltd., September.

TCI (The Children's Investment Fund). (2007) Letter from the Children's Investment Fund to ABN Amro, 20 February 2007.

Thanh, V.T. and Bartlett, P. (2006) *Ten Years of ASEAN Framework Agreement on Services: An Assessment*, ASEAN-Australia Development Cooperation Program, Regional Economic Policy Support Facility Project No. 05/004. Online. Available HTTP: <http://www.asean.org/aadcp/repsf/docs/05–004-FinalReport.pdf> (accessed 1 October 2012).

Thomson Reuters. (2011) Deals Business Intelligence Quarterly Reviews, Full Year 2010 (Global Investment Banking. Global Syndicated Loans, M&A, Debt Capital Markets, Equity Capital Markets). Online. Available HTTP: <http://online.thomsonreuters.com/DealsIntelligence/Reviews AndAnalysis/RecentQuarterlyReviews> (accessed 1 October 2012).

Tickell, A. (1998) Creative Finance and the Local State: The Hammersmith and Fulham Swaps Affair, 17 *Political Geography* 7, 865.

Tongurai, J. (2005) Bank of Thailand's Swap Operations in 1996–97: Viewpoints of the Bank of Thailand and the Nukul Commission, 16 *Osaka City University Business Review*, 25.

Torstensson, J. (1994) Property Rights and Economic Growth: An Empirical Study, 47 *Kyklos*, 231.

Towers Watson. (2011a) Top 300 Pension Funds 2010. Online. Available HTTP: <http://www.tower-swatson.com/research/5351> (accessed 1 October 2012).

—— (2011b) The World's 500 Largest Fund Managers 2010. Online. Available HTTP: <http://www.towerswatson.com/assets/pdf/5707/PI500-Analysis-YE2010.pdf> (accessed 1 October 2012).

Treasury Select Committee (UK). (2011) Competition and Choice in the Banking Sector, Oral and written evidence, London, House of Commons.

Trebilcock, M. and Leng, J. (2006) The Role of Formal Contract Law and Enforcement in Economic Development, 92 *Virginia Law Review* 7, 1517.

Triffin, R. (1978) *Gold and the Dollar Crisis: Yesterday and Tomorrow*, Princeton NJ, Princeton University Essays in International Finance No. 132.

Trollope, A. (1875) *The Way We Live Now*, London, Chapman and Hall.

Truman, E. (2011) Sovereign Wealth Funds: Is Asia Different? Washington DC, Petersen Institute for International Economics, Working Paper No. 11–12, June.

Tsai, E., Yuan, H.E. and Liu, J. (2006) Taipei, China, 154 in *Asian Development Bank*, *Asia-Pacific Restructuring and Insolvency Guide*, London, Globe White Page.

Turner, A. (2009a) *The Turner Review: A Regulatory Response to the Global Banking Crisis*, London, Financial Services Authority.

—— (2009b) How to Tame Global Finance, *Prospect*, London, 162, 27 August.

—— (2010a) After the Crises: Assessing the Costs and Benefits of Financial Liberalisation, 14th Chintaman Deshmukh Memorial Lecture, Reserve Bank of India, Mumbai, 15 February. Online. Available HTTP: <http://www.fsa.gov.uk/pages/Library/Communication/Speeches/2010/0215_at.shtml> (accessed 1 October 2012).

—— (2010b). The Future of Finance, speech to The Future of Finance Conference, London, 14 July.

Twining, W. (1996) Globalization and Legal Theory: Some Local Implications, 49 *Current Legal Problems* 1, 9.

UN (United Nations). (undated) United Nations Statistical Databases. Online. Available HTTP: <http://unstats.un.org/unsd/databases.htm> (accessed 1 October 2012).

UNCITRAL (United Nations Commission on International Trade Law). (2003) *Draft Legislative Guide on Insolvency Law*, A/CN.9/WG.V/WP.70 (I and II).

—— (2005) *Legislative Guide on Insolvency Law*. Online. Available HTTP: <http://www.uncitral.org/pdf/english/texts/insolven/05–80722_Ebook.pdf> (accessed 1 October 2012).

Underhill, G. (2006) Theorizing Governance in a Global Financial System, in P. Mooslechner, H. Schuberth and B. Weber (eds.) *The Political Economy of Financial Market Regulation: The Dynamics of Inclusion and Exclusion*, Cheltenham, Edward Elgar.

UNIDROIT (International Institute for the Unification of Private Law). (1988) *Convention on International Factoring*, May 28. Online, Available HTTP: <http://www.unidroit.org/english/conventions/1988factoring/main.htm> (accessed 1 October 2012).

—— (2001) *Convention on International Interests in Mobile Equipment*. Online. Available HTTP: <http://www.unidroit.org/english/conventions/mobile-equipment/main.htm> (accessed 1 October 2012).

US Senate Committee on Governmental Affairs. (2002) Financial Oversight of Enron: The SEC and Private-Sector Watchdogs, Staff Report, Washington DC, 8 October.

Valukas, A. (2010) Lehman Brothers Holdings Inc. Chapter 11 Proceedings Examiner's Report. Online. Available HTTP: <http://lehmanreport.jenner.com/> (accessed 1 October 2012).

Van Boom, W. (2008) Insurance Law and Economics: An Empirical Perspective, Rotterdam Institute of Private Law Accepted Paper. Online. Available HTTP: <http://ssrn.com/abstract=1290237> (accessed 1 October 2012).

Van der Wee, H. (1977) Monetary, Credit and Banking Systems, in E. Rich and C. Wilson (eds.) *The Cambridge Economic History of Europe, Vol. V, Economic Organization of Early Modern Europe*, Cambridge, Cambridge University Press.

Van Niekerk, J.P. (1998) *The Development of the Principles of Insurance Law in the Netherlands from 1500 to 1800*, Kenwyn, Juta.

Vander Weyer, M. (2000) *Falling Eagle: The Decline of Barclays Bank*, London, Weidenfeld and Nicolson.

Vassiliou, L. (2003) The Asian Recovery: Progress and Pitfalls, presentation to Global Forum on Insolvency Risk Management, Washington DC, 28–29 January.

—— (2006) The Restructuring Revolution in the Asia-Pacific Region, in *Asian Development Bank*, *Asia-Pacific Restructuring and Insolvency Guide*, London, Globe White Page.

Viksnins, G. and Skully, M. (1987) Asian Financial Development: A Comparative Perspective of Eight Countries, 27 *Asian Survey* 5, 535.

Vincent, S. (2011) Is Portfolio Theory Harming Your Portfolio? Online. Available HTTP: <http:// papers.ssrn.com/sol3/papers.cfm?abstract_id = 1840734> (accessed 1 October 2012).

Vo, T.T. and Bartlett, P. (2006) Ten Years of ASEAN Framework Agreement on Services (AFAS): An Assessment. Online. Available HTTP: <http://www.aseansec.org/16945.htm> (accessed 01 October 2012).

Vogel, F. (1998) The Islamic Law of Finance, 17 in F. Vogel and S. Hayes *Islamic Law and Finance: Religion, Risk and Return*, The Hague, Kluwer.

Wade, R. (2004) *Governing the Market: Economic Theory and the Role of Government in East Asia*, Princeton NJ, Princeton University Press, 2nd edn.

—— (2007a) Globalization as the Institutionalization of Neoliberalism: Commodification, Financialization, and the Anchorless Economy, 250 in W.R. Garside (ed.), *Institutions and Market Economies: The Political Economy of Growth and Development*, Basingstoke, Palgrave Macmillan.

—— (2007b) Ngaire Woods, The Globalizers: The IMF, the World Bank and Their Borrowers, 12 *New Political Economy* 1, 127.

Walker, G. and Blair, M. (2007) *Financial Markets and Exchanges Law*, Oxford, Oxford University Press.

Wall Street Journal. (2009) Paul Volcker: Think more boldly, 14 December.

Wang, Q. and Yam, D. (2007) China Economics: What is the Risk to China's Economy if the A-share Market Bubble Bursts? Morgan Stanley Research, 28 May. Online. Available HTTP: <http://www. morganstanley.com/views/gef/archive/2007/20070529-Tue.html#anchorf3a1aa3e-419e-11de-a1b3-c771ef8db296> (accessed 1 October 2012).

Warde, I. (2012) Status of the Global Islamic Finance Industry, 1 in C. Nethercott and E. Eisenberg *Islamic Finance Law and Practice*, Oxford, Oxford University Press.

WFE (World Federation of Exchanges). WFE Database. Online. Available HTTP: <http://www. world-exchanges.org/statistics> (accessed 1 October 2012).

Weber, M. (1930) *The Protestant Ethic and the Spirit of Capitalism*, trans. T. Parsons, London, Allen and Unwin.

Weber, R. and Arner, D. (2008) Toward a New Design for International Financial Regulation, 29 *University of Pennsylvania Journal of International Law*, 391.

Wei, S. and Zhang, X. (2009) The Competitive Saving Motive: Evidence from Rising Sex Ratios and Savings Rates in China, National Bureau for Economic Research Working Paper No. 15093.

Weisbach, M. (1988) Outside Directors and CEO Turnover, 20 *Journal of Financial Economics*, 431.

WCCU (World Council of Credit Unions). (2010) *2009 Statistical Report*. Online. Available HTTP: <http://www.woccu.org> (accessed 1 October 2012).

Wheatley, M. (2012) *The Wheatley Review of LIBOR: Final Report*, London, HM Treasury.

Williamson, J. (1990) What Washington Means by Policy Reform, in J. Williamson (ed.) *Latin American Adjustment: How Much Has Happened?* Washington DC, Institute for International Economics.

—— (2000) What should the World Bank think about the Washington Consensus? 15 *World Bank Research Observer* 2.

Wilson, B. (2011) On the Information Content of Ratings: An Analysis of the Origin of Moody's Stock and Bond Ratings, 18 *Financial History Review* 2, 155.

Wolf, M. (2008a) Asia's revenge, *Financial Times*, 9 October.

—— (2008b) *Fixing Global Finance*, Baltimore MA, Johns Hopkins University Press.

Wood, P. (2007a) *Comparative Law of Security Interests and Title Finance*, London, Sweet and Maxwell, 2nd edn.

—— (2007b) *International Loans, Bonds, Guarantees and Legal Opinions* 2, London, Sweet and Maxwell, 2nd edn.

World Bank. (1989) *World Bank Development Report*, Washington DC, World Bank.

—— (1993) *The East Asian Miracle: Economic Growth and Public Policy*, New York NY, Oxford University Press.

—— (2001) *Principles and Guidelines for Effective Insolvency and Creditor Rights Systems*, Washington DC.

—— (2002) *World Bank Development Report*, Washington DC, World Bank.

—— (2003) *World Bank Global Development Finance Report*, Washington DC, World Bank.

—— (2006) Global Financial Stability Report, April. Online. Available HTTP: <http://www.imf.org/external/pubs/ft/gfsr/2006/01/index.htm> (accessed 1 October 2012).

—— (2010) Principles and Guidelines for Effective Insolvency and Creditor Rights Systems. Online. Available HTTP: <http://web.worldbank.org/WBSITE/EXTERNAL/TOPICS/LAWAND JUSTICE/GILD/0,CONTENTMDK:20086184~menuPK:146153~pagePK:64065425~piPK:16215 6~thesitePK:215006,00.html> (accessed 1 October 2012).

—— (2012) Per Capita Gross National Income 2010. Online. Available HTTP: <http://siteresources.worldbank.org/DATASTATISTICS/Resources/GNIPC.pdf> (accessed 1 October 2012).

—— (undated) Bretton Woods 60th Anniversary. Online. Available HTTP: <http://jolis.worldbankim-flib.org/Bwf/60panel4.htm> (accessed 1 October 2012).

—— (undated b) Financial Structure Database: Bank-based vs. Market-based Financial System. Online. Available HTTP: <http://econ.worldbank.org/WBSITE/EXTERNAL/EXTDEC/EXTRESEARCH/ EXTPROGRAMS/EXTFINRES/0,contentMDK:20292122~menuPK:546160~pagePK:64168182~ piPK:64168060~theSitePK:478060,00.html#database> (accessed 1 October 2012).

Wurgler, J. (2000) Financial Markets and the Allocation of Capital, 58 *Journal Financial Economics*, 187.

Yam, J. (1998) Hong Kong Monetary Authority speech, Coping With Financial Turmoil, 23 November. Online. Available HTTP: <http://www.info.gov.hk/hkma/eng/speeches/speechs/joseph/ speech_231198b.htm> (accessed 1 October 2012).

—— (2010) Remarks for High-level Policy Panel on the Development of Financial Markets, 215 in BIS Papers No. 52, *The International Financial Crisis and Policy Challenges in Asia and the Pacific*, July.

Yeyati, E., Schmukler, S. and van Horen, N. (2006) International Financial Integration through the Law of One Price, World Bank Policy Research Working Paper No. 3897.

Yip, C. (1983) Four Major Buildings in the Architectural History of the Hongkong and Shanghai Banking Corporation, 123 in F. King (ed.) *Eastern Banking: Essays in the History of the Hongkong and Shanghai Banking Corporation*, London, Athlone Press.

Young, A. (1995) The Tyranny of Numbers: Confronting the Statistical Relationship of the East Asian Growth Experience, 110 *Quarterly Journal of Economics* 3, 641.

—— (2003) Gold into Base Metals: Productivity Growth in the People's Republic of China during the Reform Period, 111 *Journal of Political Economy* 6, 1220.

Yu, G. (2009) The Role of Mortgages: A Case for Formal Law, 26 *Journal of Contract*, 45.

Yunus, M. (1998) *Banker to the Poor: The Autobiography of Muhammad Yunus, Founder of the Grameen Bank*, London, Aurum Press.

Zhou, X. (2009a), Reform the International Monetary System, People's Bank of China, 23 March. Online. Available HTTP: <http://www.pbc.gov.cn/english//detail.asp?col=6500&ID=178> (accessed 1 October 2012).

—— (2009b) Some Observations and Analyses on Savings Ratio, People's Bank of China, February. Online. Available HTTP: <http://www.pbc.gov.cn/history_file/files/att_19482_1.pdf > (accessed 1 October 2012).

—— (2010) Remarks to High-level Policy Panel on Financial Stability Issues, 376 in BIS Papers No. 52, *The International Financial Crisis and Policy Challenges in Asia and the Pacific*, July.

—— (2011) On Savings Ratio, People's Bank of China, 165 in Banque de France, *Financial Stability Review* No. 15, February.

Index

Note: Tables are indicated in bold; figures in italics.